REA LIBRARY

ACPI ITEM
DISCARDED

SO-BLA-117

261.873 P31   7117628

PEACE IN A NUCLEAR AGE

DO NOT REMOVE
CARDS FROM POCKET

ALLEN COUNTY PUBLIC LIBRARY

FORT WAYNE, INDIANA 46802

You may return this book to any agency, branch,
or bookmobile of the Allen County Public Library.

DEMCO

Peace in a Nuclear Age

Peace in a Nuclear Age

The Bishops' Pastoral Letter in Perspective

edited by Charles J. Reid, Jr.

The Catholic University of America Press
Washington, D.C.

Allen County Public Library
Ft. Wayne, Indiana

Copyright © 1986
The Catholic University of America Press
All rights reserved
Printed in the United States of America

LIBRARY OF CONGRESS CATALOGING-IN-PUBLICATION DATA
Main entry under title:
Peace in a nuclear age.
  Bibliography: p.
  1. Peace—Religious aspects—Christianity—Addresses,
essays, lectures. 2. Nuclear warfare—Religious
aspects—Christianity—Addresses, essays, lectures.
3. Catholic Church. National Conference of Catholic
Bishops. Challenge of peace—Addresses, essays,
lectures. 4. Catholic Church—Doctrines—Addresses,
essays, lectures. I. Reid, Charles J.
BT736.4.P42 1986   261.8′73   85-27974
ISBN 0-8132-0624-3

Contents

71176528

III. Religious Ethics

Editor's Preface

The project that led to the publication of these essays on the war and peace pastoral letter was conceived of and organized by The Catholic University of America's Center for Law and Religious Traditions, whose members share a commitment to the study of the interaction of law and religion. The project consisted of three symposia and several individual lectures during the academic year 1983–84 on the "Tradition of the Church," the "Formation of Public Policy," and the Judeo-Christian ethical responses to war. The structure of the book mirrors this original arrangement, with the addition of Part IV, which examines more specifically the implications of the pastoral letter for American Catholics. The Rev. J. Bryan Hehir's paper was originally published in R. C. Johansen, ed., *The Nuclear Arms Debate: Ethical and Political Implications*, World Order Studies Program, Occasional Paper No. 12, Center of International Studies, Princeton University, 1984, pp. 7–40. We gratefully acknowledge permission to reprint this paper. In addition, the Rev. Robert Drinan, S.J., and General Russell Dougherty (U.S.A.F.-Ret.) presented talks but were unable to contribute papers. We gratefully acknowledge their participation in the series and interest in the subject. From different ends of the spectrum, their careers reflect an enduring commitment to peace.

A project of this sort inevitably generates many debts. Dean Steven P. Frankino of The Columbus School of Law of The Catholic University of America generously provided both tangible and intangible support. Professors Robert A. Destro, the center's faculty advisor, and William J. Wagner contributed a great deal of their time and much sage advice. Monsignor Frederick McManus made several substantive suggestions, the fruits of which can be found in these pages. The Rev. Thomas Halton of CUA's Greek and Latin Department also made substantive suggestions incorporated into the volume as well as extended much moral encouragement. Dr. David McGonagle, director of The Catholic University of America Press, proved to be as much a teacher as a publisher in the assistance he gave the novice editor of this volume. The Rev. Anthony Giaquinto, rector of the Theological College Seminary and a most gracious host, allowed visiting scholars to reside at Theological College while presenting their papers. Craig Parker, assistant dean of CUA's Law School, helped to overcome many administrative hurdles.

Mrs. Monica Rohner and Mrs. Joan Sheehan Vorrasi oversaw the technical operation of the lecture and symposium series and were instrumental in assuring that many vital matters were properly managed. Ms. Gayle Campbell, the office manager for CUA's Law School, and her secretarial staff provided prompt and skilled word-processing services. Ms. Katie Noone was especially helpful in preparing the final proofs of the volume.

Funding for the project was contributed by The Columbus School of Law, the Departments of Canon Law and Theology, the Graduate Student Association, the Undergraduate Student Government, and The Catholic University of America's Peace Studies Group. John McCarthy and Brian Corbin were especially helpful in securing crucial assistance from the graduate and undergraduate student governments. Special thanks goes to The Columbus School of Law's Interdisciplinary Program in Law and Religion and the Henry F. Luce Foundation, which provided funding for support services.

Individual members of the Center for Law and Religious Traditions were also vital to the success of the series. Patrick Viscuso and Carla Perantoni contributed many hours of time. They were present from the earliest organizing stages, and the format and substance of this volume reflect many of their ideas. Ms. Tammy Edgerly-Dowd saw to many of the administrative details, such as travel arrangements, and also assisted in editing. Ms. Maureen Keashon managed the publicity for the series. Mark Kreder and Ms. Ann Stuart also assisted with many administrative details. Ms. Marlyn Banks and Ms. Erika Lert assisted in the editing. Wes DeMarco and Ron Pagnucco of the Peace Studies Group and many other individuals also provided advice and support and contributed to the success of the series. A heartfelt thanks is extended to all of them, even though it is not possible to name everyone. Finally, however, my deepest gratitude is reserved for my wife, Mrs. Cheryl Thorgaard-Reid, who showed limitless patience and good humor in the face of the daily impositions a series of this sort presented.

Washington, D.C.   CHARLES J. REID, JR.
August 6, 1985

Introduction

England's Coventry Cathedral is more than a mere building. It is part of history. Destroyed in the ravages of World War II, its structure was rebuilt as a symbol of humanity's quest for peace. Benjamin Britten wrote his renowned "War Requiem" for its rededication, using the dissonance of many voices to achieve an eloquent plea for an end to war. In 1982, Pope John Paul II visited Coventry and reminded us: "Like a cathedral, peace must be constructed patiently and with unshakeable faith."

If the pastoral letter *The Challenge of Peace: God's Promise and Our Response* is to continue its contribution to the dialogue of peace, then it is necessary to listen to the voices that challenge the bishops to build on the ideas that the letter presents. It is also important to listen to the voices disagreeing with the letter in order to test its ideas and to refine it.

In this series of papers on *The Challenge of Peace* from The Catholic University of America Press, the reader encounters a diversity of opinion about constructing peace in our times. Although no one can agree with all the views expressed, the many voices of agreement and disagreement give evidence of a sincere attempt to build an authentic peace.

These papers mirror the original work that shaped the pastoral letter. The task of the drafting committee began rather quietly upon its appointment during the 1980 annual meeting of the National Conference of Catholic Bishops. In the course of its deliberations, the committee clarified why the bishops were addressing the question of war and peace. The committee also spent many hours attempting to understand the Church's long tradition regarding this complex subject. Then, looking at the contemporary world situation, the committee began to assess what the bishops needed to say from the perspective of faith in the Risen Lord.

During the letter's development, experts in theology, technology, and political science provided rich resources for the committee. The three drafts of the letter also provided an opportunity for comment by a wide range of interested people. In short, the pastoral letter developed from a study of our tradition, an analysis of the present situation, and broad-based consultation. Its purpose was to address one of the most critical issues of our day from the viewpoint of religious and moral analysis.

Many of the papers in this book seek to deepen our understanding of the tradition out of which the bishops speak in the letter. The Church has not been, nor can it be, silent about the subject of war and peace. Even within the context of a violent world, the vision of the Kingdom remains a vision of peace. Despite a history too often written in battles and wars, the authentic tradition of the Church has been to limit the destruction and killing of war. At this new moment in history, it is our responsibility to take full advantage of the insights and challenges of our Scripture and tradition in building a true and lasting peace for future generations.

Some contributors to this volume disagree with the letter's strategic analysis or with the conclusions the bishops reached. Some argue against the emphasis the bishops gave to certain situations.

The bishops wrote the pastoral letter precisely as bishops in a nation that ranks as one of the world's two superpowers. This circumstance has to be acknowledged. Questions of counter-population strikes, first use of nuclear weapons, limited nuclear warfare and deterrence cannot be resolved in a moral vacuum. The arms race presents us with questions of conscience we cannot avoid. They demand a response.

Other authors challenge us to move forward, to consider the next steps that must be taken to build an authentic peace. The pastoral letter clearly calls for ongoing education and continuing dialogue. The needs for international discussion and commitment to control of nuclear arms are obvious. The issues of justice and development, especially in the Third World, are key components in building peace. The pastoral letter, building on recent papal teaching, makes it clear that, without justice, there can be no authentic peace. Completion of the pastoral letter merely marks a particular moment in the necessary, ongoing work for peace.

At the beginning of the fifth century, the Church faced a new moment in its history. It was no longer a Church at odds with the Roman Empire. It became a Church seeking to preserve civilization in the face of great changes and challenges. The work of St. Augustine reflects a Christian response to the circumstances of those times. From his genius emerged the just-war theory that has been further developed in the intervening years to our own time.

As the pastoral letter states, we too face a *new* moment in our history. With advances in technology and science, we are truly capable of threatening the very existence not only of our civilization but of the entire planet. At the same time, we are also able to transform these advances into resources for building a true and lasting peace. We can use our science and technology to build our world into a "cathedral of peace," constructed patiently and with unshakeable faith.

This volume of reflections on various aspects of the pastoral letter offers a valuable contribution to peace making at this new moment in our history. As we consider the weighty and complex questions of war and peace, the genius of our age is located, not in a single individual, but in the many voices engaged in the dialogue seeking peace. This series of papers serves as a model to encourage others to speak, to listen, to become aware of the deep yearning for peace in the human heart. Pope John Paul II said it best in his 1983 World Day of Peace Message:

Now I am deeply convinced that dialogue—true dialogue is an essential condition for such peace. Yes, this dialogue is necessary, not only opportune. It is difficult, but it is possible, in spite of the obstacles that realism obliges us to consider. It therefore represents a true challenge, which I invite you to take up.

JOSEPH CARDINAL BERNARDIN
Archbishop of Chicago

I The Tradition of the Church

QUENTIN QUESNELL

1. Hermeneutical Prolegomena to a Pastoral Letter

Pre-note: Everything that I will say about the bishops' pastoral on peace and war should be understood in the context of my immense gratitude to the bishops for producing it. It is by far the best thing we have so far.

This series is undertaking a serious, detailed study of the pastoral, and for that I shall focus on just one point: its grounding in the Scriptures. That not unnaturally results in some critical observations.

Text/Countertext

In the 1520 tapestry illustrations of the Apocalypse by Bernard van Orley, the 19th is a brightly colored representation of Christ on horseback, on his head a combination battle helmet and tiara, in his hand a long, two-edged sword raised to strike. The horse is galloping; the Lord is shouting a battle cry. Surrounded by hosts of Christian knights, he is charging against his enemies. The text is Revelation 19:11–16: "Then I saw heaven opened and behold, a white horse. He who sat upon it is called Faithful and True, and in righteousness he judges and makes war. His eyes are like a flame of fire, and on his head are many crowns. . . . He is clad in a robe sprinkled with blood, and the name by which he is called is the Word of God."

The paragraph immediately preceding this one is the text we quote before Communion: "Blessed are those who are invited to the marriage-supper of the Lamb."

This juxtaposition and contrast raise the question that must face any bishop setting out to construct a pastoral: "What about the fact that the devil can quote Scripture?" On any subject, there are always texts and countertexts. One side quotes: "I have said this that you may have peace," and the other replies: "I have come to bring not peace but a sword." One says: "Peace I leave with you, my peace I give to you," and the other quotes: "Nation shall rise against nation and kingdom against kingdom."

3

If, instead of merely hurling words back and forth, one tries to do a little thinking as well, to set the texts in their contexts, to see their implications, the situation often grows worse instead of better. Thus Paul exhorts the Ephesians to "Put on the whole armor of God . . . the breast-plate of righteousness and the shield of faith, the helmet of salvation, the sword of the Spirit. . . ." One may reasonably comment in a pacifist sense: "The text is merely figurative. Those are purely metaphorical weapons."

The comment is true enough. But a just-war proponent replies: "Is it likely Paul would use such a metaphor for the Christian life if he thought it was sinful to wear armor, carry weapons in real life? You would not expect Paul to compare Christian life to an orgy or to operating a brothel. So why should he compare it to soldiering, if he thought military life immoral?"

"But," the first side could retort, "in this very same chapter of Ephesians, Paul advises slaves to 'be obedient to your masters with fear and trembling, in the simplicity of your hearts as to Christ,' apparently seeing no incompatibility between the Gospel and the institution of slavery. Perhaps then Paul is not a good guide to the social implications of the Gospel he preached." And so it goes.

In another example, one may note that the centurion of Matthew 8 is praised by Jesus for his faith, without a word of criticism for his profession as a Roman soldier. But another points out that in the same Gospel Jesus is "the friend of publicans and sinners" (Matt. 11:19), who tells the Pharisees, "The tax collectors and the harlots go into the kingdom of God before you" (Matt. 21:31) without any negative comment about how they make their living. There seems to be not much likelihood of certainty coming out of this kind of debate.

Scripture in the Pastoral

Yet no bishop wants to write a pastoral without laying a strong foundation in Scripture. As the text of this pastoral says, the bishops want to speak "precisely in light of the Gospel" and to contribute to a theology of peace "solidly grounded in the biblical vision."[1] They believe "the Sacred Scriptures provide the foundation for confronting peace and war today."[2] They "recognize in the Scriptures a unique source of revelation, a word of God which is addressed to us."[3] They find that "The sacred texts have much to say to us about the ways in which God calls

---

1. *The Challenge of Peace: God's Promise and Our Response* (Washington, D.C.: United States Catholic Conference, 1983), n. 25.
   2. Ibid., n. 27.   3. Ibid., n. 29.

us to live,"[4] and that it is "the Gospel vision of peace which guides our work in this letter."[5]

Yet surprisingly after such strong words the section on the Bible, Old and New Testament (I, A.), seems to conclude little more than that peace is ultimately desirable and the not exactly astounding revelation that the Bible thinks peace is better than war.

But such a conclusion implies that the Bible is not really going to be terribly important in the body of the pastoral. And so it seems to turn out. In 283 paragraphs that follow Chapter I, A., the Bible is quoted eight times, three of those times merely as part of a quotation from a papal document. If every mention of the word *Gospel* or *Scriptures* is included, as well as every possible allusion to them, there are perhaps 20 mentions within the same 283 paragraphs. Scripture seems not to have been exactly the focal point of the pastoral message.

Let us take a closer look at the Scripture section of the pastoral. It is the first half of the first chapter of the letter (I, A: Peace and the Kingdom, nn. 27–55). It begins by noting that the Scriptures "contain no specific treatise on war and peace." The word *peace* in the Bible has, it specifies, at least four senses, and "cessation of armed hostilities" is only one of them. The others are an individual's sense of well-being, a right relationship with God (justification), and eschatological peace, that is, the full salvation of the last days, the end time, the world to come. Of these four, two are predominant: the individual's right relationship with God and the peace of the world to come. Neither of those applies directly to the question of war.

So the beginning of the biblical discussion prepares the reader not to expect too much. What about the end? The conclusion of the section repeats that the Bible tells of peace as the individual's right relationship with God and of the peace of the end of the world and that these two senses of peace, taken together, "provide us with urgent direction when we look at today's realities." That is, because Christians possess their own inner peace and look forward to eternal peace, Christians feel called to help make peace in the world.

Now, motivation to work for peace in the world is no small thing. But it is a good deal less than many people have always thought they were finding in the Scriptures of the New Testament. And it is very interesting that the bishops at several places later in the pastoral show a nagging awareness of the existence of these unnamed "some people" and of the much more specific message that "many" think they get from the Gospel. At one point, for instance, the pastoral says: "*Some* understood the

---

4. Ibid., n. 29.   5. Ibid., n. 125.

Gospel of Jesus to prohibit all killing."[6] And later: "*Some* insist on conclusions which may be legitimate options, but cannot be made obligatory on the basis of actual Church teaching."[7] And in n. 111 again: "Moved by the example of Jesus' life and by his teaching, *some* Christians have from the earliest days of the Church committed themselves to a non-violent lifestyle."[8] The bishops also state: "For *many* the leaven of the Gospel and the light of the Holy Spirit create the decisive dimension of this new perspective."[9] And finally: "In *some* cases they are motivated by their understanding of the Gospel and the life and death of Jesus as forbidding all violence."[10]

They even hint at their own moderate approval and agreement: "We recognize the intellectual ground on which the argument is built, and the religious sensibility which gives it *its strong force.*"[11] They also say: "Each increase in the potential destructiveness of war serves to underline the rightness of the way *that Jesus mandated* to his followers . . ."[12]; "Spiritual writers have helped trace the theory of nonviolence to *its roots in Scripture.* . . . Christ's own teachings and example provide *a model way of life* incorporating the truth, and a refusal to return evil for evil"[13]; and, "We believe work to develop nonviolent means of fending off aggression . . . best *reflects the call of Jesus.* . . ."[14]

How does this happen? The bishops know there is an interpretation of the New Testament that makes nonviolence a part of Jesus' teaching, a mandate of Jesus, a call to his followers; they seem to grant the interpretation is well grounded; but in their section on the New Testament (I, A. 2), they never say that there was a mandate or call or teaching, and they do not make it a part of their conclusions from a study of the New Testament. Why not?

Perhaps they felt frustrated by the game of texts/countertexts. They may have hesitated to commit themselves to one firm, clear meaning for those texts because they knew the havoc the devil, and others, can play with any texts. Someone would surely complain that the texts on which they relied were negated by some other text or were historically unreliable or did not actually say what they seem to. They may, like others before them, have felt they were faced with only two possible recourses: either follow blindly some one exegete or school of exegesis—which would limit the broad appeal of the pastoral—or settle

6. Ibid., n. 111.
7. Ibid., n. 283.
8. Ibid., n. 111.
9. Ibid., n. 125.
10. Ibid., n. 173.

11. Ibid., n. 198.
12. Ibid., n. 78.
13. Ibid., n. 226.
14. Ibid., n. 78.

for some bland generality not too clearly tied to any text and not too likely to offend anyone—which is the choice they in fact made.

Hermeneutics

Could there be any other escape from the frustrating game of text/ countertext? I think there is. I think a bishop who wanted to use Scripture seriously in a pastoral can find a way out by reflecting for a while on some principles of hermeneutics. Hermeneutics is not exegesis. *Exegesis* is the concrete wrestling with texts: What does this one mean? What does that? *Hermeneutics* asks what *anything* means, what it means "to mean," how it is possible to transmit meaning from one person to another, and the rules for finding meaning correctly.

There are standard canons of hermeneutics, but I do not wish to linger over those here, because they can be found in many manuals: standard summaries of how one must try to pin down the time, the place, the reason for writing, the author, the recipient, the language, the cultural background, the state of the text. Allow me rather to focus on three hermeneutical issues that are not usually treated in manuals, but on which everything can depend.

These issues are among the basic realities that, as Lonergan shows us, precede and condition one's fact-finding. They are issues so basic that they must ultimately be settled by decisions. The decisions are not only within the competence of anyone who is about to attempt exegesis; they are in fact inescapable decisions. No one ever does exegesis without having made them. But there is a world of difference between making them implicitly and making them consciously, deliberately, in full awareness of their implications.

There are at least three decisions called for before anyone starts looking for the meaning of Scripture: one dealing with the source of meaning, another with limits to the meaning, a third with possible effects of the meaning. But since it will be clearer if I treat the third first, I will proceed in this manner.

What decision is needed concerning the effects of meaning? Very simply, you ask yourself, suppose I were sure what the text meant. What effect would that have on me in reality? What would follow? Would I then simply possess more information about the New Testament Church? Or would I feel I had received a compelling revelation from God?

This is not trying to determine ahead of time what I would actually do if the text clearly called for action; because many of us fail to do things we feel we ought to do. But it is asking, if I were sure what the text meant, would I feel an obligation to try to live up to it? It is a question about what importance Scripture has for me, to what extent I would consider it normative, if I were sure of its meaning. And such a question is not to be answered without a decision.

A second decision to be made concerns the source of meaning. It is quite simply to ask: Where will I look for the message? For, even though the canon of Scripture is handed to me without my asking, from there on it is a matter of choice. How much of it will I read? How often? Will I allow for "epistles of straw"? Will I interpret by a "Gospel within the Gospel"?

Most particularly, will I use the Bible only as a storehouse of possible pearls of wisdom, where each verse, like the memory unit of a computer, is as likely as any other to have been used for storage by the Divine Programmer? Or will I listen and watch, in continuous, connected, patient reading, for the internal structures of emphasis that the authors themselves have built into their human literary compositions, attending above all to what the authors, one after another, are trying to tell me?

Without being able to provide full justification for it here, I suggest that by this kind of patient, connected reading of large pieces of Scripture, the normal reader—and certainly a bishop—can grow aware of the internal emphases of the documents themselves and can compare them with one another to obtain a sense of what the bishops here call "the word of God which is addressed to us."[15] As they try for this, I suggest—again without being able to provide the justification for it here—that one would not go far wrong in deciding that the words "teaching of the New Testament" be used, not for anything that happens to be found written in any biblical author, but reserved strictly for that which clearly, unmistakably reveals itself as a central and thematic literary concern of at least two different canonical New Testament books; which is fully developed in at least one of them; which is not in obvious conflict with the central and thematic concerns of any other New Testament book; and which is supported by reasonably frequent allusions in at least several New Testament books.

If we reserved the phrase for such items, the list of doctrines supposedly "taught by the New Testament" would be a fairly short one, but the list would certainly include one doctrine that does directly apply to the question of war and peace people are asking today.

The third decision that must precede any significant use of Scripture is, What are the limits of the meaning itself? That is, what possibilities of meaning am I going to allow? The answer depends on how big my

15. Ibid., n. 29.

universe is, how big my view of the world, how big my life. It may be very large indeed—but it always has limits. It is good to force myself to be aware of what those limits are.

For instance, Sir Arthur Conan Doyle believed in fairies and spent years collecting scientific evidence of their existence. Now Conan Doyle may present his evidence, but I, for one, will never believe him. My mind will follow the pattern of Hume's position on miracles: that it is always more probable the witness is lying or deceived than that these events, so completely outside his universe, should actually have happened. I will find it impossible to forget that Conan Doyle is also a writer of fiction when I read his reports. I stick with Scrooge in reflecting that the spirit he sees before him could be "an undigested bit of beef, a blob of mustard." So there are *a priori* limits to what testimony and text can mean.

Thus the Gospel is full of direct statements that are so far from ordinary life that one has to ask oneself seriously what possibilities of meaning one will grant them. The Witnesses of Jehovah read Matthew 5: "I say to you not to swear at all," and they feel bound by it literally, so they refuse to take oaths in court or even to pledge allegiance. I was always taught that that was a ridiculously extreme interpretation. Yes, the words are in Scripture, but they *couldn't* mean that. Tolstoy, on the other hand, insisted that the words certainly meant precisely what they said. Fully aware that forbidding all oaths would make an organized state impossible—no courts, no military, no police, and very few lawyers—he made the words a keystone of his anarchic Christianity.

The question of whether we can swear or not cannot really be settled on the basis of the words of the text. The words are unmistakably "Do not swear at all," but the issue is, by a prior decision, one's setting limits or not setting them as to what the words can possibly mean.

Take another example: Catholics teach that the marks of the Church are four: one, holy, catholic, apostolic. A good case can be made for these on the basis of Scripture. But a much better case can be made for five quite different marks of the Church on the basis of Mark 16:17 ff.: "These signs will follow those who believe; in my name they will cast out demons; they will speak in new tongues; they will pick up serpents; and if they drink any deadly thing, it will not hurt them; they will lay their hands on the sick and they shall recover."

Now I cannot in my wildest dreams imagine myself joining a sect of Kentucky snake handlers. It is not in my universe and it will not be. Modern scholarly agreement that Mark 16:9–20 is not part of the original Gospel, if it did not exist, would have to be invented. Still, at least since Trent, that text is certainly canonical.

"It is easier for a camel to go through the eye of a needle than for a rich man to enter heaven," Jesus says. Exegetes have invented a gate in Jerusalem called "eye of the needle," so low that a loaded camel had to stoop and squirm to get through; or they have noted that *kamelos*, camel, could be a mistaken copying of *kamilos*, a rope. In both cases they would corrupt the uproarious but shocking image of the camel and the needle into situations of difficulty and effort instead of absolute impossibility.

Luke 14:33 says, "Whoever of you does not renounce all that he has cannot be my disciple." Can this mean what it says? It certainly seems a serious statement. The doctrine recurs often enough in Luke, as in 6:30: "Give to everyone who asks of you"; 6:35: "Lend, expecting nothing in return"; and finally the words in Luke to a certain ruler who had observed all the commandments from his youth: "One thing you still lack. Sell all that you have and distribute it to the poor . . . and come, follow me."

I must ask myself, if I would approach the Scripture looking for guidance as the bishops are doing, Will I allow the text to mean that? Or will I, knowing in my heart that God couldn't really ask that much of me, reject that meaning *a priori* and keep looking until I find one better suited to my life-style? Francis of Assisi heard those texts and was able seriously to envision a life lived with them as his standard. Most of us are content to move with the eye-of-the-needle exegetes. But my point is only that before asking Scripture to teach me, I must decide how much I am willing to let the Scriptures teach.

Back to War and Peace

When one consults the New Testament about peace and war, after having made the three hermeneutical decisions just described, one does find oneself confronted with a doctrine centrally, emphatically stated and developed in at least one work, centrally stated and emphasized in more than one work, put in the mouth of Jesus more than once in the most universal forms in the great discourses, and in a prominent position within them. I refer of course to the texts already classic in most peace-war discussion, the words of the Great Introductory Sermon of the Gospels of Matthew and of Luke.

In Matthew: "You have heard that it was said, An eye for an eye and a tooth for a tooth. But I say to you, Do not resist one who is evil. But if anyone strikes you on the right cheek, turn to him the other also; and if any one would sue you and take your coat, let him have your cloak as well; and if anyone forces you to go one mile, go with him two miles. Love your enemies and pray for those who persecute you."

In Luke: "Love your enemies. Do good to those who hate you. Bless those who curse you. Pray for those who abuse you. To him who strikes you on the cheek, offer the other also. From him who takes away your cloak, do not withhold your coat as well. Of him who takes away your goods do not seek them back again. Love your enemies, and do good and lend, expecting nothing in return."

That these teachings are made central and emphatic in these two Gospels cannot be seriously denied. They are underlined by the story of the Passion itself, Christ's suffering and death, around which the Gospels are constructed. But their theme stands among the central concerns of the moral-exhortation sections of several epistles: Romans 12: "Repay no one evil for evil" (v14); "Never avenge yourselves" (v17); "If your enemy is hungry, feed him; if he is thirsty, give him drink . . . ; do not be overcome by evil, but overcome evil with good" (20 ff.). And nine verses later: "You shall love your neighbor as yourself; love does no wrong to a neighbor" (13:9 ff.).

The same idea of the characteristically Christian way of life is exemplified in the typical lists of Christian virtues, for instance, that of Galatians 5:22–3. To be convinced of that, recall first the classical, pagan virtues: prudence, justice, fortitude, temperance. Then compare those to the Gospel sayings: "Do not resist; turn the other cheek; give up your coat and cloak as well; go an extra mile; do not seek your belongings back. . . ." Prudence? Justice? No. Fortitude? Temperance? Hardly. But the gospel sayings do cohere perfectly with the Christian virtues listed in Galatians: "peace, patience, kindness, goodness, faithfulness, gentleness, self-control."

The Gospel sayings could also explain the list of virtues in Colossians 4:12–15: "compassion, kindness, lowliness, meekness and patience; forbearing one another and, if one has a complaint against another, forgiving one another; as the Lord has forgiven you, so you also must forgive. And above all these, put on love, which binds everything together in perfect harmony."

These different New Testament writers have at heart a distinctive way of life, of which the general features are not obscurely stated. Another frequently recurring formulation of the essence of that life is forgiveness, as in the Gospel sayings, "Forgive seventy times seven times," and "Unless you forgive your fellows from the heart, neither will your heavenly Father forgive you." Another formulation of it is the call for perfect love of one another thematically developed in I John 2–4.

This theme cannot be explored more fully here, but the texts already cited show well enough that we are dealing with a pattern that is central in more than one New Testament book. Its clarity and importance is witnessed to further by many of the earliest pieces of Christian literature outside the canon. When the first-century Didache and the second-century letter of Polycarp present the heart of Christian teaching, they start from these teachings of the Great Sermon of the Gospels.

The texts are no secret. They are the lines of the New Testament most people think of when questions of peace and war are raised. They have been appealed to by the historic peace churches for centuries. But in this pastoral the bishops have avoided focusing their readers' attention on them.

I have tried to show that this fact cannot be accounted for simply by a concern about the clarity or obscurity of those texts, for they are no more obscure or unclear than any other texts regularly used in Christian teaching. And they are certainly not incidental. If they cannot safely be used in a pastoral, then no text of Scripture can ever be used in Christian teaching: not "Thou art Peter, and upon this rock I will build my Church"; not "He who hears you, hears me"; not "He who divorces his wife and marries another commits adultery"; not "This is my body; this is my blood." The problem is not one of clarity or historical reliability. The problem is one of prior decisions as to what the texts can be allowed to mean and what effect in life that meaning will be allowed to have.

Gospel or Law?

Now I would like to turn to another reason that might make one hesitate about calling attention to these texts when facing the peace/war questions of today. This is the distinction between Gospel and law, and the ease with which that distinction can be forgotten.

Concern over this point is indicated when the pastoral mentions "conclusions which may be legitimate options, but cannot be made obligatory on the basis of actual Church teaching." The words of the Gospel are peremptory: "I say to you, do not resist one who is evil." "If any one strike you on the right cheek, turn to him the other also." They are stated as commands. They look like laws. If those sayings were quoted in the pastoral's New Testament section, people might understand them as laws. If they appeared again in the New Testament summary, it might look as if the bishops were imposing them as laws. Conclusion: Everybody has to be a pacifist to be a Catholic; a government that is not pacifist is simply immoral and un-Christian. The bishops knew they did not want to say that.

I have argued elsewhere[16] that sayings of this kind in the Gospels are

---

16. Quentin Quesnell, "Made Themselves Eunuchs for the Kingdom of Heaven (Matt. 19: 12)," *Catholic Biblical Quarterly* 30 (1968), 335–358; 357–358; Quesnell, *The Gospel of Christian Freedom* (New York: Herder and Herder, 1964), pp. 63–65; Quesnell, "Beliefs and Authenticity," in Mathew Lamb, ed., *Creativity and Method: Essays in Honor of Bernard Lonergan* (Milwaukee: Marquette University Press, 1981), pp. 173–183; p. 179.

not laws and that they actually lose in power rather than gain when people try to turn them into laws. Let me summarize that briefly here:

Laws are binding on all those to whom they are addressed. Those who break them are liable to punishment. Laws are defined as precisely as possible, for people must know exactly what is expected of them. Laws are orderings of reason, based on the best available knowledge of the real world, of human probabilities, with reasonable hope of improving the welfare of the community by them. Laws support the structures of the community and make possible their orderly functioning.

Naturally a believing person who loves the Gospel and also appreciates the value of law is tempted to search out ways to turn the Gospel into laws; to make it precise, easily and widely available; to widen its influence from haphazard, occasional inspiration for individuals into a stable influence on the culture, supported and promoted by all the resources of society. This has long been a tendency of the Church as civilizer, which has done much good, as well as some possible harm.

But, granting the good that may result for the structures of society, there is along this route a danger of losing the essence of the Gospel. For laws operate within the limits of the society for which they were written. But just as the measure with which to love God is to love God without measure, so the Gospel challenges are phrased in terms that always drive beyond all limits. There cannot be a law that means one must always do more—a law of which everyone would always be in violation. But that is precisely what is demanded by challenges like, "Do not resist the evil person," and "Give to everyone who asks," and "If someone takes your cloak, give him your coat as well."

You cannot have a law that shatters the temporal order. But the value of the Gospel is to keep the believer always open to new possibilities and to that extent to being ready to step outside of any existing arrangement. The Gospel statements are not precise. They have no punishment attached to their violation, except that intrinsic punishment of losing the good they promise. They do not bind all to whom they are addressed, but only those who hear, understand, and believe them. And above all, they are not ordinances of reason; they are entirely based on faith.

The Gospel sayings on nonresistance are no more calculated to make us win the next war than the Gospel sayings on poverty are calculated to make us rich. They are themselves, in fact, a call for faith. They are small embodiments in specific areas of the central Christian faith that Vatican II calls "the Paschal mystery." That is the faith that in Christ's defeat was his triumph; that dying with him, we rise; that if, in practicing the Gospel we lose our lives, we gain eternal life.

But none of that is built upon the best human probabilities. Nor does any of it guarantee the future welfare of the community, except perhaps in a happy day when every member of the world community would share and practice that same faith. A criticism directed sometimes against Gospel morality is that it is an individual morality; it does not address social institutions, except insofar as they are made up of individuals. Whether it merits criticism or not, this is certainly a fact about Gospel morality. The Gospel sayings place each person who hears and believes in front of major decisions, decisions that cannot be made by any person for another person. This is the real reason why such decisions cannot ever be made by the government either. A decision to implement the Gospel for the entire nation—by, for instance, giving away all the wealth of the country—would be moral only if each and every citizen, including the aged, the infirm, and the children, gave 100 percent enthusiastic consent because of their own love of the Gospel. But there has never been and never will be a Christian commonwealth that consisted entirely of the wholly committed, with every person in it eager to die for Christ.

The Gospel sayings are indeed proposed in the Gospel as true—as the surest way to happiness—which is why they stand in close connection with the beatitudes. They are challenges, invitations, messages of eternal life to all who hear and believe. They are themselves gospel in the sense that one who believes and lives them will find in them a revelation of good news; but, because their good news is beyond nature and only available by a step that nature dreads taking, they cannot be imposed on anyone. They must be proposed to everyone.

Now that may be hard for some bishops to agree with. It seems to reduce their role to that of preachers of the Gospel. Yet preacher of the Gospel, according to Vatican II, is precisely the most honored function of the bishop: "Among their tasks, one stands out above the rest: To preach the Gospel."

Another Kind of Pastoral

The bishops could conceivably fulfill their essential teaching task by preaching the Gospel without laying down laws, leaving the decisions about action to the individuals who would hear and believe. There seems to be no hesitation in conceding that in regard to the Gospel sayings about possessions. When Jesus in Luke 14 teaches: "Unless you renounce all your possessions you cannot be my disciple," and in Luke 18: "Sell all you have and distribute it to the poor," the Church proposes these sayings to the world as true and does so in such a way that everyone understands Francis of Assisi was a disciple of Jesus in a fuller way than the rest of us because Francis did devote his life to taking them seriously, whereas most of us do not.

Most of us tend to hear those sayings, admire someone like Francis who practices them, feel moved by them as long as we are thinking about them, and perhaps for a time even hold our own possessions just a bit more loosely than we would otherwise have done. When the sayings are proposed to us seriously as part of the Gospel, they make us uneasy. We have, as believers, a right to that uneasiness. The bishops should foster it in us, as Kierkegaard cries, not protect us from it. There is nothing shameful in admitting we are unable to live up to what the Gospel proposes; but if we pretend the challenge does not exist, or if we turn it into something trivial, something perfectly compatible with ordinary, comfortable bourgeois living, we are, Kierkegaard insists, making a fool of God.

So, what might a different pastoral be like? It too would have an introductory chapter on Scripture. But that chapter would focus as strongly as possible on the New Testament passages we have just been discussing. In particular, it would not fail to present the texts in full citation.

It would try to make Catholics vividly aware of the importance of these texts. It would remind them that these Gospel words of Christ demand faith in the same way as other verses of the same chapters, like, "Every one who looks at a woman lustfully has already committed adultery with her in his heart" (Matt. 5:28), or "whoever marries a divorced woman commits adultery" (Matt. 5:32).

Around them, it would group supporting texts from other parts of the New Testament, to confirm how central is the way of life there described. Particularly effective for this might be selections from I Peter, showing the connection between Christ's suffering and the suffering of Christians, and I John, showing the connection between the Christians' love and the love that took Christ to the Cross.

The new pastoral would be deliberately directed to individuals, even as the Gospel challenges themselves are. The bishops would make clear the obligation they feel, as authorized ministers of the Word, to make these texts present to the faithful. They would explain that they themselves cannot add anything to them, but that they simply strongly desire that each person make them their own and then act as they feel called to act in faith.

In a second chapter they would address themselves to the concrete problems that Catholics who hear these words have to face. That is, they would make every effort to clarify for their readers the areas of life in which these Gospel texts call for a decision. This is important. The decision for Catholics reading the pastoral is not whether nuclear wars shall be begun or what targets the Pentagon will pick out. The actual decision for Catholics will be whether to cooperate with the actions being taken in their name by their democratically elected government.

Therefore a major concern of the pastoral would be to lay the facts before the faithful so that they can apply the Gospel texts to the facts and decide for themselves.

For instance, facts like those in the present letter about the extent of the American arsenal, the number of weapons we have, the number of soldiers, and the number of people our government will surely kill when it eliminates the 60 military targets it has identified within the city of Moscow alone, the numbers of people we will kill[17] when we hit the 40,000 military sites targeted for nuclear destruction in the entire Soviet Union. Facts like these from the present letter, but presented in vivid juxtaposition with the Gospel texts—perhaps set up on parallel pages— would prompt believing readers to serious reflection and would invite them to draw their own conclusions, each according to the extent of their faith and their circumstances.

The real-life decisions for the readers of the pastoral are decisions whether to vote for certain candidates; let our representatives know we are for or against certain policies; whether to accept positions in the military as volunteers or as draftees; whether to cooperate by working in industries that produce weapons or poison gas or chemicals to be used in killing; or in universities that accept government contracts to do research on such things for the military; whether to instruct others in the Gospel as we know it; perhaps above all the decision whether to continue paying the thousands of dollars annually that each of us contributes by our taxes to the government's preparations for future wars.

In connection with each of those decisions, Catholics should find themselves confronted by the Gospel texts about enemies, about forgiveness, about resistance, about giving your attacker freely more than he tries to take from you. So confronted, they will still make their own decisions. No doubt most who read such a pastoral will act just as they always have acted—like most other Americans. But if a few are moved to make a different decision, the Gospel will begin to be noticed in a new way and may produce a still larger effect.

This is still individual morality, but it can sway nations. Actually, if the Gospel addressed collectivities, you would never be sure to whom it was being spoken or who was called on to make the sacrifice. Since it addresses individual persons, you can aways be quite sure: "Thou art the man." You're the one. Do your part then, without reservations. Don't wait to see if the rest follow. And do not wait for the other person to make the first move. If you do, we shall all be here until Doomsday.

The state, democratic or otherwise, is still made up of individual persons. If no individual will kill or cooperate in killing, the state will not be able to kill in our name. In the present pastoral, the bishops praise

17. *Challenge of Peace*, n. 180.

conscientious objectors and say that, in the name of the Gospel, they want to stress their support for a pacifist option for individuals.[18] If all Catholics did become conscientious objectors, a quarter of the potential armed forces of the country would be cut off. That would certainly be an event of enormous significance, but it would happen entirely by the working of individual consciences.

But even that might be only stage one. Suppose a campaign for *full* conscientious objection rights were launched by the American bishops, still addressed only to individual consciences? In a completely logical follow-through on principles laid down in this first letter, they would say that a "financial conscientious objector" status should be available for the millions of Americans whose consciences will not allow them to be a part of current plans to destroy our enemies. In the name of freedom of conscience, the bishops would urge Catholics to press Congress to pass laws making possible such "financial conscientious objection."

It is after all perfectly logical: If 20 year olds can apply for alternative service outside the military for the sake of conscience, why should the 40 to 60 year olds not be able to put their tax money to alternative purposes outside the government's war program in order to spare their consciences too? Surely a list of acceptable charitable organizations could be drawn up to which the money could be given with full government sanction. The fact that allowing this would impose additional financial burdens on those who do agree with the government's defense program is no different from the fact that granting alternative nonmilitary service to some young men also imposes a greater burden, a larger share of the fighting, on those who do serve as soldiers.

There is great power in the call to the individual, and preachers of the Gospel, of all people, should exploit that power to the maximum.

Reason and Faith

Would the new pastoral then leave no room for discussions of the kind that make up the bulk of this one? Discussions about the morality of specific acts of war? Is prophetic denunciation to be the only mode of discourse in the future, leaving those who will not accept total pacifism to plan apocalypses without criticism? Is shelling a naval base really no different from obliterating New York City or Moscow, so that Christians cannot henceforth be bothered with drawing rational moral distinctions? That conclusion would mean not only scrapping the entire tradition of Catholic moral theology but also overlooking the distinction between reason and faith.

In its time and at its best, just-war theory was the answer of reason to

18. Ibid., n. 119.

certain difficult situations. When rightly expounded, as it is here in the pastoral, just-war doctrine states only what is *allowed*. One may defend and cooperate with the defending of the innocent—even defending oneself, if one is oneself innocent—against unjust attacks. Preaching the Gospel need not mean denying that such limited responses with force might be sometimes the most reasonable thing to do. But preaching the Gospel would always deny that that was the most Christian thing for a person to do or that it was what Christ urged his followers to do according to the Gospel.

No one has any trouble admitting that holding a good job, with a little money in the bank, and slowly paying off the mortgage on one's house is not the same as "No one can be my disciple unless he renounces all he possesses." It is hardly the fulfilment of "Sell what you have and give it to the poor." It is not "Take no thought for tomorrow." It is not the life described in the Gospel. It is not what Christ in the Gospel tells us is the key to true happiness. But it is reasonable and normal and natural, and 99 percent of us do it.

So here, waging a restrained response to an attacking aggressor might have been reasonable and just and even been done out of a motive of love of those near and dear. But it was never a way of fulfilling "Love your enemies; do good to those who hate you," and there is no use pretending that it was. If you are going to modify the call to love your enemies every time that loving would conflict with loving your family or friends, then you will never love your enemies at all. That is why the Gospel includes sayings like, "If any one comes to me and does not hate his own father and mother and wife and children and brothers and sisters, yes and even his own life, he cannot be my disciple" (Luke 14:26). The love of those close to us will always interfere with efforts to love our enemies, just as it will always interfere with our giving away everything we have. To choose to modify the teaching on nonresistance in order to return "just this one restrained bit of evil for evil just this once in order to protect the innocent" was always a temptation to which it was perfectly normal and reasonable to yield. But it was not the Gospel.

In other words, just-war doctrine never was the Gospel. The Gospel has always been what it is today: a challenge to *more* in the name of faith. But when for centuries moral theology became separated from ascetical-mystical or spiritual theology, bishops as teachers, not as preachers of the Gospel, became gradually used to laying down the minimum necessary rather than proclaiming the Gospel call to ever more. Just war—that is, a tolerable minimum of self-protection according to right reason—gradually became so identified with Church doctrine that so orthodox and conservative a publication as the *New Catholic Encyclopedia* (1967) could state flatly in its article on "Morality of War" that in Catholic teaching "conscientious objection is morally indefensible."[19]

The irony is that, since the introduction of nuclear weapons, an ever larger number of ethical philosophers, working purely from reason, have been deciding that just war is immoral because it is no longer a reasonable solution to anyone's problems. The bishops started out to write a Catholic position in this new context. But they did not carefully distinguish their sources of knowledge and when they were speaking from reason and when from faith.

If they had carefully distinguished them, the bishops could have faced the question of whether just-war doctrine had to be abandoned completely in this nuclear age and could have given their nuanced, reasonable answer according to their best lights and best information. But giving that answer would not have kept them from confronting their readers with the uncomfortable words of the Gospel.

Summary

The pastoral as it stands makes a great contribution: It clearly gives nonviolence equal status with just war as an optional means to peace. It grounds both options in what it calls "the Christian presumption against all war." But it hesitates to use the key Scripture texts to ground that presumption, probably because using the texts would make it clear that nonviolence and just war are not two equal options according to the Gospel. One is—or at least was—the voice of reason; the other is one of the hard sayings of the Gospel, challenging every individual to believe that the way to life lies beyond reason in faith in Christ's nonviolent Cross.

19. *New Catholic Encyclopedia* (New York: McGraw-Hill Book Co., 1967), Vol. 14, p. 804.

JOSEPHINE MASSYNGBAERDE FORD

2. Cursing and Blessing as Vehicles of Violence and Peace in Scripture

Jesus taught us that the kingdom of God is like a mustard seed, which, although minute, grows into a large, yet not majestic, shrub.[1] *Mutatis mutandis* Jesus' parable might be accommodated to the pursuit and/or teaching of peace in the early Christian Church. Its growth is not instantaneous. It is not uniform. The biblical evidence is difficult to interpret.

It is with this point in view that I should like to comment on the pastoral letter of the American bishops.[2]

First, the New Testament was written and redacted in a disturbed era, especially in view of the catastrophic war between the Jews and the Romans (66–74 C.E.). At this time the question of violence and peace became as vital an issue as it is in our world. Second, it must be noted that not all the teaching in the New Testament is irenic. Third, there is a clear maturing of thought *vis-à-vis* nonviolence in the New Testament. Fourth, it would seem that the Gospels have a different message from much of the rest of the New Testament, especially the primo-Pauline epistles and the Book of Revelation.

However, before we address the New Testament a few remarks on the Old Testament and so-called late Judaism are relevant. The pastoral letter statement "Violence and war are very much present in the history of the people of God particularly from the Exodus period to the monarchy" is correct but needs some clarification. There were no full-scale wars in the patriarchal/matriarchal period.[3] In fact, it was a remarkably peaceable age with amicable agreement concerning essential amenities, such as water and land.[4] Furthermore, during much of Israel's history the

1. The mustard seed grows into a large shrub, not a majestic tree.

2. *The Challenge of Peace: God's Promise and Our Response* (Washington, D.C.: United States Catholic Conference, 1983).

3. Millard Lind, *Yahweh Is a Warrior: The Theology of Warfare in Ancient Israel* (Scottdale, Pa: Herald Press, 1980).

4. For example, the division of land between Abraham (Abram) and Lot (Gen. 13:1–18); see especially, vi: "So Abram said to Lot: 'Let there be no strife between you and me, or between your herdsmen and mine, for we are kinsmen.'" Compare also Genesis 21:22–32, the pact between Abraham and Abimelech about the well.

fighting was hand to hand.[5] Moreover, the classical prophets, in contrast to the preclassical ecstatic prophets, as a general rule are those who espouse nonresistance to the national enemy but not necessarily toward personal enemies (cf. the conflict between Jeremiah and Hananiah).[6] I think that I am right in saying that none of the classical prophets advocates aggressive war. The Wisdom literature gives some shrewd insights into keeping domestic and local peace. All this, however, is not to deny the theology and practice of holy war. The entry into Canaan appears to be aggressive war as does the expansion of David's kingdom. However, the Deuteronomic code forbids the king to multiply horses, that is, instruments of war (Deut. 17:16). On the whole, war in the history of Israel is defensive, not aggressive. I believe that this forms quite a sharp contrast with the nations surrounding Israel. Therefore the seeds of the peace ideology lie in the Hebrew tradition.

Furthermore, in the late centuries B.C.E. and the early centuries C.E. the quietist Pharisees[7] resume the nonresistant peace policies of the classical prophets. They are mainly a lay movement, and they are followed by the peace-seeking Hillelites.[8] It is the peace policy of Hillel that triumphs in the academy established at Jamnia after the war.[9] Jamnia was the center of Judaism after the Fall of Jerusalem in 70 C.E. The quietist Pharisees are to be contrasted with the Maccabees and other later revolutionaries who inherit the Maccabean theology of the holy war and come to the foreground in the two great rebellions of 66–74 and 132–135 C.E. These two groups, the quietist Pharisees (mainly the Hillelites) and the revolutionary parties (of which the Zealots were a very small faction arising in the year 67/68 C.E.) offer a live option between violence and nonviolence in the century when the New Testament was written and redacted. It was an option both for Jews and Christians. The peace-seeking Pharisees do not extol the Maccabees.[10]

Hesed

I should add one further remark to the bishops' comment on covenant and community.[11] This is the importance of the study of *hesed*, that

---

5. Roland de Vaux, O.P., "Single Combat in the Old Testament," in *The Bible and the Ancient East* (Garden City, N.Y.: Doubleday, 1967), pp. 122–135.

6. For the dispute between Hananiah and Jeremiah, see Jeremiah 28.

7. N. N. Glazer, *Hillel the Elder: The Emergence of Classical Judaism*, rev. ed. (New York, New York: Schocken Books 1966), pp. 66–73.

8. Cf. D. M. Rhoads, *Israel in Revolution, 6–74 C.E.* (Philadelphia: Fortress Press, 1976), pp. 63–64; pp. 67–68; p. 71, and p. 91.

9. For, example, as represented by Johannan ben Zakkai.

10. For a brief summary of the situation, see the preface and first chapter of my book, *My Enemy Is My Guest* (Maryknoll, N.Y.: Orbis Books, 1984).

11. *The Challenge of Peace*, nn. 32–38.

untranslatable Hebrew word that embraces love, loyalty, faithfulness, compassion, all that is good in relationships both human and divine. It is the quality that binds covenant members together. A good starting point for this study would be the monograph of Nelson Glueck.[12] Integral to the whole concept of *hesed* is its persistence both on the part of God and of human beings even in the face of deception, e.g., the covenant between Joshua and the Gibeonites (Josh. 9) and, on the part of God, the covenant kept even in the face of woeful irresponsibility and breach of promise by human beings. Implicit, yet vivid and arresting, is the fact that God is prepared to face death to keep the covenant inviolate (sacrosanct). This appears to be the narrator's meaning when he describes the Pact of the Pieces in Genesis 15. Here it is God who walks through the lane of animals.[13] God is symbolized by the smoking brazier and the flaming torch. Abraham sees this while he is in a trance.

Jesus may be referring to this vision in John 8:56: "Your father Abraham rejoiced to see my day. He saw it and was glad." The necessity of keeping *hesed* explains the necessity of (*dei*) the passion and death of Jesus.[14] Jesus was prepared to undergo death to keep the *hesed* of the covenant.

Yet, as we see very plainly from Deuteronomy 27 and 28 (and elsewhere in Scripture and in other ancient cultures), human beings who break the covenant are cursed—in multifarious ways. Those who are faithful to the covenant and keep *hesed* are blessed. Von Rad[15] defines blessing as the *transmission of divine vitality*. Cursing is the withdrawal of divine vitality. Cursing was a common, realistic, efficacious, and terrifying phenomenon in the ancient world—indeed in many parts of the world today. The agent of the curse might be God or might be a human being, but often no external agent is needed. "The curse was automatic or self-fulfilling . . . the very words which were thought of possess reality and the power to effect the desired results."[16] Our own insensitivity

12. Nelson Glueck, *Hesed in the Bible*, transl. A. Gottschalk (Cincinnati, Ohio: Hebrew Union College Press, 1967).

13. E. A. Speiser, *Anchor Bible Commentary on Genesis* (Garden City, N.Y.: Doubleday, 1964), discussing the sacrifice described in Genesis 15 says: "The contracting parties—so at least in an agreement between equals; otherwise perhaps only the weaker of the two—passed between the sections of the dismembered animals (cf. Jer. 19 ff.) and thus left themselves open, by extension, to the fate of the sacrificed victims in the event of future violation" (p. 112).

14. The necessity of the passion occurs in all the Gospels, for example, the three predictions of the passion and death (Mark 8:31, 9:31, and 10:33–34 and parallels; cf., John 12:23–26.)

15. G. Von Rad, *Genesis*, rev. ed., transl. John Marks, (Philadelphia: Westminster Press, 1961), pp. 276–277.

16. S. H. Blank, "The Curse, Blasphemy, the Spell, and the Oath," *Hebrew Union College Annual* 23 (1950–51), pp. 73–95; the quotation is from p. 78.

to this is egregiously lamentable. For Jesus' teaching to bless, not curse, our enemies and those who maltreat us (cf. the Sermon on the Mount and Luke 6:28 ff.) is a radical break with tradition in the ancient world and with traditions in many parts of the contemporary world. Blank[17] sees the oath as a conditional curse (cf. Jesus' prohibition of oaths in the Sermon on the Mount).

Brichto[18] avers that blessing and cursing are contagious: One blessed can transfer blessing; one cursed is a danger to the whole land. He[19] describes the content of blessing as:

life, vitality, and everything making for them: victory, fertility of land and livestock, numerous progeny, longevity, heroism. The life-force of one man [sic] can be transferred to another, as revealed in the kiss attending Isaac's blessing of his son; . . . The all embracing expression for the content of blessing is *shalom* which means the absence of danger and disability, the presence of tranquility, security, good-fortune and well-being in the highest degree; hence its use in greeting. The content of curse, by contrast, is death, illness, childlessness, miscarriage, drought, pest, disturbance of corpses, and peripeteia: man becoming woman [-like], the free man becoming a slave etc.[20]

(For the Hebrew God as the source of the blessing and of the curse see Deut. 27–28.[21])

A curse might be neutralized by destroying the words (Jer. 36:23), by destroying its source (2 Sam. 16:9), by deception (in 2 Kings 22:11, Josiah tears his garments, symbolically dying so that the curse cannot take effect), or by administering a blessing as an antidote (Judges 17:2, 1 Kings 2:45, 2 Sam. 21:1–3, and Exod. 12:32).

This is one way of looking at Christian soteriology. Jesus neutralizes the curse of our disobedience by his own life, death, and the giving of the Holy Spirit.

Paul has grasped the situation when he proclaims in Galatians 3:10–14:

. . . It is written, "Cursed is he who does not abide by everything written in the book of the law and carry it out. . . ." Christ has delivered us from the power of the law's curse by himself becoming a curse, as it is written, "Accursed is everyone who hangs on a tree." This has happened so that through Christ Jesus the blessing bestowed on Abraham might descend on the Gentiles

17. Ibid., p. 87.
18. Herbert C. Brichto, *The Problem of "Curse" in the Hebrew Bible*, Journal of Biblical Literature Monograph Series, no. 13 (Philadelphia: Society of Biblical Literature and Exegesis, 1963), p. 5.
19. Ibid., p. 6.
20. Ibid., p. 7. See also Delbert R. Hillers, *Treaty-Curses and the Old Testament Prophets* (Rome: Pontifical Biblical Institute, 1964).
21. Brichto, p. 10.

in Christ Jesus, thereby making it possible for us to receive the promised Spirit through faith.

The deutero-Pauline epistles strongly affirm this, e.g., Colossians 2:14: "He (Jesus) cancelled the bond which stood against us with all its claims, snatching it up and nailing it to the cross. Thus did God disarm the principalities and powers."

Paul

Thus for Paul through faith in Jesus we are delivered from the curse of the Law and brought into the blessing of life and *shalom*.

Yet, I have said that the seeds of peace mature slowly. This is true in the case of Paul. Despite his openness towards the Gentiles, at least in his earlier epistles, he is almost inflexible towards sinners. Examples of this are:

1. His condemnation (*in absentia*) of the man living in incest with his mother-in-law (1 Cor. 5:1–5);

2. His shunning sinners (1 Cor. 5:9–13 and 6:9–20);

3. His dualism and elitism of 2 Corinthians 6:14–7:1 (if this is to be attributed to him);

4. His harshness and sarcasm—with verbal violence—towards his opponents (2 Cor. 10–13);

5. His severe confrontation with Peter over the question of table-fellowship (Gal. 2:11–14);

6. And, last, the complex text of Romans 13:1–7, where he appears to accept the use of the sword by civil authorities and the payment of secular taxes by Jews and Christians, some of which monies would certainly support military operations.

We may compare also his bellicose portrayal of Christ in 2 Thessalonians 1:7–10 and 2:8.

What Paul has not learned in his earlier letters is true love of opponents. This is a situation in which we frequently find ourselves, e.g., advocating world peace and yet being ruthless towards our personal foes. But in the case of Paul it is important to remind ourselves continually that the apostle may never have seen or heard the Gospels that are now contained in our New Testament canon.

Acts

We may take a similar view of the Acts of the Apostles, at which we must now glance.

It may be a surprise to realize that Acts imputes (and I say imputes) violence and/or destruction to God, much in the tradition of parts of the Hebrew Scriptures and the Book of Revelation.[22] It is not a question of whether the violent incidents recorded in Acts are historically accurate; rather our concern is to understand how the early Christians in Acts thought of the deity—was there still a trace of the warrior god?

An indication of this is found in the very beginning of Acts, as the following examples show.

1. The gruesome and gory death of Judas is considered a just reward for his mendacity (Acts 1:18–19). Marshall[23] remarks that this does not seem part of Peter's speech, as there is a change of person in v19. Accounts of Judas' death differ in Matthew and Acts, but in Acts it is seen more as an act of God than as suicide. The field bought with the betrayal money is cursed so that no one lives there. Thus the account of the death of Judas in Acts may be the work of a redactor.

2. Ananias and Sapphira (Acts 5:1–11) are hardly given time to realize the precipitous and lethal consequences of their pecuniary concupiscence. Marshall[24] states

It is certainly true that the story introduces us to a different world of thought from that of today. It is a world in which sin is taken seriously, and in which a person convicted of sin against the Spirit might well suffer a fatal shock at the thought of having broken a taboo. . . . More plausible is Derrett's[25] view that a sinner such as Ananias was shown to be [sic] by his divinely inflicted death would have been buried forthwith without ceremony or mourning. The early church accepted the possibility of serious judgments following acts of sin (1 Cor. 5:1–11 and 11:27–32, Jas. 5:14–16), and this is the background to the story.

3. Peter's retort to the avaricious desires of Simon Magus are egregiously irascible: "May you and your money rot with you—thinking that God's gift can be bought! You have no portion or lot in this affair. . . . I see you poisoned with gall and caught in the grip of sin" (Acts 8:20). Peter's reply constitutes a curse both upon Simon and his money. Peter's subsequent admonition that Simon should seek forgiveness, if forgiveness is possible, implies that there is a chance that God

22. In a paper presented at Pittsburgh Theological Seminary this October I read a paper on peace in the Johannine corpus with special reference to the Book of Revelation and the Farewell Discourses in the Gospel of John. This now appears as "*Shalom* in the Johannine Corpus," *Horizons* 6/2 (1984), pp. 67–89. I have also addressed the issues of the malevolent miracles in Acts in a Festschrift for Professor Horton to be edited by Paul Elbert.

23. I. H. Marshall, *The Acts of the Apostles: An Introduction and Commentary* (Grand Rapids, Mich.: W. B. Eerdmans Publishing Co., 1981), p. 64.

24. Ibid., pp. 110–111.

25. Duncan J. Derrett, "Ananias, Sapphira, and the Right of Property," *Downside Review* 89 (1971), 225–232.

will *not* forgive (v22). (With the "gall of bitterness" we may compare Deut. 29:18, Lam. 3:15, and Isa. 58:6.)

4. In the three accounts of the conversion of Paul recorded in Acts a destructive miracle is imputed to the Lord Jesus. Stanley[26] has seen the association of this "curse" with the curse in Deuteronomy that results in blindness at midday (Deut. 28:29).

5. Herod's sudden demise is attributed to a blow from the Angel of the Lord (Acts 12:20–23). Marshall refers to Josephus' *Antiquities* 19:343–350, which appears to refer to the same event. Luke seems to have added that the death was due to the angel of the Lord. Marshall[27] says, "Here the phrase is applied to the ultimate divine origin of a natural disease. . . . The point is that God acts against those who usurp his position. Eaten by worms is a stock phrase for the death of tyrants."

6. A similar fate meets the magician, Bar Jesus or Elymas.[28] When he seeks to impede Paul's mission at the court of Sergius Paulus, he is struck blind (Acts 13:4–12). Paul calls Bar Jesus "son of the devil" (cf. Jer. 5:23, Gen. 32:11, Prov. 10:9, and Hos. 14:10).

7. A more deleterious consequence ensues upon the Jewish exorcists who apparently infringe on the prerogatives of Christians by using the name of Jesus in their ministry (Acts 19:13–19). Marshall[29] remarks:

In a situation where people were gripped by superstition, perhaps the only way for Christianity to spread was by the demonstration that the power of Jesus was superior to that of the demons, even if those who came to believe in Jesus were tempted to think of his power and person in ways that were still conditioned by their primitive categories of thought; it took time for the church to purify its concept of God from pagan ways of thinking, and the tendency to let our ideas of God be influenced by contemporary, and sometimes misleading, trends of philosophical and scientific thinking is one that still confronts the church.

I venture to suggest that in these incidents—not necessarily historically accurate—we have the theology of curse, which is characteristic of much of the Old Testament, especially the Psalms, which were used enthusiastically in its emphasis on retribution. It is a curse for violation of the covenant and the laws arising from the covenant responsibility.

It is only in the light of these texts, cursing the opponent, that we can understand the revolutionary aspect of the nonresistance texts in the New Testament, e.g., the Sermon on the Mount and the Sermon on the Plain.

---

26. David Stanley, "Why Three Accounts?" *Catholic Biblical Quarterly* 15 (1953), 315–338.

27. Marshall, *Acts*, p. 212.

28. Two stories may be fused here. This would explain the use of the two names.

29. Marshall, *Acts*, p. 312.

However, side by side with the curse texts in Acts we find blessing texts, that is, where divine vitality is given, restored, or increased. We find the wheat growing among the tares.

The mission to the Gentiles is, of course, the central theme of Acts. Yet it gains in importance when we see it side by side with the theology of curse. The non-Jews were an accursed race, upon whom no strict Jews expected the Holy Spirit to descend. They were cursed because they were excluded from covenant and *hesed*.

This is radically changed in Acts. The spectacular novelty of the mission gains in importance when we see it side by side with the theology of the curse for in the first century C.E., especially in the light of the Roman oppression, the Gentiles were anathema to most Jews and early Christians.[30]

The most graphic instance of the giving of *hesed* in Acts is the descent of the Holy Spirit on the Jewish Feast of Pentecost. She descends on Jerusalem Jews and Jews from the Diaspora but not upon Gentiles (Acts 2).

The giving of the Spirit is an essential (ontological) source of unity. This fact is emphasized dramatically on the occasion of Pentecost. The event is the reverse of the myth of Babel.[31] The fruits of the Spirit are resplendent in the Christian communities as portrayed in early Acts, which gives a somewhat idealistic picture of early Christians as contrasted with the portrayal in the Pauline epistles where communities are sometimes divisive and acrimonious. Acts presents communities that appear to have no problems in relationship to finance, sex, or leadership, the three primary causes of conflict in communities. But it is important to remark that the early Christian community is *entirely Jewish*.

It is with this in mind that we approach the problem of tablefellowship with non-Jews. When the community was entirely Jewish the question of tablefellowship did not arise. In Acts there are four major issues of tablefellowship, which problem is directly associated with covenant because of the sacredness of the meal in the ancient world. These are:

1. the Samaritans in Acts 8:4–25;
2. the eunuch in Acts 8:26–40;
3. the Jewish uncircumcised proselytes in Acts 10–11:18;
4. the pagan Gentiles from the time of Paul's first mission, whose status is discussed in Acts 15.

30. Although one must concede that the first century B.C.E. and the first century C.E. were periods of avid proselytism among the Jews, especially in the Diaspora and among women.

31. J. D. Davies, "Pentecost and Glossolalia," *Journal of Theological Studies* 3 (1952), 228–231, finds verbal affinity between the Greek translation of the story of the Tower of Babel and the account of the first Pentecost by Luke.

Now all these are discrete problems but what is common to all of them is the eventual sharing of *hesed* and a covenant relationship through baptism, meals, and the Eucharist. These questions are peculiarly pertinent to the last aspect of peace mentioned by the bishops, namely, ". . . a right relationship with God which entails forgiveness, reconciliation and union."[32] They also illustrate dramatically the bishop's statement that: "Peace and war must always be seen in light of God's intervention in human affairs and our response to that intervention. Both are elements within the ongoing revelation of God's will for creation."[33]

It was God who intervened and brought the Ethiopian eunuch[34] and Philip together. It was the persecution of Stephen that scattered the Christians and caused missionary activity among the Samaritans, and it was the Holy Spirit who intervened to make certain that they would be at peace with the Jerusalem Jews.

The Samaritans were not left to become an isolated sect with no bonds of union with the apostolic church in Jerusalem. If a Samaritan church and a Jewish church had arisen independently, side by side, without the dramatic removal of the ancient and bitter barriers of prejudice between the two, particularly at the level of ultimate authority, the young church of God would have been in schism for the inception of its mission. The drama of the Samaritan affair in Acts 8 included among its purposes the vivid and visual dismantling of the wall of enmity between Jew and Samaritan and the preservation of the precious unity of the church of God through the unique divine "interception" and then prompt presentation of the spirit in the presence of the apostles.[35]

It was the intervention of the Holy Spirit falling upon Cornelius' household that signified the ending of separation between Jew and Gentile. Peter's response, and later that of his colleagues in Jerusalem, was highly appropriate, a positive response to the new intervention. God repeated Pentecost for Cornelius' household. It might be noted that Cornelius was a prominent "officer" in the Roman army. Nothing is said of his relinquishing his career after his conversion.

It is in these three incidents, that come to a climactic fruition in Paul and his companions' mission to the Gentiles, that Acts gives us a blue-

---

32. *Challenge of Peace*, n. 27.

33. Ibid., n. 28.

34. Luke may be seeing a fulfillment of Isaiah 56:3–4: "Let not the foreigner say, when he would join himself to the Lord, 'The Lord will surely exclude me from his people.' Nor let the eunuch say, 'See, I am a dry tree.' For thus says the Lord: 'To the eunuchs who observe my sabbaths and choose what pleases me and hold fast to my covenant, I will give, in my house and within my walls, a monument and a name better than sons and daughters; an eternal, imperishable name will I give them.'"

35. F. E. Bruner, *A Theology of the Holy Spirit* (Grand Rapids, Mich.: Eerdmans, 1970), p. 176.

print for accepting novel revelation and creating entirely new forms of bonding with people who were once alien to us.

This is a practical example of the love that is dominant in the Kingdom of God, a love that goes beyond "family ties and bonds of friendship to reach even those who were enemies" (Matt. 5:44–48, Luke 6:27–28). It has been intimated already in the Gentile mission in the Gospel of Mark.

It is with these thoughts in mind that I should like to conclude my paper with some reflections on what one of my graduate students felicitously called the "culinary" Jesus. Jesus' interest in tablefellowship is a highly important part of his ministry, especially to ostracized persons. Jesus is a god of conviviality.

The reader will appreciate that there are nine great meal scenes in Luke's Gospel. Some of these I have discussed in my text *My Enemy Is My Guest*.[36] They are not mere literary devices or elaborations of the symposium motif. They are essential to understanding the theology and praxis of tablefellowship that has already become a vital issue in the early Church. More especially they are pivotal for understanding the Lukan concept of *hesed* in the early Church, of reconciliation, of forgiveness, and of community.

Luke intimates his ideology of tablefellowship and the provocation that it will cause in Jesus' inaugural homily at Nazareth (Luke 4:16–32). Jesus quotes the maxim that a prophet is not without honor except in his own country and follows this with a reference to Elijah and Elisha *who cured, dined, and lodged with Gentiles*. At this point the Nazarene congregation expel Jesus and try to assassinate him by pushing him over a cliff. Dining with the spiritually and socially ostracized was an important aspect of the "favorable year of the Lord" for Jesus.

Meal with tax collectors (Luke 5:27–39)

Thus we are not surprised when we find Jesus taking his first public meal (a great banquet as recorded by Luke) with a large number of tax collectors and others ("sinners" in Matthew and Mark). His host is a tax collector, Levi. His fellow guests are marginal people from the religious point of view who would be drawn from despised occupations and trades. What is happening here is that Jesus is dining with those who "lifted their heels" against his coreligionists, namely, the tax collectors. This increases in importance when we consider that Judas the Galilean stirred up the rebellion in 6 C.E. *precisely* on the point of taxation. Jesus

---

36. See my monograph *My Enemy Is My Guest* (Maryknoll, N.Y.: Orbis Books, 1984), pp. 70–78.

did not rebel against tax collectors but formed a quasi-covenant relationship with them. If we wished to find an analogy today, we could suggest that Jesus' action is equivalent to dining with Godfather 1 and Godfather 2 and their associates in organized crime. But Jesus' action led to conversion—perhaps not only of Levi but of hundreds of others—and also to winning a close disciple, who together with others may have committed his teaching to writing.

A meal in association with a prostitute (Luke 7:36–50 and par.)

The second meal is with a marginal or, rather, ostracized woman. Derrett[37] would suggest that her gift may have involved her colleagues in her occupation. It is important to note that according to Luke, Jesus' host is a Pharisee—in Matthew and Mark it is Simon the leper. Jesus receives a gift that is bought through filthy lucre (ill-gotten gains), he allows impure perfume to enter his body and a woman with flowing hair (the sign of a prostitute) to kiss his feet. What could have been a greater horror to a practicing Pharisee, even a Hillelite! Luke alone of the evangelists adds the parable about forgiveness that depends wholly upon *hesed*. The woman is told that her faith has saved her and to go in *peace*.

The multiplication of loaves (Luke 9:10–17)

This occurs at Bethsaida (v10). There is little to say about this meal save that it is a public one. The crowd is large, 5,000, and yet there is no discrimination against any member of the crowd. I doubt whether a first century orthodox Jew would have kept such company. Mark records a feeding of 4,000 that appears to be in Gentile territory (Mark 8:1–10).

The meal with Martha and Mary (Luke 10:38–42)

This is very important from an ecclesiological point of view. It is a discipleship text. I am attracted to the thesis of Gerhardsson,[38] namely, that Luke is influenced by the Jewish concept of the two lots that fell to people, the lot of the Torah and the lot of manual labor. I am also interested in his parallel (to some extent verbal) with Acts 6:1–6. Both texts involve food and serving but also responsibility for the Torah; in the second text the apostles are seen to have the lot of Torah and the seven men the lot of manual labor. It is interesting that the men serve the

37. Duncan J. Derrett, "The Anointing at Bethany and the Story of Zaccaeus," *Law and the New Testament* (London, England: Darton, Longman, and Todd, 1970), pp. 267–268.

38. Birger Gerhardsson, *Memory and Manuscript: Oral Tradition and Written Transmission in Rabbinic Judaism and Early Christianity*, transl. Eric J. Sharpe (Uppsala: Almqvist and Wiksells, 1961), pp. 234–245.

widows, men serving women. The texts are antidiscriminatory on two levels, the feminist and racial (Hellenistic widows are involved).

Meal with a Pharisee (Luke 11:37–54)

Jesus takes a meal with a Pharisee who is surprised that Jesus does not wash before the meal. Jesus criticizes the Pharisees (Shammaites) for cleansing vessels but not giving alms and also for tithing small produce and taking front seats in synagogue. He also reprimands the lawyers who place heavy burdens on people and who murder the prophets. This meal is important for its teaching against class distinction and purity laws that burdened the poor.

Humility and inclusiveness in meals (Luke 14:1–24)

Here again Jesus is dining with a Pharisee.[39] Luke describes this individual as one of the leading Pharisees. Jesus interrupts the meal to cure a man with edema on the Sabbath, thus provoking comments. What has this pericope to tell us about healing, forgiveness, reconciliation, and inclusiveness? First, physical health is given precedence to keeping human tradition about the Sabbath, even though the condition is not life threatening. Second, Luke places in the mouth of Jesus a parable that appears to be related because it speaks about meals but does not appear to be directly connected to the healing of the man with edema. However, the parable is addressed to the guests. It concerns taking the lower seats at a banquet although the motive for so doing is not of the highest. Third, Jesus addresses counsel to his host, the leading Pharisee. He advises him not to invite to his table his relatives, friends, and opulent neighbours but, rather, marginal people, beggars, handicapped, lame, and blind. Jesus strengthens his teaching by the parable of the great Supper to which not only these marginal people but also those from the highways and from the hedgerows (symbolically, the Gentiles) are invited.

This is a very important, indeed, arresting teaching on tablefellowship; the Gospel goes further than Acts. It illustrates a "love which goes beyond family ties and bonds of friendship to reach even those who" are outcast. The inclusion of the handicapped is diametrically contrary to the teaching from Qumran:

And let no person smitten with any human impurity whatsoever enter the Assembly of God. And every person smitten with these impurities . . . and every (person) smitten in his flesh, paralyzed in his feet or hands, lame or blind or deaf or smitten in his flesh with a blemish visible to the eye, or any aged

---

39. Cf. Eli Springs Steele, "Tablefellowship in Luke," unpublished doctoral dissertation (South Bend, Ind.: Notre Dame University, 1980).

person that totters and is unable to stand firm in the midst of the Congregation; let these persons not en[ter] to take their place in the midst of the Congregation of men of renown. . . .[40]

Meal with Zacchaeus (Luke 19:1–10)

Here Jesus invites himself to the table of a chief tax collector. This narrative brings to a climax many Lukan themes. It ends with a Son of Humanity pronouncement, "The Son of Man has come to search out and save what is lost." This statement is the epitome of those who keep *hesed* and work for the things that make for peace.

The Passover (Luke 22:14–38)

This is the meal par excellence where Jesus gives hospitality to his enemy, his betrayer Judas, although Luke does not record the giving of the morsel. Quesnell[41] has argued convincingly for the presence of women at the Passover. The meal is definitely a covenant meal.

Thus the meal texts in Luke illustrate Jesus' ministry of peace, in which he expected his disciples of his and future generations to follow. It is a peace that builds up an individual's sense of well-being, which ministers forgiveness, reconciliation, and union. It is a peace that is extended to people in seven important social arenas:

1. With criminals and those belonging to despised trades;
2. With street girls;
3. With a large crowd of people from diverse ways of life;
4. With a woman disciple, or implicitly, a woman apostle;
5. The advocacy of meals with the sick, handicapped, and economically underprivileged;
6. A meal with abundantly affluent business and/or government officials; and
7. A meal with a treacherous disciple who was responsible for one's own torture and capital punishment.

Conclusion

In conclusion I should say that as a complement to the section on peace in Scripture in the bishops' pastoral, *The Challenge to Peace*, we should emphasize more strongly the gradual growth of the concept of

---

40. 1 *QSa.* 2:10, translation in Andre Dupont Sommer, *The Essene Writings from Qumran*, transl. G. Vermes (Cleveland, Ohio: World Publishing Co., 1961), pp. 107–108.

41. Quentin Quesnell, "Women at Luke's Supper," in R. Cassidy and P. Scharper, eds., *Luke and Political Issues* (Maryknoll, N.Y.: Orbis Press, 1983), pp. 59–79.

non-violence within the Christian communities and also recognize the following points:

The choice between nonviolence and war was a live option in the first century C.E. when the New Testament was being written;

All the books in the New Testament do not advocate peace to the same degree;

There is a pacifist element running throughout the Hebrew Scriptures and Judaism;

The concept of *hesed* (*chesed*) deserves further study with respect to the peace issue;

The Jewish people and Christians are called to fullfill the promise made to Abraham and to bring blessing (divine vitality) to all nations;

The example of the apostle Paul should encourage us to see the gradual growth of *hesed* in ourselves and in our neighbors;

The Acts of the Apostles, where we see the consequence of both blessing and cursing, may furnish us with a blueprint for the pursuit of peace;

Tablefellowship is a priority when we wish to be bonded together in peace, especially in respect of erstwhile enemies.

Finally, I should like to end with two quotations from Pedersen.

Close to sin lies the *curse*. . . . The sinner is charged with the curse, for the curse is the dissolution which takes place in the soul of the sinner. It is as a poisonous, consuming substance that destroys and undermines, so that the soul falls to pieces and its strength is exhausted. This poisonous consuming substance which spreads about is in Hebrew called 'ala. It consumes the earth, which loses its power of germination; the plants fade, towns collapse, the inhabitants wail and disappear from the surface of the earth (Is. 24, 6–12), the whole country decays, all pastures are dried up. . . .

The whole of this concept of life (of righteousness and peace) presupposes the harmony supplied by the covenant, in that all its members support each other and uphold the community with their blessing. . . . But the harmony must go so deep that it includes the underlying forces of existence. Behind the community stands its god in whom the covenant rests. He is with the righteous and lays the blessing into him. On his justice the Israelite bases his confidence in the subsistence of the harmony, in the development of every man [sic] to the measure for which he [she] is qualified. The strength of the members of the same covenant and of the god of the covenant is the man's soul when he acts; if they fail his energy of action is gone. But they cannot fail as long as the man is righteous; that would be contrary to the very laws of life.[42]

42. Johannes Pederson, *Israel: Its Life and Culture* (Oxford: Oxford University Press, 1964, reprint ed.), Vol. 2, p. 437; p. 362.

JOHN HELGELAND

3. The Early Church and War: The Sociology of Idolatry

They found comfort for death in murder.
—Tertullian, *On the Shows*, 12.

The topic of the relationship between the early Church and the Roman military has itself been somewhat of a battleground. In this
struggle the contestants have fallen into two camps; on the one hand we
have representatives of the European state churches—Lutheran and Roman Catholic—and on the other there are the heirs of protest communities that grew up after the Reformation. To a considerable extent, in
the documents from the first three centuries, both groups saw reflections
of their own teachings on war and military service.

Recently, however, two diverse developments have pureed the historic configurations and have brought about many fresh insights. First,
the threat of nuclear annihilation has introduced into global culture the
sardonic commonality that we may all perish together. Accordingly, the
impact of this awareness has dwarfed the significance of the pacifist-
state Church styles of interpreting the ancient texts. Second, there is the
rapid growth of the field of religious studies, a field supposedly dog-
matically disinterested in the ascendency of one religious community
over another. Religious studies has the object of looking at many kinds
of religious experience in the context of social, psychological, economic, and other fabrics. Gone are the days when a historian could be
content with merely expositing the thoughts of the great writers of the
Church and then claiming that the picture was in focus.

It is the pacifist perspective that is, for various reasons, the most
troublesome. Largely the creation of two persons, C. J. Cadoux and
Roland Bainton,[1] this interpretation has a host of lesser lights who followed them like the dogs that followed the wagon trains across the prai-

1. C. J. Cadoux, *The Early Christian Attitude to War* (London 1919, reprinted, New
York: The Seabury Press, 1980). Ronald Bainton, *Christian Attitudes Toward War and
Peace* (Nashville, Tenn.: Abingdon Press, 1962). For further documentation and argu-
ment in support of this paper, see Helgeland, "Christians and the Roman Army From

34

rie. Many of these followers satisfied themselves with mining Cadoux and Bainton as though they were primary sources. Historiographically speaking, the problem with the pacifist perspective, as well as with most other Church historians who worked on this subject, was that they quoted the Fathers out of context and cared to learn only a few aspects of the Roman military system. They passed quickly over the subject of the religion and the religious policies of the Roman army. Consequently, the Fathers' objection that the Roman army was idolatrous receives scant treatment, suggesting that it was merely a religious anachronism. There is a ticklish problem, too, of what is meant by the term pacifism.

Nobody has accused the early Christians of being warmongers. The fact that many of the Church Fathers detested war and its aftermath proves nothing. Many great generals, with the egregious exception of George Patton, have abhorred the destruction of war yet energetically pursued it when ordered to do so. General William Sherman said, "War is hell." And if this recollection is correct, no Church Father condemned the empire's wars categorically. But this is not to say that war went without criticism; in some writers there was a great deal of it. They were, however, acutely aware of the danger posed by peoples outside the empire and would, as did Tertullian and Origen, pray for victorious armies. We must remember, too, that the empire ceased to expand early in the second century; Rome's wars from then on were defensive.

Many have debated whether the early Church had a policy of prohibiting Christians from enlisting in the army. Answering this question is more complex than it might seem at the outset. Only three Fathers of the pre-Constantinian Church had anything to say on this subject—Tertullian, Origen, and Hippolytus. None of these writers can claim to represent anyone beyond themselves. All were on the borders of the Church and sometimes beyond it. Further perspective comes with the observation that, of the more than 5,000 pages of the series *The Ante Nicene Fathers*, 20 pages would easily contain the statements of these three that relate to specific evils of Christians in the service. It is clear, therefore, that any claim that there was a general policy of pacifism during the first three centuries is vastly overstated.

Pacifist theologians have argued from silence that the lack of statements on this subject indicate that the Church took for granted that its members would not enlist.[2] The army, as they saw it, was forever fighting fierce battles, and no Christian would ever be involved with this violence. That was because the Gospel stories of Jesus' nonviolent conduct reverberated so loudly that no Christian would be so faithless as to

Marcus Aurelius to Constantine," *Aufstieg und Niedergang der Römischen Welt* (Berlin, 1979), II, 23, 1, pp. 724–834. (hereafter *ANRW*).

2. Bainton, pp. 67–68.

enlist in that fighting machine. Even if we ignore the fact that many soldiers could spend their 20 years in the army without ever striking a blow outside a tavern, as Ramsay MacMullen put it, there are other considerations.[3]

There are, for instance, the Apocryphal Gospels, which convey the impression that Jesus was full of revenge.[4] He killed playmates who irritated him. And every student must have had the fantasy of killing an oppressive teacher as did the schoolboy Jesus. It is doubtful that these were stories included in this literature to counteract any pacifist leanings of the Church. Rather they glory in the super-Jesus, the divine kid who performed many amazing feats, some of which were violent. Naturally, historians of dogma have passed over stories about the Jesus who made clay sparrows and then had them fly; we can agree that such tales are vulgar and play to the most primitive of emotions. And they certainly reflect the love for violence in Roman society. But historians trained in the social sciences will see more there. These stories, first of all, enjoyed riding the crest of waves of oral tradition; some of the violent stories are to be found in several sources, for example. And second, it can be argued with some confidence that we are dealing with an uneducated stratum of the population that would be the most likely candidates for enlistment. Unless one wants to raise from the dead that quest for the "essence" of Christianity, it will not do to pass these people off as not quite Christian. Or as one pacifist historian suggests, there are two grades of Christian conduct, one for clergy and one for the laity. Once again, the interpreter takes his material out of context.[5] That is, Eusebius, from whom he quotes, meant the distinction between clergy and laity to be ontological rather than ethical or moral.

Yet another consideration is the sociological situation of Jesus and his immediate followers. They were, as Gerd Theissen put it, wandering charismatics. Characteristic of such movements is an almost stateless existence wherein the members travel from place to place without giving any thought to violence and little to self-defense. Their very security is the consequence of their refusal to return insult for insult. As Theissen argued it, their refusal to retaliate was a strategy to use the attacker's guilt against himself.[6] Wanderers, in addition, have no homes or property to defend. In retrospect, this segment of the Church's initial history was relatively short and concluded with the disappearance of Palestinian

3. Ramsay MacMullen, *Soldier and Civilian in the Later Roman Empire* (Cambridge, Mass.: Harvard University Press, 1967).

4. *Infancy Gospel of Thomas*, 3, 4, and 11.

5. Bainton, p. 84.

6. Gerd Theissen, *Sociology of Early Palestinian Christianity*, transl. John Bowdon (Philadelphia: Fortress Press, 1977), pp. 103–108.

Christianity. New sociological configurations of later years brought forth a whole new complex of relationships as the Church began to merge into the bloodstream of the Roman empire.

While many have taken the early Church experience as normative for their own times, the assumption that the early Church is to be a model for our own time presents enormous problems for those who take history seriously. What we have already discussed and what continuing research brings to light discloses a checkerboard of belief and practice. Which square shall be our model? And how can we furnish warrants for such a selection? But some will still try. This is how Cadoux did it 60 years ago.

But over against all this we have to set the facts that the first three centuries were the period in which the work of the Church in morally and spiritually regenerating human life was done with an energy and a success that have never since been equalled, where the power springing from her Founder's personal life pulsated with more vigor and intensity than was possible at a greater distance when incipient decay was held in check by repeated purification in the fires of persecution, and when the Church's vision has not been distorted or her conscience dulled by compromises with the world.[7]

It is difficult to see how one could write something like this even 60 years ago. Nonetheless, we must strike out in different directions. The early Church can teach us valuable insights even if we cannot copy its model directly.

Since the preceding views of the relationship between the Church and the military have proved unsatisfactory or incomplete, we now turn our attention to sketching out the outlines of our view of it. We begin first with the topic of military analogies.

Military Analogies

Around the turn of the century, Adolf Harnack was the first historian to devote attention to a series of metaphors that began in the New Testament and continues to the present day.[8] While one may find these analogies sprinkled throughout the New Testament, with the exception of the Gospels, none is so striking as the one from Ephesians 6:10–17. Here one is encouraged to put on the whole armor of God to fight the devil. In this extended metaphor the military belt is likened to truth, the breastplate is righteousness, the boot is the Gospel of peace, the shield is faith, the sword is the spirit, and the helmet is salvation. In opposition Satan fires flaming darts. Echoes of this analogy appear in other New

7. Cadoux, p. 3.
8. *Militia Christi*, transl. D. M. Gracie (Philadelphia: Fortress Press, 1981), pp. 27–64.

Testament literature. There are, for example, other expressions in 2 Corinthians: "weapons of righteousness" (6:7) and "not carrying on a
worldly war, for the weapons of our warfare are not worldly but have
divine power to destroy strongholds" (10:3–5). In all the military analogies from the New Testament we find no exhortation to actual violence; rather, the emphasis is intended to conceptualize spiritual warfare. All these metaphors are written to give structure and insight to the
individual Christian in his or her private expressions of faith.

It is Clement of Rome who first applied these analogies to internal
relationships in the Church. Here we find an exhortation to Church
members to obey their superiors in the Church as soldiers are expected
to obey their commanders (I Cor. 37). Clement gave us this metaphor
as a means of arguing that there was a structure of relative importance
in the Church as in the army. Shortly after we find Ignatius of Antioch
arguing for the monarchical episcopate. In his *Letter to Polycarp* (6:2)
he asserted that Christians must obey the bishop as soldiers are responsible to their commanders. Owing to his experience of being transported
across the empire at the hands of a detachment of Roman soldiers, he
added that heretics were *deserters*, and he transliterated the Latin *de-
sertor* into Greek.

Tertullian and Cyprian extended the use of military analogies to cover
the relationships between the Church and the world outside. For these
writers the Church has become the camp, persecutions are battles, the
battleground is the world, and the devil commands the opposing army.
In addition to suffering as martyrs, Christians fight the spiritual battle
by avoiding vices such as avarice, ambition, drunkenness, envy, pride,
and the lure of the world. Cyprian described the *lapsi*, those who betrayed the Church during the persecution of Decius in 250, as rebels
who had deserted the camp.[9]

To be sure, military metaphors were not the only models the Church
Fathers used. Also popular were those taken from agriculture, meteor-
ology, navigation, the athletic field, and the arena. But the military ones
appear to be the most prominent. Harnack pointed out that these metaphors not only had a vital part to play in communicating the faith but
also actually became a model for Church life: The Church actually became an army of Christ.

Yet war is one of the basic forms of all life, and there are inalienable virtues
which find their highest expression at least in the warrior's calling: obedience
and courage, loyalty unto death, self-abnegation and strength. No higher religion can do without the images which are taken from war, and on this account
it cannot dispense with "warriors."[10]

9. Cyprian *Epistles*, 10, 1; 13, 2; 25, 1; 28, 2; 57, 4–5; 58, 3; 72, 2. *On the Exhortation to Martyrdom* 10 and 13.
10. Harnack, pp. 27–28.

Harnack went on to say that the metaphorical *Militia Christi* of the early Church went on to become the armies of the Crusades nearly a millenium later, so powerful was its logic. What he passed over was the manner in which this logic functioned during the first three centuries.

To understand the place of these metaphors in a larger context it is necessary for the time being to leave this line of thought suspended. We turn next to the thought of the Church Fathers.

The Church Fathers and the Roman Military System

Of the short list of early Church writers who criticized Christians for enlisting in the Roman army, Tertullian had the most to say. His statements, always rigorous, must themselves be divided into two periods—that of the *Apology* dated about 197 and the treatise *On the Military Crown* of somewhat later date and regarded by many to be from approximately the time he became a Montanist. These two documents are points on a line tending toward increasing suspicion of Roman culture if not downright hostility to it.

First, then, the *Apology* takes up a defense against the accusation that the Christian community was disloyal to the empire. The Roman antagonist of the Christians, Celsus, had made that precise charge a generation earlier; part of his grounds for his statement was that Christians would not take part in the defense of the empire. Tertullian never mentioned Celsus, but the *Apology* could easily serve as a refutation of his complaint. In an often-quoted passage, Tertullian claimed exactly the contrary: "Without ceasing, for all our emperors we offer prayer. We pray for life prolonged; for security to the empire, for protection to the imperial house; for brave armies, a faithful senate; a virtuous people; the world at rest, whatever, as man or Caesar an emperor would wish."[11] Tertullian's support of the empire was tempered with criticism, saying that it was a shame that Rome had grown great as a consequence of war and its aftermath. Nevertheless, he was proud that the Christians were everywhere supporting the empire, including the army. A case in point was the Thundering Legion, which, the story goes, was composed of Christians and was responsible for the victory over the Quadi on the Danubian frontier. These Christians prayed for rain at a time when the army was surrounded and cut off from its water supply. The rain came in time and in the form of a thunderstorm, which both refreshed the Roman soldiers and blasted the enemy with lightning bolts. Interestingly enough, the story was fact, as the Column of Marcus Aurelius in

---

11. *Apology* 30, 4. "We have filled every place among you—cities, islands, fortresses, towns, market-places, the very camp, tribes, companies, palace, senate, forum—we have left nothing to you but the temples of your gods." 37,4.

Rome indicates even today.[12] Tertullian reported this story with pride and without any criticism of the Christians enlisted in it.

Fourteen years or so later, Tertullian wrote three synoptic treatises: *On Idolatry*, *On the Shows*, and *On the Military Crown*. Their focus is idolatry. It is clear that here he is writing for the sake of the Church and not the empire. It is interesting to us today that the chief sin of mankind, in Tertullian's mind, is idolatry. "The principal crime of the human race, the highest guilt charged upon the world, the whole procuring cause of judgment, is idolatry."[13] His view is far more sophisticated than merely the practice of worshiping wooden or stone gods: ". . . for idolatry is more easily carried on without the idol."[14] Accordingly, he gave a list of what he considered idolatrous: worship of non-Christian deities, astrology, magic, reading and teaching classical literature, the gladiatorial shows, holidays, the toga, military service, taking oaths, contracts under an oath to some deity, and so on. In a word, idolatry was Roman culture.

The treatise *On the Military Crown* (*De corona militis*) is the only work before the time of Constantine devoted solely to the topic of the military. It continues the criticism of idolatry by showing the dimensions of that sin in the military. The occasion for the treatise was the martyrdom of a Christian soldier who refused to wear his military crown while being given a donative. Along with him were other Christian soldiers who complied with military custom and wore their crowns and presumably escaped martyrdom. From this short introductory chapter, Tertullian discussed how idolatrous were crowns in all areas of Roman society, only to return, in the last few chapters, to the specifics of the army life. He mentioned killing just in passing. The sense of the whole treatise is to show how the army was completely infected with idolatry and how it is idolatry that causes, among other things, killing. The crown, of course, but also military uniforms, flags, trumpets, camp regulations, and guarding Roman sanctuaries are the effects and symbols of the idolatrous army life. At the end of his treatise he furnished us with the only extant literary description of the Mithraic initiation rites. Although Mithraism was not an official part of army religion, Tertullian made no such distinction; probably he knew from experience its close association to military life. Referring to the subterranean chambers in which Mithraism was practiced, Tertullian coined the dichotomy— camp of light (the Church) and camp of darkness. By association, the whole of army life became a camp of darkness.

The other Church Father who dealt, in more than a passing way, with

12. *Apology*, 5, 6, and *Ad Scapulam* 4, 6.
13. *On Idolatry* 1, 1.
14. Ibid., 11.

the topic of enlistment was Origen. Because he quoted Celsus as he refuted him we know something of Celsus' arguments against Christians. Celsus said that Christians would destroy the empire if all people were to follow their example of refusing enlistment. Just why they refused is never explained. Like Tertullian, Origen argued that Christians were loyal to the empire because they prayed for the victories for the armies.

And like Tertullian, he explained his position in terms of religious symbolism—the demons. It was the demons who were responsible for all war and strife. The whole Christian life is a battle against them. He said:

We do not, then, deny that there are many demons upon the earth, but we maintain that they exist and exercise power among the wicked, as a punishment of their wickedness. But they have no power over those who "have put on the whole armor of God," who have received strength to "withstand the wiles of the devil" and who are ever engaged in contests with him, knowing that "we wrestle not against flesh and blood, but against principalities, against powers, against the rulers of the darkness of this world," against spiritual wickedness in high places.[15]

Origen believed that, if the demons were defeated, the peace of God would be restored to the world. One must understand that Origen was a serious Platonist: Christian battles are allegorical and not against only flesh and blood. In this perspective, he believed that the battles recounted in the Old Testament were both real battles, in our sense of "real," and spiritually significant as well. Since God, like a true Platonist, was leading people from the material to the ideal, so too the Judeo-Christian tradition was a line of succession from the literal and material toward the allegorical and the ideal. So when the Israelites conquered the land of Canaan, the Christian reader should understand that one's purpose, in a spiritual sense, is to overcome the world. In this way, too, he intended to quiet Roman fears of a Christian insurrection: Christians were fighting battles against demons, not emperors.

Origen objected to Christians enlisting. His grounds were that Roman priests never served in the army because their role was to offer sacrifices for victory. Christians, he thought, should be in a similar category. Not only do they pray for victory, but their prayers are more effective than adding more soldiers to the army. And, as we have seen, Christians work toward the ending of war by removing its cause—the demons. The implication is that, if the world were to become Christian, there would be no more war. Origen laid down one condition for the emperors to receive the support of Christian prayers: They must fight for a righ-

15. *Contra Celsum* VIII, 34.

teous cause in a righteous manner. Then those who are in opposition will be destroyed. We have here the just-war theory *in semino*. Unfortunately, Origen never put any flesh and blood on the bones to tell what he meant by "righteous" in connection with war.

Like Tertullian's, Origen's objection to Christians enlisting in the army is based on religious grounds, that is, to the extent one can separate ethics from religion. Though he did not use the term nearly as frequently as Tertullian, one might be confident that they would have agreed substantially on the reason for Christians to stay out of the service.

Probably we can count Hippolytus in as well. He too was a rigorist and on the edge of his ecclesiastical community if not beyond. Only in the *Apostolic Tradition* did Hippolytus have anything to say on the subject of enlistment. The context where the particular canons discussing the military appear is a list of occupations and activities that Hippolytus regarded as either idolatrous or personally immoral. Catechumens may not come from any of these walks of life: keeping harlots, being a sculptor or painter of idols, being an actor in the theater, teaching children worldly knowledge, being a charioteer in the games, being a gladiator or a trainer of gladiators, being a priest or a keeper of idols. Then came three canons on the military followed by prohibitions against being a harlot, speaking about defiled things, being a magician, an astrologer, an interpreter of dreams, or a maker of amulets. With the exception of being a pimp all the rest involve some idolatrous activity.

The three military canons are:

17. A soldier who is in authority must be told not to execute men; if he should be ordered to do it, he shall not do it. He must be told not to take the military oath. If he will not agree, let him be rejected.
18. A military governor or a magistrate of a city who wears the purple (toga), either let him desist or let him be rejected.
19. If a catechumen or a baptised Christian wishes to become a soldier, let him be cast out. For he has despised God.[16]

There is, interestingly enough, not one word here referring to Christians in combat. The context, with the exception of the reference to execution, refers to cultural distinctions between Church life and Roman customs. Execution could take place anywhere, but primarily this is more a civil than a military action. Given his references to the games we could conjecture that it means to kill in the arena where a great deal of executions took place and where soldiers were called upon to be in attendance. The only significant feature of army religion here is the oath

16. Gregory Dix, ed. H. Chadwick, *The Treatise on the Apostolic Tradition of St. Hippolytus of Rome* (London: Society for Promoting Christian Knowledge, 1968).

of military allegiance required of every soldier to be recited several times annually.

Two minor writers join the discussion at this point—Minucius Felix and Arnobius. Minucius criticized the fears of the Romans for destroying, of all things, the religions and temples of other peoples. Presumably he had in mind the destruction of the temple in the war against the Jews. We cannot tell if he read Tertullian, but his criticism of features of Roman army religion are *déjà vu*. Arnobius censured the warlike character of Roman deities, Mars in particular. He gave several lists of the various calamities that arose from war, all the killing and destruction. Mars is an ineffective deity because, contrary to Roman views, he could not control war. Arnobius did not list any specific problems Christians had with war and the army, but rather criticized the military mentality that infected Roman religion generally. On those grounds he evaluated Roman religion as false.

It is in Lactantius that we find disgust with killing most graphically stated. To understand him it is necessary to divide his career into periods reflecting his thought before and after Constantine's accession to power. The *Divine Institutes* from early in his life opposes violence and killing in any form. He despised the doublemindedness of Roman culture, which could look at the killing of a single man as a contaminated and wicked act, but celebrate a general who "has inundated the plains with blood." Where he became explicit about connecting killing with warfare is, interestingly enough, in a chapter devoted to the undesirability of the gladiatorial shows. In this he parallels Tertullian. Anyone who watches the killing of a man is sprinkled with blood just the same as if he had made the sword thrust, even if it is the killing of one justly condemned to die in the arena. One's mind becomes contaminated by it; it pollutes the conscience.[17]

Lactantius' later career took a striking turn. In his *On the Deaths of the Persecutors* we find the rhetoric dripping with revenge toward all who have persecuted the Church. He recounted with relish the demise of emperors who were leaders against the Christians—Nero, Domitian, Decius, Valerian, Galerius, and Maximin Daia. Decius, for example, met death at the hands of barbarians, "nor could he be honored with the rites of burial, but, stripped and naked, he lay to be devoured by wild beasts and birds—a fit end for the enemy of God." Violence directed against the enemies of the Church apparently belonged in a special category.

At this point we have covered almost all the explicit comments on the relationship between the early Church and the Roman military. It is nec-

17. *Divine Institutes* VI, 20.

essary to put these comments in the context of Roman life. First, the religion of the army.

Roman Army Religion

About 15 years ago Robert Bellah began the now famous discussion of American civil religion. Every nation has a civil religion of some sort. Less well known, however, is that every army has a military religion. Many will say that it is not a religion but a pastiche of rituals, traditions, and stories, or, in other words, a religion. Among the many functions of military religion is to connect the army religion to the civil religion; certainly, that is the case both for the United States and for Rome. It is impossible to give here much of the rich detail of the religion of the Roman army but we can give enough of it to demonstrate that, for those in the army, it was a religious system that comprehended nearly every facet of the soldiers' life in the service.[18]

Upon induction the soldier first took the military oath, the *sacramentum*. In it, the soldier gave his pledge that he would never desert and that he would honor the emperor as the highest authority. Not only was the oath recited on induction, it was repeated several times a year and always on January 3, the army's new year. This was the *sacramentum* to which Tertullian objected.

The Roman army is famous for its standards, replicas of which can be seen in the photos of the Nazi Nuremberg party rallies of the 1930's. It was the eagle that is most remembered, the standard of the legion. The Romans thought of it as receiving the divine power, *numen*, from the emperor and which gave the spirit for victory and well-being. On the march, this standard sanctified the space around the legion. There were standards of lesser importance, for example, the *vexillum*, which was the standard for a cohort.

In the camp, the Romans housed the standards in the *aediculum* next to the *praetorium*, the commander's headquarters. This complex was the sacred center of the camp and a symbolic replica of the Capitoline hill in Rome, the seat of the Roman government. Accordingly, the camp itself was Rome in symbol; the walls around the camp were sacred as were those around Rome itself. Inside the camp every soldier had his own special place, one he shared in common with seven other men in a *contubernium*; hence the army camp was a fact of sacred space.

It was also a fact of sacred time. Every year the authorities sent out from Rome a *feriale*, a calendar of sacred days; it specified what festi-

---

18. For further detail see Helgeland, "Roman Army Religion," *ANRW* II, 16, 2 (Berlin, 1978), pp. 1470–1505.

vals were to be celebrated, the nature of the celebration, whether it called for sacrificing a bull or simply burning a pinch of incense. In the 1930's the Yale expedition to Dura Europos dug up one of these calendars, and from it we learn that there were approximately 43 celebrations of various sorts during a Roman liturgical year, in this case the year A.D. 226. Since this document was mailed to every encampment, we can see that it meant to bind together the various army posts in a sacred synchronicity no matter where the post might have been. We can see too that many of the festivals specified in the document were civil ones, much like our Thanksgiving or Fourth of July, and some of them went way back into Republican times, a fact illustrating the conservatism and traditionalism of the Roman army.

We could go on to describe the religious symbolism of the uniform or of certain other rituals.[19] For our purposes, however, it is enough to jump to the conclusion that the religion of the army was a thoroughgoing system that created, in the words of Erving Goffman, a total institution.

Total Institutions

Goffman's well-known work *Asylums* explored the social institutions that comprehended the totality of a person's life—mental institutions, prisons, monasteries, and armies.[20] In each case the object was to mold the individual to conform to the institution; one might say there was in each of them a crusade against individuality. In the end, a good inmate (or patient, or soldier) was one whose identity was the institution's identity and whose personal goals belonged to it as well. Uniforms, walls, isolation, rituals, public demonstrations—all did their part in shaping the consciousness of the inmate.

Certainly this was the Roman army. The army was considered idolatrous and demonic because it was a total institution bound together by an entirely different consciousness from that in the Church. As a matter of fact, soldiers could worship in their own way so long as it did not

---

19. It is significant to point out that, in every martyrdom of a soldier, the conflict bringing about the soldier's execution was some transgression of Roman religious policy. One never finds any soldier being disciplined for a refusal to kill in combat or in a police action. This observation holds true even for accounts of martyrdoms that are partly or completely fabricated. A convenient place to look is in Herbert Musurillo, *The Acts of the Christian Martyrs* (Oxford: Oxford University Press, 1972), in particular, Marinus (pp. 240–243), Marcellus (pp. 250–259), Maximilian (pp. 244–249), Julius the Veteran (pp. 260–265), and Dasius (pp. 272–279). For the description and location of doubtfully accurate accounts, see the appendix in Helgeland, "Christians and the Roman Army."

20. Erving Goffman, *Asylums: Essays on the Social Situation of Mental Patients and Other Inmates* (Garden City, N.Y.: Anchor Books, 1961), pp. 1–121.

preclude the rites and duties that were a regular feature of army life. But since part of Church life was meeting with the Christian community, at least for eucharistic services, services a Christian soldier could not expect to attend except when his leave fell at a convenient time, a certain tension was inherent between the Roman military and Christianity.

The logic of the military metaphor moved the Church toward becoming a total institution of its own. As a minority group in the empire the Church had to be careful for its own boundaries lest it find itself compromised by a culture oriented in radically different directions. Once the logic of the military metaphor had come to maturity it presented problems for the minority Church. The army had a sacrament; so did the Church; both also had camps and battles. In Tertullian's writing we have a glimpse of a Church descending into a battle of symbols with the army. The danger the army presented was "demonic plagiarism" where a common shared symbol could be the corridor out of one religion into another.[21] It was a problem for other early Christian writers such as Justin Martyr, who complained that the demons were busy imitating the faith in order to cause confusion. Idolatry was the word for the potential disintegration of the Christian group identity, and it was the symbol of the infiltration of the Church with concepts and symbols from the army similar to those in the "army of Christ" analogy. These Christians were confused at the similarities and identities in symbolism. What then were the Christians afraid of getting involved with?

Death Culture

Even though the armies of Rome probably never surpassed a half million men at any one time, we are probably correct in calling it a "garrison state," as Harold Lasswell meant the term, a world in which the warrior was a "star." "The distinctive frame of reference in a fighting society is fighting effectiveness."[22] Rome with its emphasis on discipline and violence fits this description precisely. Violence had penetrated to every crevice of the Roman world. But how?

Keith Hopkins in a recent essay on the gladiatorial shows provides us a view of how the violence generated in defending the borders of the empire was brought to the heart of most of Rome's major cities.[23] Ever

21. Jonathan Z. Smith, "Demonic Powers in Antiquity," *ANRW* II, 16, 1 (Berlin, 1978), pp. 425–439; pp. 428–429.

22. Harold Lasswell, "The Garrison State," in *War: Studies from Psychology, Sociology, Anthropology*, eds. Leon Bramson and George Goethals (New York: Basic Books, 1968), pp. 317–328; p. 319.

23. Keith Hopkins, *Death and Renewal: Sociological Studies in Roman History* (Cambridge: Cambridge University Press, 1983), pp. 1–30.

since Republican times, the gladiatorial shows had been the major form of public entertainment. Violence had taken the popular form of a pastime and became so seductive that even nobles and children would imitate particularly effective gladiators. The scale of it is impressive: 600 died in the games Julius Caesar gave to honor his father's death. Executions took place in the arena; we have several authentic accounts of Christians dying there: for example, the acts of *Perpetua and Felicitas* and the account Eusebius gives in his *Church History* about the persecution in Lyons-Vienne under Marcus Aurelius in the year 177.[24]

Particularly in peacetime the games were vehicles for maintaining military skill. Soldiers fought in them and were there also to keep the condemned from escaping. These "little wars" gave the populace a model to emulate. The games frequently featured Mars, the god of war. The religion of the Roman army followed the soldiers everywhere they went; the Roman clergy had front-line seats and cheered the contestants on, sometimes demanding that a gladiator at bay be killed.

It is a small wonder, then, that so many Church Fathers should have criticized Christian involvement with the military and condemned the games in the same breath. Tertullian, Lactantius, and Hippolytus, we remember, all made these connections. This is an explanation of why we find an objection to the idolatrous nature of the Roman army on the one hand and not one explicit comment, on the other, about having to kill in the defense of the empire. While admitting the legitimate necessity of defense, these writers objected strenuously to the "death culture" in which death and violence were regarded as the path to a strong, viable society. In this respect, we see Origen as speaking metaphorically when he saw the demons as the cause of strife. He was searching for a new road to a society built on something other than brutality, discipline, and death. So when the Church replaced the demons everywhere, the need for war would cease.

The problem for the Church, insofar as these writers spoke for it, was not defense. It was, as William James put it, "militaristic sentiment" that was truly idolatrous.

24. For the *Acts of Perpetua and Felicitas*, see Musurillo, pp. 106–131. For the persecution in Lyons-Vienne, see Eusebius, *Ecclesiastical History* V, 1.3–2.8, or Musurillo, pp. 62–85.

LOUIS J. SWIFT

4. Search the Scriptures: Patristic Exegesis and the *Ius Belli*

Given all the complexities of modern war and diplomacy, one is increasingly tempted to relegate early Christian statements about armed conflict to the antiquarian bookshelf. But if political and military conditions in our own day are remarkably more sophisticated than they were in the early centuries of Christianity, there is one problem that the Fathers of the Church share with anyone seeking to develop a Christian response to violence, that is, the problem of what one should say about Christian participation in war on the basis of Scripture. In this matter patristic writers as a group were no more successful than the American Catholic bishops in finding univocal solutions to specific questions.[1] Nonetheless, by carefully following how some of these writers enlisted the aid of the Old and New Testaments in articulating their views on war and peace, we can see a bit more precisely the ambiguities involved in this question and the need for circumspection in making any generalization about war and the Christian conscience.

Until about the year A.D. 170 there is precious little evidence of Christian sympathy for war and military service anywhere in the Roman Empire.[2] In fact, the triumphant declaration is repeatedly sounded that Christians are now living in the age prophesied by Isaiah 2:3 and Micah 4:2: "We who were filled with war, mutual slaughter and every other form of evil," says the apologist Justin to his Jewish opponent Tryphon, "have everywhere transformed our instruments of war, fashioning our swords into plow-shares and our spears into farm tools" (*Dialogue with*

1. *The Challenge of Peace: God's Promise and Our Response* (Washington, D.C.: United States Catholic Conference, 1983), n. 55.

2. During this period the few specific references in our sources to Christians in a military context come from the New Testament itself. See, for example, Matthew 8:5–13 (the centurion at Capernaum), Acts 10 (the centurion Cornelius whom Peter baptized), and Luke 3:14 (the soldiers who came to John the Baptist). Although the last group were not actually Christians, they are treated as such by the early Church Fathers when the topic of military service is discussed. It should be noted that until the end of the second century the whole question of Christians serving in the army was a highly speculative one since there was no involuntary conscription, and anyone who had problems of conscience in this area could easily avoid the problem.

48

Tryphon 110:3). Irenaeus talks in the same vein and suggests that Christians "know nothing about fighting; when struck they turn the other cheek" (*Adv. Haer.* 4:34.4).[3] Even when changes in Christian practice were occurring at the end of the second and during the third century, the refusal to engage in bloodshed is characterized by Origen as one of the features that distinguishes Christians from Jews. "For we no longer take up the sword against any nation, nor do we learn the art of war any more. We have become sons of peace through Jesus our leader" (*Against Celsus* 5:33).[4] Thus, if Old Testament warriors are sometimes viewed with approval or are seen as foreshadowing the works of Christ and his Church,[5] the necessity to abstain from all forms of violence is considered an essential part of the new dispensation.

However deeply felt or eloquently expressed such sentiments were among Christian writers of the ante-Nicene period, it is clear that they were not universally persuasive. Toward the end of the second century there is evidence that increasing numbers of Christians were joining the army or were being converted to the faith while in service,[6] to such a degree, in fact, that in the first decade of the third century A.D. the North African apologist, Tertullian, felt it necessary to address the problem in two separate works.

Although Tertullian sometimes boasts that Christians are to be found among the Roman soldiery (*Apol.* 37:4) and that they sail the sea, serve

3. Cf. Athenagoras, *Plea for Christians* 1:4. It is remarkable that even in the late fourth and early fifth centuries, when political and social conditions within the empire were scarcely peaceful, some Christian writers continued to speak of these prophecies as being fulfilled. Cf. John Chrysostom (*Expos. in Ps.* 45:3) and Cyril of Alexandria (*In Isaiam I; Oratio II, ad. vers. 4; Comm. in Micah,* 39), and consult G. Zampaglione, *The Idea of Peace in Antiquity*, transl. R. Dunn (Notre Dame, Ind.: University of Notre Dame Press, 1973), pp. 274–277.

4. Cf. Tertullian who cites Isaiah and then continues: "For the practice of the Old Law was to avenge itself with the sword, to take an eye for an eye and to repay injury for injury. But the practice of the New Law was to focus on clemency and to turn bloodthirsty swords and lances to peaceful uses and to change warlike acts aginst rivals and enemies into the peaceful pursuits of plowing and farming the land" (*Against the Jews* 3:10). For the problems of authorship here see the comments of A. Kroymann in *CCL* 2, 1338, and of E. Evans in his edition of the *Adversus Marcionem* (Oxford: Clarendon Press, 1972), pp. xix–xx.

5. For New Testament evidence along this vein see Acts 7:45, and especially Hebrews 11:32–34. Moses stretching out his arms to aid the Israelites in their battle with Amalech was frequently seen as a symbol of Christ crucified. See Justin, *Dial.* 131; Irenaeus, *Adv. Haer* 4:24.1; and Tertullian, *Adv. Marc.* 3:18.6.

6. The most obvious example was the presence of Christians in the *Legio XII fulminata* and their supposed role in saving the Roman army from defeat on one particular occasion (see Tertullian, *Apol.* 5:6, and *Scap.* 4:6; Eusebius, *Eccles. Hist.* 5:5; cf. Dio Cassius 71:10; *SHA*, M. Antoninus 24:4). Whatever credence one places in the miracle of the rain, the presence of Christians in the army is incontestable, and it is significant that the Christian writers who recount the incident do not suggest that this fact was reprehensible.

in the army, farm the land, and buy and sell like the rest of men (*Apol.* 42:3), when he comes to deal specifically with Christians in military service, he leaves little doubt about his misgivings. In the treatise *On Idolatry*[7] he first discusses the question whether Christians no less than Joseph or Daniel in the Old Testament could hold public office if they kept themselves free from idolatry. Tertullian's ironic answer is that they could indeed hold office provided they avoided all the normal coercive duties that fall to such an official, such as passing sentence on criminals and/or imprisoning and torturing individuals. With respect to Joseph or Daniel he says that "old things are not always to be compared with new . . . what is enslaved with what is free. For [Joseph and Daniel] were slaves despite their position, whereas you [being Christian] are nobody's slave inasmuch as you ought to pattern yourself after Christ who has freed you from the captivity of the world" (18:4–5). Clearly the Old Testament patterns have been broken. For Tertullian the Christians' role is to stay free of all temporal entanglements that threaten the faith. It is as simple as the difference between being slave and being free.

The same is true for soldiers in the ranks, for whom the problem of idolatry was not a pressing one.

The soul cannot be beholden to two masters, God and Caesar. Moses, to be sure, carried a rod; Aaron wore a military belt and John had a breast plate. If one wants to play around with the topic, Jesus, son of Nun [i.e. Joshua] led an army and the Jewish nation went to war. But how will a Christian do so? Indeed, how will he serve in the army during peacetime without the sword that Jesus Christ has taken away? Even if soldiers came to John and got advice on how they ought to act, even if the centurion became a believer, the Lord, by taking away Peter's sword disarmed every soldier thereafter. We are not allowed to wear any uniform that symbolizes a sinful act (19:2–3).[8]

Here Tertullian covers all bases in rejecting any kind of Christian participation in war or military service. Old Testament warriors carry no weight; the witness of soldiers in the New Testament is mooted by Jesus' action in the garden. In disarming Peter, the Lord disarmed every soldier thereafter.[9]

---

7. Although there is considerable debate about the date of the *De Idololatria*, it probably was written between A.D. 203–206; the *De Corona* was composed in 211. For the chronology of Tertullian's work see C. Rambaux (*Tertullien face aux morales des trois premiers siècles* [Paris: Société d'édition Les Belles Lettres], pp. 425–426) where pertinent bibliography can be found.

8. The terms *exarmando* and *discinxit* in this passage may, of course, refer to the removing of military insignia as signs of public office and the idolatrous worship associated with public functions. In the context of the whole passage, however, I think it is far more likely that these terms refer to weapons as symbols of bloodletting. Thus, Tertullian's argument here is based as much on his opposition to Christian participation in violence as it is on anything else.

9. Cf. Tertullian's remarks in the *De Patientia*, which was composed about the same time as the *De Idololatria*. Here the apologist talks about the forebearance of Christ and

In rejecting specific models from both the Old and the New Testament, Tertullian attests to the fact that a debate on the issue of military service was occurring in the Christian community of his day and that Scriptural precedents were being cited by those who were following a path different from his own. Similar ideas are seen at work in the apologist's treatise *On the Crown*, where Tertullian honors a legionnaire for rejecting the military crown as being incompatible with his Christian faith.[10] On this occasion Tertullian distinguishes between Christians who join the army and those who are converted while in the service. With respect to the first there is no doubt that the law of Christ is being violated.[11] With respect to the second he cites the examples from the New Testament we have seen earlier and seems to admit at least the theoretical possibility that one can be both a soldier and a Christian.[12] In practical terms, however, that prospect is hardly conceivable, and Tertullian rails against the plea of necessity that is often raised in connection with service in the army. "No . . . necessity for wrongdoing is incumbent on those for whom the only necessity is to avoid wrongdoing. . . . We must either refuse offices in order to avoid falling into sin or we must undergo martyrdom in order to be freed from these obligations" (11.6). This is Tertullian at his rhetorical and intransigent best. We should note, however, that his choice of proof texts from the New Testament is highly selective. Thus, he finds support for his position in a literal reading of passages such as Matthew 26:52 ("All those who take the sword shall perish by it") and Luke 16:13 ("No servant can serve two masters"), but he dismisses as irrelevant other references that do not sit comfortably with his views.

In addition to suggesting that the law of the Old Covenant has been superseded by the law of peace, Tertullian argues that certain Old Tes-

---

says (3:7–8): "When he was betrayed, when he was led to the slaughter like a lamb—'for he opened his mouth no more than a lamb in the hands of the shearer' (Is. 53:7)—he who with a single word could have had legions of angels from heaven, did not condone the avenging sword of even one disciple. The patience of the Lord was wounded in Malchus, and so he cursed the works of the sword for ever after. . . ."

10. For an excellent running commentary on this treatise see the edition of J. Fontaine (Paris: Presses Universitaires, 1966), where many specific points are dealt with in detail.

11. "Is it right to make a profession of the sword when the Lord has proclaimed that the man who uses it will perish by it? Will a son of peace who should not even go to court take part in battle? Will a man who does not avenge wrongs done to himself have any part in chains, prisons, tortures and punishments?" (11:2)

12. 11:4–5: "The situation is different if the faith comes to a man after he is in the army, as with the soldiers whom John admitted to baptism, the converted centurion whom Christ praised, and the one whom Peter instructed in the faith. Nonetheless, once a man has accepted the faith and has been marked with its seal, he must immediately leave the service, as many have done, or he has to engage in all kinds of quibbling to avoid offending God in ways that are forbidden to men even outside the service. Or, finally, he will have to endure for God what civilian members of the faith have been no less willing to accept. Military service offers neither impunity for wrongdoing nor immunity from martyrdom. The Gospel is one and the same for Christians everywhere."

tament references to warfare are intelligible only in terms of the Gospel. This point is made more than once in his treatise *Against Marcion* where, like Augustine later, he attempts to demonstrate the unity of the God of the Old Testament with the God of the New.[13] He insists, for example, that in Psalms 44:4 ("Gird thy thigh with a sword") the context demands that we interpret the sword as a figure for the word of God,[14] and later in the same treatise (4:16.1–7) he argues at length for a nonviolent interpretation of the principle, "an eye for an eye."[15] Comparing this principle with what is found in Old Testament passages that enjoin forbearance,[16] and working on the assumption that contrary stipulations cannot come from the same God, Tertullian suggests that the concept of an "eye for an eye" was not designed "to permit a second injury of retaliation. . . ." Its purpose was, in fact, to deter the initial injury "since God knows that violence is more readily restrained by the spectre of retaliation than by the promise of future punishment. . . ." In other words, the principle was directed both to the man who had a strong faith in God and to the one who did not. The former would trust God to exact vengeance; the latter would not resort to violence because of the prospect of retaliation.[17] Tertullian argues that Christ's words about turning the other cheek (Matt. 5:39) were actually meant to clarify and to reinforce this understanding of the principle of "an eye for an eye," which had remained obscure in the Old Testament (4:16.4–7). Thus, the single verity in both covenants is that vengeance is to be left

13. For Tertullian's exegetical principles see H. Karpp, *Schrift und Geist bei Tertullian* (*Beiträge zur Förderung christlicher Theologie*, 47 [Gütersloh: Bertelsmann, 1955]), pp. 21–29, pp. 32–46; T. P. O'Malley, S.J., *Tertullian and the Bible* (*Latinitas Christianorum Primaeva* 21 [Nijmegen: Dekker & Van de Vegt, 1967]), 117–172. More recently consult J. F. Jansen, "Tertullian and the New Testament," *The Second Century* 2 (1982), 191–207, and for bibliography see the helpful survey of R. D. Sider in the same fascicle, 244–247.

14. 3:14. So, too, with reference to the following verse ("Stretch forth and prosper and reign because of truth, gentleness and justice") Tertullian asks, "Who is going to produce these results with the sword and not rather deceit, harshness and injustice, which are the proper business of fighting?" The final version of the *Adversus Marcionem* was probably published between 207–208 A.D. See the critical edition of E. Evans (n. 4 above), p. xviii, and Rambaux, op. cit., p. 426.

15. 4:16.1–7. In his *Against the Jews*, which was composed around A.D. 197, Tertullian (or a redactor) had suggested that the principle of an "eye for an eye" had been abrogated by the law of Christ. See n. 4 above.

16. E.g., Zachariah 7:10, 8:17 (in the Septuagint version).

17. 4:16.5: "For he [i.e. God] is aware that violence is more readily restrained by the immediate application of retaliation than by the promise of future revenge. Both of these had to be provided for, to meet human nature and men's faith, so that the man who believed God might expect God to exact vengeance, while the man who was deficient in faith should have respect for the laws of retaliation" (Evans' translation). Thus, it would seem that for Tertullian the principle of "an eye for an eye" in the Old Testament was not an endorsement of retaliation but an acknowledgment that it would occur. Here, I think, the apologist comes close to the modern concept of deterrence.

in God's hands; man's responsibility is to practice patience and forbearance.

Tertullian's whole approach to Scripture comes down to two points: Either the Old Testament, when read correctly, says much the same thing about violence and war as does the New, or, if there is a difference, the military ethic of the old dispensation must give way to the Gospel message of peace. In neither case do we find support for Christian participation in the exercise of coercive power.

It is fair to say, I think, that Tertullian is not much concerned about integrating his own Christian values into those of contemporary society, and for this reason he is inclined to speak on the issue of violence and war in apodictic, almost defiant terms. Such an approach, however, is not the only possible one for a pacifist, as we learn from examining the views of Origen, who was the most sophisticated theologian and Scripture scholar of the ante-Nicene age. Origen shared Tertullian's adamant opposition to Christian participation in war, but he had, I believe, a broader understanding of the issues involved and a greater sensitivity to the dilemma created by the demands of the temporal order. By facing some of the problems of statecraft more candidly than Tertullian, he became the most articulate exponent of pacifism in the early Church.

Origen's clearest statement of where he stands on the issue is to be found in a long passage of his *Against Celsus*, which was composed toward the end of his life[18] and which was designed to counter objections raised against Christianity by the pagan writer Celsus some 70 or 80 years earlier. One of Celsus' complaints was that by refusing to worship the emperor and to fight on his behalf the Christians were exposing the realm to "the ravages of lawless and uncivilized barbarians." Origen replies that if all followed the Christian example, the barbarians would be converted and the prospect of war removed.[19] In more immediate terms, however, he argues that the Christian citizens, no less than the pagan priests, wield spiritual weapons against the enemies of Rome:

Though they keep their right hands clean, the Christians fight through their prayers to God on behalf of those doing battle in a just cause and on behalf of an emperor who is ruling justly in order that all opposition and hostility toward those who are acting rightly may be eliminated. . . . We do not go out on the campaign with him [i.e. the emperor] even if he insists, but we do battle on his behalf by raising a special army of piety through our petitions to God (*Against Celsus* 8:73).

18. I.e., in A.D. 249. See P. Nautin, *Origène. Sa vie et son oeuvre* (*Christianisme Antique*, 1 [Paris: Beauchesne, 1977]), pp. 375–376, p. 381.
19. *Against Celsus* 8:68.

Although just wars are possible,[20] and the need to defend the empire's borders is openly acknowledged, the responsibilities of pagans and Christians in all such activity are quite distinct. For Origen, as one modern critic has expressed it, Christians are "the entering wedge of the eschatological kingdom,"[21] and as such they are engaged in combat with those forces that stir up wars and prevent a lasting peace. In their role as a "chosen generation, a royal priesthood, a holy nation" (1 Peter 2:9) their contribution to the temporal order must remain strictly in the area of prayer and asceticism.[22]

Any claim by Celsus that there are Old Testament precedents for Christians' taking up arms is rejected as quite irrelevant. On this matter what comes into play is Origen's abiding predilection for interpreting the Scriptures in an allegorical or tropological sense,[23] for such a reading, as we have seen, makes it possible to handle Scriptural passages that are troublesome from a pacifist perspective. Thus, the sword that Phineas used to slay Zimri and the harlot (Numbers 25:1–15) might have been a source of edification for the Jews, but for Christians it must be transformed into the sword of the spirit, for Christ has taken away the physical sword.[24] Words like those of the psalmist, "Each morning I slew all the sinners on earth" (Psalms 100:8) are to be understood as referring to the destruction of "fleshly desires," and the line "Blessed is he who takes hold of thy [i.e. Babylon's] infants and dashes them against the rock" (Psalms 136:8–9) is really talking about removing "confused thoughts caused by evil which have been implanted in the

20. Cf. 4:82, where he suggests that the life of the bees is a lesson to man that "if wars are ever necessary, they ought to be just and ordered."

21. G. E. Caspary, *Politics and Exegesis: Origen and the Two Swords* (Berkeley, Calif.: University of California Press, 1978), p. 128. This work is an excellent study of the interrelationship between Origen's exegetical principles and his political views.

22. In doing so the Christians are following the advice of Scripture and serving the state as effectively as any soldier: ". . . When the occasion arises, we provide the emperors with divine assistance, as it were, by putting on the armor of God (Eph. 6:11). We do so in obedience to the voice of the Apostle who says, 'My advice is that first and foremost you offer prayers, supplications, petitions and thanksgiving for all men, especially for the emperors, and all those in authority' (I Tim. 2:1–2). To be sure, the more pious a man is the more effectively does he assist the emperors—more so than the troops that go out and kill as many of the enemy as possible on the battleline" (*Against Celsus* 8:73).

23. The literature on Origen's exegesis is extensive. Among the most helpful works are the following: J. Daniélou, *Origen*, transl. W. Mitchell (New York: Sheed & Ward, 1955), pp. 133–199; H. de Lubac, *Histoire et Esprit. L'Intelligence de l'écriture d'après Origène* (Paris: Aubier, 1950); R. P. C. Hanson, *Allegory and Event. A Study of the Sources and Significance of Origen's Interpretation of Scripture* (London: SCM Press, 1959); and M. F. Wiles, "Origen as Biblical Scholar," in P. R. Ackroyd and C. F. Evans, *The Cambridge History of the Bible*, I (Cambridge, England: Cambridge University Press, 1970), pp. 454–489. For additional bibliography see Caspary, op. cit. 7, n. 12.

24. See Caspary, op. cit., pp. 34–39.

soul and are developing there" (*Against Celsus* 7:22). In talking about "the letter that kills" and the spirit that gives life, Origen insists that Christ's words "Let him who does not have a sword sell his tunic and buy one" (Luke 22:36) can be lifegiving only if they are understood *spiritaliter*.[25] As we shall see, it is Augustine's failure to read the passage in this way that made Jesus' words unintelligible to him.

The whole pericope about the two swords in the Garden of Gethsemane (Matt. 26:52; Luke 22:35 ff.) is, in fact, critical for understanding Origen's ideas about the differences between the Old and the New Testament on the matter of violence. Going beyond Tertullian's remark that Christ disarmed every soldier in disarming Peter, Origen sees the actions of the Apostle and of Jesus as symbolic of the two dispensations.[26] When Peter wielded the sword "he clearly had not yet internalized either the evangelical patience given him by Christ nor the peace which Christ gave to his disciples." Instead, he was using "the power given the Jews by the Law regarding their enemies."[27] The advent of the new dispensation, however, is signaled by the words "put up thy sword into its place." The rebuke is clear enough, says Origen: "We must avoid unsheathing the sword under pretext of being in the army or of avenging injuries or for any other reason. All of these reasons the Gospel of Christ holds in abomination. . . . We ought not to use the sword against any man."[28] Indeed, Christians are forbidden to offer resistance even when suffering persecution at the hands of the legitimate authorities, as Origen makes clear when commenting on Romans 13:2: "If we assume . . . that those who believe in Christ are not subject to temporal powers, do not pay the tribute, do not pay taxes, fear no one, honor no one, do they not bring upon themselves the weapons of the rulers and princes thereby absolving the persecutors and condemning themselves."[29]

---

25. *Hom. Lev.* 7:5. Theoretically the distinction between letter and spirit applies equally to the Old and to the New Covenant; thus, what gives life and what brings death should be equally present in both Testaments. In fact, however, Origen does not seem to oppose letter and spirit in reference to the New Testament. See Caspary, op. cit., pp. 49–51.

26. See Caspary, op. cit., p. 38. For a discussion of the whole pericope see pp. 42–101, and for recent interpretations of this difficult passage consult G. W. Lampe, "The Two Swords (Luke 22:35–38)" in E. Bammel and C. F. D. Moule, eds., *Jesus and the Politics of His Day* (Cambridge, England: Cambridge University Press, 1984), pp. 335-351.

27. *Commentariorum Series* 101:221.

28. *Commentariorum Series* 102. For the *catena*-fragment (*Frag. Matt.* 537), which suggests that soldiers are exempt from this injunction, see Caspary, op. cit., p. 92, whose explanation seems reasonable enough. The fragment is so short, however, that it is difficult to build any kind of argument upon it.

29. *Comm. Rom.* 9:29. Earlier (9:27) Origen suggests that resistance is in order against persecutors, but it seems that such resistance can be only passive. See Caspary, op. cit., pp. 147–149.

The problem of Old Testament wars, however, remains intractable, and Origen attempts to deal with it in two different ways. In typical fashion he suggests that the battles of the Israelites are, in fact, to be read as wars of the spirit. "All those nations of vices are within ourselves," he says in his *Homilies on Joshua* (1:7); ". . . the Canaanites are within ourselves, and so too the Perizzites and Jesubites. . . ."[30] He admits quite frankly that these events have to have a spiritual sense in order to be incorporated into the Scriptural canon:

Unless those carnal wars [i.e. of the Old Testament] were a symbol of spiritual wars, I do not think that the Jewish historical books would ever have been passed down by the Apostles to be read by Christ's followers in their churches because he came to teach peace. . . . Thus, the Apostle, being aware that physical wars are no longer to be waged by us but that our struggles are to be only battles of the soul against spiritual adversaries, gives orders to the soldiers of Christ like a military commander when he says, "Put on the armor of God so as to be able to hold your ground against the wiles of the devil" (Ephes. 6:11) (*Hom. on Joshua* 15:1).

In his *Against Celsus*, however, Origen provides a more historical reason for the acceptance of war in the Old Testament and the rejection of it in the New. Celsus had claimed that Christians were caught in a contradiction since God enjoined the Jews to take up arms, whereas his son enjoined his followers to turn the other cheek. "Who is wrong?" asks Celsus, "Moses or Jesus?" (*Against Celsus* 7:18). After replying that the Old Testament has both a literal and a spiritual meaning and that certain passages of the Old Testament (e.g. Lamentations 3:27–29)[31] are very consonant with Christ's advice, Origen explains the new law of peace in terms of political developments:

Denying to the Jews of old, who had their own socio-political system and their own territory, the right to march against their enemies, to wage war in order to protect their traditions, to kill, or to impose some kind of punishment on adulterers, murderers and others who committed similiar crimes would have been nothing short of consigning them to complete destruction. . . . But Providence, which in an earlier time gave us the Law and now has given us the Gospel of Jesus Christ, did not want the Jewish system perpetuated and so destroyed the city of the Jews and their temple along with the divine worship that was celebrated there through sacrifices and prescribed rites (*Against Celsus* 7:26).[32]

30. Cf. *Hom.* 5:2: "The battle which you are to wage is within yourself; the edifice of evil that must be overthrown is within you; your enemy originates in your heart." See H. de Lubac, op. cit., pp. 187–191, and Caspary, op. cit., pp. 18–20.

31. The text of Lamentations reads: "It is good for a man when he bears a yoke in his youth. . . . He will give his cheek to the man who strikes him and shall be filled with reproaches." Thus, Origen suggests, even when we read the Old Testament on a literal level, the "Gospel does not lay down laws in contradiction to the good of the Law" (*Against Celsus* 7:25).

32. Earlier in his *Against Celsus* Origen emphasized the contrast between Jews and Christians on the matter of violence and war when he replied to Celsus' charge that the

Here is the clearest statement of what Origen meant by the old dispensation's giving way to the new. For the Jews, religious and political values were two aspects of the same reality. Without the right to use force both the temporal and the spiritual lives of God's chosen people were at risk. In the new dispensation, however, God's people, which now included Gentiles, were not to be identified with any nation; hence they had no need for a distinct political identity or for the accoutrements of power. Whatever coercive measures were required for the maintenance of civic order could and should be exercised by the forces of Rome; the Church should be free to pursue its own life and growth in a nonviolent fashion.

Thus, while adopting the same position on war and violence as Tertullian did, Origen more clearly acknowledges the separate roles to be played by the state and the Christian community in God's plan of salvation. What should be noted here is that neither author entertained the idea of the empire's being converted; a division between the Church and its larger environment was taken for granted. Not surprisingly, then, there was a tendency for Christians to look inward and to be preoccupied with the problems and expectations of their own communities. Larger responsibilities could be left to others.

Such a stance could hardly survive the political, social, and religious developments that were initiated by the advent of Constantine. It is hard to overestimate the impact of Constantine's reign, for what Tertullian thought impossible had indeed come to pass: The emperor had been converted (at least in his sentiments and outlook), and the relationship between the Christian community and the pagan world was radically altered. One effect of this change was that Christian loyalties to Rome that had welled up for centuries now "flooded the whole Empire like a high wave."[33] Conflicts that had marked Tertullian's day died away, and Christians began to assume responsibilities in public life that were heretofore unimagined. There were, of course, new problems. The most significant of these was the need to preserve the integrity of the Gospel message and to avoid merging the identity, interests, and needs of the

---

Christian Church originated in a revolt against the Jews. "If a revolt had indeed given rise to the Christian community, if Christians took their origin from the Jews, who were allowed to take up arms in defense of their possessions and to kill their enemies, the Christian Lawgiver would not have made homicide absolutely forbidden. He would not have taught that his disciples were never justified in taking such action against a man even if he were the greatest wrongdoer [Jesus] considered it contrary to his divinely inspired legislation to approve any kind of homicide whatsoever. If Christians had started with a revolt, they would never have submitted to the kind of peaceful laws which permitted them to be slaughtered 'like sheep' (Ps. 44:11) and which made them always incapable of taking vengeance on their persecutors because they had been taught not to requite enemies, and they followed the law of gentleness and love" (*Against Celsus* 3:8).

33. K. Aland, "The Relation between Church and State in Early Times: A Reinterpretation," *Journal of Theological Studies*, 19 (1968), 125.

Christian community with those of the Roman state. Along these lines the question of war and military service in a Christian context was very much to the point.

The constant interweaving of civic and ecclesial affairs in the fourth and fifth centuries as well as certain explicit statements of writers like Eusebius, Ambrose, and Orosius would lead one at first to conclude that the problem of violence and the Christian conscience was rather quickly resolved in favor of the state, that Christians adjusted quite easily to the new politics, and that they developed a new reading of Scripture to accommodate their new position. In fact, however, there was no simple turnabout on these matters as a cursory look at Augustine's writings will attest. It is appropriate, then, to consider how his reading of the Old and New Testaments affected his views on war and how that reading was itself informed by his own political ideas.

To understand Augustine, however, we need to look very briefly at Eusebius if only because the Bishop of Caesarea *did* see the problem of Christian participation in war in simplified terms, *did* interpret Scripture in quite unheard-of ways, and *did* adopt a position *vis-à-vis* temporal power that was the antithesis of Tertullian's. Eusebius not only shares with earlier writers (such as Melito of Sardis and Origen) the conviction that the *pax Romana* initiated by Augustus was God's way of clearing the path for the preaching of the Gospel,[34] he is convinced that both the monarchy itself and the spread of the Christian message were, in fact, the fulfillment of Old Testament prophecies.

By the command, as it were, of the one God, two blessings sprouted forth simultaneously, that is, the Roman empire and the doctrine of true piety. . . . Thus, the pronouncements of the ancient oracles and the sayings of the prophets were fulfilled. . . . "He will rule from sea to sea and from the rivers to the ends of the earth" (Psalms 72:8). And again, "In his days righteousness and fullness of peace shall spring up" (Psalms 72:7). "And they beat their swords into plowshares and their spears into pruning hooks. Nation shall not lift sword against nation, and they will no longer learn the arts of war" (Is. 2:4.) (*In Praise of Constantine* 16:3.7).[35]

This confidence in being able to recognize the will of God in the world of time is not limited to earlier stages of the empire. Constantine himself can be identified as God's instrument in defending orthodoxy. As the Savior keeps at bay rebellious spirits that fill the air and attack men's souls, so too his "friend, armed as he is against his foes with the

34. See the text of Melito cited in Eusebius, *Ecc. Hist.* 4:26.7–8, and for Origen see *Against Celsus* 2:30.

35. For a good short analysis of Eusebius' views on the significance of Constantine and his reign, see G. Chesnut, *The First Christian Histories* (Paris: Beauchesne, 1977), pp. 133–166. Consult also the excellent study of T. D. Barnes, *Constantine and Eusebius* (Cambridge, Mass.: Harvard University Press, 1981), especially pp. 245–260.

standards given him by [the Saviour] from above, subdues in battle and chastens the visible enemies of truth" (*In Praise of Constantine* 2:3). Even in the more mundane business of war and conquest, the Bishop of Caesarea is no less certain when and where the hand of God is visibly present. In describing Constantine's victory over Maxentius at the Milvian Bridge, Eusebius brings the Old Testament into play:

Just as in the time of Moses himself and the ancient God-fearing race of Hebrews the chariots and army of Pharao, the pick of his horsemen, were hurled by God into the Red Sea and drowned there and covered by the depths (Exod. 15:4–5), so, too, Maxentius "plunged into the depths like a stone," together with his soldiers and bodyguard as he was in the act of retreating before the divine power accompanying Constantine and was crossing the river in front of him (*Eccles. Hist.* 9:9.5).[36]

In a context like this, Old Testament wars are not a problem for Christian readers; they are a precedent. God's ties with his servant Constantine are as close as they were with the heroes of Israel, and in Eusebius' writings such analogies are not occasional flourishes of rhetoric but an integral part of his vision of the interworkings of the celestial and terrestrial cities.[37] If Constantine prays to Christ, "his ally," before going into battle (*Eccles. Hist.* 9:9.2), and if he puts the Christian labarum on his soldiers' standards, any concern for reconciling the peaceful import of the Gospels with the demands of statecraft or of understanding Old Testament wars in light of the Sermon on the Mount is clearly superfluous.

But not permanently so. In the West, at least, Eusebius' facile identification of the spiritual and temporal orders did not prevail, and if the pacifism of Tertullian and Origen was no longer an adequate response to the exigencies of statecraft, any attempt to merge the interests of the Christian community with those of the ruling power appeared equally simplistic and inappropriate. What was needed was a middle ground in which the legitimate claims and inherent limits of both the civil and the religious traditions were recognized. That ground was provided by St. Augustine, whose reputation as the architect of what has been called the just-war theory often obscures the fact that his position on war repre-

---

36. Cf. *Life of Constantine* 1:39.
37. See *Life of Constantine* 1:6: "He accomplished this and publicized it like a good and faithful servant, openly proclaiming himself a slave and freely acknowledging that he was subject to the Ruler of All. God soon rewarded him by making him lord and master, the only victor among all those who had held power, who was unconquered and unconquerable. God made him such a consistently triumphant ruler and glorious victor over his enemies that no one ever heard the like of him in human memory. Beloved by God and supremely blessed, he was so reverent and fortunate that he subdued with greatest ease more nations than any previous emperor, and he kept the realm intact up to the very end."

sents a compromise between the absolute rejection of violence that we find in writers of the ante-Nicene period and a rather uncritical acceptance of it such as Eusebius exhibits.

From the time of his conversion in A.D. 386 to the end of his life, Augustine remained remarkably consistent in his views about war and military service, although his concerns in this area and the reasons underlying his position shifted a bit from one period to another.[38] In an early work, *On Free Will* (1:4.9, 1:5.11–13), he makes a fundamental distinction when he claims that a private individual is never justified in killing even to save his own life,[39] whereas the soldier who is acting as "an agent of the law" is in a different position. Shortly after being ordained a priest, Augustine comes to grips with the problem again when commenting on Christ's words about turning the other cheek (Luke 6:29). He says,

This text does not forbid punishment which serves as a corrective, for, in fact, such punishment is a form of mercy. . . . The only one suitable for inflicting punishment is the one whose love has driven out the normal hatred which rages in us when we have a desire for revenge. We do not have to fear, for instance, that parents hate their young son if he has done wrong, and they box his ears to prevent a recurrence. . . . There are two things, then, that we ought to look for: first, that the one punishing has been given the authority to do so by the natural order of things, and, second, that he inflict punishment with the same kind of feelings that a father has toward his son. . . . This example is the best illustration of the fact that one can love and punish a son all at the same time

---

38. See R. A. Markus, "Saint Augustine's Views on the 'Just War,'" in *The Church and War*, ed. W. J. Sheils (*Studies in Church History* [London: Nelson, 1983]), pp. 1–13. Markus argues that Augustine's thought developed in three stages. In the first (ca. 386 to the mid 390's A.D.) the bishop was preoccupied with the notion of a rationally ordered universe, and he saw the just war in that context. In the second stage (i.e., during the late 390's) Augustine shared Eusebius' confidence about the fulfillment of Old Testament prophecies in the temporibus Christianis, and during this period the significance of Old Testament wars in the Christian scheme of things comes to the fore. In the third stage (i.e., from the early 400's until the end of his life) he was most impressed by the "precariousness of human order, the threat of dissolution and the permanent presence of chaos just beneath the surface of things" (p. 10). In this last context, Markus argues, the institutions of political and judicial authority played a much more critical role in Augustine's thinking than ever before. Certainly there was a shift in Augustine's thought away from a belief in a rationally ordered universe toward a much more pessimistic view of the temporal order (cf. P. R. Brown, *Augustine of Hippo: A Biography* [Berkeley, Calif.: University of California Press, 1969], pp. 147–157). However, whether Augustine ever shared Eusebius' enthusiasm for the temporal order is a matter of debate. For a different view on this point see G. Madec, "*Tempora Christiana*," in *Scientia Augustiniana*, eds. C. P. Mayer and W. Echermann (Wurzburg: Augustinus-Verlag, 1975), pp. 112–136.

39. In this he follows the views of Ambrose (*On the Duties of the Clergy* 3:4.27). For Ambrose's views on the whole question of warfare see L. J. Swift, "St. Ambrose on Violence and War," *Transactions of the American Philological Association* 101 (1970), 533–543.

rather than just letting him go undisciplined. The purpose, of course, is not to make the wrongdoer miserable through punishment but to bring him happiness through correction. (*On the Lord's Sermon* 1:20.63–64).

Most of what Augustine has to say about the morality of Christian participation in war is an expansion or clarification of these early ideas. The underlying preoccupation in all his statements is, of course, a vivid awareness of sin and of man's limited capacities to control its effects. The vision of the human race as a *massa damnata* (*Enchiridion*, 27; *To Simplicianus* 1:2.16, *City of God*, 21:12) in which the lust to dominate (*cupido dominandi*) threatens to dissolve the social fabric permeates the bishop's thought and deeply colors his views on the role of temporal power in society.[40]

Perhaps his most telling description of the human dilemma, which the American bishops themselves refer to as "the melancholy state of humanity"[41] is to be found in a well-known passage of *The City of God* where Augustine lists the woes and failings of society and the inevitable acts of objective wrongdoing with which even the public official becomes involved. He then goes on to ask: "Amidst all these dark corners of public life in society will the wise man sit as a judge or not? Undoubtedly he will. For society, which he considers it truly immoral to separate himself from, constrains him and forces him to fulfill this obligation." Augustine details such horrors as false confessions, false accusations, the torture and execution of innocent men, and then he concludes:

All these dreadful things the wise man does not consider sins inasmuch as he does them not out of a desire to do harm but because of unavoidable ignorance and a judgment that he cannot shirk because society requires it of him. This is the kind of misery in the human condition that I am talking about even though no evil intent is involved. If the wise man's inescapable ignorance and the necessity of passing judgment forces him to torture and punish innocent men, is it not enough that he be considered guiltless without needing to be happy as well? On the contrary, how much more sensitive and more in tune with his humanity is it for him to recognize the misery involved in that necessity, to loathe it in himself, and, if he is reverent and wise, to cry to God, "Deliver me from my necessities" (Psalms 25:17) (*City of God* 19:6).

Nothing in Augustine's writing, I believe, indicates more vividly than these words the difference between Tertullian's world and that of the fourth and fifth centuries. To be sure, judicial tragedies like those listed

---

40. For a good general discussion of Augustine's anthropology and its impact on his political theory see the remarks of E. L. Fortin in *The History of Political Philosophy*, eds. L. Strauss and J. Cropsey, 2nd ed. (Chicago: Rand McNally, 1972), pp. 151–181, where many of the basic texts are cited.

41. *Challenge of Peace*, n. 71.

here were no less present in the second century than in Augustine's time. But for Tertullian, as we have seen, the notion of *necessitas* was quite unintelligible. There was one thing necessary, and whatever activities in human society were incongruent with such a goal had to be repudiated. For Augustine the problem was not that simple; *necessitas* was an inescapable dimension of living in a world that acknowledged Christian principles and yet remained imperfect, where believers responsible for holding things together shared the limitations of all men. Often in such circumstances the most that can be done is to maintain a spirit of love while attempting to control the effects of wrongdoing through restraining actions that sometimes entail physical force.[42] "Surely it is not in vain," Augustine says in one of his letters,

that we have such institutions as the power of the king, the death penalty of the judge, the hooks of the executioner, the weapons of the soldier, the stringency of the overlord and even the strictness of a good father. All these things have their own method, reason, motive and benefit. When they are feared, evil men are held in check, and the good enjoy greater peace among the wicked (*Letter* 153:6.16).

And in the matter of waging war, as Augustine makes clear in his *City of God*, this principle of limited choices, of needing to achieve what one can in less than ideal circumstances, is very much part of the human condition.

Waging war and expanding the empire by conquering other peoples strikes evil men as a fortunate thing, but to good men it is simply a necessary one. Since, however, it would be worse for good men to be under the thumb of wrongdoers, it is not out of line to describe such necessity as "fortunate" (*City of God* 4:15).[43]

42. See Fortin, op. cit., p. 158: "Through sin man's lust and overweening desire to assert his dominion over his fellow men have been unleashed. The present economy is marked by the anarchy of man's lower appetites and an invincible tendency to place one's selfish interests above the common good of society. It is a state of permanent revolt, which has its source in man's initial revolt against God. The prototype of this revolt is original sin, the sin committed by Adam, and transmitted in a mysterious way to all his descendents. As a result, the freedom that man once enjoyed in the pursuit of the good has yielded to oppression and coercion. Coercion is apparent in the most typical institutions of civil society, such as private property, slavery, and government itself, all of which are necessitated and explained by man's present inability to live according to the dictates of reason. The very existence of these institutions is a consequence and a permanent reminder of man's fallen condition. None was part of the original plan of creation and all of them are desirable only as a means of inhibiting man's proneness to evil." Cf. *The Challenge of Peace*, n. 61: "Christians will find in any violent situation the consequences of sin: not only sinful patterns of domination, oppression or aggression, but the conflicts of values and interests which illustrate the limitations of a sinful world."

43. Not unlike the American bishops' acknowledgment (n. 78) that perfect peace in this world is a utopian ideal, Augustine argues more than once that wars are, in fact, inevitable. See *City of God* 17:13, and *Letter* 199:10.35.

Such general principles and convictions, however, do not remove the difficulty of reconciling the warlike sentiments and practices of the Old Testament with the spirit of the Gospels. Augustine's most sophisticated attempt at resolving this issue appears in his *Against Faustus* (22:73–79), which was composed around A.D. 400. The major purpose of the treatise is to demonstrate the unity of the God of the Old and the New Testaments against the counterclaims of the Manichaean Faustus. Among other points of disparity between the two covenants, Faustus had insisted that Moses' actions in slaying the Egyptian, in ordering the destruction of idolatrous Israelites, and in leading wars were so out of tune with the Gospels as to be clear evidence that we are dealing with quite disparate divinities. Augustine will have none of this. Working on the principle that God cannot command anything immoral,[44] he attempts to explain what is at work in the actions of the Israelite leader. Admittedly there are difficulties in understanding Moses' attack on the Egyptian. Unlike Ambrose, who saw the incident as a model for protecting the innocent,[45] Augustine is disturbed by the fact that Moses had received no injunction to take up the sword. The most the bishop can say is that like Peter's action against Malchus, Moses' violence sprang not from some deplorable savagery but from a hatred of wrongdoing and from a kind of anger that is susceptible to being redirected toward better ends (*Against Faustus* 22:70).

With respect to leading Israelites in war, however, the situation is quite otherwise. On this point Augustine argues that

he [i.e. Faustus] ought not to be surprised or horrified at the wars waged by Moses because even in that case Moses was following God's instructions and in doing so was acting out of obedience rather than a spirit of savagery. Nor was God's action in ordering such wars inhuman. He was inflicting just punishments and striking terror in the hearts of those who deserved it (*Against Faustus* 22:74).

Augustine suggests that physical death is not the thing that is most blameworthy in war.

What rightly deserves censure in war is the desire to do harm, cruel vengeance, a disposition that remains unappeased and implacable, a savage spirit of rebel-

---

44. See *Questions on the Heptateuch* 6:10, where the bishop argues that a war enjoined by God is undoubtedly just, "for there is no evil in him." Cf. *Against Faustus* 22:75: *Bellum autem quod gerendum Deo auctore suscipitur recte suscipi dubitare fas non est* (CSEL 25:673).

45. See *On the Duties of the Clergy* 1.36.178. Ambrose used Moses' action as an illustration of his point that anyone who does not prevent an evil when it is within his power to do so is as guilty as the perpetrator of the evil. Augustine's scruple, of course, is in line with his principle that violent action is warranted only when one is obeying or exercising legitimate authority. See *On Free Will* 1:4.9, *City of God* 1:12 and 26, *Against Faustus* 22:75, and *Letter* 47:5.

lion, a lust for domination and other such things. The reason why good men in the face of violent resistance even undertake wars at God's command or the command of legitimate authority is to inflict just punishment on things like these. That is to say, when they find themselves in the kind of situation in human affairs that rightfully constrains them to initiate such wars or to follow the commands of others in this regard (ibid).

War, as we have seen earlier, functions much like the father punishing his son; it is the correcting hand of God working through history, the result of *necessitas*. Indeed the New Testament itself is witness to the fact that wars are sometimes unavoidable and justified.

If this were not true [Augustine says to Faustus], when the soldiers came to John for baptism and asked, "What are we to do," he would have replied, "Throw down your arms; leave the service. Do not strike, wound or kill any-one." But recognizing that when they do such things as part of their military duty they are not guilty of homicide but are administering the law, that they are not avenging private wrongs but protecting the safety of the state, he re-plied, "Do not strike anyone; do not make false accusations. Be content with your pay" (Luke 3:14). But since the Manichaeans are in the habit of openly reviling John, let them listen to the Lord Jesus Christ himself commanding us to render to Caesar these very funds which John says the soldiers should be content with. "Render to Caesar what is Caesar's," he said, "and to God what is God's" (Matt. 22:21). Providing salaries to soldiers who are required for war is one of the things taxes are paid for (ibid.).

Clearly Augustine is reading both the Old Testament and the New in a way quite different from that of Tertullian and Origen. Old Testament wars are not to be interpreted as allegories of spiritual battles or as a stage in salvation history that is now superseded by a law of love that demands abstention from bloodshed. The *necessitas* of war is thrust upon man in every age. What is important in both the old covenant and the new is a man's internal motives and the role he plays as minister of the law. Private vengeance and cruelty have no place here, and despite appearances to the contrary, the use of force must be motivated by love and carried out for the public good by those charged to do so.[46]

How steeped Augustine was in this notion of punishing wrongs in the public sphere as a way of controlling the effects of sin is evident in what he has to say later in his remarks to Faustus about Moses' slaying the Israelites who had worshipped the golden calf.

What was cruel about Moses' command or his action . . . when he provided a salutary warning for the people of that time and established a precedent for handling such matters in the future? When one reads Moses' prayer for the

---

46. See *Letter* 47:5, where Augustine says that Christ's injunction about not resisting evil was intended to forestall our taking the kind of delight in revenge that feeds on another's misfortune; it was not meant to encourage us to neglect the correction of others.

sinful Israelites, who would not conclude that he did what he did out of deep love rather than any cruelty. "If you are willing to forgive them their sin, forgive them. Otherwise blot me from your book" (Exod. 32:32). Anyone who compares with sensitivity and reverence the execution [of the Israelites] and the prayer [of Moses] sees this point very clearly. When he observes a man loving so deeply and raging so violently, he sees how harmful to the soul it is to commit fornication through idols (*Against Faustus* 22:79).[47]

But the mystery of violence in a Christian context is not so easily solved for Augustine. If an internal spirit of love and the use of force are not inherently contradictory for him, he could hardly avoid the almost embarrassing contrast between the aggressive military victories of God's people in the Old Testament and the passive acceptance of martyrdom by God's people in the New. Augustine's response to this anomaly is that the two *populi* performed different roles in the divine scheme of things. The success of the Israelites was intended to demonstrate that all earthly goods, including kingdoms and conquests, are ultimately in the hands of the one true God. In the fullness of time, however, when the veil covering God's truth was removed in the New Testament, the words and life of Christ, as well as the death of the martyrs, were intended to show that God is to be served not for the sake of temporal happiness but for happiness in the next life:

Thus, the patriarchs and prophets ruled here on earth to make it clear that it is God who gives and takes away kingdoms. The Apostles and martyrs took no part in earthly rule so as to make it clear that the kingdom of heaven should be our primary goal. The former fought wars so that it would be clear that even those victories are the working of God's will; the latter, by offering no resistance met death to teach us that dying for one's belief in the truth is a greater victory (*Against Faustus* 22:76).

Thus, if there is nothing in Augustine like the abrogation of the Old Law that we find in Tertullian and Origen, there is a kind of progression in what God, as lord of both Testaments, seeks to reveal in the two dispensations. This is the closest Augustine ever comes to distinguishing the two covenants on the matter of violence and war, and he acknowledges that the change he describes occurred by reason of a *certum mysterium* (22:77).

Indeed, in recognizing that God's purpose is not entirely clear he turns the argument back on the Manichaeans by pointing to seeming contradictions within the New Testament itself. Christ's advice, "Let him who has no sword sell his tunic and buy one" (Luke 22:36) seems

---

47. Using apocryphal texts that were acceptable to the Manichaeans, Augustine goes on to argue that the patience enjoined by Christ's words about turning the other cheek could, in fact, be present in the heart "even if it is not evident in what one says or does" (681–682).

to gainsay his earlier disregard of "purse or wallet or sandals." And the Lord's response, "It is enough" when he was told in the garden that two swords were at hand seems to contradict his subsequent repudiation of violence (Matt. 26:52). In the latter instance Augustine admits that, for him at least, Christ's intention lies hidden since Jesus ordered swords to be carried but forbade their use (*Against Faustus* 22:77). In sum, God's actions spring from causes "that are just but obscure to man." In different but equally commendable ways Old and New Testament heroes, that is, the faithful Israelites and the Christian martyrs, serve the one God whose message is twofold: First, "that temporal goods are to be sought from God and on his account to be disdained," and second, "that physical sufferings can be enjoined by God and on his account must be endured."

Augustine's subsequent comments on the Scriptural foundations of justifiable war do not add a great deal to what has been said in his treatise *Against Faustus*. About a dozen years later in the opening book of the *City of God* he iterates the point that there is a difference between the soldier and the private individual, and that "men who have waged war at God's command or who have put criminals to death in their capacity as agents of the state in accordance with its laws . . . have not violated the commandment, 'Thou shalt not kill'"(1.21).[48] And in a letter written about the same time to the imperial tribune, Marcellinus, he repeats a point made earlier in his commentary on the Sermon on the Mount. Precepts like that of turning the other cheek, while obviously intended to enjoin patience in the face of others' malice,

pertain more to the interior disposition of the heart than to external actions, the idea being that we should maintain an interior spirit of patience and benevolence but do what seems most beneficial for those whose welfare we are bound to look out for. This point is evident from the reply made by Christ the Lord Himself, a singular example of patience, when he was struck in the face. "If I have said something wrong, then point it out. If not, why do you strike me?" (John 18:23). Thus, he did not follow his own command if we take that command literally because he did not turn the other cheek to his assailant but told him not to compound the injury (*Letter* 138:13).[49]

About a half dozen years later, in A.D. 418, he addresses himself to the Roman general Boniface, who had developed scruples about whether his military profession was compatible with the spirit of the Gospels. Augustine's answer, at a time when North African communities sorely needed protection from barbarian attacks, was quite unequivocal.

48. Cf. *Against Faustus* 22:70.
49. Cf. *On the Lord's Sermon* 1:19.57–58.

Do not believe that it is impossible for anyone to serve God while on active duty in the army. Holy David, whom God was most pleased with, was a military man, and so were a good many just men of his time. The same is true of the centurion who said to the Lord, "I am not worthy that you come under my roof. . . ." The same is true of Cornelius to whom the angel sent by God said, "Cornelius, your acts of charity have found acceptance and your prayers have been answered. . . ." And then we have the men who came for baptism to John, the Holy precursor of the Lord and friend of the Promised One. . . . When these men asked John what they should do, he replied, "Do not strike anyone or make false accusations. Be content with your pay." If he told them to be content with their pay, he certainly was not telling them that they could not be soldiers (*Letter* 189:4–6).[50]

Augustine might just as well have had Tertullian's *On Idolatry* in front of him. The very exempla that the apologist had specifically rejected as valid arguments for Christian participation in war are here put forth as precedents for justifying such action. What is significant, of course, is that Augustine, no less than Tertullian, has peace as the primary goal. Thus, after assuring Boniface that a soldier can be a good Christian, he goes on to speak in terms of ultimate aims in the face of practical necessities:

Peace should be your aim; war should be a matter of necessity so that God might free you from necessity and preserve you in peace. One does not pursue peace in order to wage war; he wages war to achieve peace. Accordingly, even in the act of waging war, be careful to maintain a peaceful disposition so that by defeating your foes you can bring them the benefits of peace. "Blessed are the peacemakers," says the Lord, "for they will be called the sons of God" (Matt. 5:9). . . . And so, let it be because of necessity rather than your own desire that you kill the enemy fighting against you (*Letter* 189:6).[51]

In the end, then, the issue is reduced to the problem of *pax* and *necessitas*. For the ante-Nicene writers, no less than for Augustine, permanent peace was scarcely attainable in the world of time where the effects of sin abounded. In light of this fact, Christians of the first three centuries were as ready to acknowledge the importance of coercive power in maintaining an earthly peace as the Bishop of Hippo was. They differed from him, however, on the role that Christians should play

---

50. Cf. *Letter* 138:15.

51. Cf. *City of God* 19:12. Augustine, it should be pointed out, is not insensitive to the tragedies involved in armed conflict. He condemns Rome's wars of conquest, and he reminds his readers more than once that war is only the lesser of evils. See *City of God* 19:7: "Let everyone grieve when he thinks about the truly shocking and cruel evils involved here, and let him acknowledge his miserable state. Any one who endures these things or thinks about them without sorrow in his heart is all the more unfortunate in considering himself happy because, in fact, he no longer possesses any human sensitivity."

in the struggle for that peace, and it was on this point that their reading of Scripture hinged. A literal as opposed to a nonliteral interpretation of the Old and New Testaments is not the dividing line between pacifist and nonpacifist writers. Both groups employed both methods; they disagreed on which method to apply to which texts. Their differences were actually predicated on how they interpreted Paul's words in Romans 13 about the state's claim on all individuals.[52] For Tertullian and Origen the limits of that claim were reached when a Christian was asked to take human life. When that occurred, one had not only the right but the responsibility to withdraw. For Augustine, who was operating in another time and circumstance, the limit was reached when the temporal power was put in the place of God or when the temporal peace was misunderstood as the ultimate goal.[53] Short of that, any decision to withdraw was a denial of the *necessitas* that rested on every man's shoulders.

Not unexpectedly, then, Scriptural interpretation in the matter of violence and war was as much a political decision—in the broad and positive sense of the term—as it was anything else; determining precisely where one's responsibility lay in the public sphere ultimately determined one's exegesis. If there was a difference on how to define that responsibility in concrete terms from one period to another—as was inevitable in changing political circumstances—we should not be surprised that Scripture did not settle the issue of violence and war for the early Christians. And on that account we can understand why neither the pacifist nor the nonpacifist tradition has been able to supplant the other during the centuries that followed.[54]

52. For bibliography on the manifold interpretations of this passage in Christian writers (including the Church Fathers), see E. Bammel, "*Romans* 13," in *Jesus and the Politics of His Day* (above, n. 26), pp. 365–383.

53. See *City of God* 15:4: "When victory goes to those who have fought in the more upright cause, who would doubt that such a victory should be celebrated. Who would doubt that the resulting peace is desirable. These are blessings and are unquestionably gifts from God. But if we overlook the higher goods which are part of the heavenly city where victory will be secure in a peace that is everlasting and supreme, and if those other goods are desired in such a way that they are thought to be the only ones, or valued more than those which are believed to be superior, then misery will surely follow, and whatever misery was there already will surely increase."

54. For the survival of pacifist sentiments in the fourth century A.D., see the enlightening article of J. Fontaine, "Le culte des martyrs militaires et son expression poétique au IVe siècle," *Augustinianum* 20 (1980), 141–171.

JAMES A. BRUNDAGE

5. The Limits of the War-Making Power: The Contribution of the Medieval Canonists

The pastoral letter on war and peace of the Catholic bishops of the United States deals with a problem that has perplexed Western Christian thinkers since the beginnings of Christianity itself.[1] The American bishops' pronouncement is only the most recent in a long chain of efforts by the authorities of the Western Church to analyze the nature of war and to spell out both its theoretical and practical consequences for believers who, however much they might wish to do so, cannot ignore the fact that socially sanctioned violence has been a feature of societies from the beginning of human history. Christian reactions to the phenomenon of warfare can only be understood, as the pastoral letter itself points out, within the historical context of the doctrinal and legal development of Christian institutions. I propose to examine one segment of that historical context, since I believe that the record of some past efforts by earlier bishops to impose moral and legal limits on the participation by Christians in warfare may provide a useful perspective in trying to understand and evaluate the American pastoral letter. The record may also raise some questions about the strengths and weaknesses of the approach that the bishops' letter embodies.

The segment of the past record that I wish to snip out and examine involves the efforts of the medieval Church's legal experts to create a system for limiting warfare, based upon the moral authority of the Church, but implemented through legal processes in the Church's courts. I shall deal with efforts to achieve this goal during roughly a 200-year period, from the middle of the 12th century to the middle of the 14th. This 200-year period was one in which the Church, along with the rest of Western society, was undergoing a fundamental, indeed a radical, transformation of its legal system. Both civil and canon lawyers during these two centuries were in the process of fashioning a broad range of new methods for dealing with some basic human problems; in

---

1. National Conference of Catholic Bishops, *The Challenge of Peace: God's Promise and Our Response; A Pastoral Letter* (Washington, D.C.: U.S. Catholic Conference, 1983; cited hereafter as *Challenge of Peace*), 1.A, "Peace and the Kingdom."

the process they created new types of social structure that have proved over the past 700 years or so to be extraordinarily durable and effective. Among their creations were the concept of the corporation, which is still very much with us, together with a corporate interpretation of government, in which are rooted our basic notions of representation and consent, of parliamentary government, of the rule of law, and of constitutional limitations on the power of rulers. Many of the basic concepts that undergird modern ideas about social structure and government, in other words, emerged from the ideas, beliefs, and intuitions of the learned lawyers of that period. Their ideas about the uses and limitations of government power still play powerful roles in shaping and conditioning the ways in which we approach many of those fundamental problems in the Western world today.[2]

It is important to realize that the men—and the fact that they were all men was a result of their society's concepts about sex roles, many features of which have unfortunately also survived to the present—were not solely academic theorists, spinning out ideas in splendid isolation from social realities. They were indeed academics for the most part, but they were also men who were often employed as counselors and advisers to monarchs and municipalities, to merchants, popes, and prelates; accordingly they were often in a position to influence and to help shape the ways in which institutions were structured and to determine the limits within which institutions functioned in the world of power, politics, and profit.

Among the many problems that concerned the civilians and canonists who taught in the law faculties of the principal European universities during this period was the problem of war and peace, more specifically the problem of the basis of the war-making power of governments, the limitations within which that power might legitimately be employed, and the consequences of its use—particularly, as we shall see, the consequences for property rights and liability for damages incurred as a result of warfare. They were engaged in constructing a law of war. The raw materials that they used consisted of some basic doctrinal concepts that they borrowed from the Fathers of the Church (principally St. Augustine), together with some notions that they found at hand in the Roman law as codified by the sixth-century Byzantine Emperor Justinian, and the usual and customary practices of contemporary armies and their commanders. This was a peculiar mixture and one might think a rather unpromising one; but despite its odd components, the structure that they fashioned turned out to be workable, if not elegant in all its details.

2. Brian Tierney, *Religion, Law, and the Growth of Constitutional Thought* (Cambridge, England: Cambridge University Press, 1982).

Now the very idea of a law of war may seem at worst absurd and at best paradoxical, since war itself results from the failure of peaceful and lawful processes to produce results satisfactory and acceptable to the parties involved in a dispute. But both medieval and modern efforts to impose some limitations on the way in which warfare is conducted testify to a persistent belief, or at least a recurrent hope, that parties to a conflict, even a violent one, can at least agree on certain fundamental conditions that will govern the ways in which that conflict will be conducted. One problem that worries critics who deny the principle that a law of war is either desirable or possible is of course the problem of sanctions and their enforcement. Who is to penalize those who break the rules? How can sanctions be imposed save by the use of force? And that, of course, means further warfare, presumably successful warfare, on the part of the enforcer.[3]

The argument that the difficulty of imposing sanctions makes a law of war impossible or fictional is flawed, however, by the fact that it rests on the Austinian assumption that only those laws are real and meaningful that carry with them readily enforceable penalties and that the purpose of law is always and necessarily to punish wrongdoers.[4] But in fact law has other functions than punishment and revenge; law also serves as a means of enunciating and defining basic social norms, of establishing and specifying standards of conduct that a community finds acceptable. Laws do not necessarily guarantee that every infraction of those norms and standards can or will be punished. We are all aware of many situations in which infraction of a statute or regulation does not regularly result in the punishment that the law provides. Further, effective legal sanctions do not necessarily rest on the use of forcible coercion—at least not unless you define forcible coercion in some very peculiar ways. If, for example, a statute provides that under certain circumstances contracts must be reduced to writing or else they will not be enforced by the courts (as did the Statute of Frauds (1677)§ 4), you have created a negative sanction that in some sense might be called coercion, but it would stretch the meaning of words rather drastically to call it forcible.

Moreover the fact that traffic regulations are often not rigorously enforced does not mean that speed limits are not worth having, nor is the

3. M. D. R. Foot, "Introduction" to Michael Elliott-Bateman, ed., *The Fourth Dimension of Warfare* (Manchester: Manchester University Press; New York: Praeger, 1970), p. ix; Georg Schwarzenberger, "Functions and Foundations of the Laws of War," *Archiv für Rechts- und Sozialphilosophie* 44 (1958), 351–369.

4. John Austin, *Lectures on Jurisprudence, or the Philosophy of Positive Law*, 4th ed., rev. by Robert Campbell, 2 vols. (London: J. Murray, 1873), especially Lectures 1 and 23 at 1:98–102, 467–469; W. Jethro Brown, *The Austinian Theory of Law* (London: J. Murray, 1906), pp. 1–3, pp. 6–14.

use of nonforcible penalties for offenders necessarily less effective than the use of force. Such laws and regulations serve two real and important functions. First, they have a deterrent function—even occasional enforcement, coupled with a reasonable fear that there might be successful enforcement in your particular case, will deter some potential offenders, though not as many as one might wish. Second, and more important, laws and regulations serve notice on all of us that society has set certain standards of conduct and that when we ignore or contravene them we are doing wrong, whether we happen to agree with the rules or not. That function of enunciating social consensus is not without utility for society at large. The law draws a line, establishes a boundary. We may trespass, of course; we may frequently trespass with impunity. But the rules make us conscious of our trespasses, while sanctions, including nonforcible ones, deter us from trespassing even more than we might otherwise do. They also instill a wholesome fear that this time, or the next, or maybe the time after that, we may get caught and that the experience will either be unpleasant or unprofitable or both.[5]

But I have ventured far from my subject, into the perilous waters of speculative jurisprudence, where no right-thinking historian is very comfortable—or very safe. Let me return to the issues at hand, in the hope that I have demonstrated that the attempt to construct laws of war may not necessarily be an exercise in futility.

The efforts of medieval jurists, and the canonists in particular, to construct a system of legal limitations on the war-making power were anchored in the Augustinian concept of the just war, as the canonists found that idea expounded in Gratian's *Decretum*, which was completed about the year 1140.[6] It is not my purpose to deal with the problems that just-war theory and its development pose for historians. I simply wish to make the point that the just war, as a juristic category, played a vital role

---

5. On the issues implied here, especially the problem of the relationship between law and coercion, see H. L. A. Hart, *The Concept of Law* (Oxford: Clarendon Press, 1961), pp. 20–25, pp. 221–226, and *Punishment and Responsibility: Essays in the Philosophy of Law* (London: Oxford University Press, 1968); Roscoe Pound, *Social Control through Law* (New Haven, Conn.: Yale University Press; London: Oxford University Press, 1942), pp. 32–33, pp. 107–108. But see also the discussion of these issues in Lon L. Fuller, *The Morality of Law*, rev. ed. (New Haven, Conn.: Yale University Press, 1969), especially pp. 133–151 and 187–242.

6. On Gratian and the *Decretum* see especially Stephan Kuttner, "The Father of the Science of Canon Law," *The Jurist* 1 (1941), 2–19, and "Graziano: l'uomo e l'opere," *Studia Gratiana* 1 (1953), 27–29; John T. Noonan, Jr., "Gratian Slept Here: The Changing Identity of the Father of the Systematic Study of Canon Law," *Traditio* 35 (1979), 145–172; Gabriel Le Bras, Charles Lefebvre, and Jacqueline Rambaud, *L'âge classique, 1140–1378: Sources et théorie du droit*, Vol. 7 of *Histoire du droit et institutions de l'église en occident* (Paris: Sirey, 1965), pp. 49–129; Gérard Fransen, "La date du Décret de Gratien," *Revue d'histoire ecclésiastique* 51 (1956), 521–531.

in the development of doctrines about the limitations of warfare, because the rules that the canonists developed for defining the consequences of actions in war were grounded on the distinction between just and unjust wars.[7] One further basic point should be stated without further elaboration, namely, that the jurists with whom I am dealing never embraced the position that it was the aim or even the business of the Church to eliminate war altogether from human affairs. They were concerned, instead, to establish limits within which war could justifiably be waged and to penalize participants in wars that transgressed those limits.[8] The canonists were not, in principle, committed to pacifism. Indeed, Giovanni da Legnano (d. 1383), the author of the earliest full-scale treatise on the law of war, argued that war stems from divine law and that God not only allows wars to happen but also made positive provision for war as an instrumentality of human government and society.[9] Giovanni further maintained that wars had their primordial origin in nature and thus that war was an element in the very fabric of the world as it came from the hand of its creator.[10] Two hundred years earlier, however, the anonymous author of the *Summa "Elegantius in iure diuino"* (written ca. 1169) had urged the view (common among the civilians) that war was a product of the law of nations (*ius gentium*), from which flowed the rules that should govern its conduct.[11] But whether war was a part of God's plan of creation or whether it arose among the practices of the *ius gentium*, the canonists did not consider warfare an aberrant kind of human conduct. It was a routine reality, and they were prepared to deal with it on that basis.

Already in the mid-12th century Gratian had inserted in his *Decretum* a descriptive analysis of the law of war, which he borrowed from St. Isidore (ca. 560–636), the learned bishop of Seville. As Isidore and Gratian described it, the law of war dealt with the formalities of initiat-

7. On just-war theory in Gratian, see Frederick H. Russell, *The Just War in the Middle Ages*, Cambridge Studies in Medieval Life and Thought, 3rd ser., Vol. 8 (Cambridge, England: Cambridge University Press, 1975), pp. 55–58.

8. Fermino Poggiaspalla, "La chiesa e la partecipazione dei chierici alla guerra nella legislazione conciliare fino alle decretali di Gregorio IX," *Ephermerides iuris canonici* 15 (1959), p. 140.

9. Giovanni da Legnano, *Tractatus de bello, de represaliis, et de duello* 10, ed. Thomas Erskine Holland, Classics of International Law, Vol. 8 (Oxford: Printed for the Carnegie Institution of Washington at the Oxford University Press, 1919), pp. 85–90.

10. Giovanni da Legnano, *De bello* 11, ed. Holland, pp. 90–91.

11. *Summa 'Elegantius in iure diuino' seu Coloniensis* 1.7, ed. Gerard Fransen and Stephan Kuttner, Monumenta iuris canonici, Ser. A, Vol. 1 (New York: Fordham University Press; Città del Vaticano: Biblioteca Apostolica Vaticana, 1969– ; in progress), 1:2; Odofredus, *Lectura super Digesto veteri* 1.1.4 v. *bella orta sunt* (Lyon: Joannes Pullon, 1552; repr. Bologna: A. Forni, 1968), fol. 7ra.

ing a state of war, with the organization, structure, and discipline of armies, and with the rules for the division of property acquired as a result of war.[12] The early commentators on the *Decretum* disagreed sharply over the question of whether the law of war should be considered part of the civil law.[13] The view that ultimately prevailed held that wars proclaimed by a prince were indeed a civil law institution. Now this labeling has more than theoretical significance. Since wars proclaimed by a prince or other lawful authority were, when fought for a just purpose, an instrument of public law, it followed that in those wars alone could adversaries be considered public enemies.[14] The importance of that, in turn, lay in the fact that as a matter of civil law there was no limit on the taking of spoils and prisoners from public enemies and property acquired in such a war was held to be acquired by a just title.[15] The courts, in other words, would recognize as rightful possessions the property acquired as a result of hostilities against public enemies, but they would not protect the title to property acquired in other types of hostilities. This definition enabled the jurists to distinguish, for example, between property acquired in just war, which was protected, and property acquired by a gang of robbers, which was not legally protected and which the courts would in due course restore to the rightful owner.

Both the army as a whole and its individual members, when fighting in a just war, were acting as agents of the ruler, and this agency conferred upon them a generous measure of legal immunity and protection.[16] Many things are lawful during a just war that are not lawful in

12. D. 1 c. 10. Gratian and the other texts of the *Corpus iuris canonici* are cited throughout from the standard edition by Emil Friedberg, 2 vols. (Leipzig: B. Tauchnitz, 1879; repr. Graz: Akademische Druck-und Verlagsanstalt, 1959), using the conventional canonistic citation system.

13. Rufinus, *Summa decretorum* to D. 1 c. 10 pr., ed. Heinrich Singer (Paderborn: F. Schöningh, 1902; repr. Aalen: Scientia Verlag, 1963), pp. 10–11; Stephan of Tournai, *Die Summa des Stephanus Torniacensis über das Decretum Gratiani* to D. 1 c. 10 v. *ius militare*, ed. Johann Friedrich von Schulte (Giessen: Emil Roth, 1891; repr. Aalen: Scientia Verlag, 1965), p. 11; *The Summa Parisiensis on the Decretum Gratiani* to D. 1 c. 10, ed. Terence P. McLaughlin (Toronto: Pontifical Institute of Medieval Studies, 1952), p. 3.

14. This concept is very ancient; an apparent reference to it appears in Gaius, *Institutes* 3.94, ed. and transl. Francis de Zulueta, 2 vols. (Oxford, England: Clarendon Press, 1946–53) 1:182. A formal definition was offered by Ulpian, *Institutiones* 1, in Dig. 49.15.24. The *Digest* and the rest of the *Corpus iuris civilis* is cited throughout from the critical edition in 3 volumes by Paul Krueger, Theodor Mommsen, Rudolf Schoell, and Wilhelm Kroll (Berlin: Weidmann, 1872–95). Ulpian's definition was familiar to the 12th-century canonists, who paraphrased it in their commentaries on the *Decretum*; see Stephen of Tournai, *Summa* to D. 1 c. 10 v. *in hostes*, ed. Schulte, p. 11; Rufinus, *Summa* to D. 1 c. 10 v. *egressio in hostes*, ed. Singer, p. 11.

15. Maurice H. Keen, *The Laws of War in the Late Middle Ages* (London: Routledge & Kegan Paul, 1965), p. 70.

16. Ulpian, *Ad edictum 6*, in *Dig.* 49.16.1.

peacetime, noted Cino da Pistoia (1270–1336/37), "because what is just depends upon the circumstances."[17] Cino's observation went straight to the heart of the matter: A just war had legal consequences that did not flow from other kinds of war. My point is that the concept of the just war, as the medieval canonists and civilians used it, was something more than simply a moral judgment. Just war created a chain of consequences that were of central importance to the participants in the conflict, for in a very practical sense the outcome of the conflict depended on those consequences.[18] Just wars vested property rights in the victor and stripped them from the vanquished; other wars did not. Just wars shielded the participants from liability for the loss of life and property in the conflict; other wars did not. The concept of just war, like many other legal concepts, was shrouded in the language of moral judgment, but for participants in these conflicts the moral overtones tended to be less immediately relevant than the tangible outcome.

The hypothesis that I wish to examine, therefore, is this: that the canonists of the classical period (i.e., between about 1140 and about 1378) sought to restrict the power to make war by imposing limitations on the definition of just war. By confining the category of just war within well-defined boundaries, they sought to circumscribe the effective power of monarchs to wage war by making the venture so potentially costly that princes would be deterred from fighting wars, save under the circumstances and within the rules that the jurists defined.

The function of law, according to the Summa "Elegantius," is to restrain violence and dispel discord.[19] In pursuit of this function, the canonists, as I have noted earlier, found at hand in the Decretum of Gratian a simplified version of the Augustinian definition of a just war: It must be proclaimed by public authority, prosecuted for a just purpose, and fought by permissible means.[20] Wars fought under these circumstances legitimized actions that otherwise would constitute crimes.[21] But not every action undertaken in a just war was permissible, for the canonists also had at hand in Gratian's work a brief catalogue of types of conduct that were not protected, even in a just war. That list included indiscrim-

---

17. Cino da Pistoia, *In Codicem et aliquot titulos primi Pandectarum tomi, id est Digesti veteris, doctissima commentaria* to Cod. 6.50.1 at 1, 2 vols., ed. Nicolo Cisnero (Frankfurt a/M.: Johannes Feyerabend, 1578; repr. Torino: Bottega d'Erasmo, 1964), fol. 423ra: "Not. primo quod aliud est ius tempore belli et aliud tempore pacis. . . . Et per hoc colligitur, quod aliud est iustum tempore guerrae et aliud est iustum tempore pacis, quia illud est iustum quod cuilibet in tempore suo expedit . . . et ita oportet legislatorem legem secundum tempora condere."

18. Keen, *Laws of War*, pp. 64–65.

19. *Summa 'Elegantius'* 1.4, ed. Fransen-Kuttner, 1:2.

20. c. 23 q. 2 c. 1–2 and d.p.c. 2.

21. c. 23 q. 1 c. 5 and d.p.c. 7; Keen, *Laws of War*, p. 65.

inate killing, atrocities inflicted as revenge, unremitting pursuit of the vanquished, and unprovoked aggression.[22] On the other hand, some types of action that in other conflicts would not only be morally reprehensible but would also create legal liabilities might be permitted in a just war, according to the Augustinian texts in the *Decretum*. Notable among these was the use of subterfuge, ambush, and surprise as tactical devices.[23]

Inherent in all this was the germ of a doctrine of limitations on the war-making power. Gratian's texts described three categories of conditions under which just war could be waged: One category defined the circumstances under which the conflict was initiated; the second limited the objectives of the warring powers; the third defined the means that might be legitimately employed in combat. But the language and the content of the texts that Gratian set forth were vague, their meanings were hard to pin down, and their implications were hazily spelled out.

Action to remedy some of these defects was soon in coming. The moving force behind one set of actions was Pope Alexander III (1159–81), the occasion the Third Lateran Council (1179). There the pope proposed and the bishops approved two canons that sought to impose limits on just wars. Both canons represented revivals of earlier efforts to limit warfare, but the new canons were designed, it appears, to specify in greater detail the implications of just-war doctrine as it appeared in the *Decretum*. The canon *Treugas autem* prescribed narrow limits on the periods of the year and even the days of the week when war could lawfully be waged. *Treugas autem* forbade combat during the penitential seasons of Lent and Advent and in addition enjoined combatants to lay down their arms from Thursday through Sunday of each week. The council commanded bishops to excommunicate those who failed to observe the prescribed truce periods.[24] The canon *Innovamus* sought in addition to prohibit attacks on certain groups of persons by warring parties: the clergy, monks and laybrothers, travelers, merchants, and peasants engaged in agricultural labor and their livestock were declared not to be legitimate targets for hostile action. Again, bishops were to excommunicate those who failed to observe this rule of immunity.[25] Shortly after the council ended, *Treugas autem* and *Innovamus* began to find their way into the law collections compiled as reference books for

22. c. 23 q. 1 c. 4.
23. c. 23 q. 2 c. 2.
24. III Lateran Council (1179) c. 21, in *Conciliorum oecumenicorum decreta*, 2d ed., by Giuseppe Alberigo et al. (Basel: Herder, 1962; cited herafter as COD), p. 198; Fermino Poggiaspalla, "La condotta della guerra secondo una disposizione del III Concilio Lateranense," *Ephemerides iuris canonici* 12 (1956), 379–386; Russell, *Just War*, pp. 183–186.
25. III Lateran Council (1179) c. 22, in COD, p. 198.

canonists and into the textbooks used for the teaching of canon law in the universities. Accordingly, these canons soon became the subject of discussion by law professors in the course of their lectures.[26]

At roughly the same time that these things were happening, some of the collections of recent law that were being compiled to supplement Gratian's *Decretum* also began to feature one further enactment that sought to impose a significant limitation on contemporary warfare. This canon, *Artem illam*, had been adopted much earlier, by the Second Lateran Council in 1139.[27] Although Gratian had not chosen to include *Artem illam* in his *Decretum*, canonists from the late 1170's onward began to insert it in anthologies of current law, and it ultimately found its way, together with *Treugas autem* and *Innovamus*, into the great official compendium of post-Gratian canons, the *Liber Extra*, promulgated in 1234 by Pope Gregory IX (1227–41).[28] *Artem illam* is particularly interesting because it represents the first and, to the best of my knowledge, the only attempt by medieval lawgivers to outlaw use of a new and, to contemporary eyes, a particularly frightening kind of weapon.

26. *Treugas autem* appears in at least a dozen early decretal collections: *1 Collectio Parisiensis* 9; *Appendix Concilii Lateranensis* 23 (21); *Collectio Lipsiensis* 21; *Collectio Bambergensis* 56.8; *Collectio Casselana* 51; *Collectio Brugensis* 23.3; *1 Collectio Alcobacensis* 10; *Collectio Ambrosiana* 65; *Collectio Floriacensis* 3; *Collectio Cusana* 176; *Collectio Dunelmensis prima* 2.45; and *Rotomagensis prima* 24.11. *Innovamus* also appears in all of these collections, save for *1 Par.* and *Cus.* (*App. Lat.* 24(26); *Lips.* 26; *Bamb.* 56.19; *Cass.* 12.4; *Brug.* 21.1; *1 Alc.* 8; *Ambr.* 71; *Flor.* 15; *1 Dun.* 2.44; *1 Rot.* 19.2). See the analyses of these collections in Emil Friedberg, *Die Canones-sammlungen zwischen Gratian und Bernhard von Pavia* (Leipzig: B. Tauchnitz, 1897; repr. Graz: Akademische Druck- u. Verlagsanstalt, 1958) and Walter Holtzmann, *Studies in the Collections of Twelfth-Century Decretals*, ed., rev., and transl. C. R. Cheney and Mary G. Cheney, Monumenta iuris canonici, Ser. B., Vol. 3 (Città del Vaticano, 1979). Both canons then appeared in the *Prima compilatio antiqua* of Bernard of Pavia; *Quinque compilationes antiquae necnon collectio canonum Lipsiensis*, ed. Emil Friedberg (Leipzig: B. Tauchnitz, 1882; repr. Graz: Akademische Druck- u. Verlagsanstalt, 1956) at 1 Comp. 1.24.1–2. From 1 Comp. the two canons passed into the *Liber Extra* at X 1.34.1–2.

27. II Lateran Council (1139) c. 29, in COD, p. 179; Paul Fournier, "La prohibition par le IIe concile de Latran d'armes jugées trop meurtrières," *Revue générale du droit international public* 23 (1916), 471–479; James A. Brundage, "Holy War and the Medieval Lawyers," in *The Holy War*, ed. Thomas P. Murphy (Columbus: Ohio State University Press, 1976), p. 115.

28. *Artem illam* was much less widely circulated than *Treugas autem* and *Innovamus*; it appears in *2 Paris.* 12.1, compiled shortly before 1179, and then turned up in *Lips.* 27.4. The canon subsequently passed into 1 Comp. 5.19.1 and thence into X 5.15.1. Russell, *Just War*, pp. 70–71, argues that Gratian omitted *Artem illam* because he disagreed with its basic premise. The argument is problematical, since it assumes that Gratian systematically left out canons that he found uncongenial; in fact, this runs counter to Gratian's method of dealing with opinions opposed to his own and, indeed, to the fundamental premise on which his work was constructed. Gratian, after all, entitled it a *Concordia discordantium canonum* precisely because its major contribution was to pose and resolve antinomies among the canons.

The weapon was the crossbow and its heavier companion, the ballista. These devices represented an innovation of considerable importance in military technology, for they were essentially armor-piercing
weapons. The crossbow was the portable version and could be used by
an individual infantryman, while the ballista was a larger scale device
of the same basic design, but mounted on a wheeled frame, something
like a caisson. Both weapons featured a metal bow, usually of steel,
with sufficient tensile resistance that the weapon had to be tensioned for
use by means of a winch, held in the ready position by a ratchet, and
discharged by a trigger mechanism. Both weapons fired pointed metal
bolts, or quarrels, with a high degree of accuracy and sufficient velocity
to penetrate most types of body armor then in use.[29] Although the crossbow and the ballista had been in limited use in Europe from the 11th
century,[30] these weapons achieved notoriety in the aftermath of the
Battle of Legnano (May 29, 1176), where the crossbows of the army of
the Lombard League inflicted a decisive defeat on the cavalry forces of
the Emperor Frederick Barbarossa (1152–90).[31] What particularly horrified contemporaries about this encounter was the fact that crossbows
and ballistas were infantry weapons. They enabled mere foot soldiers,
who were not members of the feudal nobility, to slaughter fully armored
knights on horseback, who up to this point had generally considered
themselves invincible against any other type of force they might meet,
an opinion that had been powerfully reinforced by the relatively consistent victories of European knights in their encounters with Turkish,
Syrian, and Egyptian forces during the first Crusade (1095–99) and its
successors. The victory of the Lombard infantry at Legnano abruptly
reversed this basic tenet of European warfare. Not for the last time, a
breakthrough in military technology carried the implicit threat of social
upheaval as well. It is no coincidence, I am sure, that within a year or
two following the battle of Legnano, the long-ignored ban on the use of
the crossbow and ballista enacted by the Second Lateran Council sud-
denly cropped up in the new lawbooks, and lawyers began to ponder
the implications of the ban on the use of these new weapons. The can-

---

29. Sir Ralph William Frankland Payne-Gallway, *The Crossbow, Mediaeval and
Modern, Military and Sporting*, 2nd ed. (London: Holland Press, 1958), pp. 4–16, 20–
21. More recently, Vernard Foley, George Palmer, and Werner Soedel, "The Crossbow,"
Scientific American 252/1 (January 1985), 104–110.

30. William the Conqueror employed crossbowmen at the Battle of Hastings, and
Anna Comnena apparently considered them such a novelty that she gave a detailed description of the ones employed by Western soldiers in the first Crusade; Anna Comnena,
Alexiad 10.8.6, ed. and transl. Bernard Leib, 3 vols. (Paris: Les Belles Lettres, 1943–
45) 2:317–18; Sir Charles Oman, *A History of the Art of War in the Middle Ages*, 2 vols.,
2nd ed. (London: Methuen, 1924) 1:137–140.

31. Oman, *Art of War* 1:445–449.

onists were not the only ones alarmed by these events. One of the demands that the English rebels forced King John to agree to in 1215 required the king to banish his foreign crossbowmen from the kingdom.[32]

One striking feature of *Artem illam* is that the canon pointedly prohibited the use of crossbows and ballistas against Christian and Catholic opponents. The clear implication was that use of these prohibited weapons against heretics and non-Christians was permissible. The canonists who commented on this text were quick to note the loophole. Bernard of Pavia, writing between 1191 and 1198, declared that under the terms of *Artem illam* Christian warriors were free to use crossbows against "pagans and persecutors of the Christian faith," and by this he clearly had in mind the Saracen opponents of the Crusaders in the Levant and perhaps also the pagan Livonians, Letts, and Estonians in the Baltic, against whom German bishops and warriors were organizing expeditions of conversion and conquest at precisely the time Bernard was writing.[33]

St. Raymond of Penyafort (ca. 1180–1275) carried the matter a bit further in his *Summa de penitentia* (1st ed., 1226/28; rev., 1234/36). After reiterating the observations of Bernard of Pavia about using crossbows against non-Christians and pagans, Raymond added: "Some people say that this weapon can be used in a just war against Christians" and then cited a passage from St. Augustine in support of this remarkable contention.[34] I call it remarkable, because it contradicts the plain language of the canon itself, language with which Raymond was unquestionably familiar, since he had edited the text of the canon as it appeared in the *Liber Extra* and had chosen to leave intact the restrictive phrase *adversus christianos et catholicos* of the original enactment. By ascribing the notion to "some people" (*dicunt quidam*), to be sure, Raymond distanced himself from it and refrained from expressing any opinion on the merits of this interpretation.

32. *Magna carta* 51, in William Stubbs, ed., *Select Charters and Other Illustrations of English Constitutional History from the Earliest Times to the Reign of Edward the First*, 9th ed., rev. H. W. C. Davis (Oxford, England: Clarendon Press, 1913), p. 299; Oman, *Art of War* 2:58.

33. Bernardus Papiensis, *Summa decretalium* 5.19, ed. E. A. T. Laspeyres (Regensburg: Josef Manz, 1860; repr. Graz: Akademische Druck-u. Verlagsanstalt, 1956), p. 244. On the Baltic expeditions see Eric Christianson, *The Northern Crusades: The Baltic and the Catholic Frontier, 1100–1525* (London: Macmillan, 1980), pp. 48–69, 89–100; as well as the more extended treatments in William Urban, *The Baltic Crusade* (De Kalb, Ill.: Northern Illinois University Press, 1975) and *The Chronicle of Henry of Livonia*, transl. James A. Brundage (Madison: University of Wisconsin Press, 1961).

34. Raymond of Penyafort, *Summa de penitentia* 2.4.1, ed. Xavier Ochoa and A. Diez, Universa bibliotheca iuris, Vol. 1 B (Roma: Commentarium pro religiosis, 1976), col. 461–62: "Item dicunt quidam, quod in bello iusto possunt officium hoc exercere etiam contra christianos. . . ."

The question naturally arises as to who were the people who were saying these things. I am aware of only two texts in which the argument that Raymond reports had been advanced unequivocally prior to the time that he wrote.[35] The Parisian theologian, Peter the Chanter (d. 1197) declared in his *Summa*:

Jerome states that it is dangerous to practice any craft that promotes pleasure or cruelty, as may be said of ballista specialists. Whence it is said, according to the Bishop of St. George, that communion is not to be given to them, unless they fight against the Saracens or in a just war.[36]

Likewise Peter the Chanter's former pupil, Cardinal Robert of Courson (ca. 1158/60–1219), commented in his theological lectures that manufacturers and users of the ballista and the crossbow stood in moral peril, unless they employed their deadly tools "for the defense of the holy land against the pagans, or even for defending their own kingdom."[37] Thus it appears that sometime during the 1190's, the decade during which Bernard of Pavia wrote his *Summa decretalium* and Peter the Chanter and Robert of Courson were delivering the lectures on which their *Summae* were based, the notion came into currency that the use of the crossbow could be tolerated in just wars between Christian opponents. Who invented this idea I cannot say with certainty; perhaps its begetter was that mysterious Bishop of St. George, mentioned by Peter the Chanter. In any case the Chanter is the earliest exponent of the doctrine known to me, and it seems probable, therefore, that it was created by the Paris theologians during the 1190's.

I should add, however, that Peter the Chanter also expressed his disapproval of the revolutionary new weapons I am discussing. In another passage of his *Summa* he railed against the manufacturers of these horrid instruments of destruction:

Again, there are certain businesses of no usefulness which present many occasions for sin to those who conduct them. They should be expelled from the Church—unless there are a great many of them. Such are the makers of ballis-

35. It seems significant that Joannes Teutonicus in his discussion of just war in the *glossa ordinaria* on the *Decretum* appears to be unaware of this argument, although it is virtually certain that he was familiar with the text of *Artem illam*.
36. Peter the Chanter, *Summa*, quoted by John Baldwin, *Masters, Princes, and Merchants: The Social Views of Peter the Chanter and His Circle*, 2 vols. (Princeton, N.J.: Princeton University Press, 1970), 2:160 n. 128: "Ieronimus: Omnis ars periculose exercetur quam luxuria vel quam crudelitas invenit, ut de balistariis. Unde dicendum secundum episcopum sancti georgii quod non est communio ei danda nisi contra saracenos vel in iusto bello pugnent."
37. Robert of Courson, *Summa* 10.10.12, in Baldwin, *Masters, Princes, and Merchants*, 2:160, n. 127: "Eodem modo dicimus de compositoribus balistarum precipue si balistas faciunt ad impugnandum christianos et ecclesiam dei, sed pro defensione terre sancte contra paganos vel etiam pro regno defendendo tolerari possunt."

tas and dice. Hence, if anyone possessed all the dice and all the ballistas that exist in the world, he ought to burn them, rather than sell them to Christians for illegal uses. Christians may, however, use ballistas against pagans and Cathars, but not against Christians.[38]

Despite these moralistic fulminations, however, the harm had been done. Peter the Chanter and his circle had perhaps invented and certainly publicized a loophole in the ban on the dreaded weapons, and it quickly passed from the theologians into the legal literature. Goffredus de Trano (d. 1245) incorporated the distinction in his *Summa super titulis decretalium* (written between 1241 and 1243):

Christians may not practice this craft [of the crossbowman] against Christians. . . . This is true if the war is unjust; but if it is a just war, any type of weapon may be employed. . . . This skill may also be employed against pagans and the persecutors of the Christian faith.[39]

The same line of argument recurred, with even greater effect, in the ordinary gloss of the *Liber Extra*, redacted in its final form by Bernard of Parma during the 1260's.[40] Since the ordinary gloss was the standard commentary on the *Decretals* and was routinely taught in the law faculties of medieval universities as the authoritative interpretation of the text, the gloss's adoption of the view that crossbows and ballistas could legitimately be used in just wars, even against Christians, effectively meant that the authoritative expositors of the law interpreted it to mean something quite different from, and in all probability diametrically opposed to, the intention of the legislators who framed this canon at the Second Lateran Council. The adoption of this interpretation by the academic lawyers ensured that the ban on the use of the crossbow would become entirely ineffective, which was precisely what happened.[41] The

38. Peter the Chanter, *Summa*, in Baldwin, *Masters, Princes, and Merchants*, 2:160 n. 125: "Item sunt quedam officia nullius utilitatis et multam occasionem prestant peccandi artifices illorum. Nisi multitudo esset in causa, essent eieiciendi ab ecclesia. Ut sunt balistarii et deciarii. Unde si quis haberet omnes decies qui sunt in mundo et omnes balistas potius deberet comburrere quam vendere christianis ad usum illicitum. Possunt tamen christiani uti balistis contra paganos et catares sed non contra christianos."

39. Goffredus de Trano, *Summa super titulis decretalium* to X 5.15.1 (Lyon: Roman Morin, 1519; repr. Aalen: Scientia Verlag, 1968), p. 430: "Christiani aduersus christianos non possunt hoc officium exercere, ut infra eodem c. uno [X 5.15.1]. Quod uerum est si bellum fuerit iniustum; nam si iustum, quelibet genere armorum est utendum. . . . Sed contra paganos et persecutores fidei christiane potest hoc officium exerceri."

40. Bernardus Parmensis, *Glossa ordinaria* to X 5.15.1 v. *christianos*: "Secus de Sarracenis a contrario sensu, et intellige debet de bello iniusto, arg. supra de iureiu., sicut si consisteret [X 2.24.29], quoniam si iustum esset, licitum esset pugnare, 23 q. 3 dominus [C. 23 q. 2 c. 2] et q. ultim. ut pridem [C. 23 q. 8 c. 17]." Likewise in the *Casus longi* to X 5.15.1: "Nota quod contra catholicos pugnare non licet, et intelige de bello iniusto, secus de iusto." Both the *glos. ord.* and the *Casus* are cited from the *Corpus iuris canonici una cum glossis*, 4 vols. (Venezia: Apud Iuntas, 1605).

41. Fournier, "Prohibition," pp. 477–479.

history of this effort to prohibit the use of the crossbow in domestic wars within Christendom is not a particularly comforting precedent, I fear, for those who hope to discourage the use of newer and vastly more destructive weapons in our own day.[42]

I shall now return to a theme that I touched on earlier, and one whose historical outcome may be slightly less depressing. In discussing the treatment of just and unjust wars in Gratian's *Decretum* and by the canons *Treugas autem* and *Innovamus* of the *Liber Extra*, I stated earlier that the net effort of these doctrines was that only just wars had legal consequences for property rights. The civilians and canonists in the law faculties did not subject this notion to detailed analysis until the mid-13th century and after. When they did so, their analyses led to some interesting, even suggestive, conclusions. Pope Innocent IV (1243–54), who was a law professor before he became Pope and who continued his scholarly writing during his tenure of St. Peter's Chair, maintained that soldiers summoned to fight in a just war had a right to claim compensation from their leader for any losses that they suffered in consequence of their military service. He based this contention on the intriguing theory that a summons to military service (save under certain exceptional circumstances) created a contract (a *mandatum*) between the summoner and those who responded gratuitously to his summons. By virtue of this contractual relationship, the summoner assumed an obligation to make good expenses and losses incurred by those who served him. If the leader failed to pay them voluntarily, Innocent continued, individual soldiers had recourse against him by an action in mandate. This recourse, however, applied only to those summoned to a just war; in an unjust conflict soldiers had no contract with their leader and hence had no right to sue to recover expenses and losses.[43] The effect of Innocent's doctrine was to shift liability for the expenses of conducting warfare to the person who proclaimed a just war, while in an unjust conflict the soldiers had to bear individually any expenses or losses they might incur and the initiator of the hostilities was freed from liability to his followers. This scheme created an economic disincentive for monarchs and other rulers to undertake just wars and for individual soldiers to fight in unjust ones.[44]

---

42. Another unsuccessful effort to limit violence was the attempt by the I Council of Lyon (1245) c. 18 to prohibit political assassination. The canon was incorporated in VI 5.4.1, but seems to have had little effect.

43. Innocent IV, *Apparatus toto orbe celebrandus super V libris decretalium* to X 2.24.9, no. 1 (Frankfurt a/M: Sigismund Feyerabendt, 1570; repr. Frankfurt a/M: Minerva, 1968), fol. 288r.

44. Innocent's argument was adopted by other canonists as well; see Joannes Andreae, *In quinque decretalium libros novella commentaria* to X 2.24.29 no. 5, 5 vols. in 4 (Venezia: Apud Franciscum Franciscium, 1581; repr. Torino: Bottega d'Erasmo, 1963), 2:197va.

The companion piece to this plan for discouraging war by economic disincentives was the treatment of liabilities resulting from hostile action. The clearest detailed treatments of this problem in the canonistic commentaries occur in the writings of Cardinal Hostiensis (d. 1271) and Joannes Andreae (d. 1348). Hostiensis based his exposition of this problem primarily on Roman law. The key concept, as he saw things, was the formal state of just war, which he called Roman war.[45] The ruler who waged war without a just and reasonable cause—as do most rulers nowadays, Hostiensis added—exposed himself to liability for any damages resulting from the actions of his troops during the hostilities. The courts should entertain individual actions against such rulers to recover the value of property lost, stolen, or destroyed as a result of the conflict. Joannes Andreae added that no such actions ought to be entertained against a ruler who was defending his domains against an aggressor, so long as the defender limited his actions to those required for strictly defensive purposes.[46] No restitution was required, either, for property damage resulting from a formally proclaimed just war.[47]

Joannes Andreae added a further qualification: The ruler who commences a conflict does so under a *prima facie* presumption that the conflict is unjust; the burden of rebutting that presumption rests on him. Further, Joannes added, jurisdiction over claims for compensation arising out of an unjust conflict and determination of the status of a conflict as just or unjust was vested by civil law in the courts of the Church, not in the royal courts or the courts of other secular authorities.[48]

In addition, Hostiensis and other canonistic writers maintained that there was a right to initiate criminal actions against those responsible for the deaths of persons killed in an unjust war. This conclusion rested on a consensus among the canonists that deaths in a just war, while regrettable, were not caused by wrongful acts.[49] There was respectable theological opinion, grounded in ideas that originated with St. Augustine, that sacred violence, which included waging just war against certain classes of enemies—notably pagans, other non-Christians, and

---

45. Hostiensis, *Summa aurea, una cum summariis et adnotationibus Nicolai Superantii*, lib. 1, tit. De treuga et pace, no. 4 (Lyon: Joannes de Lambray, 1537; Aalen: Scientia Verlag, 1962), fol. 59ra.

46. Joannes Andreae, *Novella* to X 4.24.29, no. 4, ed. cit., fol. 197va.

47. Hostiensis, *In quinque decretalium libris commentaria* to VI 5.4.1, 6 vols. in 2 (Venezia: Apud Iuntas, 1581; repr. Torino: Bottega d'Erasmo, 1965), 6:29va.

48. Joannes Andreae, *Novella* to X 2.24.29, no. 3 and X 5.12.24, no. 2, ed. cit., 2:197va and 5:65rb.

49. E.g. in the *Quaestiones Bambergensis I*, ed. Alfons M. Stickler, in "De potestate gladii materialis ecclesiae secundum 'Quaestiones Bambergenses' ineditae," *Salesianum* 6 (1944), 121–124, and a 12th-century Anglo-Norman gloss to C. 23 q. 5 c. 9 v. *si non licet*, in MS. C.III.1, fol. 213ra, of Durham Cathedral Library: "Tribus modis fit licite homicidium, scilicet cum inspiratur aliquis deo occulte ut aliquem interficiat, uel cum iudex habens potestatem gladii aliquem interfici, uel cum precepto principis miles interficit hostem."

heretics—was an act of love and hence morally virtuous.[50] Thus Hostiensis could conclude that "A layman who slays anyone in a just war is without fault," and *e contrario* that those who caused deaths in an unjust war were criminally guilty of homicide.[51]

Giovanni da Legnano, the author of the first full-fledged treatise on the law of war, as I mentioned earlier, drew upon these teachings of Innocent IV, Hostiensis, and Joannes Andreae in his work and summarized the conclusions that I have set forth here as his definitive statement of the doctrine of liability and redress for actions perpetrated in war.[52] In Giovanni's presentation it became obvious that there was only one type of war, the just war, that made economic sense, either for rulers or for their soldiers. The liabilities incurred by participants could potentially cripple the victor in an unjust conflict. Even if his victims proved ultimately unable to collect all their claims against him, the law, as Giovanni summarized it, provided victims of an unjust conflict with ample opportunity for almost endless legal harassment that might well strip victory of its savor and its profit.

One further class of questions remains to be considered here, namely, property rights accruing to the victors in a conflict. Roman law had forbidden private individuals to acquire property as a result of their participation in a conflict, save for the stipends that they received from the state for their services.[53] This prohibition was taken into Gratian's *Decretum.*[54] The 12th-century decretists taught it as a regular part of their treatment of the law of war.[55] In the 13th century, however, there was a change of attitude. The ordinary gloss on the *Liber Extra* asserted that the title to property captured in war depended upon the nature of the war in which it was captured. In an unjust war, the victor lacked legal title to any property he acquired in the conflict, but property acquired in a just war belonged to the victor.[56] Innocent IV expanded on this idea and declared that both persons and property captured in a just war rightfully belonged to the captor. On the other hand, Innocent continued, those who lost property as a result of actions in an unjust war were entitled to legal redress through an *actio vi bonorum raptorum* for the recovery of movables or an *actio rei vindicatio* for the recovery of im-

---

50. Jonathan Riley-Smith, "Crusading As an Act of Love," *History* 65 (1980), 177–192.

51. Hostiensis, *Summa aurea*, lib. 5, tit. De homicidio, no. 2, in ed. cit., fol. 241va.

52. Giovanni da Legnano, *De bello* 42, ed. Holland, pp. 115–116.

53. Dig. 49.16.9 (Marcianus).

54. C. 23 q. 1 c. 5.

55. Paucapalea, *Summa* to C. 23 q. 1 pr., ed. Schulte, p. 99; *Summa Parisiensis* to C. 23 q. 1 c. 5 v. *militare* and v. *sed id agere*, ed. McLaughlin, p. 211; Rufinus, *Summa* to D. 1 c. 10 v. *item modus stipendiorum*, ed. Singer, p. 11.

56. *Glos. ord.* to X 2.24.29 v. *restituat.*

movables.[57] Joannes Andreae developed this notion further. In just wars, he taught, the victor has a right to retain not only property captured from his foe—that is, the ruler against whom he waged the war—but also property captured from the enemy's vassals, subjects, and allies. But this right was subject to three restrictions, according to Joannes. First, it applied only to persons and property captured during the course of hostilities. Second, it applied only to property belonging to those who actually participated in the war. Third, it applied only to property that belonged to persons over whom the victor had legitimate jurisdiction.[58] Thus property that belonged to persons who lived in the kingdom of the victor in a just war might rightfully be seized by the ruler if the owners cooperated with the enemy during hostilities, provided that the seizure took place while hostilities were still in progress. A king had the right, in other words, to confiscate the property and imprison the persons of those who rebelled against him and who gave aid to his enemies in a just war. A king did not have the right, however, to confiscate the property or to hold the persons of his opponents who lived in the enemy kingdom, although he might hold captured opponents as hostages to guarantee specific performance, say, of provisions in a peace treaty.[59]

Thus the distinctions between just and unjust wars and between private and public hostilities that feature so prominently in medieval jurists' discussions were not simply abstract legal theorizing about the moral merits of specific kinds of conflicts.[60] The economic consequences of war depended directly upon these juristic categories, and both rulers and soldiers were certainly aware of them.[61] The speculations of the lawyers had considerable practical importance for those who engaged in war and those who declared it. This segment of legal history merits reflection, even in the 20th century, when we ponder the problems of war and peace. If the venerable tradition of just war is to have any current value, save as a rhetorical device for slandering our enemies, it may lie in the suggestion that it might be wise to use incentives and sanctions other than physical force to discourage military adventurism. If we want to make war unattractive as a policy option, perhaps the best strategy for achieving that goal may be to find ways to make it unprofitable as well.

57. Innocent IV, *Apparatus* to X 2.24.29, no. 5, in ed. cit., fol. 288 v.
58. Joannes Andreae, *Novella* to X 2.13.12, no. 20-22, in ed. cit., 2:82ra–rb.
59. Joannes Andreae, *Novella* to X 2.24.29, no. 9, ed. cit., 2:198ra.
60. Keen, *Laws of War*, pp. 70–71.
61. Keen, *Laws of War*, pp. 82–100.

FREDERICK H. RUSSELL

6. The Historical Perspective of the Bishops' Pastoral Letter: The View of One Medievalist

Confronting the bishops' pastoral letter on war and peace is a difficult task for a 20th-century medievalist, for it involves me on two levels: that of a medieval historian, and that of a 20th-century Christian. The historian in me wants to scold the bishops for their distortion of the historical record of the Church's positions on just-war theorizing and the role of the Church in warfare. The modern Christian in me wants at once to congratulate the bishops on their accomplishments and also to take issue with some points in the bishops' letter with which I disagree.

In this paper I hope to interweave these two components of my reaction. I should make clear some of my points of departure. While I am not an expert on nuclear weapons or contemporary politics, I think that in terms of nuclear war there are no *bona fide* experts, for nuclear weapons have been used only twice; the rest of the debate is speculative, so everybody can be an expert, and nobody is an expert. From the purported experts it is, however, clear to me that nuclear wars cannot be won in any traditional sense. Thus the survival of human values would be, as the pastoral letter indicates, very much at risk. With all its faults, the bishops' pastoral letter must be accorded great respect; it must also be subjected to serious and nonbombastic debate.

The literature on the justification of warfare is too immense for any one person to control. Even getting a representative sample is a formidable task. The literature, both medieval and modern, is not only vast and repetitive, but uneven in quality. We are, intellectually, what we read. Thus a modern systematic ethicist will see the problems far differently than I do. Different approaches that appear antithetical may often turn out to be complementary. I know of no one way that deals sufficiently with the problems of warfare in the modern world. Thus the bishops' pastoral letter, in its eclecticism and scholarship, compels my admiration and respect even where I do not agree with its documentation and recommendations. My remarks will proceed by a comparison of then and now, that is, by juxtaposition of warfare and its justification in the medieval Church with the views expressed in the bishops' pastoral letter. I hope to show what has changed and what has remained constant in Catholic teaching.

The most crucial part of the bishops' pastoral letter for me is the first chapter dealing with the just-war theory. To launch my observations I will look at the range of possible Christian attitudes toward warfare and survey the major late antique and medieval formulations of the right to wage war. In the late ancient world and in the Middle Ages there were, broadly, three Christian attitudes toward warfare.[1] The first was the just war, which, under Augustine's influence, came closest to the official position of the Church. The second was the holy war, undertaken on God's authority or inspiration, for the purpose of punishing sin and disbelief. This stance was fostered by Pope Gregory I and under the medieval popes led to the crusades. In a sense the holy war was a special form of just war. The third was some sort of pacifism, the conviction that recourse to violence contradicted the Christian duty of charity. This last attitude was unofficial and was for the most part condemned by the Church.

The bishops' pastoral letter treats the first and the third of these attitudes and attempts to link them, but passes over the holy war-Crusade tradition in silence. The linkage it makes between just war and pacifism is almost wholly unprecedented and takes the form of an official tolerance for selective conscientious objection within the Catholic community. This tactic of consolidation is new, fruitful, and problematical.

I

The Christian just-war theory originated with St. Augustine, whose thought developed during the decline of the Roman Empire and in an atmosphere of anxious spiritual crisis. How could a Christian pursue perfection in this world, when being a Christian no longer made any visible difference?

---

1. Much of what follows is based on my *The Just War in the Middle Ages* (Cambridge, England: Cambridge University Press, 1975). Other perspectives are offered in James A. Brundage, "The Holy War and the Medieval Lawyers," in T. P. Murphy, ed., *The Holy War* (Columbus, Ohio: Ohio State University Press, 1976), pp. 99–140; and his article in this volume, "The Limits of the War-Making Power: The View of the Medieval Canonists." The most recent treatment of the medieval just war is Jonathan Barnes, "The Just War," in N. Kretzmann, A. Kenny, and J. Pinborg, eds., *The Cambridge History of Later Medieval Philosophy* (Cambridge, England: Cambridge University Press, 1982), pp. 771–784. Special thanks are owed to Professor Robert Markus, of the University of Nottingham, who helped shape my ideas for this paper, and whose article "Saint Augustine's Views on the 'Just War,'" *Studies in Church History* 20 (1983), 1–13 shows how intellectuals often distort the ideas of any one thinker so as to make them fit into an overall scheme. As I hope to show, this is just what the bishops have done. I must emphasize as in my title that the ideas expressed here are solely my own.

Augustine's responses to this question included his teaching on war and coercion that here I will break down into five clusters of ideas: love, the definition of a just war, the requirement of authority, religious persecution, and the proper means of fighting.

According to Augustine, the private person could not fight without loss of love. It was better to be killed than to kill. In regard to private violence, Augustine was a pacifist. The situation was different, however, for public officials, who in performance of their duties could kill with impunity provided they were motivated by charity. The precepts of patience in the New Testament were to be maintained by these officials in their "inward disposition," however violent and savage their outward acts might be. Officials must guard against acting out of hatred, cruelty, and vengeance. Thus killing could be motivated by love, the love for a criminal or sinner that sought to prevent him from sinning further. The evangelical precept of charity was not abrogated but located primarily in the inward disposition.[2]

Augustine succinctly defined the just war as one that avenged injuries, such as when an enemy government refused to restore stolen goods or to punish the evil deeds of its subjects. This definition was to prove so durable that St. Thomas Aquinas and many others quoted it in their own definitions of the just war.[3]

For Augustine, princes alone among mortals had the authority to declare and wage wars. But he also showed, on the strength of Old Testament examples, that God could be the ultimate Author of a just war that would further divine purposes and providentially punish evil-doers. Wars undertaken on divine inspiration, such as the Crusades, could by this reasoning be at least potentially unlimited in ends and means.

In the course of coping with the threat to Christian orthodoxy posed by the Donatist heresy, Augustine elaborated a doctrine of religious persecution that required bishops to invoke state coercion to force heretics back into the orthodox fold. This is his famous doctrine of *compelle intrare*, "compel them [the heretics] to come in [to the Church]."[4] While this doctrine developed apart from Augustine's just-war theory and never advocated the killing of heretics, it did in the Middle Ages become grafted on to the just-war theory and was used to justify wars and Crusades against infidels, heretics, and enemies of the Church.

Augustine's thoughts on how properly to wage war consist of isolated

2. Russell, *Just War*, pp. 17 ff.
3. Ibid., pp. 18–21; pp. 267–271.
4. A good discussion of the evolution of Augustine's thought on the matter of religious coercion is found in Peter Brown, "St. Augustine's Attitude to Religious Coercion," *Journal of Roman Studies* 54 (1964), 107–116.

passages that he did not form into a systematic position. On one hand, Augustine followed Cicero in holding that faith once promised to an enemy should be maintained, while elsewhere he held that, once a war was just, it could be fought by any means, either openly or by means of ambushes and clever ruses.[5] And, while he recommended that mercy be shown to a defeated enemy population, the war was still just even if such mercy was not shown. Augustine betrayed no sense of outrage at the killing of innocent noncombatants, for after all, as sinners they were being punished for sins committed in some other connection unrelated to the war.

I hope this brief survey shows that all three medieval attitudes toward warfare took nourishment from the Bishop of Hippo. I will mention two other medieval formulations of the just war. The first is that of the canonist Raymond of Penyafort, writing about 1225. For him, a war was justified by five conditions:

1. The persons doing the fighting must be laymen.

2. There must be a just cause, such as recovering lost goods or defense of the *patria*.

3. Recourse to war must be unavoidable.

4. The intention must be proper, that is, the war should not be waged out of hatred or vengeance.

5. The war must be waged on the authority of the Church or a prince.

All five criteria must be met for the war to be considered just.

The medieval formulation of the just war best known to most of us was that of St. Thomas Aquinas, writing about 1270. For Thomas, a just war must meet three criteria: legitimate authority, just cause (the prior guilt of the enemy), and righteous intention (to promote good and avoid evil). The formula thus stated was formal, general, and abstract; it provided little substantive guidance on causes and conduct of a just war.

Medieval support for a doctrine of noncombatant immunity, such as that contained in the bishops' pastoral letter, is to be found, if at all, in notions expressed outside the formal confines of the just-war theories. It should be noted here that the limited protection of noncombatants in medieval scholastic thought was not usually extended to nonorthodox Christians. To be sure, there was the peace of God that sought to exclude certain classes of people from violence, in effect, a sort of limited noncombatant immunity. But the peace of God was not formally incor-

5. Russell, *Just War*, pp. 16, 23, 70 ff. Cf. James Turner Johnson, *Just War Tradition and the Restraint of War: A Moral and Historical Inquiry* (Princeton, N.J.: Princeton University Press, 1981), p. 123.

porated into just-war formulas, was not extended to non-Christians, and was more often honored in the breach than in the observance. I know of no medieval opinion that explicitly stated that breach of the peace of God rendered unjust a war otherwise considered just. That development would have to await the very different conditions of modern warfare.

There was also the truce of God, which attempted to shut down all violence during certain periods of the liturgical week and year. Canonists distinguished between this canonical truce and conventional truces arranged by both hostile parties and then concluded that the canonical truce was a moot issue because it was not usually observed by the parties directly concerned. As support for this position they referred to a papal letter stating that a just war could be waged any time, while an unjust war should not be waged at all, especially during the time of a canonical truce. And the canonists often cited Augustine's opinion that all means of fighting a just war were licit, while all means of fighting an unjust war were obviously illicit. Scholastic opinion also tried to restrict the use of especially lethal weapons such as crossbows to wars against infidels and heretics, but again this attempt was undercut by Augustine's opinion.[6]

Where is there in this line of thinking any doctrine of noncombatant immunity similar to that in the bishops' pastoral letter? Where is there any clear and explicit prohibition on certain means of conducting a war? I find none, although I would suggest that there are elements in the medieval scholastic analysis of warfare that could be and were used in the early modern and modern periods to develop a doctrine of noncombatant immunity. These elements were, however, not used for this purpose until at least the late Middle Ages.

By way of contrast, let us briefly consider the modern formula of the just war as found in the bishops' pastoral letter.[7] Here there are seven criteria, not the five of Raymond of Penyafort, nor the three of Thomas Aquinas. There is first a just cause, to protect human life and the conditions necessary for a decent human existence. Second comes competent authority, now a much easier criterion to meet, at least in wars between legitimate sovereign states. Third is the difficult test of comparative or relative justice inherent in each side. Fourth is the criterion of right intention, related to the just-cause criterion. Fifth, the war must be the last resort (shades of Raymond of Penyafort's criterion of cause as unavoidability). Sixth is another test that is difficult to apply, the

---

6. Russell, *Just War*, pp. 34–36, 70 ff., 156, 183–186, 194, 246, 272 ff., 298.

7. *The Challenge of Peace: God's Promise and Our Response. A Pastoral Letter on War and Peace* (Washington, D.C.: United States Catholic Conference, 1983), nn. 80–100. (Hereafter cited as *Challenge of Peace*).

probability of success. Seventh and last, is proportionality between potential gains and losses, both for the belligerent and for the international community.[8]

Whence come these criteria? I can ask, without being able to provide an answer here. The criteria are certainly post-medieval, and much has changed in both moral theory and military practice in the interim. I do note that the bishops' pastoral letter does not cite any authority writing in the long period between Thomas Aquinas and the 20th century, thus neglecting the crucial adjustments to the medieval theories of the just war made by such late scholastic thinkers as Vitoria and Suarez, not to mention Grotius. Note also that the criteria have become even more abstract than those in the Thomistic formulation and show a heavy reliance on the speculative Thomistic philosophy. Perhaps the new criteria are logically embedded in the medieval just-war teaching, but the lens of time and history employed by the American bishops has led to a distortion of the historical record, to reading history backwards, to projecting our present moral convictions back onto the thought of Augustine and Aquinas. Furthermore, the complex record of the medieval Church in preventing, regulating, and encouraging warfare has been overlooked. The medieval clergy did participate, often directly, in warfare.[9] Much of the historical material in the bishops' pastoral letter is not historically accurate. For the best of motives, the historical record has been distorted.

II

Will this selective use of the historical tradition undermine the credibility of the bishops' pastoral letter? I hope not, and I doubt that my

8. On the modern requirement of proportionality in the nuclear age, see Johnson, *Just War Tradition*, p. 337, and Michael Walzer, *Just and Unjust Wars. A Moral Argument with Historical Illustrations* (New York: Basic Books, 1977), pp. 276–280 *et passim*. One wonders why the bishops' pastoral letter makes no reference to Walzer's troubling and very different treatment of the just war.

9. To illustrate this point, one need read only the following passage from the *Alexiad* of Anna Comnena, paraphrased by Roland Bainton, *Christian Attitudes Toward War and Peace* (Nashville, Tenn.: Abingdon Press, 1960), p. 114: "A certain priest stood on the stern and discharged arrows. Though streaming with blood, he was quite fearless, for the rules as to priests are different among the Latins from ours. We are taught by the canonical laws and the gospel that the priest is holy—but the Latin barbarian will handle divine things and simultaneously wear a shield on his left arm and hold a spear in his right. At one and the same time he communicates the body and blood of God and becomes a man of blood, for this barbarian is no less devoted to sacred things than to war. This priest, or rather man of violence, wore his vestments while he handled an oar and was so bellicose as to keep on fighting after the truce." The medieval military orders are a second instance of clerics and religious engaging in combat. See Desmond Seward,

historical quibbles will seriously compromise the bishops' effort. Yet as a historian I feel bound to point out their somewhat skewed treatment of the tradition. Still, what contribution can a historian make to the debate over logical and juridical perspectives of modern Catholic just-war theories?

One staple of modern thought on justifiable war, enshrined in the bishops' pastoral letter, is the distinction between the *ius ad bellum*, the right to go to war, and *ius in bello*, proper conduct of hostilities. This is a post-medieval distinction, one that is very difficult to make both in the abstract and in the concrete. In the medieval just war, what would become the *ius ad bellum* took precedence over the *ius in bello*. Modern theories reversed this emphasis until the thinking that led to the bishops' pastoral letter. This shift came about because of the varied and often contradictory legal systems of the post-medieval world, in which situation there could be no general consensus about the *ius ad bellum*, the legitimate reasons for recourse to force. Thus the traditional just-war formulas became merely a formalistic set of criteria that did not meet the aspirations of modern nations or would-be states. Substantive justice could therefore not be realized through the traditional *ius ad bellum*. Hence many modern theorists have focused their attention almost completely on the *ius in bello*, on that complex of rights deemed applicable to a war that each side had an equal right to wage, provided it respected the rights of those somehow involved on the other side.[10] As a result, the status of non-combatants and the morality of nuclear weapons have received much attention and little consensus. The state of the question shows the futility of a *ius in bello* detached from a *ius ad bellum*. I suggest that we need to look at the *ius ad bellum* with renewed vigor, for without it the *ius in bello* becomes morally stranded, terrifying to contemplate, and intractable to consider. The potential destructiveness of nuclear warfare indeed makes this reconsideration of the *ius ad bellum* imperative. For what goals could we possibly be willing to risk a nuclear holocaust? We must refine our understanding of the specific antecedent conditions that would legitimate a nuclear war while we are able, for once engaged, there will be no time for us to weigh the moral dimensions of our actions.

An even more important mainstay of modern just-war debate is the

---

The Monks of War: The Military Religious Orders (Hampden, Conn.: Archon Books, The Shoestring Press, 1972).

10. The foremost recent exponent of the *ius in bello* theory is Paul Ramsey. See, for example, his *War and the Christian Conscience* (Durham, N.C.: Duke University Press, 1961) and his *The Just War: Force and Political Responsibility* (New York: Charles Scribner's Sons, 1968). The shift in emphasis from *ius ad bellum* to *ius in bello* is still incompletely documented; on this issue see Walzer, *Just and Unjust Wars*, pp. 21–23, 38, 41, 108, 195, 283, and Johnson, *Just War Tradition*, pp. xxxi, 177 ff., 209, 352.

distinction between licit self-defensive and defensive war on the one hand, and illicit aggressive or offensive warfare on the other. In their letter, the bishops seem to elevate the immunity of defenseless noncombatants into a clear moral principle and to assume, somewhat simplistically, that defensive war is justified and that offensive war is never licit. Here we are all at the mercy of the terms we use. Claims to be acting only defensively may make good propaganda, but, given the complexity of modern warfare, with its mixture of rights, interests, ideologies, and threats, such claims are simplistic and unrealistic. The concepts of aggression and defense suffer from a kind of "definitional uncertainty." Or, to paraphrase John Courtney Murray writing a quarter century ago, an aggressive war is merely the contrary of a war of self-defense.[11] This brings us no closer to a viable distinction. The Reagan administration has used the term "preemptive counterattack" to describe what appears to be preventive first-strike aggression. By contrast, the medieval just war did not view self-defense as the only just cause, nor the first crossing of borders as an automatically unjust cause. Indeed, the prior guilt of the enemy, however defined, made a war justifiable. This effectively excluded preventive wars from being just wars. On the other hand, self-defense against a just attack was not justifiable.[12] In this context the recent debate over whether to renounce in advance the right of first strike becomes useless. I cannot clear this linguistic jungle; the bishops and others have not either.

Yet this reliance on the seemingly common-sense distinction between aggression and defense may have shaped what is perhaps the most controversial contention of the bishops' pastoral letter: the very grudging, excruciatingly qualified justification of the policy of deterrence as a temporary expedient.[13] Here I must return to medieval just-war theory because I do not accept the possibility of a clear distinction between a defensive and an offensive war. There are simply too many possible claims and counter-claims to prior justice or to partial justice. The evidentiary problems of many charges of aggression are indeed formidable in the real world, and an international judicial body would have a hard time finding unambiguously for one party.[14] So we are left with deter-

11. John Courtney Murray, "Remarks on the Moral Problem of War," *Theological Studies* 20 (1959), 40–61, at 45 and n. 10. For modern critiques of the attempt to distinguish aggression from defense, cf. Walzer, *Just and Unjust Wars*, pp. 23, 62, 74; Johnson, *Just War Tradition*, p. 262, n. 44, pp. 328, 360; James F. Childress, "Just War Criteria," in Thomas A. Shannon, ed., *War or Peace. The Search for New Answers* (Maryknoll, N.Y.: Orbis, 1980), pp. 40–58, at p. 46.

12. Barnes, "The Just War," p. 780.

13. *Challenge of Peace*, nn. 188–199.

14. This problem gives rise to what Johnson (*Just War Tradition*, p. 178) calls "simultaneous ostensible justice."

rence as a dangerous but unavoidable strategy for the foreseeable future.[15]

The bishops' pastoral letter updates the traditional just war by "relativizing" claims to absolute justice, so that wars can be partially just on both sides.[16] The medieval canonists wrestled with this problem without success. In a sense Augustine's answer is the best we can hope for: When the "juster" side wins, it is to be congratulated; and it is worse when the injurious party prevails over the "juster" party. Augustine was aware that a war could morally be partially just on both sides, although this aspect of his thought slumbered in obscurity until the modern age. It is, of course, very difficult for a statesman or government leader to relativize his own claims.

When torn from its medieval historical context, the just war is shown not to be a legal concept, but a moral and theological concept surfaced with an often thick veneer of legalism. In legal perspective, many wars amount to "self vindication without due process of law."[17] In a just war, the justified prince was both judge and party in his own cause, hardly a defensible jurisprudential position. Agreement as to a broad and abstract definition of just-war criteria is irrelevant to an actual hostile situation. The only ability of the just-war theory to restrain unjustifiable wars lies in its support by custom and precedent and in its powers of moral suasion as an influence on the practical virtue of politics. At best, the just war is a structure of temporal order, not of substantive justice. I think this is where some segments of Catholic reaction have missed the point, for they expect too much from just-war theory. They expect it to defend and avenge the moral order.[18] As a tool of true justice, the just war is badly deficient. St. Augustine recognized this in the *City of God*, where he showed that politics on earth could not achieve true justice and that earthly institutions were in constant danger of decay.

The bishops appear to have recognized these limitations by omitting a large part of the Catholic historical experience, such as the Crusades and the holy war. Perhaps this recognition is why the bishops call for an international body to resolve international conflict. I must note, how-

15. In this context it seems somewhat perverse for Walzer (*Just and Unjust Wars*, pp. 270–274, 283) to assimilate deterrence to terrorism. After all, the inward disposition of those carrying out a policy of deterrence is surely quite different from that of terrorists.

16. *Challenge of Peace*, nn. 92–94. The modern just war serves as a guideline for making relative moral decisions: Johnson, *Just War Tradition*, pp. xxxiii ff., Childress, "Just War Criteria," pp. 42, 53. For the ancient and medieval debates, see Russell, *Just War*, pp. 21, 89–92.

17. Roland H. Bainton, *Christian Attitudes Toward War and Peace* (New York: Abingdon Press, 1960), p. 240.

18. See, for example, the rhetorical exaggeration and bombast of Michael Novak, "The Bishops Speak Out," *National Review* 35, 11 (June 10, 1983), 674–681.

ever, that the medieval papacy attempted to play a similar role, and failed. In its attempt, it also initiated major wars to prosecute its version of justice, with disastrous consequences.

III

The strengths of the bishops' pastoral letter are many and manifest, however much we can quibble with specific positions it takes. The bishops took historical change from the Middle Ages to the onset of the nuclear age into account. Wars now involve much more of the population much more catastrophically. Nuclear weapons do not allow us the luxury of passing over the issue of noncombatant immunity in relative silence. The bishops have given us a comprehensive overview of modern problems of warfare. They have also rectified many of the deficiencies of the medieval just war, such as the strong emphasis on war as a punishment for prior guilt and sin and the rather callous disregard for the fate of noncombatants. The modern just war had become reduced to an abstract, impoverished formula irrelevant to the nuclear age until the bishops breathed new life into the moribund tradition. The pastoral letter is based on much of the best of Catholic thought in the nuclear era. The bomb has changed the way we think about war; no longer do we have the luxury of splitting hairs about the *ius in bello*. In a sense, the just-war tradition has been outmoded by modern history, and the bishops recognize this transformation.[19] One major part of the Christian experience, the Crusade, has been omitted because it is no longer viable morally or militarily, however much historians might fuss.[20] Punishing religious or political heterodoxy is now disproportionate to its ends. One major part of the Christian experience heretofore denied official tolerance has been added: pacifism, especially selective conscientious objection.

By reinstating the just war as a tool of moral suasion, the bishops have encouraged discussion and the education not just of the clergy but also of the laity. They are nondogmatic on the concrete applications of their moral principles and seek to open dialogues with all concerned parties. The pastoral letter diminishes blind unreasoned deference to authorities lay and spiritual, thereby overcoming the heavy emphasis on authority in the just-war tradition.

In the drafting process the bishops harmonized an incongruity of recent Catholic attitudes. Thirty years ago prelates could support saber-

19. Cf. Walzer, *Just and Unjust Wars*, pp. 276, 282; Johnson, *Just War Tradition*, p. 327.

20. Jonathan Riley-Smith has shown how Crusade preachers preached hatred under the guise of love: "Crusading as an Act of Love," *History* 65 (1980), 177–192.

rattling rhetoric and massive retaliation directed against perceived Communist threats here and abroad. (This was perhaps a vestige of the holy war tradition.) At the same time the hierarchy condemned abortion in no uncertain terms.[21] Now, with the publication of the *Challenge of Peace*, *all* life is sacred, including that of fetuses and that of Soviet leaders. This is a step forward in consistency.

The bishops also realize that in a democracy all citizens have some responsibility for the decisions of their leaders. This places a burden on all of us, whereas in the Middle Ages subjects were supposed to defer to legitimate authority in doubtful cases. Now that culpability and innocence are more widely diffused, the bishops recognize that we possess both the theory and the practice to implement the rights of citizens against governors. In the times of Augustine and Thomas Aquinas, subjects had few rights against rulers. Modern states provide means for holding rulers accountable for their offenses against our moral sense. At the same time, the notion of popular sovereignty places a heavier burden on us as citizens. If, as good citizens, we obey officials who are acting immorally in matters of war, then we participate somewhat in their guilt, and so the distinction between combatants and noncombatants is in danger of disappearing. This is a very dangerous line of argument, one I would like to avoid, but the fact remains that in a democracy we do have some responsibility for the leaders we elect, and for their decisions.[22]

IV

I hope in my concluding assessment of the bishops' pastoral letter to block out avenues for further debate. We ought to rethink how we apply the categories of *ius ad bellum* and *ius in bello*, aggression and self-defense. From Grotius to the present, distortions of the historical context and of the textual basis of the medieval just-war theories have skewed our understanding of the theories themselves. Yet on balance the bishops were probably wise not to be bound by tradition, for there are many problems lurking within the just war tradition. The bishops uprooted the medieval tradition from the historical context in which it arose, for perhaps the best of motives, in order to construct a homoge-

21. About the atmosphere surrounding the testimony before Senator Joseph McCarthy concerning Owen Lattimore's alleged Communist ties by Louis F. Budenz, Lattimore later remarked: "[t]he mood of the crowd that came to listen to Budenz was quite different. There was a strong representation of Catholic priests, whose black garb made them stand out conspicuously": *Ordeal By Slander* (Boston, Mass.: Little, Brown & Co., 1950), p. 120; cf. ibid., p. 132. For the bishops' statement linking the condemnation of abortion with the peace movement, see *Challenge of Peace*, nn. 284–289.

22. Cf. Walzer, *Just and Unjust Wars*, pp. 296–299.

nized tradition. This uprooting is most clearly shown in the prominence accorded to noncombatant immunity and in the neglect of the crusading tradition. The bishops may have had the hidden agenda of discouraging any vestiges of crusading fervor in the nuclear age. Their accomplishment testifies to today's crisis of conscience: What does it mean to be a Christian in today's world? We have come from the late antique crisis of Augustine's day in which the world was ostensibly Christian to our world, one now ostensibly less Christian.

Neither the traditionalists nor the nuclear freeze advocates conclusively proved their respective cases before the bishops. The result, the bishops' pastoral letter in its third and final version, is a dialectical compromise in the best tradition of Catholic scholarship. As a viable moral restraint on warfare, the just war remains the only game in town. We cannot know the proximate, much less the distant future; if we so claimed, we would thus ape God and commit the sin of pride. Is deterrence a morally defensible long-run posture? I cannot say. But if our cause can be justified, we must be prepared to defend it. The bishops' pastoral letter is positive, provocative, and flawed. If it were really definitive, it would have been shorter. This situation shows the limitations of deriving concrete policies from abstract principles or the obsolete casuistry of the medieval just war. By their hesitations and willingness to accept compromise the bishops have reminded us of the need for humility. They broke the lockstep of tradition under pressure from the necessities of the nuclear age. The tone of the bishops' pastoral letter, both firm and yielding, insistent and inconclusive, is a hopeful sign for the near future. The bishops realize that no single person can unequivocally resolve all the moral and military issues.

Let the debate go forth.

WILLIAM AU

7. Papal and Episcopal Teaching on War and Peace: The Historical Background to *The Challenge of Peace: God's Promise and Our Response*

🎋

🔲 When the American bishops issued their historic pastoral letter on war and peace—*The Challenge of Peace: God's Promise and Our Response*—in May 1983, many American Catholics expressed a sense of surprise or bewilderment as to why the bishops were addressing this controversial political topic and how they arrived at their stance toward nuclear weapons and deterrence. Much of the reaction to the pastoral letter reflected a lack of historical awareness among many American Catholics of the developments within modern Church teaching on the issues of war and peace. In fact, the bishops' 1983 pastoral can only be properly understood if it is seen as the culmination of positions that had been developing within the hierarchy over the previous 20 years.

The decades of the sixties and seventies were a time of significant and unprecedented development in official Catholic teaching on the issues of war and peace. Papal and conciliar teaching in this period was both a stimulus and a support for American Catholics in considering anew the problem of war, and it formed a basic framework for their moral debates on the subject. Under the spur of this teaching and the domestic turmoil and internal Church division caused by the Vietnam War, the American bishops began a renewed effort to address the issues raised by American defense and foreign policies. Their attempts to address these issues in light of the principles set down by recent Popes and the Second Vatican Council constitute an essential element for understanding the perspectives determining the American Catholic approach to war in these years.

As the official stance of the American bishops, the statements dealt with in this essay can, in a sense, be seen as reflecting the mainstream of development in American Catholic thought on war. It must be quickly added, however, that the bishops' positions did not necessarily always reflect the majority sentiment of American Catholics, whose nationalism did not always keep pace with the stated positions of their bishops.

Historically, the American bishops have cast the image of a nationalistic body uncritical of the government's defense policy and unwilling to oppose the government in this area. Yet in their statements over the past 20 years the bishops have shown an unprecedented willingness to examine the issues of war and peace more critically in response both to the developments in papal teaching and the demands of their own constituents. Episcopal statements of these years do not consist of a systematically thought-out or articulated social analysis, which could be placed in any particular school of thought. Rather, episcopal teaching consisted of a more *ad hoc* approach to various issues of world peace and justice. Yet episcopal teaching during these years exhibits a growing internal tension between the moral principles enunciated by the bishops and their critical implications for American policies.

This paper will briefly present the major themes on which papal and episcopal teaching have concentrated in treating issues of war and peace from 1960 to 1980. It will first present the papal and conciliar teaching that formed the framework of episcopal declarations. The subsequent treatment of the bishops will focus on those major statements of the hierarchy that reflect the developing themes of episcopal teaching that form the background of *The Challenge of Peace*.

Papal and Conciliar Teaching

The immediate background for the most recent developments in Catholic teaching on war and modern society was the work of Pius XII. Pius was sufficiently horrified by the destructive dimensions of modern warfare to limit the just causes for resorting to war to that of a defense against overt armed aggression. Pius' concession of the right to defensive war, however, was predicated on the absence of an international authority with the power to adjudicate disputes and protect the rights of nations. In this sense, his granting the right of national self-defense was articulated in the context of a critique of the inadequacy of the present international order based on the unlimited sovereignty of nation states. This system Pius deemed anachronistic in the face of the increasingly global nature of the world's problems and the globally destructive potentialities of modern warfare. In Pius' vision, the need for a world authority to eliminate war went hand in hand with the need for a new world economic order to ensure the prosperity of all peoples and thus eliminate a major cause of war. Four years before the formation of the United Nations, the Pontiff warned against "narrow egotistical calculations tending to corner sources of economic supply and basic material to the exclusion of nations less favored by nature."[1]

In applying the right of self-defense to the present situation, Pius stood as a classic expositor of the just-war theory. His teaching on the use of modern ABC weapons (atomic-biological-chemical) measured their use by traditional just-war standards. That is, their use was not proscribed as intrinsically evil, but their use must be so limited as not to fall under the ban on weapons whose effects go beyond the human ability to keep them within the bounds of proportionality and discrimination. Thus, the Rev. J. Bryan Hehir interprets Pius as not seeing in the use of nuclear weapons a situation qualitatively different from the use of other modern weapons. It is also true that Pius was speaking at the beginning of the nuclear era when the full effects of nuclear war had not permeated the public consciousness and the present nuclear arsenals had not been constructed.[2]

Pius XII also represented the tradition of just-war thinking in making no provision for pacifism or conscientious objection. In 1956 he stated:

If therefore, a body representative of the people and the government—both having been chosen by free election in a moment of extreme danger decide, by legitimate instruments of internal and external policy, on defensive precautions, and carry out the plans which they consider necessary, they do not act immorally; so that a Catholic citizen cannot invoke his own conscience in order to refuse to serve and fulfill those duties the law imposes.[3]

While not granting the right of conscientious objection, however, Pius upheld the obligation of the individual to military service within the context of a democratic government acting in the purely defensive manner that he taught to be the only just recourse to war. Thus Pius XII stands as both a classic expositor of just-war theory and an articulator of major themes to be developed by his successors: the unprecedented danger of modern war, the need to establish a world authority to eliminate the right and need to resort to war, and the reconstruction of the world economic order to ensure mutual prosperity and eliminate the major causes of war.

1. Joseph Gremillion, ed., *The Gospel of Peace and Justice—Catholic Social Teaching Since Pope John* (Maryknoll, N.Y.: Orbis Books, 1976), p. 47.; Pope Pius XII, "Christmas Message," *Statements of Popes, Bishops, Councils and Churches* (New York: Paulist Press, 1982), p. 13.

2. J. Bryan Hehir, "Foreword: Reflection on Recent Teaching," in Robert Heyer, ed., *Nuclear Disarmament: Key Statements of Popes, Bishops, Councils, and Churches* (New York: Paulist Press, 1982), pp. 3–4. Hehir is associate secretary of the Department of Social Development and World Peace of the United States Catholic Conference.

3. Pope Pius XII, "Christmas Message," 1956, cited in James R. Jennings, ed., *Just War and Pacifism—A Catholic Dialogue* (Washington, D.C.: United States Catholic Conference, 1973), p. 8.

The teaching of John XXIII built upon that of Pius XII but made a transition in thinking that launched the latest phase of development in Catholic teaching on war and peace. From John XXIII through the encyclicals of Paul VI there emerged six themes that have characterized universal Church teaching on these issues in the past 20 years. Together, these themes mark the parameters of an emerging vision in papal teaching that has sought to challenge Catholics and all people of good will to a fundamental reexamination of their thinking on the most threatening problem of modern civilization.

The first theme, which was set forth most forcefully in the teaching of John XXIII, is the call to adopt a global perspective on issues of war and peace. In *Mater et Magistra* (1961) John recognized that the consideration of questions of social justice in the present situation must be done in a global context, focusing on the development and distribution of the world's resources. The encyclical also represents a shift in tone and approach from the previous hostile or defensive attitudes of papal pronouncements on the modern world and industrial society. John welcomed the advances that the development of technology had brought, but focused on the disparity of wealth between rich and poor nations, which industrialism and colonialism had wrought, and termed this the most pressing problem in the world. He also warned against the false economic development and assistance that only replaces the older political colonialism with the neocolonialism of economic control and dependency.[4]

In thus placing the Church's traditional teaching in a global perspective, John called the world's peoples away from the ideological conflicts shaping international relations to look at the objective requirements of their common good and to create a new world order to attain these requirements. This tone and perspective were continued in *Pacem in Terris*, which many believe was issued in response to the Cuban missile crisis, and has been credited with launching a planetary Catholic peace movement.[5]

Pacem in Terris did not employ the just-war method of approaching the issue, nor did it even directly apply just-war categories as such to evaluate specific weapons or policies. It is also the only major papal document on war and peace not to mention the right of self-defense of

---

4. *Mater et Magistra*, nn. 157–159. Since the major papal encyclicals and other documents cited are printed in numerous collections and journals, citations here will refer to the paragraph numeration of the documents. All the documents cited here can be found in Gremillion, ed., *The Gospel of Peace and Justice*. A second collection including some of these documents is David J. O'Brien and Thomas A. Shannon, eds., *Renewing the Earth—Catholic Documents on Peace, Justice and Liberation* (Garden City, N.Y.: Image Books, 1977).

5. Gremillion, *The Gospel of Peace and Justice*, p. 69; p. 71.

nations. Following the perspective of *Mater et Magistra*, the encyclical viewed the world as evolving into an ever greater interdependency, which required a greater world unity to meet human needs. A tragic part of this present development of the world is the technological capability for mass destruction. It was this awareness of the potential destructiveness of modern war that led John to conclude, ". . . it is hardly possible to imagine that in the atomic era war could be used as an instrument of justice."[6]

This statement cannot be seen as an explicit rejection of Pius XII's recognition of the right of self-defense, or an endorsement of pacifism as some have claimed. Without addressing that specific question, John spoke on a different level to the reality of war in the modern world, as something that that world could not afford to countenance. Father Hehir would seem correct in interpreting John XXIII as differing from Pius XII in making the substantive judgment that nuclear weapons present a qualitatively new reality. In the face of this reality, John's emphasis was not to seek to apply the just-war doctrine, but to focus on the imperative to abolish war.[7]

To achieve this end John insisted on the inescapable necessity of establishing a world federal government. He praised the United Nations' Declaration of Human Rights and called for the mutual trust and initiatives necessary to make of that world body a real government.

Thus in *Pacem in Terris*, without rejecting the just-war tradition, John shifted Catholic thought to a reconsideration of war with the "entirely new attitude" that the Second Vatican Council would encourage. In this perspective, war is intimately linked with the task of establishing an order of justice within and among nations. Essential to such a task is the willingness to view the issues affecting the world's peace, not from the perspective of national interests, but from the perspective of the requirements of the common good of the human race.

Three other elements characterizing recent universal Church teaching on war and peace appeared in the teaching of Vatican II. In its document *Gaudium et Spes* (G. S.) under the section "The Fostering of Peace and the Promotion of a Community of Nations," the Council set the moral context for the Catholic debate on war for the following two decades. The Council's teaching also reflects elements of ambiguity and conflict that would characterize American Catholic efforts to grapple with the dilemma of war during these years. The three themes of the Council's teaching that are of concern here are the recognition of both pacifism

---

6. *Pacem in Terris*, n. 127.
7. Hehir, in Heyer, *Nuclear Disarmament*, p. 4.

and the just-war tradition, the condemnation of "total war," and the ambiguity toward deterrence.

The Council made a significant step beyond previous papal teaching in both affirming the right of self-defense in the absence of a world authority and also recognizing those who have dedicated themselves to nonviolent means of defense, "provided that this can be done without injury to the rights and duties of others or of the community itself."[8] While not a ringing endorsement, it was the first official recognition in modern Church teaching of pacifism as a legitimate option for Catholics.

Similarly, while commending those in military service as agents of peace and freedom, the Council also called for legal acceptance of conscientious objectors. This, together with the acceptance of pacifism, signaled a significant change in Catholic teaching on war, which was seen by many as traditionally allowing only for the just-war theory. With this change the Council was now seen as endorsing a pluralism of conscientious positions that Catholics could take.[9]

The recognition of conscientious objection was part of the Council's upholding of the rights of the individual conscience against totalitarian claims of the state. In the same spirit the Council stressed the responsibility of individuals to refuse to obey orders to commit crimes such as genocide, which was specifically condemned.[10]

In addressing the question of the use of force in war the Council reaffirmed the condemnation of "total war" found in Pius XII and John XXIII. It also specifically spoke to the use of modern scientific weapons in stating that "any act of war aimed indiscriminately at the destruction of entire cities or of extensive areas along with their populations is a crime against God and man himself. . . . The unique hazard of modern warfare consists in this: it provides those who possess modern scientific weapons with a kind of occasion for perpetuating just such abominations."[11] This clearly constituted a rejection of nuclear "counter-city" warfare, as well as conventional "obliteration bombing" as practiced in World War II. This condemnation, however, did not resolve in many minds the question of whether *any* use of nuclear weapons was to be morally banned.

On the issue of nuclear deterrence the Council reflected an ambiguity that has marked official Church statements since then. The Council recognized that the stockpiling of massive nuclear weapons was being done with the intention of deterring war and that many see this as the best

8. *Gaudium et Spes*, n. 78.
9. Ibid., n. 79.
10. Ibid.
11. Ibid., n. 80.

available means of preserving a peace of sorts. It did not directly judge this deterrent possession of nuclear weapons, despite the fact that the present deterrence system rests upon the threat to do what the Council had just condemned as morally unthinkable. Instead, the Council passed over the question of deterrence with the conclusion, "Whatever be the case with this method of deterrence, men should be convinced that the arms race in which so many countries are engaged is not a safe way to preserve a steady peace. Nor is the so-called balance resulting from this race a sure and authentic peace. Rather than being eliminated thereby, the causes of war threaten to grow gradually stronger." This arms race was further condemned as a treacherous trap for mankind, which injures the poor to an intolerable degree by diverting resources away from human needs.[12]

Thus, in its stated desire to look at war with an entirely new attitude,[13] the Council endorsed John XXIII's rejection of war as a rational instrument for justice in the nuclear age and reinforced his call for changes in the international system to effect its elimination. Yet in its specific moral precepts the Council could not get past the tension and ambiguity of effectively outlawing the actual use of most nuclear weapons that were designed for mass destruction, while tolerating a system of deterrence based on the threat of such usage. It is clear, however, that the Council held that the present state of deterrence cannot be accepted as a permanent state of affairs and must be eliminated by a negotiated movement toward disarmament.

Following the Council, Paul VI devoted much of his ministry to the cause of peace, the theme of which was summed up in his address to the United Nations on October 4, 1965. Here Paul reaffirmed the right of self-defense as justified by Pius XII, but he also chose to focus on the emphasis of John XXIII that the modern world can no longer afford war as a means of justice and political policy:

It suffices to remember that the blood of millions of men, that numberless and unheard of sufferings, useless slaughter and frightful ruin, are the sanction of the past which unites you with an oath which must change the future history of the world: No more war, war never again![14]

Most significantly Paul developed two themes that also had their roots in the teaching of his predecessors and Vatican II: the linkage of

---

12. Ibid., n. 81. John XXIII also treated the issue of deterrence in a similar manner, by acknowledging that the intentions of statesmen were to deter war, but that the result of the stockpiling of modern weapons was only a climate of fear and insecurity. *Pacem in Terris*, par. 109–119.

13. Ibid., n. 80.

14. Pope Paul VI, "Address to the General Assembly of the United Nations," October 4, 1965, n. 19.

the issue of war with that of world economic reform and development, and the development of a new appreciation of politics. In *Populorum Progressio*, Paul stressed the need for reform of the world economic order, for the social question of the 19th century had become a global question of survival and justice in the 20th. He stressed that all people had the right to development and that in the present era *development* is actually the new word for peace.[15]

By development, however, Paul meant not purely economic development, but rather an integral development that addressed the spiritual and cultural needs of people as well as material well-being. He also adamantly stressed that development did not mean absorption of the poor nations into the Western industrial-cultural system. True human development required respect for the higher cultural values and expressions of the world's peoples and these should not be traded off for the material prosperity of the richer nations.[16] In this Paul VI clearly tried to distinguish his definition of "development" from the way that word was normally used in Western industrial nations to equate development with economics, and therefore to imply the cultural superiority of the West over the so-called underdeveloped countries.

In this presentation of the necessity of world development Paul removed the focus of Church teaching on peace and justice from the ideological East-West conflict and placed it on what was called the North-South conflict between the industrialized and the nonindustrialized nations (the so-called Third World). In so doing Paul wished to place the Church on the side of the "South" in calling for greater justice in the world economic system. In his address to the 1974 World Food Conference in Rome, Paul VI expanded on the linkage of the development question and war by referring to the perverted "aid" programs of the industrial nations as a new way of making war on the world's poor. These were seen as substituting birth control for economic justice and even using food as a weapon, designed to limit the population of the poor so as to keep them from their fair share of the world's goods.[17]

This shift of focus to the problem of development and the North-South conflict also entailed an effort on the part of Paul VI to move the Church away from its historical identification with the West. Paul took care to criticize Western liberalism and materialism along with Marxist atheistic socialism. In *Populorum Progressio* he charged that Western liberalism, through its exaggerated individualism, was responsible for perverting industrialization into a profit-seeking system based on what

15. *Populorum Progressio*, n. 6.
16. Ibid., nn. 14; 40–41.
17. Pope Paul VI, "Address to the Participants of the World Food Conference," Rome, November 9, 1974, n. 6.

Pius XI had condemned as the "imperialism of money."[18] In 1971 Paul sought to add his own contribution to the teachings of *Quadragesimo Anno* and *Mater et Magistra* with his encyclical *Octogesima Adveniens*. In this letter Paul attacked the dehumanizing character of ideological conflict in the modern world and charged that both Marxism and Western liberalism falsified life by imposing their incomplete visions upon it.[19] Clearly, the duty of the Christian for Paul was to view issues of war and world development not from the perspective of either ideological camp, but rather from the perspective of the concrete common good of humanity. To this end Paul saw the Church as giving the ideologically divided world its most precious gift, a universal vision of the nature of man and the destiny of the human race.[20]

An important aspect of Paul's linkage of world development with the establishment of world peace was his call for a renewed appreciation of politics and political power. For Paul it was essential to break the control of society by economics and to destroy the psychological atmosphere of fatalism that stemmed from viewing the world as controlled by impersonal "forces" (for example, the laws of the market). This fatalism and the economic imperialism that fed upon it had to be countered by a renewed personal and collective sense of the responsibility and competence of the individual conscience, and the belief that people can change the world which people created. This meant a renewed sense of politics as the public realm in which the human will directed the social enterprise. As Paul defined it:

> To take politics seriously at its different levels—local, regional, national and worldwide—is to affirm the duty of man, of every man, to recognize the concrete reality and the value of the freedom of choice that is offered to him to seek to bring about both the good of the city and of the nation and of mankind. Politics are a demanding manner—but not the only one—of living the Christian commitment to the service of others.[21]

The particular style and content of this political engagement of Christians was left by Paul to each local church to discern.[22] Yet the need for a revival of personal responsibility in the political realm was, for Paul, an essential element in the modern papal call for reform of the international order. The Roman Synod of 1971 reaffirmed this theme in its statement that working for justice was a constitutive element of preaching the Gospel to the world. In the Synod's view, embracing the world's struggle for justice and infusing politics with a sense of responsibility for the common good are a vital service of Christians to a world caught

---

18. *Populorum Progressio*, n. 26.   21. *Octogesima Adveniens*, n. 46.
19. *Octogesima Adveniens*, nn. 32–35.   22. Ibid., n. 4.
20. *Populorum Progressio*, n. 13.

in the paradox of a simultaneous emergence of a planetary society and the increase of forces of division and antagonism.[23]

Thus papal and conciliar teaching over the past 20 years set forth major themes that greatly influenced and shaped the Catholic debate on war and peace. The global vision expressed in this teaching obviously posed special challenges to the American hierarchy, as it faced the task of applying that vision to its own national situation and the issues to which American defense and foreign policies gave rise.

American Episcopal Teaching

This paper will next focus on the teaching of the American bishops as they addressed issues of war and peace in four major areas: the Vietnam War, conscientious objection, the linkage of war with international reform and development, and nuclear weapons.[24] In particular, attention will be given to the tensions within the bishops' teaching as they addressed these issues, and the tension between the positions taken by the bishops and the policies of the U.S. government.

Vietnam

A series of episcopal statements from 1966 to 1971 became progressively more skeptical of the morality of the American intervention in Vietnam. In these statements the bishops reflected a desire both to uphold the general principles expounded by Vatican II and to grant a presumption of justice to American policies. Their first joint statement on the war in November 1966 was in fact a juxtaposition of these two factors. The bishops listed the principles of the teachings of Vatican II that they held must be used to evaluate the morality of the war. These were the distinction between true and false patriotism; the right to legitimate self-defense; the necessity to keep the waging of war within moral limits; the knowledge that the arms race is not a safe way to preserve peace; the requirement that people in the armed forces must act as agents of security; and the need to provide for conscientious objection.[25]

They followed the listing of these principles with an assertion of confidence in the intentions of American leaders and supported the justice

---

23. Synod of Bishops—Second General Assembly, "Justice in the World," November 30, 1971, nn. 6–9.

24. Episcopal statements cited here may be found in J. Brian Benestad and Francis J. Butler, eds., *Quest for Justice—A Compendium of Statements of the United States Catholic Bishops on the Political and Social Order 1966–1980* (Washington, D.C.: United States Catholic Conference, 1981). The documents cited here will be cited according to their paragraph enunciation. Those documents not published in this form will be cited according to the page number of the collection in which they are found.

25. *Peace and Vietnam*, N.C.C.B., November 18, 1966, nn. 5–9.

of the government's decision. The bishops, however, gave no argument on how this conclusion was reached. They further insisted that the government had an obligation to keep the people adequately informed on the war and that citizens had a duty to protest when the war threatened to exceed moral limits. Support for the war, the bishops argued, must be accompanied by support for peace negotiations. The bishops' chief fear was that the war could lessen the American people's sensitivity to the moral evils of war.[26] A year later, the bishops reaffirmed their 1966 statement and encouraged the government to continue to pursue negotiations "despite the rebuffs to these efforts."[27]

In 1968 the bishops issued one of their major pastoral statements, *Human Life in Our Day*. Without altering their previous judgment on the war the bishops raised the question of whether the war had exceeded the bounds of proportionality in the destruction it was causing, assuming the justice of the American cause and intentions. The bishops recalled the teaching of Pius XII in 1953, stating that even a legitimate war of defense can cross the point of proportion where the destruction wrought is disproportionate to the injustice otherwise to be tolerated. This question the bishops left unanswered.[28]

The doubts that the bishops exhibited in 1968 on the continuing justification of American involvement in Vietnam grew until finally in 1971 the bishops stated that, "at this point in history it seems clear to us that whatever good we hope to achieve through continued involvement in this war is now outweighed by the destruction of human life and moral values which it inflicts." The bishops therefore called for an end to the conflict without further delay, but did not demand immediate withdrawal. They did, however, go on to stress that the United States had an obligation to help rebuild Southeast Asia as it had for Europe after World War II. They also called for higher G.I. benefits for veterans and pardon for draft resisters.[29]

It is significant for understanding the bishops' stated perspective that their final rejection of the war was based on the principle of proportionality and not any judgment of the justice of America's role in Indochina. The rejection of the morality of the war was somewhat expanded in the 1973 statement of the United States Catholic Conference (U.S.C.C.) Committee on Social Development and World Peace, which responded to the expansion of the war into bombing raids on Cambodia. The state-

26. Ibid., nn. 11–16.

27. *On Peace*, N.C.C.B., November 16, 1967, nn. 2–3.

28. *Human Life in Our Day*, nn. 137–138.

29. *Resolution on Southeast Asia*, N.C.C.B., November 1971, in Benestad, *Quest for Justice*, p. 78. The call for negotiations was repeated in November 16, 1972 in the N.C.C.B. *Resolution on Imperatives for Peace*, in Benestad, pp. 80–81.

ment lamented that the general climate of uncertainty about moral issues in the United States had created a vacuum in which political and military decisions became the moral judgments of the moment. The committee rejected the bombing as immoral on three counts. The committee found, first, that the bombing rested on dubious legal authority given the repeal of the Gulf of Tonkin resolution and various congressional resolutions against it; second, the use of force to uphold a shaky government in Cambodia was found to be of doubtful utility; and third, the tactic of "carpet-bombing" entire areas was condemned as the sort of indiscriminate warfare rejected by recent Popes and Vatican II.[30] This statement was one of the most specific criticisms of the United States' military policy in Southeast Asia issued by the U.S.C.C. during the war. Yet even in light of the National Conference of Catholic Bishops' (N.C.C.B.'s) rejection of the morality of continuing the war, this criticism was never expanded into a consideration of the wider dimensions of the purposes and goals of American policy in the continuance of the war.

Conscientious and Selective Conscientious Objection

As part of the debate on Vietnam the bishops also had specifically to deal with the issue of conscientious objection, especially in response to the growing number of men who refused to serve in the war effort and the ever-widening general opposition to the war. In their initial 1966 statement the bishops simply made note of Vatican II's call to make provision for conscientious objectors. In their 1968 statement, *Human Life in Our Day*, they went much further and were probably in advance of much of their own flocks in calling for recognition of both conscientious objection and selective conscientious objection to particular wars, as well as an end to the peace-time draft.

The bishops recognized that the present and future generations of young, who bear the burden of fighting wars, will be less willing to leave the decisions regarding issues like Vietnam entirely to political and bureaucratic processes. They further asserted that if war is ever to be outlawed and international institutions established on a belief in the universal common good, it will be because of those citizens who reject exaggerated nationalism and insist on principles of nonviolent political and civic action in both domestic and international affairs. The bishops joined with Vatican II in praising those who renounced the use of violence and took up methods of nonviolent defense. In this spirit the bish-

---

30. *Statements on U.S. Bombing Operations in Cambodia*, U.S.C.C. Committee on Social Development and World Peace, July 15, 1973, in Benestad, *Quest for Justice*, p. 82.

ops called for modification of Selective Service laws to allow recognition for those selective conscientious objectors refusing to serve in particular wars they believe to be unjust, as well as those who reject participation in all war.[31]

This position was reiterated in a 1971 declaration of the U.S.C.C. that stressed the Church's traditional teaching on the central importance of conscience. It argued that while the Church's insistence on serving the common good included participation in a just defense, it was also in conformity with Catholic moral teaching to refuse participation in military efforts either totally or in reference to a particular war judged to be unjust. The declaration recognized the administrative difficulties in allowing selective conscientious objection, but urged the government to accept the task of working to reconcile the demands of the civic and the moral orders on this issue.

Yet in their recognition of both complete and selective conscientious objection the bishops did not recognize or address certain serious implications of their position regarding the question of the individual's relationship to the state and the manner in which this relationship is mediated by the Church. The problem posed by selective conscientious objection is more complex than the bishops' statements acknowledged. Total conscientious objection does not pose a direct challenge to the competence or justice of the state's exercise of its prerogative to make decisions regarding the public defense. From the state's perspective the pacifist has absented himself from the realm of political decision making in which the state claims sovereignty. Selective conscientious objection, however, challenges the state precisely in the area where the state claims sovereignty by challenging the morality or legality of a particular decision of the state on the use of armed force. To grant the right of selective conscientious objection thus extends by implication beyond the waging of war to all other exercise of political power by the state. In effect, the demands of selective conscientious objection would have the state grant the individual in advance the right to disobey the law, which the state, *qua* state, cannot do.

Selective objection to particular wars deemed unjust follows directly from the just-war tradition of the Church, and the bishops logically defended it. The Christian must dissent from unjust wars as he must refuse to obey unjust laws. On the other hand, it is also true that the state, *per se*, cannot be expected to grant the right of disobedience. Thus, the problem of how to recognize selective conscientious objection and still

31. *Human Life in Our Day*, nn. 143; 148–149; 151–152. The bishops' position on conscientious and selective conscientious objection led to a debate sponsored by the USCC in 1973. The proceedings of this debate can be found in James R. Jennings, ed., *Just War and Pacifism—A Catholic Dialogue* (Washington, D.C.: United States Catholic Conference, 1973).

reconcile the individual's obligations to the state remains unaddressed in the bishops' teaching. The 1971 U.S.C.C. declaration recognized that implementing their recognition of selective conscientious objection would bring great problems, but perceived these as problems of administration, not of fundamental public theory.[32]

Part of the problem entailed in the bishops' position on conscientious objection was a dilemma long associated with the just-war tradition, namely, how to apply against the state a negative moral judgment concerning a war in which the state is engaged. The implication of selective conscientious objection is the possibility of a clash between the state and individual Christians or even large segments of the Christian community, if not the official Church structure itself. Implicit in the efforts of the bishops to gain recognition for selective as well as total conscientious objection was an effort to diffuse the potentialities of such a clash by providing legal protection for all conscientious dissent from the government's defense policies. This effort, however, presupposed the protection of all positions of the individual conscience, without addressing the inherent conflict between these positions or the state's ability to accommodate them. Most significant, it also took the focus off consideration of the bishops' own role in pressing moral judgments against the state by placing the bishops in the role of guardians of the individual conscience, whose primary task was to provide a place for each conscience rather than prophetically to pursue their own moral judgments on public policy.

The desire of the bishops to recognize total and selective objection to war was part of their desire to follow Vatican II's recognition of both the just war and pacifist positions within the Church.[33] The unaddressed conflicts in the bishops' stance on conscientious objection reflected the tension involved in their attempting to mediate these divergent positions within the ecclesial community, as well as the tension of balancing their own role of moral leadership with the desire to avoid the possibility of a radical confrontation with the government.

The Linkage of War with World Development

Another major theme of the bishops' statements on war and peace was their affirmation of the internationalist ideals that were such a clear part of modern papal teaching. In *Human Life in Our Day* (1968) and

32. A discussion of the problems of selective conscientious objection as it relates to the bishops' teaching can be found in John A. Rohr, *Profits Without Honor—Public Policy and the Selective Conscientious Objector* (Nashville, Tenn.: Abingdon Press, 1971).

33. *The Gospel of Peace and the Danger of War*, U.S.C.C. Administrative Board, February 15, 1978, in Benestad, *Quest for Justice*, pp. 84–85. The bishops stated here that in their statements on war and peace, they would draw from both the just-war and pacifist positions.

Human Solidarity (1970) the bishops urged support for the United Nations and other international agencies and followed the papal lead in strongly linking the solution to the problem of war with reform of the world economy. The bishops specifically laid responsibility on the United States, because of its immense power, to work with the United Nations to eliminate the unilateral use of force. In 1974 the bishops issued several statements stressing the theme of world development and America's role in it. The thrust of these statements reflected again internal tensions in the bishops' attempt to evaluate American policies and goals while not denying their intrinsic justice. In October 1974, the U.S.C.C. Executive Committee issued a statement on the global food crisis. The committee asserted that the United States must treat its food resources as a sacred trust and not as a weapon or as merely a matter of markets and money. It insisted that "the law of the market" is a human invention that must recognize moral limits. If it denies food to the starving it must be changed. The committee further urged the government to approach the upcoming World Food Conference with an open policy supporting an international food reserve for global emergencies, an increase in short-term emergency relief to threatened areas, and an offer of technical assistance to nations in need of increasing their food supply.[34]

The food crisis and its relation to world development, the bishops asserted, posed serious implications for the United States both at home and abroad.[35] These implications were in part articulated in a statement of the U.S.C.C. Department of Social Development and World Peace in August 1974, entitled *Development—Dependency: The Role of Multinational Corporations*.[36] The statement referred to the encyclical *Populorum Progressio* and its recognition of the historical emergence of industrialization as providing the potential for both true human development and for what Pius XI called the tyranny of the "international imperialism of money." The statement also cited the fact that recent efforts of Latin American bishops to address the problems of their countries usually focused much of their criticism on the effects of Western capitalism. The committee lamented that in hearing the words of the

34. *Statement of Global Food Crisis*, U.S.C.C. Executive Committee, October 1974, in Benestad, *Quest for Justice*, p. 101. The bishops also stressed that the burden of economic change here should not fall on the independent farmer.

35. *Statement of the World Food Crisis: A Pastoral Plan of Action*, N.C.C.B., November 21, 1974, in Benestad, *Quest for Justice*, pp. 102–105. The bishops also iterated their call with specific proposals in 1975, *Food Policy and the Church: Specific Proposals*, U.S.C.C. Administrative Board, September 11, 1975, in Benestad, pp. 113–116.

36. *Development—Dependency: The Role of Multinational Corporations*, U.S.C.C. Department of Social Development and World Peace, August 1974, in Benestad, *Quest for Justice*, pp. 105–106.

Pope and Christians from other countries, Americans could not perceive the full truth being expressed because their perceptions were filtered through the culture of capitalism.[37]

The committee felt that the crisis of the present moment was clearly reflected in the 1974 United Nations session called to hear the complaints of the nations of the so-called Third World about the international economic system. This session served to dramatize the increasing concentration of power and wealth in relatively few multinational corporations and banks. This fact, the committee argued, deterred real international development and justice.[38]

The committee argued that Americans must realize that the multinational corporations that dominate the international economy also control their domestic economy. Many domestic economic problems resulted from the service that the political and economic system renders to the needs of the multinationals to the detriment of Americans just as to the detriment of foreign populations. The committee was glad that many Catholics in the world were becoming increasingly aware of the interlocking of American domestic and foreign policies to serve the interests of transnational business enterprises.[39]

Most emphatically, the committee argued that the time had now come to question the motivation as well as the possession of such power by these institutions. "For the motivation continually to increase profit emerges from values which promote excessive individualism, unnecessary consumption, and disregard for the quality of human life, all of which are contrary to the deepest values of the Judeo-Christian tradition." Consequently, the committee maintained that the American Church must come to see itself as a prophetic voice apart from the forces controlling society, and that it could learn much on how to function in this way from the experience of the Church in the so-called Third World.[40]

The questions raised in this statement about American foreign, military, and economic policies and goals were extremely pointed and carried a strongly negative implication for the moral and human value of America's role in the world. Here again, however, this questioning of America's influence on world development was not pursued into more specific judgments on American policies that could have opened the possibility of a direct confrontation between the Church and the government. Yet this statement remains one of the sharpest indications among the documents issued under episcopal auspices that the government's policies were in direct contradiction to the values the bishops upheld as

37. Ibid., pp. 107–108.
38. Ibid., p. 107.

39. Ibid., p. 110.
40. Ibid., p. 112.

fundamental to global human welfare. Two years later in a pastoral letter of the N.C.C.B., *To Live in Christ Jesus*, the section on world development did not continue this more pointed line of criticism. Rather, it reasserted the more general principles of world development, and the criticisms of the present international system, which the bishops had previously made.[41]

The principles the bishops upheld for international development and justice, then, were a judgment on American policies and goals, but these criticisms were only a bit stronger than their commentary on Vietnam. The bishops moved from their strongest indictment on American economic practices to a more general statement of principles and exhortations.

Nuclear Weapons

It was on the issue of nuclear weapons that the bishops moved the furthest in approaching a confrontation with the government over fundamental national defense policies. In 1968 *(Human Life in Our Day)* the bishops reiterated Vatican II's condemnation of the arms race and questioned the rationality of seeking security through the threat of mutual social destruction.

The bishops recalled that Vatican II, while not condemning nuclear deterrence in itself, had gone on to condemn the arms race and the balance of terror as a means of preserving peace. In that spirit, the bishops did not address the issue of deterrence, but expressed hope that the Partial Test Ban Treaty would help lead to a cessation of arms development; they also urged the Senate to ratify the Nuclear Non-Proliferation Treaty between the United States and the Soviet Union, which committed the signatories to balanced reductions of nuclear weapons and the peaceful use of nuclear energy. Further, the bishops urged the United States to take initiatives in reducing tension and building a climate of trust by inviting the United Nations' Atomic Energy Commission and other world agencies to inspect U.S. nuclear facilities.[42]

The bishops seriously questioned the basic policy of seeking superiority in the capacity for mutually assured destruction (MAD) as a means of security. They argued that although for some years there had been an effective parity in MAD capability between the superpowers, the result had been less security, not more. They also specifically addressed the American decision to deploy a "thin" antiballistic missile (ABM) system. They deplored this decision as the latest act in the arms race and

41. *To Live in Christ Jesus—A Pastoral Reflection on the Moral Life*, N.C.C.B., November 11, 1976, in Benestad, *Quest for Justice*, pp. 41–43.
42. *Human Life in Our Day*, nn. 105–109.

prelude to an even bigger ("thick") ABM system. Although the ABM was deemed a purely defensive weapon, the bishops labeled it as dangerously destabilizing to the "balance of terror" and likely to cause the other side to increase its offensive capability.[43]

In this, the bishops did not go beyond what Vatican II had stated on the question of nuclear arms. When the bishops did eventually move to address more specifically the issue of nuclear deterrence and the use of nuclear weapons, their statements must be understood in the context of a new phase in the "nuclear debate," which arose in the mid-seventies.

The structure of the renewed debate on nuclear weapons strategy actually emerged in the mid-sixties but was obscured by the furor over Vietnam. A chief factor in its emergence was the desire of the superpowers to stabilize their relations so as to lessen the danger of all-out nuclear war. Another factor was the development of weaponry that made arms control more difficult, notably ABM defense systems and MIRV warheads (multiple independently targeted reentry vehicles— more than one warhead in a missile, each capable of being released and directed at a separate target).[44]

The introduction of MIRV's allowed the superpowers to increase their striking capability geometrically, which development threatened to destabilize the balance of terror by creating in the adversary's mind the fear of an imponderable striking power in his opponent. ABM systems, while a defense for cities against enemy missiles, would also destabilize the nuclear deterrence system by promising to limit the threat of MAD. The SALT I agreements of 1972 limited the deployment of ABM systems but solidified the superpowers' deterrence posture on the use of offensive weapons employing MIRV's.[45]

The debate over the ABM system and SALT I also raised renewed questions about the morality of attacking cities and about the MAD doctrine that was the basis of nuclear deterrence. In this context President Ford's Secretary of Defense, James R. Schlesinger, revived earlier proposals of Secretary Robert McNamara to move the United States to a "counterforce" nuclear strategy, that is, a more flexible nuclear capability with which the United States could engage in a limited nuclear war with the Soviet Union. The reasons given as motivating the shift of policy were the immorality of indiscriminately striking cities, a dissatisfaction with not being able to limit and control a nuclear exchange, and the desirability of matching the Soviet capacity for selective attacks on a variety of targets. To keep this counterforce strategy in perspective, it

43. Ibid., nn. 110–112.
44. Robert A. Gessert and J. Bryan Hehir, *The New Nuclear Debate* (New York: Council on Religion and International Affairs, 1976), pp. 53–55.
45. Ibid., pp. 55–56.

must be understood that counterforce would not eliminate MAD. Rather it would presuppose a MAD capability as the ultimate threat designed to keep any limited nuclear exchange limited. Therefore, the role of city-hostages remained at the heart of nuclear policy.[46] It was within the context of this technological escalation and a conceptual shift of strategic policies to fighting a limited nuclear war that the American bishops were to address the problem of nuclear deterrence in the late 1970's and early 1980's.

Episcopal statements on nuclear deterrence during these years reflected a position developed for the bishops by the Rev. J. Bryan Hehir of the United States Catholic Conference. Hehir's position was that of a nuclear pacifist focusing on three operating principles: first, the distinction between possession and use of nuclear weapons and allowing their interim possession for deterrence purposes while prohibiting any use; second, a rejection of any weapons development that destabilizes the balance of terror or promises a "limited" use of nuclear weapons; and third, the necessity to be seriously committed to negotiations for arms reduction and elimination of nuclear weapons.

In effect Hehir sought to sever the linkage by which one's response to the matter of deterrence is governed by one's prior judgment on the use of nuclear weapons. Hehir stressed that consideration must be given not only to the physical but also to the psychological impact of nuclear weapons. He argued that even if tactical nuclear weapons could be controlled within the limits of proportionality and discrimination, the psychological impact of moving from conventional to nuclear weapons was immense. Such a shift introduced a new order of combat with continuing potentialities for levels of escalation far exceeding all proportion and discrimination and therefore constituted a qualitative breach in the use of force that should be transposed into an ethical limit: no use of nuclear weapons.[47] Yet Hehir accepted the position that today nuclear deterrence functions as a legitimate instrument of policy and in the present international system serves to prevent the outbreak of a major world war. To reject deterrence immediately in such a system would practically be tantamount to unilateral disarmament. As Vatican II asserted, however, deterrence as a long-term goal leads to a high risk of nuclear war. Therefore, Hehir concluded nuclear deterrence is acceptable as an *interim* instrument of policy, not as a permanent state of affairs. The implication here is the necessity of seriously pursuing negotiations for arms reduction and elimination of nuclear weapons.

It also followed from Hehir's position that the only legitimate use of

46. Ibid., pp. 56–58.
47. *New Nuclear Debate*, pp. 35–46.

nuclear weapons was to deter. If deterrence failed, another policy of response not employing nuclear weapons would be morally required.[48]

In January 1976, the same year in which Hehir's views were published in a volume entitled *The New Nuclear Debate*, Archbishop Peter L. Gerety of Newark testified before the U.S. Senate Foreign Relations Committee. His testimony on American strategic policy reflected the influence of Hehir's position. Gerety stated the three principles laid down by Vatican II regarding nuclear weapons: Their use against population centers is forbidden; their possession for deterrence is not condemned; deterrence is unacceptable as a permanent state of affairs.[49]

Gerety concluded on the basis of government statements that both the United States and the Soviet Union are prepared to use nuclear weapons against cities. He claimed that not only is this intention condemned by the Vatican Council, but the use of most of our nuclear arsenal that is designed for obliterating large areas would seem banned by the Council's teaching. Furthermore, Gerety argued that the clear intent of the Council was to keep as high as possible the barrier against the use of nuclear weapons.

Therefore, he contended, even the use of tactical nuclear weapons, which otherwise might be discriminate, is highly questionable. It was also Gerety's judgment that the counterforce strategic concept lowered the barrier to the use of nuclear weapons and made war more likely. Gerety insisted that the Council's position required negotiations to move away from nuclear deterrence altogether by eliminating such weapons.[50]

The following November, the N.C.C.B.'s pastoral *To Live in Christ Jesus*, in referring to deterrence, stated that it was immoral to threaten to do what could not be morally done, such as the destruction of cities. Yet the bishops did not forthrightly condemn U.S. defense policy, but instead stressed the need to pursue negotiations for nuclear disarmament. In April 1978, Archbishop John Quinn of San Francisco, speaking as president of the N.C.C.B., seemed to reflect Hehir's reasoning in applauding President Carter's decision to defer production of a neutron weapon. His reason centered on the destabilizing effect such a weapon would have on the present deterrent system and the probability that it would escalate the arms race.[51]

48. Ibid., pp. 50–51.

49. Archbishop Peter Gerety of Newark, "Testimony before the U.S. Senate Foreign Relations Committee," January 21, 1976, in Heyer, *Nuclear Disarmament*, pp. 87–88.

50. Ibid., pp. 88–90.

51. *To Live in Christ Jesus*, in Benestad, *Quest for Justice*, p. 44. Archbishop John Quinn of San Francisco, "Remarks as President of the NCCB, on President Carter's decision to defer production of neutron warheads," April 14, 1978, in Heyer, *Nuclear Disarmament*, pp. 95–96.

The most refined episcopal statement on the issue of nuclear weapons by the end of the decade, which clearly reflected acceptance of Hehir's position, was the 1979 testimony of John Cardinal Krol of Philadelphia to the Senate Foreign Relations Committee on behalf of the U.S.C.C. Krol stated that the American bishops believed that we have too long been preoccupied with preparations for war, guided by false criteria of equivalence or superiority in armaments. It was time, he insisted, to take the first steps toward peace and negotiated bilateral disarmament.[52]

Krol stated that while legitimate just-war defense was allowed, this could not include nuclear war. The primary imperative of the nuclear age, he argued, was to prevent the use of strategic nuclear weapons. Thus, in nuclear deterrence is found the paradox of war prevented by the threat of doing what the Christian conscience could not tolerate. Krol clearly stated that the bishops accepted nuclear deterrence only as a lesser evil and only as long as the hope of a reduction in weapons is possible. He made clear the implication of this qualified acceptance in stating that if negotiations for disarmament do not seriously proceed, then the Catholic Church would have to move officially to condemn the possession as well as the use of nuclear weapons.[53]

The SALT I treaty had given the hope of leading to actual reductions in nuclear arms, Krol observed, but that hope had not materialized in SALT II, which was only a deceleration, not a reversal of the arms race. It was for this reason that some bishops would not even support SALT II, seeing it as substituting the illusion of arms control for a serious effort at disarmament. Krol rejected the view of those who felt that SALT II would weaken the United States and allow the Soviets a first-strike ability. He further specified that if the United States used SALT II to expand strategic and conventional forces it would eliminate any reason for the bishops to continue their qualified acceptance of deterrence. Krol claimed that "strategic equivalence" was only the new name for the arms race and that it would distort the bishops' support of SALT II to link this with new military expenditures within the terms of the treaty. He also urged the United States to consider the new MX missile and Trident submarine programs as negotiable in return for Russian concessions and to work to eliminate MIRV's, which SALT I had failed to do.[54]

Thus Krol's testimony shows that the bishops' position on nuclear weapons had been brought by 1979 to the near breaking point of con-

52. John Cardinal Krol, "Testimony on Behalf of the USCC Before the Senate Foreign Relations Committee," September 6, 1979, in Heyer, *Nuclear Disarmament*, p. 101.
53. Ibid., pp. 103–104.
54. Ibid., pp. 105–110.

frontation that they had avoided on other issues of war and peace. The clearly conditional acceptance of deterrence recognized the incompatibility of present American policy and Christian moral principles. It also clearly served notice to the government that if changes were not made the Church would have to officially dissociate itself from American nuclear defense policies. Since such a stance of condemnation could be seen by many as morally obliging Catholics to "get out of the defense business," the implications of Krol's warning were far reaching. The bishops' pastoral statement of 1983, *The Challenge of Peace: God's Promise and Our Response*, did not go beyond Krol's statement on nuclear deterrence, and somewhat mitigated his warning. Yet the explosive potential of the direction that the development of episcopal teaching has taken had been demonstrated. Where it will go remains to be seen.

II The Making of Public Policy

MICHAEL NOVAK

8. Realism, Dissuasion, and Hope in the Nuclear Age

I wish to make two points on the bishops' pastoral letter. Before proceeding to these two points, however, I wish to make clear that a statement by the bishops on nuclear war was, if anything, overdue. A good number of my friends, from Gordon Zahn and James Douglass to James Finn and William O'Brien, have argued for many years that the bishops should address this issue. In fact, over these many years the great experts on this question were not bishops, or even clergymen, but laymen, including those I have mentioned, who wrote many books and articles on this subject and accomplished much good work.

All such experts have long argued that the bishops *should* address the issue of nuclear war. There is absolutely no disagreement on this point, in principle. We who are Catholic believe that the faith touches every part of human life, both social and political, as yeast in dough, and we therefore believe that both we and our religious leaders are obliged to examine every aspect of life from the point of view of our faith. Much, however, depends on our *execution*. Good intentions are not enough. High moral aims are not enough. Prudent action, that is, good action, requires hitting the mark exactly, in the right way, at the right time, and to the right effect.

The bishops themselves realized that they might be unable to hit the mark exactly. They realized they could not speak on all points for the entire Catholic community, and so they encouraged argument. I think at times they regretted they received as much argument as they did, but they did in fact invite it, more in the final draft than in the first draft. The bishops went out of their way to stress their own fallibility. They distinguished at least eight times in the final document between those matters upon which they were delivering the burden of the Catholic faith as it has been delivered from generation to generation, which it is their special responsibility to hand on intact, and those other matters requiring interpretations of present circumstances and containing propositions about what we are to do, propositions that are contingent, and about which human beings of good will are bound to disagree.

I submit that the bishops undertook the proper task, but that they failed to ask, in terms of time and in a prudential sequence, the proper question. To a large extent (but not entirely), they asked the question, "What is the moral obligation of any nation 'x' that has nuclear weapons?" This might be Brazil, the Soviet Union, or any other nation. The bishops did not ask a specifically American question; instead, they inquired generally into the morality incumbent on any nation possessing nuclear weapons.

The bishops' question is an important one, but in a certain sense it is atemporal, out of time. Certainly, it is a question that moral theologians and others ought to be addressing. But there is a much more urgent ethical question that if left unanswered will not permit us time to resolve the first question. This more urgent question is how, in the mid-1980's, is the Soviet Union to be deterred? In several key aspects, the Soviet Union now possesses the most powerful nuclear force in the world. In almost every area the Soviet Union is capable of taking an initiative to which we must be able to respond in order to survive. The next four or five years may be the most critical in the history of the Republic. Thus the more important question must be, *How is nuclear war to be prevented,* given *who* possesses nuclear arms? This is an urgent ethical and political question. It is also prior in the prudential order to the critical question the bishops do pose.

Before developing this thought further, however, I would like to discuss the other point to which I alluded. I would like to address the temptation that the bishops confronted and to distinguish what the bishops accomplished from this temptation, for the two are quite different.

The Temptation Faced by the Bishops

The process the bishops engaged in was a highly public one and well covered by the various news media. As a result, the first two drafts of the bishops' letter and, in particular, some of the more extreme sentences of these preliminary drafts, became the first public fact known throughout the world. I traveled a great deal in 1982 and 1983, and I realized that people, from Europe to Asia, were aware that the American bishops were saying something on nuclear weapons. What were the bishops perceived as saying? They were understood to be advocating unilateral disarmament and pacifism.

In fact, the bishops never advocated either of these courses of action. One must keep in mind the nature of the mass media. The media create facts of an important order that are quite different from the final fact of the actual execution of a group preparing a document of 110 pages. One may publish a document of 110 pages but lack any control over the three or four lines the television news highlights. Thus, there are two very different realities, the public perception and the actual execution.

The bishops' actual execution is tremendously better than the public impression even many intellectual leaders have formed about what they have said. Many learned critics, for example, hold that the logic of the bishops' position entails unilateral disarmament, whereas the bishops themselves eschew this position.[1] Bruce Russett, one of those who assisted in the drafting of the original document, indicated in a debate the two of us had at Stonehill College (Mass.) that the bishops at the outset excluded the notion of unilateral disarmament.

Nonetheless, if one is so inclined, one can find evidence, especially in the preliminary drafts, that the bishops were tempted toward unilateral disarmament and pacifism. The bishops spoke in these early drafts of both a pacifist and a just-war tradition and seemingly regarded these as co-equal. This position was altered when the Vatican intervened and pointed out that these traditions are not co-equal and that the pacifist tradition in particular does not apply to states or societies, but only to individuals.[2] In their final draft, the bishops avoid placing these traditions on the same level, but it is still fair to say that those who interpret the bishops' document as tempted toward unilateral disarmament and pacifism can find evidence, especially in the early drafts, that this was indeed a temptation.

It is also important to distinguish, as Reinhold Niebuhr does in his 1939 book, *Christianity and Power Politics*, why the Church is not pacifist.[3] In this essay, Niebuhr demonstrates that there is an orthodox and a heretical conception of pacifism. The orthodox conception is the statement of an eschatological symbol, the fact that we are not meant for this world alone, but for the coming world as well. For this reason, some persons, acting in the full charity of the Gospels, commit themselves, as it were, to a life lived according to the law of the endtime and not by the laws of ordinary human life. In this vein is the tradition of celibacy, in which ordinary men and women live as men and women will live in the Kingdom of Heaven and forego marriage and having children. They absent themselves from the social and political obligations of procreation in order to live as a symbol of the fullness of the Gospel, in poverty, chastity, and obedience. Simultaneously, such persons have been paci-

---

1. See Albert Wohlstetter, "Bishops, Statesmen, and Other Strategists on the Bombing of Innocents," *Commentary* 75 (June 1983), pp. 15–36; and Robert Jastrow, "Why Strategic Superiority Matters," *Commentary* 75 (March 1983), pp. 27–32.

2. *Origins* 12 (April 7, 1983), pp. 691–695.

3. New York: Charles Scribner's Sons, 1940.

fists. It has always been thought wrong for the Christian clergy, or men and women religious, committed as they are to eschatological witness, to bear arms.[4] Niebuhr further points out that other individuals in the history of the Church, such as Menno Simons, deliberately eschewed the social and political vocation to live the eschatological one. As long as this selection flows from personal choice, and as long as such persons are clear about the way their own personal statement fits the Gospels, Niebuhr believes (and I think he is correct in this) that such persons are orthodox.

But the overwhelming teaching of Judaism and Christianity, which Niebuhr calls "biblical realism," is that the world as a whole remains riddled with sin and human imperfection. This world is one of ignorance and evil, in which passion, enthusiasm, and even idealism regularly darken our intellects. Those who in the 1930's on many campuses and in many churches in America demonstrated for peace intended that there be no war, but Hitler and Tojo, reading of these demonstrations, believed they were a sign of weakness and that victory would be easy. Massive invasions were launched, in consequence of which 56 million people in Europe died. It was to prevent this type of slaughter from occurring that Niebuhr very early argued that the Church should not be pacifist. Yet so unwelcome were his articles in *The Christian Century* that he founded his own journal, *Christianity and Crisis*.[5] His was a lonely voice.

Nothing is clearer in Judaism and Christianity, Niebuhr believed, than the effects of the ravages of sin. Every human being sometimes sins. No one of us, and no human being in history save two, has not on occasion betrayed both reason and our highest ideals. Niebuhr went through a basic conversion in his life while reading St. Augustine. What particularly struck him in Augustine was the political and social sense of the ravages of sin. Augustine wished that human beings would act from reason and virtue and that public authority would do likewise. But humans do not so act, and thus public authority cannot.

From his meditations on Augustine, Niebuhr formulated what I think is a true proposition. Every peace in history rests on a "balance of power." All normal human behavior supports our own awareness that reason is not to be trusted. When we see the Pope, the representative of

4. See John Vigilante, "The Prohibition Against the Bearing of Arms by Clerics: An Historical-Canonical Survey of the Tradition of the Church up to the *Decretum* of Gratian," unpublished J.C.L. thesis, The Catholic University of America, 1984. The March 1984 issue of *Catholicism in Crisis* contains a symposium on "The Christian Soldier."

5. "Our civilization was built by faith and prayers and hard work—it was also built by fighting." Reinhold Niebuhr, "The Crisis," *Christianity and Crisis* 1 (February 10, 1941), p. 1.

the Prince of Peace, we find him surrounded by Swiss Guards who pound their halberds on the floor with the sense of physical sanction. Even at the most peaceful parades, armed mounted policemen are present. The belief is that the presence of policemen or Swiss Guards deters the wildest irrationalities. Even so, we have learned that not all terror is deterred, that terrorists do break through, and that walled cities are required in every place and time.

Thus, the overwhelming weight of Christian orthodoxy maintains that most Christians cannot be pacifist. In the very name of justice and in the very name of peace, we are required to defend the innocent, and to defend justice itself, from the violence and aggression so regularly used by the unjust. Force without justice is blind, the thought may be summarized, but justice without force is like an empty wind.

Niebuhr argued that the Gospel's eschatological witness is crucial because it gives us the image of the impossible possibility toward which we strive, the Kingdom of God on earth, which is never built on earth. It is with God's light that we see the inadequacies and sinfulness of our own system, that justice in this world is always only an approximation to true justice, and that all steps forward in peace depend on an appropriate balance of power. It is normal to expect that reason follows power in this balance and that when there is too much power on one side and too little on the other, reason is seldom served. This is the other side of Theodore Roosevelt's famous maxim, "Speak softly but carry a big stick." When you carry a big stick, you *can* speak very softly. Often you do not have to say anything at all. The number of persons who will call you "Sir" is amazing. Equality, peace, and justice, then, depend in a sinful world upon a certain balance of power.

The just-war theory arose from the perception that at times peace in an evil world is unjust. It is wrong to be on the streets of New York City and hear a young woman cry for help and simply walk by while she is stabbed to death. Those who do not help her are culpable, just as nations that stand by while innocent neighbors are violently attacked are culpable. There are times when war is just, that is, obligatory, although the initial presumption is always against war.

With the foregoing as a theological excursus in support of my position, I reluctantly judge that the bishops' final statement, good as it is, falls short of sufficient theological realism. The bishops advance orthodox arguments on behalf of pacifism, for example, but fail to voice the real arguments against pacifism. The Christian tradition has always had theological, moral, scriptural, and political arguments against pacifism. These are not rehearsed in the document. Only the rosy side of pacifism is discussed, whereas, when the just-war theory is mentioned, a number of objections are raised. Nonetheless, the final draft provides a good treatment of the just-war theory and might some day even rank as a classic treatment. The final draft has flaws, but it is better than many expected.

The Morality of Deterrence in the 1980's

As alluded to earlier, the question the bishops should have addressed, but did not, is how in the mid-1980's any use of nuclear weapons can be prevented, given the current list of possessors of nuclear arms. When we say "use of nuclear weapons," it is important to recognize that nuclear arms have *two* uses. They may be exploded, or they may be used as weapons of intimidation.

General Andrew J. Goodpaster has stated that the SS-20's that ring Europe like 320 silent oaks, growing at a rate of almost one per week, capable of reaching almost any city in Europe in five or six minutes, have become, since 1979, the most effective weapons system he has ever seen and perhaps the most effective ever built.[6] Without ever being fired, they have come close to splitting the Atlantic Alliance. They have brought, on a given weekend, more than a million Europeans into the streets protesting, not against the Soviets who installed those missiles, but against the United States. They have made the people of the United States suspect that it is foolish to ally themselves with Europe, because if Europe is attacked and the United States defends Europe, the United States will be destroyed. Why should we be destroyed for Europe? The Soviets do not understand why we have not grasped this logic, since the whole thrust of their policy is to see to it that we accept it and thus to decouple us from Europe.

At least unconsciously many European leaders have recognized this basic goal of Soviet policy. In the mid-1970's, left-wing European governments, the Labor Party in Britain and the Social Democrats in Germany, urged President Carter to prepare to deploy the Pershing and cruise missiles in Europe in response to the Soviet Union's deployment of the SS-20. Such a deployment would relieve the current long-distance reliance on the American strategic arsenal. It would also result in the presence in Europe of a nuclear force with a weight and range comparable to that of the SS-20 and able to reach at least parts of the Soviet Union and Eastern Europe—one weapon system with an answering weapon system.

The deployment of the SS-20's is a case in which the Soviets have taken an initiative and compelled us to respond. The SS-20 is a very effective weapons system. Even if it is never used, strategically it has

---

6. Michael Novak, "Arms and the Church," *Commentary* 73 (March 1982), pp. 37–41.

achieved more than many weapons systems that have been used militarily. As was mentioned, nuclear weapons have two functions: one explosive, the other intimidation. The Finlandization, or perhaps more accurately, the Swedenization, of entire regions testifies to the reality of intimidation. Simply by possessing nuclear weapons, one could force other nations to surrender without occupying them, and, while not actually running them, have them serve your will while you humiliate them at your leisure. If I were a member of the Soviet leadership, that is the policy I would advocate in Europe. I would never occupy Europe or socialize it. If the Sahara were socialized, in 20 years there would be a shortage of sand. Why socialize Europe? That would only bring long lines and poverty. No, the intelligent approach to making Europe accede to your demands is to make it a vassal. Frighten the people, and oblige them to send to Moscow only Communist Party members. Make criticism of the Soviet Union something disapproved of at first and then later a crime. Demand that Americans remove themselves from Europe. And insist on very favorable returns for every economic exchange between the Soviet Union and Europe. Within 50 years, Europe could then be sucked dry.

The great religious prophet Aleksandr Solzhenitsyn has warned us that the Soviets believe that the fundamental law of history is not morality, but power, and that their aim is superiority in every field.

At one time there was no comparison between the strength of the USSR and yours. Then it became equal to yours. Now, as all recognize, it is becoming superior to yours. Perhaps today the ratio is just greater than equal, but soon it will be two to one. Then three to one. Finally it will be five to one. . . . With such a nuclear superiority it will be possible to block the use of your weapons, and on some unlucky morning they will declare: "Attention. We're marching our troops to Europe, and if you make a move, we will annihilate you." And this ratio of three to one, or five to one will have its effect: you will not make a move.[7]

I think Solzhenitsyn is absolutely accurate about what is happening. The question now before us is how a Soviet takeover is to be prevented, and how it is to be prevented with neither an explosive nor a political use of nuclear weapons. Implicit in Solzhenitsyn's remark is the simple observation that after World War II, American and European leaders decided it was best not to allow Germany to rearm. Twice already in the 20th century, we had had to go to Europe to fight wars begun by Germany. It was decided, therefore, that the United States should provide the defensive cover for Europe and Japan.

At the time, the consensus was that it would be more humane and more efficient to provide this defense through the imposition of a nu-

7. Aleksandr Solzhenitsyn, *Warning to the West* (New York: Farrar, Straus, and Giroux, 1976), pp. 76–77.

clear shield than through the maintenance of large armies in the field. Since the Soviets had more than 12 million men under arms, a conventional deterrent would have had to be in the range of 8 to 10 million men. To maintain such an army and, in time of peace, their families, in the youngest and most delicate years of their lives, would have been inhumane. It would have resulted in the militarization of Europe. Everywhere one turned there would have been soldiers. The maintenance of such a force would also have been enormously expensive. Therefore, the choice was made to concede to the Soviet Union an immense conventional superiority. Why concede such superiority? The reasoning for this decision went as follows: Since we do not intend to invade the Soviet Union, we do not need large conventional armies. What we do need are small conventional forces sufficient to deter the Soviets and to let them know that we would give them a real fight if they invaded. Meanwhile, we would hold in abeyance our nuclear force and hope that this would ultimately balance the conventional forces of the Soviet Union.

We still live by this theory of defense. We maintain a minimal conventional force in Europe, a force that almost certainly is no longer able to halt a conventional invasion by the Soviets. It would not be an unduly difficult task to upgrade NATO's conventional forces to meet the Soviet conventional threat. A special study conducted by *The Economist* has indicated that with only a small increase in the defense budget, about 4 to 6 percent more than the United States and the European nations currently spend, a conventional balance with enough power to deter a Soviet invasion could be attained.[8] Since we do not plan to invade the Soviet Union, we need only to be able to deter a Soviet attack. The configuration of Soviet forces is entirely offensive in structure, in nature, and in order of battle. Further, the Soviets, to maintain this offensive posture, require a great deal more in military hardware, many more tanks, many more fighters and bombers, than NATO does. A defensive force, to provide an effective deterrent, does not need as much hardware, or even the same types, as an offensive force.

During the last few years, permit me to repeat, the Soviets have also achieved a superiority over NATO forces in theater nuclear weapons. The Soviets have begun to ring Europe with SS-20's and other missile systems of a theater type, to which we have only recently begun to respond.

Furthermore, our strategic forces no longer possess superiority: Optimists claim parity, pessimists rather less. In 1968, Secretary of De-

---

8. "Without the Bomb," *The Economist* (July 31, 1982), pp. 11–12. See also, Committee on the Present Danger, *Is the Reagan Defense Program Adequate?* (Washington: Committee on the Present Danger, 1982).

fense Robert McNamara imposed a weapons freeze on the American triad. He froze our nuclear bomber, the B-52, at 340. The current number is considerably smaller. The total number of aircraft is now approximately 314, while those capable of a strategic mission total approximately 200. While the oldest of these aircraft is more than 30 years old, the average age is approximately 20. In fact, many of the B-52's are now older than the pilots flying them. One leg of the triad has been exceedingly weakened since 1968.

The number of land-based missiles was also allowed to remain constant. When nuclear weapons are counted, warheads and delivery systems are frequently confused. The delivery system, the missile, is essential. The warhead reaches its target only because of the delivery system. The total number of delivery systems remains at 1,052. They have been MIRVed, which means that more than one warhead can be launched from each missile, but the number of launching pads has remained the same. This situation has created the problem of "vulnerability," the theoretical ease with which 1,000 missile sites, locations of which are very well known, can be targeted by weapons sufficiently accurate and powerful to destroy them.

Finally, Secretary McNamara froze the submarine fleet at 36, approximately two-thirds or fewer of which are on station at any one time. McNamara's theory with regard to this weapons freeze was that if we freeze our weapons, the Soviets would match us and then stop. But as Harold Brown, Secretary of Defense under President Carter, observed, "When we build, they build; when we stop building, they build."

It is difficult to ascertain the exact status of our systems *vis-à-vis* the Soviet Union's. Some commentators convincingly argue that we are number two in most key defense areas. Others maintain, for various reasons, that we are at parity with the Soviet Union. We were told at the signing of the SALT accords in 1972 and again at the Vladivostok agreements in 1974 that we are at "essential parity." But unlike the Soviets, we have not built a new bomber nor have we added a single new missile system since that time. (The B-1 and the "stealth" bomber are now in early preparation.) Our Polaris submarine system is only slowly being replaced by the Trident. Moreover, since 1967 we have reduced, and I think for very good reason, the number of warheads we own by a fifth. Since 1962 we have reduced the total throw weight of our nuclear forces by more than half.[9]

I wish to emphasize what Solzhenitsyn meant when he said that the Soviets will continue to pursue weapons superiority. I also wish to

9. Albert Carnesale et al., *Living With Nuclear Weapons* (New York: Bantam Books, 1983), p. 103. Cf. Michael Novak, Letter to the Editor, *The Record* (St. John's University), March 22, 1984.

underscore his point about the political utility of such a pursuit. The American national game at the moment is football. The great dramatic play in football is the long forward pass. Drama and suddenness in war, as in football, mesmerize our imagination. The Soviet national game is chess. In chess you do not have to remove your opponent's pieces from the board to win. You simply have to produce a situation in which your opponent is placed in checkmate. The odds will be two to one, then three to one, then five to one, and then some fine morning the Soviets will announce, "Attention. Today, we are doing thus and so." And we, recognizing the odds, will do nothing whatever. Checkmate.

If one considers how to prevent checkmate from occurring, one may be led by two different routes to the same conclusion. The first involves the principles of the just-war theory. This approach questions whether there is a just cause for the military response. Who is it, and what is it, that one is attempting to deter? Why have a deterrence system at all? One cannot argue in the abstract whether a deterrence system is good or bad. Its value, in this approach, depends precisely on what is being deterred.

The second line of thought, a line that eventually leads to much the same conclusion, involves the notion of deterrence itself. The French term, *dissuasion*, better brings out the sense of what it means to "deter" than the English word. *Dissuasion* highlights the psychological element in "deterrence." The meaning of "deterrence" differs, depending upon whom and what it is one is trying to deter. A teacher deters students in one way, a parent deters children in another, while the state deters a madman in yet a third. Although Great Britain and France have nuclear weapons, we do not deploy a deterrence system against them. Our own deterrence system, and that of those nations, is directed at the same force, the Soviet Union. Whether one approaches deterrence from the point of view of the just-war and just-cause theory, or from the point of view of *dissuasion*, it is essential to possess an accurate understanding of the Soviet Union.

To form such an accurate understanding, a reasonable person must look at three things. First, one must look at "strategic potential." This consists of knowing what the Soviets actually can do and really which exact weapons are to be deterred. In analyzing strategic potential one must consider the Soviet weapons systems. Soviet conventional forces are in an offensive configuration. While the Soviet Union itself is land-locked, it operates an offensive navy in every ocean. The number of Soviet submarines off the American coast has recently been increased. Soviet submarines have been known to come as close as 300 miles to the South Carolina coast. Soviet submarines in trouble have surfaced in Tokyo Bay and in Swedish fjords. This worldwide offensive potential was beyond the Soviet naval capacity 10 years ago, but today it is in operation. As I argued before, we do not need to meet the Soviet configuration weapon for weapon. Our purpose is quite different from theirs. Nonetheless, the Soviet strategic potential must be considered. This means having an accurate knowledge of the capacities of each system. At this level of analysis, we should disregard Soviet statements of intent, examining instead only the actual capabilities of the weapons themselves.

Strategic potential is only the first level of analysis needed to gain an exact understanding of the Soviet Union. One must also consider the proclivities of its people. By this I mean national doctrines and ideologies. If one were to attempt to understand the proclivities of the citizens of the United States, one would need to know something about Judaism and Christianity. What do Jews and Christians think about the peace movement? The right to life movement? Similarly, when one considers the Soviet Union, one would want to understand Marxism.

To assess the proclivities of a people, one must also consider how they act culturally and habitually. The other side knows Americans are very vulnerable to propaganda. The leader of Nicaragua was quoted in *Newsweek* as stating that the "war for Nicaragua is being fought in the United States, not in Nicaragua." The Soviets are certainly aware of this vulnerability. Furthermore, the attention span of democratic peoples tends to be very short. It is exceedingly difficult for democratic peoples to maintain a military force of any kind when they are not actually at war. Adam Smith was aware of this tendency. As a people becomes capitalistic, he saw, they lose the sense of sacrifice and willfulness upon which martial cultures thrive. No democratic population in the world today, for example, neither French nor German nor American, desires greater defense spending.

In assessing Soviet proclivities, it is comforting to see that the Soviets typically are cautious both in their doctrine and in their character. Leninism itself is calculating. It imposes on socialism the obligation to make socialism triumphant in history. To bring about this triumph requires accurate information concerning the correlation of opposing military forces. When the correlation of forces is favorable, the socialist is morally obligated to attack. When the correlation is unfavorable, the socialist is morally obligated not to attack to prevent socialism from being weakened. There is a strong doctrinal motivation for the Soviets to be very cautious about the balance of power. Typically, they act according to this motivation.

Culturally, too, for reasons having to do with the political and social nature and history of Russia, and with the operations of Soviet collective leadership, political decisions tend to be made quite cautiously. The

Korean Airline incident is a good example of how long it takes the Soviets to know what has happened, who is responsible, and what to say about an international incident. It was a week before the Soviets were able to make up their minds about how to proceed. This is typical behavior on the part of the Soviets. The wheels do not turn quickly in their system.

The third level of analysis involves examining Soviet intentions. What do they say they are going to do? For obvious reasons, this is the most problematic level of analysis. It is hard to read peoples' minds. It is difficult to know whose words carry weight. It is also difficult to trust their words. Because of these ambiguities, I consider strategic potential and Soviet proclivities to be the more significant elements.

The bishops have urged us to think of deterrence as a step along the road to negotiation. The difficulty, however, is that there are just and unjust negotiations.[10] Negotiations are subject to the same standards of morality as is war. In the fall of 1983, we believed the Syrians when they said they would withdraw from Lebanon if Israel would also withdraw its forces. But what we got for our gullibility was a 5,000-pound bomb driven into the bivouac of 250 sleeping Marines and no Syrian withdrawal. Someone was duped. History will not judge kindly those who were taken in. Chamberlain, who claimed that he had achieved peace in his time with Hitler, certainly has not been judged kindly. We should pause when considering the nature of negotiations with the Soviet Union, since three years ago the Soviet negotiator in the Demilitarized Zone between the two Koreas returned to Moscow to receive an award, Hero of the Soviet Union. He was praised because he had been a negotiator for 18 years and had never agreed to anything.

Despite the pessimism, one should always maintain hope for the future. President Kennedy once said that a special sacrifice is demanded from each generation. His generation, one that had sacrificed much in World War II and Korea, knew exactly what he meant. The generation President Kennedy visited in Berlin, isolated from the West and still living in the relative poverty that followed World War II, knew what he meant.

The sacrifice asked of today's generation, in both Europe and America, is a peculiar one. The new generation, in both Europe and America, has experienced greater affluence and liberty than any previous generation in history. This affluence is recent. Even 10 years after the close of World War II, poverty was common, and many countries had regressed to a more primitive standard of living. I recall that when I first lived in

10. Michael Novak, *Moral Clarity in the Nuclear Age* (New York: Thomas Nelson Publishers, 1983), pp. 125–134.

Rome in 1956, I was moved to go into the countryside and to imagine traveling back in time to the 14th century. In the midst of the very affluence and liberty that surround today's generation, an affluence that offers to everyone the chance to think and to ponder moral issues, is a military force superior to that of Adolf Hitler at the very height of his power, and possessing a doctrine more directed and systematic. The burden to be carried by this generation is that of resisting this force, the Soviet Union, in small issue after large issue, day after day, year after year. This constant resistance, a dull and jading task, is the most difficult burden for any democratic country to assume.

On the other hand, the present moment itself is fleeting. When I was a child, our most terrible and hated enemies were the Japanese and the Germans. In my lifetime, they have come to be numbered among our closest friends. There is no reason why the Soviet Union cannot make this same transition. The East European people, of whom I am one, love their nieces and nephews, sons and daughters, as we love our nieces and nephews, sons and daughters. East Europeans love life; they drink hard and eat heartily. But they happen to be caught up in one of the most corrupt political systems ever devised by the human mind.

Yet there are rays of hope. It is exceedingly hard for intelligent and sensitive people in the Soviet Union to convince themselves that the only law of history is power, not morality. They may be taught never to apologize, since socialism as the key to history can never commit wrong, but people can never be made to believe this teaching or honestly to live by it. Most people do, despite themselves, love other people and they do, despite themselves, know the difference between right and wrong, truth and lies, honesty and dishonesty. A regime based on lies and systematic deception, lying even when the deception is pointless, cannot be tolerated by sensitive and intelligent human beings. As Solzhenitsyn and others have shown, no one believes the Soviet regime anymore—except in the West.

I see a second ray of hope in the development of "new technologies." Scientists are exploring the possibility that present ballistic missiles can be rendered obsolete. What we live in greatest terror of is the long-range intercontinental ballistic missile, a missile able to be shot like a bullet into the sky, and to fall with great accuracy on its target. These missiles are potentially vulnerable to destruction, and if some means could be discovered to destroy them as they rise from their launching pads, they will become a greater threat to the country that has them than to their foreign foes. Such a defensive system has at least two advantages. It is more in accord with just-war thinking, which has as its premise the validity of defense against aggression. Moreover, the secrets of such a defensive system can be shared with the other side, since the need to maintain secrecy is not as acute as with an offensive system. If such a defensive system is implemented, the ballistic missile will go the way of the dinosaur, and entire generations will be freed. I do not wish to raise false hopes, but the human capacity for invention is limitless. Such a system can become a reality.

Senator Henry Jackson once gave me a metaphor that I have always valued. The Soviets, he said, are like hotel burglars, burglars whose doctrine states that they must test every door in the hotel every night, and when they find one open, they must go through it. But as long as they find the doors locked, they are obliged to keep out. Our task is really a very simple one, although difficult for a democratic society to accomplish. We must keep the doors locked. We must block aggressive moves on the international chessboard. We do not need superiority, but we do desperately need sufficiency. This is an urgent moral responsibility. We must deter any use of nuclear weapons, whether explosive or political, and we must continue to do so steadily, consistently, year after year, until we can contrive to remove this shadow fallen on the face of mankind.

J. BRYAN HEHIR

9. The Context of the Moral-Strategic Debate and the Contribution of the U.S. Catholic Bishops

The purpose of this paper is to situate the pastoral letter of the U.S. Catholic bishops, *The Challenge of Peace: God's Promise and Our Response*,[1] within the framework of the broader argument about ethics and nuclear strategy. This essay will examine examples of moral positions that had been developed before the pastoral letter and then look at some of the responses generated by the U.S. bishops' position.

The paper will address four topics: the relationship of strategic and ethical arguments in the nuclear debate; a spectrum of moral positions on ethics and strategy; an analysis of the pastoral letter; and some initial reactions to the pastoral.

The Relationship of Strategic and Ethical Arguments

The intensity of public discussion of both nuclear strategy and the ethics of strategy in the 1980's should not obscure the fact that both subjects have a rich history in the nuclear age.[2] The present stage of the argument can be assessed more adequately if the relationship to previous chapters in the debate are kept in mind. One characteristic of this history is particularly interesting. It is the parallel quality of the strategic

This paper is reprinted with the permission of the Center of International Studies, Princeton University. It originally appeared in R. C. Johansen, ed., *The Nuclear Arms Debate: Ethical and Political Implications*, World Order Studies Program, Occasional Paper No. 12, 1984.
1. National Conference of Catholic Bishops, *The Challenge of Peace: God's Promise and Our Response* (Washington, D.C.: U.S. Catholic Conference, 1983).
2. For literature on the strategic debate consult, among others, J. M. Mandelbaum, *The Nuclear Question: The United States and Nuclear Weapons 1946–1976* (Cambridge, England: Cambridge University Press, 1979); J. H. Kahan, *Security in the Nuclear Age: Developing U.S. Strategic Policy* (Washington, D.C.: Brookings Institute, 1975); B. Brodie, "Development of Nuclear Strategy," *International Security*, 2 (1978), pp. 65–83. For literature on ethics and strategy, no single history is available, but consult: A. Geyer, *The Idea of Disarmament: Rethinking the Unthinkable* (Elgin, Ill.: The Brethren Press, 1982); P. Ramsey, *The Just War: Force and Political Responsibility* (New York: Scribners, 1968).

and ethical debates. This parallel quality is particularly striking in view of the fact that strategists and moralists worked in different forums with only rare instances of in-depth exchange. Even a brief review of the literature, however, illustrates a structural similarity of the arguments among strategists and those among moralists.

One of the themes that has cut across both disciplines is an assessment of the nature of the nuclear revolution, what degree or kind of change it has created in the world of politics and strategy. In the strategic literature two broad positions emerge: One defines nuclear weapons in a special category requiring a transformation of political and military thinking, while the other acknowledges the difference of nuclear and conventional weapons, but contends it is both possible and necessary to stretch the traditional categories of strategic thought to include nuclear weapons. Representatives of the two positions can be identified, recognizing that they share some common ground in spite of differing evaluations of the character of nuclear policy.

Nuclear Weapons as a Unique Case

The first school found an early, eloquent, and authoritative spokesman in Bernard Brodie, one of the most prolific authors of the nuclear age. In one of the first major essays on the significance of nuclear weapons, Brodie wrote: "Thus far the chief purpose of our military establishment has been to win wars. From now on its chief purpose must be to avert them. It can have almost no other useful purpose."[3]

Brodie saw fit to repeat this text and expand on its significance in one of the last essays of his life.[4] Although he was deeply involved for more than 30 years in the intellectual and political world that shaped U.S. strategic policy, he sustained throughout this period a conviction that fighting a nuclear war was not a reasonable policy.

Brodie's position has found many adherents throughout the nuclear age, both in and out of government. Certain aspects of it could be found in the theory and practice of the McNamara years at the Defense Department (1961–68).[5] At the end of the McNamara period, McGeorge Bundy restated the Brodie thesis after two decades of experience in the nuclear age:

In light of the certain prospect of retaliation there has been literally no chance at all that any sane political authority, in either the United States or the Soviet Union, would consciously choose to start a nuclear war. This proposition is true for the past, the present and the foreseeable future. For sane men on both

3. B. Brodie, ed., *The Absolute Weapon* (New York: Harcourt, Brace, 1946), quoted in B. Brodie, "Development of Nuclear Strategy," cited p. 65.
4. B. Brodie, "Development of Nuclear Strategy," cited pp. 65–83.
5. For analysis of the McNamara years, cf. Mandelbaum, cited; Kahan, cited.

sides the balance of terror is overwhelmingly persuasive. . . . There is an enormous gulf between what political leaders really think about nuclear weapons and what is assumed in complex calculations of relative "advantage" in simulated strategic warfare. Think-tank analysts can set levels of "acceptable" damage well up in the tens of millions of lives. They can assume that the loss of dozens of great cities is somehow a real choice for sane men. They are in an unreal world.[6]

The Bundy position of 1968 reflected the mainstream of strategic thought, although his article sharpened the edge of some of the accepted premises. In the 1970's, however, a new challenge to the consensus emerged: the idea of usable nuclear weapons was revived. In response, two seasoned veterans of the nuclear debate, Wolfgang Panofsky and Spurgeon Keeny, restated the Brodie position.[7] Finally, in 1983 former Secretary of Defense McNamara joined the debate himself. In the face of a variety of arguments asserting the need for a usable nuclear strategy, McNamara set forth the most explicit contrary case yet to appear in print from a person of his experience:

Having spent seven years as Secretary of Defense dealing with the problems unleashed by the initial nuclear chain reaction 40 years ago, I do not believe we can avoid serious and unacceptable risk of nuclear war until we recognize—and until we base all our military plans, defense budgets, weapon deployments, and arms negotiations on the recognition—*that nuclear weapons serve no military purpose whatsoever. They are totally useless—except only to deter one's opponent from using them.*[8]

Nuclear War as an Instrument of Policy

The counterpoint to the Brodie position also has roots early in the nuclear age; essentially it holds that nuclear weapons mark a decisive step in the history of strategy but do not constitute an essentially different problem than statesmen and strategists have faced in the past. Moreover, the emphasis placed on continuity leads this school to argue that a rationally defensible policy of use of nuclear weapons, and, *a fortiori*, a defensible strategy of deterrence can be designed. Within the framework of this general position three distinct groups can be identified: the limited nuclear war theorists, the counterforce constituency, and the advocates of defensive systems.

The policy debate about the possibility and meaning of "limited nuclear war" is woven through the history of the nuclear age. One of the first exponents of the position was Henry A. Kissinger, in *Nuclear*

6. M. Bundy, "To Cap the Volcano," *Foreign Affairs* 47 (1969), pp. 1–20.

7. S. M. Keeny, Jr., and W. F. H. Panofsky, "MAD vs. NUTS: The Mutual Hostage Relationship of the Superpowers," *Foreign Affairs* 60 (1981/82), pp. 287–304.

8. R. S. McNamara, "The Military Role of Nuclear Weapons," *Foreign Affairs* 62 (1983), pp. 59–80.

Weapons and Foreign Policy[9] Kissinger later retreated from his belief that placing limits on nuclear weapons was feasible,[10] but other advocates have appeared, ranging from James Schlesinger to Richard Pipes. The purpose of all these authors has not been to encourage the use of nuclear weapons, but to argue that a credible deterrence strategy must include a convincing plan to use nuclear weapons if necessary.

Closely allied to limiting nuclear war at the theater level by using weapons with small yield has been the counterforce position at the strategic level. Counterforce targeting sought to make strategic nuclear exchange politically and morally tolerable by diverting attacks from populated areas to military targets. The counterforce option has been a persistent theme in the strategic debate. McNamara proposed a counterforce option in 1962, then moved away from it; Schlesinger revived the idea in his "Selective Options" proposal of 1974;[11] Fred Ikle, present Under Secretary of Defense for Policy, has long advocated a counterforce capability for political and moral reasons.[12] The Carter Administration moved in a counterforce direction with "PD59"; the Reagan Administration has, if anything, accentuated this trend. Like the limited nuclear war doctrine, counterforce seeks to contain the new reality of nuclear weaponry within the traditional logic of war and politics.

The third position that stresses continuity between a pre- and post-nuclear age conception of warfare involves advocates of a defensive nuclear strategy. Here again several versions of the same theme have been proposed. The Nike-Zeus air defense option entered a new stage of sophistication in the late sixties with the proposal to deploy "ABM's" or ballistic missile defenses. Supporters of the proposal, preeminently the late Donald Brennan, have always argued its strategic and moral superiority, since its purpose is to *prevent* attack and its targets are missiles, not people.[13] The SALT I treaties sharply curtailed a defensive option for either superpower, but the idea has now been resurrected by President Reagan's support for a major research and development effort on defensive systems.[14]

This neat categorization between those who find nuclear weapons un-

9. H. A. Kissinger, *Nuclear Weapons and Foreign Policy* (New York: Doubleday Anchor, 1958), Ch. 6–7, pp. 114–168.

10. H. A. Kissinger, *The Necessity for Choice: Prospects of American Foreign Policy* (New York: Doubleday Anchor, 1962), pp. 59–101.

11. James R. Schlesinger, *Annual Report to the Congress on the FY 1975 Budget and FY 1975–1979 Defense Program* (March 4, 1974).

12. F. Ikle, "Can Deterrence Last Out the Century?" *Foreign Affairs* 51 (1973), pp. 267–285.

13. D. G. Brennan, "The Case for Missile Defense," *Foreign Affairs* 47 (1969), pp. 443–448.

14. For text of Reagan speech, *The New York Times* (March 24, 1983), p. A20.

fit for use and those who propose means to contain them so they can be used is too clear and too air tight. But it serves to highlight a real and significant difference of emphasis among strategic theorists and policy-makers, a difference that has consequences for force structure, deployment, and targeting policy and/or arms control strategies. Moreover, this division among the strategists is replicated by the moralists.

Ethics and Strategy: A Spectrum of Views

The transposition from the strategic to the moral debate means distinguishing between those moralists who have concluded that any use of nuclear weapons would necessarily exceed the permissible limits of war and those who seek to tie a concept of "limited war"—at the theater or strategic level—to the idea of "justifiable war." The debate among these moral positions was well established before the pastoral letter was prepared. An understanding of how the debate evolved will enhance an appreciation of where the pastoral fits as a moral response to the nuclear age. Each of the positions outlined in the following paragraphs has contemporary advocates who sought to convince the bishops to adopt their specific position.

The 1960's: Deciding About Deterrence

In the 1960's the first in-depth moral analysis of the nuclear age was made. Two major positions emerged. They were both rooted in a just-war moral perspective, but the exponents recognized that the application of the traditional doctrine to the nuclear reality required a close examination of the new weapons and strategic concepts. The two positions used identical principles (i.e., noncombatant immunity and proportionality), but they moved to quite different conclusions.

Professor Paul Ramsey, emeritus professor of Christian ethics at Princeton University and the most prolific contributor to the nuclear debate, developed a position legitimizing both limited nuclear war and a limited deterrent.[15] Ramsey began with the premise that nuclear weapons were new and different but not so revolutionary that they constituted an essentially different political-moral question from the past. The basis of Ramsey's position is his conviction that a morally justifiable use can be determined for nuclear weapons. The parameters of legitimate use of nuclear weapons are set by the twin principles of discrimination and proportionality. These principles are used to design a morally acceptable counterforce nuclear strategy. Such a position consists of an absolute prohibition against any countercity use of nuclear weapons supple-

15. Ramsey, *The Just War*, cited, pp. 211–258, 314–366.

mented by a complex calculus regulating the use of nuclear weapons against legitimate military targets for limited political purposes.

This specification of conditions indicating how and where nuclear weapons might be used is designed to dissolve the ambiguity surrounding strategic policy in which no clear line is drawn distinguishing counterforce and countervalue targets. A summary statement of the Ramsey position on permissible use of nuclear weapons is contained in the following passage:

> This nation should announce that as a matter of policy we will never be the first to use nuclear weapons—except tactical ones that may and will be used, against forces only and not strategically against an enemy's heartland, to stop an invasion across a clearly defined boundary, our own or one we are pledged to defend by treaty. This would make it unambiguously clear that tactical nuclear weapons will be used if need be against any invasion even by conventional forces.[16]

The moral limits placed on the use of nuclear weapons set the moral limits for deterrence. Any deterrence policy that, in intention or implementation, would exceed these boundaries is proscribed. The moral dilemma of deterrence is that it has preserved a limited peace, but the suspicion remains that it is being purchased at the cost of a conditional or actual intent to do evil. Ramsey poses the moralist's ultimate question for deterrence policy in terms of whether the deterrence that is needed to enforce restraints on war necessarily and unchangeably depends on an actual present intent to commit murder or upon a present murderous intention.

Ramsey's response to his own question involved an articulation of three distinct (and independent) reasons by which deterrence could be morally justified. The three reasons were deterrence from disproportionate combatant damage, deterrence from disproportionate collateral damage, and deterrence from the inherently ambiguous operational capabilities of nuclear weapons (i.e., they could be used against cities even if the possessing nation never threatened or intended to use them in this way).

Ramsey regarded nuclear weapons as the extension of the continuum of force legitimately available for defensive purposes by a state under prescribed ethical conditions, established by the principles of noncombatant immunity and proportionality. Consequently, Ramsey argued for the legitimate use of nuclear weapons either in defense against aggression or as a counterforce weapon, again for defense purposes, against tactical objectives. In summary, the Ramsey position is that of limited use and counterforce deterrence.

16. Ibid., p. 237.

At the very time Ramsey was developing his position, others were moving in a diametrically different direction. An anthology of English Catholic authors, edited by Walter Stein and published under the title *Nuclear Weapons and the Christian Conscience*,[17] stated the case for nuclear pacifism. Using the same principles employed by Ramsey, these authors consigned nuclear weapons to a status beyond the limits of justifiable warfare. In a sense they shared Brodie's premise but moved well beyond Brodie in their policy conclusions. Walter Stein exemplifies the perspective of his colleagues, making the case against nuclear weapons in terms of the principle of proportionality:

This is why nuclear warfare is immoral. It could hardly achieve a just balance of consequence; and the hugeness of its evils—which of course might extend to the entire destruction of civilization, grave and permanent harm to future generations, and, potentially, even the total extermination of the species—reduces the notion of "unintended effects" to parody; whilst it is, above all, absolutely clear that its indiscriminate terrors must in fact be directly willed, since "deterrence" ultimately rests on the possibility of massive retaliation.[18]

Others in the volume, like R. A. Marcus, argue that any use of nuclear weapons will inevitably violate the principle of noncombatant immunity.[19]

Although the authors do not discuss the question of limited nuclear war explicitly, the whole theme of the volume is an indictment of nuclear weapons. The position is exemplified in Marcus' treatment of the crucial distinction between possessing nuclear weapons and using them. Some things, he argues, are open to good and evil uses (e.g., guns) so that it is impossible to say *a priori* that a gun is evil; the judgment turns on its use. Possession of nuclear weapons does not fit in the same category, since "they have only one use and that is large-scale indiscriminate destruction"; "in any situation we can envisage, the use of the H-Bomb is morally inadmissable."[20] This absolute proscription of any use of nuclear weapons structures the response given to the question of deterrence.

The argument of Stein and his colleagues against deterrence is radically simple in its structure. It depends upon the prior judgment that the very nature of nuclear weapons fits them only for indiscriminate use; since it is wrong to use them, it is wrong to intend to use them. Since deterrence rests in part upon the intention to do what one threatens, the possession of a nuclear deterrent is immoral. Marcus summarizes the case: "If exploding nuclear weapons is morally wrong in any circum-

17. W. Stein, ed., *Nuclear Weapons and the Christian Conscience* (London: Merlin Publishers, 1961).

18. Ibid., p. 29.   20. Ibid., p. 65.

19. Ibid., p. 65.

stances it is morally wrong to intend exploding them in any, no matter how carefully circumscribed circumstances."[21]

The premise that a new moral problem exists, requiring a clear break with prior evaluations of restraint on the use of force, keeps appearing in the Stein volume. The position of proscribing any use of nuclear weapons prevents these authors from accepting a Ramsey-style argument for deterrence. The use of nuclear weapons is wrong *in se*; calculation of direct and indirect effects is unnecessary. Moreover, since the indiscriminate nature of the bomb makes it evil, its ambiguous operational character is irrelevant. On all counts the Ramsey deterrence position fails for the authors of the Stein volume. For them, no use of nuclear weapons can be morally justified; therefore, deterrence policy that "rests in the end on the intention to use nuclear weapons" also must be morally proscribed.

These two positions, a just nuclear war argument and nuclear pacifism, reflect much of the content of the ethical analysis of the 1960's.

The 1970's: Doubt About Deterrence

In the 1970's positions were developed on the relationship of ethics and nuclear policy that were neither as absolute as nuclear pacifism nor as optimistic about containing nuclear war as Ramsey's. While not condemning deterrence these positions came to the brink of doing this. In this sense they prefigured the pastoral letter of the U.S. bishops in the 1980's.

Indeed one persistent source of doubts about deterrence was the evolving position of the bishops in the 1970's. In a pastoral letter in 1976, *To Live in Christ Jesus*,[22] and then in congressional testimony presented by John Cardinal Krol in 1979 during the SALT II ratification debate, the bishops set forth their initial reservations about nuclear policy. In 1976, the bishops used one brief section of a broad-ranging pastoral message to focus on the relationship of intention and action in deterrence policy. The emphasis they placed on the role of intention in moral action reflected the concerns of the Stein volume but also presented a traditional concern of Catholic moral thinking. This particular facet of policy receives much less attention in the secular strategic debate. By focusing on intention, the bishops foreshadowed one of the characteristics that would give their pastoral letter a well-defined place in the debate of the 1980's. The 1976 statement said in its central passage:

21. Ibid., p. 65.
22. National Conference of Catholic Bishops, *To Live in Christ Jesus* (Washington, D.C.: U.S. Catholic Conference, 1976).

With respect to nuclear weapons, at least those with massive destructive capability, the first imperative is to prevent their use. As possessors of a vast nuclear arsenal, we must also be aware that not only is it wrong to attack civilian populations but it is also wrong to threaten to attack them as part of a strategy of deterrence. We urge the continued development and implementation of policies which seek to bring these weapons more securely under control, progressively reduce their presence in the world, and ultimately remove them entirely.[23]

This statement can be evaluated by situating it in light of the two moral positions outlined in the previous section of this paper. The bishops' statement has some affinity with nuclear pacifism in its emphasis on preventing the use of nuclear weapons. At the same time it stops short of an absolute prohibition on nuclear weapons by the qualifying phrase "those with massive destructive capability."

Paradoxically, the caution in the judgment on the use of nuclear weapons is matched by a startling clarity of judgment about deterrence policy. The bishops' statement acknowledges none of the ambiguity inherent in the linkage between intention and use in deterrence theory. The statement simply applies the classical theory of intention to condemn deterrence policy. In summary, the surprising character of the bishops' declaration is that it has more of an absolute character concerning deterrence than it has about use.

A more complex and detailed exposition of doubts about deterrence is found in Cardinal Krol's 1979 testimony before the Senate Foreign Relations Committee.[24] The testimony built on the 1976 statement but confronted more clearly the paradoxical problem that deterrence poses for both strategists and moralists. It argued that deterrence could be "tolerated" as a framework within which steps must be taken to reverse the dynamic and direction of the arms race. The Krol testimony clearly sided with those in the strategic debate who classify nuclear weapons as unusable instruments of policy; the testimony argued that the primary moral imperative of policy should be to prevent any use of nuclear weapons.

It was precisely the importance given this imperative that forced the Krol testimony to probe more minutely the political paradox and moral dilemma of deterrence. On one hand there are empirical indications that the strategy of possessing nuclear weapons and threatening to use them has been one reason why the superpowers have avoided nuclear confrontation even though they have had several political clashes. At the same time this strategy of threat and counterthreat is risky, not a stable

23. Ibid., p. 34.
24. Cardinal John Krol, Testimony on SALT II, *ORIGINS* (Documentary Service of the U.S. Catholic Conference) 9 (1979), pp. 195–199.

basis for peace, and, in the view of some observers, may involve a conditional intention to kill the innocent. Krol reviewed these contrasting features of deterrence and then made the following assessment:

This explains the Catholic dissatisfaction with nuclear deterrence and the urgency of the Catholic demand that the nuclear arms race be reversed. It is of the utmost importance that negotiations proceed to meaningful and continuing reductions in nuclear stockpiles, and eventually to the phasing out altogether of nuclear deterrence and the threat of mutual-assured destruction.

As long as there is hope of this occurring, Catholic moral teaching is willing, while negotiations proceed, to tolerate the possession of nuclear weapons for deterrence as the lesser of the two evils. If that hope were to disappear the moral attitude of the Catholic Church would certainly have to shift to one of uncompromising condemnation of both use and possession of such weapons.[25]

Other analysts of the problem also had doubts that began to appear in the secular literature. The most penetrating moral argument was made by Professor Michael Walzer in *Just and Unjust Wars*.[26] Walzer's argument begins by placing nuclear weapons in a category apart from other forms of warfare. He then argues, in a manner akin to the authors of the Stein volume, that nuclear weapons do not fit the categories of legitimate use: "Nuclear weapons explode the theory of just war. They are the first of mankind's technological innovations that are simply not encompassable within the familiar moral world."[27]

Having set himself against Ramsey's position, Walzer then refused to move to the conclusion of the nuclear pacifists regarding deterrence. Impressed by the paradox of deterrence, Walzer formulated a moral argument legitimizing the strategy of deterrence:

Supreme emergency has become a permanent condition. Deterrence is a way of coping with that condition, and though it is a bad way, there may well be no other that is practical in a world of sovereign and suspicious states. We threaten evil in order not to do it, and the doing of it would be so terrible that the threat seems in comparison to be morally defensible.[28]

When the American bishops began the drafting of their pastoral letter in 1981, each of the positions outlined here (and others analogous to them) set an intellectual framework for their work. To some degree each of the positions described can be found partially reflected in the pastoral letter; yet the conclusion reached in the pastoral is distinct from any of the earlier positions. The precise nature of the Catholic bishops' response to nuclear weapons and nuclear strategy needs to be examined now.

25. Ibid., p. 197.
26. Walzer, *Just and Unjust Wars: A Moral Argument with Historical Illustrations* (New York: Basic Books, Inc., 1977).
27. Ibid., p. 282.   28. Ibid., p. 274.

The Challenge of Peace: A Commentary

The pastoral letter is a moral-religious analysis of several of the principal political and strategic questions of the nuclear age. In Part I of the letter the bishops set forth the component elements of the Catholic vision: its biblical foundations, ecclesiological framework, and moral principles. In light of this complex fabric of moral-religious criteria the letter then moves to the policy analysis in Parts II and III. Central to the policy section of the letter is a just-war analysis of the use of nuclear weapons, the strategy of deterrence and arms control in the nuclear age.

Establishing the Moral Perspective

All the positions examined in this paper have been rooted in the just-war ethic. This is also the dominant perspective of the pastoral letter. The twin premises of this position are that in a sinful, still decentralized world of states, some use of force may be politically necessary and is open to moral justification; and that any justifiable use of force must be a limited use. The destructive capacity of nuclear weapons poses a qualitatively new challenge to the concept of a limited use of force. The strategist's concern with limits is intensified by the moralist's concern for justification.

The bishops wish to make clear at the outset of their analysis that they recognize the essentially different challenge posed by nuclear weapons. The dimensions of the challenge were concisely captured by Pope John Paul II in his address at Hiroshima: "In the past it was possible to destroy a village, a town, a region, even a country. Now it is the whole planet that has come under threat."[29]

Faced with this threat, the bishops seek to make clear that they are opposed to conceptions and descriptions of the nuclear question that fail to convey the radically new issues posed by nuclear weapons and nuclear strategy. The coming of the nuclear age has transformed the doctrine of Clausewitz that war is a rational extension of politics. As the pastoral phrases the question:

We live today, therefore in the midst of a cosmic drama; we possess a power which should never be used, but which might be used if we do not reverse our direction. We live with nuclear weapons knowing we cannot afford to make one serious mistake. This fact dramatizes the precariousness of our position politically, morally and spiritually.[30]

The precariousness of the nuclear age has both a political and a strategic dimension. The political problem is the fact of an international

29. John Paul II, *Address to Scientists and Scholars* (1981), cited in *Challenge of Peace*, n. 122, p. 39.
30. *Challenge of Peace*, n. 124, p. 40.

system not only decentralized in its structure but divided by a super-power competition that permeates every dimension of global politics. This bipolar competition, in itself, is hardly new; it is woven through history from the Peloponnesian Wars to the present. The unique character of the present dilemma is that political competition is pursued through nuclear means. Complicating both the political and strategic dimensions is the technological revolution that drives the arms race on both sides of the ideological revolution.

The premise of the bishops' just-war analysis is that limitation of the use of force means addressing the question of whether nuclear weapons can be controlled at any level of use. The issue of control was a major theme in the preparation of the several drafts of the pastoral letter, in the literature consulted, and in the extensive dialogues the Bernardin Committee had with the Reagan Administration.

The result of this detailed process of research and discussion was an attitude in the letter that is radically skeptical about the possibilities of controlling nuclear war. The pastoral stands in the line of the strategic theorists who stress the drastic discontinuity of nuclear and conventional weapons. Because of their profound skepticism about control, the bishops say "No" to the idea of nuclear war and set themselves against the careless rhetoric used at times about "winnable" nuclear wars or "prevailing" in nuclear war. Against this pattern of thought the bishops seek to build a political-moral barrier against any use of nuclear weapons and to resist the rhetoric that would lead us toward use.

Assessing Cases of Use and the Character of Deterrence

The pastoral letter comments on *three cases of use* of nuclear weapons. First, directly intended attacks on civilian populations or "Counter-Population Warfare"; this case is considered for two reasons: the moral principle at stake, noncombatant immunity, is central to the just-war ethic; and at various times in the nuclear age the direct targeting of civilian centers has been considered or planned. The basic judgment of the letter is to rule out, absolutely, direct attacks on civilian populations. The judgment is based on the just-war tradition that found forceful expression in the Second Vatican Council's statement against "destruction of entire cities or of extensive areas along with their population. . . . It merits unequivocal and unhesitating condemnation."[31]

The bishops illustrate the power of this principle by specifying its meaning in two ways. First, they rule out retaliatory action against ci-

---

31. Vatican II, *The Pastoral Constitution on the Church in the Modern World*, n. 80; cited in *Challenge of Peace*, n. 147, p. 46.

vilian centers even if our cities have been hit first. Second, anyone asked to execute strikes against civilian centers should refuse orders.

The second case, "The Initiation of Nuclear War," is the question of first use of nuclear weapons. The significance of this issue is twofold; the possibility of "first use" is still a central piece of NATO strategy and there is now a renewed debate about the strategy underway.[32] The bishops do not address the political debate as such; their purpose is to isolate the moral question in it. Briefly stated, is there a specific moral issue involved in the willingness to be the first party to move warfare from the conventional level to the nuclear level?

The pastoral finds a specific moral responsibility here and its judgment is one of the more controversial sections of the letter. The bishops say: "We do not perceive any situation in which the deliberate initiation of nuclear warfare, on however restricted a scale, can be morally justified. Non-nuclear attacks by another state must be resisted by other than nuclear means. Therefore, a serious moral obligation exists to develop non-nuclear defensive strategies as rapidly as possible."[33]

The rationale of the pastoral's prohibition of first use should be seen in light of a general theme of the letter. In a series of judgments the bishops seek to build a multidimensional barrier against resort to nuclear weapons, to insulate them, as much as possible, from quick, early, or easy use. The specific support the bishops give to a "no first use" position should be seen as a dimension of this larger theme in the letter.

The third case is "Limited Nuclear War." Here again, the bishops enter, as we have seen, a much disputed technical question with a long history in the strategic and ethical literature. They are aware that they cannot "settle" the empirical debate of whether a limited nuclear exchange can be kept "limited." Their approach in the pastoral is to raise a series of moral and empirical questions that express their radical skepticism about controlling such an exchange. Having pressed the question of what "limited" really means, they make the following assessment: "One of the criteria of the just-war tradition is a reasonable hope of success in bringing about justice and peace. We must ask whether such a reasonable hope can exist once nuclear weapons have been exchanged. The burden of proof remains on those who assert that meaningful limitation is possible."[34]

---

32. M. Bundy, G. F. Kennan, R. S. McNamara, and G. Smith, "Nuclear Weapons and The Atlantic Alliance," *Foreign Affairs* 60 (1982), pp. 753–768; K. Kaiser, G. Leher, A. Mertes, and F. J. Schulze, "Nuclear Weapons and the Preservation of Peace," *Foreign Affairs* 60 (1982), pp. 1157–1170.

33. *Challenge of Peace*, n. 150, p. 47.

34. Ibid., n. 159, p. 50.

To summarize the pastoral letter's position on the use of nuclear weapons:

1. The letter raises and responds to *three* distinct cases of use.
2. The letter sets forth moral principles of limitation (noncombatant immunity, proportion, and reasonable hope of success) by which *any* case of use should be judged.
3. The letter does not consider *every* case of use.
4. The letter does not conclude that the use of nuclear weapons is intrinsically evil.
5. There exists, therefore, a centimeter of ambiguity regarding the general question of the use of nuclear weapons.

This purposeful ambiguity about use is less specific than Ramsey, Stein, or Walzer, but is much closer to Stein and Walzer than to Ramsey. In light of this intricate position on use the bishops address *the strategy of deterrence*. Religious-moral analysis does not dissolve the formidable empirical challenge posed by deterrence. The paradox of deterrence was captured by a phrase used by the Second Vatican Council: "the stockpiling of arms which grows from year-to-year serves, in a way hitherto unthought of, as a deterrent to potential attackers. Many people look upon this as the most effective way known at the present time for maintaining some sort of peace among nations."[35]

Embedded in this cryptic description is an acknowledgment of the new reality already outlined in this chapter. The result of deterrence, "some sort of peace," is described here in language meant to convey the unsatisfactory basis of our present security. The difficult political and moral issue is whether any other available means would even preserve a "sort of peace." Not specified in Vatican II's early and brief analysis of the problem of deterrence are the following questions that have structured the post-conciliar analysis of deterrence and have been reflected in the analysis of Ramsey, Stein, and Walzer:

1. Does effective deterrence involve a "formed intention" to do evil?
2. How should threat, intention, and possible use be related?
3. How do we weigh morally the argument that deterrence has served the function of preventing any use of nuclear weapons?
4. Would less reliance on nuclear deterrence, its moral delegitimation, have the effect of "making the world safe for conventional war"?

In addition to the extensive theological-ethical literature of the 1960's and 1970's, a central force in shaping the U.S. bishops' analysis of

---

35. *The Pastoral Constitution*, n. 81; cited in *Challenge of Peace*, n. 167, p. 52.

deterrence was the statement of John Paul II in his Message to the Second Special Session of the United Nations on Disarmament in 1982:

In current conditions "deterrence" based on balance, certainly not as an end in itself but as a step on the way toward a progressive disarmament, may still be judged morally acceptable. Nonetheless in order to ensure peace, it is indispensable not to be satisfied with this minimum which is always susceptible to the real danger of explosion.[36]

The pastoral letter cites the papal text, summarizes a commentary on it provided for the American bishops by Cardinal Casaroli, the Vatican Secretary of State,[37] and then proceeds to use the Holy Father's carefully circumscribed approval of deterrence in its assessment of U.S. strategic policy. Since deterrence was perhaps the most complex and controversial topic of the entire pastoral, the bishops went to some length to understand the nature of U.S. deterrence policy.

Discussions with the U.S. government centered on questions of both strategic doctrine and targeting policy. Since the bishops had staked out such a clear and firm position against targeting civilian centers, the Reagan Administration, in a series of letters to Cardinal Bernardin, went on record saying, "For moral, political and military reasons, the United States does not target the Soviet civilian population as such."[38] The bishops received this statement (and others like it), acknowledged that such a statement responded to their concerns about the *intent* of U.S. policy regarding civilians, but did not settle the question of the *morality* of U.S. deterrence policy as a whole.

The next issue involved what kind of "indirect" or "unintended" damage would follow from striking the urban-industrial targets that every U.S. administration has openly said we target. In two of the more important sentences of the entire pastoral the bishops say:

A narrow adherence exclusively to the principle of noncombatant immunity as a criterion for policy is an inadequate moral posture for it ignores some evil and unacceptable consequences. Hence, we cannot be satisfied that the assertion of an intention not to strike civilians directly, or even the most honest effort to implement that intention, by itself constitutes a 'moral policy' for the use of nuclear weapons.[39]

---

36. John Paul II, *Message to the Second Special Session of the United Nations General Assembly Devoted to Disarmament*, No. 3; cited in *Challenge of Peace*, n. 173, p. 54.

37. Report on Meeting to Discuss War and Peace Pastoral, *ORIGINS* 12 (April 17, 1983).

38. Letter of William Clark, National Security Adviser, to Cardinal Bernardin (January 15, 1983) cited in *Challenge of Peace*, fn. 81, n. 179, p. 56.

39. *Challenge of Peace*, n. 181, p. 57.

These considerations plus a further discussion of the moral issues raised by even a well-intended "counterforce" strategy brought the American bishops to their judgment on the strategy of deterrence:

These considerations of concrete elements of nuclear deterrence policy, made in light of John Paul II's evaluation, but applying it through our own prudential judgments, lead us to a strictly conditioned moral acceptance of nuclear deterrence. We cannot consider it adequate as a long-term basis for peace.[40]

Devoid of all modifiers, the judgment on deterrence is "acceptance," not "condemnation." But the acceptance is "strictly conditioned"; this phrase places two kinds of restraint on the strategy of deterrence. The first is "temporal" in nature; both John Paul II and the American bishops tie the justification for deterrence to an understanding that it be used as a framework for moving to a different basis of security among nations. This temporal assessment means that the "direction" of deterrence policy has moral significance—are steps being taken to move away from this fragile, paradoxical basis for interstate relations or is the direction of policy simply reinforcing the present state of affairs?

The second restraint concerns the "character" of the deterrent. The strictly conditioned justification of the deterrent rests on its role of "preventing the use of nuclear weapons or other actions which could lead directly to a nuclear exchange."[41] The point here is to limit the role of nuclear deterrence to a very specific function in world affairs; the posture of deterrence is not to be used to pursue goals other than preventing nuclear war. To give specific content to this limited conception of deterrence the bishops make a series of concrete proposals:

1. *They oppose*: extending deterrence to a variety of warfighting strategies, a quest for strategic superiority, any blurring of the distinction between nuclear and conventional weapons, and the deployment of weapons with "hard-target kill" capability.

2. *They support*: immediate, bilateral, verifiable agreements to halt the testing, production, and deployment of new nuclear systems; negotiating strategies aimed at deep cuts in superpower arsenals; conclusion of a comprehensive test ban treaty; and strengthening of command and control systems for nuclear weapons.

These last comments on strategies for arms control lead logically to a discussion of the political perspective of the pastoral letter.

Political Vision in a Divided Nuclear World

To raise the political issues is to return to the perennial questions of international relations. As complex as the technological and strategic

40. Ibid., n. 186, p. 58.   41. Ibid., n. 185, p. 58.

issues are, they cannot be examined in a vacuum. The threat of nuclear conflagration is so clear that it would seem to create an automatic identity of interest among those threatened. The persisting competition, in spite of the nuclear threat, testifies to the irreducible complexity of the problem we face.

In the eyes of some observers the political division between the superpowers is the primary fact of the political and moral dilemma of the nuclear age. The French Catholic bishops, in a statement on the nuclear age published six months after the U.S. letter, gave primacy of place to the Soviet threat[42] and some American critics of the U.S. bishops argued that they concentrated too exclusively on the strategic questions.[43] The American letter did purposely stress the unique characteristics of the nuclear age: The bishops wanted to assert that alongside the classical questions of ideological competition there is today a qualitatively new danger posed by new means of warfare. But the U.S. bishops' letter did not ignore the political context of the nuclear competition. It dedicated a special section to U.S.-Soviet relations.

The pastoral's perspective on superpower relations is described in one phrase as "cold realism." The phrase highlights the fact that the pastoral addresses the strategic dilemma of deterrence in a politically divided world. The division of the world is two dimensional: First, it remains a world composed of sovereign nation states; second, two of the states are superpowers divided, as the pastoral says, "by philosophy, ideology and competing interests."[44] These divisions, each of which could be placed in historical perspective and elaborated at some length, lie at the root of the dilemma of deterrence. In the words of the pastoral: "Deterrence reflects the radical distrust which marks international politics. . . ."[45]

The "realism" of the pastoral begins with an assessment of the division of East and West. It does not assume, however, that realism compels us to transform this division into a description of the world as good vs. evil (with the former conveniently wedded to our side), nor to conclude that no common interest exists between the superpowers. On the contrary, the political response of the pastoral is based on the conviction that the United States and the Soviet Union share at least one objective demonstrable common interest—that nuclear weapons never be used. Such a view is hardly euphoric or suffused with facile optimism. It does not presume that either superpower is saintly, only that both are governed by people who recognize that in the nuclear age war is more likely to be the destruction of politics rather than its extension.

---

42. Joint Pastoral Letter of the French Bishops, *Winning the Peace*, in J. V. Schall, ed., *Out of Justice, Peace and Winning the Peace* (San Francisco: Ignatius Press, 1984), pp. 101–120. (These are the German and French Catholic bishops' statements.)

43. M. Novak, "Moral Clarity in the Nuclear Age," *National Review* (April 1, 1983).

44. *Challenge of Peace*, n. 245, p. 76.   45. Ibid., n. 174, p. 55.

This truth, that the means of warfare in the nuclear age threaten to destroy the values that in the past made resort to force a reasonable policy, lies behind Bernard Brodie's quote at the beginning of the nuclear age. The threat of nuclear destruction creates a common interest, even though other competing interests still persist.

It is on the basis of this narrow but crucial common interest that the pastoral proposes a series of diplomatic measures and arms control initiatives. While the focus is on controlling nuclear forces, the pastoral extends its concern to various measures of conventional arms control as well. In addition to these standard diplomatic concerns, the pastoral letter proposes efforts to make nonviolent means of defense and conflict resolution more applicable to personal activity and public policy.

The overriding perspective of the pastoral letter is that precisely because in the nuclear age war threatens to destroy politics, the means of politics and diplomacy and the power of public opinion must be used creatively to eliminate the threat of nuclear war.

Response to *The Challenge of Peace:* Themes and Issues

The U.S. bishops' letter had both a pastoral and a policy purpose. Pastorally, it was designed as a teaching document to assist Catholics in the formation of conscience on questions of modern warfare. The policy purpose was to create space in the public argument about defense policy for an explicit analysis of moral issues. Responses to the pastoral letter have focused on the *role* of religious argument in the public debate and the *content* of the Catholic contribution to the debate.

The Church-State Question

Just below the surface of the intricate ethical and technical arguments about deterrence, limited nuclear war, and arms control runs the question of the role of religion in the public life of the nation and the right of the Church to enter the delicate arena of "national security" questions. James Reston described one passage in the second draft of the pastoral letter as "an astonishing challenge to the power of the state."[46] *Washington Post* columnist Steven Rosenfeld was even more detailed in his assessment of the challenge the Catholic bishops were positing for the nation:

The Catholic bishops are doing a brave yet questionable thing. They are forcing a public debate on perhaps the most perplexing nuclear question of them all, the morality of the doctrine of nuclear deterrence. . . . The bishops,

46. James Reston, "Church, State and the Bomb," *The New York Times* (October 27, 1982), Op Ed.

speaking for and to a large mainstream mass-membership institution, are pressing an anxious public and a reluctant government to treat explicitly a question that has heretofore been left in the shadow and that may have no new satisfactory answer now.[47]

The Church-state argument involves both a constitutional and a theological question. The constitutional issue is whether an "activist" Church policy on national security violates the meaning of the First Amendment. The theological issue is whether an "activist" posture corrupts the religious meaning of the Church's ministry. A response to the constitutional question requires an evaluation of the political meaning of the "separation clause" in the First Amendment. Essentially, the separation clause holds that religious institutions should expect neither favoritism nor discrimination in the exercise of their civic or religious responsibilities. Religious organizations must earn their way into the public debate by the quality of their positions, but the First Amendment is not designed to silence or exclude the religious voice. This interpretation finds support from two other themes in the constitutional tradition of the West. First, the fundamental distinction between society and state supports the right and responsibility of religious groups to participate in the public arena; separation of the Church from the state can be firmly asserted without arguing that the Church should be separate from the life of society. Second, within the wider society the constitutional tradition reserves a crucial role for voluntary associations; these groups, organized for public purposes but independent of the state, play an essential role in a democracy. In the American political system, religious organizations are classified as voluntary associations. They bring the specific quality of a disciplined tradition of moral-religious analysis to bear on both personal and public issues. It is precisely this role that the Catholic bishops envisioned in writing the pastoral letter.

The theological question in the Church-state argument often arises from within the Church. The concern expressed is whether sociopolitical involvement is in accord with the religious ministry of the Church. The answer lies with *how* the Church pursues its public engagement on issues. The Church has no special political or technical wisdom on complex public topics. It should have a capability to analyze public issues precisely in terms of how moral and religious themes (values, principles, rules of action) can illuminate and direct policy choices. The premise supporting such a role for the Church is a fundamental idea: It affirms that the moral law extends to every dimension of human life—personal and social, local and international. Within the Catholic

---

47. Steven Rosenfeld, "The Bishops and the Bomb," *The Washington Post* (October 29, 1982), Op Ed.

tradition this affirmation of the public meaning of morality extends from the patristic period to modern papal teaching. The Catholic bishops, from a theological perspective, were not acting *ultra vires* but simply extending this public moral teaching when they scrutinized the moral meaning of the nuclear age in their pastoral letter.

Politics, Strategy, and Ethics

The impact of the pastoral letter on the strategic debate is manifested in part by the range of commentary it has generated. The successive drafts of the letter produced an enormous amount of media commentary; in addition, the drafts and the final document have been analyzed in more extensive articles within the theological and strategic communities. My purpose at this point is not an extensive analysis of this literature but simply to cite examples that provide a flavor of the strategic-moral debate.

One group of commentators focused on politics and ethics, i.e., on the political context of the arms race—the U.S.-Soviet relationship—and how that should be evaluated. The criticism made of the U.S. bishops was that they focused too exclusively on nuclear weapons as an ethical problem and failed to grasp the ideological divide in the world that generates the arms race. Critics of the U.S. letter found the French Catholic bishops' statement, *Winning the Peace*, more persuasive. The French built their analysis around the theme, "Between War and Blackmail,"[48] which highlighted the *political use* the Soviets can make of the nuclear threat. In the United States Michael Novak continually stressed this line of argument: "Among these and other possibilities, how should we judge the purposes and character of the leadership of the Soviet Union? That is the factual question on which subsequent ethical judgment turns."[49]

The U.S. letter did not reduce the moral dilemma of the nuclear age to the question of nuclear weapons alone. The concerns expressed in the French letter and the problem of the nature of the U.S.-Soviet relations are identified as essential components of the dilemma we face. The U.S. bishops did wish to stress, however, that the distinctively new aspect of our time is not the classical problem of states and ideologies in conflict and competition, but the contemporary problem that the age-old competition (from Sparta and Athens to Moscow and Washington) is today conducted with threats that could destroy the political and human values each side seeks to defend with its arsenal. The American letter does not say "means" are the only problem; it does say the prob-

48. *Winning the Peace*, cited, pp. 101–104.
49. Novak, *Moral Clarity in the Nuclear Age*, cited, p. 370.

lem of means is qualitatively different in the nuclear age. The argument of the U.S. bishops is that the distinctiveness of the means question should be clearly acknowledged, that the control of the arms race should be given priority in superpower relations, and that other dimensions of the political relations do not have to be settled before steps are taken to contain the nuclear danger.

Precisely because of the stress on an ethic of means in the pastoral letter, the major responses to it have focused not on politics and ethics, but on strategy and ethics. In a detailed assessment of this question Professor Albert Wohlstetter takes the bishops to task for squandering a significant opportunity.[50] In his view the moral principles of the Catholic tradition, especially noncombatant immunity, provided the conceptual basis for guiding U.S. strategic policy toward objectives that are both strategically effective and morally sound. But the bishops missed this opportunity, argues Wohlstetter, because they listened to the wrong technical advice. The advice they heeded is too skeptical of our ability to control the use of nuclear weapons; such advice makes the bishops reticent to endorse a strategy that can convincingly threaten the Soviet political and military structure. These are the "values" the Soviets seek to protect; a forthright challenge to them would be an effective deterrent, and a force structure designed with highly accurate, miniaturized warheads would be morally defensible.

Although the pastoral letter agrees that some form of counterforce targeting policy is the only one Catholic moral principles could accept, the bishops exhibit little of Wohlstetter's confidence about controlling the use of nuclear weapons. The pastoral is much closer to former Secretary of Defense Harold Brown's assessment of our ability to control nuclear weapons:

None of this potential flexibility changes my view that a full-scale thermonuclear exchange would be an unprecedented disaster for the Soviet Union as well as for the United States. Nor is it all clear that an initial use of nuclear weapons—however selectively they might be targeted—could be kept from escalating to a full-scale thermonuclear exchange, especially if command-and-control centers were brought under attack. The odds are high, whether weapons were used against tactical or strategic targets, that control would be lost on both sides and the exchange would become unconstrained.[51]

A quite different critique of the pastoral came from Leon Wieseltier in one of the most literate essays in recent strategic literature, *Nuclear War, Nuclear Peace*. Wieseltier shares the pastoral letter's skepticism

---

50. A. Wohlstetter, "Bishops, Statesmen and Other Strategists on the Bombing of Innocents," *Commentary* (June 1983), pp. 15–35.

51. H. Brown, *Department of Defense Annual Report FY 1979* (Washington, D.C.: Government Printing Office, 1978), cited in *Challenge of Peace*, n. 144, fn. 61, p. 45.

about control of nuclear war, and he also agrees with most of the policy specifics of the letter. His dissent lies with the letter's critique of the concept of deterrence. In Wieseltier's view, the bishops have done much "to bring deterrence into disrepute."[52] This is the fundamental flaw in the letter because "The disparagement of deterrence in the present intellectual and political climate is more than a little irresponsible."[53]

Wieseltier correctly grasps a basic theme of the pastoral letter. The bishops did not intend to make the Church or the state comfortable with the idea of deterrence, politically or morally. Their purpose, however, was not "the disparagement of deterrence," but an analysis of how fragile an instrument we rely on to keep the peace in the nuclear age. The letter does seek to raise doubts about the long-term viability of deterrence; it does try to catalyze both intellectual and political forces that can move the strategic balance beyond deterrence. To highlight the fragility and risk of deterrence policy is not, however, simply to disparage it or to advocate dismembering it immediately. The purpose of the letter is to press the public debate beyond tactical issues to a fundamental assessment of security in the nuclear age. Failure to examine the risks of deterrence can be as "irresponsible" as undermining it without providing an alternative.

Indeed in the long run, the contribution of the Catholic bishops to the strategic debate may lie precisely in the capacity of a religious-moral critique to push the daily debate beyond tactical choices and specific decisions to the level of fundamental ideas. Commentators as different in their policy views as Jonathan Schell,[54] Senator Daniel Moynihan,[55] and the editors of the *New Republic*[56] have argued that the pastoral letter moves the nuclear debate back to "first principles." Given the danger the nuclear age holds for all of us, this surely is where the public debate should be conducted.

52. L. Wieseltier, *Nuclear War, Nuclear Peace* (New York: Holt, Rinehart Winston, 1983), p. 74.
53. Ibid., p. 74.
54. J. Schell, "The Abolition," *The New Yorker* (January 2, 1984), p. 66.
55. D. P. Moynihan, *Loyalties* (New York: Harcourt, Brace, Jovanovich, 1984), pp. 27–30.
56. "Antinuclear Spring," *The New Republic* (May 30, 1983), p. 8.

EDWARD N. LUTTWAK

10. Catholics and the Bomb: The Perspective of a Non-Catholic Strategist

Our subject is a very distressing episode, the statement of the U.S. Catholic bishops on the matter of nuclear arms. I would like to begin with some comments on the nature of strategy. Strategy is made of paradoxes: The logical action fails, often merely because it is logical, and thus anticipated and so countered. It is the contest of opposed wills interacting perversely. Strategy possesses inherent tension, for there are always at least two sides involved and often more.

What makes strategy unique is not, however, the contention alone. Any number of the circumstances of daily life involve the struggle of opposing wills. For example, most religions at some point, usually at a central point, presuppose a tension between man's animal nature and that side of man as fashioned by God, which is designed to allow him to rise above his instincts, to control his sensual impulses, or otherwise to achieve the spiritual rewards offered by divinity. There is certainly tension in the religious understanding of man's nature.

The tension of strategy is different. As in the contest between base and noble instincts in man, it is a contest of opposed wills. But it also has the quality of maneuver. For the religious, God is not a malevolent force scheming to cheat him of the rewards that God himself has promised in return for adherence to a certain moral code. The religious person understands God as having made man with the capacity to behave both in a base, sensual sort of way and in a noble, altruistic manner. He also understands God as engaging in a certain degree of temptation to test the noble side of man. But the religious person would not understand God as actively trying to subvert man's will to be good.

In strategy, on the other hand, subversion is the permanent state of things. A simple example demonstrates the point: A general is planning a campaign. He must move his army from point A to point B. There are a number of different routes available. One route crosses a waterless desert; another leads through high mountain peaks; a third traverses a swamp. There is also a fourth route, a very well made road through easy terrain. This last is the best route. But if this best route is used, it becomes the worst route, because the enemy expects it to be taken. In strategy, the best course is almost always the worst course.

Strategic thinking therefore demands the ability to think paradoxically. Linear thinkers, the sort of person who would try to go from point A to point B by the most comfortable route, should avoid strategy. Similarly, weapons designers, who design for optimality, who want a missile to lock onto the absolute peak point of heat emission, defeat themselves—because that will facilitate countermeasures. Weapons designers, untaught by strategy, had to learn from trial and error that the best heat-seeking missile is not the one that goes for the focus of maximal heat, but the one that goes for the lesser surrounding heat, because that is off target, and much more difficult to counter.

It is a failure to engage in strategic thought that I see as the fundamental flaw in the bishops' action. When one enters the field of strategy with linear thoughts, such as, "I don't want war; I want peace; I will achieve peace by not fighting," one inevitably fails in one's goals. This is equivalent to the general who takes the best road only to discover that it is the worst road.

The bishops engage in an error of linear thought in issuing their call for "negotiations to halt the testing, production, and deployment of new nuclear weapons systems,"[1] and for "effective arms control leading to mutual disarmament, ratification of pending treaties [and] development of nonviolent alternatives. . . ."[2] This portion of my paper will focus on the fallacy in the bishops' case for arms control. An example from recent history illustrates the flaw in such thinking.

Approximately a decade ago, a new technique for the delivery of nuclear weapons was offered. This was the cruise missile. The cruise missile flies like an airplane, not ballistically; it is not thrown in a parabolic trajectory as are ICBM's. When the cruise missile appeared on the scene almost all the arms controllers pronounced against it. Now, it is important to remember how arms controllers operate. They are not disarmers; their goal is to maintain arsenals in a context where the chances for mechanical conflict will be minimized; where, furthermore, should there be a conflict, a lesser amount of destruction will ensue. Arms controllers do not oppose all weapons. They oppose mainly weapons thought to be "destabilizing," that is, weapons whose deployment would lead to "hair-trigger" situations.

Why did arms controllers oppose the cruise missile? At the time the cruise missile was first deployed, the United States and the Soviet Union

1. *The Challenge of Peace: God's Promise and Our Response* (Washington, D.C.: United States Catholic Conference), n. 204.
2. Ibid., n. 202.

were in the midst of negotiations intended to limit strategic arms. These negotiations were predicated on ballistic missiles. The emergence of the cruise missile upset the process.

The arms-control interest being a powerful one, it succeeded in delaying greatly the deployment of cruise missiles. Arms controllers resisted this development for several reasons. First, cruise missiles were not of classic form, they do not have the stable and recognizable shape of a ballistic missile in the ground. Therefore, satellite photography, which is the primary means of verification, upon which all arms control is predicated, could not see the cruise missile unambiguously and clearly, in the way in which a ballistic missile could be seen. With a minimum of countering effort by the other side, cruise missiles cannot be detected at all. Since cruise missile limits cannot be verified, it is impossible to write an arms control agreement around them. Hence, the only recourse was to ban them, to have none at all (which allows verification by observing testing).

The second negative aspect arms controllers saw in the cruise missile was the fact that each unit is inexpensive. A nation could manufacture large numbers of cruise missiles without great cost. Therefore, the natural control on weapons systems ultimately imposed by the size of a nation's gross national product did not function in the case of the cruise missile.

It is important here to rehearse the purposes of arms control. The primary purpose is to avoid destabilizing relationships of weapons. What is meant by a destabilizing weapon depends on the state of technology. At about the time the cruise missile was being developed, ballistic missiles were becoming destabilizing. This was because their precision had increased to the point where it became practical to target another nation's ballistic missiles. Therefore, a situation prevailed where stability was no longer automatic, as it had been originally, but was instead becoming impossible. Moreover, ballistic missiles were being MIRVed, thus multiplying the number of warheads available. While each side might have only 1,000 land-based ICBM's, an aggressor nation could act with 5,000 to 10,000 warheads, depending on the number of warheads on each MIRVed missile. Therefore, a built-in incentive arose to act as the aggressor.

It is in this context that the cruise missile emerged. The chief characteristic of the cruise missile is that an opposing side cannot target it; one cannot write an attack program into the navigation systems of a ballistic missile force to destroy a diversified cruise missile force. Therefore, in substantive terms, the cruise missile was a heaven-sent opportunity to restabilize the arms relationship. A diversified cruise missile force cannot destroy another like force. Therefore, had the arms controllers been pursuing the *substance* of their purposes, namely, the avoidance of war triggered by mechanical imbalance, they would have embraced the cruise missile. But the arms controllers were locked into a procedural track, whereby they ignored arms control in substantive terms, and instead busied themselves with its procedural aspects. Looking at existing legal categories for arms limitation, they discovered none were applicable to the limitation of cruise missiles, and so they rejected the missile entirely.

Arms controllers in acting this way were not thinking strategically. In fact, their error occurred at a much lower level of thought. They simply confused form and substance. But let us now take a broader view of arms control, operating without the crude error committed by the arms controllers in the case of the cruise missile. We shall hypothesize an ideal world and see exactly what the final outcome will be if all the steps the arms controllers consider positive come to pass.

Let us imagine a hypothetical two-power world in which the means of verification are what they are now, primarily satellite photography, but in which the two participants in the arms control process are much more comparable. Let us also imagine a Congress where there are no players with political motives to oppose the arms control agreement at hand, and no grandstanding demagogues apt to discover one problem or another. Let us also assume that the normal tendency of the armed services' bureaucracies to prefer the conventional forces over the nuclear is even more pronounced than it is today. Let us finally assume that the Soviet leadership is altogether comparable, that the Soviets do not have the bureaucratic problems they have and that Soviet leaders have no hidden agendas. Everything is fine.

What happens? Instead of having protracted SALT negotiations over extended periods of time, very intense negotiations take place. Every few months another treaty is signed. Limits are placed on every weapon that it is possible to verify. SALT I is signed in the spring, SALT II in the summer, and SALT III by autumn. But the outcome of all these "arms control breakthroughs" is paradoxical: Funds for research and development are now diverted from weapons that are subject to verification and limitation to weapons that cannot be verified at all. One moves from the large, fixed ballistic missile, the slowly built submarine that can be photographed in construction, and the massive bomber that can be photographed from early prototype stage onward to weapons much more difficult to verify. The result of all these agreements will be forces made of supersonic cruise missiles, stealthy aircraft of one type or another, particle and laser beam weapons, and so forth. We are now in a much more dangerous world full of invisible weapons and massive uncertainty. The limits of arms control are illustrated by this ideal case:

Arms control is fully successful, but it produces the normal paradoxical result that results in strategy wherever one moves in a straight line.

The impulse in this nation (as the bishops amply demonstrate) has always been to press forward with arms control negotiations. These negotiations have not resulted in the panoply of agreements of my hypothetical case, but they have resulted in some agreements. Moreover, there has been the imminent prospect of further agreements. The logical extension of these agreements and expectations was that resources were diverted from weapons of classic form, that at least could be seen and counted and that offered a theoretical potential for stability, to weapons not of classic form, that have wholly new appearances and dimensions and that cannot be recognized or verified. We therefore find ourselves in a situation in which the patterns of armaments are far more likely to be destabilizing than before the advent of arms control.

Weapons that cannot be verified are destabilizing in more than one way. To be sure, such weapons are destabilizing because they cannot be counted or verified for purposes of a treaty. But they are destabilizing in a much more fundamental way, because one side cannot count the other side's unverifiable weapons when it comes to war planning. Thus, much more generous allowances must be made for the other side's threat capability. Both sides must behave much more prudentially. And prudential war planning by each side leads to a very nonprudential outcome. In other words, arms control, given this dynamic impulse, ends by completely subverting its purpose, for the same basic reason that the general who takes the best route is actually taking the worst route. Arms control is internally subversive of its own purposes, whether with respect to a single weapon, such as the cruise missile, or with respect to the entire process. Arms control does not fail because the baser, warlike instinct prevails over the better instincts; it fails because it is programmed to fail.

The world has not seen a great deal of arms control. But it has seen enough of it to have left us with the present state of "strategic parity." Before the United States entered the house of arms control in the middle 1960's, American strategic nuclear armaments were greatly superior to the Soviet's. That condition reflected the American comparative advantage in developing such weapons. The Soviet comparative advantage, on the other hand, is in conscripting people, teaching them relatively simple but sound techniques of warfare, and mass producing medium-technology weapons, typically tanks and other armored vehicles. The closer the Soviets remain to medium-level technology, the better off they are. As the Soviets approach higher technology weapons, their skill level is not nearly so great.

The United States lacks the basic attributes to compete with the Soviet Union in the arena of Soviet comparative advantage. Periodically, the United States has instituted drafts, but these were rather partial social mechanisms, opposed by many. In addition, this country lacks a tradition of continental land warfare. The American army has no expertise to speak of in continental, armored warfare. The American army experienced armored warfare only briefly between the summer of 1944 and the spring of 1945, in contrast to the Soviet army, which fought a sustained land war for several years, first losing, then finally prevailing against the German army. This experience taught the Soviets valuable lessons; they learned how to put together an operational plan for war, how to accumulate military forces, and how to train troops. These experiences gave the Soviets a comparative advantage in land warfare that they have not yielded.

The American comparative advantage has been in innovation and high technology, in techniques of electronic control, precision navigation, and long-range delivery. These advantages correspond to the requirements of nuclear delivery. Until the mid-1960's, there was, therefore, a natural equilibrium between American and Soviet comparative advantages, and Europe and the world experienced peace and security.

If one travels through Europe today, one finds many people who believe that war is now once again possible. Such political movements as the Greens in Germany might be viewed as a product of newly vivid fears of war. But in the 1960's, Europeans would have laughed if it had been suggested to them that war was an imminent possibility, even though the 1960's were not peaceful elsewhere in the world. A major war was being fought in Indochina, and briefer but sharp conflicts in the Middle East. Europeans maintained this attitude because even the most casual observer understood that there was a stable, asymmetrical balance between Soviet superiority on land and American superiority in nuclear weapons. This balance was stable precisely because neither side was acting against the grain of its comparative advantage. Each side's behavior was compatible with its culture, propensities, and natural drives.

At present we have lost this stability. The present bequeathed to us by arms controllers is "strategic parity." Strategic parity is essentially the product of the renunciation of America's comparative advantage. This renunciation was inevitable as soon as arms control became policy. In the mechanism of negotiations between sovereign states, explicit, formal inequalities are unacceptable. When inequalities are necessary they are extremely difficult to impose. Even the largest state has enormous difficulty in imposing inequality on the smallest power, if such inequality must be formalized in the body of a treaty.

One must understand strategic parity in this context. Strategic parity offers equality only where the United States possesses a comparative advantage, while promising no equality in land forces. No "conventional arms limitations talks" or "armored division limitation talks" were ever held. The Soviets were therefore left free to retain their comparative advantage.

Strategic parity has had effects beside the surrendering of the American comparative advantage. Once parity became American doctrine, it was no longer possible, bureaucratically, within the Pentagon to write program memoranda advocating the construction of weapons systems for the purpose of maintaining superiority. Had the bureaucracy made such requests, Congress would have disapproved them. Hence, the decline of American military power in the 1970's did not result from the Soviet ability to outmaneuver the United States in the process of negotiations. It was the logical result of the negotiations themselves.

As I have indicated, the United States has had a comparative advantage in innovation. That comparative advantage was not completely suppressed. New inventions emerged from time to time. The cruise missile is a case in point. No general ever placed an order for a cruise missile. The technology for the cruise missile had its origin with an army idea to equip infantrymen with jetpacks to allow them to "hop around" on a battlefield. A research contract was signed, some breakthroughs occurred, and the end product, after much interservice infighting, was the cruise missile. So, it is clear that innovation is not entirely suppressed once one embarks on the path of arms control, but the logical basis for demanding such innovation is undercut.

The United States thus entered the 1980's, having adopted arms control and the parity doctrine, and so lacking its formerly large, natural superiority in nuclear arms. At the same time, the Soviet Union has retained its superiority in the means of land warfare. The result is destabilization and fear in the streets of West Germany that a nuclear war might be imminent.

Destabilization is thus the outcome of our good intentions in the realm of arms control. The maxim states that good intentions randomize behavior. But not so in the field of strategy. In strategy, the outcome of good intentions is almost always perverse. Arms control has left us with such a classic paradoxical outcome. Having entered the process of arms control to reduce the danger of war, which was not then large at all, we now find ourselves in a far more dangerous situation. The only means by which to extricate ourselves from this dangerous situation is to take some very risky steps. What must be done is to reestablish a series of broad American superiorities in the field of nuclear weapons so that an equilibrium can once again exist between a greatly superior American nuclear force and a correspondingly greatly superior Soviet conventional force.

The advocacy of more asymmetrical arms control is not the only fallacy in the bishops' reasoning. But before commencing an analysis of these other fallacies I must make some preliminary statements on theology. My knowledge of Christian theology is limited largely to some texts of the Church Fathers, such as Basil, Eusebius, and Augustine, that I read in preparation for a book on Byzantine military strategy. (I read these texts primarily to search for incidental statements on the condition of the empire.)

The authors of the early Church lived in very different conditions in widely scattered locations and wrote over a span of several centuries. One of the great dividing lines in the thought of these writers is the fourth century, the time of the consolidation of the Christian Empire under Constantine and his successors.

The attitude adopted by the post-Constantinian authors toward war and violence appears to be very different from that which preceded it. It would take a suspiciously sophisticated reader to find in the original Christian revelation, the sayings and *exempla* of Jesus Christ, any approval for the use of force. Church Fathers, such as Augustine, working under the enormous pressures of a collapsing political order and responding to still-vocal pagan critics who blamed Christianity for the catastrophes that had befallen the empire, offered a compromise. Augustine, for example, while stating his preference for the removed, spiritual existence, also allowed those who did not wish to adopt a withdrawn life, and so married, had children, and engaged in secular affairs, to serve in the Roman army insofar as there were barbarians that needed to be contained.

Augustine's position evolved into that of the courtier-theologians. Even so, the Augustinian position carefully circumscribed the areas in which killing was permitted. Augustine allowed killing for defensive purposes, not to dominate others. (See, for example, *City of God*, 3, 14, where Augustine criticizes aggressive war waged to obtain glory.) Augustine's position would not entitle one to attack third countries for the sake of advancing whatever the latest captain of horse deemed the imperial interest.

The courtier-theologians, however, had their freedom constrained by their relationship to the royal courts. They were no longer close to the Christian revelation in the way the pre-Constantinian writers had been. Responsibilities of state intruded. Just-war theories and other rationalizations were produced.

Theologians in the United States no longer need feel the constraints of political pressure. They are free to regain a certain closeness with the original revelation. Being closer to the text, the simple position to take, the position not subject to counterinterpretation, is that no Christian can kill, especially to advance something like national security, which is really only a collection of perceived interests in other nations' affairs. I wonder, therefore, why the pastoral letter had to be so complicated. The bishops could have said that in this emancipated, pluralistic society they no longer need to fear the wrath of kings or emperors and are free to speak the truth: Christian revelation forbids the taking of life.

The outcome of unilateral disarmament would not be as drastic as many people think. At the most, the United States would be placed under Russian governance. Catholics should not be frightened by such a prospect. The goal of Catholic faith is to provide those who adhere to it a means of achieving heaven. Given this goal, it would seem the ideal state for Catholics is Poland. Poland, after all, is the country in the world with the highest percentage of the population in compliance with the rules for admission into heaven. If a deal were offered to the Soviet Union to allow the United States a Polish-style government in return for disarmament, I am sure that the Soviet leaders would be very liberal in their terms.

The bishops, however, chose not to adopt this position. They decided instead to intrude into the domain of strategy, first of all, by advocating arms control rather than astrategical disarmament.

The bishops also manifest a puzzling ambivalence toward deterrence. They condemn any actual use of the nuclear arsenal.[3] They assert that planning for counterstrikes or other means of prevailing in a nuclear war is unacceptable; that nuclear "sufficiency," not superiority, should be American policy; and the maintenance of deterrence must be coupled with "progressive disarmament."[4] In essence, this means the United States may have a deterrent but may not intend its use should deterrence fail. This is where the bishops have stepped on the razor-sharp edge of the paradoxes of which strategy is made.

Deterrence cannot work the way bishops would like. Deterrence works only so long as the enemy believes not only that the threat is real but also that the potential adversary is eager to carry out the threat and so able to overcome all the obstacles that would otherwise prevent the use of the deterrent. It must be kept in mind that the obstacles to any use of nuclear weapons would be enormous. Communications systems will fail; military personnel may resist or simply prove unable to carry out their tasks; missiles will break down. These are all the frictions of war. Everything in war is simple when viewed on the analyst's desk,

3. Ibid., n. 150.   4. Ibid., n. 188, pp. 1–3.

but is greatly complicated in reality, because it depends on a huge number of tasks being performed properly in a precise sequence. The popular perception of nuclear warfare would have one believe that the president could casually drop a book on "the button" and thereby launch all the missiles. The reality is very different. It is extremely difficult to launch a nuclear strike. Everything will conspire against it. Therefore, to have a credible deterrent, a nation must demonstrate an intense commitment to follow through with the retaliation.

The bishops reject this position. Their approach to deterrence would displace the United States from its deterrent posture. Not only would the Soviets no longer be dissuaded from aggressive conduct at places and times of their choosing, other consequences would follow as well. Congress will reject new weapons systems, since such development would be unnecessary in the light of an acknowledgment that the United States would never follow through. The next time an administration would ask for funds to construct yet another communications device to withstand some further nuclear effect, Congress, if influenced by the letter, would have to say no. The American comparative advantage in innovation would be further suppressed. One wonders, if all the bishops were concerned with was the appearance of deterrence, why they did not advocate a *papier maché* MX missile.

Another conclusion the bishops come to is a demand for the creation of an international authority that can impose limits on armaments. The international authority the bishops propose would be one in which national sovereignty would *not* be surrendered. They suggest the United Nations as a model for this authority.[5] No strategist can oppose the principle of a unitary world government. The moment a unitary government is adopted, the unopposed will disappears. The bishops however, do not go this far. They favor only the half-measures of international organizations, which again would produce results paradoxical to the bishops' desires; as the U.N. itself shows, the provision of a venue for altercations duly evokes them.

Consistent with Christian revelation, the bishops might have made the following statement: "No Catholic should participate in murder, which is the business of the armed forces. But given the reality of armed conflict, we advocate the strengthening of conventional forces in order to reduce the likelihood of nuclear murder, which is the worst form of murder, because of its vast size." The bishops grudgingly give some lip service to the relationship of nuclear deterrence to conventional forces, but in the bishops' own words this is done "reluctantly."[6] The bishops could have urged Catholics aggressively to enlist in the armed forces,

5. Ibid., nn. 241–244, 264–269.   6. Ibid., n. 215.

or called for greatly increased conventional defense spending, or advocated the various other steps that could prevent the danger they seek to avert, that of nuclear war.

By not calling for such actions, the bishops fail to respond to the salient fact of our strategic predicament: The principal mechanism for nuclear war is precisely American conventional weakness. Popular perceptions notwithstanding, nuclear war will come about because somewhere or another there is an interest that we are trying to protect with conventional means failing in a debacle then redeemed by nuclear war. A hypothetical case illustrates how the mechanism might work. The Soviet Union places four divisions in Iran. If they traverse Iran, 1,000 kilometers or so, they reach the Persian Gulf and directly threaten some very important interests. American planners have prepared for this contingency with the Rapid Deployment Force and other means. So, the United States responds by placing four divisions in southern Iran. The Soviets see the United States is serious and move in 25 divisions. At this point, we could no longer respond by conventional means. We are left with two alternatives: to withdraw, allowing the Soviets to travel to the Persian Gulf, erect their tents and summon the local potentates to sign on the dotted line; or, to inform the Soviets that any further advance across Iran will be met with a nuclear response. In all theaters of possible conflict this same mechanism would lead to nuclear war; the essential element in the equation is the inadequacy of our conventional forces.

Paradoxically, if the Soviets were to do us the favor of invading Iran with 40 divisions (which they could do) we would be spared the danger. Even members of Congress know that we do not have 40 divisions worldwide; there would be no attempt to respond and thus no danger of escalation. If the Soviets invade a nation in which there is an American defensive presence, where, say, an American division is surrounded and about to be destroyed, or if the United States succeeds in meeting a Soviet attack, as in the Iranian hypothetical case, and the Soviet response is overwhelming, then the mechanism to trigger nuclear war is primed.

The bishops pay lip service to this reality but evade its implications. If they actually wished to reduce the menace of nuclear war they would have favored the creation of a conventional force symmetrical to the Soviet Union's, thereby removing the mechanisms that, all are agreed, are most likely to trigger nuclear war.

When I read the pastoral letter I see, before me, one of those "faddish" documents that are produced by people who succumb to surrounding social pressures and accept opinions not their own. Because of the bishops, others will fall into error. This will weaken the state. The state having been weakened, a war is made more likely. And, in the course of the war, if not fatal, literature will be produced by those who once took the faddish position but who now wish to recant. A whole record of such literature exists in Britain, churned out by those who, in 1940, 1941, or 1942, were red faced over what they had written in 1936, 1937, or 1938. In this instance, however, I fear that the error of the bishops may not be exposed, at least not in any useful manner. For if we find ourselves again in a 1940 situation, it will not be possible for those who had fallen into error to atone for their mistake.

GEORGE WEIGEL

11. The Bishops' Pastoral Letter and American Political Culture: Who Was Influencing Whom?

Seven months after the adoption of the pastoral letter *The Challenge of Peace: God's Promise and Our Response* by the National Conference of Catholic Bishops, Joseph Cardinal Bernardin, archbishop of Chicago and chairman of the N.C.C.B. Ad Hoc Committee on War and Peace, which had drafted the pastoral, gave the Gannon Lecture at Fordham University. The lecture, entitled "A Consistent Ethic of Life,"[1] caused considerable comment because of its seeming attempt to "link" the issues of abortion, capital punishment, and nuclear weapons (a linkage that did not find a consistently favorable response from the right-to-life movement, nor among moral theologians). But the Gannon Lecture was also interesting and important in that it reflected the Cardinal's assessment of the intention of the pastoral letter *The Challenge of Peace*, as well as his judgment of the impact of the pastoral letter to date.

Cardinal Bernardin's generic statement of the pastoral's purpose was that the bishops wrote their letter ". . . in order to share the moral wisdom of the Catholic tradition with society."[2] But, within the next two paragraphs of his lecture, the Cardinal made it clear that it was a very particular part of "society" that was the object of the bishops' attentions: "We wanted to provide a moral assessment of existing policy which would both set limits to political action and provide direction for a policy designed to lead us out of the dilemma of deterrence."[3] In other words, the bishops' primary intention was to make a difference within the actual public-policy process, rather than at the more general level of "society" and its moral values.

The bishops were able to speak as forcefully as they did in *The Challenge of Peace*, Cardinal Bernardin went on to suggest, because there was, as the pastoral itself argued, a "new moment" in the strategic de-

---

1. Joseph Cardinal Bernardin, "A Consistent Ethic of Life: An American Catholic Dialogue," The Gannon Lecture, Fordham University, December 6, 1983; reprinted in *Thought* 59 (1984), 99–107.

2. Ibid., p. 100.   3. Ibid., p. 101.

bate. How do we know? "The public sense of the fragility of our security system is today a palpable reality."[4] And how do we know that? "The interest in the TV showing of *The Day After* is an example of how the public is taken by the danger of our present condition."[5] But the "new moment" is not merely a result of public nervousness, the Cardinal argued; it has to do with debates in the strategic arena as well. "Ideas are under scrutiny and established policies are open to criticism in a way we have not seen since the late 1950s. From the proposal of 'no first use,' through the debate about the MX, to the concept of a 'nuclear freeze,' the nuclear policy question is open to reassessment and redirection."[6]

Cardinal Bernardin then concluded with an analysis of the relationship between the bishops' pastoral and the "new moment" in the peace-and-security debate: "The fundamental contribution of *The Challenge of Peace*, I believe, is that we have been part of a few central forces which have created the 'new moment.' We have helped to shape the debate; now we face the question of whether we can help to frame a new consensus concerning nuclear policy."[7] Again, it is quite clear from the Cardinal's remarks that the bishops' intention goes far beyond setting the moral framework for the strategic debate, but includes an active role at the policy-formulation and implementation levels as well.

Cardinal Bernardin's Gannon Lecture epitomizes in a few brief paragraphs what one might reasonably call the "Catholic Establishment" view of *The Challenge of Peace*. According to this view, a brave group of bishops, often beset by conservative lay opposition and stoutly resisting government pressure, applied the age-old wisdom of the Roman Catholic tradition to the moral, strategic, and technical complexities of the nuclear weapons issue and pointed the way beyond our present peace-and-security dilemma to a strategy that is more congruent with Catholic social ethics than current U.S. policy. The pastoral, on this view, was an exercise of the bishops' "prophetic" office and set an admirable model for the Vatican II-mandated dialogue between the Church and the modern world.[8]

Within this "Establishment" view, as it was within Cardinal Bernardin's Gannon Lecture, the central claim is this: The pastoral decisively shaped the current nuclear strategy discussions, at least in terms of de-

4. Ibid.   6. Ibid.
5. Ibid.   7. Ibid.
8. Cf. Jim Castelli, *The Bishops and the Bomb: Waging Peace in a Nuclear Age* (New York: Doubleday, 1984), for a chronology of the process leading up to the adoption of "The Challenge of Peace," written from well within the "Catholic Establishment" viewpoint. Philip Murnion's introductory chapter to *The Challenge of Peace: A Commentary on the U.S. Catholic Bishops' Pastoral Letter on War and Peace* (New York: Crossroad, 1983) is another statement from this perspective.

fining the key questions that must be answered by policymakers interested in forging enough public consensus to sustain a coherent strategic policy over time.

I do not wish to dispute that particular claim in this paper; in fact, I really doubt that the claim is susceptible to meaningful assessment today. Only much more time will tell whether the bishops have made the kind of fundamental impact on the public-policy process that the claim implies.

But what I do want to suggest in this paper is that the *trajectory of influences* that precipitated the bishops' pastoral letter, and that shaped the content of *The Challenge of Peace*, was in no way as unilinear as Cardinal Bernardin's lecture at Fordham suggested. My hypothesis, in fact, is rather the opposite: In answering the question of "The bishops' pastoral and American political culture: Who was influencing whom?" there was considerably more influence *from* the political culture *on* the letter than is allowed for in the "Establishment" view of the pastoral. Moreover, I want to argue, as a second hypothesis, that a number of these influences from the political culture are in tension with, if not actually contradictory of, the social-ethical tradition that the bishops rightly sought to bring to bear on the central issue of our time.

(The times being what they are, a brief excursus on what I am *not* arguing is required here. I am not arguing that "the bishops have no business in the strategic debate." At the level of enunciating the relevant moral norms that should guide that debate, the bishops not only have a right, but a responsibility, to speak their minds clearly and forcefully. At the policy level, the bishops are also within their rights to suggest what, in their prudential judgments, the appropriate applications of these moral norms require of U.S. foreign and military policy. The bishops have as much right to enter this prudential level of the discussion as any citizen of our democracy; but they have no *more* right to a presumption of wisdom on these prudential matters than any layman whose conscience has been properly formed by the moral norms established by the magisterium of the Church and the consensus of theological opinion. I am also not arguing that there is anything wrong, in principle, with the bishops arguing that the strategic debate, often thought to be merely technical and political, has a third, moral leg; on the contrary, I think the bishops' insistence that all decisions in this complex policy arena inevitably involve moral choices, and that clarity about the nature of those choices is as important as clarity about the circular error probable of a Trident C-4 missile's warhead, is both welcome and overdue. As I shall point out, the bishops' entry into the strategic debate as the third leg on the triad of strategic decision-making sets up a dialectical process of mutual influence between the Church and the political culture, and here, too, I see nothing methodologically inappropriate, in principle. The issue, as I shall argue, is how the dialectic is weighted.)[9]

There are four areas of concern to me in *The Challenge of Peace* where, in my judgment, the trajectory of influence is far more conspicuously *from* the political culture *to* the bishops, rather than a matter of the bishops actively shaping the public debate.

The first area of concern has to do with the entry point the bishops chose for articulating their emergence into the public-policy arena on this issue. In the sixth sentence of *The Challenge of Peace*, we read that the bishops share the "terror" they perceive in the minds and hearts of their people as we face the threat of nuclear holocaust.[10] The choice of vocabulary here is important (as is the fact that the vocabulary was rather consistent on this point throughout the three drafts of the pastoral); the bishops do not speak of "concern," or "fear," or even "anxiety." They speak of "terror."

Why is this alleged "terror" among the Catholic population (and, presumably, everyone else) the entry point for the bishops' discussion? Why start *here*? Is this a reflection of a renascent, New Testament-based apocalypticism within the National Conference of Catholic Bishops? Is it an attempt to bring the eschatological teachings of the Judeo-Christian tradition to bear on contemporary issues (no easy task, given the complexities of that tradition)?

Or, much more likely, is the bishops' use of the term "terror" and their use of this allegedly widespread experience among their people (for which no evidence is produced) as the entry point for their moral analysis a reflection of those survivalist currents in American political culture that had played such a notable role in shaping the new nuclear nervousness of the 1980's? Absolute clarity is impossible on these

9. My own views on the pastoral, in draft and in final form, can be found in "The Catholic 'Peace' Bishops," *Freedom at Issue* (July/August, 1982); "The Bishops' Role," *Catholicism in Crisis* (November 1982); "An Open Letter to Archbishop Bernardin," *Catholicism in Crisis* (February 1983); "The Bishops' Pastoral: Beginning, Not End," *Catholicism in Crisis* (June 1983); "The Challenge of Peace: Reflections on the Open Church," *Catholic Northwest Progress* (June 9, 1983); "Read the Whole Letter, Please" *Catholic Northwest Progress* (June 2, 1983); "Peace Pastoral: Points to Ponder," *Catholic Northwest Progress* (June 9, 1983); "Beyond 'The Challenge of Peace': *Quaestiones Disputatae*," *Center Journal* 3 (1983), 101–121. My small book, *The Peace Bishops and the Arms Race* (Chicago: World Without War Publications, 1982) gives the flavor of the argument in American Catholicism as the Ad Hoc Committee on War and Peace began its work. My earlier essay, "The Catholics and the Arms Race: A Primer for the Perplexed" *Chicago Studies*, 18 (1979), 169–195, is an interesting artifact in that a rereading of it today suggests, to me at least, how much the bishops were reflecting currents of thought in the existing argument, rather than shaping a more adequate, new discussion.

10. *The Challenge of Peace* (Washington, D.C.: United States Catholic Conference, 1983), Introduction, n. 2.

points, of course; but it does seem more than a coincidence that the bishops adopt language and imagery that had been so successfully used for the purposes of antinuclear publicists like Jonathan Schell (in his *The Fate of the Earth* phase) and Dr. Helen Caldicott, the nuclear Cassandra of Physicians for Social Responsibility (whose exploits received Academy Award notice with the film *If You Love This Planet*).[11]

The worst example of the bishops' adoption of this essentially pagan theme of survivalism was not in the final text of *The Challenge of Peace*, but in the second draft (subject of debate at the November 1982 N.C.C.B. annual meeting), where the bishops claimed, astoundingly, that mankind's stupidity in blowing up the planet, if matters should come to that disastrous end, would "threaten" the "sovereignty" of God.[12] As I remarked publicly at the time, perhaps more flippantly than the moment demanded, I was sure that this would come as news to God. The passage was subsequently, and mercifully, deleted from the third draft of the pastoral; but the fact that it was there at all, in the crucial second draft, is cause for alarm.

Survivalism, the notion that sheer, physical survival—in either personal or species terms—is the highest moral good to which all other goods must be subordinated, is not compatible with Judeo-Christian ethics. Yes, we are called to be the stewards of creation, to gentle the earth, and to work for the coming of the Kingdom among us. But, from the first, Christianity has taught that we have here no earthly home, that we are a pilgrim people, living in the tension between that which is revealed in the Resurrection of the Lord and that which will be completed in glory in the final establishment of the Kingdom. It seems highly curious, to say the least, that the senior leadership of a Church that flowed from the blood of Christ on the Cross, and that regularly celebrates its martyrs in the rhythm of its liturgical year, should adopt language and imagery that is utterly at cross-purposes with basic Christian insights into the human condition and the moral norms that can be read from that condition.

It can be argued that I am making too much of a single word in the final draft, and an unfortunate phrase in the second draft, of *The Challenge of Peace*. But it is not an accident, as the Marxists would say, that these things happen. It suggests the degree to which powerful themes in the political culture could shape the bishops' reflections—even when

11. A particularly sharp critique of Schell may be found in Max Lerner's review of *The Fate of the Earth*, entitled "Visions of the Apocalypse," which can be found in *The New Republic*, April 28, 1982. Adddressing cognate issues, Glenn Tinder also criticized Schell's survivalism in "The Secular City" (*The New Republic*, August 16–23, 1982).

12. *Challenge of Peace*, second draft, p. 32, lines 4–5 (U.S.C.C. typewritten version).

those themes were, at bottom, flatly contradictory of basic Christian understandings.

But the problem with the survivalist entry point the bishops chose extends beyond these concerns. Fear is the worst possible basis on which to build that political action, which, as Cardinal Bernardin makes clear, was the bishops' intention. For fear does not stay fear when it enters the contest for power, which is to say, when it enters politics; fear becomes hate. The results of a fear-based politics, on our own political culture and on the boat people of Southeast Asia, should have been clear from the Vietnam era. When Americans turn on their political community, not much good results. How much more should we worry about this when the issues at stake do not have to do with a somewhat peripheral international arena like Indochina, but with the central security dilemma in world affairs today?

Finally, the bishops' tacit embrace of the survivalist *ethos* is bound to have unhappy results on the formation of individual conscience. One might wonder what has happened when the bishops of the United States publicly confess to being in the thrall of "terror" over the facts of nuclear weapons, and the atheist political philosopher Sidney Hook supplies the appropriate response:

It is better to be a live jackal than a dead lion: for lions, not for men. Men who have the moral courage to fight intelligently for freedom have the best prospects of avoiding the fate of both jackals and dead lions. Survival is not the be-all and end-all of a life worthy of man. Sometimes the worst thing we can know about a man is that he has survived. Those who say life is worth living at any cost have already written for themselves an epitaph of infamy, for there is no cause and no person they will not betray to stay alive. Man's vocation should be the use of the arts of intelligence in behalf of human freedom.[13]

These are the sentiments that one might reasonably have expected to come from the National Conference of Catholic Bishops—particularly if the bishops really believed that they were confronting congregations of terrorized Catholics. Rather than sensitively rearticulate the Catholic tradition on these matters—that human life is sacred and that it is not ultimate in the secular-survivalist sense that Schell and Caldicott would make it—the bishops succumb, perhaps unwittingly, perhaps not, to the political culture they claim to want to challenge and shape.

So on this vital question of the ground on which one enters the new nuclear debate, the bishops show tell-tale signs of being the influenced much more than the influential. Given the survivalist influences at work here this is not a happy conclusion to have to reach.

---

13. Sidney Hook's famous riposte to survivalism, now widely quoted, is the sole citation from his voluminous writings in his entry in *Who's Who*.

This question of the entry point for the discussion is closely related to a second cluster of concerns I have with *The Challenge of Peace*, which have to do with the bishops' seeming abandonment of the classic form of just-war analysis, in which the first order of business is to establish the "just cause" that would permit a resort to the use or threat of armed force. The bishops correctly observe, in *The Challenge of Peace*, that the classic just-war theory is not a blanket endorsement of mass violence; on the contrary, the formulation of the question on just war in St. Thomas ("Is war ever justifiable?")[14] suggests that the burden of proof must lie with those who would argue for the permissibility of the resort to violence in particular circumstances. The just-war theory emerged, the bishops contend (correctly), as a means of limiting the sway of war in the affairs of men. Since the presumption, in just-war theory, is *against* the use of violence, it is imperative that the first thing to be settled in a just-war moral analysis is the "just cause" that would make the resort to violence or its threat (as in deterrence) permissible.

Under contemporary conditions, the "just cause" that would presumably be invoked in a moral analysis of deterrence is the moral requirement to defend innocent life against an aggressive, totalitarian enemy, the Soviet Union.[15] And the bishops do discuss the Soviet threat—but far, far back in the pastoral letter, in fact, *after* the main discussion of deterrence and the establishment of criteria for guiding prudential decision-making on the structure of deterrence, nuclear targeting, and so forth. The bishops' statement on the Soviet Union, when one finally reaches it in *The Challenge of Peace*, is unexceptionable; it acknowledges the hard facts of contemporary Soviet intentions and capabilities, although the bishops cannot seem to bring themselves to make the conceptual linkage between the problem of totalitarianism and the problem of nuclear weapons as their German confreres did. Moreover, the section on the Soviet threat in the final version of *The Challenge of Peace* is significantly more persuasive to experienced students of world affairs than the milder formulations of the first and second drafts of the pastoral; it should not go unremarked that this toughening of analysis and language followed the Vatican consultation between certain key American bishops, their advisor Father Hehir, European bishops and experts, and Vatican officials. So one cannot reasonably argue that the bishops *ignore* the necessity of establishing "just cause" in *The Challenge of*

---

14. St. Thomas Aquinas, *Summa Theologiae*, II-II, 40:1, "*Utrum aliquod bellum sit licitum.*"

15. For an analysis of how *Challenge of Peace* handles the question of the moral duty to defend innocents, and what this portends for future dialogue between pacifists and just war theorists, cf. Stanley Hauerwas, "Surviving Justly: An Ethical Analysis of Nuclear Disarmament," *Center Journal* 3 (1983), 123–152.

Peace, even if one can raise hard questions about the methodology that led to the analysis of the Soviet threat being positioned in the letter the way it was.[16]

Still, it is instructive to remember Cardinal Bernardin's exegesis of the pastoral's view of the "signs of the times" in the Gannon Lecture, particularly as the Cardinal's remarks bear on this question of "just cause." The most significant thing about Cardinal Bernardin's brief list of the most important "signs of the times" is that it does not take account of the most salient strategic fact of both international life and today's American debate on nuclear weapons: namely, that the current wave of nuclear anxiety followed hard on the heels of the Soviet Union's achievement of parity with the United States in strategic nuclear weapons, and superiority in certain classes of nuclear weapons in Europe. This surely is among the most important "signs of the times" to be read in discerning the contours of the "new moment" in which we debate these matters, but it is not mentioned once in *The Challenge of Peace*, nor is it referenced in Cardinal Bernardin's Gannon Lecture.

What one finds, to get to the point, is a kind of ideological selectivity in defining the "new moment." This selectivity does not derive from the Roman Catholic social-ethical tradition; the filters at work are not theological, but political. The principles of selectivity that seem to guide both the pastoral's reading of "the signs of the times" and Cardinal Bernardin's definition of the key issues in today's "new moment" come from a certain part of American political culture, a rather easily recognizable subset of the actors in the current strategic debate. Who defines the "signs of the times" as the nuclear freeze debate, the MX debate, and the argument over no first use of nuclear weapons in Europe? Who, in defining the "signs of the times" in those ways, also tends to ignore or minimize the fact of Soviet strategic parity and theater superiority in certain indices? Certain elements in the professional arms control community do. Organizations such as Physicians for Social Responsibility, the American Committee for East/West Accord, the Center for Defense Information, and the Nuclear Weapons Freeze Campaign do. One wing, now dominant, in the Democratic Party does. The bishops' fellow leaders at the National Council of Churches do. These are all important actors in the current strategic debate, to be sure, and I do not mean to minimize their importance. But they hardly represent the sum total of wisdom on these matters, and in fact are more noteworthy for their own

16. *Challenge of Peace*, III, B, 2. "The Superpowers in a Disordered World." Cf., as complement and counterpoint, the German bishops' pastoral letter, *Out of Justice, Peace* (San Francisco: Ignatius Press, 1984). At the end of their letter, the Germans state forthrightly that the problems of nuclear war and the problem of totalitarianism cannot be disentangled, and that their solutions will be mutual, if at all.

commitment to certain orthodoxies about the world, the "arms race," "the superpowers," and the "military-industrial complex" than for their willingness to engage in the kind of reconstituted public debate the bishops claim as being one of their principal goals.[17] In these circumstances, one is at least entitled by circumstantial evidence to ask who is influencing whom. More important, for those concerned with the integrity of Catholic social ethics, at both the level of theological speculation and the level of authoritative teaching, there ought to be legitimate concern when the range of influences from the political culture on the triadic dialogue the bishops wish to foster is so narrow. When "the signs of the times" are read, not through the lenses of faith and theological reflection but through particular political binoculars with a tendency to screen out certain disharmonious facts, the "new moment," which I, too, believe is upon us, is not being well served.

The third cluster of concerns I would raise about the reciprocal influences operating between *The Challenge of Peace* and American political culture has to do with the pastoral's address to strategic theory and to specific policy options in the field of nuclear force modernizations. From what one can gather from the pastoral itself (prescinding here from the equally interesting, and perhaps more important, question of what is going on in the minds of the key staff members responsible for these issues at the United States Catholic Conference), the Roman Catholic leadership of the United States is willing to give a "strictly conditioned moral acceptance" to a form of minimum deterrence. The bishops would seem to prefer that this deterrent be constructed of single-warhead ICBM's or SLBM's targeted on military installations alone, and the bishops hint that such a scaled-down nuclear deterrent should be complemented by some conventional force upgrading so that a "no first use" of nuclear weapons policy in Europe (and presumably, elsewhere) would be militarily credible.[18] (Here, too, we will prescind from the question of how the bishops, deeply worried about the amount of federal dollars being spent on defense and thus diverted from domestic programs, would have us pay for the kind of conventional upgrading required.)

This strategic posture has drawn both applause (from McGeorge Bundy) and severe criticism. In the critics' camp, Albert Wohlstetter offered the most trenchant critique, in his June 1983 *Commentary* essay,

---

17. Cf. my chapter, "Intellectual Currents in the American Public Effort for Peace, 1930-1980," in *The Nuclear Freeze Debate* (Paul Cole and William J. Taylor, Jr., eds., Westview Press, 1983), for a tracing of the origins of these themes in citizen peace activism, and a call for the peace effort to reject the neo-isolationist base of its analysis as well as its one-eyed focus on resistance to American military programs alone.

18. *Challenge of Peace*, II, D, 2, "The Moral Assessment of Deterrence."

"Bishops, Statesmen, and Other Strategists on the Killing of Innocents," and the subsequent exchange of correspondence on that essay in
the November 1983 *Commentary*.[19] In brief, Wohlstetter argues that the
bishops, wittingly or not, have settled for a "bluff deterrent" that an
adversary knows we cannot use and thus is rather unlikely to be deterred
by. This, in Wohlstetter's judgment, makes nuclear war more likely,
rather than less, and makes the escalation to nuclear weapons within a
conventional conflict more probable rather than less. The nub of Wohlstetter's criticism comes not so much from the bishops' seeming preference for a minimum deterrent (although Wohlstetter would surely find
much wrong with that on maintenance-of-deterrence grounds), but from
the bishops' statement that they find it hard, indeed almost-but-not-
quite impossible, to imagine the circumstances in which a resort to even
modest use of nuclear weapons would be justifiable. In the words of
Father J. Bryan Hehir of the U.S.C.C. staff, the bishops are "agnostics,
bordering on atheists" on the question of the possibly justifiable use of
any nuclear weapon.

The Wohlstetter/N.C.C.B. argument is a fascinating one that is sure
to be pursued vigorously over the next few years;[20] that Wohlstetter's
critique closely follows the oft-repeated reasoning of some Catholic
just-war theorists like William V. O'Brien will help guarantee a lengthy
dispute. But that is not the line of argument I wish to take up in this
paper. So let us return to our major concern, which is the question of
reciprocal influence between the bishops and the political culture, on
this matter of strategic theory and specific policy options.

I must confess, after two years of involvement with the process leading up to *The Challenge of Peace* and more months of reflection on the
finished product, that it remains unclear to me how the strategic vision
the bishops propound (which has numerous critics both left and right)
can claim to be a more legitimate expression of the Roman Catholic
social-ethical tradition than, say, O'Brien's view on "usable," low-yield,
high-accuracy nuclear weapons as a deterrent, or the view of the President's Commission on Strategic Forces (the Scowcroft Commission,
which recommended de-MIRVing, a return to single-warhead missiles,

19. Bundy's remarks may be found in *The New York Review of Books* (June 16, 1983),
in an article entitled "The Bishops and the Bomb" (the entire process surrounding *The
Challenge of Peace* may have set a new world's record for unimaginative essay titles).
Wohlstetter's essay, as noted, may be found in the June 1983 issue of *Commentary*; the
exchange of correspondence on the essay appeared in the November issue of the same
journal and is in some ways more critically telling in its analysis of *The Challenge of
Peace* than the original article.

20. Cf. my own effort to sketch the current terrain of debate in "The New Nuclear
Debates," *Catholicism in Crisis* (June 1984).

and the use of a modest number of MX's as political levers for getting Soviet agreement to such a fundamental restructuring of nuclear forces around the concept of "stability"—neither side having even the theoretical capability of launching a crippling first strike on the other).[21] Given the strategic vision and arms control approach implicit in the bishops' letter, it is fairly certain that the bishops will oppose even serious research on ballistic missile defense systems; is this refusal to defend innocents, or to maintain stable deterrence, if that should involve major force modernizations, as in the Scowcroft Commission recommendations, congruent with the Catholic social-ethical tradition?

These are immensely complicated questions, and reasonable people of good will can differ on them, and differ dramatically. Still, it is worth observing, on the question of reciprocal influences, that however difficult it may be to find the bishops' approach clearly implied by the norms the bishops establish, it is rather easy to find that part of the political culture in which the bishops' views have great resonance—and that is in a fairly narrow band of what we might call the "institutional arms control fraternity." This is a fascinating, and crucial, sect within contemporary American political culture. It comprises theorists, academics, occasional government officials, and publicists who have abandoned work for general and complete disarmament (or even nuclear disarmament) and have opted for arms control as a means of "managing" the inevitable weapons competition between the United States and the Soviet Union so that it becomes as "safe" as possible under the prevailing technological and political circumstances. To describe these men and women this way may sound deprecating; that is not my intention. Many of them have labored hard in the heat of the day; many of those in this fraternity with whom I have had the opportunity to work are people of moral sensitivity and deep commitment to peace. But they are not persuaded of the possibility of disarmament, conventional or nuclear; they are highly skeptical of grand improvement schemes for conducting international affairs; they are largely wedded to the notion of deterrence through mutual assured destruction (assured second-strike capability on industrial and population "assets" of the enemy); they tend to believe, on the basis of MAD theory, that weapons aimed at people are stabilizing while weapons aimed at weapons are destabilizing; and they are the inheritors of a certain set of credal propositions about nu-

---

21. For O'Brien's view, cf. "A Just-War Deterrence/Defense Strategy," *Center Journal* 3 (1983) and "The Failure of Deterrence and the Conduct of War," an as-yet unpublished paper delivered at Georgetown University's conference on "Justice and War in the Nuclear Age" (March 15, 1984). The Scowcroft Commission Report is available from the Government Printing Office, or through any member of Congress.

clear strategy that tend to make them extremely nervous about the development of counterforce capabilities and defensive capabilities.[22]

This is the part of the American political culture from which the bishops seem to have drawn most of their strategic vision and policy options; yet it is interesting to note, on the question of reciprocal influences, that the standard history of thought on these matters, Lawrence Freedman's *The Evolution of Nuclear Strategy*,[23] barely mentions the moral arguments at play in its detailed analysis of the history of strategic thought. Would a new edition of Freedman's book be any different, given the new fact of *The Challenge of Peace*? Who is influencing whom?

The final draft of the bishops' pastoral correctly distinguished between those principles the bishops were enunciating with the full weight of their teaching authority and those prudential judgments about which the bishops were less certain, or which fell outside the scope of their proper teaching authority. The pastoral's sections on strategy, force modernizations, and arms control approaches surely fall within this latter category of nonbinding prudential judgments. But it must be admitted that it is precisely at this level that the pastoral letter has had its major impact. To read any of the major newspaper accounts of the May 1983 N.C.C.B. meeting, to listen to the radio and television discussions at the time, to read the flood of study materials published since the adoption of the letter—is to see my point. The "common wisdom" understanding of *The Challenge of Peace* is that it "rejected American national security policy" and that the bishops' letter is to be primarily understood as an element within a broader, renascent antinuclear effort.[24]

That the bishops would deny this to be their intention does not minimize the fact that such has been the public impact of their work; con-

---

22. What I term the "institutional arms control fraternity" is hardly monolithic; it has interesting intellectual cross-currents and eddies in its pool. Still, it is the same pool, essentially. Some representative examples of recent thought within this highly influential grouping: Theodore Draper's assault on counterforce, in an exchange of lengthy public correspondence with Secretary of Defense Casper Weinberger, which may be found in *The New York Review of Books* (November 4, 1982; August 18, 1983; and January 19, 1984). Cf. also Leon Wieseltier's *Nuclear War, Nuclear Peace* (New York: Holt, Reinhart, and Winston, 1983); Wieseltier, interestingly enough, is also nervous about the influence of the nuclear freeze movement on the bishops. Cf. also the Harvard Nuclear Study Group's book, *Living With Nuclear Weapons* (Cambridge: Harvard University Press, 1983). The cross-currents and disagreements within the fraternity make it intellectually stimulating, but these cross-currents do not involve fraternity challenges to the major premises noted in my essay.

23. Lawrence Freedman, *The Evolution of Nuclear Strategy* (London: St. Martin's, 1982).

24. Cf. my analysis of several post-pastoral study guides in *The National Catholic Register* (May 6, 1984).

trolling the hermeneutics of Church documents by the mass media is a mission impossible for any institution, even the N.C.C.B. But one could still wonder, granting the essential truth of the bishops' claims about their intention, just how sorry some elements in the N.C.C.B. were to have their carefully crafted document reduced to such simplifications. An example from the process leading up to the May 1983 N.C.C.B. meeting illustrates my point. The second draft of *The Challenge of Peace* was widely, and accurately, portrayed as being in support of a nuclear freeze. Under the weight of criticism from several sources—intra- as well as extra-ecclesiastical—the third draft of the pastoral eschewed the freeze language imagery, and talked of "curbing" the arms race. *The New York Times*, among others, immediately interpreted this as the bishops backing away from "the freeze." At the Chicago N.C.C.B. meeting to consider the third draft, Bishop Malone of Youngstown, soon-to-be president of the N.C.C.B., urged his brother bishops to eliminate the word "curb" and substitute the word "halt," since this "curb/halt" matter would "set the tone" for the entire document. Given the political-media context in May 1983, it cannot be doubted by any sophisticated observer that what Bishop Malone (and others) had in mind by "setting the tone" for *The Challenge of Peace* was bringing the document back into line with freeze orthodoxy, from which it had presumably strayed under the impact of the Vatican consultation and argument within the Ad Hoc Committee on War and Peace. In any case, whatever the internal dynamics of the N.C.C.B. debate on "curb/halt," the media unanimously interpreted the substitution of "halt" as a victory for pro-freeze forces in the N.C.C.B.—and this point was never persuasively denied by official or semiofficial N.C.C.B. spokesmen after the adoption of the pastoral letter. Various bishops would claim that the document did not endorse any one approach (i.e., the bishops did not flat-out endorse "the freeze" *as such*), but neither did these bishops distance themselves from the now-standard media hermeneutic of their document as part of the freeze movement.[25]

Now, on the question of who is influencing whom here: The fact is, that by May 1983, "the freeze" had been sharply criticized by more than a few serious arms control experts, and not a few Congressional Democrats who, having originally seen the House of Representatives' freeze resolution as a means of holding the Administration's toes to the arms control fire, were privately quite dissatisfied with the freeze as arms

---

25. Castelli, op. cit., traces the semantic/political contest between "curbers" and "halters," which I find quaintly and ironically reminiscent of the battle between "Ditchers" and "Hedgers" in the early-20th-century battle over the reform of the British House of Lords; Barbara Tuchman provides the relevant narration in *The Proud Tower: A Portrait of the World Before the War* (London: H. Hamilton, 1966).

control, and increasingly upset with the rigidity of the orthodoxy-guardians among the leaders of the freeze movement, who refused, at that time, to countenance the prospect of *any* nuclear force modernizations. The participants in the May 1983 N.C.C.B. meeting seemed largely unaware of these beyond-the-freeze dynamics at work in the country, but the bishops seem to have been led by what they perceived to be a public wave of pro-freeze sentiment to give tacit endorsement to a specific policy option that was increasingly seen as being of dubious arms control merit.[26] The tacit freeze endorsement in *The Challenge of Peace*, then, is not a conclusion drawn from an analysis within the Catholic social-ethical tradition, but an accommodation to pressures working outside that tradition and its institutional bearer. No doubt that here, as elsewhere, dialectical influences are at work. But it seems easier and more persuasive to argue that the trajectory of influence on questions of strategy and arms control was *from* the political culture on to *The Challenge of Peace*, in terms of relative weights and impacts.

A fourth set of concerns about the question "Who was influencing whom?" in *The Challenge of Peace* revolves around the pastoral's minimal attention to world-order issues, i.e., to the question of how we solve today's peace-and-security dilemma in ways that are morally and politically sound and that defend and advance democratic values and human freedom in world affairs.

The paucity of attention paid to these questions of the international system and its possible reform is particularly odd in a Roman Catholic document, for among the crown jewels of the Catholic social-ethical tradition is a vision of law and political process as alternatives to mass violence in the resolution of conflict. This Catholic vision of world order is not a utopian expectation involving the fundamental alteration of human nature so that conflict is no more; rather, it is a vision within the Catholic social-ethical tradition of "moderate realism"—sober about the abiding reality of conflict in the world (the political meaning of the doctrine of original sin), but affirming of the possibility that human beings can create institutions of law and governance capable of processing that conflict without mass violence. The contemporary high point of this Catholic world-order tradition (vigorously provided by the American hierarchy in its April 1945 and November 1946 statements on the kind of peace that ought to be the goal of U.S. policy in the

26. For representative liberal critiques of the freeze, cf. Albert Gore, Jr., "Cold, Hard Facts About the Freeze," *The Washington Post*, (December 7, 1982); and "In Defense of Deterrence," *The New Republic* (December 20, 1982). The latter article has several interesting critiques of the bishops' second draft, which still seem sound to me in light of the final draft of *Challenge of Peace*.

aftermath of World War II) came in 1963 with Pope John XXIII's encyclical *Pacem in Terris*, in which the Holy Father argued that the "universal common good" required international legal and political institutions to perform the function now reserved, at the bottom line, to war or to its threat: the resolution of international conflict. John's teaching stood squarely in a line with the moderate-realist school of Catholic social-ethical thought, and reflected, in contemporary terms, Augustine's axiom that peace is the "tranquility of order." It should be emphasized that what Pope John had in mind was not Jonathan Schell's "reinvention of politics," which the *New Yorker* writer called for in *The Fate of the Earth* (and abandoned in his sequel, *The Abolition*). Pope John saw no need to "reinvent" politics; what was needed was to apply already known procedures and institutional arrangements to the problem of international conflict. In the Pope's view, the world had become a political arena, but was not yet a political community. Bridging that gap between arena and community was required of us by the principle of the universal common good.

The bishops do discuss world-order issues at the close of *The Challenge of Peace*,[27] but they do so with nowhere near the amount of attention to detail that is paid to the finer points of nuclear weapons targeting doctrine. Moreover, when the bishops do tackle world-order questions, they do so in an unfortunately weak-minded and intellectually limp way. The bishops' discussion of the U.N., for example, is light years closer to the attitudes and analyses one would find in the publications of the United Nations Association, for example, than to the more critical view taken by, say, Daniel Patrick Moynihan in his U.N. memoirs.

The fact that the bishops pay relatively little attention to world order questions, and the judgment that they pay attention limply when they do briefly address these issues, suggest that two influences, both of which we have already seen in this paper, were at work from the political culture on the formulations of *The Challenge of Peace*.

The relatively minimal attention paid to the broad question of legal and political alternatives to war in the pastoral closely parallels the predilections of the liberal arms-control community, which is not really interested in world-order issues for a variety of reasons, some having to do with analytic judgments, others reflecting the caste concerns of the arms-control fraternity. But when international legal and political institutions are discussed in that part of the liberal internationalist political culture that still worries about these matters, the tendency is to say soothing things and not to face the harsh fact that, for example, the

---

27. *Challenge of Peace*, III, B, 3, "Interdependence: From Fact to Policy."

U.N. General Assembly is, in its daily operations today, an actual obstacle to peace.[28] The parallels between these inclinations of, first, the arms-control fraternity and, second, the liberal internationalist/world-order community, and the line taken by *The Challenge of Peace*, is too close to be coincidental.

During my own testimony before the Ad Hoc Committee on War and Peace, and in subsequent commentaries on the first and second drafts, I emphasized what seemed to me to be the importance of reclaiming the Catholic world-order tradition in meaningful contemporary terms; I saw no way the bishops could intelligently address the symptom—weapons—without first setting a credible framework for addressing the disease—international anarchy, in a nuclear-armed world whose landscape is shadowed by the dark specter of armed totalitarian power. So I suppose I was, to a very modest degree, pleased in May 1983 that world-order issues got treated at all in *The Challenge of Peace*. But my modest satisfaction has given way, over time and reflection, to dismay: For the only way even to begin to think clearly about legal and political alternatives to war is forthrightly to acknowledge, and try to do something about, the mendacity and hypocrisy that characterize much of international organizational life today. Only then can we define the needed tasks, and set the policy direction, for achieving Pope John's vision of a world, not without conflict, but without mass violence as the *ultima ratio* in resolving conflict. The bishops' failings here, which once again reflect influences from outside the specific purview of the Roman Catholic tradition (which in this particular instance has a rich and complex heritage of reflection to bring to bear on contemporary problems), seem to me, over the long haul, to be as important as their adoption of a survivalist entry point for the discussion. That the bishops fail, for example, to discuss the relationships among the defense and advance of democracy, the cause of peace, and the possibilities of arms reduction and disarmament—at a time when parts of the political culture to which the bishops seem oddly unattuned were joining forces to create a National Endowment for Democracy, which, if successful, would broaden that part of the globe in which conflict could be settled without mass violence—seems not merely unfortunate, but almost negligent. It further illustrates the degree to which the dialectic of influences operating

28. The ambassadorship of Donald F. McHenry to the U.N. was the quintessential expression of this "speak softly and carry no stick" approach to international organizational life. The counterarguments are made compellingly by Daniel Patrick Moynihan (in recent days, an impassioned defender of international law) in his U.N. memoir, *A Dangerous Place* (Boston: Little, Brown and Co., 1978). Whatever else has changed about Moynihan, his approach to the U.N. remains constant, as is demonstrated in his recent book *Loyalties* (New York: Harcourt, Brace, Jovanovich, 1984).

on *The Challenge of Peace* was weighted in a particular direction: from a narrow band of the political culture, on to the N.C.C.B.

By Way of an Inconclusive Conclusion . . .

These four clusters of worries make it reasonably clear, to this observer at least, that Cardinal Bernardin's and others' claim that *The Challenge of Peace* has had a major impact on the American political culture could just as easily be inverted, and in a way that ought to provoke serious examination of conscience among bishops, social ethicists, publicists, and the concerned Catholic population. As I said at the outset, it is too early to tell what middle- and long-term impact the bishops' pastoral will have on American political culture; I will even admit, quite cheerfully, that that impact *could* be great, and *could* be in ways wholly surprising (and thus reassuring) to me. Only time will tell on that score.

But what does seem more, rather than less, certain is that in the short term the bishops' primary impact has not been to help launch a reconstituted and better discussion on the problem of peace, security, and freedom, but to lend the weight of their public credibility to factions within the already existing argument. Moreover, these factions seem to have had an inordinate impact on the bishops' own reflections, which, when they descend from the articulation of general moral norms to the development of strategic approaches and arms-control proposals, exhibit a high degree of similarity to particular arms-control orthodoxies as expounded in certain seminars at Harvard, M.I.T., and Stanford and that, in determining the entry point for the discussion, seem remarkably similar to some pages of *The New Yorker*. Now it is conceivable that we have here a natural congruence between the applications that any thoughtful person would draw from within the Catholic social-ethical tradition and the approaches taken by certain factions in American political culture; it is conceivable, but it is highly unlikely. The more tenable hypothesis is that the dialectic of reciprocal influence was not evenly weighted, but heavily canted *from* Palo Alto, Manhattan, and Cambridge *to* 1312 Massachusetts Avenue, N.W., in Washington, D.C., to adopt symbolic referents for a moment. That may be agreeable to those who would argue, reasonably enough, that the views adopted from the wider political culture are in all particulars congruent with Catholic social-ethical norms. It is less comforting to those of us who are convinced, precisely from a peace-concerned base that takes the threat of totalitarianism as seriously as the threat of nuclear weapons, that the Cambridge/Manhattan/Palo Alto orthodoxy has lost intellectual and moral steam and is in no position to create the kind of reconstituted public debate about the contemporary peace, security, and freedom dilemma that the bishops quite rightly want to launch.

If I am right in my basic hunch about the way the dialectic of influence operated in *The Challenge of Peace*, or even if I am only pointed in the correct hermeneutic direction, the really interesting question is, "Why?" Why did the bishops seemingly succumb to Schellian apocalypticism, when they were the bearers of an eschatological tradition more than two and a half millenia old? Why did the bishops abandon the traditional method of just-war analysis, thereby implicitly accepting the view that the threat posed by nuclear weapons is of such horror that it relativizes the threat posed by totalitarian power? Why did the bishops fail to see that such a relativizing of the totalitarian dimension of the problem could (as it did in the 1930's) help make war more likely, rather than less, were its net impact to be the reinforcement of a psychology of appeasement already well advanced in some elite circles? Why did the bishops tacitly endorse an arms-control approach—"the freeze"—that almost no serious student of arms-control accepts (even those students of arms control on whom the bishops lean most heavily for strategic and policy advice)? Why did the bishops diminish the importance of the classic Catholic perspective on alternatives to war?

I have no answers to these questions yet, or, rather, I have no answers that I find intellectually satisfying. One could speculate endlessly about the impact of the dominant ideological currents within the U.S.C.C. staff on the perceptions of the staff's episcopal masters in the N.C.C.B; but bureaucratic answers only touch the surface of the needed exploration (and examination of conscience). Supposing that some clarity could come from an analysis of U.S.C.C. staff perspectives, one would still have left unanswered the question as to why the staff had come to hold those particular views. What is most peculiar about all this is the kind of breathlessness that the bishops and their staff brought to the discussion. After all, the Catholic Church is hardly a Johnnie-come-lately to the moral analysis of war and peace issues; we've been doing it, in one form or another, since Paul wrote the 13th chapter of the *Epistle to the Romans*.

It is these questions, which bear, at bottom, on the vulnerabilities of Catholic social ethics when confronted with the tangled conditions of modernity—and particularly with the inescapable nexus of the problem of nuclear weapons and the problem of totalitarianism—that are urgently in need of exploration in the aftermath of *The Challenge of Peace*. Such an exploration is an essential component in creating that "theology of peace" the pastoral mandates. Thoughtfully conducted, the exploration could lead, in time, to the pastoral letter that remains to be written: one in which the dominant focus would not be on weapons, but on the problem of political community amid diversity. As American bishops speaking to Americans—bearers of a precious tradition of just such political community—the bishops would challenge the Church in the United States to think past the present, polarized discussion to explore, for example, how U.S. policy might work to alter the present dynamic of Soviet policy through helping facilitate a process of pluralization and humanization within the U.S.S.R. That pastoral letter, as I say, remains to be written. Whether such a task is undertaken, or whether American Catholicism will devolve into simply one more marketeer of policy options in the public arena, will tell us much about the state of the Church in the United States as we approach the bicentennial of the originating Diocese of Baltimore.

12. Revisionist History: A Catholic Perspective on the Nuclear Freeze Movement

Interpreting the morally binding teachings of the Catholic Church is difficult. It is certainly controversial. But interpreting what Church doctrine advises Catholics to do about national security issues, such as the policy of deterrence, nuclear arms, and conventional weaponry, can divide parishes, study groups, and families. Conviction of one's opinion runs that deep. I, for example, do not expect agreement on each and every thought I will put forward. But I hope that many of you will come to realize and understand the reasons for my position. Understanding and tolerating differences continues to be one of the great strengths of our faith.

As is well known, some prominent clergy in the Catholic Church have been actively supportive of recent pacifist movements in the defense debate. Their participation in the nuclear freeze movement—as well as other "peace" activities—is a reflection of their judgment that it is their moral obligation, as emphasized by Church teaching, to speak out on these issues.

However, the basis of this authority is somewhat clouded. Without clarification of Church teaching—or lack of Church teaching—behind these judgments, there is a risk that the layperson will believe it is a moral and religious obligation to support pacifist movements. This—in my opinion—represents a very dangerous situation, because I believe that the teaching of the Church does not spell out a clear policy. Catholics may not be able to speak with one voice on specific policy recommendations aimed at achieving peace.

A recent statement of Auxiliary Bishop Thomas Gumbleton of Detroit reveals one view of the Church's position: "The decisions that we make on deployment and use of [nuclear] weapons are moral decisions. There is much evil in them. That evil is destructive, as evil always is, to the perpetrator as well as the victim. . . . The intent to use nuclear weapons necessarily includes the intention to do destruction on a scale the world has never known before . . . that is an evil on a scale that surpasses any former concept of sin."[1]

Surely, Bishop Gumbleton believes a Catholic must oppose nuclear weapons on all terms. But, this is only his opinion.

Bishop Roger Mahony, from Stockton, California, interprets the Second Vatican Council as saying, ". . . any use of nuclear weapons, and by implication, any intention to use them, is always morally—and gravely—a serious evil. No Catholic can ever support or cooperate with the planning or executing of policies to use, or which by implication intend to use, nuclear weapons even in a defensive posture, let alone in a first strike against another nation."[2]

Bishop Mahony is surely as strongly opposed to the use of nuclear weapons as Bishop Gumbleton; however, again, this opposition is dependent on prudent judgment and not on Church doctrine.

Nuclear freeze advocates within the Church may decide that American nuclear arms policy is morally wrong. But, and this point is very important, the Catholic Church has not taken a stand on any particular American arms policy. The Catholic Church has not embraced the nuclear freeze movement. To say it has would mean accepting a revision of Church history.

Just what do I mean by "prudent judgment"? It is defined as forming an opinion based on reason and a personal interpretation of the facts. It is separate from Church doctrine. Bishop John O'Connor, one of the writers of the American bishops' pastoral letter, has pointed out that there was not unanimity by the conference of bishops to put prudential judgments in the letter.[3] But they were added anyway. This is a point I will stress repeatedly. It is extremely vital to know the difference between Church teaching and interpretation of Church teaching. Informed people of good faith and good will can disagree on all opinions presented.

Cardinal Bernardin articulated this difference between teaching and opinion in an article published in early February 1984. He said:

> . . . When it comes to such matters as the initiation of nuclear war and the merits of a "no first use" pledge, whether it is possible to confine the use of nuclear weapons within morally acceptable limits, whether and how deterrence can be morally justified—then reasonable people, working within the

1. "Should Church Oppose Nuclear Arms?" *U.S. News and World Report* (December 20, 1982), p. 47.

2. Bishop Roger Mahony, "The Case for Nuclear Pacifism," *The Apocalyptic Premise*, eds. Ernest W. Lefever and E. Stephen Hunt (Washington, D.C.: Ethics and Public Policy Center, 1982), p. 282.

3. Unpublished text of Archbishop John J. O'Connor's address to the American Bar Association, November 18, 1983.

framework of Catholic teaching, can and do differ in their conclusions because of differences concerning facts and their evaluation of the facts.[4]

I believe it is of utmost importance that the Catholic layperson distinguishes between the opinions of certain Church leaders and the morally binding teachings of Church authority. If one accepts the challenge set out by the American bishops' pastoral letter to make policy judgments based on an informed conscience, then one must study Catholic Church doctrine. One must go beyond opinion. The sincere Catholic must also look to non-American Catholics who have commented on this issue. In this presentation, I will quote the letters by the German and French bishops, who have methodically researched and reflected on nuclear conflict, to enhance the universal Church teachings on this issue.

In examining the teachings of the Catholic Church in the nuclear era, there are four principles that are morally binding when applied to national security issues. These can be traced through the years. Catholics are morally obligated first to defend against unjust aggression; second, to respond to a threat with proportional means; third, to avoid directly intending the death of the innocent (in nuclear terms, this means avoiding the targeting of civilian populations); and fourth, to oppose the intrinsic evil of totalitarian regimes that deny the basic freedoms and rights of human beings (in the contemporary international order, this means Marxist-Leninist regimes).

In his address before the American Bar Association on November 18, 1983, Bishop O'Connor remarked: "Bishops can fool around with a lot of things, but they cannot fool around with straight papal teaching."[5]

O'Connor reminds Catholics that Church authority states several principles that have stood the test of time. He iterates that one may never "directly, deliberately, intentionally," take an innocent life, and one may never use "disproportionate means" when responding to the moral duty to defend against unjust aggression.[6]

The history of Catholic Church doctrine on war and peace and the history of American nuclear arms policy are not contradictory to these principles. Anyone who attempts to state otherwise is revising history based on his or her own judgment, not based on the theology of the Church.

The history of the early Christian Church teaches us that a restrained use of force is morally justified. This teaching is a result of the growing involvement of Christians in the secular world. Early Christians, while proclaiming pacifism as a way of life, adopted this belief because they

---

4. Joseph Cardinal Bernardin, "What I Said at Fordham," *The Chicago Catholic* (February 10, 1984), p. 2.
5. O'Connor, American Bar address.   6. Ibid.

were excluded from the Roman world and were able to withdraw from conflict. Over time, Christians became more involved in the secular world. They had to face the sin of man. Furthermore, the Christian faith was growing and becoming more influential in the daily lives of soldiers.

As the number of Christian soldiers increased at the end of the third century, the wall dividing Christians from the world fell. The German bishops, in their pastoral letter *Out of Justice, Peace*, write that "The exceptional situation which they had once been able to afford as a small minority was no longer possible for them. They now began themselves to share the responsibility for what they had previously accorded to the emperor. . . , namely the right to wage just and controlled wars."[7]

With this responsibility came the duty to respond to the "sin of man" within the morality of the Christian faith. The Synod of Arles (A.D. 314) declares that Christians have a role in protecting the state, but they can question taking another human life in war.[8]

References in the Holy Bible reinforce this issue of man using force as a means to an end. Violence occurs in an imperfect world. One finds a history of conflict in the Bible as man falls through his imperfections to sin. In fact, as will be remembered from the Old Testament, our God often used force to teach his Chosen People lessons.

In the story of Noah, God destroys the wicked on earth who have forsaken His laws. The evil ones are again destroyed in the cities of Sodom and Gomorrah by God's hand.

In the New Testament, Jesus tells us in Mark 14:27 that His peace is not of this world. Because sin is such a part of earthly life, true peace cannot exist. The New Testament further examines the role of the military in the Christian tradition when Roman centurians became Christians. As described in the German bishops' letter, the Romans are not asked to give up their careers in the military by Jesus in Matthew 8:5–13, by John the Baptist in Luke 3:14, or by St. Paul in Acts 22:25. The Bible teaches that while Christians on earth must accept the existence of war and conflict, they must still work for peace in their lives.

Through the ages, Christian thinkers explored this seemingly paradoxical link. St. Augustine was but one. When he heard that Rome had been sacked, he said: "'There has to be an end to every earthly kingdom.' Then he devoted the remaining seventeen years of his life to the deeper question of the relation between earthly cities like Rome which

7. Joint Pastoral Letter of the German Bishops, *Out of Justice, Peace: The Church in the Service of Peace*, ed. James Schall, S.J. (San Francisco: St. Ignatius Press, 1983), pp. 25–26.
8. Ibid., p. 26.

men build and then destroy, and the city of God, which men did not build and cannot destroy."[9]

In A.D. 430, St. Augustine described the relationship between God and man in his work, *The City of God and the City of Man*. Because sin existed in the world, Augustine reasoned that Christians were justified in using force to defend their faith. Furthermore, he believed that God's peace would not be achieved in this world.[10]

St. Augustine also formulated a "just war" theory for Christians to follow in deciding how to respond to aggression. "A war was only 'just' if it: (i) served the cause of peace; (ii) was directed against an injustice (which one's adversary was not prepared to terminate or to rectify); (iii) if the legitimate authorities ordered the waging of war; and (iv) if the war did not infringe the word of God."[11]

Clearly, the Christian tradition acknowledges that conflict and force will play a role in life on earth. Catholics have the guidance of the "just war" theory to respond to worldly imperfection. From the evidence presented, no one can argue that the Catholic faith is a pacifist faith.

As I mentioned earlier, the true meaning of the pastoral letters, whether it be from the American, the German, or even the French bishops, strongly depends on understanding the difference between morally binding teachings and judgments.

The definition of "morally binding" involves the imposition of an obligation that has been conformed to a standard of right behavior. The Ten Commandments are a distinct example—something that cannot be argued within the Church, and where there is an obligation to obey.

Another example of a morally binding teaching can be found in the issue of abortion. The Pastoral Constitution of the Church in the Modern World states that "God, the Lord of life, has conferred on men the surpassing ministry of safeguarding life, a ministry which must be guarded with the greatest care, while abortion and infanticide are unspeakable crimes. . . . The Church has always taught that abortion, whether performed early or late, is a grave evil. . . ."[12]

Cardinal Bernardin also uses this example as a morally binding teaching. He argues that "Abortion, the direct taking of innocent life, is intrinsically evil and must be categorically condemned."[13]

9. Malcolm Muggeridge, "Muggeridge Sees Deliverance Despite West's Despair," *Los Angeles Times* (June 17, 1979), p. 27.

10. German bishops, *Out of Justice, Peace*, p. 27.

11. Ibid., p. 26.

12. "Abortion and the Catholic Church," N.C.C.B. Committee for Pro-Life Activities, 1312 Massachusetts Ave., N.W., Washington, D.C. 20005. 1983/1984 Respect for Life Manual, p. 16.

13. Bernardin, "What I Said at Fordham."

While the Church teaches all Catholics to oppose abortion, Catholics may choose different methods to oppose it. They may choose to oppose politicians who support abortion, they may work for the passage of a Human Life Amendment, they may volunteer at a Birthright office, or may choose many other options that protect the unborn.

The Rev. Robert Drinan, S.J., consistently cast his vote to support federal funds for abortion when he was a member of Congress. While I cannot agree with his decision to use taxpayers' money to destroy the unborn, presumably Father Drinan believed his vote upheld his moral obligation to oppose abortion. As is evident, if Father Drinan is required to oppose abortion as an "intrinsic evil," but supports public funding of abortion, Church teaching certainly allows flexibility in making and judging other public-policy decisions. I would not hesitate to say that the Church's position on abortion is much more easily understood by a Catholic than the Church's position on the issue of war and peace.

As stated before, the pastoral letters on war and peace reaffirmed four morally binding teachings. As quoted in the American bishops' pastoral letter, Pope Pius XII strongly asserts that "A people threatened with an unjust aggression, or already its victim, may not remain passively indifferent, if it would think and act as befits a Christian." [14] The letter goes on to say that "The council and the popes have stated clearly that governments threatened by armed, unjust aggression must defend their people. This includes defense by armed force if necessary as a last resort." [15]

The first morally binding teaching, that one has a duty to defend against unjust aggression, is constrained in the pastoral letters by two other morally binding teachings: Defense must not involve the direct targeting of civilian populations, nor be of unproportional means. The nondiscrimination principle ". . . prohibits directly intended attacks on non-combatants and non-military targets." [16] The proportionality principle ". . . means that the damage to be inflicted and the costs incurred by war must be proportionate to the good expected by taking up arms." [17]

The French bishops' letter, *Winning the Peace*, is especially significant in providing Catholics with the insight of the fourth morally binding teaching, which is the present-day barrier to the ultimate goal of every Christian—the Marxist-Leninist threat to peace. Marxism-

---

14. The Pastoral Letter of the U.S. Bishops on War and Peace, *The Challenge of Peace: God's Promise and Our Response* (Washington, D.C.: United States Catholic Conference, 1983), n. 76.

15. Ibid., n. 75.   17. Ibid., n. 99.
16. Ibid., n. 107.

Leninism is the universal threat to Christians because it is intrinsically evil. Official Catholic Church teaching obligates us to oppose this evil. Let me explain this further.

The Church, based on natural law, has historically defined intrinsic evil as something that denies freedom of conscience, freedom of worship, freedom to "be open to graces," and ultimately denies Christians their reason for life—"union of the soul."[18] As I stated before, abortion is considered intrinsically evil because it takes life.

The ultimate threat facing Catholics today is not the threat of war, but the threat of Marxist-Leninist doctrine conquering the free world. The French bishops in their pastoral letter write that ". . . it would be unjust to lump everybody together and close one's eyes to the domineering and aggressive character of the Marxist-Leninist ideology. For it, everything, even the peoples' aspiration to peace, must be used for conquest of the world."[19] The threat of this "conquest" is explicitly defined by both Marxists and by papal teaching.

Lenin's hostility toward religion is clear. He wrote that "All religious ideas . . . are an unspeakable abomination." He also wrote, "We must combat religion: this is the ABC of all materialism and consequently of Marxism."[20]

Pope Pius XI presented the historical position of the Church when he wrote, "Whether (Marxist) socialism is considered as a doctrine, or a historical fact, or as a movement, if it really remains socialism it cannot be brought into harmony with the dogmas of the Catholic Church, . . . the reason being that it conceives human society in a way utterly alien to Christian truth."[21]

As quoted in the Connecticut bishops' letter, *The Communist Doctrine of Marxism-Leninism*, Pope Pius XI continues: "See to it, venerable brethren, that the faithful do not allow themselves to be deceived. Communism is intrinsically wrong, and no one who would save Christian civilization may collaborate with it in any undertaking whatsoever."[22]

The pastoral letters then leave Catholics with four morally binding teachings on which to rely in their journey toward "true" peace. But then we must ask ourselves, What is "true" peace?

The German bishops make a significant contribution in defining this

18. Quotes from a meeting with Matthew F. Murphy, a specialist in the area of arms control and Catholic Church teaching and a public information officer with the U.S. Arms Control and Disarmament Agency.

19. French bishops' statement, *Winning the Peace*, reprinted in *The Wanderer*, transl., the Rev. Michael J. Wrenn (December 8, 1983), p. 442.

20. The Connecticut Catholic bishops' statement on *The Communist Doctrine of Marxism-Leninism* (The Connecticut Catholic Conference, February, 1982), p. 2.

21. Ibid., p. 5.   22. Ibid., p. 6.

concept, stating that the proper role of the Church in this journey is theological. The German bishops base their letter on the biblical definition of peace. They write, "When the Holy Scriptures in the Old and New Testaments speak of peace, they do not limit it to the resolution of disputes between nations or the settlement of hostilities and wars among states. On the contrary, they testify to the history of God's relations with mankind and they show in the light of that testimony by what means God's desire for peace among humankind and through human beings can be realized."[23]

The German bishops go on to say that the absence of war does not mean peace: "The Christian testimony to peace must be verified and supplemented by active service on behalf of that righteousness which alone permits and sustains lasting peace."[24]

The German bishops call Christians seeking unity with God to a concern even more important than establishing earthly peace: "When we as Christians speak of peace, then we are speaking of more than simply the peace which can be maintained, safeguarded, endangered or destroyed in political or military terms . . . the closer peace of God can never be so personally and effectively felt as in the celebration of the Eucharist."[25]

A Catholic in the modern world, then, is called to look beyond the limited offerings of the earthly life and seek a peace that is wholly satisfying and "true" to the ultimate goal of a Christian—to be united with his Creator. Striving for this spiritual unity, and not earthly peace, must be the ultimate goal in a Catholic's life in order to achieve God's peace.

But Catholics must still live with the imperfections of this world. Church teaching is a guide to help us respond to this challenge. But, in using these teachings in their response, the Catholic is given the responsibility to use God-given "free will" and to make judgments that are consistent with his conscience. In this light, a Catholic who wants to make an informed judgment about concrete issues, such as nuclear arms policy, must examine Church history and Catholic teaching. This history is the measurement that must be applied to current policies.

The American bishops, in reaffirming the Christian moral duty to defend, to use proportionate means and nondiscriminate strategy in this defense, and to oppose the "intrinsic evil" of Marxism-Leninism, also include many judgments in their letter. The bishops regard "no first use" of nuclear weapons as the morally correct defense policy, they question the morality of deterrence to defend our freedom, and they view the possible use and/or threat of nuclear weapons as evil as using them. The

23. German bishops, *Out of Justice, Peace*, p. 11.
24. Ibid., p. 46.   25. Ibid., p. 66.

bishops, however, point out that these decisions are judgments. They write, "Readers should be aware . . . of the distinction between our statement of moral principles and of official church teaching and our application of these to concrete issues."[26]

The policy has been to resist aggression and protect freedom in accord with what Pope John Paul II calls the Christian ". . . right and duty . . . to protect their existence and freedom. . . ."[27]

President Harry S. Truman said in 1952, "The new emphasis on military preparedness reflects the necessities of the world situation today. It reflects no shift of purpose. Our purpose remains to secure and strengthen peace. We are determined to seek peace by every honorable means—mindful of our responsibility to ourselves, to our friends and allies, and to humanity everywhere to spare the world the tragedy of another world war. We are likewise determined to spare ourselves and the world the even deeper tragedy of the surrender of justice and freedom."[28]

In abiding with this obligation to oppose unjust aggression, American defense policy has transformed with the changing conditions the Catholic Church has placed on this teaching.

Under John F. Kennedy, the only Catholic U.S. President, American policy was to follow the mutual assured destruction (MAD) doctrine—to target and threaten civilian populations with "devastating" power.

President Kennedy said in 1961:

Our strategic arms and defenses must be adequate to deter any deliberate nuclear attack on the United States or its allies—by making clear to any potential aggressor that sufficient retaliatory forces will be able to survive a first strike and penetrate his defenses in order to inflict unacceptable losses upon him . . . what we have and must continue to have is the ability to survive a first blow and respond with devastating power.[29]

During the Carter Administration, we began to move away from the MAD doctrine. This movement was consistent with Catholic teaching because the MAD doctrine advocated the targeting of civilian populations and massive means of retaliation. President Reagan continues to direct American nuclear policy in accord with Catholic teaching. His Administration is the first to state categorically that the United States does not intentionally or directly target Soviet cities.

President Reagan, in a speech on March 23, 1983, remarked, "What if free people could live secure in the knowledge that their security did

26. U.S. bishops' Summary of "War and Peace," *ORIGINS*, Vol. 13, No. 6 (June 23, 1983), p. 101.

27. *The Challenge of Peace*, n. 106.

28. President Harry S. Truman, *Public Papers of the Presidents*, 1952 Annual Budget Message to the Congress (January 15, 1951), pp. 61–62.

29. President John F. Kennedy, *Public Papers of the President* (1961), p. 231.

not rest upon the threat of instant U.S. retaliation to deter a Soviet attack; that we could intercept and destroy strategic ballistic missiles before they reached our own soil or that of our allies? . . . Would it not be better to save lives than to avenge them? . . ."[30] Ironically, this proposal, known as the "Strategic Defense Initiative," has incurred the wrath of the nuclear freeze movement, even though it is absolutely consistent with Catholic Church teaching.

While many Catholics may still have doubts about the morality of American nuclear arms policy, they cannot ignore the fact that we have a moral obligation to oppose the "intrinsic evil" of Marxism-Leninism. American policy has been consistent with this teaching.

President John F. Kennedy in 1963 described Communism as the "selling out of the soul." He went on to conclude that,

If there is one fact, it seems to me, larger than any other, it is that the last decade has proved that those who sell their souls to the Communist system under the mistaken belief that the Communist system offers a quick and sure road to economic prosperity have been proven wholly wrong. . . . The fact is that the last decade has conclusively proven that communism is a system which has outlived its time, that the true road to prosperity, the true road to progress, is by democratic means. . . . It seems to me incumbent upon us all to make that promise bright in the remainder of the sixties. . . .[31]

President Reagan has been even more specific about the evil of Communism. It is vitally important to note that he quotes directly from the creators of this system:

During my first press conference as President . . . I pointed out that as good Marxist-Leninists the Soviet leaders have openly and publicly declared that the only morality they recognize is that which will further their cause, which is world revolution. . . . I was only quoting Lenin, their guiding spirit, who said in 1920 that they repudiate all morality that proceeds from supernatural ideas or ideas that are outside class conceptions . . . everything is moral that is necessary for the annihilation of the old exploiting social order and for uniting the proletariat.

Reagan went on to say, "Let us be aware that while they preach the supremacy of the state, declare its onmipotence over individual man, and predict its eventual domination of all peoples of the Earth—they are the focus of evil in the modern world."[32]

President Reagan has been ridiculed for being so consistent with Catholic teaching. Yet, even Popes have identified this Marxist-Leninist state as the "evil empire."

---

30. President Ronald W. Reagan, Presidential Address (March 23, 1983).

31. Kennedy, *Public Papers* (1963), p. 549.

32. President Ronald W. Reagan, Presidential Speech to the National Association of Evangelicals (March 8, 1983), Orlando, Florida, p. 4.

Allow me to repeat the words of Pope Pius XI: "See to it, venerable brethren, that the faithful do not allow themselves to be deceived. Communism is intrinsically wrong, and no one who would save Christian civilization may collaborate with it in any undertaking whatsoever." No one would dare ridicule Pope Pius for such a harsh statement, much harsher than calling the Soviet Union an evil empire.

These historical facts clearly indicate that American nuclear arms policy has been developed on judgments consistent with Catholic moral teaching. Catholics can be proud of America's commitment to abide by Church policy.

Yet despite the historical record, nuclear freeze advocates within the Church continue to question this consistency and commitment. In particular, the religious leaders holding a "pacifist" stance accuse the United States of leading the arms race, being insincere in arms talks, threatening the human needs of all people, and exaggerating the threat of Marxism-Leninism. Let us examine each charge.

Bishop Roger Mahony, in "The Case for Nuclear Pacifism," wrote in 1981, that, "With each new American acquisition the Soviets rushed to catch up and vice versa. Now we are making an unprecedented leap in arms expenditures a precondition for any arms-limitation talks with the Soviets."[33]

This is a judgment that ignores the facts.

The U.S. expenditures on defense since the 1970's show remarkable restraint. It is remarkable because the United States clearly had the opportunity to "outrace" the Soviet Union in weapons, both nuclear and conventional. Yet, we chose to make reductions in missiles, bombers, and nuclear warheads throughout the 1960's and the 1970's.

In 1968, we unilaterally froze the number of land-based missiles at 1,054; the number now stands at 1,045. Sea-launched missiles remained constant at 656 from 1972 to 1980. By 1981, their number decreased to 576. The fleet of ballistic missile submarines was held steady at 41 boats throughout the 1970's, and then shrank to 31. The strategic bomber force stood at 1,364 in 1964. Today, it stands at 316. The number of interceptor aircraft assigned to the strategic defense of the continental United States dramatically decreased from 1,800 in 1964 to 312 in 1982. Moreover, the United States initially deployed only one of two possible antiballistic missile sites allowed under SALT I, and dismantled it in 1975.[34]

The number of weapons tell only part of the story. Defense spending

---

33. Mahony, "The Case for Nuclear Pacifism," p. 288.

34. For additional information see "On Myth and Peace," Terry Hall, *National Catholic Register* (August 1, 1982).

has also fallen with respect to total budget expenditures. In 1962, defense made up 45.9 percent of the budget; by 1978 it had declined to 23.3 percent. The 1983 budget increased defense spending to 26.4 percent, and the 1985 budget proposes to increase it to 27 percent.[35]

Funds specifically for atomic weapons are only a fraction of this budget. According to the Department of Defense figures for the $305 billion fiscal year (FY) 1985 defense budget (which has already been reduced by the House and Senate), $152 billion is estimated to be spent on conventional weapons, while $31.6 billion is estimated to be spent on strategic weapons. This means only 10 percent of the budget will actually be spent on strategic weapons; 10 percent of the less than 27 percent of the entire FY 1985 defense budget.[36]

Furthermore, less than 50 percent of this budget will be for the procurement and research/development of all weaponry. More than 57 percent of the defense budget is devoted to military pay, retirement, and the maintenance of existing forces.

Michael Novak, in his book *Moral Clarity in the Nuclear Age*, wrote:

The total money spent on nuclear weapons and their technology has been a very small fraction of U.S. economic resources. Expenditures on the research and production of nuclear weapons by the U.S. since 1945 have been estimated to be less than $400 billion, about $12 billion a year. In FY 1983, U.S. expenditures on nuclear weapons constituted 9% of the military budget, 2.9% of the entire federal budget, and about 0.6% of the GNP.[37]

This voluntary restraint on defense spending continues under the Reagan Administration. NATO announced a plan in November 1983 to eliminate more than 23 percent of its arsenal of tactical nuclear arms. NATO will also withdraw 1,400 nuclear warheads from European soil over the next several years, reducing NATO warheads to 4,600 when combined with the 1,000 warheads already withdrawn.[38]

But, while we show restraint, the Soviets relentlessly continue to build up their defense capabilities. They are the ones fueling a single-nation arms race. The NATO Nuclear Planning Group writes, "In recent months the Soviet Union has continued construction of at least three new SS-20 bases east of the Ural Mountains, in addition to the already deployed 351 operational SS-20 launchers comprising 1,053 nuclear

35. "Rebuilding Our Defenses: The Reagan Administration's Record on Defense Issues" (Washington, D.C.: Republican National Committee, September 1983), p. 5.

36. For additional information, see *Fiscal Year 1985 Department of Defense Annual Budget*.

37. Michael Novak, *Moral Clarity in the Nuclear Age* (New York: Thomas Nelson Publishers, 1983), pp. 43–44.

38. Charles Corddry, "NATO Planning to Eliminate Nuclear Anti-Aircraft Missiles," *Baltimore Sun*, (November 10, 1983), p. 14.

warheads."[39] The Soviets are also retaining a large number of SS-4 and SS-5 missiles and replacing older systems with a new generation of more accurate systems, namely, the SS-21, SS-22, and SS-23.[40]

The Soviet Union expenditures on defense show that since the 1970's, they have been outspending the United States on strategic forces by a factor of three-to-one. The U.S.S.R. surpassed NATO in total destructive power in its strategic systems in the late 1960's and in the number of strategic nuclear delivery vehicles in 1973.

The Soviets have concentrated most of their nuclear warheads in their land-based missiles, the most lethal weapon—the intercontinental ballistic missile (ICBM). Sixty-two percent of the Soviet warhead stockpile is maintained for ICBM's, while the United States designates only 31 percent.[41]

The Soviets also hold a monopoly on the largest and most powerful missile—the SS-18, and they continue to build on the average one missile per day. The Soviets build even while negotiating—or demanding reductions in U.S. weaponry.

Even if we ignore the nuclear stockpiles of each nation and focus on conventional weaponry, the Warsaw Pact countries (the Soviet Union and their communist allies), have a huge lead on NATO allies. The Warsaw Pact has a total of 42,500 tanks to our 13,000, 31,500 artillery and mortars to our 10,750, 173 manpower divisions compared to our 84, and 4,370 tactical interceptor aircraft to our 740.[42]

Finally, the Warsaw Pact has a chemical weapons advantage that ranges from a factor of 10 to 1 to a factor of 100 to 1. The biological weaponry advantage is incalculable. The United States has destroyed all its biological weapons.

If one argues that the United States is "racing" with the Soviet Union in an arms buildup, then these figures showing a decline in our weapons arsenal, and a unilateral build-down in certain categories, are being ignored. In fact, the Soviet Union has been racing all by itself.

Nuclear freeze advocates within the Church also accuse the United States of being a stumbling block to arms talks. Yet, historically the United States has been sincere in arms treaties.

Probably the most famous arms-control treaty is the Baruch Plan, introduced in 1945 by the United States. It is the first and only proposal to eliminate entirely "the use of atomic energy for destructive pur-

39. NATO Press Release, "NATO Nuclear Planning Group: Final Communique" (October 28, 1983), p. 1.
40. Ibid.
41. *NATO and the Warsaw Pact: Force Comparisons* (Washington, D.C.: Government Printing Office, 1983), p. 25.
42. "Rebuilding Our Defenses," p. 22.

poses." Unfortunately, the Baruch Plan was rejected by the Soviet Union because it opposed placing control of nuclear weapons in the hands of an international body.[43]

Although some have argued that the United States should share the blame for the collapse of the Baruch Plan, the historical record tells a different story. In fact, the Soviets did not want to give up the future possibility that they could have the technology to develop nuclear weaponry. The Soviet Union advanced counterproposals to the Baruch Plan aimed to leave control with national governments, making it almost worthless because it could not be verified.

The Antarctic Treaty, introduced by the United States in 1958, was a precedent in arms agreements because it closed off the region to military purposes. Its goal was to keep the Antarctic continent open to scientific and other peaceful projects. This has been a success and is an excellent example of exercising foresight to avoid future conflicts.

Further, the U.S.-initiated "Hot Line" Agreement in 1961 was also a first in relations between any country in the world. The United States proposed a group of measures to reduce the risk of war, including plans to allow for advanced notification of military movements and maneuvers as well as establishing a system of "rapid and reliable communications."

The Nuclear Non-Proliferation Treaty was introduced by the United States in 1965 to prevent the spread of nuclear weapons. To date, this has been very successful in keeping nuclear power and control out of the hands of terrorists.

The current Strategic Arms Reduction Talks (START), initiated by President Reagan, are additional sincere efforts to address the long-range intercontinental weapons systems. The U.S. goal is to make "real reductions" in the number of nuclear warheads, ballistic missiles, and throw-weight of both sides. These talks have been stymied because the Soviet Union has proven to be intransigent at the bargaining table.

The Intermediate-Range Nuclear Force talks (INF), based in Geneva, are stalled because the Soviet Union walked out, a fact that is not disputed. The U.S. goal is to reduce the number of intermediate-range nuclear forces deployed in Europe by both sides.

President Reagan has also continued the Mutual and Balanced Force Reduction talks (MBFR), based in Vienna. These talks are to increase the security of Europe by decreasing the number of troops and conventional armaments deployed by NATO and the Warsaw Pact.

The United States has also gone the extra mile in arms negotiations,

---

43. *Arms Control and Disarmament Agreements: Texts and Histories of Negotiations* (Washington, D.C.: Arms Control and Disarmament Agency, 1982), p. 6.

offering confidence-building measures to improve the "Hot Line" agreement and to reduce, through peaceful means, the risk of war. No other nation has been so involved in controlling and reducing nuclear weaponry.

The advocates of "pacifist" efforts within the Church have also accused the United States of spending too much money on defense, thereby depriving people of essential human services. The facts do not support this accusation.

Defense outlays as a percentage of federal outlays were 23.8 percent in FY 1981, while 76.2 percent were for nondefense outlays. In FY 1984, the percentage devoted to defense is 27.1 percent, while the remaining nondefense percentage is 72.9 percent.[44]

The 1984 Department of Defense Annual Report to Congress stated that

The defense share of federal outlays has dropped from an average of 48% in the 1950s to about 30% today. Even with the continuing buildup, defense spending will account for only one-third of the federal budget in FY 1989. Non-defense spending, on the other hand, constituted about 50% of total federal outlays in the 1950s, but now represents more than 70% of the budget.[45]

Let us look at it another way. Using current prices, the federal government spent $195.7 billion in total budget outlays in 1970: $81.7 billion was for defense and $66.1 billion was for direct payments to individuals, including such programs as Social Security, AFDC, child nutrition programs, and Medicare. By 1980, total budget outlays had increased to $576.7 billion, with $134 billion for defense and $283.1 billion for direct payments to individuals.[46] Defense spending has not even doubled in this 10-year period, whereas entitlement programs have more than quadrupled. The present Administration will continue to spend more on these programs, estimating $237.5 billion for defense and $413.2 billion in 1985 for social programs.[47]

The issue least raised by nuclear freeze advocates is their opposition to the intrinsic evil of Marxism-Leninism. Some even question any opposition.

In an interview with *U.S. News and World Report* on December 20, 1982, Thomas Gumbleton, auxiliary bishop of Detroit, was asked if he would ". . . deem it preferable for Russia to dominate the U.S. and the West rather than for those democratic countries to possess and use nuclear weapons in self-defense." Bishop Gumbleton's response was that

44. For additional information, see *Fiscal Year 1984 Department of Defense Annual Report to the Congress* (Washington, D.C.: Government Printing Office), p. 65.
45. Ibid.
46. Ibid.   47. Ibid.

"It would be preferable to me; and not only preferable, but it is the only choice I could make—to choose to do what is right, even if it meant the loss of my freedom. I am not saying I'd rather be red than dead. I wouldn't choose either one, but I will choose to do what I know is morally right at whatever cost."[48]

Bishop Roger Mahony states in *The Apocalyptic Premise*: "We must not evade the real danger posed by Soviet policy, but we must refuse to 'demonize' them and caricature their views and aspirations."[49] Kay Camp, the 1979 international president of the Women's International League for Peace and Freedom (WILPF), goes further when she regards the Soviet invasion of Afghanistan as a reasonable reaction to border relations. She writes that "While military intervention is always regrettable, the Soviet interest in having close relations with a neighboring country with which it shares a 2,000 mile border is understandable."[50] Unfortunately, the close relationship between the Soviet Union and Afghanistan has been documented to be in the form of yellow rain.

The massacre of 269 passengers on board the Korean Airliner, KAL 007, indicates that Soviet policy needs to be taken seriously. Secretary of State George Shultz, quoting Foreign Minister Gromyko on September 7, 1983, provides a haunting reminder to any country that dares to enter the Soviet territory uninvited: "We state . . . in Soviet territory the borders of the Soviet Union are sacred." The White House further details this threat by quoting from the government-run Soviet Tass news agency: "Their commentator, Yuriy Kornilov, writes that his country will continue to act 'in compliance with Soviet laws' calling for the shooting down of unarmed aircraft which may chance to fly over their airspace."[51] By their actions, we must acknowledge the intrinsic evil of a Marxist state.

The Connecticut Catholic bishops' letter, *On the Communist Doctrine of Marxism-Leninism*, states, "Indeed, even some clergy and religious have been duped into advocating Marxism. They forget, or choose not to realize, that Christianity—which they espouse—and Marxism are antithetical: one cannot at the same time believe in God and deny Him."[52]

Marx wrote, "Religion is the opium of the people. . . . The first requisite for the happiness of the people is the abolition of religion."

48. "Should Church Oppose Nuclear Arms?" *U.S. News and World Report*.

49. Mahony, "The Case for Nuclear Pacifism."

50. Rael Jean Isaac and Erich Isaac, "The Counterfeit Peacemakers," *The Apocalyptic Premise*, p. 160.

51. Department of State Bulletin, 83: No. 2079, White House Statement (September 7, 1983), p. 12.

52. Connecticut bishops, *The Communist Doctrine of Marxism-Leninism*, p. 2.

Lenin wrote, "Communism will never succeed until the myth of God is removed from the minds of men."[53]

Aleksandr Solzhenitsyn, the exiled writer of the Soviet Union, and a survivor of the Gulag camp, has a much more direct explanation of the threat of Marxism-Leninism to the Christian faith. He said in his book, *The Dawn of Hope*:

> Within the philosophical system of Marx and Lenin and at the heart of their psychology, hatred of God is the principal driving force, more fundamental than all their political and economic pretensions. Militant atheism is not merely incidental or marginal to communist policy; it is not a side effect, but the central pivot . . . Communists proclaim both of these objectives openly, and just as openly put them into practice.[54]

Perhaps, then, the most important obligation of a Catholic who seeks peace is not to judge American policy, but to pray for peace and for the conversion of Russia.

> No one can properly understand the dramatic change in Catholic thinking on war and peace without first considering the tradition of Fatima in twentieth-century Catholicism. The message given to the three children by the Virgin at Fatima in 1917 was that World War I would soon end, but another more horrible war would follow, and another still more horrible war loomed in the future. Russia would succumb to atheism and "spread her errors throughout the world," ushering in a conflagration that would destroy two entire great nations. All this could be avoided, Mary told the children, only by prayer. . . . In the United States . . . , Catholic priests and bishops offered a steady drumbeat of advice to their parishioners who were worried about nuclear war: "Pray the rosary. Pray for peace. Pray for the conversion of Russia."[55]

Unfortunately, in writing the American pastoral letter, the assembled bishops refused even to mention Fatima in the 100-page final text.

Catholics are obligated to reflect seriously upon the opinions of the American bishops in their pastoral letter, as well as the morally binding teachings of the Church. Catholics will differ on specific policy recommendations and strategy. But all must unite in their defense of their Christian faith in a world of conflict. Solzhenitsyn writes of the experience of his countrymen, leaving us with a challenge and hope.

> It is true that millions of our countrymen have been corrupted and spiritually devastated by an officially imposed atheism, yet there remain many millions of believers. . . . It is here that we see the dawn of hope: for no matter how

---

53. Ibid., p. 4.
54. Aleksandr Solzhenitsyn, "The Dawn of Hope," *Soviet Analyst*, Vol. 12 (May 18, 1983), p. 8.
55. Philip Lawler, "Guarded Prophecies: The Bishops Hedge Their Nuclear Bets," in *The Ultimate Weapon* (Chicago: Regnery Gateway, 1984).

formidably communism bristles with tanks and missiles, no matter what successes it attains in seizing the planet, it is doomed never to vanquish Christianity.[56]

Catholics can be proud that American nuclear arms policy has been both consistent with Church teaching and responsive to the conflict all Catholics face in their journey toward true peace. Those who dispute this conclusion are, indeed, engaging in revisionist history.[57]

56. Solzhenitsyn, "The Dawn of Hope," p. 4.
57. For further reading on the issue of Christian morality and nuclear weapons, see *The Apocalyptic Premise*, eds. Ernest W. Lefever and E. Stephen Hunt (Washington, D.C.: Ethics and Public Policy Center, 1982); *The Challenge of Peace: God's Promise and Our Response* (Washington, D.C.: United States Catholic Conference, 1983); Connecticut Catholic bishops, *The Communist Doctrine of Marxism-Leninism* (1982); French bishops' pastoral letter, *Winning the Peace* (1983); German bishops' pastoral letter, *Out of Justice, Peace: The Church in the Service of Peace* (1983); Malcolm Muggeridge, "Muggeridge Sees Deliverance Despite West's Despair," *Los Angeles Times* (June 17, 1979); *Abortion and the Catholic Church* (Washington, D.C.: United States Catholic Conference, 1983/84); Michael Novak, *Moral Clarity in the Nuclear Age* (New York: Thomas Nelson Publishers, 1983); Aleksandr Solzhenitsyn, "The Dawn of Hope," *Soviet Analyst* (May 18, 1983); *Arms Control and Disarmament Agreements: Texts and Histories of Negotiations* (Washington, D.C.: United States Arms Control and Disarmament Agency, 1982).

ROBERT R. REILLY

13. In Proportion to What? The Problem with the Pastoral

One is obliged to take into consideration the massive presence of violence in human history. It is the sense of reality in the service of the fundamental concern for justice which forces me to maintain the principle of legitimate defense in this history.
—John Paul II, World Day of Peace Message (January 1, 1984)

However much the power of the West may have declined, however great the dangers to the West may be, that decline, that danger, nay, the defeat, even the destruction of the West would not necessarily prove that the West is in a crisis: the West could go down in honor, certain of its purpose. The crisis of the West consists in the West's having become uncertain of its purpose. The West was once certain of its purpose—of a purpose in which all men could be united, and hence it had a clear vision of its future as the future of mankind. We do no longer have that certainty and that clarity. Some among us even despair of the future, and this despair explains many forms of contemporary Western degradation.
—Leo Strauss, *The City and Man*

At the outset I wish to make clear that I do not share the opinion of those who say the bishops have no right to address the issue of justice and war in the nuclear age. They have every right to address this issue, indeed an obligation to do so. Morality infuses every part of man's life and is an element in almost all his choices, most certainly in those deciding war and peace. Every choice one makes is a selection for better or worse ultimately judged against a standard of what is good. And what is good in the eyes of the Church resides finally in the judgments on faith and morals made by the Magisterium, the teaching office of which the bishops are a part.

The pastoral letter, *The Challenge of Peace*, reiterates the just-war teaching of the Catholic Church. The just-war teaching is a constant of Church doctrine since at least the fifth century, having been begun by St. Augustine, developed by St. Thomas Aquinas, and elaborated upon by moralists in our own day. Certainly insofar as the pastoral letter reiterated the just-war teaching it performed an extremely valuable service.

The traditional just-war teaching forbids us to defend ourselves with destructive force when the evil or "harm" from such a defense would be greater than the good achieved. This is the principle of proportionality. To apply the principle of proportionality one must know what is at stake. The larger the value of those things at stake, the greater the exertions permitted in defense of them. As Pope Pius XII made very clear, the principle of proportionality is not to be applied in merely quantitative terms of physical destruction. The question Pius XII posed was: What would be the loss in the moral order if self-defense is not undertaken? Pope Pius XII even spoke of the "absolute necessity of self-defense against a very grave injustice that touches the community, that cannot be impeded by other means, but nevertheless must be impeded on pain of giving free field in international relations to brutal violence and lack of conscience."[1] War, then, can be a moral obligation if employed in defense against evil, if that evil cannot be prevented by other means and if there is a fair chance of success in the effort. This does not, of course, mean that once one has conscientiously established the justice of one's cause that there are no limitations to what can be done in defense of it. This is precisely what would be limited by the principle of proportionality.

However, after adopting the just-war teaching, the bishops engage in a series of "prudential moral judgments," applying the traditional teaching of the Church to the particular problems of today. The bishops had been instructed, during the drafting of the letter, to distinguish very carefully between that part of the letter that iterated traditional magisterial teaching and that part of the letter that reached prudential moral judgments, about which reasonable men can disagree. The prudential moral judgments reached by the bishops concern quite complex issues of strategic weapons systems, geopolitical realities, the features of nuclear deterrence, and the proper role of tactical nuclear weapons.

I disagree with a number of the bishops' prudential moral judgments. As a reasonable man, I think those judgments are erroneous. They do not reflect a complete understanding of what is at stake nor of the strategic situation but, more important, they do not show a firm grasp of what is at risk in the moral order.

These deficiencies can be clearly revealed by transposing the claims made by the pastoral letter to the pre-World War II period to examine them in historical perspective. If one substitutes the words "aerial bombardment" for the word "nuclear" in *The Challenge of Peace*, one would almost duplicate the arguments and rhetoric of the peace movement of the 1930's. At that time it was anticipated that the new technology of heavy aerial bombardment was so potentially destructive that its

---

1. Pope Pius XII as quoted in John Courtney Murray, *We Hold These Truths* (New York: Sheed and Ward, 1960), p. 259.

use must either be prevented or the end of civilization would follow. The charge was that aerial bombardment was not simply a difference in size but that this new size of destructive force represented a difference in *kind*. And it was this different *kind* of war that made war impossible because its consequences were unthinkable. In a way, of course, this was true: The destruction caused by World War II was beyond imagination. That, however, was not the point. It was thought that potential destruction on the scale made possible by aerial bombardment was so great that it demanded disarmament and a new world order that would ensure against its use. This universal moral obligation superseded politics itself. Certainly it was not for the outmoded sovereignty and selfish interests of petty nation-states to stand in the way of this demand for a new world order. It was as if, in the very threat of massive destruction, people were finally to discover their universal humanity through the epistemology of horror.

The only problem with these horror-induced arguments for universal disarmament and a world state is that they were made without reference to the threat of Adolf Hitler and Nazi Germany. In other words, they were totally divorced from the political realities of their day.

It was precisely the proponents of these arguments in the 1930's who unwittingly promoted accommodation to Nazi ambitions. They thought that the phenomenon of Naziism could be understood in traditional Wilhelmian terms, that Hitler could be treated like Bismarck, and that Nazi goals were limited. Some even claimed that "there is more real Christianity in Germany today than there ever was under the Weimar Republic."[2] They therefore thought the Nazis could be negotiated with and placated. If the Nazis wished to rearm the Rhineland, they had best be allowed to do so, even though a treaty was violated in the process. Perhaps peace would follow. Similarly, Austria and Czechoslovakia were taken without serious resistance. Surely, that would be the limit of Hitler's appetite. In addressing his High Command before the Polish operation, Hitler assured his officers of Allied impotence: "Our opponents are little worms. I saw them in Munich."[3] Nourished by this appeasement, Hitler's appetite grew. Hitler was not immobilized by an obsession with air-raid terror; rather he was energized by its paralytic hold on the allies. He proclaimed before invading Poland: "The stronger is the right."[4] Only with the invasion of Poland was action finally taken against the Nazis.

Thus, an unnecessary war became a necessary one. Hitler himself admitted, "If the French had marched into the Rhineland we would have

2. Paul Johnson, *Modern Times* (New York: Harper and Row, 1983), p. 306.
3. Ibid., p. 360.   4. Ibid.

had to withdraw with our tails between our legs."[5] Hitler was encouraged precisely by those who failed to appreciate what was at stake, who failed to grasp the totalitarian nature of Naziism and the mortal threat it presented to the moral order. Traumatized by visions of massive destruction, they were blinded to the true causes of the conflict.

The American Catholic hierarchy was not among those so deluded. They had a clear appreciation of Naziism's threat as America entered the war. In their joint pastoral letter, *Victory and Peace* (November 14, 1942), the bishops wrote:

> Some nations are united in waging war to bring about a slave world, a world that would deprive man of his divinely-conferred dignity, reject human freedom, and permit no religious liberty. . . . We are associated with other powers in a deadly conflict against these nations to maintain a free world. This conflict of principles makes compromise impossible.

This assessment corresponded with reality and forcefully expressed the magnitude of what was morally at stake in World War II. One wishes for a paragraph of such clarity in the new pastoral letter in the application of moral principles to political reality. Unfortunately, it is not possible to find a similar expression of the stakes in the current conflict. Why? The reason seems to be that the bishops have allowed themselves to be victimized by nuclear terror in much the same way as were those who fell victim to fear of aerial bombardment in the 1930's.

For instance, the bishops seem to accept the same inverted view of the relationship between military technologies and politics that persisted in the pre-World War II peace movement: as if the weapons themselves give rise to the threat, rather than being mere expressions of it. The bishops seem to be unaware that the political realities of today are not shaped by the nuclear bomb, but the bomb by political realities. The possession of atomic weapons by France or Great Britain does not threaten our own security because the political realities of our relationship are such as to make their use against us inconceivable. We worry about the bomb because the Soviet Union has it, because of the moral character of the Soviet regime. These political and moral realities give nuclear weapons their relevance—of and by themselves they are meaningless.

The bishops do mention certain deficiences in the Soviet Union, but they neglect any substantive analysis of totalitarian ideology and the nature of the threat it represents. Instead, like the pacifists of the 1930s, they dwell at length on the moral obligations that this new kind of nuclear weapon seems to present. Those obligations are the same as before: disarmament and world government, made imperative by the ob-

5. Ibid., p. 352.

session with nuclear terror. The only alternative to movement toward these goals is that "we shall destroy one another."[6]

Contrast the following excerpt from the present pastoral with the previously quoted passage from *Victory and Peace*:

> No relationship more dramatically demonstrates the fragile nature of order in international affairs today than that of the United States and the Soviet Union. These two sovereign states have avoided open war, nuclear or conventional, but they are divided by philosophy, ideology, and competing ambitions. Their competition is global in scope and involves everything from comparing nuclear arsenals to printed propaganda. Both have been criticized in international meetings because of their policies in the nuclear arms race.[7]

From this statement it would be very difficult to ascertain who is at fault for this state of affairs. Indeed, both nations are considered from a shallow neutrality above the clamor of the "competition" in which they are engaged. The word *competition* (which recurs, as in "East-West competition," throughout the letter) implies contestants in a game. The language used here gently nudges the reader into assuming a moral equivalence between the Soviet Union and the United States, as if both nations were directed to the same ends, as in any competition, and were using the same means to reach them. Both are subject to the same international obloquy. Differences between the two are not stated in terms of moral principle but rather are demoted to the level of "competing ambitions," or, even worse, of "ideologies."

This implied equivalence is strongly disavowed in several places in the letter but never quite convincingly. The disavowals are always followed by quick qualifications that *whatever* the differences between the two "ideologies," they can and must be overcome because of the transcending threat of nuclear war. No worries are expressed about a "slave world . . . that would deprive man of his divinely-conferred dignity, reject human freedom and permit no religious liberty." In fact, the word "evil" appears only once in the section on "The Superpowers in a Disordered World," in a papal quotation, and, even then, not in regard to the principles of the Soviet Union. Yet "evil" is the only possible word to encompass and make comprehensible the horrors visited upon the world by Marxism-Leninism. Certainly, it is difficult to admit to the nature of the struggle because it is difficult to acknowledge the existence of evil; so much follows from it in terms of moral obligation. "Seeing creates responsibility," as Archbishop Sheen used to say. Willful ignorance in the face of evil is what Solzhenitsyn calls "the desire not to know."

6. *The Challenge of Peace: God's Promise and Our Response* (Washington, D.C.: United States Catholic Conference, 1983), n. 244.
7. Ibid., n. 245.

The implied moral symmetry between the United States and the U.S.S.R. is illustrated in the following passage, which refers, even more significantly, to Christianity itself:

In a 1980 pastoral letter on Marxism we sought to portray the significant differences between Christian teaching and Marxism; at the same time we addressed the need for states with different political systems to live together in an interdependent world: "The Church recognizes the depth and dimensions of the ideological differences that divide the human race, but the urgent practical need for cooperative efforts in the human interest overrules these differences."[8]

There is a curious but consistently ambiguous use of language here. The differences between Christianity and Marxism are said to be "significant," rather than essential. Significant differences, after all, can be overcome, but not essential ones, not the kind of "conflict of principles" of which the bishops spoke in 1942. The gravity of these differences is "overruled" and therefore minimized. This demotion undercuts what could be morally justified in defense of the United States because it puts at risk in the conflict only a "competing ambition," as the letter calls it earlier, rather than a moral principle. According to the principle of proportionality, the defense of a "competing ambition" would be morally dubious at best, while the defense of moral principle would be almost morally mandatory. This deflation of the moral nature of the conflict seems rooted, not in some transcending moral good, but in fear of physical extinction.

This deflation also incapacitates one from making sound moral judgments. To transpose to another time again, it is as if an observer were dropped out of the sky at the Battle of the Bulge. What would he see? He would see the Nazi army engaged in mortal combat with the Allied forces. He would see tank battles, howitzer duels, hand-to-hand combat, with soldiers of both sides thrusting bayonets into the bodies of the other side. From such a close-hand observation, the observer would see that one side behaved pretty much as did the other. In his eyes both sides would be interchangeable but for their different uniforms. If the observer were morally sensitive he might be moved by the destruction he witnessed to say, "A pox on both your houses; one side is as bad as the other." In other words, from observing the Battle of the Bulge at such close quarters, he would learn nothing about the justice of the causes for which the Battle of the Bulge was fought. To learn about the justness of the two sides' respective causes, he would have to examine the principles of the Nazi regime and the principles of the Allied nations. It would be only on this basis that he could judge whether the differences were essential, nonnegotiable moral issues, whether the war was just,

8. Ibid., n. 246.

and which was the right side. From observing the battle he could learn not a thing. This is the sort of neutral observer stance that permeates the pastoral letter.

Here are several more examples of the incapacity this detached observer status confers.

For most Americans, the danger of war is commonly defined primarily in terms of the threat of Soviet military expansionism and the consequent need to deter or defend against a Soviet military threat. Many assume that the existence of this threat is permanent and that nothing can be done about it except to build and maintain overwhelming or at least countervailing military power.[9]

Notice that the truth or falsity of these assumptions is never itself addressed. The bishops themselves are not asserting these opinions but assigning them to "most Americans." Or they simply tell us that "many assume. . . ." Then, while admitting that there is, in fact, a Soviet threat, the permanence of which is dubious, the letter goes on to say, "The history of the Cold War has produced varying interpretations of which side caused which conflict, but whatever the details of history illustrate, the plain fact is that the memories of Soviet policies in Eastern Europe and recent events in Afghanistan and Poland have left their mark on the American political debate."[10]

No sides are being chosen here as to which of the "varying interpretations" might be true in describing the causes of the Cold War. When it seems as if the letter may take a side on this issue by acknowledging a "plain fact," the fact turns out to be nothing more than that the "memories" of certain people engaged in the American political debate have been affected by the recollection of Soviet behavior. But are these memories correct? Have they affected the American political debate in an adverse or a beneficial way?

The closest we come to an answer to these questions is provided in the next sentence. "Many peoples are forceably kept under Communist domination despite their manifest wishes to be free. Soviet power is very great."[11] Finally we have the outright assertion of fact.

However, the next sentence lapses back into ambivalence. "Whether the Soviet Union's pursuit of military might is motivated primarily by defensive or aggressive arms might be debated, but the effect is nevertheless to leave profoundly insecure those who must live in the shadow of that might."[12] Here we have moved from the mnemonic to the psychological. It appears the important thing is not whether the arms of the Soviet Union are defensive or aggressive, but the fact that people are left "profoundly insecure" by those arms, as if the problem were pri-

---

9. Ibid., n. 248.   11. Ibid.
10. Ibid., n. 249.   12. Ibid.

marily a psychological one. If so, is the psychological response neurotic or healthy? The answer must depend on the actual fact as to whether the arms of the Soviet Union are primarily defensive or aggressive, but we are left with the impression that this remains a matter of debate, not yet settled, despite 68 years of Soviet imperial expansion. The letter's indecision notwithstanding, students of military strategy are agreed that the majority of Soviet arms are deployed in an offensive posture. Large armies of tanks, for instance, are *designed* for offense.

The letter continues in the next paragraph: "Americans need have no illusions about the Soviet system of repression and the lack of respect in that system for human rights or about Soviet covert operations and pro-revolutionary activities."[13] One is led to expect here a hard-headed approach to the Soviet Union, but the imprecision and diction in this sentence can lead to the illusions that it is supposedly preventing. For instance, the problem in the Soviet system is not "the lack of respect for human rights," but rather the explicit denial of their very existence. This "repression and lack of respect," then, is not an exception to, or a flaw within, the Soviet rule but rather an expression of its basic principles. It is to the principles of the regime that the letter so often fails to speak, thus neglecting the ends the regime serves.

The next sentence contains the usual qualification that this neglect of principles leads to: "To be sure, our own system is not without flaws. Our government has sometimes supported repressive governments in the name of preserving freedom, has carried out repugnant covert operations of its own and remains imperfect in its domestic record of insuring equal rights for all."[14] Having made this "invidious comparison," the letter in the middle of the next paragraph admits: "The facts simply do not support the invidious comparisons made at times even in our own society between our way of life, in which most basic human rights are at least recognized even if they are not always adequately supported, and those totalitarian and tyrannical regimes in which such rights are either denied or systematically suppressed."[15] This last statement, as well as several others, considerably relieves the impression of moral equivalence between the superpowers that is conveyed by the rhetorical weight of the rest of the document. Such exemplary statements, however, do not seem an integral part of the document because they are not coherently developed or steadfastly maintained. They seem to be concessionary, inserted perhaps to placate those on the committee who objected to the rest of the document.

Troubles arise again by the end of the paragraph in which it is as-

13. Ibid., n. 250.
14. Ibid.

15. Ibid., n. 251.

serted: "Many attempts to justify, for reasons of state, support for regimes that continue to violate human rights is all the more morally reprehensible in its hypocrisy."[16] Here again is neglected the distinction
between regimes that acknowledge but fall short of human rights, and
those whose abuses are an expression of their denial of the very existence of human rights. That this quoted statement is foolish, if not indeed hypocritical itself, can be seen in the attempted application of its
litmus test to: the Shah of Iran versus Khomeini in Iran; Lon Nol versus
Pol Pot in Cambodia; President Thieu versus Ho Chi Minh and his successors in South Vietnam. Rather than "morally reprehensible," the
choice of a lesser evil in political life is morally obligatory. The sentence
quoted is quite dangerous in its failure to distinguish between totalitarian and authoritarian regimes, a distinction that will be discussed later.
Nor does it acknowledge the need for statesmanship, which is the art of
prudence.

One of the most sensible parts of this section of the letter is an extensive quotation from Pope John Paul II from his 1983 World Day of
Peace message, in which he speaks of ideologies "that see in force the
source of rights," rather than in the laws of nature and nature's God.
The "cold realism" of this text however is immediately translated by the
bishops into their conclusion that despite

all the differences between the two philosophies and political systems, the
irreducible truth is that objective mutual interests do exist between the super
powers. Proof of this concrete if limited convergence of interest can be found
in some vitally important agreements on nuclear weapons which have already
been negotiated in the areas of nuclear testing and nuclear explosions in space
as well as the SALT I agreements.[17]

The extremely limited way in which this statement may be true can only
be understood if one at first realizes that the Soviet Union itself vehe-
mently denies the existence of "objective mutual interest" with the
West. Marxism-Leninism denies the notion of a shared common good
with non-Marxists because it denies the existence of human nature. To
suppose that Soviet dread at the prospect of total nuclear war is based
on some sudden apprehension of the common humanity of all people is
a grievous error. Soviet motivation for avoiding such a total nuclear
exchange is not based upon moral principle but on the fear that the revolution itself may be physically destroyed. This would represent the
total repudiation of Marx and his historical materialism. It is illusory to
claim that this reluctance to sacrifice their revolution constitutes "objective mutual interests" with the West. This illusion also ignores two
things: that the Soviets operate with a strategy of fighting and winning

16. Ibid.   17. Ibid., n. 255.

a nuclear war, if possible, and that the Soviets have violated almost every treaty in which they have been engaged. These "agreements" do not represent a "convergence of interest," but a cynical affair of convenience that the Soviets have used to enhance their strategic goals. Noting the aggressive and dominating character of Marxism-Leninism, the French bishops in their pastoral letter remarked: "In this ideology, everything, even the aspirations of nations for peace, must be utilized for the conquest of the world."[18]

Also, the apocalyptic attitude the bishops adopt toward nuclear weapons prevents them from understanding the political functions nuclear weapons serve. A recent example is provided by the tremendous political influence over Western Europe that the installation of more than 370 SS-20 triple warhead missiles gave the Soviet Union. The political purpose of these weapons will be more fully addressed at the end of this chapter.

The last paragraph of this section of the letter closes with the following advice: "Soviet behavior in some cases merits the adjective reprehensible, but the Soviet people and their leaders are human beings created in the image and likeness of God."[19] This insight follows the advice that the United States should seriously consider a *modus vivendi* in political, economic, and scientific areas with the Soviet Union.

One can demonstrate the distance from political reality this document achieves by substituting the word *Nazi* for the word *Soviet* wherever it appears. Of course this exercise will have effect only if one accepts the moral equivalence of Naziism and Marxism-Leninism. For the time being only let Molotov's statement after the signing of the infamous Nazi-Soviet pact in 1939 stand for the compatibility that the Nazis and Communists themselves accepted: "As for whether one is a Communist or a Nazi, that is a matter of taste."

One can imagine the insipidity of being reminded that the Nazis are people too. But it is no less ridiculous than to be reminded that the Soviets are people. What does our recollection that the Soviets are people help us to do? Properly understood, it would help us make the vital distinction between the people and the regime and appreciate that the Soviet peoples are the first and most long-suffering of the victims of the Soviet regime that enslaves them. However, our attention is not drawn to this fact, but away from it, as if the Soviet regime and the people it rules were indistinguishable. (Indeed, the Soviet rulers are people too.) It invites us to humanize the Soviet regime on the ironic basis that the subjects it oppresses are human.

18. J. V. Schall, ed., *Out of Justice, Peace, and Winning the Peace* (San Francisco: Ignatius Press, 1984), p. 104.
19. *The Challenge of Peace*, n. 258.

The counsel that we transcend our differences with the Nazis to reach an economic, political, and scientific *modus vivendi* with them would have been found morally repugnant by the bishops who signed the joint pastoral letter of 1942. They understood what the loss of the principles they were prepared to defend would mean for mankind. The current pastoral letter on war and peace neglects to explain adequately the differences in moral principle between the United States and the Soviet Union and therefore is an insufficient guide in answering the vitally important question of what is at stake in the conflict. This is a grievous omission because it makes it impossible to apply the principle of proportionality prudently.

To apply the principle of proportionality in today's world, one would have to answer Joseph Cropsey's question, "Do we have any reason for believing that the Sovietization of the world is an evil commensurate with the peril of opposing it?"[20]

To appreciate what the Sovietization of the world would mean requires an understanding of totalitarian ideology. At the beginning of the pastoral letter there is the statement: "Peace is the fruit of order: order and human society must be shaped on the basis of respect for the transcendence of God and the unique dignity of each person. . . . "[21] What must be addressed is the problem posed by a regime that denies this "transcendence of God" and the unique dignity of each person and therefore makes impossible the order of justice.

This antipathy between peace and injustice is clearly seen in the period since 1945, which has witnessed a "peace" in which there have been more casualties to state violence than in either world war or all subsequent conflagrations. The body count in the Soviet Union exceeds 60 million, gone in Lubyanka Prison, in the forced starvation campaigns of the Ukraine and in the Gulag. Gone, too, is a third of the population of Cambodia, and no one knows how many Chinese have fallen victim to state violence since 1949.

How is it, under conditions of "peace," that casualties of this enormity occur? The answer lies in the nature of modern totalitarian ideology, the two most virulent manifestations of which are Naziism and Communism. What both of these ideologies did or do, one on the basis of race, the other on the basis of class, is to allow the dehumanization of human beings.

How these ideologies function cannot be understood unless one realizes that the fundamental act at the root of all civilization is the recog-

20. Robert A. Goldwin, ed., *America Armed* (Chicago: Rand McNally and Company, 1963), p. 83.
21. *The Challenge of Peace*, Summary.

nition of another person as a human being. As simple as this may sound, it is profound. The tribal societies of the ancient, prephilosophic world were incapable of this act, as are tribal societies that exist today. A Spartan, for instance, could not conceive of himself as a human being, but only as a Spartan in service to the gods of his city. When he attacked Athens, the Spartan could ransack it, rape the women, enslave the children, and kill the men, all in service to the gods of Sparta, the gods of Athens having just been defeated.

Greek philosophy, however, came to recognize that all men are constituted in the same essential way and are directed toward a common good, transcending all differences. With the discovery of human nature came the recognition that there is a single standard of justice for all men. One could no longer have one standard of justice for Spartans and another for Athenians. Justice would henceforth demand equality of rights. A Spartan must treat an Athenian in the same way he would a Spartan because they are essentially the same. This was a tremendously revolutionary assertion to make in the ancient polis because it undermined the gods upon which the polis was founded. If a standard of justice transcended the city, it also transcended the gods of the city. Socrates, accused of impiety, had to forfeit his life as the price for making this claim.

Eventually, this understanding of human nature fused with the monotheism of the Judeo-Christian tradition as it spread throughout the Hellenistic world. It became clear that the justice above man and above the city, the good to which man was directed, was God Himself who was to be reached through the saving sacrifice of Jesus Christ.

This view of man and his relationship to God had within it a restricted view of politics. The political order could not bring about the ultimate good of salvation that belongs to the order of grace. Rather the role of politics within this hierarchy of values was to ensure those material and temporal conditions of life necessary to the practice of virtue and the achievement of the good. Augustine and orthodox Christian writers always recognized that perfection could not be attained on earth. This is the basis of Augustine's distinction between the City of God and the City of Man.

The contention of modern ideology as it came to be expressed as early as Rousseau, but most especially by Nietzsche, and, of course, by Marx and then Lenin, was that the source of disorder in human life, that is, the cause of human unhappiness, is something other than sin, the dislocation in the relationship between God and man, which Christ had overcome. Their aim was to heal man without God. In fact, these writers contended that the existence of God itself sets limits to man's greatness and robs mankind of the opportunity of attaining perfection. They believed in the reverse of the Promethean myth: It was not man who stole fire from the gods, but God who stole fire from man. Their project was to restore divinity to man. The engine of that restoration was to be the state, the new vehicle for salvation.

Modern ideology therefore found Augustine's distinction a false dichotomy. These ideologues sought the creation of the city of God, without God, here on earth. Two things alone, they contended, were required to attain the perfection of total happiness: First, the idea of God must be eliminated; second, a formula must be devised by which one could come to control history, to absorb within history man's transcendent end, or, in the words of Eric Voegelin, "to immanentize the eschaton." Their revolution against the very structure of being is obviously not a political enterprise but a metaphysical one.

God had to be eliminated from the scheme of things becase He is the source of Nature, which determines what man can and cannot do. With the disappearance of God, man's essential nature would disappear and man could be remade in a fundamental way. The formula to be devised was not the same for all the ideologues. For some, it entailed the elimination of inferior races; for others, the elimination of other classes. But the goal was the same: to gain control of all the conditions of man's life and so transform man in a fundamental way. This, for modern ideologues, was the ground for a temporal hope that supplanted the theological virtue of the same name.

The difficulty with the modern project, philosophically and intellectually, is that once the concept of God is removed, there is nothing in theory to prevent some men from degrading others to the level of subhuman.[22] Among the essentials of man's nature that were to disappear in modern ideology were reason and free will. Marx did not believe that man's reason is sufficiently independent of material forces and the particular conditions under which he lives to apprehend the truth. All that man's mind can know is class interests. Those class interests are determined by the means of production. If one changes the means of production, one changes the way man thinks. Thus man's mind is the excrescence of material forces, unable independently to come to know the truth. (This is the obverse of Pope John Paul II's assertion that ". . . man is not a being subjected to economic and political processes; these processes are subject to him.")[23]

If man cannot know the truth, what meaning is left to free will? Man has no basis of judgment with which to exercise his free will. He cannot

22. Paul Eidelberg, *Beyond Detente* (LaSalle: Sherwood-Sugden, 1977).

23. Pope John Paul as quoted in Kerry J. Koller, "Economics and Creation," *Idea Inc.* 2/4 (December 1983), p. 7.

choose unless he knows true from false, good from evil. Man in Marxist analysis is thus found bereft of reason and free will, totally conditioned by his place in society. To affect man's transformation, the state must assume control over every element of man's being, social, psychological, economic, and religious. All moral restraints are removed in order that the state might more easily bring about this transformation. As Lenin said, "We reject any morality based on extra-human and extra-class concepts. . . . We say that our morality is entirely subordinated to the interests of the proletariat's class struggle."[24] It is with this absolution that the Gulag opens its giant maw and consumes millions upon millions of human beings, all in the name of a new humanity.

Within the perspective of Naziism or Communism there are no means by which one can come to recognize another person as a human being. That faculty of recognition has been deliberately destroyed. That destruction has caused the rebarbarization and dehumanization of man. Hitler exulted: "We are barbarians; we want to be barbarians. It is an honorable title." Hitler was precisely aware of how modern ideology reduces man to the new barbarian. This new barbarian is distinct from the Spartan who sacked Athens. The new barbarian could be a product of the highest culture, could be conversant with the latest scientific technologies, and could simultaneously lack any respect for other persons as human beings. The new barbarian could wear a lab coat at Dachau, take a Jew and submerse him repeatedly in ice water until he expired, to satisfy the needs of some experiment, and could then return home, put on a recording of Schubert, and weep over the delicate beauty of it.

What has happened here? This was not an impassioned barbarian riding as part of the horde through the steppes, cutting down an enemy tribe. This was a German, a product of one of the most highly cultured civilizations the world had seen. That well-educated and cultured Germans could descend to such conduct illustrates the dramatic dehumanization brought about by modern ideology in its effort to transform the world.

In light of the nature of modern totalitarian ideology, we must look again at the letter's claim that U.S. support for regimes that continue to violate human rights is "morally reprehensible in its hypocrisy." The distinction that the pastoral neglects between a totalitarian and an authoritarian regime is simple yet profound. As indicated, the former denies the existence of normative human nature and therefore has made itself the dehumanizing vehicle for man's secular redemption and requires total control of the intellectual, moral, and social life of man. An

24. V. I. Lenin, *Selected Works* (New York: International Publishers, 1971), Vol. I, p. 613, as quoted in Eidelberg, p. 62.

authoritarian regime makes no such claims and therefore at least tacitly acknowledges the essential permanence of human nature and at least some of the limits that nature places upon the exercise of its power. Consequently it does not try to relegate to itself man's final end, but leaves his salvation to the transcendent order outside of history. This is not a difference of degree, that one is more or less repressive than the other, but a difference of kind, a metaphysical difference.

"Right is the rule of the stronger" was a refrain familiar to the ancient world as found in Thrasymachus' defense of it in Plato's *Republic*; it was updated for the modern world by Machiavelli, enshrined in the all-powerful state of Hegel, incarnated in the 20th century by Lenin and Hitler, who repeated the refrain exactly: "The stronger is the right." The status of this dictum changed, however, from the cynical observation of the success of tyrants to a metaphysical postulate. In the ancient world, tyranny was limited by the reach of the tyrant's will: It was a moral disorder. In modern ideology, this disorder is not only moral, it is intellectual and metaphysical. That is why it is systematized and affects all aspects of life. It is an inversion of reality that is insisted upon not only by the will but by the mind. It is the product not only of disordered appetite but of mental derangement.

Selective condemnation of human-rights abuses is the proper response to an authoritarian regime's policy. The condemnation must be strong but not subversive of the regime lest the way be paved for the extinction of human rights altogether, à la Vietnam, Cambodia, Iran, etc. Likewise, when abuses are denounced in totalitarian regimes, it should be done in such a way as to make clear that those regimes are abuses in and of themselves.

Since modern ideology demands for its success the total metaphysical transformation of the world, it is not difficult to conclude that the foreign policy goals of a nation whose animating principles arise from modern ideology are similarly unlimited. As *Pravda* of March 25, 1983, informs us, the present era is the "age of the formation of a Communist future for all mankind." Philosophically, those foreign policy objectives must be unlimited, otherwise they would be inconsistent with the ideology itself. And we know from experience that modern ideology demands the internal consistency of a total lie. As Edward N. Luttwak said with masterful restraint, "The only destructive thing about the Soviet Empire is that it is an empire with no natural limits."[25]

If the foreign policy objectives of the Soviet Union are unlimited,

25. Edward N. Luttwak, "Question and Answer: The Soviet Union Seen as a Classic Land Empire," *The Washington Times* (September 16, 1983), p. 4C.

then American defense policy must be formulated with this fact in mind. If we fail to do so, if we delude ourselves into thinking we can understand Soviet policy in some conventional geopolitical way, we would be making the same error as those who thought Nazi Germany could be similarly understood.

The principles upon which the Soviet Union is based are evil, in conception and in execution. Traditional moral theology teaches us that once an evil is recognized, appropriate steps must be taken for its elimination. This does not mean we are required to go to war with the Soviet Union. The dictates of prudence and the principle of proportionality tell us that we are not to set about eliminating an evil by creating an evil worse than the first. Obviously, the dictates of prudence would forbid us to make any such attempt to eliminate the Soviet Union through nuclear warfare.

However, this understanding of modern ideology should provide us with our basic orientation toward the Soviet Union and toward the right of the United States and Western Europe to engage in measures of self-defense. In fact, we not only may; we *must* defend ourselves. The pastoral letter, it should be fairly stated, is extremely forthright in holding that this defense is not only a right but a moral duty.

But the bishops also argue that this defense cannot be undertaken in a nuclear way. The bishops are correct insofar as nuclear weapons are to be used within the parameters of mutual assured destruction, but are mistaken in their prudential moral judgment that the tactical use of nuclear weapons could probably never conform to the principles of the just-war teaching.

To understand this latter point properly, one must first briefly examine the state of strategic doctrine. The popular culture of the West, in films from *Dr. Strangelove* and *Failsafe*, to *The Day After* and *Wargames*, has cultivated the impression that our nuclear arsenal and nuclear policy exist as the result of some sort of chance or accident and that these weapons might, through some sort of accident or some mindless inattention, be set off and destroy civilization. In fact, what we see depicted in the popular culture is not the result of happenstance, but the product of a deliberately and carefully thought out strategic doctrine known as "mutual assured destruction," the acronym of which is, appropriately, MAD. I would assert that mutual assured destruction is both morally and strategically corrupt.

I regret that the bishops did not write their letter in the 1960's, at a time when more attention could have been paid to the moral inadequacies of mutual assured destruction. The so-called countervalue use of nuclear weapons, the targeting of civilian populations, the intention to build weapons that have the capacity not to hit hardened military targets, but simply to serve as "apartment-busters," to obliterate cities, is morally and strategically unacceptable.

To whatever extent mutual assured destruction was once the strategic doctrine of the United States, there is serious question whether the Soviets ever accepted the premises of this doctrine. Mutual assured destruction assumes as a premise that, to work, each nation must be willing mutually to terrorize the other. It also contains within it the total abrogation of the state's traditional responsibility to protect its own population instead of leaving it hostage to the good will of its adversary.

The United States has shifted away from mutual assured destruction at the level both of strategic planning and the level of weapons design. President Carter, for example, signed a national security directive continuing the retargeting of American nuclear forces from civilian to military targets. To accommodate this shift in strategic doctrine, a new generation of nuclear weapons is required. The development and application of this new technology is already taking place. The direction in which nuclear technology is currently moving is toward smaller warheads of vastly reduced megatonnage. Over the last 20 years, the megatonnage of American nuclear forces has declined 75 percent. This is because, as the accuracy of the warheads increased, a smaller megatonnage could be employed to the same effect upon a target.

As accuracy increases, megatonnage goes down. The Soviets, because they were behind in the technology of accuracy, have much larger rockets to carry much larger warheads of vastly greater megatonnage. It was hoped that if the destructive area were large enough the target would be destroyed, despite the missile's inaccuracy. These kinds of large dirty weapons now make sense only within the context of a doctrine of mutual assured destruction that we no longer accept and the Soviets may never have accepted. It is for this reason, among many others, that the basic premise of the nuclear freeze movement is flawed. The nuclear freeze would block the current development of smaller, more accurate weapons that would have greater ability to differentiate their targets and that would be able to hit a military target with little collateral damage to civilian centers. The point should not be lost, however, that the speed and accuracy of these weapons combine to provide a more credible deterrent and thus make nuclear war much less likely. Given the demise of the MAD doctrine and the ascendancy of new strategic doctrines and sophisticated technologies, traditional principles of proportionality can again govern strategic considerations and deterrence. President Reagan's Strategic Defense Initiative, for instance, would seem to meet every moral criteria of the just war teaching.

Finally, one must consider at this point the conventional military situation in Europe. The Soviet Union has 42,500 tanks facing west, 20,000 deployed within the last decade. The tank, it is well known, would be the basic ingredient to any Soviet offensive in Europe. The NATO powers have 13,000 tanks. No one disputes any longer the immense conventional military superiority of the Soviet Union. The only open question currently is how long it would take the Soviets to reach the Rhine, and this depends more on Soviet logistics than NATO defense capabilities. General Bernard Rogers has estimated that European forces could not withstand a full-scale onslaught from the East for more than 7 to 10 days.[26]

This overwhelming conventional superiority does not translate necessarily into military use, but it does translate into tremendous political power. It must be remembered that military power has influence well short of any actual utilization of it. As Frederick the Great said, "Diplomacy without arms is like music without instruments." And as James Billington has suggested, ". . . the continuing Soviet threat is not military attack so much as the classic Stalinist conversion of military power into political pressure against and within free societies."[27] Certainly the political effect of the deployment of SS-20's is ample illustration of this equation. Some think the nature of nuclear weaponry obviates any political expression of it since it is so "horrible." But thinking so is exactly the political effect of nuclear terror that the Soviets wish to induce in the first place. This effect is seen in the pastoral letter's extremely deficient understanding of the tremendous power the Soviets can exert politically when they have strategic superiority. As Solzhenitsyn warns us:

At one time there was no comparison between the strength of the USSR and yours. Then it became equal. . . . Perhaps today it is just greater than equal, but soon it will be two to one. . . . With such nuclear superiority it will be possible to block the use of your weapons, and on some unlucky morning they will declare: "Attention. We're sending our troops into Europe, and if you make a move, we will annihilate you." And this ratio of three to one, or five to one, will have its effect: you will not make a move.[28]

The Soviets do not wish war; they wish the fruits of war. Nuclear terror is one of the means used to obtain them. Unfortunately, the bishops have succumbed to this terror without reflecting on the political consequences achieved by their doing so. Currently Soviet political power is seriously attenuated by the knowledge that should Soviet tanks

26. General Bernard Rogers as quoted in William Drozdiak, "NATO Weighs Non-Nuclear Strategies," *The Washington Post* (September 26, 1983).

27. James Billington, "Who Andropov Was, What He Did," *The Washington Post*, Outlook (February 12, 1984).

28. Aleksandr Solzhenitsyn, *Warning to the West* (New York: Farrar, Straus, and Giroux, 1976), pp. 76–77.

ever move, NATO forces and the United States might employ tactical nuclear weapons against them. One such weapon is the neutron warhead, which we now possess, although it is not deployed in Europe. I would contend that the utilization of the neutron warhead against a massed Soviet armored attack could meet every criterion of the just-war teaching and that furthermore there is at present no other way to halt an armored Soviet blitzkrieg. The neutron warhead is a weapon that would have only limited collateral effects. The fallout is minimal and quickly dissipated. The warhead can be used discretely in the field by our armed forces. It is capable of being fired from the ground by artillery shell and aimed precisely where the Soviet offensive would appear most threatening.

It is the Soviet realization that the United States has not renounced and will not renounce first use of nuclear weapons in Europe that diminishes the political influence that vast Soviet military superiority would otherwise accord them. What does this diminution in influence translate into? Freedom for the West. Without the presence of our nuclear arsenal in Europe, the nations of Western Europe would find themselves under overwhelming pressure to accommodate Soviet power and to make whatever internal political changes would be needed to remain in Soviet good graces.

PETER J. HENRIOT, S.J.

14. Disarmament and Development: The Lasting Challenge to Peace

Is it possible simultaneously to increase military spending and commit ourselves to meeting the needs of people? Can we continue to fuel the global arms race and still attempt to meet the challenge of global poverty? Can we have "guns and butter"?

The thrust of these questions focuses my topic for this essay, an exploration of the linkage between disarmament and development.

I wish to treat four points in this paper. First, I pose a *thesis* regarding the link between disarmament and development. Second, I review the *focus* of the U.S. bishops' peace pastoral's discussion of this topic, found in Part III of their document. Third, I propose three *areas of response* that we need to make. Fourth, I offer a *challenge* to the academic community concerning this topic.

Thesis

Today the world moves toward the year 2000 faced by two terrible threats: war and poverty. These threats, of course, have been the twin scourges of humankind since the earliest days. But both modern technology and the rapid growth of population have meant that today, to a degree never before experienced in history, these threats pose serious uncertainty as we move into the future.

The possibility of massive nuclear destruction is heightened when we consider the consequences of proliferation of nuclear arms.[1] At this time, five nations publicly hold nuclear weapons—the Soviet Union, the United States, the People's Republic of China, Great Britain, and France. A sixth, India, has publicly detonated a nuclear device. But

I acknowledge my appreciation for assistance in preparing this article to two of my colleagues at the Center of Concern, Jane Blewett, staff associate, and Brian Corbin, research assistant.

1. See *World Armaments and Disarmaments: The SIPRI Yearbook*, published annually by the Stockholm International Peace Research Institute (Cambridge, Mass.: Oelgeschlager, Gunn and Hain).

privately, three or four other nations probably have nuclear weapons or near capability: Israel, Brazil, South Africa, and possibly Iraq, Argentina, and Pakistan. In another 10 to 15 years, another 10 to 15 countries may possess nuclear weapons and possibly one or two terrorist bands.[2] This is hardly an encouraging picture to contemplate.

The challenge of global poverty is perhaps most graphically presented in the crisis of hunger around the world. In 1974, the United Nations World Food Conference was held in Rome and drew the world's attention to the widespread problem of malnutrition, hunger, and starvation. Today, 10 years later, that problem is stll as severe. Heightened by extended drought in Africa, poor farming techniques in other parts of the world, inequitable food distribution patterns, basic lack of resources, and rapidly increasing population in the poor countries, the problem of hunger has not gone away. The United Nations estimates that the absolute numbers of those who face hunger and malnutrition apparently have not diminished over the last decade: 400 to 600 million people are considered chronically hungry. Approximately 15 million people a year—44,000 a day—die of hunger and hunger-related problems.[3]

As we move toward the year 2000, our future is indeed challenged by these twin problems of war and poverty. They represent structural challenges along East-West and North-South lines. Our response to these challenges will determine whether we reach the year 2000 in any human and humane fashion.

In this context, then, it is important to probe the connection between the promotion of peace and the eradication of poverty. This connection has long been recognized in discussions of global order. One direction of this connection was enunciated succinctly by Pope Paul VI in his 1967 encyclical, "The Development of Peoples" (*Populorum Progressio*). According to the Pope, "Development is the new name for peace." Unless the vast numbers of poor in the less developed countries (LDC's) are able to provide the basic necessities of life—food, clothing, housing, health, education—for themselves and their families, there is little hope that global unrest and even massive warfare can be averted in the future. Peace is gravely threatened by the lack of progress in development.[4]

But there is another and even more important direction in the connec-

2. See Robert A. Friedlander, "The Ultimate Weapon: What If Terrorists Go Nuclear?" *Denver Journal of International Law and Policy*, 12 (1982), 1–11.

3. United Nations World Food Council, "Programs Toward the Eradication of Hunger: A Multilateral Decade for Food, 1974–1984," WFC/1984/2 (February 1, 1984).

4. For latest figures on world poverty, see World Bank, *World Development Report*, 1984 (New York: Oxford University Press, 1984).

tion between peace and poverty. It has become increasingly clear in a world deeply divided not only between the rich North and the poor South but also between the militaristic superpowers of the East and the West that Pope Paul's maxim can rightfully be recast for today: "Peace is the new name for development." That is to say, *either* the global community continues to pursue the arms race and builds ever-larger and more deadly weapons, *or* it shifts direction and moves with determination toward global socio-economic development. *It cannot do both.* There is an absolute competitive relationship between the arms industry and the ability to invest in the life and future development of the peoples of the world.

The clear understanding of this latter direction in the connection between disarmament and development is comparatively recent. It is certainly true, of course, that a linkage between the effort spent on armaments and the effort spent on meeting people's basic needs has always been acknowledged. We can simply recall the words of Isaiah 2:4, "They shall beat their swords into ploughshares and their spears into pruning hooks." But what is new in this discussion is that today there exists a solid body of research and information not previously available to support what had been a rather weak proposition linking the two in the past.

Two significant research reports were released in 1982 that gave greater substantiation to the link between disarmament and development. The first, "A Study on the Relationship between Disarmament and Development," had been mandated by the First U.N. Disarmament Session in 1978 and was presented at the Second U.N. Disarmament Session in 1982.[5] The study was chaired by Inga Thorsson, Swedish Undersecretary of State. The second, "A Report of the Independent Commission on Disarmament and Security Issues," came from a group of international political leaders chaired by Olof Palme, Prime Minister of Sweden.[6]

The conclusion of both these extensively researched reports is very much the same. There can be no effective movement toward meeting the basic needs of the human family unless there is a significant shift away from the massive worldwide efforts of raising armies and building armaments. The commitment to the arms race is having ever-more serious consequences on the essential building blocks of the human society. All the following are affected:

---

5. United Nations, *The Relationship Between Disarmament and Development*, A/36/356 (New York: United Nations, 1982).

6. *Common Security: A Blueprint for Survival* (New York: Simon and Schuster, 1982).

1. Resources—economic, physical, intellectual.

2. Institutions—international relations, United Nations and other multilateral agencies, domestic policies.

3. Spirit—imagination, creativity, human energy.

A look at just one of these areas, resources, demonstrates the devastating consequences of the arms race. The use of resources for military purposes means, in the simplest terms, that they are not available to address the great human problems of the world community. This is not to say that freeing up these resources through steps toward disarmament would *automatically* make them available for development purposes. It is necessary to be clear about that. There is no political guarantee that this would be the case. But until a halt is called to the squandering of scarce resources in the arms race, then no talk of meeting development needs is realistic. Expressed in rather traditional philosophical terms, disarmament is the *necessary* but not *sufficient* cause of development. Why this is so can be seen from a brief look at five dimensions of this issue.

1. *Capital.*—Total military spending around the globe is now more than $650 billion. The United States alone, in President Reagan's proposed military budget for the next five years, would spend more than $1.5 trillion. We live in a "capital short" world economy, an economy heavily dependent on borrowed funds and hence an economy always at the mercy of such factors as rising interest rates and availability of funds. Expenditures on arms divert funds that otherwise could be used to meet human needs. Ruth Sivard, in her annual *World Military and Social Expenditures*, has demonstrated dramatically the extent of this diversion of resources through a series of comparisons.[7]

The global military budget of $650 billion is more than the entire income of 1.5 billion people living in the 10 poorest countries. The price paid for a single modern fighter would be sufficient to pay for inoculating 3 million children against major childhood diseases. The price of one nuclear submarine with all its missiles would provide 100,000 working years of nursing care for the elderly. In 32 countries, governments spend more on military purposes than for education and health care combined. The world's average annual expenditure per soldier is about $20,000, but only $380 for a school-age child. For every 100,000 people worldwide, there are only 85 doctors, but 556 soldiers. The world spends $22 on military purposes for every $1 on development aid given to the LDC's. Since FY 1981, the Reagan Administration has added $8 in security assistance to every $1 in development aid.

7. Ruth Leger Sivard, *World Military and Social Expenditures 1983: An Annual Report on World Priorities* (Washington, D.C.: World Priorities, 1983).

2. *Human labor.*—Approximately 50 million people worldwide are currently engaged in military-related activities. This number includes some 25 million serving in the armed forces of different nations, civilians employed in defense departments, more than 500,000 scientists and engineers engaged in research and development for military purposes, and another 5 million workers involved in weapons production. It is a major concern that these numbers have been increasing in recent years. For example, 1980 figures show that the world's regular armed forces are 10 percent larger than in 1970 and almost 30 percent larger than in 1960.

3. *Military industrial production.*—An estimated 28 percent to 32 percent of all industrial production in the world is absorbed by the military. In some industries, the percentage is even higher. For example, in the United States in the mid-1970's, military demand accounted for 45 percent of the total sales of the aircraft industry and 74 percent of all new construction in the shipbuilding industry. The skewing of industrial production so heavily in the direction of military purposes has definite harmful effects on the economy. The greater part of military production is capital intensive and thus does not really boost employment. Moreover, military production tends to be a major factor in inflation, since it adds to demand but, unlike spending on roads, schools, or hospitals, does little to improve productivity in the long run.[8]

4. *Raw materials.*—The magnitude of the consumption of energy and minerals for military purposes worldwide takes on new significance for two reasons. First, in recent years there is an increasing awareness of the scarcity of nonrenewable resources in the globe.[9] This is true not only of oil but also for the 16 basic minerals most needed by industrialized economies. Second, as more and more Third World nations advance along the continuum of industrialization, demand on limited supplies will heighten. This raises the fear of increased tensions and possible "resource wars." Western Europe, North America, and Japan already consume more than two-thirds of the annual production of nine of the leading minerals. The developing countries, on the other hand, consume percentages like 7 percent of the world's aluminum production, 9 percent of its copper, and 12 percent of its iron ore. In fact, in the case of aluminum, copper, nickel, and platinum, estimated global consumption for military purposes is greater than the demand for these minerals for all the purposes in Africa, Asia, and Latin America combined.

8. See Seymour Melman, *The Permanent War Economy* (New York: Simon and Schuster, 1974).

9. See Donella H. Meadows et al., *The Limits to Growth* (New York: Universe Books, 1972).

5. *Research and development (R and D)*.—Perhaps nothing more strikingly indicates the hold the military/defense complex has on the world than to realize that the largest single objective of all scientific inquiry and technological development worldwide is for military purposes. In the face of tremendous global needs for food, clean water, housing, health care, etc., the scientific-technological community is overwhelmingly focused on refining instruments of death and destruction. Global expenditures on military R and D in 1980 were approximately $40 billion, or approximately 25 percent of all monies spent on R and D in the world. The budgets for health, energy, agriculture, and pollution control combined were only 23 percent of the total. Of the world's qualified scientists and engineers, 20 percent were engaged in military work in 1980; in the United States, the percentage was much higher—close to 50 percent. The average military product is 20 times as research-intensive as the average civilian product.

A look at these five areas indicates the serious questions regarding the link between disarmament and development and the impact of the arms race on the poor of the world. But there are deeper *structural* problems to which we must also turn our attention. These can be summed up in the phrase used by Andre Gunder Frank: "The progressive militarization of global society and growing arms economy in the Third World." [10] These structural problems are seen in at least four areas.

First, North-South issues of development are continually subordinated to East-West issues of strategic-political conflict betwen the superpowers. This is evident in the current disputes in Central America and in Africa, where socio-economic problems take second place behind ideological disputes between the Soviet Union and the United States.

Second, military solutions are offered to an increasing number of issues, at times overriding ordinary diplomatic relations. One thinks of the British-Argentine confrontation in the Malvinas/Falkland Islands and the Israeli invasion of Lebanon in 1982, or of the invasion of Grenada in the fall of 1983. The recent report of the Kissinger Commission (1984) reveals very well these first and second structural problems. According to the report, the internal conflicts in Central America are seen through the filters of an ideological struggle of democracy with Marxism, and military assistance is promptly increased to right-wing dictatorships even while economic aid for development is proposed with some difficulty. [11]

10. Andre Gunder Frank, *Crisis: In The Third World* (New York: Holmes and Meier, 1981), p. 280.
11. "Report of the National Bipartisan Commission on Central America," January 1984 (Washington, D.C.: Government Printing Office, 1984).

Third, arms sales to the Third World countries have a massive impact on development. In 1983, arms sales by the industrialized nations to the Third World amounted to $24.7 billion. This is the lowest level since 1976. And for the first time in that seven-year period, the U.S. share of those sales was more than double that of the Soviet Union's.[12] Scarce foreign exchange of many poor countries is eaten up by the purchase of arms, purchases that have frequently been pressured by one or more of the superpowers.[13] (Particularly disturbing in the arm sales field today is the action of Israel of selling to many military dictatorships with extremely oppressive human-rights records, for example, in Central America and Iran.)

Fourth, there is the human tragedy of the refugee problem throughout the Third World, directly influenced by military policies. In South Asia, Central America, and the Horn of Africa, millions of refugees flee their homes because of military action.[14] Driven violently from their homes, these refugees face danger and death in the process of relocating and bigotry and isolation wherever they happen to settle.

Focus

Most of the public commentary on the pastoral letter on peace, *The Challenge of Peace: God's Promise and Our Response*, has focused upon the military-strategic-political debate found in Part II. It is there that the particularly controversial topic of deterrence is discussed, with specific judgments and evaluations made of current U.S. military policy. As important as this part is, however, I feel that the more important part in the long term will be Part III, which bears the title, "The Promotion of Peace: Proposals and Policies."

In a very striking fashion, this part turns our attention to the structural relationships between disarmament and development. It recalls the devastating impact of the arms race on the poor, as described by *Gaudium et Spes* in 1965. This great statement of the Second Vatican Council called the arms race: "one of the greatest curses on the human race and the harm it inflicts upon the poor is more than can be endured."[15] In a statement before the U.N. in 1976, the Holy See expressed a judgment on the arms race in commenting that even though these arms may never

12. "U.S. Share of Arms Sales to Third World Called Twice That of Soviets,'" *The Washington Post* (May 10, 1984).

13. See Andrew J. Pierre, *The Global Politics of Arms Sales* (Princeton, N.J.: Princeton University Press, 1982).

14. See Michael J. Schultheis, S.J., "Refugees: The Structure of a Global Justice Issue," *Occasional Paper* No. 2 (Washington, D.C.: Center of Concern, 1983).

15. *Gaudium et Spes* ("The Pastoral Constitution on the Church in the Modern World"), n. 81.

be used they have already caused the deaths of hundreds of thousands of people by depriving them of scarce resources.

In Part III, the pastoral letter begins its discussion of the promotion of peace by reminding us that peace is not simply the absence of war but also the presence of the structures of peace and the structures of justice. It quotes the message of Pope Paul VI from his *Development of Peoples*: "Peace cannot be limited to a mere absence of war, the result of an ever precarious balance of forces. No, peace is something built up day after day, in the pursuit of an order intended by God, which implies a more perfect form of justice among men and women."[16] Another expression of this important theme can be found in the homily that Pope John Paul II delivered at Coventry Cathedral in 1983, also cited by the pastoral letter:

Peace is not just the absence of war. It involves mutual respect between peoples and nations. It involves collaboration and binding agreements. Like a cathedral, peace must be constructed patiently and with unshakable faith.[17]

In developing this theme of the link between peace and justice—central to the linkage of disarmament and development—Part III of the pastoral letter mentions at least seven relevant points.

1. The structures of "global order" must be promoted, since the universal common good can be achieved only by an international cooperation that is effectively institutionalized (nn. 241–242).

2. The interdependence of nations obliges us to acknowledge that poverty is caused not just internally but in the international structures of trade, monetary relationships, investments, and aid (n. 260).

3. It is necessary to translate charity into structural policies, by meeting the needs of people in ways other than simply relief and emergency assistance (n. 263).

4. It is imperative to support the United Nations, and the United States should take a more positive and creative role in its participation in this international institution (n. 268).

5. A broader understanding of "security" is necessary so that we recognize that such global difficulties as environmental problems are genuine threats to "security" but cannot be met by military means (n. 270).

6. Economic resources must be converted away from military production, to the production of the goods necessary to meet basic human needs. Persons displaced from military jobs should receive some help from the community to ease transition into the civilian sector (n. 271).

16. *Populorum Progressio* ("The Development of Peoples"), n. 76.
17. *Origins* 12 (1982), 55.

7. Effective economic planning must be based on a global community where a mutuality of interests is respected (n. 272).

These topics from Part III indicate clearly that in the building of peace, development issues must play a central role. It is noteworthy that this emphasis on the link between development and disarmament is repeated in the testimony offered in June 1984, by Joseph Cardinal Bernardin of Chicago and Archbishop John O'Connor of New York before the Committee on Foreign Affairs of the U.S. House of Representatives.[18] Both bishops, prominent members of the committee that drafted the pastoral letter, suggested that one of the major criteria for evaluating weapons systems relates to the cost of the arms race. This testimony is significant as an update of the teaching of the pastoral letter. Therefore it is important to note the strong emphasis put on the impact on the poor of the continuation of the arms race.

Areas of Response

I want briefly to suggest three major areas of response that we need to make if we are to be sensitive to the link between disarmament and development. Each of these responses gets progressively more difficult but also progressively more important in changing the direction of current policy.

The first response is simply recognizing that "guns and butter" is not possible. It was not possible when first suggested by Lyndon Johnson at the height of the Vietnam War, when he struggled to continue to fight the domestic war on poverty. Scarce capital, human labor, industrial production, raw material, and research and development simply cannot be oriented primarily to armaments without serious consequences affecting development efforts. One simple example can be added to the many instances cited. The National Science Foundation's 1983 "Compilation of Federal R and D Funding for Fiscal Years 1980–1984" reveals that federal funding for research and development for military purposes has increased sharply in recent years, while federal funding for the rest of the nation's R and D efforts has considerably decreased.[19] In 1980, for example, of the total R and D budget of $39 billion, $19.4 billion went to national defense purposes and $19.6 billion to all other R and D. In 1982, of the total budget for R and D of $39.6 billion, $24.2 billion went to national defense and $15.4 to all other purposes.

18. Testimony of June 26, 1984. *Origins* 14 (1984), 1954.
19. F. A. Long, "Federal R & D Budget: Guns Versus Butter," *Science*, 223, 4641 (March 16, 1984), 1133.

And in 1984, of the $45.7 billion of total R and D, $32 billion went to national defense and $13.7 to all other purposes. This is but one of many examples that can be cited to reinforce the conclusion that "guns and butter" cannot simultaneously be offered either to the United States or the world.

A second response calls on us to redefine "security" and what it means to speak accurately of the "national security." We must emphasize quite strongly that national security is inseparable from global security and that it is something that cannot be achieved by military means alone. Our security at the global level is guaranteed by the viability of three interrelated systems.[20] The first is the global environmental system, for we live in a world that has a unitary nature. Issues of ecology, toxic wastes, acid rain, oxygen depletion, law of the seas, all point to the importance of paying attention to this unitary nature. The second global system is the communication and transportation network that makes possible so much of how we identify with modern civilization. The third global system is the integrated world economy, which means, for example, that if Brazil suffers financial collapse because of its massive debt crisis all the industrialized nations of the world will be profoundly shaken. Each of these three global systems presents problems for which there are no military solutions. To guarantee our security we must pay close attention to these systems lest highly unstable conditions bring about greater insecurity.

The third response relates to our stance toward change in the modern world. The military mind set is simply unacceptable in dealing with the various problems facing the globe today. Political responses that are primarily military can achieve neither the development that is necessary nor the peace longed for. This means that we must evaluate all budget proposals, for example, in terms of their true impact on meeting the most serious issues of the day. It is not inappropriate, in a United States that seems perennially preoccupied with the campaigning process for president, for me to say that when I speak today of the option for the poor I always emphasize that it implies an option for peace and that both options imply very strongly the option for politics. We must translate our concern for development and peace into political choices.

Challenge

In concluding my presentation on the linkage between development and disarmament I would like to offer a challenge to the academic com-

---

20. See Michael J. Schultheis, S.J., "Search for Security in the Nuclear Age," *Occasional Paper* No. 9. (Washington, D.C.: Center of Concern, 1983).

munity represented at this forum at The Catholic University of America as well as the broader readership of this volume.

It is critically important that we reject out-of-hand any value-free approach to the topic of war and peace that abstracts from the real-world situation. The bishops' pastoral letter should once and for all have discredited discussions of such topics as military budgets, arms strategies, and potential destruction measurements of weaponry (in any fashion) which would ignore the ethical questions involved in each of the topics. Persons engaged in the pursuits of teaching and research who would also promote peace must therefore always strive to keep the two issues of disarmament and development closely linked. Persons concerned with world-development issues must not talk as if this were possible without addressing the questions of the impact of the arms race on the poor and on any adequate responses to the problems of poverty. Persons involved in peace studies must never forget the linkage to justice issues.

It seems to me that this is especially important at The Catholic University of America. As the university sponsored by the U.S. Catholic hierarchy, this institution has particular responsibility to assist the U.S. bishops in implementing the peace pastoral. That is my understanding of the rationale behind holding this specific forum. It seems to me that one of the key ways that this assistance can be offered here at CUA might be to explore the intimate connections between the topic of the peace pastoral and the topic of the upcoming pastoral letter being prepared by the U.S. bishops on Catholic social teaching and the American economy. Surely the issues of war and peace and the issues of the operation of our economy are intimately entwined. Here at this university, the issues of disarmament and development should always be closely connected. In this fashion, the twin scourges of war and poverty will be more directly and effectively addressed.

III   Religious Ethics

ARTHUR WASKOW

15. Nuclear War or Nuclear Holocaust: How the Biblical Account of the Flood Might Instruct Our Efforts

In this paper I would like to shed light on the issue of nuclear arms and war by using the classical Jewish process called *midrash*. Midrash, drawn from the verb meaning "to search," is the process of looking into the Torah to arrive at an accurate understanding of the spirit of the text. It is the effort to understand the meaning contained within the text, although not at an explicit level. As the rabbis of the Talmud said, the text of the Torah is not written in black ink on white parchment; it is written in black fire on white fire. There is as much truth in the white fire, that is, the spaces, as there is in the black fire, the letters themselves. This ancient rabbinic process has reawakened in considerable richness within American Jewish life, for various complicated reasons. But midrash has always been present. Through the ages, it has been the process by which generation after generation of the Jewish people coped with the transformations of Jewish life and of the larger society within which they lived.

The Torah is central to this process. The study of the Torah is itself a form of prayer, a direct contact with God. The blessing with which we traditionally begin the process—and which I shall repeat here—is: "Blessed is the Holy One of Being, Who is the Breath of Life, Who makes us holy by means of the study of the Torah."

Three years ago when the people of the Jewish community first began in a serious way to ask the question, "What would Jewish tradition have to teach about the possibility of nuclear war?" the passage that surfaced and we found ourselves responding to was not the passage concerning just or unjust wars. What arose in this context was the passage that describes the Flood, Noah's Ark, and the Rainbow. Given that this passage came to us almost like a dream arising from the unconscious, we asked, "What does it mean for us that this is what arises? What would it mean for our generation to study this text carefully?"

It should be added that in classic rabbinic writing the Noah text, which sets forth the three-cornered covenant between God, Noah, and all human life, is the origin of most Jewish thought regarding the obligation that *all* human beings have to God, to each other, and to the created universe. The Noah text is, in classical Jewish thought, the text from which questions of the universal character of the human race arise.

Upon examination of the Noah text, it was obvious to us why it had arisen. This is the one passage of the Torah that talks about the danger of the destruction of all life on the planet. Within the text are some extraordinarily powerful symbols, such as the Flood itself, the Ark, the Rainbow, and the dove. However, we were not satisfied with simply the possibility of the power of these symbols, even though that power could awaken our own and others' spiritual energy toward dealing with the danger of the destruction of all human life. We wanted more than that as a teaching from the text..

The initial two levels of learning are fairly obvious. The first is the obligation of all persons to deal with the potential of the destruction of all life on the planet. The command to Noah is to protect every species of life on the planet, not just the human race or one section of the human race. Although only one portion of the human race was preserved in the Noah account, one realizes in reading the story that it was God's intent to make possible the re-creation of the entire human race and all the rest of life. For us it is clear that when the destruction of all life is threatened, we are commanded to preserve life. We must also take seriously our knowledge that there is no Ark capable of preserving all life—except this planet. No area smaller than the planet can do this; no cavern under the Smokies with corporate records, no concrete-lined bunker under the Rockies designed to protect some faint part of the Strategic Air Command, no fallout shelter will suffice. Only the planet will do.

The second level of learning from the text teaches us that God's command comes to a very "special" unspecial type of human being. The "specialness" of Noah is that he is unspecial. Noah is not an expert. He is not an expert on rain or on animals. The rabbinic midrash contains wonderful accounts of the difficulties Noah had dealing with all the animals on the Ark. Nor is Noah an expert at shipbuilding. He has to be told how to build his very peculiar ship. Noah is simply a reasonably righteous individual. In fact, the rabbis question how fully righteous an individual he was. They compare Noah to Abraham and Moses, who, when there were threats of destruction, as at Sodom and Gomorrah, and at Mt. Sinai, argued with God and prevailed. Noah never argued. So, the rabbis conclude, Noah was righteous for his generation, but when measured against others, he was not "super"-righteous.

This "unspecial" quality to Noah should serve as a powerful reminder to us not to defer to experts on the question of nuclear arms. Many of us have the habit of saying, on the question of nuclear weapons, that this issue is so complicated and advanced in its technicalities that it should be left to generals, or scientists, or international diplomats, or priests, rabbis, and theologians. Our typical reaction often is: "Don't come to me! What do I know?" But our understanding of Noah should refute this reaction.

We should also remember that Noah was not the leader of any government. Noah was, in a sense, a private citizen of the earth. This also raises some profound questions. To whom is the Noah text directed? Only to private citizens? To government leaders? Or to both? If to private citizens, what should be the impact on public policy?

As we studied the text further, an unexpected teaching came from it. The question we had put to the text was, What does it have to teach us about nuclear war? In the process of studying and reflecting on the text, we realized that the text rejects, through a very powerful silence, talking about war at all. The text does not want to deal with the danger of the destruction of all life on the planet as if it were a war. So, we asked ourselves, of what use is this teaching? One use of the teaching is to raise a profound question as to whether war is the appropriate category to apply to exchanges of nuclear weapons.

This question strikes at the logical root of the bishops' pastoral letter. The dominant logic of the pastoral letter is centered on the issue of just and unjust wars. Nonetheless, the pastoral letter also alludes to other ways of thinking about this issue. One strain of the bishops' thought approaches the understanding that has evolved for us. This strain of thought is found in the references in the letter to the fact that what is at risk is the whole of God's creation.[1] The insight is, however, weakened

---

1. The pastoral letter, in its discussion of the Pontifical Academy of Sciences' "Statement on the Consequences of the Use of Nuclear Weapons," recognizes that what is at risk in the nuclear age is the survival of the entire planet. The pastoral moves from this recognition to the conclusion that the appropriate moral corollary is the prevention of nuclear war. (See *The Challenge of Peace*, nn. 126–131.) The pastoral, however, somewhat anomalously given this recognition, also maintains a just-war analysis.

Moreover, the anomaly is not just theoretical—but goes to the heart of certain policy issues. In addressing *how* to prevent nuclear "war," the pastoral letter does not examine the possibility that if in the real world any use of nuclear weapons is very likely to result in world nuclear holocaust, then the proclamation of this fact by nuclear powers as truth and even its translation into weapons targeting may be a less immoral version of "deterrence" than false and phony claims that nuclear weapons are not being targeted on civilians.

To make that point more precise: The pastoral letter, out of a just-war analysis, says that any version of deterrence based on an explicit intention and warning of the deliberate destruction of cities is immoral. I would suggest that if *any* version of nuclear deterrence is less immoral than any other—itself a doubtful proposition—the version most likely to be least immoral is one that says: "Since any nuclear war is very liable to turn into a world holocaust, and since attempting to prepare for a 'limited nuclear war' is liable to bring one on and therefore liable to bring on a world nuclear holocaust, we will eschew all rhetoric or practical steps looking toward a 'limited nuclear war' altogether. We are

in that the letter fails to use it as the basis for any call to action or for the development of any new systematic ethics, any new approach to knowing what action to take. It remains as powerful rhetoric. There may be an implicit connection between this insight and ideas of proportionality or the pursuit of justice, but such connections are not made explicit.

To return to the Noah text: We concluded that there was a serious danger in using the category of war, even when framed in terms of just or unjust war, when dealing with the issue of nuclear arms. The primary danger is that the category of war is one that the human race is accustomed to controlling. We have traditionally thought of war in terms of justice and injustice, in terms of gain and loss, and in terms of proportionate damage for the gain. It appeared to us that by pushing the category of war to its limits we had perhaps pushed beyond its limits. Some of us have become accustomed to saying that in nuclear war there would be no winners. Far fewer of us are accustomed to saying and absorbing the statement, "In a nuclear war there might be no losers." Although some political leaders have said such words in public, these concepts have not *in fact* been absorbed into the strategic theories and operational plans of either the United States or the Soviet Union; both nations' strategic plans still seek to "prevail" in nuclear war. What strategists and most of the rest of us have failed to internalize is the essentially different character of nuclear war. Once one realizes that in a nuclear "war" there might be no winners or losers, one questions the very usefulness of the category of war.

It is not only "winners" and "losers" that might be missing in a nuclear "war," but also "justice" and "injustice." For if no human community remains after a nuclear exchange, can there be justice or injustice? Or, are the standards dissolved and the category of war inappropriate? This question cuts close to the heart of the logic of the pastoral letter, which has at its root a call for justice.

A third aspect of this problem of the inadequacy of the category of war deals with our attitudes toward the weapons of war. Keeping in mind that the human race is accustomed to war and knows the painful consequences that ensue from both winning and losing a war, the human race in its various parts, when it notes an advantage, still prepares to

---

therefore abandoning all but a small number of weapons, and these are targeted on cities, purely to deter anyone from using nuclear weapons against us. We invite all other nuclear powers to do the same, but this is not a precondition. We will pursue with great vigor the elimination of these remaining weapons by all nuclear powers." The explicit statement that a "minimum deterrent" is targeted on cities seems to be excluded by the pastoral letter—which I think is the (unwise) result of its inappropriate use of just-war theory.

win the war. The way to win a war ordinarily is to have a greater number of weapons, and more powerful weapons, than the anticipated opponent. This is the source of arms races. Such actions make sense if one thinks in the category "war." The notion that there might emerge a weapon that, given a certain number, would obliterate life on the planet has been a difficult notion to absorb. We now know that the number beyond which nuclear bombs cease to be weapons is considerably lower than we had surmised 20 years ago. Scientists have reported that there is clear evidence that perhaps as few as 100 one-megaton nuclear bombs detonated on major cities might create a dust cloud so thick that sunlight could not reach the earth for an extended period of time. This period of time would be long enough to cause the cessation of photosynthesis and the death of all life on the planet. One hundred is a small number, taking into account that at present there are 50,000 nuclear "bombs" in the arsenals of the two superpowers.[2]

In the light of the foregoing, we must ask ourselves whether the Noah text is teaching us to leave the category "war" altogether. The text might powerfully be teaching us to stretch ourselves, to think in different categories. If one thinks in the category of war, one is much more likely to participate in that category. Employing the category "war," nations are prone to go forward with the nuclear arms race, as such a race makes sense within the category "war." One is also prone to attempt fine-tuned analyses of just and unjust war. The high probability that such a "war" would result in universal destruction does not enter the equation.

The Noah text and traditional midrash on it intimates at the destruction that would follow a nuclear exchange. In the text, humanity is destroyed by a flood of water. Paralleling this text, however, is an ancient rabbinic midrash that notes that while God promised not to send a flood of water at the end of the world, God did not promise that the world would not end in fire. This midrash has even entered southern Black culture in a song that says, "God gave Noah the rainbow sign—no more water—the fire next time."

We shall now attend to the text. The text first conveys the fact that *khamas*, i.e., violence, corruption, and ruination, were appearing

---

2. There is now very persuasive evidence on the devastating effects of the detonation of even the "small" number of 100 megatons of nuclear bombs. See, R. P. Turco, O. B. Toon, T. P. Ackerman, J. B. Pollock, and C. Sagan, "Nuclear Winter: Global Consequences of Multiple Nuclear Explosions," *Science* 222, 4630 (December 23, 1983), pp. 1283–1292; P. R. Ehrlich, J. Harte, M. A. Harwell, P. H. Raven, C. Sagan, G. M. Woodwell, J. Berry, E. S. Ayensu, A. H. Ehrlich, T. Eisner, S. J. Gould, H. D. Grover, R. Herrera, R. M. May, E. Mayr, C. P. McKay, H. A. Mooney, N. Myers, D. Pimentel, and J. M. Teal, "Long Term Biological Consequences of Nuclear War," *Science* 222, 4630 (December 23, 1983), pp. 1293–1300. See also Scientists' Report to Pope John Paul II, "The Nuclear Winter," *ORIGINS*, Vol. 13, 38 (March 1, 1984), pp. 625, 627.

everywhere on earth. God is still present in this process, however, maintaining that what the human race sows, so it shall reap. If humankind floods the earth with violence and corruption, then this violence and corruption will overflow and the world will be flooded.

The text, however, refuses to do what the category of war would require, i.e., define a "them" and an "us," a good side and a bad side. The Noah text refuses to have a good side and a bad side. There is only a tiny family. This family is not defined politically or ethnically. Noah and his family are not Jewish. Neither is it suggested that they are set against the rest of the human race. One might conclude that where the destruction of all life is threatened, the text cautions us not to expend energy searching for a bad side or a good side.

There is a strong tendency in every culture to find a good side and a bad side. This is seen even in peace movements. Among some of those active in the peace movement in this country, there is sometimes a tendency to say that since the United States is building nuclear bombs, the United States must be at fault. Among Americans who favor building more bombs, there is a tendency to say that the United States is morally superior to the Russians. (Among Soviet dissidents and apparatchiks there are obverse reactions. Soviet dissidents tend to identify the U.S.S.R. as the uniquely evil power; Soviet apparatchiks see the U.S.S.R. as uniquely good.) The Torah warns against all these outlooks. Rather than attempting to fix blame, the text teaches us to be on guard for the springs of violence that can overflow in every human society.

When we began dealing with the concept, "flood of fire," it echoed, especially for Jewish ears, with the modern English word "holocaust," which literally means the burning of everything. Flood of fire—Holocaust—in the life experience of the Jewish people brings to mind the fact that a "high civilization," the society of Goethe and Beethoven, acted not only brutally but irrationally in its decision to try to obliterate the Jewish people even at great cost to itself. In trying to come to terms with the historical record, one realizes that the Nazis' decision to implement the Holocaust was made despite the fact this diversion of resources, labor, and energy made their victory in World War II less likely. By normal definitions this is not rational behavior. The notion that a government of a highly "advanced" and "civilized" Western society might commit an act of extraordinary evil ultimately harmful to itself is difficult to believe. But the Jewish people is a witness to this action, not in a vague sense, but in the tangible sense of having had the crime perpetrated on its own body. As a result, the Jewish people is available to state to the world: "We know that *the* most dangerous statement that can be made in the face of danger is that nobody would ever do such a crazy thing, that acts of supreme irrationality can never be committed." This is the most dangerous statement that can be made because it weakens efforts to prevent the "unthinkable" from being *done*.

We discovered not only an unexpected silence, but an unexpected speaking in the text, as well. The Noah text is full of dates. In the entire book of Genesis, no dates are provided for some very important events. There are no dates provided for the creation of the world, or for Abraham's departure for and arrival in Canaan, or for Joseph's journey to Egypt and his appointment as prime minister of Egypt. In contrast, there is a plethora of dates in the Noah story. There is a date for the beginning of the Flood. We learn not only that the rain falls for 40 days and nights, but also how much time elapsed before the water reached its crest. There are dates for the receding of the water, for the appearance of the mountain tops, and then the appearance of dry ground on the rest of the planet, and finally the exit from the Ark and the experience of the Rainbow. We were startled to realize the presence of all these dates and the extraordinariness of this in the context of Genesis.

In Jewish tradition, as in all religious traditions, it is clear what is to be done with important dates. They are made into moments in the cycle of the year, in which the event is re-addressed and re-experienced. Thus, the date of the Exodus is made into Passover and the date of the rededication of the Temple is made into Hannukah. In the Christian tradition, the use of dates is seen with the Crucifixion, the Resurrection, Advent, and so forth. The Passover Haggadah, the service read on the first night of Passover, teaches that the Passover event is not to be taken only as history. The participants themselves in their own lives each year re-experience the liberation from slavery.

There was, however, no observance of the dates of the Flood, either its beginning or its end. It became clear to us why this lack of observance was so. There was never any generation of the human race that had faced the practical possibility of the destruction of life on the planet— until our own. So it seemed to us that these dates had been "stored away" by the Torah to address our present generation, which faces this danger. Taking into account the way religious traditions deal with dates, we are now to understand a command to experience this danger, this deliverance, and to participate in the Rainbow Covenant, in order to make the deliverance a reality.

Jewish communities began to respond to this command in 1982. That first year, possibly 20 communities observed the call. I would estimate that in 1984, 1,000 communities have held or will hold observances. Increasingly, Jewish communities holding such observances, recognizing that the Flood was a universal event and nuclear holocaust a universal danger, are inviting other religious communities to join them.

These observances must not simply be "faddish" events. They must be built into the liturgy, the life cycle, of the people. I have visited synagogues where the reaction has been, "We covered the nuclear issue last year." Compare this response to Passover. We "did" liberation from Pharaoh last year and we will "do" it again this year, and 1,000 years from now, until the Messiah comes. It is now clear that the danger posed by nuclear bombs will be with us just as long a time. Even if all the bombs were physically eliminated, we would still have to deal with the fact that the knowledge to produce these bombs will always be with us.

Such an incorporation into the liturgical calendar means that the nuclear issue can never be avoided. It is a means of defeating the American tendency to deal with issues only periodically, while it is fashionable to do so. In the period 1959–64, nuclear arms was an important question on the agendas of the two superpowers. It was in this period that the heads of the Soviet Union and the United States agreed that general and complete disarmament was essential. The deputies of these two leaders initialed an agreement on the general principles of how to proceed toward disarmament. (See the McCloy-Zorin Pact.) But beginning in 1964, disarmament fell out of fashion and little else was done. Placing this concern in the liturgy of the people will help prevent any future loss of interest and will teach our bodies, our emotions, and our spirits—as well as our minds—to go deeper into the Wellspring of Life in order to prevent the flood of fire. For these reasons, I hope the Church as well as the Synagogue will create such liturgies.

The liturgy that we feel is called for is a flexible one and is based around the Rainbow Sign. The Rainbow is a powerful element in the midrash on the Noah text. The Rainbow represents a covenant between God and humankind promising the preservation of all life. The giving of the Rainbow Sign to Noah was accompanied by the following passage: "While the earth remains, seedtime and harvest, cold and heat, summer and winter, day and night, shall not cease." This passage evokes a concern with cycles. It suggests that one of the things that had gone wrong in the period leading up to the Flood was that the cycles had been disrupted.

The concern for cycles is strengthened by other elements in the account. If one adds up the periods of time mentioned in the text, one finds that it equals a Jewish lunar year, plus 11 days. This is precisely a solar year. Hidden within the text are other indications of a concern for cycles. When the Flood waters abated, Noah sent forth a raven and a dove to search for land. The word raven in Hebrew is *arvah*, very close to the Hebrew word *erev*, "evening." And the Hebrew word for dove, *yonah*, is very close to the Hebrew *yom*, "day." So first Noah sends out the dark of night and then the light of day. Heightening this symbolism, it should also be noted that the raven is a bird of carrion that would bring to a full end the last cycle of time before the Flood, by eating the carcasses bestrewing the flooded earth; and the dove returns with the olive branch, the first growth of the new cycle. The use of the raven and the dove at this point suggests that Noah knew that the cycles had been disrupted, both the micro-cycle of day and night, and the macro-cycle of life and death.

We realized that this insight has application to today. One of the great failings of the modern period is its destruction of the cycles of life. Modern society no longer considers the cycles important. Modern society has become so skilled at creating things, manufacturing things, that the notion of sacred time, a time where you stop producing and rest—contemplate—meditate—has been obliterated. We no longer know how to make sabbath. Both Jewish life through the great festivals and Christian life through feast days and saints' days respected the fact that there are times and days that are sacred and holy. This sacred time was recognized through ceasing the normal daily routine and meditating. But the modern Western world of the last several hundred years has forgotten how to do this.

What is the connection between this loss of sacred time and the bomb? The connection is that when you produce, and make, and manufacture, and never rest, the result is destruction. Artists recognize this fact of life. Artists begin a painting with great creativity, but if the artist works too long, if the artist makes one brushstroke too many, the painting is not finished, it is finished off. One act of creativity too many leads to ruination.

One can compare the flood to the story of creation. The creation account illustrates that it is necessary not to create in order to create. The crucial final act of creation was the Sabbath, the day on which God rested. God's rest sealed creation.

Cycles are crucial in both a large sense and a small sense. These last 500 years, we have done some extraordinary things. We have invented technologies that have transformed the planet. The oceans are chemically different from what they were 500 years ago. The face of the moon has been touched. The human life span is appreciably longer. New elements, such as californium, which have not existed since the first few minutes of creation, have been created. We must now stop, catch our breath, and make sabbath. Failure to do so will finish off the painting that is the earth.

Modernity and religious traditions must become reconciled. Our religious traditions have been very skeptical toward the technological and scientific developments of the last 500 years. It is now time to integrate what the human race has learned these last 500 years into the religious traditions. If one sees the last 500 years as a moment in the cycle of a great harvest of human knowledge, then the thing to do after the harvest is to recognize that last year's growing season is dead and that all that is left are seeds. It is a time for taking stock, the close of one harvest and the beginning of another season.

The Rainbow itself also provides important symbolism. It is an extraordinary symbol of unity in diversity. The Rainbow is not white light; if it were, it would be invisible. The Rainbow is a pattern made from all the colors of the spectrum, red, orange, yellow, green, blue, indigo, violet. It is infinite variety.

But the Rainbow is not merely infinite variety. There is also an aspect of unity: a pattern. A nuclear-age midrash illustrates this point. People who have seen the hydrogen bomb tested say that the mushroom cloud is a thing of terrifying beauty. The bomb so disrupts the electromagnetic patterns that it creates sparks and flashes of all the colors. All the colors of the Rainbow are found in the mushroom cloud, but shattered into a billion pieces. This suggests that only seeing the diversity is not enough, just as seeing only a unity is not sufficient. There must be a way to recognize that the Rainbow unites dissimilarities.

Related to this is the role Mt. Ararat plays in the account. Ararat was for the writers of the Torah what satellites are to us—the satellites from which the entire Earth could be seen as a ball of blue and white. From Ararat, the entire Middle East—the "world" of the Torah—can be seen as a unity. In fact, the Middle East forms a sort of great arc, the great fertile crescent. The Rainbow might be seen as a reflection in the sky of this crescent of many cultures. From Ararat, one would see the whole of the great crescent in the sky.

I wish to close by reflecting on Noah. Noah, as mentioned earlier, is not a political leader. This raises the question, how are we called to act against the flood of *khamas*, violence, on the planet? What does it mean that *each* human being is obligated to act to prevent the destruction of all life on the planet and is obligated not to cooperate with the structures and rules that proceed inexorably toward this destruction? What does it mean that every human being is obligated to build the Ark that is this planet?

The bishops' pastoral letter takes only tentative steps toward addressing this question of personal responsibility, although a number of bishops have begun to set honorable personal examples. I hasten to add that most other communities—including the organized Jewish community—have not yet done any better. I should also add that the publishing of the pastoral letter may prove to be one of the key moments of world history—even of "Earth history," defined more broadly than the history of the human race alone. It will not be the only key moment, however; standing alone, it is not enough. It is now our duty, acting in fraternal/ sororal unity—in the tradition of the Rainbow—to push beyond this noble beginning.

STANLEY HARAKAS

16. The N.C.C.B. Pastoral Letter, *The Challenge of Peace*: An Eastern Orthodox Response

The Christian world in general, and the Christians in the United States in particular, it seems to me, must receive the National Conference of Catholic Bishops' pastoral letter *The Challenge of Peace: God's Promise and Our Response* with much gratitude.

Even though the pastoral letter commends the work of theologians and exhorts them to continue studies so as to deepen Christian understanding of the issue of peace, it is quite another thing when the hierarchy of the U.S. Roman Catholic Church, after years of study and debate, issues an official pastoral letter on the topic of peace.

It is important, because, regardless of the wisdom, erudition, insight, and sophistication of theologian-scholars, it is not possible for this segment of a Church to exercise the same impact on the mind and heart of the people inside and outside the Church—especially on the ecumenical, cultural, social, and political scenes—as can the combined voices of the hierarchy of a Church so large and so pervasively present as is the Roman Catholic Church.

Certainly, the approach taken, rooted as it is in a particular theological and moral tradition, will not be fully accepted by Christians whose approaches historically are at variance with the Roman Catholic view. But as the bishops themselves recognize, the most important and significant fact is that by their concerted action, by the seriousness with which they have addressed the issue, and by the importance they have attached to the issue of peace, they have in a most decisive way brought to mind the moral and spiritual dimensions of the issue of peace in our day. Further, having addressed the pastoral letter not only to their own flock, but to Christians of other traditions, non-Christians, and officials in the public sphere, they have furthered a valuable dialogue and discussion. This bold contribution has significantly helped move the role of religious values and perceptions from the backwaters of private opinion into the mainstream of discussion on the issue of peace in our day.

Although episcopal conferences of other countries heavily populated by Roman Catholics, such as Ireland, Germany, and France, have issued similarly focused pastoral letters and statements, the issuance of such a document in the United States has special significance. Providing religious leadership for a large and influential segment of the population of one of the two superpowers in the nuclear standoff, the Roman Catholic bishops have influenced the public debate in a way that religious leaders in other nations cannot.

So it is with basic and general appreciation that I accepted the invitation to reflect on the document from the perspective of Eastern Orthodox Christianity, the historic "sister church" of Roman Catholicism with which we have shared more than a thousand years of common history. First, a *caveat*. I speak only for myself, not as a representative of any specific bishop or hierarchy of the Orthodox Church. I speak as a student and teacher of the Eastern Orthodox Christian ethic, with the same kind of reservations for my place in my Church, as I indicated regarding the theologian's place in the Roman Catholic Church.

My approach will be, first, to discuss similar, although far less extensive statements emanating from Eastern Orthodox sources, with some observations about their significance *vis à vis* the N.C.C.B. pastoral letter. Second, I will seek to address some specifics of the moral reasoning of the pastoral on peace from an Eastern Orthodox ethical perspective, with special application to the major question of deterrence as an ethical question. Finally, I will briefly conclude this offering to the discussion with a word on peacemaking, especially as it is embodied in the nuclear confrontation between the two superpowers.

Recent Statements on Peace from Eastern Orthodox Sources

The National Conference of Catholic Bishops' pastoral letter on war and peace is a statement for peace and against nuclear war. It steers a course that recognizes the alternatives for individuals of pacifism or a just-war stance, but as for public policy it clearly opts for a just-war approach to the issue of peace and war. However, it is tempered by a realism that progressively narrows the circumstances that would ethically endorse belligerency in our age and says a powerful "No" to nuclear war.

Among the major positions supported by the pastoral letter are the following: rejection of the use or intended use of nuclear or conventional weapons primarily against civilian populations; no initiation of nuclear or conventional warfare; a highly skeptical attitude toward the possibility of a "limited nuclear war"; rejection of the idea of a "winnable nuclear war" as a presupposition for policymaking; and rejection of the concept that one or another side in the nuclear confrontation should seek "superiority." The arms race is perceived as a crime against the poor, hungry, and suffering of the world as well as an effective denial of the genuine human needs of all nations and peoples of the world.

I iterate these positions only in order to lay the ground for a general comparison of the positions in the N.C.C.B. pastoral letter and some statements from Eastern Orthodox sources. What follows in this section of my paper is discussed both for purposes of general information, and also for purposes connected with positions I want to develop later on in this paper.

Recently, a volume of mine was published that describes the development of social concern in the Greek Orthodox Archdiocese of North and South America. It draws primarily from encyclical letters, keynote addresses of the biennial Clergy-Laity Congresses of the Church, and from the decisions of those Congresses arising out of the work of their social and moral issues committees covering the last 25 to 30 years. Among the many topics discussed in these sources are the issues of war and peace in our day.[1]

Under different circumstances and with varying goals in mind, the Clergy-Laity Congresses of the Greek Orthodox Church in this country addressed the issues of world peace, war and the arms race at every session, save one, from 1966 to 1984.

Preceding these committee-inspired decisions was a "statement of purposes" issued by Archbishop Iakovos at the beginning of his service as leader of the Greek Orthodox Church in this country, which was issued following the 15th Clergy-Laity Congress in 1960. In this statement, the archbishop twice referred to peace and war questions, on the one hand expressing a "determination to fully support the policies of our government for the securing of the peace of the world and justice," and on the other with the prayer that "lasting peace is attainable only through the prevalence of humility, love and obedience to the divine will and law."[2]

The major work of the Clergy-Laity Congresses is done through its various committees whose deliberations are brought to the floor of the plenary for debate, acceptance, revision, or rejection. The topic of peace was treated, for example, in 1980, at the 25th Clergy-Laity Congress in Atlanta when a resolution on peace was adopted that included the following affirmations:

. . . It is a fundamental Christian axiom that there is only one war which a Christian can fight: that "against the principalities, against the powers, against the rulers of the darkness of this world, against spiritual wickedness in high

1. Stanley S. Harakas, *Let Mercy Abound: Social Concern in the Greek Orthodox Church* (Brookline, Mass.: Holy Cross Orthodox Press, 1983), pp. 18, 28, 29, 64, 70, 71, 72, 74, 94, 95, 96, 98–99, 109, 120, 124, 129, 140, 142, and 156.
2. Ibid., pp. 113–114.

places" (Eph. 14:9). . . . Christ blesses the peacemakers and calls them the children of God (Mt. 5:9) and the Bible further exhorts us to "follow after those things which make for peace;" (Rom. 4:19). . . . As St. John Chrysostom has said, "It is certainly a greater and more wonderful work to change the minds of enemies bringing about the change of soul, than to kill them." . . . Peace is the goal and hope of mankind but peace to be real and lasting . . . must be a peace based on mutual cooperation—not blind trust. . . . (We resolve to) dedicate ourselves anew to the cause of peace and condemn and abhor all armed aggression. . . . (In order) to prevent the ultimate destruction of mankind we call upon the leaders of all nations to exert every effort to deescalate the arms race, and to work ceaselessly toward the goal of peace.[3]

Ten years earlier at the 20th Congress in New York City in a statement calling for the end of the war in Southeast Asia, the Congress said:

Peace on earth stands, perhaps, as the single, most desired objective of decent good people the world over. Yet it appears that this goal seems more remote and illusive today than at any other time in the history of man. The last fifty years have witnessed the greatest carnage and destruction of human life and the unleashing of demonic forces unparalleled in any other period of man's life on earth. What we must never for a moment forget, is that those secularist, demonic anti-human forces, both of the Right and the Left have in no way been contained. This Congress goes on record to commend every effort and every movement to terminate war and hostility in every area, whether it be Southeast Asia, the Middle East or anywhere else.[4]

Most recently, the 1984 Clergy-Laity Congress also dealt with issues of world peace and the arms race. Three items of interest were produced:

1. The pre-congress workbook included in the "Church and Society" section a subsection on "War" decrying the evils of war but recognizing as well that the "alternatives are sometimes a nightmare beyond comprehension." The sixth proposed study question in the section asked the delegates to discuss the complexities of nuclear disarmament and how the Church "should respond to the threat of nuclear war?"[5]

2. In the keynote address we find a call for "the condemnation of nuclear armaments and the arms race" together with a call for justice for those deprived of "life's essential needs," and for those suffering the "abridgement of political and religious freedom."[6]

3. The proceedings of the 27th Clergy-Laity Congress have not as yet been published. However, there exists in the Holy Cross School of The-

3. Ibid., pp. 156–157.

4. Ibid., p. 129.

5. *Delegate Workbook: 27th Biennial Clergy-Laity Congress*, July 1–5, 1984 (New York: Greek Orthodox Archdiocese, 1984), pp. 40–41.

6. Archbishop Iakovos, "Keynote Address," 27th Clergy-Laity Congress (New York: Greek Orthodox Archdiocese, 1984), p. 12.

ology Library a copy of the original "Report of the Committee on Church and Society," chaired by Bishop Maximos (Aghiorgoussis) of Pittsburgh, with Evan Alevizatos Chriss, Rapporteur. On p. 6 of the duplicated report is a section entitled "Nuclear Armaments and Nuclear War." It speaks of the impossibility of considering nuclear war as an alternative for the resolution of international disputes, decries the proliferation of nuclear arms, and calls for "meaningful and substantive negotiations to stop the increase of nuclear weaponry, to reduce nuclear arsenals, to resume serious negotiations to eliminate their use, "and also calls for a pledge by all nuclear powers "not to use or threaten to use nuclear weapons against each other for any reason."

Such statements, although much more limited in purpose and scope than the N.C.C.B. pastoral letter, express a shared sense of values and, more than any other consideration, focus on the end result sought— peace, not war. They represent a desire for peace emanating from one of the many religious and spiritual traditions within one of the two superpowers of the day. Surely, similar statements could be presented from nearly all other faith traditions in our country.

However, another set of quotations, interesting in comparison, have recently come forth from the Soviet Union. In July 1981 the Primate of the Russian Orthodox Church, His Holiness Patriarch Pimen of Moscow and all Russia, issued an invitation for a world congress of religious leaders on the question of peace. With the concurrence of religious leaders of many different religions, the meeting was held in Moscow in May 1982. Characteristically, this world conference carried the quite Soviet-sounding title of "Religious Workers for Saving the Sacred Gift of Life from Nuclear Catastrophe."

The western, and particularly the American, reaction to such a conference is predictable. It would seem to be another example of the subservience of religion to the propaganda interests of the Soviet Union, that is, until one reads the documents produced by the conference. In addition to the "Communique" there were "Appeals" to religious leaders and believers, to all governments, and to the United Nations 1982 Session on Disarmament.[7] I wish to share with you just a few of the statements articulated in these "Appeals" for I believe they are pertinent to our discussion here.

Early in the "Appeal to the Leaders and Followers of All Religions" the conference, chaired by Patriarch Pimen, presumed on the moral and spiritual power and authority of religion.

---

7. *The Journal of the Moscow Patriarchate* Special Issue, 11 (1982). For a balanced critical assessment see Max Stackhouse, "Moscow Peace," *Christian Century*, 100 (June 8–15, 1983), 584–586.

We appeal to you, dear brothers and sisters of all faiths in all countries of the world, because taken together we account for the majority of the world's population and because by assuming moral obligation to work together we can alter the course of history by appealing to the conscience of mankind and to those who make decisions on behalf of states, on the basis of our common love of mankind.[8]

The statement continues by pointing to the need for common purpose in the area of peace concerns "because a nuclear catastrophe threatens all of us in an equal measure." There is an admittance that "Therefore . . . there can never and under no circumstances be any justification for a nuclear war, which represents the gravest threat to mankind today."

The "Appeal," directed to all those who hold religious belief, then counsels the following, in its second part. It positions all its argumentation on the moral requirement to "save life." Toward this purpose it is necessary to "abandon the false understanding of national security and narrow national interests." Mankind, it is said, must concern itself with the "security of the whole of mankind," must divest itself of the "false idea of security as resting on the force of arms . . . and trying to establish one's own security by destroying the other" and "the false ideas that greater amounts of weapons produce greater security." The statement deplores the arms race, numerous forms of injustice seen as the sources of international conflict, as well as "the lust for power, the desire of one country to gain superiority over others and dominate them." It is affirmed that "in order to save life, peace must not be separated from justice for all; it is only peace with justice that can be a durable peace."

All who are religious are urged in the "Appeal" to work together as well as to work with nonbelievers to "put pressure on the decision-makers, and government leaders." The goal of this pressure is to foster negotiations, "abandon confrontations," "work out, on the basis of a program of action for disarmament, an effective time-scale with fixed deadlines for the different stages of a new comprehensive program of disarmament," adopting a nuclear freeze so as to "begin destroying a considerable part of the currently available arsenals of nuclear weapons," both unilaterally and multilaterally, "on the principle of equal security for all." In addition the "Appeal" calls for a massive peace-education program, rejecting the ideas that a nuclear war is "survivable," that there is even the possibility of a limited nuclear war, that "security can be gained by a pre-emptive strike capability," or that nuclear superiority offers greater security.

Toward the conclusion of the "Appeal," this judgment is made on the moral status of nuclear weapons:

8. Ibid.

But first and foremost, religions of the world should condemn with one voice as a moral evil the production, development, testing and deployment of all types of nuclear weapons by any quarters. This is not a political, but above all a moral issue. Religions must speak in a humble tone, being mindful of the fact that in the past they were parties to wars and violence. But they must speak out clearly, loudly, and unambiguously, since it is saving the gift of life which is at stake.[9]

The "Appeal" ends with a call to prayer for the aversion of world nuclear catastrophe, expressed with confidence that "He Who is the Beginning and the Ground of all that exists and of all life cannot fail to hear our prayers."

The same basic points are repeated in the "Appeal to All Governments" and to the "Appeal to the Second Special Session of the U.N. General Assembly on Disarmament."[10] There is therefore no need to elaborate on these documents.

My purpose in presenting these references is not to relativize the N.C.C.B. pastoral letter. On the contrary, I wish to show that in the conclusions supported by the pastoral letter there exists a shared and common support by spokespersons from Eastern Orthodoxy, both in the United States and in the Soviet Union. We find a commonly held perception about the total unacceptability of nuclear war and of the several policy positions that seem to increase its possibility. It would seem to me that this is a hopeful sign and an encouragement for the future of peace for the world. As I hope to show, however, such shared views do not resolve the issue of peace in its concreteness. I shall now briefly discuss the moral reasoning of the pastoral from an Eastern Orthodox ethical perspective.

Some Comments on the Pastoral Letter's Moral Reasoning

While conclusions of the pastoral letter and the representative statements from Eastern Orthodox sources share a remarkable harmony, it is perhaps of interest to speak to a few of the differences of methodology that lead to these conclusions and perhaps to point to some of the unresolved tensions that arise from these different approaches.

The first and major comment on the ethical argumentation has to do with the just-war theme. I would like to begin with a brief statement of what appears to me to be the consistent Eastern Christian ethical stance on questions of war and peace.

It seems to me that it is not possible to understand war in whatever form as a moral good. Given the presuppositions of an ethical requirement that human beings acknowledge the rights of the neighbor, some

9. Ibid.   10. Ibid.

of these most elementary rights are violated by the simple exercise of war. The life of the neighbor is the first and major good of human existence. Without it none of the other values can be realized in this life. But the first responsibility of war is to destroy the life and power of the enemy in order to prevail.

On the level of international relations, nations generally respect the rights of others by resolving conflicts through diplomatic means. When nations are at peace, it is recognized as a moral responsibility and duty toward other nations to accord respect to their territorial integrity, the lives of their citizens, and the inviolability of their property. However, what are acknowledged as elemental rights and duties in peace time immediately suffer a reversal in war time. When a nation enters a war, it rejects the normal moral claims previously placed on it by the now-enemy nation. Thus, formally speaking, war may be understood as the refusal of one nation to accord to another nation the rights it normally acknowledges, while at the same time refusing to acknowledge the duty it normally recognizes to respond to those claims. By such a definition no war could claim to fulfill criteria of the good.

When the consequences of even conventional warfare are counted, the evil of warfare is even more strongly punctuated. In another context, ecumenical in nature, I expressed a view on the unmitigated evil of war in the following words:

The huge toll of human life, evil, injuries, destroyed families, material destruction, social dislocation and widespread immorality condemn war from the point of view of its consequences . . . Even survivors are brutalized by it. Even the progress which comes from war in the technological field must be seen as totally out of proportion to the cost. Thus, one of the early Fathers of the Church wrote in a somewhat sarcastic vein: "All the world is wet with fraternal blood and murder. When it is committed by private citizens, it is a crime; if it is committed by the state, it is called valor; this means that it is not the stamp of innocence but the vastness of slaughter which bestows impunity on crimes."[11]

For Eastern Orthodox Christian ethics, the primary metaphor is growth toward God-likeness by the individual and growth toward the Kingdom of God in social relations. The primary model for the Christian ethic is the life and teaching of Jesus Christ.[12] It is impossible for us to conceive of Christ as actively encouraging warfare. The message of Christ was repeatedly couched in the themes of peace and love, and

11. Stanley S. Harakas, "Foundations of Orthodox Christian Social Visions," *Diakonia* 18 (1983), 178–188.

12. Stanley S. Harakas, *Toward Transfigured Life: The "Theoria" of Orthodox Christian Ethics* (Minneapolis: Light & Life Publishing Co., 1983), pp. 199–205.

I find it impossible to believe that Christ-likeness—which is the image of the good in human relations—could call war, any war, a moral and spiritual good.

In the imperfect world in which we find ourselves, given our human sinfulness and the perversion of structures in the condition of fallenness in which the whole world resides, wars of defense may sometimes have to be fought, and we may in one way or another have to legitimize our involvement in war. My point is that the defense of the innocent, the protection of the rights of others under our care, the restitution of injustice, the protection of "civilization" or the making of the world "safe for democracy" may provide *justification* for involvement in a war situation. But it appears to me that this acceptance cannot and should not be made into a virtue, into a moral good, and given the status of a moral good by being called a *just war*.

The recognition that the Church at times has blessed arms, has approved the raising of armies, has prayed for victory, and has celebrated that victory should not be understood as providing a moral judgment of *goodness* on warfare. It must—when ethically evaluated—be seen rather as a necessary, sometimes unavoidable, and thus tragic, evil, to which we are pushed as a result of the imperfection of our fallen and distorted condition. Given the conflict of duties and responsibilities, we may find it necessary or even obligatory to go to war—but going to war will never be a moral good that, in Eastern Orthodox terms, needs to be reflective of God-likeness and the values of the Kingdom of God.

Contrary to Augustine, who "called it a Manichaean heresy to assert that war is intrinsically evil and contrary to Christian charity,"[13] the Eastern Patristic tradition rarely praised war and, to my knowledge, never called it "just" or a moral good. The *locus classicus* is the 13th canon of St. Basil from his *First Canonical Letter to Amphilochius*. The canon struggles to free killing during war from the ethical judgment of being equivalent to murder, while concurrently refusing to call the act good, or just. Here is the text:

Our Fathers did not consider murders committed in the course of wars to be classifiable as murders at all, on the score, it seems to me, of allowing a pardon to men fighting in defense of sobriety and piety. Perhaps, though, it might be advisable to refuse them communion for three years, on the ground that they are not clean handed.[14]

---

13. *The Challenge of Peace*, n. 82, fn. 31.

14. *The Rudder* (Chicago: The Orthodox Christian Educational Society, 1957), p. 801.

The major (if only) early patristic passage that Basil may have been referring to is found in St. Anthanasius' *Epistle to Amun*.[15] In passing, and by way of illustration, as he seeks to show that circumstances serve to modify moral judgments, St. Athanasius refers to killing in war: ". . . thus it is not right to commit murder, but to kill enemies in war is lawful and praiseworthy."[16] His conclusion, however, does not place him so far from Basil as might first appear. "Therefore, the same thing on the one hand according to which at one time is not permitted, is, on the other, at appropriate times permitted and *is forgiven*."[17]

The emphasis on "forgiveness" is reflective of the strong tradition in Eastern Christianity on the concept of "involuntary sin." This teaching acknowledges the lack of direct and willed responsibility for an act, while concurrently acknowledging the involvement of the moral agent in an act that in itself is not good. In fact, St. Basil's 13th canon follows on a canon where this concept is discussed in the context of "involuntary murder." In the case of "involuntary murder," Basil imposes a penance of abstinence from communion for 11 years (not a small period, compared to 20 years for a voluntary murderer), because "the man who struck had no intention of killing him." Nevertheless, he adds, "we deem the assailant a murderer, to be sure, but an involuntary murderer."[18]

Clearly, Basil, like Athanasius, evaluates killing in war to be less of an evil than a face-to-face killing, albeit involuntary, since in canon 13, he provides for three years of abstinence from Communion, rather than 11 years of abstinence in the preceding canon.[19] Other Eastern Patristic sources for the concept of "involuntary sin" are the fifth canon of St. Gregory of Nyssa,[20] and Canon 23 of the Council of Ancyra (c. 314–315).[21]

This view is characteristic of Byzantine society, even the military establishment. In an anonymous manual of strategy, written in the sixth century during the reign of Emperor Justinian I (whose military exploits were rather significant), war is acknowledged to be "the greatest of evils," though often necessary.

I know well that war is a great evil, even the greatest of evils. But because enemies shed our blood in fulfillment of an incitement of law and valor, and

---

15. Migne, *Patrologiae Cursus Completus, Series Graeca* (166 vols., Paris, 1857–1887), 26, cols. 1169–1170.

16. Ibid., 1173B.

17. Ibid. Emphasis mine.

18. Canon 11, as quoted in *The Rudder*, p. 800.

19. For more on "involuntary sin," see Harakas, *Toward Transfigured Life*, p. 84.

20. The "Canonical Epistle to Letoius, Bishop of Melitine," *The Rudder*, pp. 874–875.

21. Ibid., p. 502.

because it is wholly necessary for each man to defend his own fatherland and his fellow countrymen with words, writings, and acts, we have decided to write about strategy, through which we shall be able not only to fight but to overcome the enemy.[22]

I believe that this passage expresses well the viewpoint of the Eastern Orthodox Church on war. Thus, in a strict sense it cannot speak of a "good war," or even a "just war."

There are, of course, problems on both sides of this issue. For example, seeing war as a necessary evil, rather than as a "just" and thus morally approved practice raises the question of motivation for the waging of war, since calling it a necessary evil can hardly be encouraging to a strong military *élan*. Consequently, some might be motivated to charge the Eastern approach as guilty of contributing to the possibility of defeat and failure by fostering the begrudging taking up of arms. It is perhaps because of some such considerations (with the possible exception of Heraclius' Persian campaign) that crusades were noticeably absent from Byzantine imperial military policy.

But in Byzantium, which endured for more than a thousand years as a political entity, concepts such as total war, and even the desirability to open and full battle, were not thought to be very good military policy. Walter Kaegi, a historian of Byzantine military strategy, summarizes a late 6th-century or early 7th-century major Byzantine strategic treatise, known as the *Strategikon of Maurice*, which shows that every means possible was used to avoid open warfare.[23]

The author of the *Strategikon* advises his readers to fashion craftiness and cunning in war and to avoid open battles, that it is often preferable to strike the enemy "by means of deceptions or raids or hunger" instead of open battle. . . .

He cautions against using open warfare. The object of warfare is the defeat and disruption, not necessarily the slaughter, of the enemy. In fact, the author of the *Strategikon* counsels against using the technique of encirclement because it would encourage the enemy to remain and to risk battle. He advises that it is better to allow an encircled enemy to flee to avoid forcing him to take a life-or-death stand, which would be costly in casualties to the encircling party. There is no more eloquent testimony to the desire to avoid decisive battle.[24]

---

22. "Des Byzantiner Anonymous Kriegswissenschaft," 4.2 in *Griechische Kriegschriftsteller mit kritischen und erklarenden Anmerkungen*, H. Koechly and W. Rustow, eds. (Leipzig. W. Engelmann, 1853–1855, 2 vols. in 3), Vol. 2, p. 56.

23. *Das Strategikon des Maurikios*, einführung, edition, und indices von George T. Dennis. Übersetzung von Ernst Gamillsheg (Wien: Osterreichischen Akademie der Wissenschaften, 1981); G. T. Dennis, transl., *Maurice's Strategikon: Handbook of Byzantine Military Strategy* (Philadelphia: University of Pennsylvania Press, 1984).

24. Walter Emil Kaegi, Jr., *Some Thoughts on Byzantine Military Strategy* (Brookline, Mass.: Hellenic College Press, 1983), p. 8.

We are not here primarily interested in Byzantine military strategy, of course. The purpose of quoting these passages is to show that, both religiously and militarily, the East recognized the necessity for war, as well as its evil. Although one might question the practical outcome of such a view, it is considered by some to have been an important contributing factor to the long life of the Byzantine Empire.[25] In the last analysis, it would appear that the Eastern approach served to limit and reduce war and its evil consequences, in practice, while neither making it into a good, nor following the path of pacifism.

The problem with a just-war approach is, perhaps, precisely opposite. I am sure that in some historic situations certain wars have fulfilled all of the criteria of *jus ad bellum* and perhaps even a few military encounters have fulfilled the requirements of *jus in bello*. But the human heart is too easily subject to self-deception and too ready to justify rationally that which it wants to do for other reasons. It seems to me that the overall effect of the just-war doctrine has been to foster the viewpoint— regardless of the objective realities—that "our side" is always justified, thus allowing the legitimization of military exploits, precisely and paradoxically as it seeks to reduce the excesses of war.

It seems to me that this point is supported by the pastoral letter itself. I see a progressive narrowing of the parameters of the possibility of a nuclear just war as the specific issues of targeting policy, the winnability of a nuclear war, "first use," and other such issues are discussed. Thus, in the section of the pastoral letter entitled "The New Moment," we hear the bishops saying ". . . in the light of our study, reflection, and consultation, we must reject nuclear war"[26] and that after all this careful study, the "'no' to nuclear war must, in the end, be definitive and decisive."[27] In addition, the bishops place the same restrictions on conventional war. In the section on "The Relationship of Nuclear and Conventional Defenses" they reason cogently that "it is not only nuclear war that must be prevented, but war itself."[28] But what then has happened to the validity of the concept of the "just war"?

In response, one could say that in fact this conclusion belies my point that the just-war approach does not function well in limiting warfare. But since the pastoral letter finally arrives at the conclusion that no contemporary war situation, conventional or nuclear, fulfills the criteria for a just war, it seems to me functionally to support the understanding of war as essentially evil. Theoretically, it seems to say, there can be a moral war, but practically, in today's circumstances, there is no such thing. In spite of this, however, were there then a consistent follow

---

25. Ibid., pp. 9–10.
26. *The Challenge of Peace*, n. 132.
27. Ibid., n. 158.
28. Ibid., n. 219.

through, it would indeed be the case and the just-war approach would be somehow vindicated.

The problem comes with the treatment of deterrence. There is need, in the just-war approach, somehow to make deterrence into a positive moral good. The result is the genuine dilemma that the just-war approach places on the bishops who must somehow relate the threat of retaliation as a defense posture with the nonintention of using the weapons. The contradiction in this position has been noted by many. "The nonintention of use" and its impact precisely on the deterrence value of the weapons are a problem precisely because there is need somehow to make the whole process "just."

On the other hand, if the ethical reasoning is not burdened with trying to make a necessary evil into a moral good, then the inner contradiction is dissolved. War is evil, and the slaughter of innocents is evil, and the loss of freedom and self-determination is evil. And the very need to defend one's self is an evil. But it is a lesser evil. And the stance of preparedness that will constrain a potential aggressor is an evil, but it is even less of an evil because the consequences are less evil.

I do not want to be misunderstood. I have little quarrel with the struggle to control the circumstances under which the Church seeks to limit the entry into war by nations with antagonistic interests. Nor could I quarrel with the kinds of considerations embodied in the *jus in bello* moral concerns. But I think that these reasonings—to which both Orthodox and Protestants in different measures are indebted—would ring more truly if they were cast in "lesser evil" categories, than in the just-war categories of this pastoral letter.

According to Richard McCormick's description of the statements and pastoral letters of the National Conferences of the Roman Catholic Bishops in Ireland, France, and Germany[29] the European approaches to the nuclear problem do take the tragic and sobering context of this approach. This is probably more acceptable from an Eastern Orthodox perspective. It seems clear to me that the just-war approach only apparently resolves the tension between the achievement of the good in human affairs and the tragic requirement that war sometimes is necessary.

Although, as the pastoral letter indicates, there might well be a difference in nature between conventional warfare and nuclear warfare, the difference arises not from the considerations of intent, if both are defensive. (Neither American nor Russian policies claim to advocate offensive use of nuclear weapons.) Rather, the qualitative difference arises from the consequences. The convergence of the conclusions of the East-

---

29. Richard McCormick, S.J., "Notes on Moral Theology: 1983," *Theological Studies* 45 (1984), 80–138; see pp. 122–138.

ern Orthodox statements on the one hand, and the bishops' pastoral letter cited above, on the other hand, it would appear, arises not primarily from the use of a just-war approach, and especially from the considerations of intent and motive, but from the self-evidently unacceptable consequences of nuclear war. Being required, practically, to hold nuclear arms for the purpose of deterrence, while hoping never to have to use them, fits into a "lesser evil" moral framework more credibly than it does into a just-war argument. The "lesser evil" approach argues that a nation holds such weapons (a bad thing in itself) in order to prevent something worse being done by the enemy (i.e., the initiation of nuclear war and the destruction of my nation). But in any case, deterrence as a policy and a practice is fraught with problems. I will address some of them in the following section.

Before turning to that task, however, there are two other brief comments I would like to make on the moral reasoning of the pastoral letter that interest me as an ethicist in the Eastern Orthodox tradition.

I was unhappy to see that the pastoral letter adopted the stance of a significant contemporary body of opinion on the interpretation of the term "violence" in moral discourse. In an otherwise quite valuable section entitled "True Peace Calls for 'Reverence for Life'"[30] there is an acceptance of the widely held view that any and all forms of injustice and evil fall under the rubric of "violence." It is clear that metaphorically such a use of the word is both understood and serves a certain emotive purpose. But it seems to me that careful use of terms is needed in specifically ethical and legal discourse. The basic sense of physical force utilized immorally, I believe, needs to be preserved in the use of this term. While not always understood as an evil, for example, the use of the word in reference to monastic spiritual formation as the exercise of force upon one's self to overcome faults, its connotations have traditionally related primarily to the use of physical force in immoral and illicit ways. Thus, when applied to abortion, it is used correctly. When used, however, to describe a host of other moral evils, in which there is no overt immoral use of force, I believe that it clouds and confuses the issues. My real concern, I suppose, is that our moral language not be further confused and diluted.

The final point in this section addresses the question of the specificity of the moral judgments in the pastoral letter. Most commentators have commended the decision of the bishops to address specifics. On the other hand, these judgments are carefully and frequently hedged with disclaimers. Thus, the bishops readily admit that they lack expertise in the details of weapons technology, and they acknowledge that they are

---

30. *Challenge of Peace*, nn. 284–289.

not privy to much technical information, while recognizing concurrently that no moral decision can be accurately made without a measure of this kind of information. The list of disclaimers could be significantly extended.

My question is then whether judgments that reach extremely concrete levels of specificity sometimes suggested by the letter are appropriate. I would ask at this point, if it were not better, more reasonable, and finally, more efficacious in influencing those who control the nuclear buttons, to keep the Church's pronouncements more on the level of "middle axioms" than on detailed specific moral judgments. For example, I stand in wonder that some people—not the bishops—are able to single out one newly created weapons system (*read*, Pershing missile) as totally, unquestionably, and unambiguously immoral, while concurrently overlooking the immorality of the rather simpler issues related with abortion.

On the other hand, I cannot accept as an Orthodox ethicist the idea that ethics remain only in the sphere of moral generalizations. Ethics, indeed, must come down to cases. But if on the level of specific and concrete moral pronouncements these are hedged about with disclaimers and the admission that "others may legitimately have differing opinions," I cannot help but wonder whether such statements have much convincing normative value. I would, in consequence, commend this question for discussion rather than take an inflexible position on it.

Peace Making in a Nuclear Confrontation Situation

The most attractive and compelling aspect of the bishops' pastoral letter is its emphasis on peace building. Both the Orthodox statements and the N.C.C.B. pastoral letter place the weight of their positive recommendations on the need for the superpowers—as the pastoral letter puts it—to "limit the use of force in a world comprised of nation states . . . but devoid of adequate international political authority."

Both sets of statements make appeals that the arms race be stopped, that arms control and arms reductions be made a priority, that injustices—perceived to be the root causes of war—be eliminated. Further, both sets of statements basically agree that the only way to achieve this is through the development of a sense of world community, the substitution of negotiation for recourse to military confrontation, and the strengthening of international structures such as the United Nations to mediate and control international conflict. At the heart of the success of this approach is the question of mutual trust, and the conditions that warrant it, especially between the two major powers.

The pastoral letter is much more realistic on this matter than is the

Moscow Patriarchate "Appeal." It is precisely the overly idealistic tone of the latter that gives a measure of justification to the charge of its being a propaganda vehicle. I prefer the realism of the N.C.C.B. assessment of the situation:

It is one thing to recognize that the people of the world do not want war. It is quite another thing to attribute the same good motives to regimes or political systems that have consistently demonstrated precisely the opposite in their behavior. There are political philosophies with understandings of morality so radically different from ours that even negotiations proceed from different premises, although identical terminology may be used by both sides. This is no reason for not negotiating. It is a very good reason for not negotiating blindly or naively.[31]

Clearly, for the American audience, the primary one for whom the pastoral letter was written, this cautionary paragraph adequately describes the communistic Soviet state. What perhaps needs to be understood by Americans, is that Soviets would regard the very same statement as justification for their own caution and suspicion of the motives and trustworthiness of the United States.

I shall provide two brief illustrations. I gave the pastoral letter to my students with an invitation to them to select it as a topic for their term papers in this semester's social ethics class. The first student to turn in a paper on the N.C.C.B. pastoral letter did not think that the letter went far enough in understanding the perfidy, atheism, and disregard for accepted moral values by the Soviets. Strongly influenced by conservative American political views, in more sophisticated and nuanced language than President Reagan's statements on the moral quality of Soviet intentions and purposes, he felt that the bishops were on the naive side by assuming that the letter could be equally received on both sides of the nuclear wall. The net effect for him is that, if accepted in the United States, the letter would only serve to weaken the negotiating position of the United States *vis à vis* the Soviets. He concludes by quoting Alexander Solzhenitsyn's 1978 Harvard address, which charged the West, and in particular its leadership embodied in "the American intelligentsia," with the loss of courage and will power. There is no willingness to trust the Soviets in this approach. It is interesting that the student is a former Anglican and a convert member of the jurisdiction known as the Orthodox Church in America—whose historic roots are in Russia.

A member of the same Orthodox jurisdiction, however, told me a story that graphically illustrated the opposite situation in Russia. This Orthodox Christian, an American priest, fluent in spoken Russian and Church Slavonic, once visited a neighborhood Orthodox Church in

31. Ibid., n. 253.

Moscow on a weekday. He wanted to make arrangements to serve the Divine Liturgy there on the Sunday following. As he went through the door in the iconostasis into the altar area he was immediately asked to identify himself, since he was wearing a roman collar, as is the custom for Orthodox priests in the United States, but not in Russia. Speaking Russian, he identified himself as a canonical Orthodox priest and requested permission to serve the Liturgy. He was then asked where he was from. The reaction to the information that he was an American, given the context of the conversation, was notable. All questions of canonicity were immediately forgotten. "We want peace!" "No war, please!" was what was addressed to him. It was clear that for these religious people it is the United States that is the major threat to world peace.

In both cases, the influence of propaganda and militarist interests may be readily identified, of course. But my point is that given these dominant realities, the sobering realism of the N.C.C.B. letter needs to be deepened and expanded even more. For all seem to agree that what is needed to break the impasse is trust in negotiations in order to eliminate the threat of nuclear conflagration. But it is precisely this trust that is missing! One is reminded of the Prophet Jeremiah's pessimistic words about peace, which can be slightly paraphrased to describe our situation: "From prophet to priest, everyone deals falsely. They have healed the wound of my people lightly, saying 'Trust, trust,' when there is no trust."[32]

Yet, in both cases, the Orthodox and the Roman Catholics have—in the final analysis—little more to counsel the powerful of the world than negotiations founded on the hope of trust. Little wonder that the "hard headed" on both sides genuinely question the relevance of our words as they call for more weapons, more sophisticated systems, more money for military purposes, all in the name of a security and a defense that increasingly appears more elusive and questionable to the rest of us.

The only way to overcome this impasse, it seems to me, is to show that the method of negotiation and the trust that it demands in the last analysis *is* workable, *is* capable of results, and *is* worth the risk, even though the risk is considerable. Clearly, the track record of our various religious traditions is not so convincing on this matter, given our own very slow and hesitating steps in the field of ecumenical relations. But the course of dialogue has at least reduced tensions and provided an opportunity for improved relations among the churches. I think that these developments serve adequately to show that in practice the spiritual and religious principles we espouse stand firm and do work.

32. Adopted from Jeremiah 6:13–14.

Perhaps the same principles that govern our thinking on such matters and have been seen to be effective in lessening tensions can be recommended for application to other apparently unrelated environments. That this is the case, in fact, is becoming clearer as scholars of another very highly competitive human enterprise seek to analyze behaviors and to recommend more successful ways for people to overcome conflict situations. The sphere I have in mind is business organization.

Recently a wide range of studies has been seeking to analyze methods of organization and functioning in the corporate world and to propose methods that help to overcome debilitating and antagonistic organizational patterns. One of these studies of corporate processes has been researched and put into practice by Christopher Argyris, James Bryant Conant Professor of Education and Organizational Behavior at Harvard University. His major work in this area is his book *Reasoning, Learning and Action: Individual and Organizational.*[33] It is not my purpose here to outline the complete approach Argyris has developed. But so that my main point might be clear, I will use some of Argyris' own words to give a brief sketch of his ideas. I believe that it will be immediately apparent how these ideas may have significance for our topic at hand. Argyris begins his book with the following statement of purpose:

The purpose of *Reasoning, Learning, and Action* is to describe the results of ten years' research on how to increase the capacity of individuals and organizations to solve difficult and underlying problems. The focus is on those problems that cannot be solved without changing basic values, policies and practices.[34]

Argyris' major premise is that

Individuals or organizations who achieve their intentions or correct an error without re-examining their underlying values may be said to be single-loop learning. They are acting like a thermostat that corrects error (the room is too hot or cold) without questioning its program (why am I set at 68 degrees?). If the thermostat did question its setting or why it should be measuring heat at all, that would require re-examining the underlying program. This is called double-loop learning.[35]

Needless to say, Argyris finds that most inefficient organizations and businesses have been caught in the single-loop learning cycle, with little or no opportunity for significant development and change through a careful examination of existing values, policies, and practices. This level of approach is retained because it is simple, easy to monitor, and provides for uncomplicated solutions. But in the process it creates more

---

33. Christopher Argyris, *Reasoning, Learning and Action: Individual and Organizational* (Washington, D.C.: Jossey-Bass Publishers, 1982).
34. Ibid., p. xi.   35. Ibid., pp. xi–xii.

problems and provides for inner contradictions when the responses and behavioral patterns are not effective or efficient. Through a sophisticated analysis of communication, the reasoning process and repeated intervention in practice, Argyris opts for a double-loop approach that calls for the constant monitoring of the interactive process by all the participants involved in it.

The aspect of his organizational theory that is most interesting to us in the context of the desire to foster peace in the relationships of the nuclear powers is that which he calls "The Unfreezing Process." Beginning with a situation he labels as "Incompetent Action, Unjust Consequences and Unawareness," he describes its immediate effects on those in the organization. These he designates with the terms "decreasing self-confidence, the increasing sense of not being in control and the increasing fear of not being in contact with reality." This leads to what he calls "Feelings of Vulnerability." It is here that the two kinds of learning come into play. Single-loop learning, or low-level learning, basically denies errors of the past, rejects new actions as impractical, and reverts to the original stand-off situation. On the contrary, the recommended method is to enter into a process of "Reflecting, Experimenting and Generating Models" of what he calls "theory-in-use." The result of this activity breaks the old patterns and encourages new actions, new competence, more just actions and organizational structures, and increases a sense of confidence. This, in turn, creates a high level of learning—double-loop learning—in which the participants become involved in "inquiring and confronting cases, leaders, participants and self."

This approach, when describing the process by which double-loop learning takes place in the corporate and organizational setting, uses what amounts to startling language when the issue before us is the question of fostering trust in negotiations for the decrease of tensions between the nuclear powers. Model II, as he calls it,[36] requires certain governing variables for action. Each of these is perceived as producing an action strategy for the actor and towards the environment. These, in turn, produce consequences for the behavioral world that are described in terms of learning consequences. The first variable described is "Valid Information." The action strategy for the actor and toward the environment related to this variable calls for the design of situations or encounters in which participants originate ideas and experience high personal causation. In the circumstance of nuclear negotiations this would appear to mean that participants would enter the talks without preconceived solutions to the questions of deterrence, arms reduction, and the like and with the expectation that something new was desired to overcome

36. Ibid., p. 102, Table 6.

the impasse. In such a situation the participants would not be defending any particular proposal and the negotiations would clearly have the character of a "brainstorming" exercise open to a certain unbinding and unpredictable conclusion.

That which keeps it from being threatening is that no participant is constrained or forced to accept the conclusions, for the second variable is free and informed choice. On this level, the action strategy calls for the task to be controlled jointly; therefore, defensiveness is minimized, and the discovery and proposal of solutions take on the characteristics of unpredictable conclusions through double-loop learning, leading potentially to increased effectiveness. Could we conceive of Americans and Soviets sitting down at a table (even in a mock negotiations setting) and deciding to find mutually acceptable ways to resolve the nuclear dilemma? Would it be possible to "think together" on these matters not in a way that sought to preserve the *status quo* but to find new resolutions to a situation that both powers recognize as untenable and dangerous in the extreme? Could not trust be fostered by such efforts? Is it not conceivable that such negotiations could produce plans that might dissolve or at least reduce the tensions inherent in our present nuclear standoff?

The final governing variable has strong resonances in the nuclear negotiations processes of the past. Argyris' phraseology is interesting: He calls it "internal commitment to the choice and constant monitoring of the implementation." This is how he describes action strategy for the actor and toward the environment: "Protection of self is a joint enterprise and oriented toward growth, together with bilateral protection of others."[37] A negotiating stance in organizational and corporate affairs that would place the protection of the other on an equal level of concern for the protection of self is here called for. Applied to nuclear negotiations it would invite and promote a mood of concern and care by the participants not only for one's own nation but for the opponent's as well! It would require that those participating in the negotiations give equal attention to the security requirements of the other nation, as they do for their own.

As such, the negotiation model would require the negotiators to assume the concerns of the other nation as well as their own on all questions. It would be a joint peace building enterprise. And it seems to me that such a negotiating model would come as close as possible to love for enemy as one could possibly come, in the sphere of international relations. The difference between this model and a full Christian understanding of love for enemy is that enemy nations would agree to act in

37. Ibid.

this way because there are no real alternatives. Their intentions would still be self-preservation, even self-enhancement. It is the consequences as relating to the mutual avoidance of nuclear annihilation that would be the goal. Clearly, however, the kind of love and caring for the other in personal relations that may require an exposure to full vulnerability is not possible on the international level, just as it is not practicable on the corporate and organizational level.

As a result there is need for constant monitoring, for openness to correction and learning, to maintaining the ongoing process by which the freedom of the participants is preserved, leading slowly and step by step to internal commitment and encouraging risk taking to help bring about the desired consequences. Such a model in the peace-negotiating process, if accepted and practiced over a period of time, might provide the possibilities for a genuine de-escalation of the arms race and provide the presuppositions for a genuine achievement of peace.

I have probably failed to convey anything more than the barest outlines of this "Unfreezing Approach," but I do not believe that it escapes the attention of those interested in peace in a nuclear age that negotiations between the nuclear powers are very much caught up in Argyris' single-loop learning cycle. Phrases such as "incompetent action," "unjust consequences," "unawareness, leading to decreasing self-confidence," "increasing the sense of not being in control," and the "increasing fear of not being in contact with reality," leading to "feelings of vulnerability," have a remarkable conformity with attitudes regarding the present nuclear standoff. Our retreat to the old patterns of the cold-war era, to solutions that demand more and more of the same nuclear deterrences in the face of their increasingly apparent impracticability, must now be evident to everyone.

Argyris' model of double-loop learning seems to be an organizational model that specifies a relatively modest level of operation that can engender the minimal level of trust for a genuine process of negotiation to take place. It may well be that in a model such as this, where all is not posturing to retain the *status quo*, the leap toward world peace may take place. The interesting thing about Argyris' model is that the process seems to work in business organizations and in other competitive situations. The shared process of inquiring and confronting of cases rather than one another might be precisely the kind of methodology that would foster the hard-headed, yet innovative, negotiating that might well produce results on behalf of lessening tensions and reducing the threat of nuclear war.

It may be argued that the West, with its more individualist, self-determining traditions, would be more ready to enter into such a process, while the more structured patterns of organization in the socialist countries, and particularly the Soviet Union, would be less amenable to change. But by the same token, the Soviets are much more vulnerable to significant change by this more open process, which, it must be remembered, is precisely understood as a learning process.

As one reflects on this model, it more and more seems to embody the values of the Gospel's approach to human relations, which focuses on the practice of love that seeks not only one's own well-being but that of the neighbor as well. What I have described here is not much more than an intuition. I would hope that those much more knowledgeable than I in these matters (including, I would hope, Professor Argyris) would investigate the application of these ideas to the sphere of nuclear negotiations. It may be the only way that the trust that the religious communities perceive as essential may be realized.

Conclusion

The National Conference of Catholic Bishops' pastoral letter on *The Challenge of Peace* as it comes toward its conclusion asks that prayer be offered for peace. I conclude this paper with portions of the litany offered at practically every service conducted in the Orthodox Church. Known as the "Litany of Peace," its first three petitions refer to peace. The liturgical response to them is "Lord, have mercy." They are as follows:

"In peace, let us pray to the Lord."
"For the peace from above and the salvation of our souls, let us pray to the Lord."
"For the peace of the whole world, for the stability of the Holy Churches of God, and for the union of all, let us pray to the Lord."

JOHN HOWARD YODER

17. *The Challenge of Peace*: A Historic Peace Church Perspective

Among the many perspectives for both affirming and challenging criticism that *The Challenge of Peace* so fruitfully provokes, my task is to identify those questions arising from the particular perspective of the nonviolent minorities within Christian history, who have recurrently challenged the dominant vision of justified violence that took over Christian moral thought in the fourth century. By "historic peace churches" are traditionally designated three denominations present in North America: the Mennonites from the 16th century, the Quakers from the 17th, the Church of the Brethren from the 18th. Fuller historical accuracy would add others; some older, like the Waldenses from the 12th century or the Czech Brethren from the 15th, and some younger like the Churches of Christ from the 19th, and from our own century early Pentecostalism, the Kimbanguist community in Zaire, and the Mukyokai in Japan.

The right of the peace churches to be heard is not based on any success they might have recorded in building world peace or in performing works of mercy, or even in merely surviving: The reason for them to be heard is only that what they say is on the subject to which the letter speaks and that they have been saying it for a long time.

The phrase "nonviolent minorities" that I first used reaches beyond sectarian Protestantism or the historic peace churches. For centuries the same moral position was prescribed for Franciscans, for pilgrims in penitence, for practically all priests, and for serfs.

Nor should we commit ourselves to any specific interpretation of the relation between minority status and nonviolence. Is it that the nonviolent position is not assumed by many people because it is costly: "It is a narrow gate and a hard road that leads to life, and only a few find it"? Or is it the other way around? Is it that only the exclusion of these people from social domination provided them the exemption or the luxury of leaving coercive social management to others? We need posit no one answer to that. Nor must one understand "minority" numerically. In any tyrannical society, the powerless people are a numerical majority.

All that my label means then is that the questions I should address to *The Challenge of Peace* are those that become visible when one does not posit the assumption that one must reason morally from and toward the widely acceptable consensus of which the dominant ecclesiastical teachers since the early Middle Ages were the spokesmen.

I therefore do not attempt to see the letter as a test of internal coherence and organic development within the just-war tradition. Such a pattern of dialogue evaluation may well be intrinsically more ecumenically appropriate, when reading a document addressed by a body of pastors to their own faithful, than my outside perspective, but the more distant critique is my assignment.

I shall therefore set aside, except for this allusion, such challenging perspectives of internal criticism as the warrants for the tripartite epistemology of paragraph 9, for the reason why moral judgments made in particular cases with regard to nuclear death do not have the authority to bind conscience[1] as those relating to fetal death, or the difference between faddist and responsible understanding of "discerning the signs of the times."[2]

Not only might the themes I am not dealing with be ecumenically more promising: They also are the points where the document seems to me to be the most disappointing. The description of the just-war tradition in general[3] is far weaker than the actual application in the later text, which applies firmly only a few of the just-war criteria. The distinction between general moral principles that may be taught with authority and practical applications that may not, without clarifying how you know which kinds of truths belong in which area, is far less clear than the drafters seem to think. Yet those are the topics obviously I must leave to critics operating within the majority tradition.

The most simple affirmations are called for on the most general level. It is enormously to be welcomed from the peace church position that the bishops picked up this question at all, that they studied it in a way that opened them to recognizing all kinds of new information, both technical and moral, that they were ready to take positions critical of presently dominant national policies, that their study process itself relativized and enriched the notion of episcopal magisterium, and that they surveyed the biblical witness in a way not typical of earlier moral theology in the field. It is great that they took seriously, at least on the surface, the invitation of Popes and councils to be original and not only respectful of tradition. My specific cavils with regard to how they car-

---

1. *The Challenge of Peace: God's Promise and Our Response* (Washington, D.C.: U. S. Catholic Conference, 1983), n. 10.

2. Ibid., n. 13.

3. Ibid., nn. 80–110.

ried out the assignment can be properly understood only against the background of this initial strongly affirmative appreciation. Nothing else that the bishops have done, and precious little that mainline Protestants and Orthodox have done in the same field, can stand any comparison with the quality of originality and synthetic vision the *Challenge of Peace* demonstrates.

Not everyone involved in ecumenical conversation has been about that task long enough to feel the freedom to be critical as well as affirmative. It therefore may be important for the readership that I state what in other connections ought better to be taken for granted: namely, that the freedom with which I proceed to a series of critical observations in detail is a part of my long-established respectful involvement in conversation with Catholic moral theology, my especially long and strong personal esteem for Bryan Hehir, and my awe at the dimensions and quality of this letter as an unprecedented event in the life of the churches (not only of the Roman obedience) in this country.

Two Languages?

By the nature of the case the items that I can lift out will not be all of the same shape or size: I renounce any vision of equilibrium or balanced coverage because of the specific selectivity assigned to me.

The first point where a doubt is provoked by the text, seen from my assigned perspective, is the sanguine confidence of paragraph 17 that two different kinds of moral discourse, although distinct, can be counted on to be necessarily complementary, when one is based on "a specific perspective of faith" and the other is addressed in its own terms to a community that "does not share the same vision of faith." From any perspective of real history or pure critical reason, it is quite unclear how we can know *a priori* that the moral discourse prescinding from the vision of faith will still be open to the same basic moral meanings. That the wider civil community is "bound by certain key moral principles" is itself a statement of faith. It is not *a priori* self-evident nor empirically verifiable by a survey of all possible civil societies and subcultures.

Paragraph 17 telescopes as if it were one statement three levels of argument: that both the community of the faithful and the civil community should be addressed on moral questions; that on "certain key moral principles" both communities are in point of fact (i.e., under God) bound by the same obligations; and that in point of fact (i.e., in empirical social experience) most communities can be addressed with the same moral imperatives. The first two statements are not specifically Catholic: They would be held to equally by Baptists and Quakers, by humanists, fundamentalists, and liberal Democrats. The third presumption, on the other hand, transposes an empirical question into what it calls "Catholic ecclesiology." The label is probably true but not in the sense the drafters intended. The social context in which one can assume that the language of the civil community and that of the community of faith will coincide on key issues is that of establishment or recent disestablishment. It is not a general fact of experience, nor a general characteristic of the fallen world. It is the social product of that particular coincidence of experiences in the medieval world, in which the civil community and the faith community were as far as possible merged: completely in theological intention and to a considerable extent in institutional achievement. Oddly, then, the credibility of the statement that the two distinct styles of communication will be complementary, when their patterns of reasoning are quite distinct, is based on the millennial heritage of times when the communities were permitted to differ from each other as little as possible. If the civil community in question were that of the Ik, of the Soviet Republic of outer Mongolia, or the Khmer Rouge, the first two affirmations would still be credible because they are a religious vision: The third would be pointless.

Of course we all want to be able to speak in such a way that people from outside our faith community can understand. There is nothing specifically Roman Catholic or even "catholic" about that intention. The question is how we go about making it possible for them to understand. Do we simply dilute the level of moral expectancy? Do we distinguish in some substantial way between different kinds of moral obligation? Do we affirm for instance that nonviolence and just war are complementary for Christians but that for pagans they are not? The simple social fact that we have to talk in the presence of non-Christian fellow citizens and make sense to them is cited at a strategic place in the beginning of the text as if it made a big difference: yet we are not told what the difference is at the concrete point of the wrongness of killing people.

This is not to call into question the fruitfulness, in the present western social mix, of our making the most of those points where there can in fact be a relatively great overlap between the value systems of the faith community and of the civil community. What is questionable is our knowing *a priori* that the overlap is assured, and what its moral content is.

This characterization of the situation is odd: It describes specifically as "Catholic ecclesiology" a situation in which the Church accepts being a minority, and accepts the terms of discourse of an unbelieving society, on the grounds that the moral truths derived from the faith need to be tailored to fit the unbelief of the "civil" listeners. Until a generation ago, that was called the sectarian position. It was the Catholics who then tended to be confident that their truth was not specifically Catholic truth.

The logic here seems to be the opposite of that which the same bishops would take with regard to the life of the fetus. The strongest spokesmen for "Catholic ecclesiology" have refused to concede that their convictions regarding the dignity of fetal life are those of a peculiar religious minority, which it would therefore be wrong to impose by law upon others. They insist that such a concession would deny precisely the Catholic quality of the claim that the truth about human nature is not sectarian but simply and naturally true. Yet truths about war, it seems, are conditioned by their derivation from religious faith, and therefore need to be translated and perhaps diluted by some kind of lower common denominator to make sense in the civil community. It would have been more helpful if the dualism here described abstractly had been permitted first to arise out of the concrete debate. To state it ahead of time leaves us not knowing whether the dualism we are being prepared for is the same as the one between nonviolence and the justified-war theory, which will be talked about later on in paragraphs 120/121, or the difference between strict and loose construction of the just-war theory as that permits tolerating deterrence, or the distance between basic moral principles and practical technical judgments,[4] or the contrast between the individual and the social.

Paragraphs 16 and 17 repeat phrases like "distinct but overlapping," "complementary but distinct." The surprise for outside observers arises when they remember that the historic origins of Catholic thought are derived precisely from a time when such a distance did not exist between the Church population and the world population. For a thousand years it was the "sectarians" who distinguished between the Church and the world, and who found that the language of faith was not understandable without translation by the rest of the population.

The Historic Shape of Pacifist Witness

Paragraphs 114 to 117 skim over history, with specific reference only to St. Francis and the 20th-century representatives Gandhi, Dorothy Day, and Martin Luther King, Jr. These figures are described representatively as "echoing and re-echoing sometimes more strongly, sometimes more faintly" the nonviolent witness of the early Christians.[5] This summary avoids specifically recognizing some of the facts that would matter the most if the historic pacifist witness were to be taken seriously:

4. Ibid., nn. 10–12.
5. One might consult on the history of the nonviolent witness of Christianity, Roland Bainton, *Christian Attitudes Toward War and Peace* (Nashville, Tenn.: Abingdon, 1961); Geoffrey F. Nuttall, *Christian Pacifism in History* (Chicago: World Without War Council, 1980).

1. That the major expressions of an alternative ethos were not heroic individuals but communities, linking rejection of war to other dimensions of radical reformation of the Church (to this community aspect we must return);

2. That their claim was regularly based on a renewed appeal to the teachings and example of Jesus Christ, against which the official Church teachers of the time regularly opposed moral doctrines appealing to "reason" and "nature" to justify war;

3. That those pacifist renewal communities were routinely persecuted by Catholic rulers, with the encouragement of Catholic clergy.

The way in which "peace" is spoken of in the pastoral, paragraph 117 notwithstanding, does not take the form of any serious attention to the witness of Christians on this subject for centuries. Between the 3rd century and the 20th, it alludes only to Martin of Tours and Francis of Assisi. Paragraph 117 would seem to allude to others when it says "the witness of numerous Christians who had preceded them [i.e., Gandhi, Day, and King] over the centuries was affirmed in a remarkable way at the Second Vatican Council."

Such a "remarkable affirmation" is, however, not present in *Gaudium et Spes*, although the pastoral constitution does open doors in the right direction. Its reference in paragraph 78 is brief and patronizing: It speaks of nonviolent means only in the present and characterizes them as "methods of defense which are available to weaker parties," in obvious reference to the experience of Gandhi and King, leaving room for those who see nonviolence rather than war as the last resort.

The Historic Shape of Nonpacifist Christendom

With this observation we move beyond the question of the place that nonviolence or pacifism had, as a minority stream within Christian history, to note that the just-war position was not in point of historical fact what Christians in government were doing.

The Challenge of Peace is more pastoral than historical in the picture it projects—more by implication than expressly—of the history of the question. It seems to be making a simple historical statement when it says that there are and have for a long time been just two ways to think about the morality of war. It can then proceed to assert that they interrelate in a mutually complementary way.[6] That is however a most inaccurate description of the real history.[7]

In terms of moral logic, the "Holy War" is a quite different moral

6. Ibid., nn. 120–121.
7. To the account of Bainton, my text may be added: *Christian Attitudes to War, Peace and Revolution* (Elkhart, Ind.: Mennonite Co Op Bookstore, 1983).

understanding. Medieval writers included the Crusade under the broader category of just war, but two different kinds of reasoning were clearly at work. Beginning with the 16th century at the latest they began to be disentangled. The "Holy War" defines just cause and just authority differently. It denies, or at least defines in a much more limited way, the rights of the adversary. It sets aside the criteria of last resort and of probable success and is less demanding in its criteria *in bello*. It provides no handles for effective political restraint. It was specifically bishops and abbots of the medieval Catholic Church who preached up the Crusades, and Popes who defined specific wars as having Crusade status by proclaiming specific indulgences. This majority tradition was not disavowed immediately by the Zwinglian reformation: It was rejected by the Lutheran Reformation, and of course by the Czech Brethren and Anabaptists. The rest of Europe disavowed that tradition by the time of the peace of Westphalia, as a decision of peoples and diplomats, sometimes without the approval of churchmen.

There is a fourth logical type that has also been present in Christian thought: namely, the notion that the political sovereign is also morally sovereign: i.e., that no higher moral authority exists or needs to or can exist than the prince (in the age of Machiavelli) or the nation (in the theory of Hans Morgenthau). Sometimes this position is called "realism" and is argued against religious moralists. At other times religious rhetoric supports this view under the heading of "divine right of kings." The concern of Machiavelli was to defend the autonomy of the prince over against any moral claims of his people or fellow princes. The same logic applies today in the claim that one nation has no obligations to the world community, or that the justified self-interest of a national community may properly be defended at the indirect cost of the welfare of the innocent.

There has always been in Roman Catholic moral teaching some concern for the wider community. In modern times there is a distinctive papal doctrine of the priority of world order. Yet nothing practical was done for centuries to prevent local preachers and bishops from affirming the sovereignty of their respective nations. Although some of his speeches entitled Benedict XV to stand in the anthologies as a "peace Pope," he appears to have been powerless to keep the episcopal leadership of Germany and France from ratifying respectively the national causes of their opposing regimes: even though neither the German government nor the French was very Catholic. It can hardly correspond to an ideal Catholic ecclesiology to let the identification of the Church with the civil community go so far as to bless both sides of a war as just; yet practically that is what most Catholics of world history have experienced.

The reason for asking questions about the past has to do with the difference between competing models of the historical faithfulness of the visible Church. The most basic identifying characteristic of what are usually called "the historic peace churches" is from the perspective of ethical epistemology, not their position on war but their view of history. They are with reason called, in the phrase made current by Professor George H. Williams of Harvard, "radical reformers." These dissenting communities arose because of the conviction that the way Christendom had evolved needed to be corrected, not just superficially but from the root. As against the vision of unbroken and organic progress presided over by a magisterium infallible in essentials, the critics I am to interpret were convinced that something worse had happened than mere frailty, inattention, or ignorance could explain. They held that the development of Christendom had not merely fallen short of the ideal, but had in fact betrayed the substance of the faith, so that what was needed was not mere revitalization or even reformation but the restoration of something essential that had been lost. Such renewal had to be prepared for by the denunciation of apostasy.

Without pretending explicitly to do so, *The Challenge of Peace* projects a vision of history that is fundamentally false, in a way that exemplifies the aforementioned criticism. It says that Catholic moral teaching with regard to war has always been in favor of peace and that this presumption in favor of peace has been implemented predominantly in the just-war tradition but also in pacifism. Thereby the document skips over a monumental opportunity to repent and to instruct. Most of the wars fought in Christian history have not met the requirements for the just-war. They have been simple expressions of dynastic or national selfishness, and yet most Catholic bishops and priests have blessed those national wars. They have not generally brought to bear upon them the discipline of just-war thinking, as this document intends to do for the present. The second category of wars that really happened were called just wars at the time but did not fit, nor did anyone claim that they could fit, the criteria *The Challenge of Peace* itemizes. They were holy wars, with bishops and abbots not merely approving but in fact often instigating them, condemning for unbelief or cowardice the populations that did not with sufficient alacrity take up arms and go off to the Holy Land. The justifiable war tradition (properly so called) was developed by theologians precisely to criticize the other two thought patterns, so that when we describe the history of critical theologies it is the just-war tradition that predominates. That is, however, not what *The Challenge of Peace* says. It does not say that the just-war tradition was articulated by a critical minority, trying unsuccessfully to bring some moral discipline to bear on the sanctified belligerence of their nations, including the episcopal shepherds of their nations.

My point in accentuating this historical corrective is not to renew an outdated pattern of interconfessional polemics, but to draw attention to the potential for learning and renewal that would reside in a more critical historiography. If it were true as claimed that the just-war position was what most Catholics were living by, and most of the hierarchy preaching, we should be hard pressed to explain how there has been so little success or even so little awareness of the need for moral restraint.

If on the other hand were we to admit that what was really going on for the last millennium and a half was that the just-war position was being taught by the moralists but sinned against by the real people, not only in the armies but also in the chanceries, then there might be a basis for recognizing how creatively original is the degree of discipline that the bishops today propose to initiate; it would also be easier to understand the mixed reaction they are getting.

The freedom, spiritual and psychological, even institutional, with which Christians and other morally concerned persons in the last sixth of our century can reopen moral questions with regard to war will depend partly on whether we can be enabled, by whatever spiritual resources it takes, to look at the story of the Crusades with that attitude that Christian faith calls "repentance," or at least what secular psychology calls learning from one's errors.

But that is not all that is missing in the learning that the past might permit. In terms of logical typology, as I said, there are not three views on the morality of war (pacifism, justifiable war, and the Crusade), but four. The fourth is what some people call "realism," articulated in early modern times by Machiavelli and in modern times by Hans Morgenthau and his disciples, according to which the interest of the nation, or of the ruling house of a nation, is itself an autonomous moral value. This has seldom been taught in normative moral theology as an accountable position: There have always been moral theologians to reject Machiavelli, as there have been morally concerned lawyers like Grotius to reject cynicism and "realism." But there have been abundant voices in the practical and pastoral theological field that did in effect ratify the thesis of the moral autonomy of one's own sovereign. The doctrine of the divine right of kings has routinely had its Catholic, Anglican, Lutheran, and Bible Belt advocates arguing with a good conscience the moral autonomy of the nation. The modern doctrine of national sovereignty, although never formally ratified in Roman Catholic moral theology, was never resoundingly questioned either until this century.

Luigi Sturzo, the Italian statesman, put part of this question bluntly:

How does it happen that the pope treats international questions so well and then when the time comes to take seriously the instruction and the warnings of the popes, the clergy and the Catholics take no account of it, as if it were not their business? Aggressive wars, breaking treaties between nations, extreme nationalism and the oppression of the poor etc . . . are condemned; but when wars break out, Catholics, with the agreement of their clergy, take sides with their respective governments, even if these governments have broken treaties, have used violence and are openly aggressive. It even appears that the pope himself not only tolerates such conduct but recognizes it as legitimate . . .[8]

The bishops' letter of 1983 is clear in its affirmation that the nation must not be an idol and that the citizen must not sell his soul morally to the government. Yet there is no depth of struggle, except implicitly, with the fact that to make that statement represents a radical reversal of the actual pastoral practice of churches throughout the West for 16 centuries.

William V. O'Brien and John Courtney Murray, who as legal and moral scholars, respectively, were writing most authoritatively on these matters during the early nuclear years, were both clear in saying that the just-war theory had been neither taught nor applied by significant numbers of Catholic clergy or citizens in recent centuries. Instead of pretending that the bishops are moderating a process of organic progress that one needs only to reformulate and update, a more accurate historical picture of the past failure of Christendom would have made much more understandable the place for repentance and renewal in authentic moral discernment and would have raised the awareness of the moral power of the whole process.

I am not prepared to argue whether this vision of history that hesitates to be judgmental is dictated self-consciously by a desire to be "Catholic" in the sense of an affirmative bias about organic history, or whether its deeper explanation is a matter of pastoral realism: i.e., the assumption that a more critical attitude toward uncritical patriotism in the recent past would jeopardize the loyalty of the Catholic people. My assignment to look at a Catholic document from outside would not best be discharged by assuming that there is such a thing as just one Catholic way to think morally. I trust the least the more abstract definitions whereby one attempts to live up to some abstract model of Catholic method, such as a particular evaluation of "nature" or of "tradition," or the treated claims to a special ecclesiology that this text makes in certain paragraphs. The most authentically Catholic moral thinking may well be done by people not trying hard to be specifically Catholic. So when I here identify a certain tension between trying to be affirmative about history to the point of misreporting it, and a pastorally concerned episcopate trying not to jeopardize the support of its people, it is not that one of those tilts is "Catholic" and the other not: They may both be specifically Catholic but in different ways.

---

8. *Les Guerres Modernes et la Pensée Catholique* (Montreal: Editions de l'Arbre, 1942), p. 77.

At another point as well I must distinguish between different modes of being Catholic. Numerous commentators have pointed out that if we were to look at *The Challenge of Peace* in the light of a standard typology like that of James Gustafson, the letter is not very Catholic. Gustafson said this himself in a paper read at Chicago on January 17, 1984:

> The most notable feature of the theology adduced in the letter is that the bishops have grounded it basically in biblical materials and in themes that are a form of biblical theology. In this respect the letter is extraordinarily different from how American bishops grounded social statements and proposals in the first half of the century. While the applications to war follow the principles of the just war tradition (always allowing for a pacifist ethic of discipleship as well), the theology is singularly devoid of traditional theological principles adduced from the divine moral ordering of the world through "nature." The title of the letter itself calls attention to this; "God's Promise and Our Response." It is noticeably not: "The Moral Order of Creation and our Obligation to Conform to It." The letter states that "at the center of all Catholic social teaching, are the transcendence of God and the dignity of the human person." Note: it does not say that at the center is the divine governance of the world through a natural moral order. "A theology of peace should ground the task of peacemaking solidly in the biblical vision of the Kingdom of God. . . ." The Kingdom and History, Jesus and the Reign of God, Promise and Response, the appeal to love, all set a theological and religious tone to the letter that is remarkably similar to some Protestant efforts to ground social ethics in some sort of biblical theology. The space given to adducing biblical materials which back the letter is itself indicative of the shift I am stressing. There is nothing in the letter about the eternal law in the mind of God, the participation of the divine revealed law and the natural law in the eternal law.[9]

The letter does seek to speak to all people (in the name of Catholic ecclesiology), but first of all it begins with Jesus' proclamation of the kingdom. Yet it still falls short of numerous of the other components of Catholic moral thought that in the lives of ordinary people have been nourished more by the lives of the saints than by either abstractions about nature or generalizations about the kingdom of God. The moral discourses of the confessional, the convent, and the spiritual exercises have contributed more—I would claim—to the moral fiber of the Catholic soul than did the academic consistency of Thomism or the casuistic refinement of the canon lawyer.

The Personal-Social Complementarity

The new formulation, according to which nonviolent respect for life and just-war respect for peace are complementary, will demand more definition if we are to be enabled to distinguish between sloppy pluralism and authentic complementarity. The simplest way to adjudicate the complementarity is to leave the nonviolence to the individual level and

---

9. *Criterion* 23 (1984), 6; quoted with permission.

maintain the just war for the social realm. This is the argument of Michael Novak in his *Moral Clarity in the Nuclear Age*. He too affirms "two vocations in the church, yet one vision . . . more than one vocation, yet one common teaching. . . ."[10]

Authentic pacifism is limited to individual vocation analogous to celibacy and most appropriate for clergy:

We sharply distinguish between pacifism as a personal commitment, implicating only a person who is not a public figure responsible for the lives of others, and pacifism as a public policy, compromising many who are not pacifists and endangering the very possibility of pacifism itself.[11]

The notion that a pacifist commitment is meaningful only for individuals, so that for societies only just war is indicated, is stated most bluntly in this anti-letter of Michael Novak, yet it is present in the bishops' paragraph 119 and by implication in 118. It is there at the crucial turns (paragraphs 62 and 75). Likewise in the vocationally focused admonitions (paragraphs 303 ff.) the assumed models of moral accountability are individual. Individual nonviolence may be thought of as an individual act of renunciation, as a special virtue in some analogy to celibacy. Historic Christian nonviolence on the other hand has been a collective and ordinary normative stance, more analogous to the commitment of marital fidelity. The dichotomy that relegates the ethic of Jesus to the symbolic irrelevance of personal idealism is like the reading of the New Testament that denied Jesus' role as historical Messiah.

This neglects the more-than-individual potential:

1. Of the *Rerum Novarum* vision of vocational communities and intermediate associations between the individual and the nation state.

2. Of the collective quality of nonviolent commitment in the peace churches, in religious communities, in Gandhi and King, Chavez and Camara: collective not only as a way of sustaining motivation but also as a way of achieving goals.

3. Of the Body of Christ as a supra-national community, not only in the eternal purposes of God but in sociopolitical realism. What the internal Roman self-definition of "ecumenical" meant in the pastoral's preparatory process was only that one supranational component of the bishops' process was their going to Rome to meet with bishops from the NATO nations. A more authentic ecumenicity would have strengthened their effort substantially.

4. Of the acceptance of Diaspora status (Rahner) or minority status

---

10. Michael Novak, *Moral Clarity in the Nuclear Age* (Nashville, Tenn.: Thomas Nelson, Inc., 1983), p. 32.

11. Ibid., p. 34.

(Segundo) in a post-establishment world. The letter does accept this new status in its [to me odd] description of a "Catholic ecclesiology" as meaning one ready to communicate to nonbelievers in their own frame of reference; but the affirmative counterpart, namely, appropriating the freedom to be *as a body* a social power in but not of the world, and therefore also in but not of the nation, is missing. Catholicism's Americanization agenda is progressing, but has not yet issued in sufficient self-esteem to be free to be "unpatriotic."

The distinction between an ethic for individuals and an ethic for communities may coincide with the distinction between an ethic based on faith and an ethic accessible to other people of good will, but the document does not say that. The bishops may be assuming that the way in which nonviolence and the just war are complementary is that one is only for individuals and the other for communities, but the complementarity argument of paragraph 121 does not say that. Thus we are left stranded in the effort to understand what the document really means about the place that it affirms for the rejection of violence as a moral imperative. But the opposite can be said as well: It presents no argument for rejecting it as a moral imperative. The just-war tradition is presumed as having always been there, but the reason it should be right in the face of the *prima facie* presumption against violence[12] is not given. The document says (quite rightly) that the two positions coincide in the rejection of nuclear war and in a presumption against the use of force. But the reason that the just-war position diverges and overrides the presumption against the use of force is not explained anywhere in the text. The closest thing there is to an argument at all is the simple historical account that: "The council and the popes have stated clearly that governments . . . must defend their people." The previous paragraph had said that "millions of men and women have served with integrity in the Armed Forces." I must respectfully and ecumenically insist that neither of these statements constitutes a moral argument. Any positive moral argument would not have been easy, after the way the biblical groundwork had been laid.

The conversation between pacifism and just war is made much more complex by being carried on in relatively similar ways at three different places in the text. First of all it comes within paragraphs 73 through 78, before the case against violence has been made. It is then simply iterated in paragraph 121 and picked up again in 221 through 230. Whereas the pacifist position as argued by Cyprian and Martin, to say nothing of the New Testament, had spoken of the question of self-defense, namely

---

12. *Challenge of Peace*, nn. 120–121; 224.

to exclude it, that theme was left out of the pastoral's biblical treatment, in such a way that when the argument for self-defense is made in 72 through 78, it appears as the thesis rather than the antithesis. Then the recognition that, after it has been overruled as a position based on the Gospel, nonviolence still has some secondary value for individuals, comes as an afterthought. When measured by earlier Roman Catholic statements, such an afterthought is already quite benevolent. I respect both institutionally and personally those who are responsible for this signal improvement. It falls far short, however, of living up to the stated intention of having the two positions be in any sense reciprocally supportive of each other or equally valid.

World Order: Vision or Obligation

I have previously described as "pastoral" the way in which Popes, conceiving of the whole world as their diocese, can call on the entire global flock to rise above factional squabbling and live in peace, without taking on the functions of legislation or adjudication. As *The Challenge of Peace* says, there is a papal vision of long standing that calls for world order. It is true that numerous Vatican texts since John XXIII give increasing recognition to peace as an imperative. It is appropriate that Joseph Fahey should have said that the position of Rome on peace is one of the best-kept secrets of our age. The acceptance of the necessity of national self-defense is regularly stated by papal documents (e.g., *Gaudium et Spes* 82) as a concession "in the absence of" or even "until we achieve" a valid international peace-keeping order.

There is strong reason for the pacifist and the papalist to join in projecting that vision. It has been a standing component of the historical eschatology of Christian sovereigns ever since the 15th century: e.g., King George of Bohemia (1464). It has been the vision of minority thinkers like the Moravian Comenius or the Quaker William Penn, of philosophers like Kant and poets like Tennyson.

But the point of apparent agreement helps us clarify the substantial disagreement that it is my assignment to articulate.

The papal vision is of a state of affairs that, if it obtained in world affairs, would enable us without too much loss to stop killing each other. When, however, such a state of affairs fails to obtain, as it has since Cain and Abel, and in the most systematic way since the Peace of Westphalia, this vision lays no claims on us that would obligate us to continue to revere the life of our enemies. Instead, it becomes a potential motivation for war, if the war we undertake can claim to be aimed at establishing such a world order, which can only be achieved by putting down our enemies.

For the minority witnesses Comenius or Penn, on the other hand, the pertinence of hope cannot thus be relegated to the category of an impossible "ideal" nor of an end to be attained by means contrary to it. To call it an "ideal," which by the very act of giving it that name we declare we are ready to act against, until God by means of his own brings about a world in which it would cost us less to obey him, is to disconnect historical project from ideal hope. To say on the other hand that we expect to achieve on God's behalf the establishment of a world order of peace by successfully subduing militarily those who threaten "peace" as we represent it is to connect project and hope backwards. Scripture rather connects project and hope in terms of first fruits, prefiguring, proleptic realization, whereby the rightness of our present activity is determined not by its bringing about with some kind of consequential certainty a better end state, but by its participating already in the nature of that end that we confess has been initiated in the Incarnation, Crucifixion, Resurrection, and Ascension of Jesus of Nazareth, and in the projection of his life into ours through Pentecost and through the ongoing mission of the people of God.

The kingdom of God is neither an ideal whose irrelevance leaves us to figure out how to run the world according to our own resources, nor an inner-worldly achievement that we are responsible to produce by our own machinations: It is an already incipient reality, which we are called to be governed by, in the face of a world whose powers continue to operate as if it were not true. If we grant that it is not true, and make our own ethical choices on the grounds of its not being true, we have platonized it into an irrelevant ideal and/or operationalized it into a justification for our own claim to be not servants but lords in the rebellious cosmos.

''Tis a Gift to be Simple'

One crux of the pastoral demands comment, despite the fact that there is no firm or agreed vocabulary in the peace church tradition to elucidate the issue. It figures here more as appendix than as conclusion. There is a very special kind of moral discourse going on when, after having said with unprecedented firmness that a massive nuclear arsenal may never be used and must in principle be dismantled, the letter goes on to say that from that strong statement there need not be drawn the commonsense conclusion that the dismantling would need to begin now or that the use of these weapons as a deterrent threat need not be renounced. The French bishops were still more blunt in juxtaposing the prohibition of explosive use with the affirmation of deterrent use. That may perhaps be read as a suggestion that something peculiarly congenial to the Latin mind is going on here. Far be it from me to determine whether there is anything specifically Germanic about the response of Mennonites and Brethren, or anything specifically British about the response of the Friends, who find this kind of distinction unrealistic with regard to the way social bodies work and dishonest with regard to the way persons make moral decisions. The bishops' second draft articulated the acquiescence in deterrence with a temporal framework, repeating the famous Krol testimony, and stating an explicit threat that *if* progress were not made rapidly and verifiably toward disarmament then the acquiescence would be revoked. That brought the discussion back into the reach of moral accountability. When the third and fourth drafts abandoned that seriousness, they also jettisoned the capacity to convince. They cannot at the same time convince the Russians that we do plan to retaliate disproportionately and indiscriminately and convince fellow Christians in North America that they have not sold out practically after having stated the firm position theoretically.

I cannot without further research state, in terms of systematic theological ethics or cultural anthropology, that this kind of complex casuistics would necessarily be incongruent with the peace church position and congruent with the "Catholic" position. Thus the correlation is impressionistic rather than systematic. That impressionistic correlation is located more on the level of truth telling ("let your 'yea' be 'yea' and your 'nay' be 'nay'") than on that of the morality of killing. Nothing in the document makes credible, or even argues responsibly in favor of the credibility of a balancing operation by pastors or politicians to make the deterrent threat credible to the Russians at the same time that the determination not to use the weapons should be credible to fellow Christians.

Fuller analysis might see in this concession one more specimen of the "pastoral" readiness to place the unity of the community above logical coherence. Or it might be a crucial test of the "double effect" tradition. For now, it must suffice to record doubts about whether such complex casuistry can be applied by real human communities.

The Abstractness of the Gospel

It is always somewhat unfair to read a document for what it fails to say: Often the hazards of redaction and compression do not reflect any intentional or even unconscious selectivity. It is, however, still notable that paragraphs 39–54, dealing with Jesus, remain hopelessly general. The themes of the proclamation of the reign of God, of resurrection and forgiveness are clear. The notion that the law is fulfilled, which is the central theme of Matthew 5, itself identifiable on literary critical grounds as the core ethical catechism of the Gospel, is not accentuated.

Neither is the way in which three of the six contrasts in the chapter have been centered on radicalizing the prohibition of killing, the end of retaliation, and radicalizing love of the neighbor into love of the enemy. The love of the enemy is referred to[13] but the radicality of the Gospel writer who framed that text to make us see it as more than just an all-inclusive love is avoided. Paragraph 37 says we are to love as Jesus loved us: The Gospel is far more radical in that it says we are to love enemies because God does.

A second significant lacuna in the New Testament interpretation is that Jesus is spoken of only as the proclaimer of the coming kingdom or as the teacher of an ideal morality. That sets aside weighty dimensions of the lived humanity of Jesus the social leader:

1. That he was discharging a messianic mission, defining in his career a response to the challenge to be a zealot liberator. Rejecting quietism he agreed to be a liberator: yet he rejected righteous revolutionary violence as well;

2. The sweeping portrayal by the entire New Testament of the sacrifice of Jesus as a paradigm for the life of the disciple. The witness of the New Testament to the kingdom of peace is thereby flattened into a long-range social idealism, the goal of a better social reality to be worked toward by whatever means we find reasonable. Jesus is flattened into a teacher of a slightly more generous and slightly more demanding moral idealism, but not different in substance from other moral idealisms.

3. The fusion of Atonement and ethics in the Cross that is *at once* divine transaction and human obedience, unique achievement, and general paradigm.

If it were not for the document's repeated appeal to the difference that a "Catholic ecclesiology" should make, it might not be appropriate to discern at this point an intentional tilt. That Jesus' life and ministry revealed God's love is said, but not that they revealed that love by refusing to lead a military campaign for a just cause.

Thus the first characteristic of this part of the text, when seen from the Radical Reformation perspective, is the thinness of its Christology. It is not avowed, but the structure of the rest of the letter nonetheless assumes that Christ's moral authority is not the last word, when it comes up against our need to defend those social values that the just-war tradition affirms.

Certainly there can be no thought that the bishops, if asked to speak about Christology in a doctrinal or liturgical context, would be satisfied

---

13. Ibid., n. 37.

with such a thin and moralistic vision of Jesus, His achievement, and His authority. The New Testament references[14] would have provided a basis to say more, although even there the themes of atonement and ascension, both politically important, are underdone, but their potential is immediately squeezed off by a systematic hermeneutical discussion about the need to keep salvation and fallenness, "already" and "not yet," in balance.[15] Already here they tip their hand by predicting compromise (before the substance of the issue calls for it), saying they will "examine both the positions open to individuals."[16]

The perspective of historical debates makes it yet more clear how the whole question of the moral authority of Jesus becomes significant. We could not tell it from the New Testament texts alone, but we know from later intellectual history that Christians differ as to whether what Jesus said and did about the love we should have for our enemies is the last word on the subject, or whether it is one word among several, needing to be complemented and even corrected by other words to be derived from reason, nature, or experience.

The Challenge of Peace makes much of a "Catholic" ecclesiology at some points. Some of its interpreters make more of a "Catholic epistemology"; namely of the importance of saying explicitly that Jesus is *not* our final guide in these matters, precisely since nature, reason, and historical experience show us the necessity sometimes of loving the enemy less because we must love more someone the enemy threatens. At this point it turns out to matter considerably whether we believe truly in Jesus as the first and last Logos of God, or as one teacher among several. When compared to documents of just a generation ago, *The Challenge of Peace* is striking in the amount of attention it gives to Jesus and to Scripture, and by the less direct and more implicit way in which "nature and reason" are allowed to speak. Yet when contrasted to the witness of the historic pacifist minority, the difference is still great in the other direction.

It is, as I said at the outset, unfair to measure *The Challenge of Peace* from the peace church perspective. From any other perspective the pastoral is a great step forward. It should be measured from its own base; by the sensitivity that in the first place opened the agenda, by the unprecedented involvement of all the bishops and all the faithful, by the growing appropriation of biblical and contemporary perspectives, by the growing confidence in local pastoral application. In all those respects it opens a new era: May its originality be worthily followed by the new kind of pastoral catechesis and community moral discernment that it implies.

14. Ibid., nn. 39–55.   16. Ibid., n. 62.
15. Ibid., nn. 57–62.

ALAN GEYER

18. Two and Three-Fourths Cheers for the Bishops' Pastoral: A Peculiar Protestant Perspective

My former colleagues at *The Christian Century* declared the Catholic bishops' pastoral letter *The Challenge of Peace* to be the number one religious story of 1983. I would venture an even more superlative judgment: The pastoral provided the most significant entry of Church leadership into American public debate on war and peace in many, many years—perhaps in the whole of American history.

In 1967–68 I chaired the Task Force on Defense and Disarmament for the National Council of Churches, which produced a policy statement still in effect as the Council's basic platform on these issues. There are many points of convergence theologically and politically between that document and the pastoral, including an emphasis on the created order and an endorsement of a freeze on the testing, production, and deployment of nuclear weapons—yes, way back in 1968. But how many Americans have ever heard of the N.C.C. statement, much less studied it? The Council never made its study process visible to its constituencies or to the general public. Nor did the N.C.C. ever muster the staff resources and competence to mobilize its member communions around the issues of nuclear disarmament.

As a witness before the bishops' drafting committee, a critic of its early drafts, and a participant in numerous forums on the pastoral, I have come to believe that the process of the pastoral's formation is as significant as its content and has been the key to its impact. It was a visible process, engaging significant leaders from many professions, demanding enormous commitments from bishops and staff over a two-year period, and open to widespread participation and criticism through four laborious drafts. Government testimony was sought, then rejected—to the consternation of some officials, especially a certain Catholic national security adviser who presumed to lecture the bishops on sound Catholic doctrine. What an extraordinary church-state confrontation it has been, to the benefit of us all! The media clearly found the debates and intramural struggles to be exciting stories. It has too often been the habit of bishops in my own denomination to concoct a brief message overnight, confer only among themselves, and dispatch it to our churches—with little if any measurable response.

The pastoral's process was also *ecumenically open*. As one of three Protestants invited to testify on ethical issues, I found myself called a "moral theologian" for the first time in my life—not only an unmerited title for a mere political scientist but an unheard-of title among mere Methodists. The awareness that the bishops were looking for help in every direction has much to do with the positive reception accorded the pastoral in Protestant and Orthodox communions.

The pastoral itself displays yet another kind of openness: an *openness to the future*. There is a becoming modesty in acknowledging that scientists and physicians, not priests, have done the most to raise public consciousness about nuclear issues. But the bishops speak of much unfinished business, even unfinished theological business, yet to be done. Three passages particularly point to the need for theological and ethical reconstruction. In Section I on "Peace in the Modern World," we read: "This pastoral letter is more an invitation to continue the new appraisal of war and peace than a final synthesis of the results of such an appeal. We have some sense of the characteristics of a theology of peace, but not a systematic statement of their relationships."[1]

Later, in outlining problems and principles for "War and Peace in the Modern World," the bishops say:

> The task before us is not simply to repeat what we have said before; it is first to consider anew whether and how our religious-moral tradition can assess, direct, contain, and we hope, help to eliminate the threat posed to the human family by the nuclear arsenals of the world.[2]

The really startling word in that passage is "whether"—a seeming confession by the bishops that the theological and moral tradition they have known may not be fully capable of coping with the novelty and enormity of the nuclear challenge.

Again, in the pastoral challenge to theological educators near the conclusion of the letter, the bishops humbly acknowledge: "We know that we have only begun the journey toward a theology of peace; without your specific contributions this desperately needed dimension of our faith will not be realized."[3]

Not the least of the pastoral's benefits has been the opening up of a new nuclear debate within the American military. On a recent cross-country flight, I fell into conversation with the two-star general next to

---

1. *The Challenge of Peace: God's Promise and Our Response* (Washington, D.C.: U. S. Catholic Conference, 1983), n. 24.

2. Ibid., n. 122.   3. Ibid., n. 304.

me who reported on intensive studies of the pastoral by senior Army officers in the Pentagon and at military colleges. Catholic leadership among Air Force chaplains has involved me in three conferences on chaplains as peacemakers, an almost unthinkable theme several years ago, but now inspired by the pastoral.

Beyond these personal testimonies, the official responses of the National Council of Churches and many of its member communions bear witness to the pastoral's ecumenical impact. The N.C.C.'s Governing Board, meeting in San Francisco just 10 days after the pastoral's adoption in Chicago in May 1983, unanimously adopted a "Resolution on Peacemaking and Ecumenism: A Celebration of the Catholic Bishops' Pastoral Letter." The opening section of that resolution reads as follows:

With deepest gratitude to God for the work of the Spirit moving among our Roman Catholic sisters and brothers, the Governing Board of the National Council of the Churches of Christ in the USA gladly joins in celebration of the Bishops' Pastoral Letter on "The Challenge of Peace: God's Promise and Our Response."

We heartily welcome:
1. The call for a new theology of peace "in the midst of a cosmic drama"— a theology which goes beyond the repetition of moral traditions, which grounds peace itself in God's Good Creation, and which views nuclear war as a most sinful confrontation with our Creator.
2. The involvement of the bishops themselves in a long, painstaking, admittedly perplexing, and disciplined process of study. . . .
3. The engagement of the bishops with a large and diverse company of witnesses. . . .
4. The courage of the bishops in assuming the burden of risk in applying Christian principles to specific policy issues, notably their opposition to first use of nuclear weapons, counter-population warfare, first strike weapons, and nuclear war-fighting strategies, as well as their strongly expressed skepticism about the concept of "limited" nuclear war.
5. The bishops' forthright endorsement of a bilateral nuclear freeze, deep cuts in nuclear arsenals, a comprehensive test ban, United States fidelity to Article VI of the Non-Proliferation Treaty, and "independent initiatives" by the United States toward reversing the arms race.
6. The bishops' advocacy of renewed "efforts to develop nonviolent means of conflict resolution," a more positive dialogue with Soviet leaders and people, and a clearer recognition of the tragic implications of the arms race for the world's poorest peoples.[4]

Now because of the rather slow, lumbering, cumbersome process of policymaking in the N.C.C., that resolution had to be formulated in January 1983, four months before the bishops actually completed their pastoral. In January, the Council was responding to the second of the

---

4. "Resolution on Peacemaking and Ecumenism: A Celebration of the Catholic Bishops' Pastoral Letter," *Center Circles* (Newsletter of Churches' Center for Theology and Public Policy) (June 1983), No. 10., p. 5.

bishops' four drafts, knowing that drafts three and four were yet to come.

The original language hailed "the courage of the bishops" in addressing what the pastoral's second draft called the "negative dimensions of deterrence." But the widely recognized problem of the second draft—the seeming contradiction between the Pope's legitimation of nuclear deterrence and the bishops' rejection of it—was solved by deleting that sharp critique of deterrence in the third and final drafts. The N.C.C. therefore continued to hail the bishops for their courage on other issues but, alas, felt it had to delete that reference to deterrence.

The N.C.C. resolution, also on the basis of the pastoral's second draft, welcomed the bishops' advocacy of "a more positive dialogue with Soviet leaders and people." But the pastoral's third and final drafts added half a dozen rather shrill paragraphs of anti-Soviet, pro-NATO sentiment.[5] In the end it was perhaps more the Council's own investment in improving U.S.-U.S.S.R. relations than approval of the pastoral's harsh and perhaps somewhat unbalanced language that inclined the Governing Board to leave its own wording intact. The N.C.C. for the past two years has had a U.S.-U.S.S.R. Church Relations Committee, growing out of the "Choose Life" consultations in Geneva in 1979 and 1980. Under that committee's auspices four exchange programs are occurring in 1984, including a massive 300-member visitation by Americans to Russian churches in June. While a goodly number of Roman Catholics are joining in the June seminar, relationships between U.S. and Soviet Catholic churches remain tenuous at best. I would hope that the National Conference of Catholic Bishops could in time develop a more positive orientation to Soviet peoples, including the tens of millions of Christians in severely constrained but growing churches.

But it was still another issue, that painfully divisive one of abortion, which evoked the only serious proposal from the floor in San Francisco to amend the draft resolution. Four rather purple paragraphs on abortion were added to the pastoral in the third and fourth drafts.[6] Pro-choice advocates were called symptomatic of a "a disease of the human spirit"—and that in the same pastoral in which it was held that justice in war might require killing "proportionate to the value defended." This seemed to some Protestants to be a dubious dualism in moral reasoning, as between abortion and war. Accordingly, the section of the N.C.C. resolution that refers to "several serious and unresolved questions" for ecumenical cooperation in peace making was proposed as the place

5. *Challenge of Peace*, nn. 245–258.   6. Ibid., nn. 285–289.

where differences of religious conviction on abortion and its ethical relation to peace making might be respectfully acknowledged. Several women on the Board rose to support such an amendment in very moderate language. However, many colleagues who might have joined them on the issue itself opposed such an amendment. They did so because the Board's discussion of the resolution followed a splendid address by Archbishop Quinn of San Francisco, and they were disinclined to disrupt the mood of ecumenical solidarity at that moment—or to give the media a sensational headline such as "NATIONAL COUNCIL BLASTS PEACE PASTORAL ON ABORTION." So the proposed amendment was turned aside. But the painful issue remains.

One further and more positive word on that San Francisco meeting: Governing Board members who had closely monitored the bishops' drafts and who were troubled by what the third draft did to the second draft were much relieved that the fourth draft seemed at several key points to return to the second draft. This was particularly the case with regard to strong language in support of the nuclear freeze and in opposition to first-strike weapons. Another change welcomed in the final draft was the reinstatement of nonviolence as a Christian moral tradition instead of the third draft's claim that just-war teaching was "*the* classical Christian position" (emphasis added). Then, too, the third draft's curious appearance of accepting at face value Caspar Weinberger's and William Clark's letters on the morality of Administration nuclear targeting policies was modified by demoting Weinberger's and Clark's comments to footnotes in the final draft. Such welcome changes as these led the Governing Board to alter the very title of its resolution from "An Affirmation" to "A Celebration" of the pastoral letter. (Of course, some zealous hearts, such as my own, would have been pleased at the excising of Weinberger's and Clark's remarks altogether.)

The rest of this commentary is a more substantive discussion of the pastoral under three headings: some unheralded issues, some neglected issues, and the central nuclear issues.

Some Unheralded Issues

The attention accorded to nuclear policy issues, not least because the pastoral itself describes the nuclear arms race as "a moment of supreme crisis" for "the whole human race," has tended to obscure other valuable portions of the text.

Section IV on "The Pastoral Challenge and Response" contains particularly helpful paragraphs aimed at the diversity of vocations and their distinctive callings to peacemaking. While priests, deacons, and religious and pastoral ministers are enjoined to cultivate "the gospel vision of peace as a way of life for believers and as a leaven in society," it is the injunctions to the laity that I find especially empowering.

Educators are asked to "teach the ways of peace" and are told that to do so is not "to weaken the nation's will, but to be concerned for the nation's soul."[7] That calling is reinforced throughout the pastoral, not only by its teachable substance but by repeated imperatives to peace education at all levels. The bishops acknowledge that questions of war and peace have a political dimension because they are embedded in public policy. But the fact that these questions are political, they say, is "no excuse for denying the church's obligation to provide its members with the help they need in forming their consciences." They add: "We reject, therefore, criticism of the church's concern with these issues on the ground that it 'should not become involved in politics.' We are called to move from discussion to witness and action." This legitimation of the political content of Christian education is a liberating gift to all churches that remain enfeebled and privatized in their education programs.

Similarly, *public officials* are enjoined to examine "with great care and objectivity every potential initiative toward world peace, regardless of how unpromising it might at first appear." One such initiative commended is "the establishment of a task force including the public sector, industry, labor, economists, and scientists with the mandate to consider the problems and challenges posed by nuclear disarmament to our economic well-being and industrial output."[8]

Men and women in *defense industries* are instructed to form their consciences by the moral principles of the pastoral. They are also promised that "those who in conscience decide that they should no longer be associated with defense activities should find support in the Catholic community."[9]

Men and women of *science* are urged to "pursue concepts as bold and adventuresome in favor of peace as those in the past have magnified the risks of war."[10]

Men and women of the *media* are told: "On the quality of your efforts depends in great measure the opportunity the general public will have for understanding this letter."[11]

Men and women in military service, parents, and youth are all empowered to fulfill their own special vocations for peace making.[12]

I share the judgment that some of these exhortations, in their content, are rather pale platitudes. But this entire emphasis on peace making as

7. Ibid., nn. 304–305.
8. Ibid., nn. 323–325.
9. Ibid., n. 318.

10. Ibid., nn. 319–321.
11. Ibid., n. 322.
12. Ibid., nn. 306–317.

an enduring vocation is a guard against mindless and momentary spasms of activism that too often have undermined the credibility and effectiveness of peace movements. We Protestants have often thought we invented the notion of the ministry of the laity but it remains a woefully undeveloped doctrine in our religious practice. The pastoral is virtually a Reformation document on this point.

The section on "Interdependence: From Fact to Policy"[13] challenges the Church and both superpowers to confront the chasm between the world's rich and the world's poor: to face up to the systemic issues of injustice in international economic power structures. Especially striking is a quotation from Pope John Paul II's 1980 encyclical, "The Redeemer of Man," which, on behalf of the poor, questions "the financial, monetary, production and commercial mechanisms that, resting on various political pressures, support the world economy."[14] The bishops go on to stress "the need to expand our conception of international charity and relief to an understanding of the need for social justice in terms of trade, aid and monetary issues."[15] Whatever the defaults of Catholicism in this matter, neither the National Council of Churches nor most of its communions have begun seriously to incarnate this conception. Charity and relief operations continue to monopolize resources. It is still more acceptable to wait for disasters to happen than to try to prevent them. Preventive policies are seen as too "political." Churches apparently have to let people suffer and die before we really get involved. Even then, the involvement is not likely to touch the terms of trade or money or insurance or shipping.

It is unfortunate that the new peace-making programs of some denominations that have at last focused on nuclear issues are viewed by some Third World groups as racist because they have not focused on North-South economic issues. The only healthy way out of this painful confrontation between so-called peace issues and so-called justice issues (which, in the roundedness of *shalom* should never be pitted against each other) is hardly to de-emphasize the nuclear threat: It must be to muster new cadres, institutions, and programs to work for justice in the world market and economic development policies. Moreover, the nuclear challenge itself is a matter of *justice*, as I shall emphasize in my conclusion.

While the pastoral discusses both the just-war and pacifist traditions, there is a very special grace in the way in which the final draft embraces these alternatives as complements to each other. While the second draft dignified pacifism by discussing it first, the third draft demoted pacifism

---

13. Ibid., nn. 259–273.   15. Ibid., n. 203.
14. Ibid., n. 259.

to last and characterized just-war theory as "*the* classical Christian position"—although additional paragraphs were added on "the value of non-violence." As a nonpacifist with some skepticism about the adequacy of just-war theory as a peace-building doctrine, I found the final draft much more peaceable in such language as this:

> . . . the "new moment" in which we find ourselves sees the just-war teaching and non-violence as distinct but interdependent. . . . They diverge on some specific conclusions, but they share a common presumption against the use of force as a means of settling disputes.
>
> Both find their roots in the Christian theological tradition; each contributes to the full moral vision we need in pursuit of a human peace. We believe the two perspectives support and complement one another, each preserving the other from distortion. Finally, in an age of technological warfare, analysis from the viewpoint of non-violence and analysis from the viewpoint of the just-war teaching often converge and agree in their opposition to methods of warfare which are in fact indistinguishable from total warfare.[16]

The pastoral persists, however, in characterizing pacifism as an "option for individuals" and not for state policy.

There remains a kind of contradiction between the bishops' heavy reliance on just-war rationalism, a philosophical style sundered from biblical theology, and the bishops' candor in acknowledging that they have only begun to imagine what a *theology of peace* might be. It is this dissociation between moral philosophy and prophetic theology that helps to account for what I believe are the inadequacies of the pastoral's approach to the central issue of nuclear deterrence, of which I shall say more later. Stanley Harakas has suggested that just-war philosophy cannot really justify deterrence, which would better be viewed as a "necessary evil"—a view he believes to be more compatible with Orthodox and Protestant theologies.[17] Joseph Boyle has employed precisely the norms of just-war philosophy, especially the moral argument of the bishops themselves concerning proportionality, to suggest that deterrence cannot rationally be regarded as "morally acceptable."[18] At any rate, the pastoral does not wholly succeed in vindicating just-war theory as the prism through which to view nuclear ethics, much less as a dynamic and rounded theology of peace making.

Some Neglected Issues

As comprehensive as the pastoral is, there are some very salient issues that are not addressed at all.

16. Ibid., nn. 120–121.
17. See Stanley Harakas, "The N.C.C.B. Pastoral Letter, *The Challenge of Peace*: An Eastern Orthodox Response," this volume.
18. See Joseph Boyle, "*The Challenge of Peace* and the Morality of Nuclear Deterrence," this volume.

One of these is the universality, the multinational reality, of the Church of Jesus Christ, transcending all nations and sovereignties and ideologies. Bryan Hehir himself on numerous occasions has offered a lucid analysis of the Church as a transnational actor—but that analysis is not adequately reflected in the pastoral. The need of American churches to have our nation-centric fixations challenged by Christians on the other side of all our conflicts—our "enemies," our economic rivals, the nuclear have-nots, and those who share "the epistemological privilege of the poor" (a phrase of Jose Miguez Bonino, liberation theologian from Argentina)—that need has given ecumenism a more fundamental meaning than ever. For ecumenism—our life together on the whole inhabited earth, our multinational community in the Body of Christ—has become synonymous with peace making. In short, the pastoral lacks a truly *catholic* ecclesiology, if a mere Methodist may be forgiven such a presumptuous judgment.

Another neglected issue is the systemic impact of military technology and the arms race on the very polity of American society. The "Star Wars" fantasy of some of our leaders hardly promises to restore the ability of this nation-state to fulfill its constitutional obligation to provide for the common defense—actual *defense*, that is. When decision-making frames are reduced to minutes, our deliberative bodies cannot deliberate and all notions of plebiscite are nullified. Elsewhere I have written:

The managerial structures of military technology have evolved a new form of government in which industrial, scientific, military and political elites collaborate in setting national priorities and allocating resources. Early bureaucratic decisions about weapons research and development become increasingly inaccessible to the public and even irreversible in the legislative process. As the U.S. approaches the bicentennial of its Constitution in 1987, we must surely take stock of all such unratified amendments imposed by military technology.[19]

It is just here we see that the Pauline doctrine of wrestling with principalities and powers and (in Colossians) of Christ disarming the principalities and powers is a necessary component of a full-blown theology of peace. But I could not find it reflected in the pastoral.

A related issue is the problem of *truthfulness* in international conflict. In my testimony before the Bishops' Committee, I said:

The nuclear arms race has become the severest test of truth in our nation's history. It is zealously promoted with false words, deceptive jargon, pretentious dogmatics, hateful propaganda, and arbitrary bars on access to truth.
    Demythologizing has become the indispensable theological tool of peace-

19. Alan Geyer, *Theology and Ultimate Violence: A New Nuclear Agenda for the Churches* (Washington, D.C.: The Churches' Center for Theology and Public Policy, May 1982), *A Shalom Paper*, n. 12, p. 7.

making: it is the empowerment of people to understand the stratagems by which inhuman and violent speech violates the word of God.[20]

The SALT II treaty's ratification, which both the N.C.C.B. and N.C.C. supported, was defeated by a combination of myths and downright lies that the Treaty's supporters largely failed to expose, preferring to try to out-tough the opposition in their so-called realism about the Soviet Union.

The French Protestant theologian, André Dumas, in his *Political Theology and the Life of the Church*, has written that the Bible portrays the lie as "the first and most poisonous source of injustice." The violence of lying destroys communication, trust, and confidence—the prime requisites of peace making—and ultimately generates hostility and death.

The Central Nuclear Issues

An unplanned ecclesiastical debate over nuclear deterrence occurred at the United Nations in June 1982. During the Second U.N. Special Session on Disarmament, the Vatican Secretary of State, Agostino Cardinal Casaroli, speaking in the name of Pope John Paul II, offered a provisional legitimation of deterrence. Nuclear deterrence, said Casaroli, might be "a step towards progressive disarmament" and therefore could be judged "morally acceptable"—although not an end in itself.

That statement was regarded by the U.S. Catholic bishops as a direct and authoritative intervention in their deliberations over their pastoral letter, then in its early stages of development. When in the second of four drafts they obediently invoked this papal language, they nevertheless proceeded to spell out what they regarded as the five "negative dimensions of deterrence." Those five dimensions were:

1. Deterrence requires the intention to use strategic nuclear weapons, which would violate traditional just-war criteria of discrimination and proportionality.

2. If deterrence fails, the human consequences of nuclear war would be morally intolerable.

3. Deterrence requires a relationship of radical distrust.

4. There is no assurance of limits on weapons use if deterrence fails.

5. Maintaining large and costly nuclear arsenals for deterrence requires the diversion of resources from compelling human needs.

This contradiction between papal legitimation of deterrence and the bishops' critique could not long endure. Following consultations at the Vatican and further deliberation by the bishops, the five-point critique

20. Ibid., p 7.

was deleted in the third and final drafts. That deletion was seized upon by Reagan Administration officials as a vindication of U.S. nuclear policy—but the bishops insisted that their tolerance of deterrence was "strictly conditioned."

At the U.N. in June 1982, the World Council of Churches was represented by General Secretary Philip Potter in a statement amounting to a categorical rejection of deterrence. Fully cognizant of the Pope's statement a few days before, and drawing upon the report of the Council's Public Hearing on Nuclear Weapons and Disarmament in Amsterdam the previous November, Dr. Potter charged that deterrence "negates the very security it seeks to achieve." He went on to say:

Deterrence offers no reliable basis for peace. . . . It can in no way be a step towards disarmament. On the contrary, it has fueled and continues to fuel the arms race at various levels. The concept of deterrence is thus politically unacceptable and morally indefensible.[21]

Thus were the lines drawn for a new moral debate between the Vatican and the World Council—but with both profoundly committed to ending the nuclear arms race.

In April 1983, an unprecedented Pan-Christian World Conference on Life and Peace was held in Uppsala, Sweden. Hosted by one of the six presidents of the World Council of Churches, Archbishop Olof Sundby, the conference brought together Orthodox, Protestant, Roman Catholic, Anglican, and evangelical bodies. In the process of drafting and deliberating over its final "Message," the Uppsala gathering also brought deterrence to the forefront of ecumenical controversy. The conflict had been foreshadowed by the U.N. debate between the Holy See and the Council. Catholics, Lutherans, and some Anglicans sought to mute the critique of deterrence that developed through four drafts. The drafting committee sought to balance its prophetic impulses with its pluralistic conferences but only partially succeeded. There were eight abstentions and one Roman Catholic negative (unofficially on behalf of the U.S. bishops) on the final draft of the Message, which read, in part:

The current military and political doctrine of nuclear deterrence must be challenged. The dangers of nuclear proliferation and accident, and the increasing sophistication of weaponry, leading to the concept of the so-called "limited nuclear war," all render the doctrine of nuclear deterrence increasingly dubious and dangerous from every point of view. Most of us believe that from the Christian standpoint reliance upon the threat and possible use of nuclear weapons is unacceptable as a way of avoiding war. Some are willing to tolerate nuclear deterrence only as a temporary measure in the absence of alternatives. To most of us, however, the possession of nuclear weapons is inconsistent with

21. Statement by Dr. Philip Potter, June 24, 1982, Ad Hoc Committee of the Special Session of the U.N. General Assembly Devoted to Disarmament (mimeographed).

our faith in God, our concept of creation, and our membership in Christ's universal body. Nuclear deterrence is essentially dehumanizing, it increases fear and hatred, and entrenches confrontation between "the enemy and us." Most of us therefore believe that the existence of these weapons contradicts the will of God. For all of us obedience to that will demands a resolute effort within a specified time limit for their total elimination.[22]

Some of that language is rather close to the bishops' second draft—but not so close to the final draft.

A third 1983 event, the Sixth Assembly of the World Council of Churches in Vancouver, also substantially addressed the topic of deterrence. Following the lead of Philip Potter and quoting the Amsterdam Report, the Assembly's major policy statement on peace and justice asserted that deterrence is morally and politically unacceptable as a basis for peace making. With Amsterdam, the Sixth Assembly declared:

We believe that the time has come when the churches must unequivocally declare that the production and deployment as well as the use of nuclear weapons are a crime against humanity and that such activities must be condemned on ethical and theological grounds.[23]

Beyond this policy statement, a Vancouver section report on "Confronting Threats to Peace and Survival" provided a more detailed critique of deterrence much in the style of the Uppsala Message of the previous spring—in fact, very much influenced by the Uppsala discussion. That report, commended to all Council churches for their study and action, offers perhaps the most substantial analysis of deterrence yet to emerge from Protestant and Orthodox communities.

The World Council and Uppsala statements highlight another aspect of this topic that was entirely neglected by the pastoral: the fact that deterrence theory has a virtually *theological* character. Deterrence-as-theology tends to convert technical and political issues into a *credo*. It becomes a whole belief system with a dogmatic style. Like most dogmas, deterrence is highly abstract and speculative: Its historic effects cannot be proved. In his 1981 book *National Defense*, James Fallows wryly observed:

The "best" minds of the defense community have been drawn toward nuclear analysis, but so were the best minds to be found in the monastery, arguing the Albigensian heresy, in the 14th century. A novel theory about how the Kremlin might respond to nuclear strikes may be advanced, may make the author's name, and may lead to billions in expenditures without entering any further

22. *The Message*, Christian World Conference on Life and Peace (Uppsala, Sweden: April 20–24, 1983), pp. 6–7.

23. "Statement on Peace and Justice," in David Gill, ed., *Gathered for Life: Official Report VI Assembly World Council of Churches* (Geneva: World Council of Churches, 1983), p. 137.

into the domain of fact than did the monks' speculations about the nature of God.[24]

Deterrence-as-theology makes fundamental claims about reality itself—so much so that some strategic analysts and even some professional theologians speak of "The Deterrent" as if it had a capital D—as if it were an objective and dominant historical force. That was one of my concerns about the early drafts of the pastoral letter, which repeatedly spoke of *the* deterrent. I complained about that, and the number of such references was at least reduced in the final draft. It still seems to me highly inappropriate for an authoritative church document to seem to baptize *the* deterrent as the historical incarnation of some presumed ultimate force.

Nuclear deterrence, after all, is a dogmatic rival to Christian faith. The challenge of nuclear weapons is not simply a rational moral choice about whether to possess or use them, or how or when to use them: It is the challenge of absolutist dogmas about our security to the foundations of our faith.

It is this idolatry of nuclear deterrence, its ritual invocation in support of every new nuclear weapon, even its apocalyptic terror that must lift our Christian critique beyond the norms of rationalistic philosophy, even just-war philosophy, to prophetic theology.

A more prophetic perspective is also reflected in the greater seriousness with which both Uppsala and Vancouver addressed the issues of nuclear proliferation and its relation to deterrence. Father Hehir has publicly acknowledged that the pastoral's brief mention of the Non-Proliferation Treaty was inadequate to the point of being a "two-line throwaway." (Actually, there were five lines on the subject.) We would do well to recognize that treaty as the most solemn moral and political covenant of the nuclear age: the absolute renunciation of nuclear weapons by 116 nations now in return for the legal obligation to nuclear disarmament and energy sharing by the superpowers. It is the breaking of that covenant by both the U.S. and U.S.S.R. that may make proliferation the terrible equalizer in the few remaining years of this millennium. It is the issue that makes nuclear weapons a matter of both peace and justice.

To reject deterrence as an idolatrous, speculative, and dehumanizing doctrine is not necessarily to insist that we can and should unilaterally get rid of all nuclear weapons by 6:00 tonight. One of the consequences of such an action would almost surely be a decision by Britain, France, and China to build up their own nuclear arsenals—and by Germany, Japan, and still other countries to go nuclear. There is simply no way to

---

24. James Fallows, *National Defense* (New York: Random House, 1981), p. 39.

escape the nuclear dilemma without acting in concert with other nations to seek common security. So we must distinguish between deterrence as an *ideology*, which I believe must be displaced, and a *prudent political judgment* as to how best to make progress toward nuclear disarmament. The pastoral, precisely because it does not expose this ideological character of deterrence, does not help us to make this necessary distinction.

But my last word is to recall the silly title of this commentary: "Two and Three-Fourths Cheers for the Pastoral." My emphasis is still upon the *cheers*. My gratitude for participation in the process and for the pastoral's redemptive influence is much, much greater than the sum of all my questions and carpings. If in this commentary I have largely focused on some of the still-debatable principles of Christian peace making, it is only in the hope of peace itself, which the pastoral has elevated so marvelously.

BRIAN JOHNSTONE

19. Noncombatant Immunity and the Prohibition of the Killing of the Innocent

In the U.S. bishops' pastoral letter on war and peace, *The Challenge of Peace: God's Promise and Our Response*, a distinction is made between universally binding moral principles and prudential applications of these principles to specific circumstances.[1] The two central principles presented as universally morally binding are the principles of noncombatant immunity and proportionality.[2] The subject of this essay is the principle of noncombatant immunity. Can this principle be upheld as universally morally binding? This paper has three parts. The first part presents the conceptual framework for an understanding of the principle and its role in moral judgments on the conduct of war. The second part provides an analysis of several contemporary positions, some challenging the principle, some supporting it. The third part is a critical analysis of these positions. In conclusion it will be argued that there are moral reasons of sufficient strength to uphold the principle as universally binding.

A Conceptual Framework

To set the context for this investigation we could begin with the following stipulations:

1. Human life is sacred; therefore the taking of even one life is of momentous importance.

2. There are two value positions following from this:

(a) Because it is sacred, human life may never be taken under any circumstances. An important stream of the Christian tradition has taken this view. If it were adopted, there would, of course, be no further place for any discussion. We would be constrained to adopt a doctrine of universal, absolute immunity of all human life. However, this has not been the dominant view taken in the tradition.

1. *The Challenge of Peace: God's Promise and Our Response* (Washington, D.C.: U.S. Catholic Conference, 1983), n. 10. Hereafter cited as *Challenge of Peace*.
2. Ibid., n. 9.

305

(b) Because human life is sacred, the presumption must be that the taking of human life is prohibited. But in certain carefully delineated, exceptional cases the presumption may be overridden. How are these exceptions to be justified?

The rationale for the exceptions has taken the following form: It is presumed that we live in a broken world where the communal pursuit of good is threatened by the pervasive human proneness to evil.[3] Thus, it can happen that a good (e.g., the lives of innocents, the existence or security of a people, the order of justice, or peace) is endangered by some violent act on the part of others. The pursuit of the good in such a case, precisely by reason of the active, violent threat, may have to take the form of violent resistance. Such violent resistance may entail the killing of the other, the active, violent source of the threat. It is the very pursuit of the good, in the circumstances of violent opposition to its attainment, which justifies the use of violence. It is the involvement in the violent opposition to the attainment of the good that renders the opponent a legitimate object of violent, even lethal, resistance. This involvement may, however, be regarded from different perspectives. If the active involvement is regarded from a subject-centered perspective, then it is the moral guilt (in the formal, subjective sense) that renders the opponent liable to resistance by violence. If the involvement is regarded from the perspective of the objective order, it is the violation of that order, the objective, material guilt of the opponent, his status as injurer, which is relevant. If the involvement is regarded from the perspective of the actual use of violence, e.g., by the bearing of arms, then it is the status of combatant that is significant. Thus, according to these different perspectives, it is the "guilty," or the "injurer," or the combatant who becomes liable to lethally violent resistance.[4] Correspondingly,

3. The good to be pursued falls within the scope of corporate or communal responsibility. This article is not concerned directly with individual pursuit of good and the question of individual self-defense that may arise from this.

4. St. Thomas' analysis focuses on *culpa*, which he understood as moral fault, in the sense of subjective moral guilt. *Summa Theologiae*, II–II, q. 40, art. 1. See Leroy Walters, *Five Just-War Theories: A Study in the Thought of Thomas Aquinas, Vitoria, Suarez, Gentili, and Grotius* (Ph.D. dissertation, Yale University, 1971), p. 111. More recent discussions of the question in the manuals of moral theology took "guilt" to mean not personal, subjective guilt but *material* guilt. This was expressed by the use of the Latin words *nocens* (injurer) as opposed to *innocens* (not injurer). This position is reflected in the article by John C. Ford, S.J., "The Morality of Obliteration Bombing," *Theological Studies* 5 (1944), 261–309, p. 272. In this sense material "guilt" is morally relevant in that the violent, unjust act prevents the defender attaining or preserving a good to which he/she has a just claim and so may be justly, and violently, resisted. In this sense it is not necessary that the guilt include criminality involving personal culpability. See George I. Mavrodes, "Conventions and the Morality of War," *Philosophy and Public Affairs* 4 (1975), 117–131, p. 123 for a contrary view. The character or quality of

the following remain within the protection of immunity: the innocent, the noninjurer, the noncombatant.

Hence, in the structure of the just-war doctrine, a basic rule for the conduct of the war requires a distinction between those who are liable to violent repression and those who are not. With this is joined a second principle, that of proportionality, according to which the response to the aggression must not exceed the nature of the aggression, or that the harms done must be proportionate to the good sought.[5] This essay will be directly concerned with the principle calling for such a distinction, or the principle of discrimination. The principle is a *ius in bello* criterion and may be applied only after the fundamental justice of going to war has been established by the *ius ad bellum* criteria.

The bishops' letter does not distinguish between the principle of discrimination, the prohibition of the direct killing of the innocent, and the principle of noncombatant immunity.[6] However, these are not necessarily identical. The category of the innocent belongs in the moral-theological tradition, and the corresponding principle prohibits the direct, intentional killing of the innocent. The category of noncombatants belongs originally to the legal tradition, and the corresponding principle prohibits the direct, intentional killing of noncombatants and the destruction of civilian targets not immediately connected with military activities.[7] The principle was developed primarily as part of the customary

---

"injurer" may be meaningfully specified by the bearing of arms or the status of combatancy. This does not imply that combatants are the *only* injurers, but specifies a category who are injurers and who can in a practicable fashion be discerned as such. There may be others who so qualify, but it would be difficult, if not impossible, to determine precisely who they are. Hence, in framing an operational norm it is reasonable to focus on this determinable category.

5. The first formula of proportionality is that used in *Challenge of Peace*, n. 103. There appear to be significant differences between the two formulas.

6. *Challenge of Peace*, nn. 103–105, 147–148, 178, 183, 185.

7. Cf. William V. O'Brien, "Proportion and Discrimination in Nuclear Deterrence and Defense," *Thought* 59 (1984), 41–52. On discrimination, see also William V. O'Brien, "Legitimate Military Necessity in Nuclear War," in William V. O'Brien, ed., *World Polity*, Vol. 2 (Utrecht: Spectrum Publishers, 1960), pp. 35–120; William V. O'Brien, "Nuclear War and the Law of Nations," in William V. O'Brien, ed., *Morality and Modern Warfare* (Baltimore: Helicon 1960), pp. 126–149; James Turner Johnson, *Just War Tradition and the Restraint of War: A Moral and Historical Inquiry* (Princeton, N.J.: Princeton University Press, 1981), pp. 121–228; Geoffrey Best, *Humanity in Warfare* (New York: Columbia University Press, 1980). On the distinction between combatants and noncombatants in international law see, for example, Lester Nurick, "The Distinction between Combatant and Non-Combatant in the Law of War," *American Journal of International Law* 39 (1945), 680–697; Ian Brownlie, *International Law and the Use of Force by States* (Oxford, England: Clarendon Press, 1963); Hans Kelsen, *Principles of International Law*, rev. and ed. Robert W. Tucker (New York: Holt, Rinehart, and Winston, Inc. 1967), esp. pp. 113–127; Sidney D. Bailey, *Prohibitions and Restraints in War* (London: Oxford University Press, 1972); Robert E. Osgood and Robert W. Tucker, *Force, Order and Justice* (Baltimore: The Johns Hopkins Press, 1967), p. 214.

law of war rather than as a rule derived from theological or philosophical principles.

The question then concerns the adequacy of the concrete material norm, noncombatant immunity, as a specification of the basic prohibition of killing the innocent. To be adequate it would need to pass certain tests:

1. The test of *specification*: Does it specify adequately who ought to be protected?

2. The test of *justification*: Can the limit it sets be supported by adequate reasons? Since it must be presupposed that the presumption must be against exceptions to the prohibition of killing, the onus of proof is on those who would argue for exceptions. Thus, the task of justification of the limits on killing is essentially one of critical examination and refutation of claims to abolish or extend such limits.

3. Critics of the norm (of noncombatant immunity) also require that it pass the test of *practicability*: i.e., Can it be followed in the real situation of war and especially nuclear war?[8] A further related test is that of feasibility, i.e., Can the norm generate sufficient acceptance on a broad range so as to enable it to become an effective rather than a merely theoretical limit?[9]

These points raise special difficulties and call for a more extended comment. There is a fundamental question to be answered: What is the function of this norm to be? There are two basic options that might be taken. The first is, granted that war is sometimes necessary as a means of attaining a good, such as (temporal) peace, how may war be waged and how may fellow human beings be attacked without incurring the inner moral devastation of sin on the part of the maker of war? St. Augustine seems to have framed the question in this way. Thus, in asking what is the real evil of war, he answered that this is not the mere death of those who will eventually die anyway, but rather the real evils are ". . . love of violence, revengeful cruelty, fierce and implacable enmity, wild resistance, and the lust of power."[10] This has remained the central question in the theological tradition: Is killing in war always a sin?[11]

Or is the function of the norm the following: Granted that war may

---

8. Cf. Richard Shelley Hartigan, "Noncombatant Immunity: Reflections on Its Origin and Present State," *Review of Politics* 29 (1967), 204–220, p. 217.

9. This is a dominant concern of international jurists. Cf. Kelsen, *Principles*, p. 113.

10. Augustine, *Contra Faustum* XXII, 74, cited in *The Political Writings of St. Augustine*, Henry Paolucci, ed. (Chicago: Henry Regnery Co., 1962), p. 164. Cf. Richard Shelley Hartigan, "St. Augustine on War and Killing: The Problem of the Innocent," *Journal of the History of Ideas* 27 (1966), 195–204, p. 198.

11. Cf. St. Thomas Aquinas, *Summa Theologiae* II–II, q. 40, art. 1. *Utrum bellare sit semper peccatum.*

sometimes be necessary, how is the lethal impact of war to be kept to the minimum? If one were addressing the holder of public power who decided on and waged the war, and those who acted under his or her authority, the first perspective would be the relevant one. But if one were among those likely to be killed in the course of the war, the matter would appear differently. She or he would be more likely to require a rule that would effectively limit the killing.[12]

There seems little doubt that the theories of the just war have been constructed from the perspective of those wielding power rather than from that of the prospective victims. It is, nevertheless, also the case that the function of just-war doctrine has been understood in this way; granted that war may be necessary, how may it be limited as far as possible? Nevertheless, the different perspectives will give a certain salience to different questions. In the first perspective, that of the agent waging war, questions such as that of intention will be paramount. The significant limits on the attendant destruction will be the proportion between this destruction and the end pursued by that agent, i.e., again, the one who wields power and control. In the second perspective, the paramount question will be the effectiveness of a proposed limit in preventing death and destruction of the "objects" of violence. If effectiveness is crucial in the norms limiting violence, then it will be important to ask: Is the norm feasible, i.e., does it have a chance of general acceptance; is it operational, i.e., is it sufficiently specific so as to provide meaningful guidance; is it practicable in the sense of being capable of implementation, rather than of being theoretically attractive, but unlikely to be followed in practice and so leave the victims deprived even of that protection they might have had from a less than ideal, but nevertheless effective, rule?

This tension could be illustrated from the bishops' letter itself. If we say, the moral duty today is to prevent nuclear war from ever occurring,[13] then the basic moral requirement is construed in terms of effectiveness. The appropriate means will then be those that most effectively prevent nuclear war. Since deterrence does this, or seems to, it may be a morally acceptable means, and perhaps morally required. On the other hand, if we approach the question in terms of the doctrine of intention, taking into account the realities of weapons policy, where threat seems to entail at least a conditional intention to use, we would be pushed in

---

12. The perspective of the victim is taken into account in *Challenge of Peace*, n. 105: "It is of the utmost importance, in assessing harms and the justice of accepting them, to think of the poor and the helpless, for they are usually the ones who have the least to gain and the most to lose when war's violence touches their lives." But precisely how justice relates to these persons is not explained.

13. *Challenge of Peace*, n. 175.

the direction of a moral condemnation of deterrence.[14] The same, or similar, tensions are present in any endeavor to develop a criterion of immunity in war.

It seems clear that effectiveness is indeed a requirement for an adequate norm. But the effectiveness may not be simply equated with or subordinated to the practicalities of technical military or political rationality. We must focus on morally relevant effectiveness. This would suggest two further tests to be passed:

1. The test of *intentionality*: Does the specific norm adequately guide intention into concrete proposals that respect the innocent, or does it, when taken up to guide specific proposals, leave room for a direct willingness to kill the innocent?

2. The test of *effectiveness*: Does the norm itself, and the theory of exceptions that go with it, adequately protect the innocent from direct attack, and also from undue, so called, "indirect" attack?

3. There is a further test, which could be called that of *viability*. The logic of intentionality seems to drive us in the direction of an absolutist position, either an absolute rejection of all killing, or the rejection of all killing in the strict sense, i.e., all direct killing. This would lead to a moral rejection of all war, or, in the second case, almost all wars that have recently been fought.[15]

The problem here is that an absolutist position leads to the conclusion that war, at least in almost all cases, is totally immoral. But then when war occurs, this will lead to the assumption that war is inevitably an immoral activity; war is hell. Thus, any attempt to subordinate the conduct of war to any moral limits will be abandoned.[16] If, then, the moral norm is to be sustained, it requires some theory of exceptions. On the other hand, if the theory of exceptions allows excessive flexibility, it can undermine the norm itself by rendering it meaningless. Critics have brought such charges against the theory of double effect, which has traditionally provided the theory of exceptions in the just-war doctrine.[17]

14. Ibid., n. 178. Cf. Germain Grisez, "The Moral Implications of a Nuclear Deterrent," *Center Journal* 2 (1982), 9–24; cited in David Hollenbach, S.J., *Nuclear Ethics: A Christian Moral Argument* (Ramsey, N.Y.: Paulist Press, 1983), p. 70.

15. Cf. Germain Grisez and Joseph M. Boyle, *Life and Death with Liberty and Justice* (Notre Dame, Ind.: University of Notre Dame Press, 1979), p. 399.

16. Cf. Paul Ramsey, *The Just War: Force and Political Responsibility* (New York: Charles Scribner's Sons, 1968), p. 146. Ramsey directs this charge against the absolutist position taken by pacifism.

17. Cf. William V. O'Brien, "Just War Doctrine in a Nuclear Context," *Theological Studies* 44 (1983), 191–220, p. 211; *The Conduct of Just and Limited War* (New York: Praeger Publishers, 1981), p. 45; Michael Walzer, *Just and Unjust Wars: A Moral Argument with Historical Illustrations* (New York: Basic Books, 1977), pp. 152–153; James Turner Johnson, *Ideology, Reason and Limitations of War: Religious and Secular Concepts 1200-1740* (Princeton, N.J.: Princeton University Press, 1975), p. 200; Elizabeth Anscombe, "War and Murder," in *War and Morality*, R. Wasserstrom, ed. (Bel-

We must distinguish between the way in which the norm was historically evolved (through a complex development influenced by cultural
circumstances and practices), the way in which a certain legal status is
conferred upon it (e.g., by pacts among nations), and the moral status
of the norm. Granted that the norm, in its historical genesis, was conditioned by multiple contingent factors, this does not necessarily mean
that it has a purely relative moral force. Granted, further, that the norm
has been given legal status by pacts among nations, this does not mean
that it has *only* the force of mutual agreements, i.e., that it is purely a
convention and thus ceases to have moral force on one party when the
other belligerent party violates it.[18]

What is in question is, rather, its derivative moral force as a specification of the general moral principle requiring the immunity of the innocent from lethal attack. Does it adequately guide agents in the construction and execution of policies so as to honor this principle? Does it
establish protective structures so as effectively to protect the immunity
of innocents? It is argued here that an adequate norm ought to fulfill the
tests described: specificity, justification, feasibility, practicability, intentionality, effectiveness, viability. In examining the arguments of some
authors who challenge the norm and propose replacements, it will be
investigated whether the proposed replacements pass these tests. If they
do not, then the replacements fail to respect the requirements of the
basic moral principle calling for the immunity of the innocent.[19] In analyzing the arguments of some who support the norm of noncombatant
immunity, it will be asked whether they pass these tests, or whether they
need to be corrected and improved.

Positions Challenging the Principles

Those who challenge the principle have offered a variety of positions.

1. Uphold the moral principle, the innocent may never be directly
slain under any circumstances or for any reason, but distinguish this

---

mont, Calif.: Wadsworth, 1970), pp. 42–53, criticizes abuses of the principle but up-
holds it as valid.

18. Mavrodes, "Conventions," p. 128, argues that the obligation to respect the immunity of noncombatants is a convention-dependent obligation, with moral force. This,
I believe, is correct. But Mavrodes derives the moral force from the function of the rule
in limiting the extent of killing in war. It is argued here that the moral force of the rule
derives not only from this desirable limiting but from the prohibition to kill the innocent,
of which the prohibition to kill noncombatants is a reasonably justifiable specification.
In other words, it has more than a consequential or teleological foundation.

19. Those who challenge the rule may be reasonably asked to supply an answer to the
question: If the line is not to be drawn here (at noncombatancy), then where? Cf. Ian
Clark, *Limited Nuclear War* (Princeton, N.J.: Princeton University Press, 1982), p. 126.
If they cannot provide an answer, then clearly no adequate protection is provided for the
innocent. If they do give an alternative proposal, this may be subjected to the critical
tests proposed here.

from the principle of noncombatant or civilian immunity—a juridic determination. The latter is contingent and historically conditioned and needs to be replaced so as to determine who is to be presumed innocent in an enemy population under modern conditions of war. This is the position advocated by Richard Shelley Hartigan.[20]

2. Retain the principle of noncombatant immunity but not as an absolute principle.[21] The absoluteness of the principle must yield to the exigencies of the effectiveness of deterrence and defense.[22] Thus, individual immunity is to be abandoned. The limit on "collateral" destruction is to be determined in terms of proportion of the collateral damage arising from military action to its military utility.[23] Approaches in terms of intention and double effect are to be set aside. This is the view of William V. O'Brien.

3. Affirm the distinction between innocent and guilty in the principle that ". . . no one can be threatened with war or warred against, unless through some act of his own he has surrendered or lost his rights."[24] However, in the face of an imminent and extreme danger of an unusual and horrifying kind, these rights may be violated. Such an extreme emergency brings us under the rule of necessity, and necessity knows no rules.[25] Nevertheless, societies have ways of rehabilitating the principle after the event.[26] This is the position of Michael Walzer who, in distinction to the other positions so far discussed, founds his position on a theory of rights. But this is not fully worked out.[27]

Positions Supporting the Principle

4. Uphold the principle of noncombatant immunity as an absolute, with no distinction between this principle and the principle of the im-

---

20. "Non-Combatant Immunity: Reflections on its Origin and Present Status," *Review of Politics* 29 (1967), 204–220.

21. William V. O'Brien, *The Conduct*, p. 45. "It is my contention that the moral, just-war principle of discrimination is not an absolute limitation on belligerent conduct. There is no evidence that such a principle was seriously advanced by the Church, and it is implicitly rejected when the Church acknowledges the continued right of legitimate self-defense, a right that has always been incompatible with observance of an absolute principle of discrimination."

22. William V. O'Brien, "Morality and War: The Contribution of Paul Ramsey," in *Love and Society: Essays in the Ethics of Paul Ramsey*, James Turner Johnson and David Smith, eds. (Missoula, Mont.: Scholars Press, 1974), 163–184, p. 174.

23. William V. O'Brien, "Proportion and Discrimination," *Thought* 59 (1984), 41–52, p. 51.

24. Walzer, *Just and Unjust Wars*, p. 135.

25. Ibid., p. 254.

26. Ibid., p. 323.

27. Ibid., Ch. 8. For a critique of Walzer's development of a theory of rights see Johnson, *Just War*, p. 20.

munity of the innocent.[28] It must be respected in its own right before any consideration of proportion. Indeed the absolute protection due to noncombatants is so fundamental that to disregard it is to deny the highest of all values.[29] This refers, of course, to Paul Ramsey's well-known "twin born" justification of and limitation of war. It is charity or, more precisely, "love informed reason" that recognizes the claims of a victim of hostile force to protection. Where there is no other way to ward off this hostile force, charity requires that a preference be made between the victim and the attacker. This preference, to be effective, may call for the use of force to repress the hostile force. It is only the call of charity that justifies the use of force and even the killing of the attacker. Therefore, there can be no justification of killing the innocent.

However, unlike O'Brien, Ramsey does make use of the principle of the double effect. Thus, he would recognize a clear moral distinction between a direct, intentional attack on a noncombatant population and an attack on combatant forces, in which some noncombatants would suffer but only as an indirect, unintentional result of the action.[30]

5. Affirm the principle of the immunity of the innocent (taken from the theological tradition), and integrate this with specific prohibitions of the war convention so as to generate the principle of noncombatant immunity. Recognize a distinction between the direct killing of the innocent-noncombatants and indirect killing. The former is prohibited as intrinsically wrong; the latter may be permitted. Set a limit to the extent of the permissible, indirect killing by the criterion of proportionality. This has been the way taken by Roman Catholic moral theology.[31]

6. Uphold the principle of the prohibition of killing the innocent, but without binding the general principle of the theological tradition explicitly to the customary law category of noncombatant. This has been the way followed in the teaching of the Magisterium of the Roman Catholic Church.[32] This being the case, then, the way in which the principle is

28. Paul Ramsey, *The Just War*, pp. 154–155.

29. Cf. Johnson, *Just War*, p. 357.

30. Paul Ramsey, *The Just War*, pp. 154–155. The principle is invoked frequently by Ramsey.

31. This was a generally accepted position. For representative statements see John C. Ford, S.J., "The Morality of Obliteration Bombing," *Theological Studies* 5 (1944), 261–309; "The Hydrogen Bombing of Cities," in *Morality and Modern Warfare: The State of the Question*, William J. Nagle, ed. (Baltimore: Helicon Press, 1960), pp. 98–103. This is essentially the position taken in *Challenge of Peace*.

32. This has left some ambiguity. See William V. O'Brien, *The Conduct*, pp. 44–45. ". . . it is significant that in the considerable body of contemporary Catholic social teaching on war, embracing the pronouncements of Pope Pius XII and his successors and of Vatican II, the principle of discrimination is not prominent in any form, absolute or conditional. When weapons systems or forms of warfare are condemned, deplored or reluctantly condoned, the rationales are so generalized that the judgments appear to be based on a mixed application of the principles of proportion and discrimination. If any-

proposed in the U.S. bishops' pastoral has a degree of clarity not present in previous magisterial statements.

Finally there should be noted an important development in the *law* of noncombatant immunity. This had been broken down by the practice of belligerents in the two world wars. But efforts have been made to bring the law back to the pre-total war practice. Thus, for example, article 48 of the 1977 Geneva Protocol I states:

> In order to ensure respect for and protection of the civilian population and civilian objects, the parties to the conflict shall at all times distinguish between the civilian population and combatants and between civilian objects and military objectives and accordingly shall direct their operations only against military objectives.[33]

Geneva Convention IV (1949), which has been in force for signatory nations since October 21, 1950, stated that human persons possess rights that are to be respected even in war time. One of those rights possessed at least by civilians is the right to be spared direct, intentional attack. This convention is closely linked with the modern movement to protect human rights and is organically linked to the United Nations Declaration of 1948.[34]

A Critical Analysis

The third part of the paper is a critical analysis of these proposals in terms of the tests of adequacy that have been explained earlier.

1. Hartigan's proposal involves the abandonment of the strict norm of noncombatant immunity and its replacement by flexible norms.[35] A first criticism could be made from the perspective of specificity and effectiveness. The flexible norms suggested are too vague to be operation-

---

thing, these pronouncements seem more concerned with disproportionate rather than indiscriminate effects." A reading of the official statements reveals a noteworthy difference between these and the treatment of the question by the moral theologians. Some of the latter, at least since the 1920's, explicitly identify the ancient distinction between innocent and guilty with the distinction between noncombatant and combatant. The official statements do not invoke the latter. The Second Vatican Council, in the *Constitution on the Church in the Modern World* (n. 80) condemns *indiscriminate* acts of war, but does not explain this in terms of the distinction combatant-noncombatant.

33. Cited in O'Brien, *The Conduct*, p. 49. However, it remains to be seen whether this will be ratified by a majority of states, including the great powers. Does a convention of uncertain legal force that is not acceptable by a significant number of states have *moral* force, and, if so, on what grounds? This problem was ignored by the moral theologians. Mavrodes has a valid point in drawing attention to this difficulty. See Mavrodes, "Conventions," p. 130.

34. On the Geneva Convention IV, see Morris Greenspan, *The Modern Law of Land Warfare* (Berkeley: University of California Press, 1959), pp. 156–196. Cf. Hartigan, "Noncombatant Immunity," p. 206.

35. See Hartigan, "Noncombatant Immunity," supra, note 8.

ally effective. What other groups are there that could be clearly specified? We must ask, if we do not draw the line here, then where shall we
draw it? The very flexibility Hartigan urges would seem to undermine
the effectiveness of any rules of limitation.[36] Further, the apparently
unavoidable tendency to undermine the rule of limitation itself would
seem to preclude such flexible norms from being viable in the sense
defined.

A second criticism could be made from the point of view of effectiveness in limiting the collateral deaths incurred. The factor governing the
degree of flexibility is the necessity of conducting the war so as to attain
the just end. But could not the concept of necessity be expanded so as
to include forms of war making that would lead to vast collateral losses?
Without any limit independent of the necessity of means to the end,
there is no significant protection of the potential victims.

Hartigan clearly wishes to retain the moral criterion of the immunity
of the innocent. This, then, would have to guide the intentionality of
those directing the making of war. But would not the vagueness of the
more concrete specific norms leave a "window of vulnerability" through
which the making of war could be directed also at the innocent? In this
case the more specific norm would allow forms of conduct that could
not be reconciled with the requirements of the fundamental moral norm.
They would not shape intentionality in such a way as to preclude an
intention to kill the innocent, if circumstances required.[37]

2. O'Brien's position is that the principle of discrimination ought to
be upheld, but not as an absolute rule in the specific form of noncombatant immunity. Rather, the principle is to remain a ". . . critical source
of both moral and legal limitations of belligerent behavior."[38] In this
argument the issue of practicability is the dominant consideration. However, the problems associated with nonabsolute, flexible norms would
remain and be subject to the same criticisms directed against Hartigan's
proposal. A norm rendered flexible for the sake of practicability may
end up being so vague as to be quite impractical.

The major difficulty, however, would lie in the justification of the
limits proposed. The actual content of the limits is to be provided by a
"balancing" of the need to protect noncombatants with the need to recognize the legitimate military necessities of modern warfare.[39] How is
the balancing to be construed? O'Brien seems to assume that, given a

36. Cf. Clark, *Limited Nuclear War*, pp. 125–126.
37. There is also a problem with the justification of the proposed limits. What the
measure of flexibility might be is not explained. Such proposals might be able to gain a
degree of support and thus be feasible, but this would be offset by the other difficulties.
38. The *Conduct*, p. 45.
39. Ibid., p. 46.

just end, the military means to this end are endowed with a legitimate necessity. Since an absolute adherence to the principle of noncombatant immunity would impede the carrying out of the necessary means, the principle must yield its claim to absoluteness in the name of practicability.

This overlooks the fundamental moral principle that a just end does not justify any means. If the only available means are themselves unjust, then the end may not be morally pursued. In establishing the criteria to govern the balancing of needs, O'Brien rejects the principle of the double effect and the notion of "indirect" killing and falls back on the criterion of proportionality.[40] This is a notoriously difficult notion to apply, above all because the more weight that is attached to the end, the greater extension allowed in the losses proportionate to this end. Without an independent limit, such calculation of proportionate balance can allow for indefinitely escalated "permissible" loss of life.[41] Furthermore, O'Brien construes proportionality in terms of military necessity. This seems to collapse the moral relationship of means to end into a purely technical relationship of means to ends. This confuses distinct levels of relationality. This proposal falls short on the ground of a moral justification of the limits it proposes and allows.[42]

3. The first problem with Walzer's theory is its fundamental justification. He sets out to derive the principle of immunity inductively from the war convention as manifested in a series of historical instances. James Turner Johnson has questioned the methodological adequacy of such an inductive process from history.[43]

However, the more immediate problems concern his theory of exceptions. Walzer explains his concept of "imminent and extreme danger" as one arising from an *ultimate* threat, from "evil objectified in history."[44] (He has in mind Nazi domination.) When there is no other way to oppose the triumph of ultimate evil, means may be followed in the "supreme emergency," which violate the principle of noncombatant immunity.

The problem is with the concept of ultimate evil. I am not sure

40. Ibid., p. 47. Cf. O'Brien, "Just War Doctrine in a Nuclear Context," *Theological Studies* 44 (1983), 191–220, p. 211.

41. O'Brien is, of course, aware of this difficulty. See The *Conduct*, p. 47. See also O'Brien, "Proportion and Discrimination," p. 44.

42. O'Brien's challenge to the absoluteness of the principle of noncombatant immunity is, in part, grounded on the lack of an unambiguous affirmation of the principle in official Catholic pronouncements. There may, however, be intrinsic arguments to support the principle. *Challenge of Peace* produces the clearest official Church statement upholding the principle. But it does not develop arguments to support its position.

43. Johnson, *Just War Tradition*, p. 21.

44. Walzer, *Just and Unjust Wars*, pp. 252–253.

whether this is an importing of eschatological concepts into historical affairs, as Johnson claims.[45] But it does raise fundamental philosophical and theological problems. Can any temporal disaster be *ultimate* evil? Or should we keep this term for the taking on of evil in free, knowing decision, which we call *sin*, or, again, restrict it to that state of definitive rejection of the good or of the source of good, God, which Christians call hell.

However, in the moral context the problem is clearer. If the evil to be repelled is ultimate, then any means would seem to be acceptable in Walzer's view. Walzer does not deny that the killing of the innocent, even in such a case, could be a crime.[46] But it is a crime that must be done. We must sin, not boldly, but grieving in ultimate necessity. This is the truly necessary sin of the people under threat. But then we must ask, necessary for what? Walzer's answer is, for the survival and freedom of political communities. The survival and freedom of such communities are the highest values in international society.[47] A challenge to these values puts us under the role of necessity, and necessity knows no rules. He does not accept an argument that communities have different and larger prerogatives than individuals. Nor does he accept that communal life has a kind of transcendent value, or that a nation may violate the rights of a smaller but determinate number of peoples.[48] Nevertheless, the ordering of values here seems to be without adequate foundation. Likewise, the relationship between the individuals, with their rights, and the communities that may destroy them is unclear. Walzer has sought to found his approach on a theory of rights. This, I believe, is a valid and necessary step. But the theory is not worked out adequately.

Thus, I would argue, Walzer's approach does not satisfy the test of justification. He is conscious of the problem of viability, i.e., how the rule is to be protected from being undermined. Thus, he envisages that the people who violate the rule of immunity might have mechanisms symbolically to restore it after the violation, e.g., by the nonhonoring of the agents it employed to do the dirty work.[49] But, one might ask, why restore it, if it is only to yield again to another supreme emergency? Walzer would no doubt reply that it would, nonetheless, be a viable and effective norm for situations this side of the emergency. But what would it mean to restore the norm after the successful repulsion of the agents of ultimate evil, if in the process of repelling the evil, the defenders had made themselves imitators of the agents of evil? Would this not represent rather a triumph of the ultimate evil in the very spirit of the defend-

---

45. Johnson, *Just War Tradition*, p. 25. 48. Ibid.
46. *Just and Unjust Wars*, p. 259. 49. Ibid., p. 323.
47. Ibid., p. 254.

ers, even though they had thrown back the actual military forces of the attacker?

In this respect, the defenders have *intended evil*. Thus, it would seem clear that this theory does not satisfy the test of intentionality. As a rule, if only for the emergency, it guides the defenders to the direct willing of the doing of evil.

4. Paul Ramsey has provided the most eloquent and compelling defense of the principle. However, there are difficulties in his argument which require analysis. A first issue here would be the problem of specification. Ramsey uses, apparently interchangeably, the concepts of the innocent and noncombatant.[50] How might he respond to the criticism previously mentioned, namely, that the two cannot be identified? As far as I know he does not directly address this precise question, but by analogy from his treatment of a similar question he would probably argue as follows. We do not need to be able to determine who precisely the innocent are, or whether this is to be precisely determined by the category of noncombatant. It is sufficient to know *that* there are definitely some who are innocent (or noncombatant). That this is so can be demonstrated by giving a list of those who clearly are in no way participating in the act of aggression, e.g., children, the helpless sick, the aged.[51] If some are present in a proposed target, then a proposal to directly attack that target is immoral. Thus, in order to frame a norm of adequate specificity to govern policies, it is not required that the categories of the immune be further specified. In this sense, if the group of the noncombatant includes at least some who are certainly not involved, it is adequately specified. No further more complex specification is necessary.[52]

The second issue would concern the question of justification. This has two aspects: How is the immunity rule itself justified? How are exceptions justified? With regard to the first, critics have argued that while Ramsey's theologically grounded, charity argument may well be convincing for religious persons, it is not likely to win assent from a wider population.[53] The rule then would be justifiable for a small group, but could hardly satisfactorily convince a nation or its policymakers. Thus, it would fail the test of feasibility. However, there does not seem to be any reason why this charity argument could not be mediated with a

50. Paul Ramsey, *The Just War*, pp. 142, 150, 153.
51. Ibid., p. 157.
52. Thus, the rule would be adequately specific in relation to the kinds of attacks likely to be proposed in nuclear war. It would not, however, provide a sufficiently specific norm for discrimination in, for example, guerrilla warfare.
53. Cf. O'Brien, "Morality and War: The Contribution of Paul Ramsey," p. 173.

theory of justice. Ramsey himself has moved in this direction.[54] However, more work needs to be done if the justification of the rule is to become capable of engendering conviction in the wider public debate.

There are problems with Ramsey's theory of exceptions. As is well known he invokes the principle of the double effect to justify counterforce use of nuclear weapons, and a policy of deterrence based on the deterrent effect of the prospect of the "unintended" collateral effects of such use.[55] Critics have challenged whether such effects can truly be said to be "unintended" when the deterrent posture is so utterly dependent on them.[56] Others argue that this application of the double effect allows such wide exceptions that it would tend to undermine the rule of immunity itself.

Thus, there would seem to be problems here in satisfying fully the tests of intentionality and effectiveness (in limiting "unintended" killing).

5. A complete study of the tradition of Roman Catholic moral theology would have to take account of the stage of foundations (Augustine, St. Thomas, the canonical tradition), the stage of formation (Vitoria, Suarez), and the stage of reception, the divulgation of doctrine in the "manuals" and text books. It will be sufficient here to sum up the accepted position of the last stage.

1. Killing of the innocent is clearly prohibited.

2. Direct killing of the innocent is absolutely prohibited. The innocent may be killed "indirectly," the limit to this being set by what is necessary for attaining the purpose of the war, i.e., victory.

3. The "innocent" are designated as those who do not bear arms and are specified in lists: children, women, agricultural folk, merchants, guests, clergy, and members of religious orders.

4. The doctrine is still developed from the perspective of those who wield power and their agents. There is no clear doctrine of the *rights* of potential victims.[57]

---

54. Paul Ramsey, "A Political Ethics Context for Strategic Thinking," in *Strategic Thinking and its Moral Implications*, Morton A. Kaplan, ed. (Chicago: University of Chicago Center for Policy Study, 1973), pp. 101–147. Cited in Johnson, *Just War Tradition*, pp. 103–105.

55. Paul Ramsey, *The Just War*, pp. 281–284, 314–366; cf. also Paul Ramsey, *War and the Christian Context. How Shall Modern War Be Conducted Justly?* (Durham, N.C.: Duke University Press, 1961), Ch. 8.

56. See Walzer, *Just and Unjust Wars*, p. 280. Cf. Clark, *Limited Nuclear War*, p. 129.

57. See, for example, John C. Ford, S.J., "The Morality of Obliteration Bombing," supra note, p. 31. This author employs the notion of the rights of noncombatants in war (p. 269), but there is no developed theory of rights or clear explanation of the concept of right.

There are some particular problems that call for explicit mention. The first concerns the issue of specification of who is to be immune. In a sense, the lists provide the specification of who is to be immune. But efforts were made to work out a more conceptualized framework of immunity. While the earlier manuals simply spoke of the innocent, later writers incorporate the categories of combatant/noncombatant. This they take over from the customary law, which they refer to as the *ius gentium*.[58] More specific norms are included from "pacts among nations," from positive international law. But there were several problems with this. The actual legal status of many of these pacts was uncertain. No effort was made to explain the precise justification for taking up these rules. In general they were regarded by the moralists as specifications of the natural law, but no detailed analysis was provided.[59]

This move to incorporate the international law was probably motivated by an interest in specification (Who is to be regarded as innocent in concrete historical conditions?) and feasibility (How is the principle of immunity to be mediated to public understanding and public structures so as to have a chance of general acceptance and influence on policies?). If the American bishops are challenged today for attempting to mediate moral-theological principles in terms of strategic doctrine, the moral theology of the recent past would have to be similarly challenged for attempting to mediate its principles in terms of international legal doctrine.

The most serious problem lies with the theory of exceptions; the justification of the indirect killing of the innocent under the limit of proportionality to the necessities of victory. Necessity was at times interpreted in far too facile a manner so that indirect killing could be too easily justified.[60] Proportionality could be applied such that where the end or goal of the war was endowed with almost ultimate moral value, the permissible indirect losses proportionate to this end could be vast, even the destruction of the race, including of course, all innocents.[61]

---

58. This is common to most authors. See, for example, Dominicus M. Prummer, O.P., *Manuale Theologiae Moralis*, t. II, eds. 4 and 5 (Friburg: Herder & Co., 1928), p. 123.

59. These difficulties are evident in Ford's treatment of the foundation of the right to immunity. He bases this on the international law, "the law of humanity," and the natural law. But the connections between these "laws" are obscure, as is their respective moral force.

60. Henry Davis, S.J., *Moral and Pastoral Theology*, 3rd ed., Vol. II (New York: Sheed and Ward, 1938), p. 149.

61. See Gustav Grundlach, S.J., "Die Lehre Pius XII zum Atomkrieg," *Stimmen der Zeit* 164 (1959), 1–13. This was an extreme view, but it illustrates the lengths to which the logic of proportionality, without other, independent limits, could be taken. Cf. *Challenge of Peace*, n. 103. "To destroy civilization as we know it by waging a 'total war' as

Such conclusions illustrate in a dramatic way the inherent weakness of the traditional theory; it is constructed from the perspective of the holders of power and their agents.[62] It is they who decide the fate of the victims. The latter have no say in it at all. The necessary corrective is to take the perspective of the victims and to give them a voice, at least vicariously, through a theory of rights. The limit of proportionality by itself is only a weak and imprecise restraint.

6. Since a detailed study of magisterial statements would be beyond the scope of this paper, only the most explicit and frequently cited texts will be considered. In the Second Vatican Council's Constitution on the Church in the Modern World it is said:

. . . this most holy synod makes its own the condemnation of total war already pronounced by recent popes and issues the following declaration: Any act of war aimed indiscriminately at the destruction of entire cities or extensive areas along with their population is a crime against God and man himself. It merits unequivocal condemnation.[63]

However, the statements of previous Popes were not as clear as the Council itself. The most explicit statement, and one referred to in the Council text, was by Pius XII.

When putting this method (ABC warfare) to use involves such an extension of the evil that it entirely escapes from the control of man, its use must be rejected as immoral. Here there would no longer be a question of "defense" against injustice or a necessary "safeguard" of legitimate possessions, but the pure and simple annihilation of all human life within the radius of action. This is not permitted for any reason whatsoever.[64]

The principles of the rights of innocence and the distinction between combatant and noncombatant receives, to say the least, no strong emphasis in this latter statement.[65] In the conciliar text the criterion of discrimination was deliberately substituted for the empirically controvertible criterion of controllability. But even in this text there is no explicit mention of the principle of noncombatant immunity. The statement may

---

today it *could* be waged would be a monstrously disproportionate response to aggression on the part of any nation." This would seem eminently reasonable. But what if the aggression included an assault on "moral" or "spiritual" values, higher than the value of life or any temporal value? What destruction would be disproportionate to the loss of such values? Some other ground of limitation is required here apart from proportionality.

62. This is expressly the perspective adopted by authors like O'Brien. See his "Morality and War," p. 168.

63. n. 80.

64. Pius XII, Allocution to the 8th Congress of the World Medical Association, September 30, 1954, *AAS* 46 (1954), p. 589.

65. See John Courtney Murray, S.J., "Remarks on the Moral Problem of War," *Theological Studies* 20 (1959), 40–61, p. 51, n. 31.

indeed be read as the conclusion that would be drawn from the application of the principle in a judgment on a certain kind of act of war.[66] But it is not clear whether such an act is condemned precisely because it violates this principle, or because the enormous losses of both combatants and noncombatants, or innocent and guilty, would be totally disproportionate to any attainable goal.

These are the two texts cited in the bishops' letter, after which they go on to affirm the principle of noncombatant immunity explicitly and apply it to judgments on the use of weapons.[67] Thus, the bishops' document is much more explicit than the previous statements.[68] The U.S. bishops have followed the lead of the moral theologians and adopted the principle of noncombatant immunity.

Conclusion

This essay has sought to demonstrate that, granted the fundamental principle of the prohibition of the killing of the innocent, there are strong moral reasons for maintaining the principle of noncombatant immunity as a concrete, nonrelative specification of that principle. The counterproposals can be shown to have serious deficiencies that would lead them to condone violations of the fundamental principle. However, the critics have presented a case that has to be answered and have pointed out weaknesses, particularly in the equating of the two principles that had become commonplace in more recent moral theology. The discussion has revealed further problems in the traditional just-war theory and its contemporary versions in their treatment of rules of immunity. In particular, there is a lack of an adequate account of the rights of the potential victims of war. As noted earlier, recent developments in international law have invoked these rights, but without providing a developed theory to sustain them. What is called for, then, is a recasting of the just-war theory in a way that takes account not only of the holders of power who wage the war but of the powerless who are likely to be its most numerous victims.

---

66. Johnson sees in this text, ". . . an assertion of the inviolability of noncombatants, of the *ius in bello* principle of discrimination, in the most absolute way against counter-city nuclear war." *Just War Tradition*, p. 345.

67. *Challenge of Peace*, n. 147.

68. One can only speculate as to the reasons for this reticence in the previous magisterial statements. Was it because the authors wished to remain on the level of general principle and regarded the principle as belonging to the sphere of international law, and so outside their specific range of competence?

JOSEPH M. BOYLE, JR.

20. *The Challenge of Peace* and the Morality of Nuclear Deterrence

In *The Challenge of Peace: God's Promise and Our Response*, the American bishops devote a section to the troubling question of the morality of nuclear deterrence. The pastoral expresses serious moral reservations about nuclear deterrence as practiced by the United States, but following the statement of Cardinal Krol in 1979, and Pope John Paul II's statement in 1982 that deterrence "can still be judged morally acceptable," the pastoral does not unequivocally condemn the present nuclear deterrence policy of the United States. Instead the deterrent is accepted as a condition for carrying on disarmament efforts and other steps toward making the world safer from nuclear war.

The issue of the morality of deterrence is clearly one of the most difficult and controversial aspects of the contemporary discussion of international affairs and modern warfare. Thus, it is not surprising that the treatment of this subject in the pastoral has occasioned at least as much criticism and commentary as any part of this document. It seems worthwhile, therefore, to take a careful look at this section of the pastoral, and I shall do so in this paper.

This seems an appropriate thing for a Catholic moralist to do, because the pastoral itself (at n. 195) calls for scrutiny of the claims of any government that its deterrent is morally acceptable,[1] and because the attempt in this direction that the pastoral presents is put forth in a tentative way that seems to welcome further dialogue and analysis.

I think that it is very difficult to see how anything like the present U.S. deterrent is in fact justified by the considerations put forth in the pastoral. For all these considerations appear to provide reasons why the deterrent should be morally rejected. Moreover, if some analytical precisions are added to the reasoning actually presented in the pastoral, the difficulty of seeing how the deterrent can be justified is increased.

---

1. All references to the pastoral letter are to the numbered paragraphs in the authorized United States Catholic Conference publication of the Pastoral: National Conference of Catholic Bishops, *The Challenge of Peace: God's Promise and Our Response: A Pastoral Letter on War and Peace* (Washington, D.C.: United States Catholic Conference, May 3, 1983).

In saying this I do not mean to suggest that the framework of the pastoral is mistaken. For I do not believe this; the framework of the pastoral, to the extent that this is clear, is largely that of traditional Catholic moral theology and casuistry and, in particular, the doctrine of the just war. I accept this framework but do not see how the pastoral or, for that matter, any argument within this framework, can justify the present U.S. deterrent or any strategy that is essentially like it. In other words, I think that the deterrent is immoral—that considerations compatible with traditional moral principles do not really justify it. But my focus here will be on the reasons actually presented in the pastoral, and not on other reasons that might be adduced in favor of the deterrent within the framework of Catholic moral principles.

Clearly, my conclusion is not a happy one, and it is not surprising that the *Challenge of Peace* refrains from drawing it. For it is a conclusion that the Pope himself seems not to have drawn or, perhaps, has even rejected. For in his 1982 statement to the United Nations, Pope John Paul II does not condemn the deterrent, but seems to give it a cautious endorsement. The approval given to the deterrent is, however, ambiguous: Does the Pope's statement that deterrence based on balance "may still be judged morally acceptable" mean that nuclear deterrence of the kind now being used by the superpowers is morally indifferent in and of itself and that its evaluation depends solely on the extrinsic purposes for which it is used—purposes that at present can still be judged legitimate? Or does the Pope's statement mean that the question of the moral character of the deterrence is an open question at the present, no one as yet having shown that it must be categorically rejected? I think that it is difficult to answer questions like these on the basis of what the Pope actually said. In any case, it seems to me that this question is an open one for Catholic moralists to consider. For surely, there is no evidence that the Pope meant his statement to close debate on this issue; indeed, serious discussion of the intrinsic moral character of nuclear deterrence of the kind the superpowers now use has hardly begun.

If the rejection of the deterrent presupposed pacifism—in the strict sense in which "pacifism" is the name of the proposition that a government may never take up arms to fulfill its obligations to defend justly its interests or those of other countries—then perhaps the issue might be a closed one. For the Church seems to affirm the obligation of political societies to defend themselves against unjust aggression.[2] The rejection of the deterrent need not be based on pacifism, but can be based instead on the conviction that the deterrent cannot be justified in terms of the relevant principles of the just-war doctrine—in terms of the traditional

2. *Challenge of Peace*, see n. 75.

casuistry of the ethics of killing and the intention to kill. To reject a particular military posture as immoral is not to say that any military posture is immoral. If a military posture is immoral, it makes no moral difference that it is the only way we have to get or protect things we are obliged to get or protect. The end does not justify the means—no matter how important the end may be.

Does the Pastoral Leave Room for a Moral Deterrent?

The answer to this question is that the intention of the *Challenge of Peace* is clearly and explicitly to allow room for the deterrent. The problem is how the argument of the pastoral does this. For the reasons given are all of a kind that makes the moral character of the deterrent doubtful, and no suggestion is given as to why these reasons do not absolutely exclude it.

After summing up the teachings of the Church bearing on the question of nuclear deterrence, including the earlier statements of the American bishops and their representatives and of Pope John Paul II, the pastoral puts forth two questions of fact that provide the focus for discussing the deterrent. The first question concerns the targeting doctrine and strategic plans for the use of the deterrent, especially their impact on civilian casualties. The second concerns the relationship of the deterrent to nuclear war-fighting capability and the likelihood that war will be prevented.[3]

The Targeting Doctrine
Targeting and the Intention to Kill Innocents

The first issue, that of targeting, is said to be morally important because it determines significantly what would happen if the weapons were ever used. Then the pastoral affirms: "Although we acknowledge the need for deterrent, not all forms of deterrence are morally acceptable. Specifically, it is not morally acceptable to intend to kill the innocent as part of a strategy of deterring nuclear war."[4]

The *Challenge of Peace* does not say explicitly how such a strategy could or might involve the intention of the deaths of innocents. The context, however, suggests that the intention to kill innocents is taken to be a matter of the targeting. For the phrase "intention to strike civilian centers" is parenthetically rendered as "directly targeting civilian populations."[5] This suggests that the two phrases might be taken as equivalent. Thus, in the language of modern philosophy, the pastoral may be

3. Ibid., n. 177.
4. Ibid., n. 178.

5. Ibid.

supposing that there is a biconditional relation between intending to kill the innocent in war and the targeting of civilian populations; on this view one intends the death of noncombatants if and only if (or just in case) one targets civilian populations. This logical relationship can be expressed in two conditional propositions. The first, stating the sufficiency of targeting civilians for intending their deaths, is: If the policy targets civilians, then it involves the intention of their deaths. The second, stating the necessity of targeting for intention (the "only if" condition), is: Only if a policy targets civilians does it involve the intention of their deaths. This last conditional can be stated in two different ways—namely, if the policy involves the intention to kill noncombatants, then it must involve targeting civilians, and (which says the same thing) if the policy does not target civilians, then it does not involve the intention to kill them.

It is worth pausing to consider these conditions. The first, stating the sufficiency of targeting for intending, is obviously the stronger, more disputable condition. This conditional, if true, would exclude any account of the deterrent as a bluff. For targeting is said to be sufficient to determine the intent of the deterrent. This conditional also excludes any account of the deterrent according to which the targeting was in some way put at a distance from the voluntary action essentially involved in the choice to deter.

This latter needs consideration, because the moral issue of the deterrent is concerned primarily with what is being willfully done to deter, and this is a matter of the human choice involved. The character of such a choice is not settled by the nature of the hardware involved; the moral significance of the hardware is determined by the use one chooses to make of it. The same thing can be said about the plans to use the hardware, although this is not so easy to see. For these technical plans do not have moral significance in and of themselves, but in virtue of the choices in which they are embedded. In general, the same plan can be good or bad depending on how a person intends to use it. So, if the *Challenge of Peace* is in fact affirming the sufficiency of targeting to settle the question of the intention of the deterrent, a number of controversial issues are being determined without any explicit argumentation. However, although this conditional is suggested by the parenthetical paraphrase of the intention to strike civilian centers as "directly targeting civilian populations," it is not actually used in the argument in which the pastoral seeks to show that U.S. policy does not involve the intention to kill innocents.

The conditional actually used in this argument is the second one— the "only if" conditional that states that the targeting of civilians is necessary for the intention to kill them—and, thus, that the absence of such targeting in the policy is sufficient for the conviction that it does not involve the prohibited intention. This conditional seems plausible—although I will argue later that it is false. It does not exclude the common attempts to justify the deterrent in the way the first condition does. The truth of this second conditional is compatible with the claim that the deterrent is a bluff and does not suggest that technical considerations about targeting settle the willing involved in the deterrent. Rather, on this condition, the targeting of civilians is reasonably understood as a necessary means for carrying out an intention to kill them.

This conditional is the one used in the argument that the U.S. deterrent does not involve the intent to kill innocents. It functions as the major premise in a simple conditional argument: If the policy does not target civilian population centers, then it does not involve the intention to kill innocents; and the evidence is that the policy does not target civilian centers; therefore, it does not involve the intent to kill the innocent.

The focus of the pastoral is on the minor, factual premise. It is supported by the testimony of high administration officials to the effect that our policy is not to target civilian populations as such. The testimony cited in fn. 81 is that of William Clark and Caspar Weinberger. Clark, in a letter to Cardinal Bernardin, denies that population centers as such are targeted as a matter of American policy, but he admits that this policy does reserve the right to attack Soviet military targets even if they are located in Soviet population centers. A letter of Weinberger to Bishop O'Connor is cited, and the following statement from his 1983 annual report to Congress is quoted: "The Reagan Administration's policy is that under no circumstances may such weapons be used deliberately for the purpose of the destroying of populations."

It seems to me that assurances of administration officials in response to the questions of citizens cannot be taken to be the same thing as the policy of the government. This is not to suggest that they are insincere; the point is only that they are reports about the policy and not definitive of it. Thus, the quoted statement of Weinberger is the most significant thing in fn. 81 for the purpose of the pastoral's argument. If that expresses U.S. policy, then it does not involve the targeting of civilian populations as such. Even here, however, there is room for doubt. For other official statements seem inconsistent with it, for example, the U.S. military posture statement for 1983 says that the retaliation threatened by the deterrent must be "focused on Soviet values."[6] In its normal meaning in strategic discussions, "values" is contrasted with "forces"

---

6. The organization of the Joint Chiefs of Staff, *United States Military Posture for FY 1983* (Washington, D.C.: United States Government Printing Office, 1982), p. 19.

and includes in its referent noncombatant lives. So it is not clear that the factual premise in the argument is true; the factual ambiguities of this question seem to be acknowledged in the pastoral.[7]

To explore the moral significance of these ambiguities about the facts would take us far afield, so instead, I will suppose that the facts are as the pastoral supposes them to be. Thus, any further question about this argument will focus on the major premise—that, in effect, the targeting of civilians is necessary if there is an intention to kill them.

A final point is in order to close this discussion of the relation of the targeting policy and the intent to kill innocents: In this complex discussion of factual and conceptual issues, it is important not to lose sight of the basic principle underlying this discussion—namely, that the intention to kill innocents must be excluded; deterrence policy must respect the immunity of noncombatants from direct attack.[8] This principle is treated as the moral absolute that the Catholic tradition has always held it to be. Thus, the pastoral suggests no possibility of calling this norm into question in the light of considerations of proportionality.

Targeting and Proportionality

Considerations of proportionality are the moral basis for the next problem the *Challenge of Peace* considers. For in addition to the question of the intent to kill the innocent, there is also a moral question about the indirect or nonintentional killing of civilians.

The problem arises because of the current placement by both sides of legitimate military targets within populated areas. The effect is that the loss of life as a side effect of the attack on military targets either in the United States or in the Soviet Union would at the present time be massive. Administration officials are cited as prepared to retaliate in a massive way if necessary, and as admitting that the loss of life in a substantial exchange "would be almost indistinguishable from what might occur if civilian centers had been deliberately and directly struck."[9]

The moral principle here is the principle of proportionality. This moral principle is described earlier in the pastoral: "the damage to be inflicted and the costs incurred by war, must be proportionate to the good expected by taking up arms."[10] This statement is followed by two comments: First, that the damages to be considered are not only the easily measurable physical harms but also the damage to spiritual values, and second, that the effect of the action on other nations and the whole world must be considered.

The principle of proportionality is taken as a principle for evaluating

---

7. *Challenge of Peace*, n. 179.
8. Ibid.
9. Ibid., n. 180.
10. Ibid., n. 99.

the side effects of otherwise good actions; it is relevant here because of the massive indirect loss of life involved in the use of the deterrent, even supposing that it involves no intention to kill civilians. Thus, as the pastoral insists, "A narrow adherence exclusively to the principle of noncombatant immunity as a criterion for policy is an inadequate moral posture for it ignores some evil and unacceptable consequences."[11]

The pastoral also notes that any judgment of proportionality is open to differing evaluations, but that some actions can be decisively judged to be disproportionate. But it does not say how one would arrive at a decisive judgment that an action is disproportionate, nor does it make clear to what extent the deterrent must be said to be disproportionate. Instead, the application of the proportionality principle to the massive loss of life involved in the use of the deterrent is stated in very guarded and conditional terms: "The location of industrial or militarily significant economic targets within heavily populated areas or in those areas affected by radioactive fallout could well involve such massive civilian casualties that, in our judgment, such a strike would be deemed morally disproportionate, even though not intentionally indiscriminate."[12]

The force of the "could" and the "would" in this paragraph is not clear. Does the conditional character of these terms make reference to factual doubts about how massive the loss of life would be? Or is the question one of how high the loss must be for it to count as disproportionate? It seems to me that it cannot be a question of the former, for the factual situation was laid out very clearly and categorically in a prior paragraph. So, what keeps the pastoral from affirming less conditionally that the deterrent is disproportionate must be—so it seems to me— some concern that this judgment is not one that can be decisively made.

But what reason is there for thinking that the massive loss of life of the kind projected would not be disproportionate? I can think of only one reason, but this reason seems to be one the pastoral excludes.

Let me begin to explain this by making a case for the deterrent's being disproportionate. Our deterrent is deployed in the face of the Soviet threat to take actions that will destroy our entire society. Thus, the use of what we threaten to do would in all likelihood take place within a context in which the values the deterrent is meant to preserve and defend were already largely destroyed and would be further damaged by further nuclear exchanges. Even if the mutual threats were limited in various ways, the possibility of escalation to full-scale destruction is very great. Thus, the actual carrying out of what the deterrent threatens would be suicidal, and, therefore, the loss of life attendant to our destruction of military targets would necessarily be disproportionate.

---

11. Ibid., n. 181.   12. Ibid., n. 182.

Of course, this argument focuses on the *use* of what the deterrent threatens and ignores the intended purposes of the deterrent, which include, of course, the prevention of the use of the weapons that is threatened in the deterrent. Why should the proportionality of the deterrent be evaluated in the light of the suicidal purpose that would have to obtain on "the day" should we ever seem required to use what we threaten? Why not measure the side effects in relation to the stated purpose of the deterrent? To restrict the consideration of the side effects of the actual use to the purpose of actual use might seem arbitrary when the willingness to bring them about is for the sake of preventing their coming about. For it does not seem to follow in any obvious way from the fact that it would be disproportionate to carry out what the deterrent threatens that the deterrence policy itself must be disproportionate. In fact, one might make a case that the deterrent itself is proportionate, since it does provide a framework for doing some good things and clearly it permits a defense of values that we have an obligation to defend.

This is the only line of reasoning that I can think of which might plausibly overturn the disproportion that seems to exist between the massive loss of life that would occur if the deterrence were actually used and any purpose that might be achieved by the actual use. Can the *Challenge of Peace* have such a line of reasoning in mind? I think not, for the following reasons.

First, the pastoral seems to exclude this line of reasoning. In the summary of this part of the document, the principle of proportionality is treated as parallel to the principle of discrimination that forbids direct killing. "No *use* of nuclear weapons which would violate the principles of discrimination and proportionality may be *intended* in a strategy of deterrence."[13] What this suggests is that, just as a deterrent strategy must be rejected if its actual use would involve the intention to kill the innocent, so also must a strategy be rejected if its actual use would be disproportionate. Just as the intent to kill the innocent that would be carried out on "the day" is the intent that flaws the standing policy, so also the disproportion of what would be done on "the day" is the disproportion that is relevant to the evaluation of the standing policy. This would be determined by relating the side effects of the use and the purpose to be achieved by the use at that time.

Second, the discussion of proportionality in the pastoral is focused on the side effects of the use of the deterrent, and the very guarded conclusion of this discussion quoted does not suggest that factors not relevant on "the day" would be part of the considerations relevant to this conclusion.

13. Ibid., Summary, I. B2.

Moreover, the parallel with intention is not implausible. For, although one does not intend the side effects, one does accept or permit them as side effects, and so in a certain way wills them. If it is wrong conditionally to intend something because of the intrinsic character of what is intended, it also seems wrong conditionally to intend something whose side effects it would be disproportionate to bring about.

This parallel suggests a moral ground for the pastoral's limiting its focus to the disproportion of the actual use of the deterrent, although the pastoral gives no hint that it has such a ground in mind. Conditionally to intend the deaths of innocents for the sake of preventing nuclear war is clearly a violation of the moral principle that one must not do evil that good might come of it. So also conditionally to intend to do something that, while not disordered in virtue of the intention itself, one believes to be significantly disproportionate—to involve massive, unjustifiable loss of life—seems to violate this principle. For the disproportion of what we are ready to do, should "the day" ever come, seems to be something we are willing as a means to maintaining our defense while avoiding nuclear war. If this relation is a means/end relationship, then the good to be achieved in the end cannot be used to offset the moral deformity of the means. That would be justifying a bad means by a good end. And it surely does seem that what we do to deter is a different act, morally speaking, from that for the sake of which we do it. If they are regarded as a single complex action, then we have a case of the traditional distinction between the object of the act—what is being done—and the further purpose or intention for the sake of which it is done. These must be evaluated independently and not merged into a single object for moral evaluation.

Whether this argument is sound, it does seem, as I noted, that the pastoral accepts the conclusion toward which it points—namely, that it is the disproportion of the actual use that is decisive. If this is true then it is hard to see how the position of the pastoral can avoid the judgment that the deterrent is disproportionate.

To sum up this section on targeting: The pastoral insists that the intention involved in the deterrent must not be the intention to kill innocents. The conclusion is that this is not the intent of deterrent policy. The intention, the pastoral supposes, is to destroy military targets, but grounds are presented for thinking that this policy would have unacceptable side effects if it ever had to be carried out. Thus, it would seem that the deterrent should be rejected as disproportionate, but it is not.

Deterrence and War-Fighting Strategies

After considering the questions surrounding targeting, the *Challenge of Peace* takes up the moral issues surrounding the relation of war-fighting capability and the deterrent. The exact moral significance of these considerations is difficult to determine, but they seem to me simply to add to the reasons for total rejection of the deterrent. These considerations focus on the dangers and consequences of moving towards a truly counterforce deterrent. Two dangers are considered: The first is that counterforce strategies are often joined to a declaratory policy "which conveys the notion that nuclear war is subject to precise rational and moral limits."[14] Earlier in the pastoral serious doubts were expressed about this idea. The second is that "a purely counterforce strategy may seem to threaten the viability of other nations' retaliatory forces, making deterrence unstable in a crisis and war more likely."[15] It seems that the concern here is about the destabilizing effects of efforts to develop a first strike capability—a point explicitly made later.[16]

If these considerations are joined to the previous discussion of targeting, it is hard to see how the conclusion can be other than a complete rejection of the deterrent. For the requirement of noncombatant immunity is taken to exclude the targeting of civilian populations as such, and the requirement of proportionality seems to exclude targeting of military installations within population areas (although this is not stated in so many words), and the dangers of moving towards a more purely counterforce strategy make that morally unacceptable as well. Yet what is concluded from all this is: "These considerations of concrete elements of nuclear deterrence policy, made in the light of John Paul II's evaluation, but applying it through our own prudential judgments, lead us to a strictly conditioned acceptance of nuclear deterrence."[17] My question is why the conditions stated do not altogether exclude it, and if not, exactly why not.

Is Targeting Civilians Necessary for the Intent to Kill Them?

In the introduction to this paper, I stated that I thought that it was hard to see how the reasoning of the pastoral could allow for the deterrent and that the difficulty was increased if certain analytical precisions were added to the reasoning presented. In this last part of the paper, I will try to add a precision of the kind I referred to there. This precision concerns the operative assumption that targeting civilians is a necessary means for carrying out the intent to kill them. As I mentioned in passing earlier, I think this claim is false. I will try to show, therefore, that the "only if" conditional in the biconditional connecting targeting and intention is

14. Ibid., n. 184.
15. Ibid.
16. Ibid., n. 190.
17. Ibid., n. 186.

false. The claim that if one does not target civilians then one must not be intending their deaths is not true.

I think that the point I wish to make is not merely an exercise in logic chopping because it is this assumption about the relationship of targeting and intention that allows the pastoral quickly to dispense with the question of whether the deterrent involves the intent to kill innocents, and go on to the less definite area of proportionality. It is in this area of proportionality, surely, that the pastoral supposes there to be some room to avoid complete condemnation of the deterrent. If the assumption in question cannot be sustained, then the move to the area where proportionality is the proper standard is not so easily made. And if the assumption is false, the possibility is stronger that the deterrent does involve the absolutely prohibited intent to kill the innocent.

The plausibility of the position that targeting civilians is necessary for the carrying out of one's nuclear planning arises in the context of military actions. In this context if one wants to destroy soldiers and positions, one must surely in some way aim one's weapons at them. But must one aim one's weapons at anyone one intends to kill? It seems not. One might want to kill some people at whom one's weapons are not precisely aimed. For example, one might discover that one's military actions were bringing about many noncombatant deaths and that this effect was significantly demoralizing the enemy population. One might rejoice in this effect and then make it part of one's reason for attacking the installations in question. This could be done without any change in the targeting; perhaps one has a legalistic fear of violating certain rules of war, or is worried about war-crimes trials.

So the connection between targeting and intention is most reasonably held to be necessary in the case of military actions, and even there it seems not to be necessary to carry out all intentions to kill. But the human action under discussion is not a military action but an act of deterrence. Here the choice is a choice to deter—not to take a military target. So the question must be what is it that we are intentionally doing to deter the other side. Surely, the targeting cannot settle the nature of that choice. For what from the point of view of the targeting might be a side effect might also be part of what we are threatening to do in order to deter.

This is not to say that everything that in fact serves to deter is part of what one chooses as a deterrent. For it seems clear that a person could be deterred without any act of deterring on the part of another. More important, one might choose something as a deterrent and know that some side effects of this would also have a deterring effect without one's choosing those side effects as part of one's deterrent. The point is simply that it is possible to choose as part of what one is doing to deter some things that, from the point of view of the targeting, are only side effects: that they are side effects of the targeting does not mean that they are side effects of the deterrence policy.

Whether U.S. deterrence policy contains as a part of what it threatens the destruction of the lives that will be lost if the deterrence is carried out is a factual question to which I do not know the answer. Surely, there is no evidence that it does not. The evidence cited by the pastoral is not to the point. Still, even those statements in which the government denies that the deterrent is aimed at civilian populations as such emphasize the fact that there will be great civilian loss if the deterrent is used. Then there are the statements that affirm the focus of the deterrent on Soviet values.

Of course, if we had a serious counterforce deterrent, one in which we could threaten to destroy the Soviet military capability before they could inflict unacceptable damage on us, then the claim that the targeting of military installations was what we were doing to deter would be plausible, but as it is, the targeting of military installations is within a framework of deterrence policy that surely is not counterforce. The pastoral warns of the dangers of attempting to develop such a strategy. At the very least, it is reasonable to question the idea that the targeting of military installations is a sign of the intentions of the deterrent when this targeting operates within a framework that cannot be counterforce.

But perhaps the facts are otherwise than I suspect them to be. Perhaps our policy is only to deter by the damage inflicted on military targets. Are we then clear of any suspicion that the deterrent involves the intention to kill the innocent? I think not. For the threat to carry out the deterrent to the last stage involves the threat to kill enemy soldiers not as those attacking oneself but simply as persons. In the last stage of the deterrent we will be attacking silos, military bases, and ships and submarines that have already disposed of most or all of their weapons. Our country will already have been destroyed; in effect the war will have been lost. The status of the enemy soldiers in this situation is that of a victorious army; the status of our remaining forces is like that of vengeful terrorists who wish to deprive the enemy of his victory.

If our threat involves the resolve to carry out the final stage, then it is hard to see how it threatens the enemy military as an aggressive force and not rather as a group of humans held hostage. This is another factual question to which I do not know the answer. But the appearances seem to be that we are prepared to carry through the deterrent to the end. We seem committed to convincing the enemy that on "the day" we will carry out the deterrent to the very end. To believe this they must be convinced that the motive of vengeance will be sufficient to carry out what would otherwise be absurd. We all hope that if "the day" ever comes, we will be human enough not to do what we threaten. But we earnestly resolve to do it and to convince the other side that we will. Can killing another out of vengeance and hatred be anything but prohibited killing? When one is killed because he is hated, is he killed as an unjust attacker? I think not. The same must be said, I fear, about the serious threat or resolve to do it. Vengeance is mine alone, says the Lord.

FRANCIS X. WINTERS, S.J.

21. The Cultural Context of the Pastoral Letter on Peace

American commentary on the pastoral letter, whether sympathetic to the letter or critical, has greeted the pastoral as an innovation in Church life. Some applaud this departure for churchmen; others challenge it. Neither of these responses to the letter, however, is adequate to the event of its publication, because both overestimate its novelty. In studying and judging the justice of the present military strategy of their nation, the bishops were merely acting out in their own day the ancient ways of western civilization itself. Precisely because they refused to innovate, that is, to remain silent in the face of injustice, precisely because they hearkened back to the Church's heritage, they have created a new political moment in the West and generated new hope. Precisely because the letter is the fruit of a timeless tradition, it is timely at present. The bishops have thrown light on the present political-military crisis precisely by reminding western civilization of its origins and central convictions. It was the historian R. W. Carlyle who captured the genius of western political culture when he remarked: "There cannot be an adequate definition of justice, but it is exactly the pursuit of justice which distinguishes the rational and moral society."[1] Perhaps he should have said, "There cannot be an adequate definition of justice, but it is exactly the pursuit of justice which distinguishes the *western* rational and moral society," because this may not be a universal phenomenon. It does, however, in my mind clearly describe the political civilization of the *West*.

The perennial quest for justice in western civilization is paradoxical, for western civilization is deeply and richly inspired by the Gospel, which makes love the touchstone of discipleship. Thus, it would surely not have been surprising if western civilization had kicked over the traces of justice and fashioned itself by the law of love. But it chose not to, perhaps because of the enormous and honorable weight of its pagan past and the richness of the Greco-Roman tradition.

1. R. W. and A. J. Carlyle, *A History of Medieval Political Theory in the West* (New York: Barnes & Noble, 1939), VI, 506.

Western politics is essentially animated by the quest for justice, the effort to assign to each one what is his due and to defend each one in its possession even by resort to coercion. Politics, as it is understood in the West, is a tapestry of rights, of capacities of individuals and communities to act in certain ways with impunity. Politics is not a mere matter of comparative strength, as some "Realists" would urge; nor is it a mere matter of trust and voluntary cooperation, as "Utopians" would assert. It is neither so base as a comparison of strength, nor so exalted as an act of trust. Rather, western politics is a matter of rights and obligations.

This formula of Carlyle's may appear vague. But it is written in the history of our civilization at certain special places and on certain special days. It is written, for example, at Runnymede, where a wayward king was corralled by a bishop, Stephen Langton of Canterbury, acting in concert with a loose coalition of eight other bishops and some barons. It was at Runnymede that King John was forced to sign a charter reaffirming the rights of the English people against their king. The quest for justice, of which Carlyle speaks, is the articulation and defense of the people's rights even against their monarch.[2]

The Great Charter, as it came to be known, was extorted from the king under threat of deposition by a superior coalition of forces mustered, paradoxically, by a bishop. The lesson of Runnymede is important. Neither the prerogatives of kingship nor the creative openness of trust are our birthright as a civilization; our birthright rather is the insistence on a signed articulation of rights extorted under the threat of force.

Not for the first time, then, in 1983 did bishops intervene in politics. While the bishops and barons at Runnymede did not seek to define justice (for, as Carlyle says, justice cannot have an adequate definition), they did make bold to list their rights and insist on a signature under pain of deposition.

Revolution is our birthright in the West. Our political system has as its source the capacity to remove an inflexible tyrant from office, by force if need be, and with moral impunity. This right of revolution springs from the conviction that man has a divinely appointed and eternal destiny that can be made virtually inaccessible by a tyrannical political regime. But since mankind's destiny is not a matter of freedom, but a matter of divine command, any human ruler blocking access to this destiny must be removed. The community has, in other words, no right to tolerate tyranny. Individuals may exempt themselves for many reasons from the burden of removing the tyrant but the community has no right to tolerate the tyrant. The community may not refuse to resist.

---

2. For the history of the events leading to *Magna Carta*, cf. Joseph Clayton, *Innocent III and His Times* (Milwaukee: Bruce, 1941), pp. 168–170.

Society's obligation to God, therefore, gives rise to the right to revolution.

One of the fundamental paradoxes of our civilization, then, is the right to revolution, the conviction that, in the absence of any external enemies, society's most gifted members, those with the most to gain from the present order, have the right (and indeed, as a group, the obligation) to engage with moral impunity in mutual slaughter in the name of justice. This is the living meaning of Carlyle's placid phrase about the quest for justice. Its meaning is seen at Runnymede. In the face of inflexible tyranny, where all other avenues of redress have been exhausted, the people have the obligation to engage in fraternal struggle to eradicate the tyrant.

From this right of revolution to the right of national self-defense is but a short step. All that is required to generate from the right of revolution the corollary right of self-defense is the appearance on the horizon of an external enemy meaning to undo the revolution won at such cost. For the people's right to revolution does not evanesce at the appearance of an invader. Rather, the right of revolution extends to the armed defense of the fruits of the revolution. There is a right to go to war, rooted in the right to revolution.

Western civilization thus has room for war. But it also has a clear and fearful notion of the historical meaning of war. War for the West is precisely an instrument in the perennial quest for justice. It is morally acceptable only insofar as it remains such a human instrument. Not every large-scale combat at arms is a war. For war is the disciplined defensive use of force to persuade an illegitimate aggressor to desist from attack or, failing such a change of will, the use of force to disarm him. War thus has a clear historical and philosophical meaning. War is not an instrument of annihilation; it is not an instrument of punishment, nor of revenge. It is only an instrument of defense, a means of dissuading or disarming the aggressor.

Therefore (and we now have come to the crux of the argument in the nuclear era), war must admit of being won, of imposing defeat on an enemy and eliciting his surrender. Military hostilities that can neither be won nor lost are not war. They cannot be an instrument of justice. A phrase that might summarize the doctrine of the bishops in their pastoral letter is the following: "Wars that cannot be won (or lost) may not be fought."

By general and official agreement, nuclear hostilities cannot be won or lost. Over the months the bishops spent preparing the pastoral letter, the views of the most senior officials of the government, everyone but the President himself, were sedulously sought out. Government officials responded; the bishops nuanced their letter accordingly. One of the great paradoxes of this preparatory period is that the government not only disclaimed any ability to control nuclear war, but every responsible official in the government said repeatedly and candidly that nuclear war cannot be won or lost in any recognizable sense.

This recognition has been a source of continuing astonishment. It can be dated back at least to 1975, when the Arms Control and Disarmament Agency published a pamphlet entitled "Some Effects of Nuclear War," in which the uncontrollability of nuclear war was admitted.[3] Since that time, the government has repeatedly and candidly expressed the view that nuclear war cannot be controlled and thus cannot be won.

The clear conclusion to be drawn from every official government document issued on this matter since 1975 is this: Although we know how to start a nuclear war, we have no idea how to stop one. Given this official and general consensus on the uncontrollability and unwinnability of nuclear war, the bishops drew a conclusion they could not have failed to draw. As Cardinal Ratzinger said in his first response to the American letter in May 1983, "given the principles of Catholic teaching, and given the nature of nuclear war, the American bishops could have come to no other conclusion."

The conclusion the bishops arrived at is a sound one, given the general and unchallenged admission by the government that nuclear war cannot be controlled or won. We must come to the same conclusion, namely, that western civilization has no room for nuclear war. Neither the ethical sense nor the strategic sense of western civilization accepts the justice of a combat at arms that cannot achieve any political purpose. Neither bishops nor generals recognize in a prospective nuclear exchange anything resembling war or any possibility of justice. Hence the bishops condemn any use of nuclear weapons. Because they continue to accept the tenets of western civilization, however, the bishops sketch the limits of warfare even in the nuclear era. For that reason, paradoxically, the bishops found themselves forced to fill the vacuum of strategic thought that has existed since 1945 on the matter of nuclear arms. This vacuum itself is attributable to two factors: First, the reliance by the superpowers on nuclear weapons, which has displaced traditional military planning, and second, our generals' continued observance of the traditional constraint that they not speak publicly on matters of foreign policy.

The bishops, therefore, in trying to bring to bear the insights of the Catholic tradition on the current situation, have found themselves com-

3. U.S. Arms Control and Disarmament Agency, "Worldwide Effects of Nuclear War . . . Some Perspectives," Report No. 81 (Washington, D.C.: U.S. Government Printing Office, 1975), p. 5.

pelled to articulate a strategy, because neither politicians nor generals have done so over the last 40 years. They found themselves, as conscientious citizens, in a strategic vacuum. Where generals fear to tread, in the modern era, the bishops, some would say foolishly, have rushed in to sketch and recommend an alternative political and military strategy adequate for the imperatives of security and faithful to the constraints of conscience.

It is unnecessary to recall here the moral content of the pastoral, which is now well known.[4] Suffice it to say that the bishops call for a unilateral renunciation of the strategy that contemplates using nuclear weapons while equally condemning the unilateral dismantling of the arsenal itself, which they expect to be gradually reduced through bilateral and verifiable arms-reduction agreements.

It is well known that this radical but rigorously logical moral conclusion was considered anathema by a highly vocal group of Catholic lay men and women. This band of dissidents sought to elicit signatures to an alternative pastoral letter drawing diametrically opposed conclusions. Among the signers to this letter, which had anticipated the endorsement of high government officials who would repudiate in advance the moral teaching of the bishops, was not a single recognized authority or responsible (civilian or military) official concerned with defense questions.

This absence of signatures to the alternative "pastoral" is significant. I submit that the reason these responsible policymakers avoided signing the alternative letter is because the traditional doctrine of the limited right to go to war, which is the starting point of the bishops' letter, is also the first principle of strategy, namely, that there is a limited right to the use of force. For both bishops and generals, therefore, war, if it is to be rational and therefore acceptable, must be *war*. It must not be something else. War must be the disciplined application of force to persuade the enemy to desist and/or to disarm him. A war must be capable of being won or lost.

Nuclear war does not meet this simple and commonsense criterion. It is, for example, technologically unlikely that one side could communicate a message of surrender to the other side during a nuclear exchange. If the Soviets were to choose, in the midst of nuclear combat, to surrender, we would have no way of learning of this decision. We would therefore go on fighting. Even if our national command center could learn of the Soviets' intent to surrender, it would be unable to communicate with our troops to tell them to stop firing. We have, in other words, no way

---

4. For a summary of the doctrine, cf. my essay, "Did the Bishops Ban the Bomb? Yes and No." *America*, Vol. 149, No. 6 (September 3–10, 1983), 104–108.

to stop a nuclear war.[5] Unlimited and illimitable nuclear exchange does not qualify as war and so does not constitute an instrument of justice. This type of exchange is therefore both militarily and morally unacceptable.

Conclusion

Earlier in this essay the thesis of Carlyle, that it is the quest for justice that defines western political civilization, was illustrated by recalling the pivotal event of *Magna Carta*. There, at Runnymede, bishops and barons conspired in extorting from King John a written affirmation of the people's traditional rights. At that moment the genius of western civilization inspired individuals to act in a way that set history on a new course. It is interesting to ask at this point in our reflections whether they knew at that time what they were doing. Were they conscious of the cardinal character of their common resolve? Did they know "they were making history"?

The same question can be asked, not without justification, of the recent process whereby the bishops prepared their letter. Responding to the inescapable challenge of questions from the faithful, and relying on their theological formation to provide the response, they moved to condemn the centerpiece of contemporary military strategy, the resort to use of nuclear weapons. Though they were conscious of the difficulties and consequences of their individual discernment on the morality of nuclear war, it is doubtful that many of them felt themselves responsible for changing the course of human history. Yet, all unwittingly, they may well have done so. Western nations seem to be turning gradually away from the present strategy that contemplates the use of nuclear weapons in war. Political leaders, at least those out of power, are beginning to speak about a return to conventional defense as the upper limit of legitimate self-defense. If this trend to accept the self-limitation of renouncing nuclear war becomes dominant, historians will recognize that the bishops of the United States were among the decisive influences reenforcing this shift away from the precipice of nuclear war.

---

5. In support of their judgment about the uncontrollability of nuclear war, the bishops' letter cites well-known works on the topic, including Desmond Ball, *Can Nuclear War Be Controlled?* Adelphi Paper, No. 161 (London. International Institute of Strategic Studies, 1981). They cite as well testimony of witnesses, such as former Defense Secretary Brown, who had admitted the uncontrollability of such a war in the text of his annual Department of Defense Report, FY 1979 (Washington, D.C.: U.S. Government Printing Office, 1979).

IV Implications for American Catholics

DAVID JOHNSON

22. Educating for Peace: Into the Mainstream

I have been asked to reflect on the significance of the American Catholic bishops' pastoral on war and peace from an educator's perspective. The viewpoint expressed here is that of a generalist, one who has for several years been working in a national office to incorporate peace and justice studies into the curricular and co-curricular activities of all departments at Catholic colleges and universities. As I am not a specialist in either moral theology or strategic politics, I will accordingly resist the temptation to critique the content of the body of the pastoral. Rather, I will deal with the bishops' particular language on educating for peace—specifically, Sections III (A)(5) and IV (B) (C) of the pastoral—and its implications for Catholic education. Forgive me, however, if my discussion centers more on higher education and less on elementary and secondary education, for the former is what I know best.

Before addressing the bishops' charge to educators, however, some preliminary comments need to be made regarding the pedagogical process of the pastoral. That process—applauded in most quarters of the Church—also has broad implications for educators. That it will receive slightly less treatment here than the specific language addressing educators reflects not a lesser importance—indeed, it may be the single most important outcome of the pastoral—but the fact that it has been dealt with quite well elsewhere.[1] The title of these reflections, "Educating for Peace: Into the Mainstream," should perhaps be followed with a question mark. Surely the bishops are telling us that educating for peace is something that Catholic educators should be about, and what could—in most cases—be more "mainstream" than that kind of endorsement from the American bishops? My hesitation at subscribing fully to such an optimistic scenario is based on two reasons. For one thing, *The Challenge of Peace* is perhaps less a "mainstream" document than it is a document of real moral leadership in both the Catholic community and the nation as a whole. The bishops may well be ahead of the faithful on

---

1. See especially Edward Vacek, S.J., "Authority and the Peace Pastoral," *America* (October 22, 1983), 225–228.

this issue. For another thing, most Catholic educators certainly have yet to accept peace education as part of *their* mainstream, as we shall see. But the bottom line, I think, is that the bishops' endorsement is having, and will have in the future, a strong effect on *bringing* peace education "into the mainstream" of Catholic education, despite the cultural lag we are experiencing today. So we'll leave the title as is; the word "mainstream" has another important connotation that will justify its use further along in these reflections.[2]

The Pedagogy of the Pastoral

In a sense, *The Challenge of Peace* does not "have implications for" Catholic education—it *is* Catholic education at its best. For those of us in Catholic higher education who still must respond (if only occasionally) to believers in George Bernard Shaw's famous statement that "a Catholic university is a contradiction in terms," the pastoral provides a clear answer. We have often spoken of Catholic education as the forum in which faith and culture interact. This pastoral, perhaps more than any other Church document, provides a fine example of both the legitimacy and the benefits of that interaction. It is an extraordinary document: It is science informed by faith, faith informed by science.

Consider first the method by which it was formulated, a method based on the academic model. Months of research and interviews with the finest minds that the committee could find, covering the broadest possible spectrum of religious and political thought, followed by two preliminary drafts to which comments were invited by colleagues, and ending with a final draft that was subject to debate before the assembled national media in Chicago.

Needless to say, this kind of open consultative process has not been the normal manner in which Church documents have been composed. Yet the direct results of the use of that process have been almost entirely beneficial:

1. It produced a tight, coherent document that has made a major intellectual contribution to the debate about nuclear warfare.

2. It simultaneously raised the level of public debate on this issue around the world, through massive and unprecedented coverage in the secular media.

3. The open consultation produced a feeling of "ownership" of the letter, not just among the bishops but among men and women of good will throughout the country.

2. See pp. 348–354 below.

4. It set the stage for further discourses of a similar nature, most notably the pastoral letter on the American economy.

Consider also the "style" of the letter as a model for Catholic education. It is both forceful and nonauthoritarian. It makes, I believe, no compromises with essential Church teachings and yet recognizes, in its distinction between fundamental moral principles and specific applications of those principles, the supremacy of individual moral conscience and the need for persons of good will to form their own conclusions within that framework of principles. It claims not to enjoy a monopoly on truth; rather, it suggests that the search for definitive answers is only beginning, and it invites others to join in that search.[3]

The document thus accepts the advantages of the academic model in the search for truth and then goes beyond that method by adding a moral dimension that lends far greater meaning to the political and strategic conclusions reached.

In so doing it reminds those of us in the educational ministry of the Church just how unique and rewarding our brand of education can be when we do it correctly. We are, as we continually say to outsiders, in the business of values education. We aim not just to teach the facts that are known and do research to discover those that are not, but also to guide—not direct—our students in the formation of their individual consciences. That is precisely what *The Challenge of Peace* accomplishes so effectively, and its style merits emulation in our schools and colleges.

Catholic Education for Peace

Let us turn now to the bishops' challenge to educators.

In Section II (A)(5), entitled "Efforts to Develop Non-Violent Means of Conflict Resolution," the bishops make a specific call for research, with these words: "With Pope John Paul II, we call upon educational and research institutes to take a lead in conducting peace studies: 'Scientific studies on war, its nature, causes, means, objectives and risk have much to tell us on the conditions for peace.'"[4] Later in the same section, after endorsing the concept of a National Academy of Peace and Conflict Resolution, the bishops say:

3. Cardinal Bernardin's December 6, 1983, address at Fordham University reinforces that invitation in the context of developing "A Consistent Ethic of Life," *ORIGINS*, Vol. 13, pp. 491 ff.

4. The National Conference of Catholic Bishops, *The Challenge of Peace: God's Promise and Our Response* (Washington, D.C.: United States Catholic Conference, 1983) n. 228.

We urge universities, particularly Catholic universities, in our country to develop programs for rigorous, interdisciplinary research, education, and training directed toward peacemaking expertise . . . No greater challenge or higher priority can be imagined than the development and perfection of a theology of peace suited to a civilization poised on the brink of self-destruction.[5]

Then, in their concluding section, "The Pastoral Challenge and Response," Part IV of the pastoral, the bishops call for a balanced education on the pastoral itself to be carried out, explaining clearly "those principles or teachings about which there is little question," and then applying those teachings to concrete situations that may present several possible legitimate options.[6] Finally, the bishops acknowledge in their message "To Educators" that the framework they have outlined for considering issues of war and peace "will become a living message only through your work in the Catholic community."[7]

Clearly then, the bishops are asking Catholic schools at all levels to begin the process of educating for peace and Catholic colleges and universities to combine that education with research initiatives in peace studies.

An examination of the implications of responding to that charge—based on my experience in monitoring peace studies at Catholic colleges and universities—will indicate that what the bishops ask is easier said than done, but clearly not impossible.

Teaching Peace

Up until now, Catholic education has not had an enviable record on teaching its students about war and peace and how moral decisions on those issues are to be addressed in the light of Church teachings. My own experience lends a case in point. I arrived at the University of Notre Dame in 1967, as the war in Vietnam was heating up rapidly. After eight years of Catholic grade school education, four years of weekly C.C.D. classes, and two full years at the university, it was (finally) in 1970, my junior year, when I first heard of the just-war theory, not in a theology class but in a seminar on the great books, strangely enough. It happened

5. Ibid., n. 229.
6. Ibid., n. 283.
7. Ibid., n. 304. It should be noted that *The Challenge of Peace* is not the first time that the American bishops have urged Catholic colleges and universities to educate for justice. Similar challenges were issued at the bishops' 1976 Call to Action Conference and in their 1980 pastoral on Catholic higher education. See the National Conference of Catholic Bishops, *To Do the Work of Justice* (Washington, D.C.: United States Catholic Conference, 1978), p. 5, and the National Conference of Catholic Bishops, *Catholic Higher Education and the Pastoral Mission of the Church* (Washington, D.C.: United States Catholic Conference, 1980), pp. 8–9.

to be the same year that I discovered that my student deferment was going to end in favor of a new lottery system for determining who was called to duty, and I was faced with the first major moral decision of my life. If called, could or should I go?

In a way I was fortunate. My friends who were considering the same question had *still* not heard of the just-war theory, simply because they hadn't taken the same class I had. Almost overnight I became my dormitory's resident "expert" on the just-war theory, and eventually we helped to set up an information center for those who were considering applying for conscientious objector status and wanted to know the Church's teachings on war.

The point is, of course, that all of us—not just those who were inclined to conscientious objector applications—needed to know the Church's teachings and should have known them as a matter of course as a result of our travels through the Catholic educational system. Instead, at the height of a war that the just-war theory clearly called into question, that crucial aspect of our moral education was left largely to chance. If my own experience and that of my colleagues at Notre Dame is any guide—and my conversations with those who attended other Catholic colleges and universities during that era convince me that it is—then Catholic education failed miserably in its responsibilities to students during this time of crisis.

It is, I think, in recognition of that earlier failure (as well as in recognition of the fact that nuclear war allows no time to apply for conscientious objector status) that the bishops so directly challenge Catholic educators to raise these questions now. Left unsaid by the bishops is "how"—How do we teach peace?

In formulating a response to that question, I make two suggestions:

1. That a good response by Catholic educators to the bishops' charge might be to introduce course requirements designed to ensure that every student who matriculates at a Catholic high school or college would examine the teachings of the Church on these matters, and particularly the bishops' pastoral; and

2. That education for peace is of limited value unless it is but part of an overall education for justice.

If carried out, the first suggestion would ensure that no Catholic student today would be left in the situation that my colleagues and I found ourselves in 15 years ago. They would at least have heard about the just-war theory and the nonviolent tradition within the Church and would have that basic information on which to proceed with their own life choices. It could be accomplished through the imposition of a required course in the junior or senior year of high school, using the pastoral as a main text. If desired, students who have fulfilled such a requirement could "test out" of a similar required course on the college level—although, frankly, considering the duplication of study that already occurs among secondary and postsecondary courses, the overriding importance of the issue, and the rapid maturation that often occurs in students of this age group, a second required course (more in the way of a seminar) on the college level would be justified, I believe.

If adding a single required course to high school and college curricula sounds like a simple and easy way for Catholic education to fulfill its responsibilities here, consider the implications in terms of the allocation of already scarce educational resources. Catholic secondary schools enrolled 788,000 students in fall 1983, roughly one-fourth of whom are seniors. If we assume 40 students per section of our required course on the Church's teachings on war and peace, then 4,925 sections are needed around the country each year to cover just the senior class.

The Catholic University of America enrolled about 600 new freshmen this year. If we assume seminar classes of 20 students, that means 30 such seminars need to be offered this year to incoming freshmen (or sophomores, etc.). It also means the equivalent of about 10 full-time faculty positions. At $20,000 per position, that amounts to roughly $200,000 in new annual expenditures at CUA, conservatively calculated. At a university of Notre Dame's size, with 1,600 incoming freshmen each year, 80 seminars, 25 faculty positions, and $500,000 would be required. Not even Notre Dame can afford such an expense with ease, if at all.

Surely these calculations can be reduced by assuming larger classes and the like, but the bottom line remains the same: If such requirements are indeed necessary to fulfill our responsibilities to Catholic students, the resource expenditures will be tremendous. And, at most Catholic institutions, those resources are not going to be "new monies" but reallocations from some other program or programs currently receiving those funds. When you add to these financial exigencies the problem of finding and training competent faculty to teach these courses, clearing space among many competitors for designation of such courses as "core" requirements, and the like, it quickly becomes evident that what I propose simply cannot be done considering the constraints under which Catholic education operates.

Fortunately, there are alternatives. Let me begin to raise some by referring back to my second suggestion and to some of the Association of Catholic Colleges and Universities' (A.C.C.U.) experiences in this area.

It was Paul VI who said, "If you want peace, work for justice." That simple statement nicely summarizes the thrust of our efforts at Catholic colleges and universities. It suggests that, as important as *The Challenge of Peace* is, it should not be isolated as an object of study. Rather, it and the Church's other statements on war and peace are but a part of a much broader and equally impressive collection of Church literature addressing justice in the world as a precondition of peace, including *Mater et Magistra, Pacem in Terris, Gaudium et Spes, Populorum Progressio*, the documents of the 1971 Synod of Bishops and the 1976 American bishops' "Call to Action" conference, and others.[8]

The position of the National Catholic Educational Association (N.C.E.A.), of which A.C.C.U. is the higher education branch, is that this entire body of Catholic thought, loosely termed the "social teachings of the Church," should be part and parcel of Catholic educational efforts at all levels. Peace education is not enough. Justice education, of which peace studies is an important component, is what our ministry calls us to do.[9]

Those who have been around college-level academics for a time know that when a new area of study is proposed, we immediately begin to think of "turf"—a new department, separate faculty and budgets, "our own" students. So it will not be surprising that many of the early proponents of justice education on the college level thought immediately of new majors and minors in "Justice and Peace Studies." Such programs are valuable in that they provide an in-depth examination of the relevant issues, but they also carry their own problems. They require the allocation of resources that many institutions do not possess. More important, I think, their value is limited in that such programs are of interest to only a few students on any given campus, particularly in a time of increasing careerism among youth. So if our goal is to expose as many students as possible to the justice teachings of the Church, then majors and minors are not going to do the job by themselves.

What we have been suggesting to the colleges then, is that rather than setting up separate programs for a few, it would be measurably better to center our efforts on incorporating justice issues into the already existing courses of study in the various disciplines, i.e., into the academic "mainstream," if you will. Rather than examining the Church documents on labor, for example, in a course on "Catholic Social Teaching," examine them in business management courses. Rather than addressing

8. For a fine collection of these documents to 1976, see Joseph Gremillion, *The Gospel of Peace and Justice* (Maryknoll, N.Y.: Orbis Books, 1976).

9. For a report on the Association of Catholic Colleges and Universities' efforts in this area, see *Occasional Papers on Catholic Higher Education*, Vol. IV, No. 2 (Winter 1978), and *Current Issues in Catholic Higher Education*, Vol. 1, No. 2 (Winter 1981), both available from the N.C.E.A. Publications Office, 1077 30 St., N.W., Washington, D.C. 20007.

The Challenge of Peace only in a separate course, as many of our institutions are doing, or only in a theology course, examine it in political science courses, in military science courses, and—especially—in teacher education courses. The issues that these Church documents address arise naturally in all disciplines, whether they be physics, biology, sociology, political science, literature or whatever.

This is not to suggest that separate majors or even separate courses on "The Church's Teachings On War and Peace," for example, are of no value. Indeed, the available literature could support several such courses, and these issues certainly deserve such treatment in depth. Rather, we're suggesting that the college can reach more students—and perhaps have a greater impact on the formation of their life and career values—if justice issues are addressed in the context of their major fields of study. And the side benefit to the college, of course, is that such an approach requires little in the way of new resource allocations.

What this method does require is a commitment on the part of faculty who teach these courses to do considerable extra reading and reflection themselves and then to alter or expand their syllabi and reading lists to consider how justice issues touch on the particular subject matter of their disciplines.

Again, those who have been around higher education for a while know that getting such a commitment from faculty is no easy task. Our tradition of academic freedom means, among other things, that neither bishops, nor college presidents, nor provosts have any right to tell a faculty member what should be included in his or her course outlines. They must be convinced, freely, that justice issues are appropriate matters for inclusion in their courses and that Church statements like *The Challenge of Peace* deserve study. Many of our faculty have yet to accept that notion.

My own argument to them runs like this: If you accept the notion that science and education are no longer value free (if indeed they ever were), then the question is simply, "*Which* values shall guide our research and teaching?" Among all the possible choices, I suggest that the values of justice for all human beings and peace in this world are simply the best and most important. I suggest that the attainment of these values would represent the highest possible achievement in humankind's search for perfection. I suggest that the Catholic Church, among many others, has something to contribute to that kind of education, a now impressive array of justice literature. And I suggest that a failure to consider these questions in the light of that Catholic heritage results in an incomplete education.

Make no mistake, however. A call for consideration of justice issues in the context of the standard academic disciplines is a call for a serious reforming of the curriculum. Many faculty still believe that their job is to teach students how an atomic bomb works and that going beyond that to an examination of the morality of the use of atomic bombs is either beyond their competence, or not their "place."

Lest there be any doubt, however, let me be clear on another matter. When we suggest that justice issues deserve to be considered in the curriculum and that the Catholic Church's statements on those issues deserve particular examination at Catholic schools and colleges, we are not saying that our Church has all the answers, or even the best answers necessarily. The bishops acknowledge just the opposite in *The Challenge of Peace*. What we are saying is that these Church documents merit serious study and reflection, nothing more or less.

I have perhaps belabored the issue of curricular reform too long here. I do so because I believe that, in the long run, a separate system of Catholic education must be distinguished by its commitment to education for justice, that we have a long way to go in this respect, and that we had better get on with it if we hope to reach the next millennium.

But, while we are about the long-term business of convincing the faculty about justice education, there are other, more immediate responses that Catholic educators can make to *The Challenge of Peace*. This series of lectures here at The Catholic University of America is a fine example of this kind of co-curricular effort. During spring 1983, A.C.C.U. sent a letter to the presidents of every Catholic college and university in the country, suggesting that they make the pastoral a specific topic of study and reflection on their campuses during 1983–84. At least 140 of them accepted that suggestion and designated one or more individuals on their campus as coordinator of activities relating to the pastoral. Many of them put together lecture series similar to this one. Others are sponsoring faculty teach-ins, speeches by bishops, film festivals, liturgies for peace, debates, conferences, special courses on the pastoral such as that offered here at CUA and all manner of other events with *The Challenge of Peace* as a cornerstone.[10] I'm convinced, from the reports we've received from these colleges, that Bishop Gumbleton and the Rev. Bryan Hehir have cloned themselves—they're speaking everywhere. So also, I'm happy to say, is the Rev. Daniel Berrigan, whose personal witness for peace continues to serve as an inspiration to many of us.

A key issue in our response to the pastoral, however, is whether these events will be continued beyond this year and into the normal course of

---

10. For a summary of activities on many of these campuses, see the A.C.C.U. newsletter *Update*, Vol. XI, Nos. 3, 4, and 5, available from A.C.C.U., Suite 650, One Dupont Circle, N.W., Washington, D.C. 20036.

Catholic education. We can ill afford to let that letter fade from our consciousness or that of our students. Its message, and the messages contained in the other Church documents to which I have referred here, must become institutionalized as part of the normal course of education in Catholic schools and colleges.

Other Implications for Educators

The challenge to educators posed by *The Challenge of Peace* has other implications beyond the actual teaching of peace and justice.

If we accept the notion that faculty are called to devote time and energy to this effort, it follows that the standard reward systems for faculty—hiring, promotion, and tenure—need also to be revised to reflect this emphasis. This can be the administration's "carrot": While faculty cannot be required to teach X, Y, or Z in their courses, the college or university *can* choose, first of all, to hire only scholars who reflect an emphasis on values education. At too many of our institutions, and for too long, hiring decisions have been based almost solely on qualifications determined by the leading secular universities—where the candidate received his or her doctorate (preferably from the Ivy League), whether the candidate's dissertation (or other writings) has been published, what the candidate's particular specialization is within that discipline. There is no legal reason why our institutions cannot (and there are compelling moral reasons why they should) also inquire of its applicants about their commitment not just to a given discipline, e.g., sociology, but to teaching sociology "as if it matters," to raising values questions with students both in and outside the classroom. Fortunately for the institution, and unfortunately for faculty today, it is a buyer's market in most fields. Our institutions can afford to be selective and to choose scholar-teachers who both possess academic credentials and reflect an emphasis on the examination and development of values. They need not all be Catholic, and they certainly need not be "liberals"—any institution that attempts to hire only from those categories will rapidly become both boring and stagnant. What the faculty should hold in common is that commitment to values education and development. Beyond that qualification, a wide range of ethical, religious, and political views should be present.

In a similar way, faculty already employed by the institution need to be rewarded for their efforts in this area. Criteria for both promotion and tenure should reflect that emphasis. The situation today is almost in opposition, I am sorry to say. Faculty who move beyond the narrow confines of their discipline to pursue interdisciplinary work with colleagues often find departmental structures unaccommodating, and those who choose to spend greater amounts of time on values development with students find that spending the same time writing for publications pays greater dividends. We need to reward such work, not penalize it. We need to encourage it affirmatively through allocation of funds for interdisciplinary research on these issues and through faculty development programs. Up until now, most of our colleges have not done so.

The pastoral also carries implications for the way the institution *qua* institution conducts itself and how its "Catholicity" is measured. It suggests that the "Catholicity" of an institution is judged unfairly if it is measured only by the number of theology courses that are required, or by the degree to which members of the academic community must conform to certain papal teachings, and not by the quality of its scholarship, its commitment to justice and peace education, or its success at raising values questions among its students.

It suggests, I think, that Catholic institutions need to pay attention to how they comport themselves in ways other than academic—in their student services, campus ministry, research contracts, investment policies, and choices for honorary degrees. These things, too, should reflect the institution's commitment to peace. In the area of research, e.g., if "offensive war of any kind is not morally justifiable," as the bishops state,[11] then it should follow that research and development of clearly offensive weapons systems should not take place on Catholic college and university campuses. What weapons should be included in that "clearly offensive" category is beyond my competence to judge. I suspect that the line is often a fine one. The neutron bomb and weapons of germ or chemical warfare—designed as they are to be counterpopulation weapons[12]—would seem to present the clearest cases for exclusion from research on Catholic college and university campuses. If the judgment is correct, it may also follow our investment portfolios should exclude corporations that manufacture such weapons.

On the other hand, the pastoral letter does not suggest that ROTC programs have no place on Catholic school or college campuses. Indeed, it suggests that the type of values education presented here would be particularly appropriate for those who intend to spend some years in military service.

As I have suggested at various points in this discussion, Catholic education has a long way to go in addressing implications of this sort. We have spent far too much of our time, energy, and spirit in an attempt to emulate secular institutions, by way of proving that we are "just as good" as they are. *The Challenge of Peace* shows us, again, how we can be better.

---

11. *The Challenge of Peace*, I, A, p. iii.

12. Counterpopulation warfare is expressly condemned in *The Challenge of Peace*, pp. 46–47.

ROBERT A. DESTRO

23. Pastoral Politics and Public Policy: Reflections on the Legal Aspects of the Catholic Bishops' Pastoral Letter on War and Peace

Taken as a whole, the Roman Catholic bishops' 1983 pastoral letter on war and peace, *The Challenge of Peace: God's Promise and Our Response*[1] has two purposes: first, to assist Catholics in the formation of their consciences; and, second, to contribute to the ongoing public policy debate concerning the morality of war in general, and of nuclear war in particular.[2] This paper will address the stated purposes of and the suggestions made in the pastoral letter from the vantage point of American statutory and constitutional law. It will make no attempt to provide definitive legal answers to the many questions raised by and in the letter, for there are none in this complex and challenging area of law. Its purpose is to raise some of the practical legal and moral questions critical to the conscientious choices of the individuals to whom the letter is addressed: government officials, citizens, members of the armed services, workers in defense industries, clergy and religious, and others.

The letter calls on each person to whom it is addressed to "probe the meaning of the moral choices which are ours as Christians"[3] respecting the issue of nuclear war and states that peace "is the fruit of ideas and decisions taken in the political, cultural, social, military, and legal sectors of life."[4] It correctly recognizes that conscientious choices are not made by individuals in a moral vacuum, but by "citizens [who] wish to affirm [their] loyalty to [their] country and its ideas" and who must also remain both "faithful to the universal principles proclaimed by the Church" and sensitive to the needs of the world as a whole.[5]

The standard citation system for legal writing is employed in this article with only slight modifications.

1. National Conference of Catholic Bishops, *The Challenge of Peace: God's Promise and Our Response* (Washington, D.C., May 3, 1983) [hereafter cited in text as "pastoral letter" or "letter"].

2. *See*, *Id*. [hereinafter cited in notes as *The Challenge of Peace*].

3. *The Challenge of Peace*, n. 67.

4. *Id*., at n. 21.   5. *Id*., at n. 326.

In keeping with this view, the first section of this paper sketches the structural framework of the American statutory and constitutional law that necessarily comes into play, formally or informally, whenever religiously motivated citizens or religious institutions act in the public sphere or explicitly take action with legal effect and defend those actions on the basis of sincerely held religious beliefs or teachings. The second section is a discussion of the constitutional and policy questions raised whenever organized religious groups explicitly seek to involve themselves in the political process. Finally, the third section is a discussion of the constitutional and statutory issues raised whenever individual believers seek exemptions from social or employer-imposed duties on religious grounds.

Religious Freedom in American Law

American law has valued religious freedom as an essential element of individual liberty and civil society from its earliest beginnings. When the Pilgrims landed at Plymouth in 1620, they intended that the newly formed Massachusetts Bay Colony would be as a biblical "city on a hill."[6] More recently, in 1952 the late United States Supreme Court Justice William O. Douglas frankly recognized that "[w]e are a religious people whose institutions presuppose a Supreme Being."[7] The American people and their leaders have defended and fostered freedom of religion and its corollary, freedom of conscience, through express legislative and judicial[8] action designed to provide maximum protection for religious belief and practice.[9]

In the early years, protection for individual religious belief and conscience was seen as the logical extension of a theological and moral imperative. In his famous "Memorial and Remonstrance Against Religious Assessments,"[10] James Madison argued that:

6. "Wee shall be [. . .] as a Citty upon a Hill, the eies of all people are uppon us; soe that if wee shall deal falsely with our god in this worke wee have undertaken and soe cause him to withdrawe his present help from us, wee shall be made a story and a byword through the world." John Winthrop, "A Model of Christian Charity" (1630), a sermon delivered aboard the Arbella, *quoted in* Daniel Boorstin, *The Americans: The Colonial Experience* (New York: Vintage Books, 1958), p. 3.

7. *Zorach v. Clauson*, 343 U.S. 306, 312–313 (1952).

8. *See, e.g.*, Virginia Declaration of Rights, Art. 16 (1776); Title VII of the Civil Rights Act of 1964, 42 U.S.C.§§ 2000e, *et seq.*, 78 Stat. 255 (employment discrimination); 20 U.S.C. § 4071, P.L. 98–377, 98 Stat. 1303 ("The Equal Access Act").

9. *See, e.g.*, U.S. Const. Art. VI, cl.3, U.S. Const. Amend I; Cal. Const. Art I § 4 (West, 1983); Fla. Const. Art I § 3, 25A Fla. Stats. Ann. Art I § 3.

10. J. Madison, "Memorial and Remonstrance Against Religious Assessments" (1785), *quoted in*, *Everson v. Board of Education*, 330 U.S. 1, 63–72 (1947) (Rutledge, J., dissenting) [hereinafter "Memorial and Remonstrance"].

[R]eligion, or the duty we owe to our creator, and the manner of discharging it, can be directed only by reason and conviction, not by force or violence. The Religion then of every man must be left to the conviction and conscience of every man; and it is the right of every man to exercise it as these may dictate. . . .

. . . It is the duty of every man to render to the Creator such homage, and such only, as he believes to be acceptable to him. This duty is precedent both in order of time and degree of obligation to the claims of Civil Society. Before any man can be considered as a member of Civil Society, he must be considered as a subject of the Governor of the Universe: And if a member of Civil Society, who enters into any subordinate Association, must always do it with a reservation of his duty to the general authority; much more must every man who becomes a member of any particular Civil Society, do it with a saving of his allegiance to the Universal Sovereign.[11]

In Madison's view, it was critical that each individual should be responsible only to God for abuses of this freedom,[12] and that the rights of all religious believers and dissenters should be placed on an equal footing.[13] This view was carried forward into his first draft of what later became the first amendment to the Constitution of the United States:[14]

---

11. *Id.*, n. 1 (note in the original to "[Va] Decl. Rights, Art 16."). *Compare The Challenge of Peace*, at n. 326.

12. *Id.*, n. 4.

13. *Id.* It should be noted, however, that Madison's express concern was for the rights of religious "dissenters," not for those who professed no religion whatsoever. On August 15, 1789, Madison said that "he apprehended the meaning of the words [of the proposed amendment] to be, that Congress should not establish a religion, and enforce the legal observation of it by law, nor compel men to worship God in any manner contrary to their conscience." 1 *Annals of Congress* at 730. Similarly, the early 19th-century legal scholar and Supreme Court Justice Joseph Story wrote that "[p]robably at the time of the adoption of the constitution, and of the amendment to it, now under consideration [the First Amendment], the general, if not the universal, sentiment in America was, that christianity ought to receive encouragement from the state, so far as was not incompatible with the private rights of conscience, and the freedom of religious worship. An attempt to level all religions, and to make it a matter of state policy to hold all in utter indifference, would have created universal disapprobation, if not universal indignation." J. Story, *Commentaries on the Constitution of the United States*, v. II, Ch. XLIV § 1874 (1851).

The importance of the distinction between a constitutional jurisprudence that both encourages religion and protects the dissenting believer from coerced religious belief or practice, and one that protects the sensibilities of the unbeliever by enforcing a strict state neutrality as between religion and nonreligion is critical to an understanding of First Amendment rulings by the United States Supreme Court since 1948. The Court's recent rulings underscore the importance of the distinction. *See, e.g., Wallace v. Jaffree*, 472 U.S. –, 105 S. Ct. 2479 (1985); *Caldor, Inc. v. Estate of Thornton*, 472 U.S. –, 53 U.S.L.W. 4853 (1985); *Aguilar v. Felton*, 472 U.S. –, 105 S. Ct. 3232 (1985). Although the implications of the Court's recent holding in *Caldor, Inc. v. Estate of Thornton* is discussed in this essay because of its direct relationship with the question of accommodation of religious belief and practice, a thorough discussion of the underlying issue of constitutional "neutrality" is beyond the scope of this paper.

14. U.S. Const., Amend. I provides, in relevant part: Congress shall make no law respecting an establishment of religion, or prohibiting the free exercise thereof; . . . .

The Civil Rights of none shall be abridged on account of religious belief or worship, nor shall any national religion be established, nor shall the full and equal rights of conscience be in any manner, nor on any pretext infringed.[15]

Although the language of Madison's proposal seems tailored specifically to accommodate the needs of the present-day conscientious religious dissenter,[16] neither its author,[17] nor the individual whose views have been most influential in shaping the contemporary American understanding of the constitutional guarantee of religious freedom, Thomas Jefferson,[18] would have given it a particularly expansive reading in cases when religious belief was in clear conflict with the requirements of either the public order or the public welfare.[19]

15. 1 *Annals of Congress* 434 (June 8, 1789), *quoted in* M. J. Malbin, *Religion and Politics* (American Enterprise Institute, 1978), at 4. This version of the proposed amendment, along with one that would have prohibited the states from "violat[ing] the equal rights of conscience or the freedom of the press, or the trial by jury in criminal cases," went through several modifications before it emerged in its present form from a House/Senate conference committee comprising Reps. James Madison (Va.), Roger Sherman (Conn.), and John Vining (Del.) and Senators Oliver Ellsworth (Conn.), Charles Carroll (Md.), and William Patterson (N.J.). The committee's language was accepted by the House and Senate on September 24–25, 1789, respectively. *See Id.*, 13–14. The Senate had rejected an amendment that would have prohibited the states from infringing on the equal rights of conscience. 1 *Annals of Congress* at 72 (Sept. 7, 1789), *Id.*, at 13 n. 34.

16. Compare note 87 *post* and accompanying text.

17. A good statement of Madison's views on the extent to which sincerely held religious belief might be set up in opposition to government authority appears in Madison's 1832 Letter to Reverend Adams, in which he stated that "it may not be easy, in every possible case, to trace the line of separation between the rights of religion and the Civil authority with such distinctness as to avoid collisions and doubts on unessential points." Letter from James Madison to Reverend Adams (November 1832), *reprinted in* IX *The Writings of James Madison* 485 (G. Hunt, ed., 1909), *quoted in* E. M. Gaffney, Jr., "Political Divisiveness Along Religious Lines: The Entanglement of the Court in Sloppy History and Bad Public Policy," 24 *St. Louis U.L.J.* 205, 223 (1980). Madison fully accepted the proposition that "no other rule exists, by which any question which may divide a society, can be ultimately determined, but the will of the majority" and felt that all believers would be best served by an equality principle forbidding the "subjecting [of] some to peculiar burdens . . . [and] granting to others peculiar exemptions." *See* "Memorial and Remonstrance," *ante* note 10, at nn. 1, 4. It is particularly relevant to the present topic that Madison chose "the Quakers and Menonists" as examples of religious groups whose beliefs ought not to "be endowed above all others, with extraordinary privileges, by which proselytes may be enticed from all others." *Id.* at n. 4. *Compare* text accompanying notes 74, 75, 78 *post.*

18. Although Thomas Jefferson was not involved in the drafting of the First Amendment, his views on the proper relationship of church and state form the starting point for contemporary analysis. Jefferson's letter of 1802 to the Danbury Baptists is the source of the now-famous metaphor, "a wall of separation between Church and State," which has influenced the outcome of nearly all cases involving the Religion Clauses since 1947. *See, e.g., Illinois ex rel McCollum v. Board of Education*, 333 U.S. 203 (1948); *Everson v. Board of Education*, 330 U.S. 1 (1947). Whether the Jeffersonian view of "separation" is appropriate given the language and history of the First Amendment is a topic beyond the scope of this paper.

19. *See generally*, D. Little, "Thomas Jefferson's Religious Views and Their Influence on the Supreme Court's Interpretation of the First Amendment," 26 *Cath. U.L. Rev.* 57 (1976); Malbin, *Religion and Politics, ante* note 15 at 25–29.

In Jefferson's view, a clear distinction could be drawn between two aspects of religious liberty: belief and action. In his 1802 letter to the Danbury Baptists,[20] Jefferson stated that because "religion is a matter which lies solely between a man and his God . . . the legislative powers of government reach action only, and not opinions."[21] This distinction between beliefs, which are deserving of absolute protection, and religiously motivated actions, which may be regulated "when [religious] principles break out into overt acts against peace and good order,"[22] has been accepted as a truism by most courts deciding cases involving religious freedom claims,[23] for Jefferson was "convinced that [man] has no natural right in opposition to his social duties."[24]

The holdings of the United States Supreme Court on the topic since 1963 are somewhat inconsistent with the Jeffersonian view of deference to be accorded to religious conscience when it comes into conflict with legislatively determined social duty.[25] Although an exhaustive treatment of this issue is beyond the scope of this paper,[26] those cases provide a

20. Letter of Thomas Jefferson to a Committee of the Danbury Baptist Association (January 1, 1802), *reprinted* in A. Koch and W. Reden, *The Life and Selected Writings of Thomas Jefferson* 332–333 (1944).

21. *Id.*

22. J. Boyd, *The Papers of Thomas Jefferson* (1950) at 545, *quoted in* D. Little, *ante* note 19 at 62 ¶¶ 27–29.

23. *See, e.g., Cantwell v. Connecticut*, 310 U.S. 296, 303–304 (1940) where the Court stated: "[The Constitution] forestalls compulsion by law of the acceptance of any creed or the practice of any form of worship. Freedom of conscience and freedom to adhere to such religious organizations or form of worship as the individual may choose cannot be restricted by law . . . [Free Exercise] embraces two concepts – freedom to believe and freedom to act. The first is absolute but, in the nature of things, the second cannot be . . . [The] freedom to act must have appropriate definition to preserve the enforcement of that protection . . . [although] the power to regulate must be so exercised as not, in attaining a permissible and, unduly, to infringe the protected freedom." Where the distinction between belief and action has been the starting point for the judicial analysis of a free-exercise claim, the result is commonly the rejection of the religious claim. *See, e.g., United States v. American Friends Service Committee*, 419 U.S. 7 (1974) (levy on Quaker funds); *Braunfeld v. Brown*, 366 U.S. 599 (1961) (enforcement of Sunday closing laws against Orthodox Jews); *Hamilton v. Regents of the University of California*, 293 U.S. 633 (1934) (military training); *Reynolds v. United States*, 98 U.S. 154 (1878) (polygamy).

24. Letter of Thomas Jefferson to a Committee of the Danbury Baptist Association, *ante* note 20.

25. *Compare, e.g., Thomas v. Review Board of the Indiana Employment Security Division*, 450 U.S. 707 (1981); *Sherbert v. Verner*, 374 U.S. 398 (1963), *with, e.g., United States v. Lee*, 455 U.S. 252 (1982); *Johnson v. Robison*, 415 U.S. 361 (1974); *Gillette v. United States*, 401 U.S. 437 (1971); *Autenreith v. United States*, 279 F. Supp. 156 (N.D. Cal. 1968), *aff'd sub nom Autenreith v. Cullen*, 418 F.2d 586 (9th Cir. 1969) *cert. den.* 397 U.S. 1036 (1970).

26. *See generally* Clark, "Guidelines for the Free Exercise Clause," 83 *Harv. L.Rev.* 327 (1969); Dodge, "The Free Exercise of Religion: A Sociological Approach," 67 *Mich. L.Rev.* 679 (1969); Giannella, "Religious Liberty, Nonestablishment, and Doctrinal Development—Part I. The Religious Liberty Guarantee," 80 *Harv. L.Rev.* 1381 (1967);

good framework for analysis of the relevant constitutional principles to be applied when a religious liberty claim based on the pastoral letter is made by a member of one of the groups specified in the pastoral letter on which this paper focuses: public officials, clergy and religious, the military, civilian employees in defense industries, and the citizenry at large.[27]

Pastoral Direction of Public Officials and Catholics as Citizens

Constitutional and Public Policy Implications

For purposes of American constitutional law, the legal principles governing the activities of religiously motivated public officials are, in large part, the same as those governing the citizenry at large. To be sure, the constitutionally prescribed oath taken by each federal official to "support and defend the Constitution of the United States"[28] imposes a higher degree of responsibility and adherence to constitutional norms upon the public official than it does on the citizen.[29] Ultimately, however, control of the acts of public officials is relegated by the Constitution to the political process.[30]

Marcus, "The Forum of Conscience: Applying Standards Under the Free Exercise Clause," 1973 *Duke L.J.* 1217.

27. *See* Parts I and II, *post*, regarding the political process and defense workers. The questions arising for military personnel are similar to those that apply to defense workers, but the room for permissible dissent and accommodation is far more narrow.

28. The presidential oath of office is set forth verbatim in U.S. Const. Art. II § 8. The oath of office for all other federal officials, including members of Congress, judges, and executive officials, and for members of every state's legislature must include an oath or affirmation to support the Constitution. U.S. Const. Art VI § 3.

29. By its terms, the Constitution speaks only to the structure and operation of the federal system: (*i.e.*, to the federal government, federal officials, the states and state officials). In only one instance does it speak directly to the rights of individuals, rather than imposing a limit on the power of government, and, even then, it does so by negative implication. *Compare*, U.S. Const. Amend. XIII (abolishing slavery and involuntary servitude directly) *with* U.S. Const. Amend. XV (right to vote shall not be infringed "by the United States or by any State"). For generalized discussion of the implications of the "state action" doctrine, *see generally*, Lockhart, Kamisar and Choper, *Constitutional Law* (5th ed., West, 1980) at 1511–1624.

30. Political control of the legislative branch is accomplished through three basic methods: election (Art. I § 2); presidential veto of enactments (Art. I § 7, cl. 2, 3); expulsion and control of members (Art. I § 5 cl. 1, 2). Political control of the executive is exercised through five basic methods: election (Art. II § 1); impeachment (Art. II § 4; Art. I § 2 cl.5;st 3 cl. 6); the power to advise and consent to nominations and treaties (Art. II § 2 cl. 2); the Congressional power of the purse (Art. I § 7 cl. 1 § 8, § 9 cl. 7); and the power to override presidential vetos (Art. I § 7 cl. 3). Political control over judicial authority is accomplished: through legislation resting on an express constitutional power, *Katzenbach v. Morgan*, 384 U.S. 641 (1966); impeachment (Art. II § 4, Art. III § 1); and control of the Supreme Court's appellate jurisdiction (Art. III § 2). Political control over the entire federal system is guaranteed through the dual method for proposing constitutional amendments provided in Article V: The first is legislative and

The question for citizens, politicians, and public officials, therefore, is the degree to which they should permit their religious views to influence their voting patterns or their official activities. Not surprisingly, this question evokes sharp responses and critical commentary whenever it surfaces on the American political scene.[31] It dominated the presidential campaigns of Al Smith in 1928 and John F. Kennedy in 1960; President Jimmy Carter was often criticized for his use of "born again" religious language and rhetoric[32] and, most recently, the 1984 presidential campaign witnessed an ongoing debate among politicians themselves[33] and among church leaders,[34] politicians,[35] and commentators[36]

---

depends entirely on the will of Congress, the second is also legislative, but rests on the authority of a special convention called for the purpose by the Congress upon petition of three-fourths of the states. No member of Congress may, at the same time, sit as a member of such a convention, Art. I § 6 cl. 2 (the Incompatibility Clause), thus assuring that "incompatible" political allegiances will not develop. In either case, proposed constitutional amendments must be ratified by the requisite number of state legislatures or state ratifying conventions, as specified by Congress, Art. V. The convention method, which has never been used *under* this Constitution, but which produced it, has become a politically controversial issue of late, in large part because approximately 32 of the 34 states needed to call a convention have petitioned the Congress to do so. *See Washington Post* (October 2, 1984), p. A4, col. 2. On the topic of the political nature of the amendment process, *see generally*, *Coleman v. Miller*, 307 U.S. 433 (1939).

31. Remarks of Senator John F. Kennedy Before a Meeting of the Greater Houston Ministerial Assn., Houston, Texas, September 12, 1960; O. Handlin, *Al Smith and His America* (1958). *See generally*, W. Berns, "The Nation and the Bishops," *Wall Street Journal* (December 15, 1982), p. 28W. col. 3; E. Goodman, "Bishops as Bosses," *Washington Post* (September 11, 1984), p. A23 col. 1; J. Kraft, "Debate Among Catholics," *Washington Post* (September 18, 1984), p. A19, col. 1; J. Lofton, "Jackson Debases Religion, Politics," *Washington Times* (September 5, 1984), p. 3A col. 1; C. Rowan, "An Unnatural Alliance," *Washington Post* (September 16, 1984), p. B8, col. 2.

32. *See* J. Johnson, "A Born Again Style at the White House," *Washington Post* (January 21, 1977), p. A18, col. 3.

33. Remarks of President Ronald W. Reagan to the Ecumenical Prayer Breakfast, Dallas, Texas, August 23, 1984; Remarks of Walter F. Mondale to the International Convention of B'nai B'rith, Washington, D.C., September 6, 1984; Governor Mario M. Cuomo, "Religious Belief and Public Morality: A Catholic Governor's Perspective," delivered to the Department of Theology, University of Notre Dame, South Bend, Ind., September 13, 1984 (Governor of New York); Representative Henry J. Hyde, "Keeping God in The Closet: Some Thoughts on the Exorcism of Religious Values from Public Life," delivered at the Thomas J. White Center on Law and Government, School of Law, University of Notre Dame, South Bend, Ind., September 24, 1984.

34. *See, e.g.*, K. A. Briggs, "Catholic Theologians Have Mixed Reactions to Cuomo's Notre Dame Talk," *New York Times* (September 17, 1984), p. B12 col. 3; H. Cox, "Our Politics Needs Religion," *Washington Post* (September 2, 1984), p. D8, col. 1.; R. D. McFadden, "Episcopal Bishop Says Officials Must Put Law Before Tenets," *New York Times* (September 17, 1984), p. B12, col. 1.

35. "Ferraro Denies Charges on Abortion," *Washington Post* (September 11, 1984), p. A9, col. 2; G. Larder, "Cuomo Urges Wider Debate of Religion," *Washington Post* (August 4, 1984), p. A5, col. 1; McNeill-Lehrer News Hour, P.B.S. (September 11, 1982), segment 2 (Robin McNeill and Charlayne Hunter-Gault interview with Archbishop Bernard Law of Boston and Senator William Mitchell of Maine).

36. *See generally, e.g.*, R. Cohen, "Religion: Reagan's Divider . . ." *Washington Post* (September 5, 1984), p. A19, col. 1; R. Evans and R. Novak, ". . . And Mondale's

on the "proper" role of religion in political action and discourse.[37]

Although phrased most often in popular parlance as a matter of "separation of church and state,"[38] the idea of "separation of church and state" is neither useful, nor particularly relevant when religiously motivated individuals seek to draw on their religious or moral belief systems as sources for public policy choices.[39] What *is* at issue is the political role of religious discourse and influence in the development of public policy on issues of great public importance.

In their letter, the bishops correctly recognize that "public opinion . . . can, through a series of measures, indicate the limits beyond which a government should not proceed."[40] This is especially true in a representative democracy such as the United States, where the electronic and print media regularly report the latest public opinion polling

Wedge," *Washington Post* (September 5, 1984), p. A19, col. 4; N. Hentoff, "Bishops, Bigots . . . ," *Washington Post* (September 21, 1984), p. A21, col. 1; J. Kraft, "Elmer Gantry Time," *Washington Post* (September 6, 1984), p. A21, col. 1; W. McPherson, "God and Man in Dallas," *Washington Post* (September 4, 1984), p. A19, col. 5; W. Pruden "The Shootout at God's Corral," *Washington Times* (September 5, 1984), p. 2A col. 1; W. Pruden "'Holy War' Pits North vs. South," *Washington Times* (September 19, 1984), p. 2A, col. 1; J. Sobran, "Of Political Piety and Pandering," *Washington Times* (September 6, 1984), p. 2C, col. 2; E. M. Yoder, Jr., "Religion's Place," *Washington Post* (August 29, 1984), p. A25 col. 6; E. M. Yoder, Jr., "The Pope's Example," *Washington Post* (September 6, 1984), p. A21, col. 1. *See also* sources cited note 31 *ante*.

37. *See also*, *Harris v. McRae*, 448 U.S. 297 (1980), *rev'g*, *McRae v. Califano*, 491 F. Supp. 630 (E.D. N.Y. 1980)(discussing the role of religion in the political process when the issue is one that is commonly identified with particular religious traditions). *See also* text at notes 65–75 *post*.

38. The United States Constitution does not contain the phrase "separation of church and state" but rather the following admonitions respecting limits on *government* activity: "Congress shall make no law respecting an establishment of religion, or prohibiting the free exercise thereof . . . ." U.S. Const. Amend. I; ". . . [N]o religious Test shall ever be required as a Qualification to any Office or public Trust under the United States." U.S. Const. Art. VI cl. 3.

39. As a practical matter, there has never been "absolute separation" of church and state in the United States. The language of the First Amendment ("*Congress* shall make no law") itself bears witness to the desire of the framers of the Constitution to leave intact then-existing state-established churches, *see*, *e.g.*, C. J. Antieau, A. T. Downey, E. C. Roberts, *Freedom from Federal Establishment* (1964), and contemporaneous statutory enactments make it clear that religion and morality were important factors influencing public discourse. *See*, *e.g.*, Northwest Ordinance of 1787, as adopted by Congress, Statutes of 1789, c.8 (August 7, 1789) ("Religion, morality, and knowledge being necessary to good government and the happiness of mankind, schools and the means of education shall be forever encouraged."); J. Story, *Commentaries on the Constitution of the United States*, vol. II, Ch. XLIV §§ 1870–1879 (1851). George Washington's farewell address also made the point: "Of all the dispositions and habits which lead to political prosperity, religion and morality are indispensable supports . . . let it simply be asked where is the security for prosperity, for reputation, for life—if the sense of religious obligation desert . . . and let us with caution indulge the supposition that morality can be maintained without religion." D. H. Matheson, *History of the Formation of the Union Under the Constitution* (1941) at 569–570, *quoted in* Antieau, *et al.*, op. cit at 188.

40. *The Challenge of Peace*, n. 140.

results on issues of importance, and politicians regularly consult the latest figures. As a result, the immediate problem *for the bishops* is how to define the permissible limits of the task they have set out to accomplish "in concert with public officials, analysts, private organizations and the media to set limits beyond which our military policy should not move in word or action."[41]

Some of the current political interpretations of American church/state principles would place severe constraints on the permissibility of such participation,[42] and events in the 1984 presidential campaign show clearly that attempts by church leaders to "encourage a public attitude which sets stringent limits on the kind of actions our own government and other governments will take"[43] on issues of major political and social importance—such as nuclear war or abortion—can have predictable consequences for both political leaders and the electorate at large.

To probe the issue of "religion in politics" in a useful way, however, it is necessary to set out a few of the constitutional ground rules governing religiously based attempts to influence the course of public policy. There are statutory rules as well,[44] but they too must be seen in light of the constitutional principles governing the discussion from the outset.

The most critical of these constitutional considerations are the other rights protected by the first amendment: the express rights of freedom of speech, press, and peaceable assembly, and the right to petition government for a redress of grievances, as well as the implied right of freedom of association.[45] Taken together, these rights serve as a powerful shield protecting almost all political speech[46] from government regulation.[47] As a result, any attempt to limit speech intended to influence public officials or public opinion on the basis either of the identity of

41. *Id.*, n. 141.
42. *See* sources cited at notes 31–37 *ante.*
43. *The Challenge of Peace*, n. 141.
44. *See* note 85 *post.*
45. U.S. Const. Amend. I. The right to freedom of association is not expressly mentioned in the Constitution, but has been implied as being a necessary to protect those rights that are express. *See generally, Herndon v. Lowry*, 301 U.S. 242 (1937); *De Jonge v. Oregon*, 299 U.S. 353 (1937); *Whitney v. California*, 274 U.S. 357 (1927).
46. *See generally, Consolidated Edison Co. v. Public Service Comm'n*, 447 U.S. 530 (1980); *First National Bank v. Bellotti*, 435 U.S. 765 (1978); *Mills v. Alabama*, 384 U.S. 214 (1966). *See also* R. Bork, "Neutral Principles and Some First Amendment Problems," 47 *Ind. L.J.* 1 (1971); J. H. Ely, *Democracy and Distrust* (1980); R. Polsby, "Buckley v. Valeo: The Special Nature of Political Speech," 1976 *S.Ct. Rev.* 1.
47. *But see, F.C.C. v. Pacifica Foundation*, 438 U.S. 726 (1978) (FCC regulators upheld, which limited the use of vulgar language during certain hours); *Lehman v. City of Shaker Heights*, 418 U.S. 298 (1974) (limitation on political advertising in public transit vehicles); *Adderly v. Florida*, 385 U.S. 39 (1966) (limitation on demonstration on jail property); *Kovacs v. Cooper*, 336 U.S. 77 (1949) stands for the general proposition that the government may impose reasonable "time, place and manner" restrictions on speech.

the speaker[48] or the content of the message[49] would be subject to the strictest judicial scrutiny.[50]

Thus, the first question for discussion is the degree to which American traditions of church/state relations[51] should limit religiously motivated speech designed to influence public policy on any question of political significance, including war and peace. Phrased in this manner, however, the question becomes not merely one of constitutional law but a political issue of major significance in and of itself.

While a discussion of the *politics* of religious influence on political debate is beyond the scope of this paper, examination of the underlying *constitutional* rules that should guide the discussion sheds considerable light on the "religion-in-politics" issues that captured so much public attention during the 1984 presidential campaign.[52] Review of the cases and relevant statutes makes it clear that the debate over religion as a force in American politics is based more on philosophical and political considerations than it is on constitutional rules.

Aside from the most obvious professional distinctions to be drawn among church leaders, politicians, and interested members of the public, all are entitled to the general political rights of citizenship: to speak out on issues,[53] to run for public office,[54] and to take an active part in political campaigns and debates.[55] Traditionally, the only constitutional

48. For purposes of this discussion, the only relevant identity-based restrictions would be limits on the ability of church officials to speak on political matters, limits on the ability of politicians to address issues, and limits imposed on the citizenry at large. Each of these is discussed, in turn, *post.*

49. Content-based regulations are presumptively unconstitutional, *Widmar v. Vincent*, 454 U.S. 263 (1981); *Carey v. Brown*, 447 U.S. 455 (1980); and the government must demonstrate a "clear and present danger of imminent lawless action" before such regulation can be justified. *See, Brandenburg v. Ohio*, 395 U.S. 444 (1969).

50. The "clear and present danger" standard represents the highest standard of judicial review in American constitutional law, for it allocates the entire burden of proving an extraordinary degree of justification to the government, which must rebut the presumption of unconstitutionality discussed in the previous note. *See generally* L. Tribe, *American Constitutional Law*, §§ 12–9 to 12–11 (West, 1978); Nowak, Rotunda and Young, *Constitutional Law* 874–886 (West, 2nd ed., 1983).

51. *See* text at notes 6–25, *ante.*

52. *See* commentary at notes 33–36, *ante.*

53. *See* text at notes 45–50 *ante.* The Speech and Debate Clause of the U.S. Constitution, Art. I § 6, confers an absolute privilege for speech by elected legislators. *See,* R. Reinstein and H. Silvergate, "Legislative Privilege and the Separation of Powers," 86 *Harv. L. Rev.* 1113 (1973).

54. Although Pope John Paul II has indicated that Catholic clergy and religious should not hold public office, W. Brown, "Pope John Paul II Bars Priests from Serving in Public Office," *Washington Post* (May 5, 1980), p. A1, col. 1, nothing in American constitutional law would prevent them from doing so. U.S. Const. Art. VI § 2; Amend I. *McDaniel v. Paty*, 435 U.S. 618 (1978).

55. There are limitations on the ability of church leaders to use church facilities and tax-exempt funds for political purposes, *see generally* materials cited in note 84 *post,* and generally applicable campaign spending limits for federal election campaigns.

arguments *against* such participation have arisen when the speaker or official is a member of the clergy,[56] or when the issue itself can be characterized as a religiously based or motivated issue, such as abortion, school prayer, or support for religiously affiliated, nonpublic schools.[57] The rationale advanced in support of constitutional restrictions in these policy areas has generally been that debates over religious issues, especially those led by clergy, are politically "divisive" and merit strict judicial oversight.[58]

In recent years, the Supreme Court has spoken clearly on the "political divisiveness" issue on two occasions. The first was a case challenging the right of a Baptist clergyman to hold elective political office.[59] The Supreme Court of Tennessee had ruled that the state constitution[60] barred clergy from holding seats in the Tennessee legislature and supported its judgment on the grounds that the participation of clergy in legislative debates could foster divisiveness along religious lines and might lead to the enactment of religiously preferential laws.[61] The Supreme Court reversed in a series of opinions that were agreed on the result, but divided as to the proper approach.[62] Of the various positions

---

Federal Election Campaign Act, as amended, 2 U.S.C. §§ 431–441, 451–455, 5 U.S.C. §§ 1501–1503, 18 U.S.C. 26 U.S.C. §§ 276, 6012, 9002–9012, 9031–9042; 42 U.S.C. §§ 312, 315, Pub. Laws 92–255, Feb. 7, 1972, 86 Stat. 3; 94–283, Title II, §§ 201–210, Title III §§ 310, 302, 90 Stat. 475–476, 94–283, Title I, §§ 101–115(f, h, i), May 11, 1976, 90 Stat. 475–496; 95–127, Oct. 12, 1977, 91 Stat. 1110; 95–216, Title V, § 502(a), Dec. 20, 1977, 91 Stat. 1504–1565; 93–443, Oct. 15, 1974, 88 Stat. 1263; 94–283, May 11, 1976, 90 Stat. 475; 96–187, Jan. 8, 1980, 93 Stat. 1339.

56. *See, e.g., McDaniel v. Paty*, 435 U.S. 618 (1978), *rev'g, Paty v. McDaniel*, 547 S.W.2d 897 (Tenn., 1977).

57. *See Widmar v. Vincent*, 454 U.S. 263 (1981) (prayer); *Harris v. McRae*, 448 U.S. 297 (1980) (abortion); *Lemon v. Kurtzman*, 403 U.S. 602 (1971) (nonpublic schools); *Everson v. Board of Education*, 330 U.S. 1 (1947) (student transportation).

58. *See* text at notes 59, 63–65. Such a theory of judicial oversight raises substantial questions regarding the role of the judiciary in a representative democracy. Such questions are, for the most part, beyond the scope of this paper. On this topic, *see generally* A. Hamilton, *et al.*, *The Federalist* (No. 78) (1788).

59. *McDaniel v. Paty*, 435 U.S. 618 (1978).

60. The Tennessee Constitution of 1796 provided: "Whereas ministers of the gospel are, by their profession, dedicated to God and the care of Souls, and ought not to be diverted from the great duties of their functions, therefore, no minister of the gospel, or priest of any denomination whatever, shall be eligible to a seat in either house of the legislature." Tenn. Const., Art. VIII, § 1 (1796). Seven of the original states (Maryland, Virginia, North Carolina, South Carolina, Georgia, New York, and Delaware) disqualified clergy from legislative office. Three of the seven (New York, Delaware, and South Carolina) barred clergy from holding any political office. *McDaniel v. Paty*, 435 U.S. 618, 622 and n. 3 (1978), *quoting* L. Pfeffer, *Church, State and Freedom*, 118 (rev. ed., 1967).

61. *See Paty v. McDaniel*, 547 S.W.2d 897 (Tenn. 1977).

62. Chief Justice Burger, Justice Powell, Justice Rehnquist, and Justice Stevens argued that the Tennessee constitutional provision impermissibly conditioned McDaniel's right to free exercise of religion on the surrender of his right to seek public office and

taken, perhaps the most succinct and relevant to the present inquiry was made by Justices William Brennan and Thurgood Marshall:

> The state's goal of preventing sectarian bickering and strife may not be accomplished by regulating religious speech and political association. The Establishment Clause does not license government to treat religion and those who teach and practice it, simply by virtue of their status as such, as subversive of American ideals and therefore subject to unique disabilities. . . .
>
> In short, government may not as a goal promote "safe thinking" with respect to religion and fence out from political participation those, such as ministers, whom it regards as overinvolved with religion. Religionists no less than members of any other group enjoy the full measure of protection afforded speech, association, and political association generally. The Establishment Clause, properly understood, is a shield against any attempt by government to inhibit religion as it has done here. . . . It may not be used as a sword to justify repression of religion or its adherents from any aspect of public life.[63]

Having disposed of the argument that clergy should have no place in legislative chambers in *McDaniel v. Paty*, it remained to be seen just how far the court's "political divisiveness" standard[64] for cases would be taken in a case involving allegedly "religious" issues or the active involvement of religious institutions or believers in the political process at large.[65] That opportunity finally arose in *Harris v.*

---

cited *Sherbert v. Verner*, 374 U.S. 398 (1963) as the controlling case. (*Sherbert* is discussed at some length in the text accompanying notes 147–159 *post*.) Justice Brennan and Justice Marshall argued that the prohibition was a religious test absolutely prohibited by U.S. Const. Act VI, cl. 3 and *Torcaso v. Watkins*, 367 U.S. 488 (1961); that it imposed an impermissible burden on the rights conferred by the Free Exercise Clause, citing *Sherbert*; and violated the Establishment Clause by establishing a religiously based classification that had a primary effect of inhibiting religion, 435 U.S. at 630. Justice Stewart argued that *Torcaso* alone controlled the case because it was directed at prohibitions that do not turn on *statements* of belief, but on action dictated by belief. 435 U.S. 643. *See also* text at notes 16–25 *ante*. Justice White argued that the prohibition violated the Equal Protection Clause of the Fourteenth Amendment and that it was both underinclusive and overinclusive. 435 U.S. at 644.

63. *McDaniel v. Paty, ante*, 435 U.S. at 641 (Brennan and Marshall, JJ., concurring) (footnote omitted).

64. The "political divisiveness" argument had its genesis in *Walz v. Tax Comm'n*, 397 U.S. 664 (1970), when the late Justice John Harlan cited Professor Paul Freund's article, "Public Aid to Parochial Schools," 82 *Harv. L.Rev* 1680 (1969), to support the idea that highly charged political controversies such as debates over the funding for church-related schools "engender a risk of politicizing religion" and that "history cautions that political fragmentation on sectarian lines must be guarded against." 397 U.S. at 695.

65. By the time the court decided *Lemon v. Kurtzman*, 403 U.S. 602 (1971), the "political divisiveness" argument had become what appeared to be an additional factor to be considered in First Amendment cases involving the Religion Clauses. In *Lemon* the court formalized what has since become known as a "three-pronged" test for "secular purpose," a "primary effect which neither advances nor inhibits religion," and lack of "excessive entanglement" between religion and government, 403 U.S. at 612–613. It also seemed to raise the "potential" for division along religious lines to the status of an independent factor in constitutional analysis, *see*, 403 U.S. at 622–624. Although the "political divisiveness" point was arguably unnecessary to the court's decision, the court

McRae,[66] a challenge to Congress' refusal to provide Medicaid funding for abortions.[67] In *McRae*, the plaintiffs, which included the City of New York, welfare rights organizations, and several religious groups,[68] argued that the statutory refusal to pay for abortions—commonly referred to as the "Hyde Amendment"[69]—imposed "one religious view" (i.e., the Catholic view) on the community regarding the humanity of the unborn and the morality of abortion. From this, it was argued that the identity of the religious view allegedly imposed could be proved by examining the religious identity, motives, and activities of the major *participants* in the political debate[70] (e.g., the tactics and positions of the major lobby groups and sponsors of the legislation).

The practical effect of accepting such an argument and allowing such "proof" as relevant evidence in constitutional litigation would have been twofold: First, the high-profile involvement of clergy and religiously motivated individuals in public policy debates involving controversial issues would become a negative factor to be considered in later constitutional controversies over the validity of the challenged legislation; and, second, religious rhetoric in political debates would be perceived as an impermissible, or at least suspicious, influence on the course of the political debate. To the degree such evidence would be considered

---

apparently felt some need to speak on the issue. Chief Justice Burger's opinion for the court states flatly that "[i]t conflicts with our whole history and tradition to permit questions of the Religion Clauses to assume such importance in our legislatures and in our elections that they could divert attention from the myriad issues and problems that confront every level of government[,]" and that it was unwise to force "candidates to declare and voters to choose" on such issues. 403 U.S. at 623. When the court was forced to consider the full implication of "the political divisiveness" argument in the context of individual participation in the political process, however, it backed away. *See Harris v. McRae*, 448 U.S. 297 (1980) (attempted invalidation of congressional spending restrictions on divisiveness grounds); *McDaniel v. Paty*, 435 U.S. 618 (1978) (exclusion of clergy from state legislative post based, in part, on potential for political "divisiveness" on religious grounds). *See also* E. M. Gaffney, Jr., "Political Divisiveness Along Religious Lines: The Entanglement of the Court in Sloppy History and Bad Public Policy," 24 *St. Louis U.L.J.* 205 (1980).

66. 448 U.S. 297 (1980) decided together with *Williams v. Zbaraz*, 448 U.S 358 (1980).

67. Act of September 30, 1976, Pub. L. 94–493, 90 Stat. 1434 (1976); Act of December 9, 1977, Pub. L. 95–205 § 101, 91 Stat. 1460 (1977); Act of October 18, 1978, Pub. L. 95–480 § 210, 92 Stat. 1586 (1978); Act of November 20, 1979, Pub. L. 96–123 § 109, 93 Stat. 926 (1980).

68. Among the plaintiffs in the *McRae* case included: Cora McRae, the Women's Division of the Board of Global Ministries of the United Methodist Church, and the Health and Hospitals Corporation of the City of New York.

69. The statute, an amendment to numerous appropriations bills in addition to the ones cited in note 67, *ante*, bears the name of its original proponent, Rep. Henry Hyde of Illinois.

70. *Harris v. McRae*, 448 U.S. 297 (1980); *See* First Amended Complaint of Plaintiffs *McRae v. Califano*, 491 F. Supp. 630 (E.D. N.Y. 1980), *rev'd sub nom, Harris v. McRae, ante.*

persuasive or relevant to the constitutional validity of legislative or other political action, overt religiously motivated involvement or overtly religious political rhetoric would be judicially discouraged.

The court responded to this novel—and constitutionally suspect[71]—application of the "divisiveness" rationale with an affirmation, albeit a grudging one,[72] of the role of religious and moral ideas in the formulation of public policy.

> Although neither a State nor the Federal Government can constitutionally "pass laws which aid one religion, aid all religions, or prefer one religion over another," *Everson v. Board of Education*, 330 U.S. 1, 15, . . . , it does not follow that a statute violates the Establishment Clause because it "happens to coincide or harmonize with the tenets of some or all religions." *McGowan v. Maryland*, 366 U.S. 420, 442, ... That the Judaeo-Christian religions oppose stealing does not mean that a State or the Federal Government may not, consistent with the Establishment Clause, enact laws prohibiting larceny. *Ibid.* The Hyde Amendment, as the District Court noted, is as much a reflection of "traditionalist" values towards abortion, as it is an embodiment of the views of any particular religon. 491 F. Supp., at 741. *See also Roe v. Wade*, 410 U.S., at 138–141, ... In sum, we are convinced that the fact that the funding restrictions in the Hyde Amendment may coincide with the religious tenets of the Roman Catholic Church does not, without more, contravene the Establishment Clause.[73]

The Pastoral Letter as a Call for Political Action

Applying these principles to the policy suggestions contained in the pastoral letter, it seems clear that the bishops were not only well within their rights as citizens to call for specific public policy responses, but were also entitled to call upon Catholic politicians to formulate public policy positions that would clearly reflect the legitimate legal needs of Catholic citizens.

71. *See* notes 46–50 and accompanying, text *ante*.

72. In his opinion for the majority in *Harris v. McRae*, Justice Stewart made the traditional comment that "[i]t is not the mission of this Court or any other to decide whether the balance of competing interests reflected in the Hyde Amendment is wise social policy[,]" 448 U.S. at 326, but added, somewhat uncharacteristically, that "[i]f that were our mission, not every Justice who has subscribed to the judgment of the Court today could have done so." *Id.* Justice Marshall was not so circumspect regarding the nature of the process and the role of the Supreme Court. Justice Marshall's dissent argued that the Court should never have permitted such a highly charged issue to be exposed to the normal political process because ". . . the Court's decisions [in *Maher v. Roe*, 432 U.S. 464 (1977), *Beal v. Doe*, 432 U.S. 438 (1977), and *Poelker v. Doe*, 432 U.S. 519 (1977)] [were] an invitation to public officials, already under extraordinary pressure from well-financed and carefully orchestrated lobbying campaigns, to approve more such restrictions on governmental funding for abortion", 448 U.S. at 337 (Marshall, J. dissenting). *But see* U.S. Const. Act I, § 7, cl. 9; Brief of Rep. Jim Wright, *et al.*, and Certain Other Members of Congress of the United States as *Amici Curiae, Harris v. McRae*, 448 U.S. 297 (1980). *See also* note 30 *ante*.

73. 448 U.S. at 319–320.

One of the most obvious areas of public policy concern for the bishops is the current illegality[74] of selective conscientious objection to selective service registration, induction, and military service involving weapons of mass destruction.[75] Traditional just-war doctrine is addressed as much to individual conscience as to government policymaking.[76] By adopting criteria by which to judge the "justness" of particular wars or the means used to wage them, the bishops have mandated that Catholics presently in the armed forces, or eligible for induction, weigh the moral consequences of their military service. Because those in the military, or of draft age, who would respond to the bishops' call to conscience would be placed at legal risk, the bishops explicitly call on Catholic politicians to work for a change in the law that would accommodate Catholic doctrine.

Needless to say, such episcopal intervention in the political process in pursuit of stated public policy goals rooted in identifiably doctrinal needs is inevitably controversial and becomes even more so when the goal requires the explicit cooperation of Catholic politicians.[77] Notwith-

74. *Gillette v. United States*, 401 U.S. 437 (1971) (rejecting "selective" conscientious objection).

75. *Id.* Protection of the right to "selectively" object to government policy would expand the scope of currently available legal protection for Catholic conscientious objectors who subscribe to traditional Catholic views on "just wars." As construed by the Supreme Court of the United States, the Military Selective Service Act of 1967 § 6(j), 50 U.S.C.App§ 456(j), *as amended*, required that the objector plead and prove that he objects to war in general. *Gillette v. United States*, 401 U.S. 437 (1971). Such a construction of the statutes raises a multitude of constitutional and statutory policy questions. *See Welsh v. United States*, 398 U.S. 333 (1970); *United States v. Seeger*, 380 U.S. 163 (1965); *Selective Draft Law Cases*, 245 U.S. 366, 389–390 (1918); Reply Brief on Behalf of Petitioner, *Negre v. Larsen*, No 70–325, *Gillette v. United States*, 401 U.S. 437 (1971)(companion case involving Catholic objector). For discussion of other critical constitutional questions raised by the selective service cases *see generally*, Donnici, "Governmental Encouragement of Religious Ideology: A Study of the Current Conscientious Objection Exemption from Military Service," 13 *J. Pub. L.* 16 (1964); Greenwalt, "All or Nothing at All: The Defeat of Selective Conscientious Objection," 1971 *Sup.Ct.Rev.* 31; Moore, "The Supreme Court and the Relationship Between the 'Establishment' and 'Free Exercise' Clauses," 42 *Tex. L. Rev.* 142 (1963); Rabin, "When Is a Religious Belief Religious: United States v. Seeger and the Scope of Free Exercise," 51 *Corn. L.Q.* 231 (1966); Schwartz, "No Imposition of Religion: The Establishment Clause Value," 77 *Yale L.J.* 692 (1968).

76. See R. Marcin, "Individual Conscience Under Military Compulsion," 57 *A.B.A.J.* 1222 (1971).

77. *Compare* Governor Mario M. Cuomo, op. cit. note 33 *ante* with Rep. Henry J. Hyde, op. cit. note 33 *ante*. It is interesting that *Catholic* politicians are most affected by this problem. President John F. Kennedy's Houston speech is a classic example of a Catholic politician forced by political forces to distance himself from his religious affinity group and its issues. Governor Cuomo's speech is similar in political motivation, although the speaker's position on the particular issue causing the most controversy is well aligned with that of the dominant forces in the Democratic Party in 1984. Perhaps the classic example of such "singling out," however, is the use of asterisks by the *Congressional Quarterly* to identify Catholic politicians in reports on congressional action on abortion-related issues. *See* note 78 *post*. One could imagine the public outcry if such "reporting" of religious affiliation—or lack of it—became commonplace.

standing this difficulty for Catholic politicians when the topic is one that has traditionally been identified by the major media as a "Catholic" issue—such as abortion or tuition tax credits,[78] it would be difficult, under any reading of the first amendment, to argue that active involvement by clergy in the fight for freedom of conscience—especially where the law itself discriminates in the protection it affords religious believers[79]—is constitutionally inappropriate.

The pastoral letter simply reflects both the bishops' willingness to join in, and to influence, the political debate by stressing the moral dimensions of political acts. That such episcopal activity might be uncomfortable for Catholic politicians who traditionally distance themselves from the official representatives of the teaching Church whenever the issues are particularly sensitive to non-Catholics[80] was clearly recognized in the difference between the second and final drafts of the letter. The bishops explicitly account for the fact that the moral responsibilities of politicians may sometimes be in conflict with the tenor of the political times, but do not absolve *any* politician from those responsibilities. "The difficult yet noble art of politics"[81] simply requires that the two be resolved.

Thus, their call in the final draft to all public officials to "[be] particularly attentive to the consciences of those who sincerely believe that they may not support warfare in general, a given war, or the exercise of a particular role within the armed forces,"[82] and the specific admonition to Catholic politicians to support selective conscientious objection that appeared in the second draft[83] are perfectly legitimate pastoral admonitions suggesting the revision of existing public policy. Specific directions to Catholic politicians regarding their own duties to "[propose] and [support] legislation designed to give maximum protection to . . . true

78. Although these are not really "Catholic" issues, as such, they have been so identified in the popular and other press. *See, e.g.*, Remarks of Senator John F. Kennedy Before a Meeting of the Greater Houston Ministerial Association, September 12, 1960, cited at note 31 *ante* (pledge regarding support for parochial schools); *Congressional Quarterly* (February 4, 1979), at 258–267 (Catholic legislators marked with an asterisk in reference to votes on abortion-related issues).

79. *See Gillette v. United States*, 401 U.S. 437 (1971); *Welsh v. United States*, 398 U.S. 333 (1970); *United States v. Seeger*, 380 U.S. 163 (1965); *Selective Draft Law Cases*, 245 U.S. 366, 389–390 (1918); Reply Brief on Behalf of Petitioner, *Negre v. Larsen*, No. 70–325, *Gillette v. United States*, 401 U.S. 437 (1971)(companion case involving Catholic objector holding traditional view).

80. *See* sources cited notes 34–36 *ante*.

81. *The Challenge of Peace*, n. 323, *quoting Pastoral Constitution* n. 75.

82. *Id.* at n. 324.

83. National Conference of Catholic Bishops, Ad Hoc Committee on War and Peace, *The Challenge of Peace: God's Promise and Our Response* (second draft), 12 *ORIGINS* 305, 325 (Washington, D.C., October 28, 1982). The second draft contained the following specific suggestion: "Catholic public officials might well serve all of our fellow citizens by proposing and supporting legislation designed to give maximum protection to . . . true freedom of conscience."

freedom of conscience,"[84] while they may be politically controversial, do not present any legal problem insofar as they are clearly within the context of pastoral teaching.[85] The Jeffersonian metaphor, "a wall of separation between church and state,"[86] is conceded by the United States Supreme Court to be a "useful figure of speech" that "is not a wholly accurate description of the practical aspects of the relationship that in fact exists between church and state." The "wall" is, in fact, only a "blurred, indistinct and variable barrier depending on all the circumstances of a particular relationship"[87] that should neither restrain Church leaders, politicians, or believing citizens from suggesting solutions based on Church teaching, nor reduce the nation's bishops to the ubiquitous political device of calling for a committee to study nuclear disarmament.[88] All who are concerned with the potential for nuclear destruction—regardless of their particular suggestions for preventing it—should heed the admonition of Professor Alexander Meiklejohn regarding the value of speech on issues of great controversy:

The First Amendment [does] not require that, on every occasion, every citizen shall take part in public debate. Nor can it even give assurance that everyone shall have opportunity to do so. . . . [What] is essential is not that everyone shall speak, but that everything worth saying shall be said. . . . And this means that though citizens may, on other grounds, be barred from speaking, they may not be barred because their views are thought to be false or dangerous. [No] speaker may be declared "out of order" because we disagree with what he intends to [say].

Conflicting views may be expressed, must be expressed, not because they are valid, but because they are relevant. If they are responsibly entertained by anyone, we, the voters need to hear them. [To] be afraid of ideas, any idea, is to be unfit for self-government. Any such suppression of ideas about the common good, the First Amendment condemns with its absolute disapproval.[89]

84. *Id. Compare The Challenge of Peace*, n. 324 (admonition to public officials generally).

85. Pastoral teaching should not be understood, however, to include the official support of particular candidates or particular pieces of legislation by the Church as an institution. Such activities, while constitutionally protected, may result in a proportionate or total loss of tax exemptions available to religious and charitable institutions under federal and state tax laws. *See, e.g.*, Internal Revenue Code §§ 501(c)(3), 511; N.Y. Real Property Tax Law § 421, N.Y. Tax Law §§ 601(d), 1116; Art. 9–A. A detailed discussion of the statutory and public policy implications of the tax exemption issue is beyond the scope of this paper. For general discussion of these issues, *see Bob Jones University v. United States*, 461 U.S. 574 (1983)(public policy and tax exemptions); *Walz v. Tax Comm'n*, 397 U.S. 664 (1970) (constitutionality of tax exemptions); *Christian Echoes National Ministry v. United States*, 470 F.2d 849 (10th Cir. 1972), *cert. den.* 414 U.S. 864 (1973).

86. *See* notes 18–20, *ante*.

87. *Lynch v. Donnelly*, –U.S.–, 104 S.Ct. 1355, 1362 (1984), *quoting Lemon v. Kurtzman*, 403 U.S. 602, 614 (1971).

88. *See The Challenge of Peace*, n. 324.

89. Alexander Meiklejohn, "Free Speech and Its Relation to Self-Government," *reprinted in part in* Lockhart, Kamisar and Choper, *Constitutional Law* (5th ed., West, 1980) at 684.

By calling for active public dialogue over nuclear war and peace, the bishops and those who debate the merits of their suggestions will be following in the time-honored American tradition of free and open discussion of important controversial ideas. Given the necessity for free and open debate on issues of public importance, even the architect of the metaphorical "wall of separation betweeen church and state" would find it difficult to question either the bishops' right to get the debate over the moral aspects started, or the right of the citizenry and its representatives to act on the principles identified in the process.[90]

Conscientious Objection and the Worker in Defense Industries

Perhaps the most difficult area in which to predict the legal impact of the pastoral letter on individuals is the situation of the worker in defense industries engaged in the production of weapons of mass destruction. For politicians and the citizenry at large, the analysis is largely one that focuses on the relationship of freedom of speech and exercise of religion to debates that, either because of the subject matter or the participants, appear to occur in the zone where religion and generalized public policy concerns intersect. For military personnel, the analysis is confined by the limits, both practical and legal, that a tightly structured and focused military command must impose on its members.[91] In the case of the worker in a defense industry, however, the analysis is complicated by the civilian status of the employee, the need of the contractor for reliable workers, inherent limitations on the reach of constitutional rights,[92]

90. *See* D. Little, "Thomas Jefferson's Religious Views and Their Influence on the Supreme Court's Interpretation of the First Amendment," 26 Cath. U.L. Rev. 57 (1976).

91. It is well settled that the needs of the military services command substantial deference in the analysis of constitutional claims that will have an impact on either military action or discipline. *See, e.g., Rostker v. Goldberg*, 453 U.S. 57 (1981) (upholding federal law requiring only males to register for the draft); *Brown v. Glines*, 444 U.S. 348 (1980)(upholding Air Force regulation requiring authorization "from the appropriate commander" before signatures could be collected on a petition); *Greer v. Spock*, 424 U.S. 828 (1976) (upholding regulations banning demonstrations, picketing, protest marches, political speeches, or similar activities on the post, and prohibiting the posting of any publication without prior written approval of post headquarters); *Parker v. Levy*, 417 U.S. 733 (1974) (upholding conviction of Army officer for urging soldiers to disobey orders to go to Vietnam under Articles 133 and 134 of the Uniform Code of Military Justice for "conduct unbecoming an officer and gentleman" and "prejudicial to good order and discipline"); *Schlesinger v. Reservists Committee to Stop the War*, 418 U.S. 208 (1974)(standing; judicial refusal to intervene in war-powers controversy), *Korematsu v. United States*, 323 U.S. 214 (1944)(Japanese exclusion cases). *See also Dronenburg v. Zech*, 746 F.2d 1579 (D.C. Cir. 1984).

92. Substantive constitutional rights that find their source in either the Bill of Rights or the Fourteenth Amendment are limitations on the powers of government. To hold a private party as being involved in "state action," a nexus must be shown between government and the private action. *Jackson v. Metropolitan Edison Co.*, 419 U.S. (1974); *Moose Lodge v. Irvis*, 407 U.S. 163 (1972); *Burton v. Wilmington Parking Authority*, 365 U.S. 715 (1961); *Civil Rights Cases*, 109 U.S. 3 (1883).

and express provisions limiting the duty of employers to accommodate employee religious practices that exist in many employment discrimination laws.[93]

To obtain a clear picture of the status of the worker in a defense industry, it will be helpful to start with the relevant text of the pastoral letter itself:

> To Men and Women in Defense Industries: You also face specific questions, because the defense industry is directly involved in the development and production of the weapons of mass destruction which have concerned us in this letter. We do not presume or pretend that clear answers exist to many of the personal, professional and financial choices facing you in your varying responsibilities. In this letter we have ruled out certain uses of nuclear weapons, while also expressing conditional moral acceptance for deterrence. All Catholics, at every level of defense industries, can and should use the moral principles of this letter to form their consciences. We realize that different judgments of conscience will face different people, and we recognize the possibility of diverse concrete judgments being made in this complex area. We seek as moral teachers and pastors to be available to all who confront these questions of personal and vocational choice. Those who in conscience decide that they should no longer be associated with defense activities should find support in the Catholic community. Those who remain in these industries or earn a profit from the weapons industry should find in the Church guidance and support for the ongoing evaluation of their work.[94]

From an examination of the final recommendations in the text, it is possible to glean several key points, which may be summarized as follows:

1. Physical or economic participation in the production of nuclear weapons raises, for each individual, the same moral questions that have been raised in the letter as a whole.

2. The teachings of the pastoral letter are a guide for Catholics involved in defense industries and should be used in the formation of a position of conscience on continued participation (to whatever degree) in the industry.

3. Diverse judgments of conscience are possible, for there are no clear answers to many of the concrete questions that will face the defense worker.

4. The Church will provide guidance and support, whatever decision is made.

Each of these points is critical to an examination of the legal rights and obligations of defense workers who elect to take a position of conscience based on the teachings of the letter and at odds with the requirements of their employer.

---

93. *See* text at notes 118–120 *post.*   94. The *Challenge of Peace*, n. 318.

Formulation of the Conscientious Position: A Legal Requirement

In any analysis of the rights of the religious dissenter, it is imperative to begin with that which is most basic: the nature and sources of the conscientious objection. For a Catholic or adherent of another religion who seeks to utilize the letter in defense of a position of conscience, it is important, for legal purposes, that the pastoral letter be seen as the teaching tool the bishops designed it to be—as a *guide* to the formation of conscience that contains both "universally binding moral principles found in the teaching of the Church" and "recommendations which allow for diversity of opinion on the part of those who assess the factual data."[95] Because it is not, by its own admission, a definitive statement of binding moral norms, but rather an invitation for extended discussion and reflection on the morality of nuclear war,[96] the person intending to rely on the text of the letter, without more, to defend himself or herself against foreseeable employer reactions, would be well advised to reconsider reliance on the text alone;[97] for the letter itself makes no meaningful distinction between the official responsibilities of government officials and the discrete obligations of individuals who are searching for the place to draw the line in their own lives and careers.[98]

What the letter appears to call for,[99] and what the law demands,[100] is a clear statement of *personal* moral principle on the part of each individual who wishes to take advantage of the limited freedom of action protected by both the First Amendment[101] and employment discrimination law.[102] It is only when the individual has formed a conscientious position—and disclosed it—that the protections of the law, to whatever extent they are applicable, come into play. The inherent limitations of the letter itself and their impact on the average Catholic are discussed in the concluding sections of this paper.

Conscientious Objection and Employment Discrimination Law:[103]
Allocating the Burdens of Conscience

Because the pastoral letter calls upon men and women in defense industries to "confront . . . questions of personal and vocational

95. *Id.*, Summary.
96. *Id.*, nn. 4, 10.
97 *See* text at notes 164–170 *post* (reference to employment discrimination cases).
98. *The Challenge of Peace*, nn. 66, 70, 75–111.
99. *See Id.*, n. 318.
100. *See, e.g., Wisconsin v. Yoder*, 406 U.S. 205 (1972).
101. *See* text at notes 25–26 *ante*.
102. *See* text at notes 117–120 *post*.
103. The materials in this section deal only with the requirements of the main *federal* employment discrimination law, Title VII of the Civil Rights Act of 1964, 42 U.S.C. §§ 2000e, *et seq.* The requirements of applicable state fair employment practices

choice"[104] that will inevitably involve either a decision to "no longer be associated with defense activities"[105] or to "remain in these industries or earn a profit from the weapons industry,"[106] it is critical that the risks and burdens that come with such decisions be analyzed. The bishops pledge their availability "as moral teachers and pastors,"[107] but what about the practical legal risks attendant on the making of a moral choice to resign, transfer, or continue employment with explicit reservations concerning the types of acceptable assignments? Surprisingly, these questions were *not* considered by the bishops in the investigative process that led to the publication of the letter,[108] even though the answers to many of them will determine the level and type of "support" the Catholic community should be expected to provide those whose actions have legal consequences such as job loss.[109]

The primary focus of this section of the paper, therefore, will be the operation of the religious discrimination sections of Title VII of the Civil Rights Act of 1964[110] and the degree to which they may be used to defend the conscientious choices of those who work in the defense industry against discrimination by employers. Also to be considered will be the level of constitutional protection afforded workers who quit or are fired from their jobs for reasons of conscience. While Title VII governs the employer/employee relationship, eligibility for unemploy-

---

laws and the application of those statutes to federal defense contractors are beyond the scope of this paper. *See, e.g.,* Arizona Rev. Stat. Ann. § 1–1463 (B)(1) (1974); Hawaii Rev. Stat. § 378–2 (1976); Maine Rev. Stat. Ann. 5 § 4572 (1964); Nebraska Rev. Stat. § 48–1104 (1943); Pa. Stat. Ann. Tit. 43 § 955(5)(g) (Purdon 1963); 4B Utah Code Ann. § 34–35–6 (1953).

104. *The Challenge of Peace*, n. 318.

105. *Id.*

106. *Id.*

107. *Id.*

108. There is no indication in either the text of the letter and its drafts or the news coverage that followed its publication that the issue was given any consideration. The only relevant portions of the letter that could be said to address the topic were the references to the *Statement on Registration and Conscription for Military Service* (Washington, D.C, 1980) and *Human Life in Our Day* (Washington, D.C., 1980), but examination of the footnote material referenced in the text of the letter indicates that they are not on point, especially with respect to the obligation of civilians in the nonmilitary context.

109. *The Challenge of Peace*, n. 318.

110. Title VII of the Civil Rights Act of 1964, *as amended,* §§ 701(j), 702, and 703(a–e), 42 U.S.C. §§ 2000e(j), 2000e–1, 2000e–2(a–e). 110. Section 701(b) of Title VII, 42 U.S.C. § 2000e(b) extends Title VII coverage to any "employer . . . engaged in an industry affecting commerce who has fifteen or more employees . . . and any agent of such person, but such term does not include (1) the United States, a corporation wholly owned by the Government of the United States, an Indian tribe, or any department or agency of the District of Columbia subject by statute to procedures of the competitive service (as defined by section 2101 of Title 5 of the United States Code), . . ." Title VII was amended in 1972 to include federal employees, P.L. 92–261, 86 Stat. 111, as amended 92 Stat. 3781 (1978), 42 U.S.C. § 2000e–16. *Morton v. Mancari,* 417 U.S. 105 (1974).

ment benefits turns on the construction of state law,[111] which has been held to be subject to the constitutional restraints of the Free Exercise Clause.[112]

Title VII of the Civil Rights Act: Narrow Protection for Religious Belief and Practice

Title VII of the Civil Rights Act of 1964 prohibits discrimination in employment on the basis of race, color, religion, sex, or national origin.[113] For purposes of the statute, the term "religion" is defined as follows:

The term "religion" includes all aspects of religious observance and practice, as well as belief, unless an employer demonstrates that he is unable to reasonably accommodate to an employee's or prospective employee's religious observance or practice without undue hardship on the conduct of the employer's business.[114]

Title VII thus defines and prohibits two distinct forms of employment discrimination based on religious factors:

1. That which is based on the identity or type of religious belief held or practiced by the employee (representation),[115] and

2. Failure to accommodate religious practices where it is possible to do so without "undue hardship" to the employer's business (accommodation).[116]

There are three related, but distinct, exceptions to the general prohibitions, but only one of them is relevant to workers in defense industries.[117] In relevant part, it provides as follows:

Notwithstanding any other provision of [Title VII], (1) it shall not be an unlawful employment practice for an employer to hire and employ employees, . . . on the basis of his religion, . . . in those certain instances where religion, . . . is a bona fide occupational qualification reasonably necessary to the normal operation of that particular business or enterprise. . . .[118]

111. *See generally, e.g.*, Ohio Rev. Code § 4141.09. *et seq.* 29 (Page, 1984); 15 Tex Civ. Stats §§ 5221b–1 *et seq.* (Vernon supp., 1983).

112. *Thomas v. Review Board of the Indiana Employment Security Division*, 450 U.S. 707 (1981); *Sherbert v. Verner*, 374 U.S. 398 (1963).

113. Section 703, 42 U.S.C. § 2000e–2.

114. Section 701(j); 42 U.S.C. § 2000(j), *as amended*.

115. *See* note 140 *infra*.

116. See note 119 *infra*. Cases arising in this category are, by far, the most common for reasons discussed in note 140 *infra*.

117. The other two sections, 42 U.S.C. §§ 2000e–1, and 2000e–2(e)(2), relate to the need for religious institutions and their affiliated educational institutions to hire on the basis of religion whenever their activities reasonably require it.

118. 42 U.S.C. § 2000e–2(e).

Taken as a whole, therefore, Title VII imposes upon employers a duty of nondiscrimination on the basis of religion *except* where the "normal operation" of the particular business or enterprise "reasonably" requires differential treatment, and where accommodation will result in an "undue hardship" on the employer's business.[119]

Given this background, the application of these rules to the conscientiously objecting worker in a defense-related industry can now be examined. Once again, the first reference is to the pastoral letter. Because the letter offers no concrete guidance to the individual who will not be involved with those activities that are deemed to be clearly immoral, such as targeting civilian populations,[120] a considerable amount of discretion has been vested in individual Catholics to form their own consciences on issues of nuclear war and peace.[121] Traditional Catholic doctrine distinguishes between "just" and "unjust" wars by reference to the *ius ad bellum* and between means of waging war that are legitimate and illegitimate under the criteria of the *ius in bello*.[122] This method of analysis presupposes that some wars are just and that some means of waging war are legitimate. It would be difficult to characterize positions that go beyond those teachings to generalized objection to all war or to *any* use of nuclear weaponry as based in what is commonly understood to be "Catholic" teaching. The bishops appear to make this clear when they stated that while "[they had] ruled out *certain* uses of nuclear weapons, [they had] . . . also express[ed] conditional moral acceptance for deterrence"[123] [i.e., other uses]. Since "different judgments of conscience will face different people" who can and should make "diverse concrete judgments" on these questions, all such individuals are entitled to support from both the clergy and the Catholic community at large as . long as they form their respective consciences in a manner arguably consistent with the language of the pastoral letter.[124] Given such flexibility of approach, the bishops' concern that the law protect "true" [i.e., selective][125] freedom of conscience is well founded. Traditional Catho-

---

119. It is significant that the statute is phrased in this manner, for it negates the applicability of the nondiscrimination provisions on the showing of "reasonable" necessity. It has been held that, for purposes of religious discrimination, all that need be shown by the employer to claim the exemption is a *de minimis* impact on business or labor contract interests. See *T.W.A. v. Hardison*, 432 U.S. 63, 84 (1977) (accommodation); Equal Employment Opportunity Commission, Religious Discrimination Guidelines, 29 C.F.R.§1605.2(e)(1)(defining "undue hardship").

120. *The Challenge of Peace*, nn. 147–149.

121. *See* text at note 93 *ante*.

122. *The Challenge of Peace*, nn. 80–111.

123. *Id.*, n. 318.

124. *Id.* This is especially true given the discussion of the value of nonviolence in nn. 111–121.

125. *Id.*, n. 324.

lic positions concerning selective conscientious objection have never been accepted by the courts in the military context,[126] and it would be devastating for Catholics as workers to face the same insensitivity to their conscientious needs. More important, however, the bishops' admission that individual Catholics may find it difficult to determine precisely how the letter applies to their own situations as workers in defense-related industries would make it nearly impossible for an individual Catholic to rely on the pastoral letter alone[127] to resolve questions of conscience that might have an impact on the "personal, professional and financial choices facing [them] in [their] varying responsibilities."[128]

For purposes of Title VII, however, the law makes it clear that providing legal protection for conscientious objection claims, even those supported by positions that are not identified with the exact teachings of a given religion, is legitimate and may be constitutionally required.[129] The "Religious Discrimination Guidelines"[130] published by the United States Equal Employment Opportunity Commission (E.E.O.C.) state that "the Commission will define [the statutory term] 'religious practices' to include moral or ethical beliefs as to what is right and wrong which are sincerely held with the strength of traditional religious views."[131] Thus, a defense worker need show only that the position of conscience taken on the basis of the teachings contained in the pastoral letter is sincerely held "with the strength of traditional religious views."

126. *Gillette v. United States*, 401 U.S. 437, *ante* notes 74, 75, 78.

127. *The Challenge of Peace*, n. 318 makes it clear that the bishops "seek as moral teachers and pastors to be available to all who confront these questions of personal and vocational choice [, and that] . . . [t]hose who remain in [defense] industries or earn a profit from the weapons industry should find in the Church *guidance and support for the ongoing evaluation of their work*." (emphasis supplied). From this it can be seen that the letter alone will not be sufficient to supply necessary answers. Reference to additional sources, in conjunction with the pastoral guidance the bishops have pledged, is necessary.

128. *Id.*

129. *See Thomas v. Review Board of the Indiana Employment Security Division*, 450 U.S. 707 (1981); *Welsh v. United States*, 398 U.S. 333 (1970); *United States v. Seeger*, 380 U.S. 163 (1965). Although *Thomas*, *Welsh* and *Seeger* were cases decided outside the scope of Title VII, they do form a legitimate basis for administrative determination of the applicable law. Of these three cases, only *Thomas* presented an actual constitutional claim. Although both *Welsh* and *Seeger* turned on determinations of congressional intent when it enacted the Military Selective Service Act, the Supreme Court made it very clear that a contrary result in either case would have raised serious constitutional questions. *See Gillette v. United States*, 401 U.S. 437 (1971), *Welsh v. United States*, 398 U.S. 333 (1970); *United States v. Seeger*, 380 U.S. 163 (1965); Reply Brief on Behalf of Petitioner, *Negre v. Larsen*, No 70–325, *Gillette v. United States*, 401 U.S. 437 (1971)(companion case involving Catholic objector).

130. Equal Employment Opportunity Commission, Religious Discrimination Guidelines, 29 C.F.R. § 1605.1, *et seq.*; CCH Employment Practices Guide ¶¶ 3970.01 *et seq.*

131. 29 C.F.R. § 1605.1

It makes no difference whether the teachings are "identifiably" those of the faith to which the worker subscribes.

> The fact that no religious group espouses such beliefs or the fact that the religious groups to which the individual professes to belong may not accept such belief will not determine whether the belief is a religious belief of the employee or prospective employee.[132]

Notwithstanding the apparent breadth of Title VII coverage in such instances, the critical factor is *not* the belief or practice of the employee, but the degree of hardship accommodation that belief will impose on the employer.[133] Because an employer may legitimately refuse to make anything more than a *de minimis* effort,[134] especially where it would involve dislocation of other employees,[135] the potential obstacles to accommodation of the conscientious objector's rights *within the workplace* will depend on whether the nature of the employer's business and labor contracts, if any, will limit or eliminate the dissenting employee's job flexibility.

An employer's duty to attempt accommodation arises at the point where an employee fulfills his or her preliminary obligation to disclose the religious need.[136] From this, it follows that an employer has the right to assume that there are no religious objections to the type of work or duties assigned, religious or otherwise, unless they are voiced by the employee. Likewise, an employer may not make blanket assumptions during the hiring or promotion process concerning adherents of a given religion—here Catholics—without first ascertaining that the individual involved would be unable or unwilling to do the job. Title VII law does not favor broad class-based assumptions about job qualifications,[137] and a defense industry employer that elected to avoid the burden of accommodation by simply refusing to hire or promote Catholics would be

---

132. 29 C.F.R. § 1605.1

133. 42 U.S.C. §§ 2000e(j), 2000e-2(e)(1).

134. 29 C.F.R. § 1605.2(c). *T.W.A. v. Hardison*, 432 U.S. 63 (1977)

135. *See* 42 U.S.C. § 2000e-2(h). *See also* text at note 119 *ante.*

136. 29 C.F.R. § 1605.2(c) provides, in relevant part: "(1) After an employee or prospective employee notifies the employer or labor organization of his or her need for a religious accommodation, the employer or labor organization has an obligation to reasonably accommodate the individual's religious practices. A refusal to accommodate is justified only when an employer or labor organization can demonstrate that an undue hardship would in fact result from each available alternative method of accommodation. A mere assumption that many more people, with the same religious practices as the person being accommodated, may also need accommodation is not evidence of undue hardship. . . ."

137. 42 U.S.C. § 2000e-1. Cf. 29 C.F.R. § 1605.1 (by negative implication). *City of Los Angeles Dep't of Water & Power v. Manhart*, 435 U.S. 702 (1978); *Griggs v. Duke Power Co.*, 401 U.S. 424 (1971); *Phillips v. Martin Marietta Corp.*, 400 U.S. 542 (1971).

guilty of a *prima facie* violation of the statute[138] unless it could be proved that the particular individual involved was unqualified,[139] or that hiring only non-Catholics was "reasonably necessary" to the conduct of the employer's business.[140]

The difficulty, if any, will arise when the defense employer learns of the employee or potential employee's objections. Assuming that an available job[141] can be located within the employer's workforce that does not compromise the employee's conscience, there is no assurance that the employer will be either willing or able to accommodate the request. Simple unwillingness, of course, is not enough,[142] but any legitimate business reason will suffice as long as it is not a pretext for discriminatory conduct.[143] Thus, it has been held that disruption of the workforce, adverse impact on morale, and simple unavailability of a suitable job are sufficient reasons.[144] When the issue is hiring or promotion, rather than accommodation, and the job or promotion would bring the candidate closer to levels of responsibility that might involve the actual planning or implementation of acts deemed by the letter to be immoral, both the employee and the employer may have legitimate reasons to discuss the situation to avoid serious future problems.[145]

138. *See generally*, B. L. Schei and P. Grossman, *Employment Discrimination Law* (B.N.A. 1976).

139. *Id.*

140. 42 U.S.C. §2000e–2(e) (BFOQ). Such a showing would be impossible under these facts, and the author has found no cases in which this section has been found to apply. The law simply does not permit such "broad brush" classification, *see, e.g., City of Los Angeles Dep't of Water & Power v. Manhart*, 435 U.S. 702 (1978) (sex-based pension annuity tables), and provides special protection in those few cases in which scrutiny of religious belief by an employer is clearly proper. *See* sources cited note 117 *ante*.

141. 42 U.S.C. §§ 2000e(j)(burden); 2000e–2(h) (seniority). *See T.W.A. v. Hardison*, *ante*.

142. *See Minkus v. Metropolitan Sanitary Dist. of Greater Chicago*, 600 F.2d 80 (7th Cir. 1979); *Haring v. Blumenthal*, 471 F. Supp. 1172 (D. D.C. 1979)(employer refusal to accommodate).

143. *See* B. L. Schlei and P. Grossman, op. cit., at 1195–1196 and sources cited. *Accord Oates v. United States Postal Service*, 458 F.Supp. 57 (S.D.N.Y. 1978), *aff'd w/o opinion*, 591 F.2d 1331 (2d Cir. 1978); *Levine v. Navapache Hospital*, 26 E.P.D. ¶ 32, 103 (D.Ariz. 1981) (anti-Semitic remark insufficient to prove religious discrimination where employee was insubordinate and disruptive; religious discrimination charge would not affect discharge for valid cause).

144. *See e.g., Palmer v. Bd. of Education of City of Chicago*, 603 F.2d 1271 (7th Cir. 1979), aff'g, 466 F.Supp. 600 (N.D.Ill. 1979) (refusal to take part in essential activities); *Howard v. Haverty Furniture Companies, Inc.*, 615 F.2d 203 (5th Cir. 1980); *Jordan v. North Carolina National Bank*, 565 F.2d 72 (4th Cir. 1977).

145. According to the dual commands of both the law and the pastoral letter, the Catholic employee's obligation in such a situation would be both legal and moral. The moral obligation would be to use the teachings of the pastoral letter to analyze the new job responsibilities and integrate them into one's conscience. *See The Challenge of Peace*, n. 318. The legal obligation would be to disclose any decision adverse to the employer's interests in order to invoke the protections of Title VII. E.E.O.C. Religious

Conscientious Objection and the Impact of Voluntary or Involuntary
Separation from Employment on Eligibility for Unemployment Benefits

Where an employee quits or is fired from a job because the employer
cannot accommodate the employee's religious needs, the former employee may wish to seek unemployment compensation pursuant to the
laws of the state in which he resides. In such cases, the immediate legal
question will be whether the individual is eligible for unemployment
compensation. This, in turn, will depend on the particular provisions of
the state statute under which application is made. In cases in which an
employee quits, or is fired for legitimate reason, many states deny unemployment compensation,[146] but in a series of cases commencing with
Sherbert v. Verner,[147] the United States Supreme Court has made it
clear that the Free Exercise Clause of the first amendment imposes important limits on this discretion. It is now virtually impossible for the
states to treat religiously based conscientious objection to continued
employment as a valid reason for denial of unemployment compensation benefits.

Where the state conditions receipt of an important benefit upon conduct proscribed by a religious faith, or where it denies such a benefit because of conduct mandated by religious belief, thereby putting substantial pressure on an
adherent to modify his behavior and to violate his beliefs, a burden upon religion exists. While the compulsion may be indirect, the infringement upon free
exercise is nonetheless substantial.[148]

The most recent of these cases is *Thomas v. Review Board of the
Indiana Employment Security Division*,[149] a case particularly relevant to
the subject matter of this paper. *Thomas* involved the refusal of an employee who was a Jehovah's Witness to transfer from a job in a defunct
roll foundry that had been turning out sheet steel for a variety of industrial uses to another of his employer's divisions that fabricated military
tank turrets. When Thomas found that his new job was related to the
manufacture of military equipment, he checked for other available plant
openings and found that all the remaining departments of his employer

---

Discrimination Guidelines, 29 C.F.R. § 1605.1, *et seq. See Chrysler Corp. v. Mann*,
561 F.2d 1282 (8th Cir. 1977), *cert. den.* 434 U.S. 1039 (1978). Such disclosure might
also be required in the course of qualification for necessary security clearances. *See* 32
C.F.R. § 156.3. It should be obvious at this point that the employer's obligations are
minimal and that the courts are unlikely to impose any obligation that would interfere
with routine operations. *See* cases cited at notes 119, 143, *ante*. It should also be noted
that actual interference with defense-related operations might be a criminal offense. *See*
18 U.S.C. § 2156.

146. *See, e.g.*, Ohio Rev. Code § 4141.29.

147. 374 U.S. 398 (1963).

148. *Thomas v. Review Board of the Indiana Employment Security Div.*, 450 U.S.
707, 718–719 (1981).

149. 450 U.S. 707 (1981).

were engaged in the manufacture of weapons. Since transfer would not solve his problem, he asked for a layoff, which would make him eligible for unemployment benefits under Indiana law,[150] but his employer refused. So he quit, asserting that he could not work on weapons without violating the principles of his religion.[151] When his unemployment claim was heard in the Indiana Employment Security Division, it was rejected on the ground that the termination of Thomas' employment was not based upon a "good cause [arising] in connection with [his] work" as required by the Indiana unemployment compensation statute.[152] On appeal, the Indiana Supreme Court upheld the decision of the Review Board, holding that "good cause which justifies involuntary unemployment must be job-related and objective in character."[153] In addition, it held that the basis and the precise nature of Thomas' views concerning his obligations as a Jehovah's Witness were unclear, apparently because Thomas' views were stricter than those of another Jehovah's Witness who had testified at the hearing and that they amounted more to a "personal philosophical choice" than a religious belief that was entitled to protection under the Free Exercise Clause of the First Amendment.[154] Nonetheless, it concluded its opinion by holding that even if Thomas had quit for religious reasons, he would not be entitled to benefits under Indiana law because termination motivated by religion did not amount to "good cause" objectively related to the work.[155]

The United States Supreme Court reversed, holding that a state court is not permitted to burden the employee's first amendment rights by conditioning the receipt of benefits on the rejection of sincerely held personal religious beliefs.[156] In this regard, the court did nothing more than reaffirm the general rule of *Sherbert v. Verner*,[157] but the case is also significant insofar as it extended the general rule against judicial inquiry into the validity or consistency of an individual's belief system[158] to the case of an individual applying for government benefits.[159] The court's words are significant given the differences in opinion that have already arisen concerning the requirements of the pastoral letter.

150. Indiana Code § 22–4–15–1 (1976 and Supp. 1978).
151. 450 U.S. at 708.
152. *Id.*
153. 450 U.S. at 712–713, *quoting Thomas v. Review Board of the Indiana Employment Security Division*, 271 Ind. 233, 391 N.E.2d 1127, 1129 (1981).
154. *Id.*, 450 U.S. at 708, 391 N.E.2d at 1131.
155. *Id.*
156. *Thomas v. Review Board of the Indiana Employment Security Division*, 450 U.S. 707, at 715.
157. 374 U.S. 398 (1963).
158. *United States v. Ballard*, 322 U.S. 78 (1944).
159. The extension of such reasoning to the provision of government benefits places the Supreme Court in an interesting constitutional quandary that it has yet to resolve. Its

Intrafaith differences . . . are not uncommon among followers of a particular creed, and the judicial process is singularly ill equipped to resolve such differences in relation to the Religion Clauses. . . . Particularly in this sensitive area, it is not within the judicial function and judicial competence to inquire whether the [individual] or his fellow worker more correctly perceived the commands of their common faith. Courts are not arbiters of scriptural interpretation.[160]

Because the states will not be free to question the interpretation of Catholic doctrine accepted by a worker who quits or is fired from a

---

decisions under the Establishment Clause indicate that the First Amendment "bespeaks a government . . . stripped of all power . . . to support, or otherwise to assist any or all religions . . . and no State 'can pass laws which aid one religion . . . [or] all religions.'" *Thomas v. Review Board of the Indiana Employment Security Division*, 450 U.S. 707, at 725 (Rehnquist, J., dissenting) (quoting *Everson v. Board of Education*, 330 U.S. 1[1947]). A long line of cases has invalidated government financial subsidies or support for religious activity, *see, e.g., Aguilar v. Felton*, – U.S. – , 53 U.S.L.W. 5013 (1985); *School District of Grand Rapids v. Ball*, – U.S. – , 53 U.S.L.W. 5006 (1985).

In *Thomas*, however, the court ruled that to deny otherwise available government benefits on the grounds that"[w]here the state conditions receipt of an important benefit upon conduct proscribed by a religious faith, or where it denies such a benefit because of conduct mandated by religious belief, [it] thereby put[s] substantial pressure on an adherent to modify his behavior and to violate his beliefs," and that such pressure constitutes a substantial and impermissible "burden upon religion" under the Free Exercise Clause of the First Amendment. 450 U.S. at 717–718 (majority opinion). The difficulty with this argument is that much of the court's teaching under the Establishment Clause also deals with conditioning otherwise available public assistance on an individual's willingness to give up the constitutionally protected right to choose to be educated in a religiously affiliated or private school rather than a public school. *Compare, Pierce v. Society of Sisters*, 268 U.S. 510 (1925) and *Meyer v. Nebraska*, 262 U.S. 390 (1923) (recognizing this right), *with e.g., Aguilar v. Felton*, – U.S. – , 53 U.S.L.W. 5013 (1985); *School District of Grand Rapids v. Ball*, – U.S. – , 53 U.S.L.W. 5006 (1985); *Witters v. State of Washington, Commission for the Blind*, 102 Wash.2d 624, 689 P.2d 53 (1984); *Thomas v. Allegany County Board of Education*, 51 Md. App. 312, 443 A.2d 622 (1982). *But cf., Mueller v. Allen, ante* (child benefit theory); *Everson v. Board of Education, ante* (same). This fact was not lost in Justice Rehnquist's pointed dissent in *Thomas*, 450 U.S. at 724, 727. It is interesting, however, that Justice Rehnquist would *not* have protected Thomas by extending the Free Exercise Clause to cover his case, but rather would have supplanted the *Sherbert* rule with that of *Braunfeld v. Brown*, 366 U.S. 599 (1961). Such a development in the law of Free Exercise would lead to a contrary result in much of the foregoing analysis.

Recent developments worthy of note as this article goes to print are the court's decisions in *Caldor, Inc. v. Estate of Thornton*, – U.S. – , 53 U.S.L.W. 4853 (1985), and *Jensen v. Quaring*, – U.S. – , 53 U.S.L.W. 4787 (1985). *Jensen*, a 4-4 tie with no binding effect, affirmed a lower court decision resting on *Sherbert*. *Caldor*, however, appears to signal a shift in the court's thinking in matters of Free Exercise. A thorough analysis of *Caldor*—which invalidated, oñ Establishment Clause grounds, a Connecticut state labor law which required accommodation of an employee's designated Sabbath— is beyond the scope of this essay. Since the case rests on Establishment Clause analysis, rather than a Free Exercise rationale, Justice Rehnquist's view of the reach of the Free Exercise Clause has gained little, if any, support within a court that seems far more preoccupied with marking the proper boundaries of religious accommodation under the Establishment Clause than making sense out of the religious freedom guarantee implicit in the First Amendment as a whole.

160. *Id.*, 450 U.S. at 716 (majority opinion).

defense-related job, it is irrelevant that the teachings of the pastoral letter may not be clear as they apply to individuals who work in defense industries. Even though "different judgments of conscience will face different people, and . . . diverse concrete judgments [may be] made in this complex area[,]"[161] the Church makes it clear that it will "be available to all who confront these questions of personal and vocational choice[,]" and will support those who "in conscience decide that they should no longer be associated with defense activities. . . ."[162] It is therefore likely that unemployment benefits will be available as at least one source of the "support" for which the conscientious objector will be eligible in the community at large.[163]

Conclusion

The purpose of the foregoing summary of the law has been to address some of the major constitutional and legal questions that arise in light of the bishops' pastoral letter on war and peace. Although no attempt has been made to address these questions exhaustively, it does seem clear that the bishops were well within their rights to sound a moral alarm over the issue of nuclear weapons and that individuals who elect to respond to the bishops' suggestions can find some support for their individual decisions of conscience in the law. Whether the bishops' teachings were justified on moral, political, strategic, or other grounds are topics that have been addressed by other contributors to this volume. The impact of these teachings on the individuals who wish to form their consciences and take concrete steps in a manner consistent with the pastoral letter, however, is a matter that was not discussed, or even considered by the bishops as they formulated their suggestions.[164] In my view, such an omission is unfortunate, not because these considerations should change the moral precepts governing the issues of war and peace—they should not—but because real people have been urged by their religious leaders to make real-life "personal, professional and financial choices"[165] with legal significance based on the teachings in the pastoral letter. Merely "rul[ing] out certain uses of nuclear weapons, while also expressing conditional moral acceptance for deterrence" does not give clear guidance to the individual who must make practical decisions that will inevitably have an impact on family and career. If the bishops did "not presume or pretend that clear answers exist to many of

---

161. *The Challenge of Peace*, n. 318.
162. *Id.*
163. *Id. Best v. California Apprenticeship Council*, 161 Cal. App. 3d 626, 207 Cal. Rptr. 863 (1984).
164. Note 108 *ante*.
165. *The Challenge of Peace*, n. 318.

these personal, professional and financial choices," perhaps they might well have stated a bit more clearly the moral principles on which the "average" Catholic worker (if such an individual exists) should base those judgments. They have done so in other contexts, including that of abortion—the other great evil condemned in the letter[166]—and it should not have been an unreasonable task for them to have done so for those who hold jobs at levels of the defense industry that are only remotely connected to that which is clearly immoral.

That such guidelines were not spelled out in the text of the letter is understandable given the breadth of the undertaking. Nonetheless, such guidance is necessary at a time when individual believers are subjected to varying interpretations of the letter's content by Church leaders, theologians, religious commentators, and representatives of the electronic and print media. Some of those interpretations appear in this volume. Whose interpretation is one to believe? This question is significant for the believer who intends to take steps that might affect his or her future.

The law requires that the individual must rely on a sincerely held religious belief in order to claim the protection of the constitutional provisions and laws of the United States that forbid discrimination on the basis of religion.[167] For Catholics who traditionally rely on their bishops to articulate the moral principles they are to apply, it will be difficult to rely on the pastoral letter unless the affected individual can articulate, even roughly, why *his* or *her* Catholic faith mandates the course of action chosen.[168] The law looks dimly on exemptions from social obligations based on mere philosophical or political points of view,[169] and Catholics who intend to rely on the text of the letter for support would be well advised to seek some pastoral guidance in the process of forming their respective consciences if they intend to take a position that goes farther than the letter itself. While civil courts may not question the veracity or consistency of a religious view,[170] it is critical that the believer be able to explain it in terms that are religious in nature. Their personal philosophy concerning nuclear weapons will not be enough.[171]

166. *Id.*

167. *See* text at notes 99–100 *ante*.

168. *See* text at notes 129–132.

169. *Wisconsin v. Yoder*, 406 U.S. 205 215–216 (1972).

170. *See United States v. Ballard*, 322 U.S. 78 (1944) and text accompanying note 158 *ante*.

171. *Thomas v. Review Board*, 450 U.S. at 797, *ante*; *Wisconsin v. Yoder*, *ante* (mere personal belief/philosophy).

CATHERINE INEZ ADLESIC

24. The Effort to Implement the Pastoral Letter on War and Peace

After several years of study, debate, consultation, and three preliminary drafts, the controversial pastoral letter, *The Challenge of Peace: God's Promise and Our Response*, was adopted by an overwhelming majority of American bishops. One of the most significant pastoral letters ever adopted by the National Conference of Catholic Bishops, its teachings and conclusions on nuclear war were not uniformly accepted by its readers. Scholars, politicians, theologians, and laypersons alike praised and criticized the letter's teachings. Many obstacles were overcome in the drafting of the letter, but one test would come only when the final document was complete: Bishops, educators, priests, and others would need to implement the letter throughout their dioceses, schools, and parishes.

Committed to reaching the Catholic community and a broader public, the N.C.C.B. for the first time voted to establish a committee of bishops to observe and guide the implementation of one of its pastoral letters. This follow-up committee was to operate one year. The late Bishop George Fulcher, Diocese of Lafayette, was selected as the chairman. Other members included Bishops Kenneth Untener, Diocese of Saginaw, and Kenneth Povish, Diocese of Lansing. In addition, an office was established at the United States Catholic Conference to monitor and assist implementation efforts. Two people were selected to staff the implementation office at the Conference. In June 1983, the Rev. Brian McCullough, S.C.J., assumed the role of director. He and I soon discovered the job would keep us very busy for the next 12 months.

From the outset the bishops' follow-up committee decided the implementation office (soon called the Pastoral Letter Clearinghouse) would act simply as a clearinghouse to disseminate information on resources and programs on the local, national, and international level to bishops, social action directors, school principals and teachers, parish leaders and others. No program or guidelines for implementation or study were produced by the committee. Rather, the bishops wanted to allow the letter to take hold at a grass-roots level. Numerous organizations and individuals were ready to meet this challenge and to begin development, production, and implementation of activities in response to the pastoral letter's call for study and discussion.

By the first weeks of July 1983, we had stacks of requests for information on educational programs. We had available study guides, videotapes and simple question-and-answer booklets. To communicate the information on hand the clearinghouse published a bimonthly newsletter entitled *Our Response*. This newsletter was intended to "periodically familiarize readers with the various programs and projects regarding the pastoral letter either developed or being developed around the world." The newsletter included brief descriptions of these educational materials. This medium and a consequent resource list proved to be a helpful and effective means of meeting the demand by thousands of people for resources and ideas.

In this article I will follow the same model. It is hoped that this article will give some insight into the types of educational courses established in the wake of the pastoral letter and their impact on Catholic laity, religious groups, public awareness and action. The clearinghouse frequently received calls from people who wanted to know the impact of the letter on the Catholic community and public policy. Questions included: What kinds of attitudinal changes have taken place? What are effective programs for a given setting (such as a diocese or a parish)? Did the pastoral influence federal legislation? and more. Those questions are difficult to answer because no quantitative or qualitative surveys of the effect of the pastoral have yet been taken. Most information, at present, is anecdotal. (Other groups are planning to do these types of surveys soon.) A study of these activities is important. The demand by the Catholic community for educational materials on the issues of peace and war has been tremendous and is bound to have had an impact on American Catholics, the general public, and the formation of public policy. The purpose of this paper is to attempt an assessment of this impact. Since no scientific analysis of the impact of the letter was available at the time this article was written, the examples discussed are anecdotal in nature and are used to give a sampling of the types of activities that occurred nationally in response to the letter.

The overwhelming response emanated from a variety of sources. Diocesan social action committees, educational departments, religious peace groups and others produced materials and organized community activities. Many of the diocesan offices and parishes structured the texts and activities to suit the needs of their area. This paper will review in turn the response to the pastoral on these various levels.

Diocesan Response

I shall cite in this section some examples of activities reported by social action directors and others with whom our office corresponded throughout the year. Each diocese has a different need, yet many of the programs shared common traits. Diocesan social action directors trained individuals to lead discussions and educational programs in the parishes. The success of those educational programs varied. Most were successful in engaging parishioners in discussion and enhancing their knowledge. Often those groups continued to study and take action based on their reflections.

In Louisville, Ky., the Archdiocesan Committee for Peace and Justice organized teams to help parishes implement the letter. These teams included members of the community who were chosen because of their leadership and knowledge of Catholic social teaching and war and peace issues. With a resource book to make planning easier, the leaders worked in different parishes. The Archdiocesan Committee found that this helped disseminate the pastoral letter on a broader scale.

Thirty-five peace volunteers were selected in Rockford, Ill., to perform a similar function in individual parishes. Each of the leaders attended an educational workshop before entering the parishes. In Little Rock, Ark., a conference was held for priests and lay and religious leaders. Discussions and lectures focused on the theology more than on the geopolitical debate. The Rev. Joseph Biltz, peace and justice director, videotaped the sessions he gave so that the tapes could be distributed for later use.

Father Biltz believed the Little Rock program successfully responded to the need for study and action. An estimated 50 percent of the parishes had some form of activity. (Each parish organized its own discussion.) At one conference, 100 people attended. Those people broke into smaller ongoing discussion groups that met for the following four or five weeks for study and discussion. The local Pax Christi chapter designated the entire year for study and provided some of the study materials. Pax Christi's assistance enhanced the overall diocesan efforts.

"Lots of interest!" That's how Ms. Rosemarie Gorman, author of an eight-part study guide on the pastoral letter, described the activities in the Diocese of Bridgeport. "For a small diocese, we do pretty well." The Peace and Justice staff developed a packet to encourage ongoing discussion groups. The small groups brought together "peace-niks" as well as those opposed to the pastoral letter, an unusual situation in previous secular or religious settings. Bridgeport's program for implementing the letter had two parts. In the first part, the Social Action Committee gave a series of eight talks to parish leaders who were members of the voluntary peace commission. After the series, the commission members set up a series of four or five talks based on the themes presented. An average of 20 to 30 people attended those parish meetings.

The second part of the Bridgeport program was designed to delve into the long-term aspects of the pastoral and aimed to increase skills for political participation. Ms. Gorman thinks the ideal situation would be to establish permanent peace and justice groups in each parish. Ms. Gorman thought that the problem would be to get people interested in reflection or action or to plan strategies. People are more interested in working directly with other people or writing letters. They are less inclined to "just study." The controversy surrounding the letter and the interest in the nuclear question attracted a broad group. Many wanted to know what to do next. Bridgeport's second step seemed to be a good framework for long-term follow-up.

John Carr, Secretary of the Social Concerns Office in the Archdiocese of Washington, D.C., enticed people of different political views to talk with one another. Group discussion was the best mode for implementation, in his mind. Preparation of parish educators increased the effectiveness of the archdiocese's parish programs that occurred in more than half of the 130 parishes. The Social Concerns Office organized *A Call to Peacemaking*, a conference to educate parish leaders and teachers. Speakers with diverse backgrounds spoke on theology and national security issues. The model allowed audience participation. Parish leaders also sharpened their conflict-resolution skills. After the conference, parish leaders sought to generate neighborhood activities.

In general, diocesan offices trained and educated leaders who were then assigned parishes. With instructional packets, educational information, and skills development, these leaders were able to create study groups committed to long-term goals. The parish leaders inspired reflection and facilitated debates (occasionally heated). The careful planning and preparation increased the overall effectiveness. Still the programs must remain in place so that more substantive action and reflection can continue. Furthermore, not only the issue of nuclear arms but the broad range of social problems, such as poverty and hunger, the resolution of which is linked to war and peace questions, must be addressed.

Ecumenical Cooperation

A strong ecumenical basis was established among Catholic, Protestant, Jewish, and various other religious groups. In many cases, the pastoral letter created a base for activities that might never have occurred if the letter had not been written. For example, a "very significant" interfaith coalition from Baptists to Catholics formed in the Diocese of Richmond. Ms. Eileen Dooley, director of the Office for Justice and Peace, at the request of Bishop Walter Sullivan, coordinated two statewide meetings in May 1984. Another was planned for fall 1984. This type of cooperation among ecumenical groups on peace issues was common.

The non-Catholic churches endorsed, supported, and praised the Catholic bishops for their boldness and courage as leaders in promoting peace. (See, for example, Alan Geyer's paper in this volume.) Some adopted the letter and mandated study of the issues in their churches. Others planned joint study guides comparing and contrasting each religious tradition's perspectives on peace.

Creating dialogue and cooperation with neighboring churches was sometimes new. It became a breakthrough for further efforts. Many churches now envision a common purpose to teach communities about the theological basis for peace making, to understand the history of war, and to examine the alternatives. They made the connections between peace and other social justice issues.

Peace with Justice Week is one example of many churches and social justice groups working together to educate the public. The National Conference of Catholic Bishops, for the first time, this year became a coalition member of the national coordination efforts. Catholic parishes and religious communities were among the most active participants.

The stronger sense of community and the realized need for cooperation among the churches were among the more significant influences of the pastoral letter. The new and intensified cooperation and support gave greater unity to interchurch efforts. One product of the pastoral letter was the birth and growth of a vast network of concerned people among the churches on these war and peace questions.

Clerical and Religious Response

Clergy naturally played a special role in the implementation process. Their responses were mixed and similar to those of the laity and general public. Priests and religious communities alike took the lead in promoting the teaching throughout parishes and schools. The parish priest often filled a primary position in reaching the parishioners. Numerous religious communities were among the chief proponents. (Often these groups have long traditions of peace and justice works.) At the same time, some members of the clergy were reluctant to take an active role.

Ideally, the parish priest would have educated his parishioners on the pastoral letter and preached on issues of war and peace. Leadership by the bishops, liturgical guides, homilies, and education days for clergy encouraged priests to lead. The role of the priest was critical to implementing the pastoral in the parishes. In many cases, his reticence or involvement made the difference between success and failure.

Priests who reacted unfavorably to the letter may have acted this way for several reasons. Some priests were individually opposed to the letter; others feared the mood of their parishioners or simply felt that the bishops had gone beyond their teaching authority. (While the bishops provided great leadership, that leadership does not ensure that the parish priest will not be "put down" by his community.) There were clerics who took on leadership roles, but sometimes found themselves without diocesan support. Finally, the clerical concern with the daily needs of the parish occasionally proved a distraction from social justice work.

Parishioners need to support the priest and exhibit a willingness to do the necessary planning of programs. A combination of parish leadership and support by the priest provides the best working environment. If the pastoral letter is to be integrated into the whole life and faith of the Church, the willingness to integrate new awareness is the task of both priests and laity.

Participation by religious communities often occurred in ecumenical settings. Their participation in symposiums, clergy-education days, and workshops was extensive on the local and national level. Intercommunity newsletters were sent out by some communities to discuss specific theological concerns on justice and peace. The Marianist Provincialate in Dayton, Ohio, distributed an interprovince newsletter entitled, *Our Response*, specifically for this task. In Kansas City, Kans., the Shalom Catholic Worker House gave workshops for "Teaching the Peace Pastoral." These presentations were designed for school and religious educators and Church ministry personnel.

Many groups such as Pax Christi and Benedictines for Peace initiated educational workshops or produced written and visual materials for their communities and the laity to use. These two groups created study guides that were available almost as soon as the letter was adopted. Pax Christi distributed a study guide, reflection guide, leader's guide, and a question-and-answer booklet. The Benedictines for Peace contributed to the retreat manual, *Women Gathered for Peace*, which was produced jointly by the National Conference of Catholic Women and the Leadership Conference of Women Religious. Catholic nuns were and are leaders in promoting peace.

Response from the Military

Discussions with parish leaders and those in the military reveal some interesting divisions in the attitudes of military personnel toward the letter. (Much of this information was derived from an in-house survey conducted by the follow-up committee.) Military personnel were active in parish discussions. Many were willing to engage in dialogue and debate the positions the bishops took. Some felt hostility or animosity toward the bishops. They were bewildered and wondered what the bishops were saying to them. At parish meetings and in group discussions, confusion subsided after the bishops' statements on the military were made known to them. Some expressed interest in disseminating the information and assessing the impact. (One colonel in the Air Force thought he might do his own research to measure public attitudes toward the letter and to evaluate the effectiveness of the educational materials.)

In some courses, military colleges incorporated the ethical evaluation of modern warfare provided by the pastoral. For example, the Air War College at Maxwell Air Force Base in Alabama included the pastoral in its ethical evaluation of warfare. Sheldon A. Goldberg, Lt. Col. U.S.A.F., chief, Department of Curricular Development, said in a letter to Father McCullough:

> While the course objective includes providing knowledge and developing understanding, the dominant aim is to develop insight, breadth of vision, a capacity for dispassionate analysis and the capability to cope with uncertainties involved in the formulation of plans and decisions affecting national security. In this respect, the pastoral provides an extremely important perspective that could not be omitted without violating our own, just mentioned, objectives and educational goals.

This type of study devoted to the letter indicates the degree of seriousness with which the pastoral was taken by those in a position to formulate public policy.

Military chaplains played a significant role in the presentation of the letter to military personnel. Using Cardinal Terence Cooke's (at the time, head of the military vicarate) letter to military chaplains, they gave workshops highlighting the significant moral and theological issues presented by the pastoral letter. This served to diffuse some of the animosity felt by military personnel and facilitated those who were supportive and wanted a greater understanding of the moral issues implicated in the nuclear arms debate. Cardinal Cooke recommended that chaplains encourage a spirit of dialogue and gave many priests the support they needed.

William J. Dendinger, Maj. U.S.A.F., member of the Chaplain Resource Board, reported in a letter to Father McCullough, S.C.J., that most chaplains planned an event. To encourage study, materials were recommended and the July edition of the clearinghouse's *Our Response* was distributed to every Air Force installation worldwide. Chaplains counsel military personnel in conscience formation, and they act as mediators in the presentation of Catholic views. Implementation of *The*

Challenge of Peace was a unique task to which they responded genuinely and generously.

Military personnel actively participated in discussions at the parish level. Some attended meetings out of fear that the military's views would not be adequately represented, while others attended to voice their concerns for peace. Once in a while, tragedy occurred when neither the "peace-niks" nor the "generals" were able to listen to one another or meetings grew tense. Misfortune fell when one or the other left the discussion in anger. Parish leaders used their conflict resolution skills to lessen such confrontation.

For a variety of reasons, therefore, military personnel participated in discussions. Most contributed much to their groups. Parish presentations cleared up many misconceptions. Consequently, some of the hostility and animosity subsided. The genuine dialogue between Christians with opposing views broadened the overall understanding of the debate for both.

Summary of Diocesan and Parish Education

Education at the grass-roots level in the dioceses was central to the implementation of *The Challenge of Peace*. The diverse backgrounds and conflicting political views of participants created challenges that sometimes led to new understandings of one another. Bishops and their social justice offices provided the leadership that assisted parishes anxious to promote peace but new to the activity. These offices produced numerous study guides, audiovisual aids, and other materials that were used for study. Symposiums, conferences, and study days were forums for discussion with experts in theology, military planning, and policy analysis. Those educational programs instigated reflection and action that will continue for years.

Ecumenical cooperation was widespread. From the cooperation a firm basis for broad educational efforts established ongoing networks. Catholics were recognized as leaders in the promotion of peace, thus creating a new perception in both Catholic and non-Catholic communities. The result was a new recognition of common goals among Catholics and those of different faiths.

Implementation of the pastoral letter in parishes presented challenges for peace activists, military personnel, moderates, and conservatives. The mutual exchanges of ideas in a sincere atmosphere achieved the basic goal of peace education, getting people to listen to one another and to cooperate for a shared goal. In fact, the discussion seemed to enhance participants' feelings of "ownership" of the letter. For many, the participation renewed waning commitments to the Church, inspired prayer for peace, and prompted them to action.

Activity in the Catholic Schools

The spring 1984 newsletter of the Association of Catholic Colleges and Universities stated that almost all Catholic postsecondary schools offered special programs of study on the pastoral letter. Many of those colleges and universities had previously developed peace and conflict studies programs, which ranged from a concentration of electives to a bachelor's degree. In response to the letter, courses on ethics and policy questions were provided. Some universities integrated the pastoral letter into their existing programs. Lectures, symposiums, and lecture series were frequent. Student groups invited speakers and sponsored debates.

Manhattan College and St. Bonaventure University (both in New York State) are models of the way in which Catholic postsecondary schools have structured peace and justice programs. Manhattan College offers a B.A. program in its Peace Studies Institute. The program is committed to the academic and moral search for solutions to the problems of war, revolution, and human justice. The program includes a core of courses that cover conflict resolution, nonviolent strategies, world order, the arms race, and social justice. Students are prepared for a variety of jobs or for graduate study.

St. Bonaventure bases its program in the Catholic and Franciscan tradition. The Peace Studies Program is interdisciplinary, with courses encompassing socio-scientific analysis and philosophical and theological perspectives. Graduates are prepared for a variety of professions in government service, public policy, and ministry. Students from both programs can also continue graduate studies in labor relations, community organizing, and the legal profession.

Many other colleges and universities, inspired by the bishops' letter, have plans to create permanent programs in peace studies. The goal is to make these courses a natural part of each student's education. Future pastoral letters focused on social issues will also be the subject of study. (See David Johnson's paper in this volume for a further discussion of peace-making activities and prospects in the nation's Catholic postsecondary schools.)

High school students received similar exposure through courses and extracurricular activities. Faculty service days focused on the theological and social questions implicated by the pastoral letter, in order to relieve anxiety among teachers unaccustomed to dealing with controversial social teachings. Educational resources were displayed at many seminars. Special councils were commissioned to evaluate and recommend resources and curricula guides.

Students at Stone Ridge High School in Bethesda, Md., studied the letter in the classroom and at a special weekend conference. Sister Barbara Rogers, a teacher at Stone Ridge, explained that her school had taught the social encyclicals for years. However, the pastoral letter brought an immediacy to the task. During fall 1983, students studied the entire document, discussed its theology, and debated public policy issues. In addition to the coursework, students took internships with local community service or peace groups.

Stone Ridge sponsored a weekend conference to study and listen to expert opinions on the theological and political problems. Two students from each of the 18 Sacred Heart schools in the United States were selected to attend. (Sacred Heart schools are those schools operated by the Sacred Heart Order of Sisters.) These students dicussed the letter with their local bishop and presented their views at the conference. The students also attended presentations by experts in theology and international politics. The students left the conference having acquired the information and skills needed to give them confidence to engage other schools and groups in their home communities.

Many high schools enthusiastically assumed the role of teaching the letter to their students. The classroom was the place for most of the reflection, although students also engaged their parents in reflections. In the end a sharing occurred between parent and child. Parents frequently raised concerns with what their children were learning about nuclear war. In recognition of the need to address this concern, the Illinois Catholic Conference created a special section in its educators' manual that gave a study program for parents. The study program explained the pastoral letter and discussed the activities and curricula in which the students were engaged. Other organizations, like the Institute for Peace and Justice in St. Louis, Mo., designed study materials specifically for families. Prominent Catholic family organizations actively sought such study guides. Family prayers and study helped youth understand their role as peacemakers.

Study in the schools on all levels should not be underestimated. As in the parishes, the response in the schools was enormous. Thorough academic study was available. Few students who attend Catholic schools will fail to receive instruction on the social teachings of the Church in the future. Peace education received serious attention. Such attention will continue to be a basic element of students' education.

On the college level, schools have created academic programs to train students for peace-related professions. Many courses and programs are in the incipient phase and are likely in succeeding years to become part of mainstream education.

Conclusion

The effect of the education process for *The Challenge of Peace: God's Promise and Our Response* is multidimensional. Catholic parishes added a new dimension to adult education and C.C.D. Catholic schools designed special courses and extracurricular activities. Special clergy education days supported priests so that they would be able to address social issues in the pulpit. Colleges and universities created or augmented programs for students, as did secondary and elementary schools. Families debated and discussed concerns about nuclear war. Many responded to the challenges they confronted by contacting their congressional representatives or other elected officials. Public officials listened carefully to moral problems on war and peace. In sum, a new consciousness on the moral questions of war and peace was formed among Catholics and others.

The pastoral letter was able to have the impact it had because of the method used by the bishops to write the letter. Every stage of the drafting of the letter received a suprising amount of media attention. This in turn created a groundswell of awareness so that when the final version was adopted, support groups were ready to put the final touches on written texts, audiovisual aids, parish strategies, and conferences. The public was anxious to participate, to hear lectures and critiques, and to apply the moral tenets of the pastoral to appropriate cases.

The long-term impact of the letter on the American Catholic community that I have described in this paper needs further evaluation. Such evaluation would assess the effectiveness, accuracy, and balance of educational materials and would test enduring public attitudes. As indicated at the time I wrote this paper, mainly anecdotal information was available. The final test of the impact would be to question whether public opinion or public policy eventually come to agree with the policy recommendations of the pastoral letter.

The historical and social value of thorough scientific study of the impact ought not to be missed. Attitudinal surveys and assessments of the educational materials ought to be done. One cannot judge with complete certainty just how individuals' perceptions were affected by this study of the issues raised by the pastoral letter. Have people changed their minds, studied more? Do they even agree with their bishops? Certainly the commitment to ongoing study indicates great concern.

The tremendous response, the unprecedented number of activities, demonstrate wide concern and interest in the problems of modern warfare. Responsible public officials must necessarily seriously consider the meaning of such intense interest at the grass-roots level. The new awareness and heightened attention can change public perception of the debate.

Bringing parishioners back to church during the week or even after Sunday Mass is often difficult. To discuss the pastoral letter, thousands of people returned to church. Not just once did they return, but for many consecutive weeks. Sometimes meetings were two or three hours long.

Entire weekends, whole days, were devoted to study. That so many individuals took the time to study peace is significant.

Why did so many citizens attend the meetings? Military personnel sometimes came to present their views and engage in the debates. Peace activists came to support the letter. Others came simply to learn more about the letter and the issues. Whatever the reasons that attracted individuals or families, the exchange of ideas provoked new thoughts among many. The moral dimension was brought to the minds of those who might never have considered the moral dimensions of nuclear warfare. People were motivated to action.

Peace groups experienced increased membership as people became aware of the letter, studied it, and then wanted to learn more and engage in action. The peace movement was supported in many ways by the position the bishops took. Secular and religious peace groups invited each other's experts to give presentations and to add to each other's effectiveness in heightening public education or changing public policy.

Although the response indicates significant impact, much work remains if the Catholic community and the public is to be reached more extensively. The peaceful ideals outlined in the pastoral need to be integrated into the whole life and faith of the Church. Implementation has two levels: study and action. It is well and good that people think about the questions, but if people do not act, the "new moment" opened by the pastoral will be lost.

Likewise, the bishops can be praised until the end of time, but without their continued scrutiny of public policy, the praise will have been deceptive and meaningless. Further testimonies and letters from the conference are necessary. (The N.C.C.B. did present testimony before the House Foreign Relations Committee on arms control issues in June 1984). Cardinal Bernardin has also made a welcome step in this direction with his Gannon address at Fordham University, in which he linked concern with peace/war issues and concern over abortion. Ongoing efforts will ensure a strong and stable future for education and change.

In his Gannon lecture in December 1983, Cardinal Bernardin said:

The fundamental contribution of *The Challenge of Peace*, I believe, is that we have been part of a few central forces which have created the new moment. We have helped to shape the debate; now we face the question of whether we can frame a new consensus concerning nuclear policy.

The question of "whether we can frame a new consensus concerning nuclear policy" will be answered with time. Framing a new consensus will depend on many factors. This challenge to frame nuclear policy has been assiduously confronted by religious and lay leaders of the Catholic Church and many other concerned individuals.

CHARLES J. REID, JR.

Selected Bibliography on Issues of War and Peace

The following bibliography is included to assist readers in locating additional materials. The bibliography is divided into three parts, the readings in each section corresponding to the subjects treated in Parts I through III of the volume. For example, materials on the patristic and medieval Church's attitude toward war are found in Part I, while readings discussing the technical aspects of arms control or deterrence strategy are found in Part II. Because of the vast quantity of literature on the topics of Christian approaches to war and peace and the conduct of war and deterrence in a nuclear age, one cannot hope to provide a comprehensive guide to the sources in a bibliography of this length. This bibliography does not pretend to be comprehensive. Rather, it is intended to offer a sampling of the available literature, thereby, perhaps, stimulating further inquiry and reflection.

The editor wishes to acknowledge the suggestions and advice received from the Rev. Brian Johnstone of The Catholic University of America's Department of Theology, Associate Dean Michael F. Noone of The Catholic University of America's Columbus School of Law, and Brian Corbin, graduate student at the Massachusetts Institute of Technology. Naturally, any omissions are the fault of the editor.

Part I

J. S. Ackerman, "Prophecy and Warfare in Early Israel: A Study of the Deborah-Barak Story," *Bulletin of the American School of Oriental Research* 220 (1975), 5–15.

K. Aland, "The Relation Between Church and State in Early Times: A Reinterpretation," *Journal of Theological Studies* 19 (1968), 15–27.

R. H. Bainton, *Christian Attitudes Toward War and Peace: A Historical Study and Critical Evaluation*, Nashville, Tenn.: Abingdon Press, 1960.

——— "The Early Church and War," *Harvard Theological Review* 39 (1946), 189–212.

P. Battifol, "Les premiers chrétiens et la guerre," *Revue du clergé francais* 67 (1911), 222–242.

J. Beeler, *Warfare in Feudal Europe: 730–1200*, Ithaca, N.Y.: Cornell University Press, 1971.

P. Biller, "Medieval Waldensian Abhorrence of Killing," in *The Church and War*, Studies in Church History 20, W. J. Sheils, ed., Oxford, England: Ecclesiastical History Society, 1983, pp. 129–146.

E. O. Blake, "The Formation of the 'Crusade Idea,'" *Journal of Ecclesiastical History* 21 (1970), 11–31.

R. Bonnaud-Delamare, *L'idée de paix a l'époque carolingienne*, Paris: les Editions Domat-Monchrestien, 1939.

———"La paix en Aquitaine au xie siècle," *Recueils Bodin* 14 (1961), 415–487.

J. A. Brundage, *Medieval Canon Law and the Crusader*, Madison, Wis.: University of Wisconsin Press, 1969.

——— "Holy War and the Medieval Lawyers," in *The Holy War*, T. P. Murphy, ed., Columbus, Ohio: Ohio State University Press, 1976, pp. 99–140.

C. J. Cadoux, *The Early Christian Attitude Toward War*, New York: Seabury Press, 1982 (first published by Headley Brothers, Publishers, 1919).

H. von Campenhausen, "Christians and Military Service in the Early Church," in *Tradition and Life in the Church*, A. V. Littledale, transl., Philadelphia: Fortress Press, 1968, pp. 160–170.

G. E. Caspary, *Politics and Exegesis: Origen and the Two Swords*, Berkeley: University of California Press, 1979.

J. Castelli, *The Bishops and the Bomb: Waging Peace in a Nuclear Age*, Garden City, N.Y.: Doubleday and Co., 1983.

M. Ceadel, "Christian Pacifism in the Era of Two World Wars," in Sheils, *The Church and War*, pp. 391–409.

M. D. Chenu, "L'évolution de la théologie de la guerre," *Lumière et vie* 7, 38 (1958), 76–97.

J. F. Collange, et al., *Résistance et soumission dans le Nouveau Testament*, Quatrième session de recherche, "Evangile et Non-violence," Poitiers: R. Macaire, 1978.

R. Coste, "Les fondements biblio-théologiques de la justice et de la paix," *Nouvelle Revue Théologique* 105 (1983), 179–217.

H. E. J. Cowdrey, "The Genesis of the Crusades: The Springs of Western Ideas of Holy War," in Murphy, *The Holy War*, pp. 9–32.

——— "The Peace and the Truce of God in the Eleventh Century," *Past and Present* 46 (1970), 42–67.

P. C. Craigie, *The Problem of War in the Old Testament*, Grand Rapids, Mich.: Eerdmans Publishing Co., 1978.

——— "Yahweh is a Man of War," *Scottish Journal of Theology* 22 (1969), 183–188.

W. D. Davies, *The Setting of the Sermon on the Mount*, Cambridge, England: Cambridge University Press, 1963.

J. R. Donahue, "The Good News of Peace," *Way* 22 (1982), 88–99.

J. von Elbe, "The Evolution of the Concept of the Just War in International Law," *American Journal of International Law* 33 (1939), 665–688.

J. J. Enz, *The Christian and Warfare*, Scottdale, Pa.: Herald Press, 1972.

J. Eppstein, *The Catholic Tradition of the Law of Nations*, London: Burns, Oates and Washbourne, Ltd., 1935.

J. M. Ford, *My Enemy Is My Guest: Jesus and Violence in Luke*, Maryknoll, N.Y.: Orbis, 1984.

F. Ganshof, "La paix au très haut moyen âge," *Recueils Bodin* 14 (1961), 397–413.

J. Genot-Bismuth, "Pacifisme pharisien et sublimation de l'idée de guerre aux origines du rabbinisme," *Etudes Théologiques et Religieuses* 56 (1981), 73–89.

S. Gero, "*Miles Gloriosus*: The Christian and Military Service According to Tertullian," *Church History* 39 (1970), 285–298.

A. Glock, "Warfare in Mari and Early Israel," unpublished Ph.D. dissertation, Ann Arbor, Mich.: University of Michigan, 1968.

J. Goldingay, "The Man of War and the Suffering Servant," *Tyndale Bulletin* 27 (1976), 79–113.

R. M. Grant, "War—Just, Holy, Unjust—in Hellenistic and Early Christian Thought," *Augustinianum* 20 (1980), 173–189.

S. Guerra, "Jesus y la violencia," *Revista de Espiritualidad* 39 (1980), 23–41.

K. Haines, "Attitudes and Impediments to Pacifism in Medieval Europe," *Journal of Medieval History* 7 (1981), 369–388.

A. von Harnack, *Militia Christi*, D. M. Gracie, transl., Philadelphia: Fortress Press, 1980 (originally published by J. C. B. Mohr (Paul Siebeck) Tuebingen, 1905).

R. S. Hartigan, "Saint Augustine on War and Killing," *Journal of the History of Ideas* 27 (1966), 195–204.

E. D. Hehl, *Kirche und Krieg im 12. Jahrhundert*, Stuttgart: A. Hiersemann, 1980.

J. Helgeland, J. P. Burns, and R. J. Daly, *Christians and the Military: The Early Experience*, Philadelphia: Fortress Press, 1985.

——— "Christians and the Roman Army from Marcus Aurelius to Constantine," *Aufstieg und Niedergang der Roemischen Welt* II. 23, 1 (1979), 724–834.

——— "Christians and the Roman Army: A.D. 173–337," *Church History* 43 (1974), 149–163.

J. Hofmeier, "Some Egyptian Motifs Related to Warfare and Enemies and Their Old Testament Counterparts," *The Ancient World* 6 (1983), 53–70.

C. J. Holdsworth, "Ideas and Reality: Some Attempts to Control and Defuse War in the Twelfth Century," in Sheils, *The Church and War*, pp. 59–78.

J. M. Hornus, *It Is Not Lawful for Me to Fight: Early Christian Attitudes Toward War, Violence, and the State*, rev. ed., A. Kreider and O. Coburn, transl., Scottdale, Pa.: Herald Press, 1980 (originally published as *Evangile et Labarum: Etude sur l'attitude du christianisme primitif devant les problèmes de l'état, de la guerre, et de la violence*, published by Labor et Fides, nouvelle série théologique, IX, Geneva, 1960).

A. Jaubert, "Les sources de la conception militaire de l'Eglise en I Clément 37," *Vigiliae Christianae* 18 (1964), 74–84.

E. N. Johnson, *The Secular Activities of the German Episcopate, 919–1024*,

402 CHARLES J. REID, JR.

University of Nebraska Studies, 30/31, Lincoln: University of Nebraska, 1932.

J. T. Johnson, *Just War Tradition and the Restraint of War: A Moral and Historical Inquiry*, Princeton, N.J.: Princeton University Press, 1981.

—— *Ideology, Reason, and the Limitation of War: Religious and Secular Concepts, 1200–1740*, Princeton, N.J.: Princeton University Press, 1975.

M. H. Keen, *The Laws of War in the Late Middle Ages*, London: Routledge and Kegan Paul, 1965.

J. Lasserre, *War and the Gospel*, Scottdale, Pa.: Herald Press, 1962.

M. Lind, *Yahweh Is a Warrior: The Theology of Warfare in Ancient Israel*, Scottdale, Pa.: Herald Press, 1980.

—— "Paradigm of Holy War in the Old Testament," *Biblical Research* 16 (1971), 16–31.

J. Linskens, "A Pacifist Interpretation of Peace in the Sermon on the Mount," *Concilium* 164 (1983), 16–25.

D. Lozada, "La paz y el amor a los enemigos," *Revista Biblica* 45 (1983), 1–15.

E. Luttwak, *The Grand Strategy of the Roman Empire: From the First Century A.D. to the Third*, Baltimore, Md.: Johns Hopkins University Press, 1976.

L. MacKinney, "The People and Public Opinion in the Eleventh Century Peace Movement," *Speculum* 5 (1930), 181–206.

R. MacMullen, *Soldier and Civilian in the Later Roman Empire*, Cambridge, Mass: Harvard University Press, 1963.

R. A. Markus, "Saint Augustine's View on the Just War," in Sheils, *The Church and War*, pp. 1–13.

A. Marrin, *War and the Christian Conscience: From Augustine to Martin Luther King, Jr.*, Chicago: Henry Regnery Co., 1971.

P. D. Miller, *The Divine Warrior in Early Israel*, Cambridge, Mass.: Harvard University Press, 1973.

W. A. Mueller, "Self-Defense and Retaliation in the Sermon on the Mount," *Review and Expositor* 53 (1956), 46–54.

T. P. Murphy, ed., *The Holy War*, Columbus, Ohio: Ohio State University Press, 1976.

A. Nussbaum, "Just War—A Legal Concept?" *Michigan Law Review* 47 (1943), 453–479.

G. F. Nuttall, *Christian Pacifism in History*, Chicago: World Without War Council, 1980.

J. F. Ortega, "La paz y la guerra en la pensamiento agustiniano," *Revista espanola de derecho canonico*, 20 (1965), 5–35.

B. Paradisi, "La paix au ive et ve siècles," *Recueils Bodin* 14 (1961), 321–394.

W. Porges, "The Clergy, the Poor, and the Noncombatants on the First Crusade," *Speculum* 21 (1946), 1–23.

G. von Rad, *Der heilige Krieg im alten Israel*, Goettingen: Vandenhoeck & Ruprecht, 1952.

J. W. Rausch, "The Principle of Nonresistance and Love of Enemy in Mt. 5:38–48," *Catholic Biblical Quarterly* 28 (1966), 31–41.

C. Reid, "Clerical Participation in Warfare: A Survey of the Canon Law From The Pseudo-Isidorian Decretals to Joannes Teutonicus," unpublished J.C.L. thesis, Washington, D.C.: The Catholic University of America, 1985.

T. Renna, "The Idea of Peace in the West, 500–1150," *Journal of Medieval History* 6 (1980), 143–167.

J. Riley-Smith, "Crusading as an Act of Love," *History* 65 (1980), 177–192.

F. H. Russell, *The Just War in the Middle Ages*, Cambridge Studies in Medieval Life and Thought, Third Series, Vol. 8, Cambridge, England: Cambridge University Press, 1975.

K. W. Ruyter, "Pacifism and Military Service in the Early Church," *Cross Currents* 22 (1982), 54–71.

E. A. Ryan, "The Rejection of Military Service by the Early Christians," *Theological Studies* 13 (1952), 1–32.

F. Schwally, *Die heilige Krieg im alten Israel*, Leipzig: Dieterich'sche Verlagsbuchhandlung, Theodor Weicher, 1901.

O. J. F. Seitz, "Love Your Enemies: The Historical Setting of Mt. V:43 ff.; Lk. VI:26 ff.," *New Testament Studies* 16 (1969), 39–54.

D. Senior, "Enemy Love: The Challenge of Peace," *Bible Today* 21 (1983), 163–169.

W. J. Sheils, ed., *The Church and War*, Studies in Church History 20, Oxford, England: Ecclesiastical History Society, 1983.

R. J. Sider, *Christ and Violence*, Scottdale, Pa.: Herald Press, 1979.

R. Smend, *Yahweh War and Tribal Confederation*, M. G. Rogers, transl., Nashville, Tenn.: Abingdon Press, 1970.

L. F. Stelton, *"Si Vis Pacem, Para Bellum,* or, If You Desire Peace, Prepare for War," *Josephinum Journal of Theology* 3 (1983), 13–19.

K. Stendahl, "Hate, Non Retaliation, and Love," *Harvard Theological Review* 55 (1962), 343–355.

B. A. Stevens, "Jesus as the Divine Warrior," *Expository Times* 94 (1983), 326–329.

F. Stolz, *Jahweh und Israels Kriege*, Zurich: Theologischer Verlag, 1972.

G. Strecker, "Compliance—Love of One's Enemy—the Golden Rule," *Australia Biblical Review* 29 (1981), 38–46.

L. Swift, *The Early Fathers on War and Military Service*, Wilmington, Del.: Michael Glazier, 1983.

———— "War and the Christian Conscience I: The Early Years," *Aufstieg und Niedergang der Roemischen Welt* II. 23, 1 (1979), 835–868.

———— "Augustine on War and Killing: Another View," *Harvard Theological Review* 66 (1973), 369–383.

———— "St. Ambrose on Violence and War," *Transactions of the American Philological Association* 101 (1970), 533–543.

J. Tooke, *The Just War in Aquinas and Grotius*, London: S.P.C.K., 1965.

A. Vanderpol, *La doctrine scholastique du droit de guerre*, Paris: A. Pedone, 1925.

J. A. Vigilante, "The Prohibition Against the Bearing of Arms by Clerics: An Historical-Canonical Survey of the Tradition of the Church up to the *Decretum* of Gratian," unpublished J.C.L. thesis, Washington, D.C.: The Catholic University of America, 1984.

J. M. Wallace-Hadrill, "War and Peace in the Early Middle Ages," in J. M. Wallace-Hadrill, *The Early Middle Ages*, New York: Barnes and Noble Books, 1976, pp. 19-39.

L. B. Walters, "Five Classic Just War Theories: A Study in the Thought of Thomas Aquinas, Vitoria, Suarez, Gentili, and Grotius," unpublished Ph.D. dissertation, New Haven, Conn.: Yale University, 1971.

M. Walzer, "Exodus 32 and the Theory of the Holy War: The History of a Citation," *Harvard Theological Review* 61 (1968), 1–14.

M. Weippert, "'Heiliger Krieg' in Israel und Assyrien: Kritische Anmerkungen zu Gerhard von Rads Konzept des 'Heiligen Krieges' im Alten Israel," *Zeitschrift fuer die altestamentliche Wissenschaft* 84 (1972), 460–493.

S. Windass, *Christianity Versus Violence: A Social and Historical Study of War and Christianity*, London: Sheed and Ward, 1964.

———— "The Early Christian Attitude to War," *Irish Theological Quarterly* 29 (1962), 235–248 (with a reply by J. Newman).

G. Zampaglione, *The Idea of Peace in Antiquity*, R. Dunn, transl., Notre Dame, Ind.: Notre Dame University Press, 1973.

Part II

R. Adams and E. Cullen, *The Final Epidemic: Physicians and Scientists on Nuclear War*, Chicago, 1981.

R. Aron, *The Great Debate: Theories of Nuclear Strategy*, E. Pawel, transl., Garden City, N.Y.: Anchor Books, 1965.

D. Ball, *Targeting for Strategic Deterrence*, Adelphi Paper No. 185, London: International Institute for Strategic Studies, 1983.

———— *Can Nuclear War Be Controlled?*, Adelphi Paper No. 161, London: International Institute for Strategic Studies, 1981.

———— "U.S. Strategic Forces: How Would They Be Used?" *International Security* 7 (1983), 31–60.

S. Bialer, "The Harsh Decade: Soviet Policies in the 1980s," *Foreign Affairs* 59 (1981), 999–1020.

C. E. Black, "The Soviet Union and Arms Control," in R. C. Johansen, ed., *The Nuclear Arms Debate: Ethical and Political Implications*, World Order Studies Program, Occasional Paper No. 12, Center for International Studies, Princeton University, 1984, pp. 101–122.

McG. Bundy, G. Kennan, R. S. McNamara, and G. Smith, "The President's Choice: Star Wars or Arms Control," *Foreign Affairs* 63 (1984), 264–278.

M. Bunn and K. Tsipis, "The Uncertainties of a Preemptive Nuclear Attack," *Scientific American* 249, 5 (November 1983), 38–47.

B. Brodie, *War and Politics*, New York: Macmillan, 1973.

———— "Development of Nuclear Strategy," *International Security* 2 (1978), 65–83.

V. Bukovsky, *The Peace Movement and the Soviet Union*, New York: Orwell Press, 1982.

W. E. Burrows, "Ballistic Missile Defense: The Illusion of Security," *Foreign Affairs* 62 (1984), 832–856.

R. Burt, *New Weapons Technologies: Debate and Directions*, Adelphi Paper No. 126, London: International Institute for Strategic Studies, 1976.

H. Caldicott, "Medical Consequences of Nuclear War," *New Catholic World* 226, 1356 (November/December 1983), 277–281.

A. B. Carter and D. N. Schwartz, eds., *Ballistic Missile Defense*, Washington, D.C.: Brookings, 1984.

A. Codevilla, "Justice, War, and Active Defense," in Philip F. Lawler, ed., *Justice and War in the Nuclear Age*, Lanham, Md.: University Press of America, 1983, pp. 61–82.

P. Cole and W. J. Taylor, eds., *The Nuclear Freeze Debate*, Boulder, Colo.: Westview Press, 1983.

F. Cross and C. V. Smith, "The Reagan Administration's Nonproliferation Nonpolicy," *Catholic University Law Review* 33 (1984), 633–665.

J. E. Dougherty, *How to Think About Arms Control and Disarmament*, New York: Crane Russak, 1973.

———— *The Bishops and Nuclear Weapons: The Catholic Pastoral Letter on War and Peace*, Hamden, Conn.: Anchor Books, The Shoestring Press, 1984.

G. I. A. D. Draper, "The Ethical and Juridical Status of Constraints in War," *Military Law Review* 55 (1972), 169–185.

S. D. Drell, P. J. Farley, and D. Holloway, *The Reagan Strategic Defense Initiative: A Technical, Political, and Arms Control Assessment*, Special Report of the Center for International Security and Arms Control, Stanford University, July 1984.

R. F. Drinan, *Beyond the Nuclear Freeze*, New York: Seabury Press, 1983.

J. Dziak, *Soviet Perceptions of Military Doctrine and Military Power: The Interaction of Theory and Practice*, New York: National Strategic Information Center, 1981.

P. R. Ehrlich, and others, "Long-Term Biological Consequences of Nuclear War," *Science* 222, 4630 (December 23, 1983), 1293–1309.

R. Falk, L. Meyrowitz, and J. Sanderson, *Nuclear Weapons and International Law*, Occasional Paper No. 10, World Order Studies Program, Center of International Studies, Princeton University, 1984.

R. Falk, "Toward a Legal Regime for Nuclear Weapons," *McGill Law Journal* 28 (1983), 519–541.

L. Freedman, *The Evolution of Nuclear Strategy*, London: St. Martin's, 1982.

R. A. Friedlander, "The Ultimate Weapon: What If Terrorists Go Nuclear?" *Denver Journal of International Law and Policy* 12 (1982), 1–11.

———— "On the Prevention of Violence," *Catholic Lawyer* 25 (1980), 95–105.

D. O. Graham, *High Frontier: A New National Strategy*, Washington, D.C.: The Heritage Foundation, 1982.

Harvard Nuclear Study Group, *Living with Nuclear Weapons*, Cambridge, Mass.: Harvard University Press, 1983.

P. Hassner, "Moscow and the Western Alliance," *Problems of Communism* 30 (1981), 37–51.

M. Hatfield and E. M. Kennedy, *Freeze! How You Can Help Prevent Nuclear War*, New York: Bantam Books, 1982.

R. G. Head, "Technology and the Military Balance," *Foreign Affairs* 56 (1978), 544–563.

S. Hoffmann, *Primacy or World Order: American Foreign Policy Since the Cold Wars*, New York: McGraw, 1978.

————— "Muscle and Brains," *Foreign Policy* 37 (1979–80), 3–27.

M. Howard, *The Causes of Wars*, London: George Allen & Unwin, 1984.

————— "On Fighting a Nuclear War," *International Security* 5 (1981), 3–17.

W. G. Hyland, "The Long Road Back," *Foreign Affairs* 60 (1982), 525–550.

————— "Soviet Theater Forces and Arms Control Policy," *Survival* 23 (1981), 194–199.

F. Ikle, "Can Deterrence Last Out the Century?" *Foreign Affairs* 51 (1973), 267–285.

R. Jastrow, *How To Make Nuclear Weapons Obsolete*, Boston: Little, Brown and Co., 1985.

————— "Reagan vs. the Scientists: Why the President Is Right About Missile Defense," *Commentary* 77 (January 1984), 23–32.

————— "Why Strategic Superiority Matters," *Commentary* 75 (March 1984), 27–32.

R. C. Johansen, ed., *The Nuclear Arms Debate: Ethical and Political Implications*, World Order Studies Program, Occasional Paper No. 12, Center for International Studies, Princeton University, 1984.

R. C. Johansen, "The Strategic and Arms Control Implications of the Bishops' Pastoral Letter," in Johansen, ed., *The Nuclear Arms Debate*, pp. 41–57.

D. Johnson, *Educating for Justice and Peace: Models for College and University Faculty*, New York: Orbis, forthcoming, 1986.

J. T. Johnson, "Applying Just-War Doctrine to Nuclear Deterrence," in Johansen, ed., *The Nuclear Arms Debate*, pp. 59–68.

J. H. Kahan, *Security in the Nuclear Age: Developing U.S. Strategic Policy*, Washington, D.C.: Brookings, 1975.

K. Kaiser, G. Leber, A. Mertes, and F. J. Schulze, "Nuclear Weapons and the Preservation of Peace," *Foreign Affairs* 60 (1982), 1157–1170.

S. S. Kaplan, ed., *Diplomacy of Power: Soviet Armed Forces as a Political Instrument*, Washington, D.C.: Brookings, 1981.

S. M. Keeny, Jr., and W. F. H. Panofsky, "MAD vs. NUTS: The Mutual Hostage Relationship of the Superpowers," *Foreign Affairs* 60 (1981/1982), 287–304.

G. Kennan, *The Nuclear Delusion: Soviet-American Relations in the Atomic Age*, New York: Pantheon Books, 1982.

R. O. Keohane and J. S. Nye, Jr., *Power and Interdependence*, Boston: Little, Brown, 1977.

H. A. Kissinger, *The Necessity for Choice*, New York: Doubleday Anchor Books, 1960.

————— *Nuclear Weapons and Foreign Policy*, New York: Doubleday Anchor Books, 1957.

J. L. Kunz, "*Bellum Justum* and *Bellum Legale*: Editorial Comment," *American Journal of International Law* 45 (1951), 528–534.

G. F. Lamberti, "Selective Service Regulations and the Ministry," *Catholic Lawyer* 28 (1983), 163–172.

E. W. Lefever and S. S. Hunt, eds., *The Apocalyptic Premise: Nuclear Arms Debated*, Washington, D.C.: Ethics and Public Policy Center, 1982.

R. Legvold, "Containment Without Confrontation," *Foreign Policy* 40 (1980), 74–98.

E. N. Luttwak, *The Grand Strategy of the Soviet Union*, London: Weidenfeld and Nicolson, 1983.

———— "Delusions of Soviet Weakness," *Commentary* 79 (January 1985), 32–38.

———— "How to Think about Nuclear War," *Commentary* 74 (August 1982), 21–28.

———— "Why Arms Control Has Failed," *Commentary* 65 (January 1978), 19–27.

R. B. Marcin, "Individual Conscience Under Military Compulsion," *American Bar Association Journal* 57 (1971), 1222–1224.

J. M. Mandelbaum, *The Nuclear Question: The United States and Nuclear Weapons, 1946–1976*, Cambridge, England: Cambridge University Press, 1979.

M. McGuire, *Soviet Military Requirements*, Washington, D.C.: Brookings, 1982.

R. S. McNamara, "The Military Role of Nuclear Weapons," *Foreign Affairs* 62 (1983), 59–80.

S. Melman, *The Permanent War Economy*, New York: Simon and Schuster, 1974.

P. L. Meredith, "The Legality of a High Technology Missile Defense System," *American Journal of International Law* 78 (1984), 418–423.

E. Meyrowitz, "The Laws of War and Nuclear Weapons," *Brooklyn Journal of International Law* 9 (1983), 227–258.

P. Nitze, "Strategy in the 1980's," *Foreign Affairs* 59 (1980), 82–101.

Office of Technology Assessment, *Ballistic Missile Defense Technologies*, Washington, D.C.: U.S. Government Printing Office, 1985.

———— *Anti-Satellite Weapons, Countermeasures, and Arms Control*, Washington, D.C.: U.S. Government Printing Office, 1985.

K. B. Payne, *Nuclear Deterrence in U.S.-Soviet Relations*, Boulder, Colo.: Westview, 1982.

———— "Nuclear Policy and the Defensive Transition," *Foreign Affairs* 62 (1984), 820–842.

T. F. Payne, "The Amorality of Arms Control," in Lawler, ed., *Justice and War in the Nuclear Age*, pp. 61–82.

A. J. Pierre, *The Global Politics of Arms Sales*, Princeton, N.J.: Princeton University Press, 1982.

N. Podhoretz, *The Present Danger*, New York: Simon and Schuster, 1980.

———— "The Present Danger," *Commentary* 69 (March 1980), 27–40.

Pontifical Academy of Scientists, Report to Pope John Paul II, "The Nuclear Winter," *ORIGINS* 13 (1984).

R. R. Reilly, "In Proportion to What? The Nature of Today's Conflict," in Lawler, ed., *Justice and War in the Nuclear Age*, pp. 5–25.

W. J. Rewak, "Universities and Weapons Research," *New Catholic World* 226, 1356, (November/December 1983), 274–276.

B. M. Russett, "The Doctrine of Deterrence," in Murnion, ed., *Catholics and Nuclear War*, pp. 149–167.

C. Sagan, "Nuclear War and Climatic Catastrophe," *Foreign Affairs* 62 (1983–84), 257–292.

J. Schell, *The Fate of the Earth*, New York: Knopf Co., 1982.

———— *The Abolition*, New York: Knopf Co., 1984.

M. J. Schultheis, *Search for Security in the Nuclear Age*, Occasional Paper No. 9, Washington, D.C.: Center of Concern, 1983.

G. Sharp, *The Politics of Nonviolent Action*, Boston: Porter Sargent Publishers, Inc., 1973.

H. Sonnenfeldt and W. G. Hyland, *Soviet Perspectives on Security,* Adelphi Paper No. 150, London: International Institute for Strategic Studies, 1979.

S. Stevens, "The Soviet BMD Program," in A. B. Carter and D. N. Schwartz, eds., *Ballistic Missile Defense*, Washington, D.C.: Brookings, 1984.

R. Strode and C. Gray, "The Imperial Dimension of Soviet Power," *Problems of Communism* 30 (1981), 1–15.

L. Sturgo, *The International Community and the Right of War*, New York: H. Fertig, 1970.

G. Treverton, *Nuclear Weapons in Europe*, Adelphi Paper No. 168, London: International Institute for Strategic Studies, 1981.

R. Tucker, "The Purposes of American Power," *Foreign Affairs* 59 (1980/81) 241–274.

R. P. Turco, and others, "Nuclear Winter: Global Consequences of Multiple Nuclear Explosions," *Science* 222, 4630 (December 23, 1983), 1283–1292.

A. Ulam, "U.S.-Soviet Relations: Unhappy Coexistence," *Foreign Affairs* 57 (1979), 556–571.

W. Ury, *Getting to Yes: Negotiating Without Giving In*, Boston: Houghton, Mifflin Co., 1981.

S. W. van Evera, "Mutual Assured Destruction: A Stable Nuclear Deterrent," in Johansen, ed., *The Nuclear Arms Debate*, pp. 85–94.

F. von Hippel, "The Prospect for a Freeze on Nuclear Weapons," in Johansen, ed., *The Nuclear Arms Debate*, pp. 96–100.

L. Wieseltier, *Nuclear War, Nuclear Peace*, New York: Holt, Rhinehart, Winston, 1983.

T. Winkler, *Arms Control and the Politics of European Security*, Adelphi Paper No. 177, London: International Institute for Strategic Studies, 1982.

G. Winter, "Nuclearism in Western Culture," in Johansen, ed., *The Nuclear Arms Debate*, pp. 69–83.

R. Woito, *To End War: A New Approach to International Conflict*, New York: The Pilgrim Press, 1982.

Part III

J. F. Ahearne, "Nuclear Deterrence: A Pragmatist's View of the Moral Issues," *Thought* 59 (1984), 78–90.

U. S. Allers and W. V. O'Brien, *Christian Ethics and Nuclear Warfare*, Washington, D.C.: Institute of World Politics, 1963.

S. B. Anthony, "Spiritual Deterrence in the Nuclear Age," *Thought* 59 (1984), 64–77.

S. D. Bailey, *Prohibitions and Restraints in War*, London: Oxford University Press, 1972.

R. Barry, "Just War Theory and the Logic of Reconciliation," *New Scholasticism* 54 (1980), 129–152.

J. B. Benestad, *The Pursuit of a Just Social Order: Policy Statement of the U.S. Catholic Bishops, 1966–1980*, Washington, D.C.: Ethics and Public Policy Center, 1982.

G. Best, *Humanity in Warfare*, London: Weidenfeld and Nicholson, 1980.

N. Blake and K. Pole, eds., *Dangers of Deterrence: Philosophers on Nuclear Strategy*, London: Routledge and Kegan Paul, 1983.

————— *Objections to Nuclear Defense: Philosophers on Deterrence*, Routledge and Kegan Paul, 1984.

D. G. Bloesch, "The Catholic Bishops on War and Peace," *Center Journal* 3 (1983) 163–176.

R. B. Brandt, "Utilitarianism and the Rules of War," in M. Cohn, T. Nagel, and T. Scanlon, eds., *War and Moral Responsibility*, Princeton, N.J.: Princeton University Press, 1974, pp. 25–45.

E. G. Brown, Jr., "Nuclear Addiction: A Response," *Thought* 59 (1983), 10–14.

R. McA. Brown, "The Religious Morality of Warfare," *New Catholic World* 226, 1356 (November/December 1983), 271–273.

C. A. Cesaretti and J. T. Vitale, eds. *Rumors of War: A Moral and Theological Perspective on the Arms Race*, New York: Seabury Press, 1982.

J. F. Childress, "Just War Criteria," in T. A. Shannon, ed., *War or Peace? The Search for New Answers*, Maryknoll, N.Y.: Orbis Press, 1980.

————— "Just War Theories: The Basis, Interrelations, Priorities, and Functions of Their Criteria," *Theological Studies* 39 (1978), 427–445.

————— "Reinhold Niebuhr's Critique of Pacifism," *Review of Politics* 36 (1974), 447–481.

Church of England, Board for Social Responsibility, *The Church and the Bomb: Nuclear Weapons and Christian Conscience*, London: Hodder and Stoughton, 1982.

I. Claude, "Just War: Doctrines and Institutions," *Political Science Quarterly* 95 (1980), 83–96.

M. Cohn, T. Nagel, and T. Scanlon, eds., *War and Moral Responsibility*, Princeton, N.J.: Princeton University Press, 1974.

C. Curran, "The Moral Methodology of the Bishops' Pastoral," in P. J. Murnion, *Catholics and Nuclear War*, pp. 45–56.

P. Deats, "Protestant Social Ethics and Pacifism," in Shannon, ed., *War or Peace?*, pp. 75–92.

J. T. Delos, "The Sociology of Modern War and the Theory of the Just War," *Cross Currents* 8 (1958), 248–265.

J. A. Devereux, ed., *The Moral Dimensions of International Conduct: The Jesuit Community Lectures, 1982*, Washington, D.C.: Georgetown University Press, 1983.

G. Doppelt, "Walzer's Theory of Morality in International Relations," *Philosophy and Public Affairs* 8 (1978), 3–26.

J. Douglass, *The Nonviolent Cross: A Theology of Revolution and Peace*, New York: Macmillan, 1968.

M. Duffey, "Reflection on the Pastoral Letter of the American Catholic Bishops," *New Catholic World* 226, 1356 (November/December 1983), 267–270.

J. A. Dwyer, *The Catholic Bishops and Nuclear War: A Critique and Analysis of the Pastoral, The Challenge of Peace*, Washington, D.C.: Georgetown University Press, 1984.

———— "An Analysis of Nuclear Warfare in Light of the Traditional Just War Theory: An American Roman Catholic Perspective, (1945–1981)," unpublished Ph.D. dissertation, Washington, D.C.: The Catholic University of America, 1983.

———— "The Role of the American Churches in the Nuclear Weapons Debate," in P. M. Cole and W. J. Taylor, Jr., eds., *The Nuclear Freeze Debate: Arms Control Issues for the 1990s*, Boulder, Colo.: Westview Press, 1983, pp. 77–92.

———— "The Morality of Using Nuclear Weapons," *New Catholic World* 226, 1356 (November/December 1983), 244–248.

E. Egan, "The Beatitudes, the Works of Mercy, and Pacifism," in Shannon, ed., *War or Peace?*, pp. 3–14.

J. Finn, "The Just War: Reviving an Old Debate," *Commonweal* 105 (August 18, 1978), 532–537.

———— "Pacifism and Just War: Either or Neither," in Murnion, *Catholics and Nuclear War*, 132–145.

H. P. Ford and F. X. Winters, eds., *Ethics and Nuclear Strategy*, Maryknoll, N.Y.: Orbis Books, 1977.

J. C. Ford, "The Morality of Obliteration Bombing," *Theological Studies* 5 (1944), 261–309.

A. Geyer, *The Idea of Disarmament: Rethinking the Unthinkable*, Elgin, Ill.: The Brethren Press, 1982.

———— "Some Theological Perspectives on Militarism," *Nexus* 59 (Summer 1980), 34–44.

D. Gill, ed., *Gathered for Life: Official Report, Sixth Assembly, World Council of Churches*, Grand Rapids, Mich.: Eerdmans, 1983.

G. Goodwin, ed., *Ethics and Nuclear Deterrence*, New York: St. Martin's Press, 1982.

G. G. Grisez, "The Moral Implications of a Nuclear Deterrent," *Center Journal* 2 (1982), 9–24.

———— "Toward a Consistent Natural Law Ethic of Killing," *American Journal of Jurisprudence* 15 (1970), 64–96.

R. S. Hartigan, *The Forgotten Victim: A History of the Civilian*, Chicago: Precedent Publishing, Inc., 1982.

———— "War and Its Normative Justification," *Review of Politics* (October 1974).

S. Hauerwas, "Eschatology and Nuclear Disarmament," *New Catholic World* 226, 1356 (November/December 1983), 249–253.

———— "On Surviving Justly: An Ethical Analysis of Nuclear Disarmament," *Center Journal* 3 (1983), 123–152.

V. Held, S. Morgenbesser, and T. Nagel, *Philosophy, Morality, and International Affairs*, New York: Oxford University Press, 1974.

J. B. Hehir and R. A. Gessert, *The New Nuclear Debate*, New York: Council on Religion and International Affairs, 1976.

J. B. Hehir, "From the Pastoral Council of Vatican II to *The Challenge of Peace*," in Murnion, ed., *Catholics and Nuclear War*, pp. 71–87.

———— "War and Peace: Reflections on Recent Teaching," *New Catholic World* 226, 1346 (March/April 1982), 60–63.

———— "Nuclear Weapons: The Two Debates," *Commonweal* 108 (1981), 135 and 159.

———— "The Just War Ethic and Catholic Technology: Dynamics of Change and Continuity," in Shannon, ed., *War or Peace?*, pp. 15–39.

———— "Moral Doctrine on Modern War: Nuclear Age-National Defense," *ORIGINS* 9 (April 1980), 675–680.

———— "The Catholic Church and the Arms Race," *Worldview* 21 (July/August 1978), 13–18.

G. F. Hershberger, *War, Peace, and Nonresistance*, 3rd ed., Scottdale, Pa.: Herald Press, 1969.

R. Heyer, *Nuclear Disarmament: Key Statements of Popes, Bishops, Councils, and Churches*, New York: Paulist Press, 1982.

D. Hollenbach, *Nuclear Ethics: A Christian Moral Argument*, Ramsey, N.J.: Paulist Press, 1983.

———— "*The Challenge of Peace* in the Context of Recent Church Teaching," in Murnion, ed., *Catholics and Nuclear War*, pp. 3–15.

———— "Deterrence, The Hardest Question," *New Catholic World* 226, 1356 (November/December 1983), 254-257.

———— "Nuclear Weapons and Nuclear War: The Shape of the Catholic Debate," *Theological Studies* 43 (1982), 577–608.

A. F. Holmes, "An Evangelical and the Bishops," *Center Journal* 3 (1983), 81–99.

J. T. Johnson and D. Smith, eds., *Love and Society: Essays in the Ethics of Paul Ramsey*, Missoula, Mont.: Scholars' Press, 1974.

J. T. Johnson, *Can Modern War Be Just?* New Haven, Conn.: Yale University Press, 1984.

———— "What Guidance Can Just War Tradition Provide for Contemporary Moral Thought About War," *New Catholic World* 226, 1346, (March/April 1982), 81–84.

———— "Ideology and the *Jus Ad Bellum*," *Journal of the American Academy of Religion* 41 (1973), 212–228.

———— "Toward Reconstructing the *Jus Ad Bellum*," *The Monist* 57 (1973), 461–488.

B. V. Johnstone, "The Right and Duty of Defense," *Studia Moralia* 22 (1984), 63–87.

———— "Nuclear War: Asking the Moral Questions," in T. Kennedy, ed., *Moral Studies: Science—Humanity—God*, Melbourne: Spectrum Publications, 1984, pp. 28–46.

M. A. Kaplan, ed., *Strategic Thinking and Its Moral Implications*, Chicago: University of Chicago Center for Policy Study, 1973.

J. F. Kealy, "Catholics in Government: In Defence of Deterrence," *Center Journal* 2 (1982), 51–56.

J. A. Komonchak, "Kingdom, History, and Church," in Murnion, ed., *Catholics and Nuclear War*, pp. 106–115.

S. E. Lammers, "Roman Catholic Social Ethics and Pacifism," in Shannon, ed., *War or Peace?* pp. 93–103.

J. Langan, "Just War Theory and Decisionmaking in a Democracy," *Naval War College Review* 38, 4 (July–August 1985), 67–79.

———— "Struggling for Moral Clarity About Nuclear Deterrence: David Hollenbach and Michael Novak," *Thought* 59 (1984), 91–98.

———— "The American Hierarchy and Nuclear Weapons," *Theological Studies* 43 (1982), 447–467.

P. F. Lawler, ed., *Justice and War in the Nuclear Age*, Lanham, Md.: University Press of America, 1983.

———— *The Bishops and the Bomb: The Morality of Nuclear Deterrence*, Washington, D.C.: The Heritage Foundation, 1982.

L. L. Long, Jr., *War and Conscience in America*, Philadelphia: The Westminster Press, 1968.

G. I. Mavrodes, "Conventions and the Morality of War," *Philosophy and Public Affairs* 4 (1975), 117–131.

R. A. McCormick, *Notes on Moral Theology, 1965–1980*, Lanham, Md.: University Press of America, 1981.

———— "Nuclear Deterrence and the Problem of Intention: A Review of the Positions," in Murnion, ed., *Catholics and Nuclear War*, pp. 168–182.

J. McKenna, "Ethics and War: A Catholic View," *American Political Science Review* 54 (1960), 647–658.

F. X. Meehan, "Nonviolence and the Bishops' Pastoral: A Case for a Development of Doctrine," in Murnion, ed., *Catholics and Nuclear War*, pp. 87–107.

———— "The Theologians' Role in Disarmament," *Proceedings of the Catholic Theological Society of America* 37 (1982), 148–154.

Y. Melzer, *Concepts of Just War*, Leyden: Sijtoff, 1975.

T. Merton, "Christian Ethics and Nuclear War," in *Thomas Merton on Peace*, essays collected by G. C. Zahn, New York: McCall, 1971, pp. 82–87.

———— "Christianity and Defense in a Nuclear Age," in *Thomas Merton on Peace*, pp. 88–93.

P. J. Murnion, ed., *Catholics and Nuclear War: A Commentary on the Challenge of Peace*, New York: Crossroads Press, 1983.

M. F. Murphy, "Why Bishops Should Not Take Sides," *Center Journal* 3 (1983), 153–162.

———— "Nuclear Weapons and the Criterion of Proportionality," *Center Journal* 2 (1982), 25–36.

J. C. Murray, "Remarks on the Moral Problem of War," *Theological Studies* 20 (1959), 40–61.

———— "War as a Moral Problem," in J. C. Murray, *We Hold These Truths*, New York: Sheed & Ward, 1961, pp. 249–274.

W. J. Nagle, ed., *Morality and Modern Warfare: The State of the Question*, Baltimore: Helicon Press, 1960.

T. Nardin, *Law, Morality and the Relations of States*, Princeton, N.J.: Princeton University Press, 1983.

———— "Philosophy and International Violence," *American Political Science Review* 70 (1976).

M. Novak, *Moral Clarity in the Nuclear Age*, Nashville, Tenn.: Thomas Nelson Publishers, Inc., 1983.

———— "The U.S. Bishops, the U.S. Government—and Reality," in Dwyer, ed., *The Catholic Bishops and Nuclear War*, pp. 65–87.

———— "Arms and the Church," *Commentary* 73 (March 1982), 37–41.

———— "The Bishops and Soviet Reality," *New Catholic World* 226, 1356 (November/December 1983), 258–261.

W. V. O'Brien, *The Conduct of Just and Limited War*, New York: Praeger, 1981.

———— *War and/or Survival*, Garden City, N.Y.: Doubleday, 1969.

———— "Proportion and Discrimination in Nuclear Deterrence and Defense," *Thought* 59 (1984), 41–52.

———— "The Challenge of War: A Christian Realist Perspective," in Dwyer, ed., *The Catholic Bishops and Nuclear War*, pp. 65–87.

———— "Just War Doctrine in a Nuclear Age," *Theological Studies* 44 (1983), 191–220.

———— "A Just War Deterrence/ Defense Strategy," *Center Journal* 3 (1983), 9–29.

———— "Morality and War: The Contribution of Paul Ramsay," in Johnson and Smith, eds., *Love and Society*, pp. 163–184.

———— "Legitimate Military Necessity in Nuclear War," *World Polity* 2 (1960), 35–120.

D. T. O'Connor, "A Reappraisal of the Just War Tradition," *Ethics* 84 (1974), 167–173.

J. J. O'Connor, "Just Peace and Just War," in Lawler, ed., *Justice and War in the Nuclear Age*, pp. 99–113.

R. E. Osgood and R. W. Tucker, *Force, Order, and Justice*, Baltimore: Johns Hopkins University Press, 1967.

T. Pangle, "A Note on the Theoretical Foundation of the Just War Doctrine," *Thomist* 43 (1979), 464–473.

B. Paskins and M. Dockrill, *The Ethics of War*, London: Duckworth, 1979.

R. L. Phillips, *War and Justice*, Norman, Okla.: University of Oklahoma Press, 1984.

R. B. Potter, *War and Moral Discourse*, Richmond, Va.: John Knox Press, 1969.

———— "The Moral Logic of War," *McCormick Quarterly* 23 (1970), 203–233.

P. Ramsey, *The Just War: Force and Political Responsibility*, New York: Charles Scribner's Sons, 1967.

———— *War and the Christian Conscience: How Shall Modern War Be Conducted Justly?* Durham, N.C.: Duke University Press, 1961.

———— "A Political Ethics Context for Strategic Thinking," in M. A. Kaplan, ed., *Strategic Thinking and Its Moral Significance*, pp. 101–147.

J. M. Rhodes, "The Kingdom, Morality, and Prudence: The American Bishops and Nuclear Weapons," *Center Journal* 3 (1983), 31–79.

R. F. Rizzo, "Nuclear War: The Moral Dilemma," *Cross Currents* 32 (1982), 71–84.

R. Roth, "Nuclear Deterrence and the Bishops' Pastoral Letter," *Thought* 59 (1984), 15–24.

E. Ruede, *The Morality of War: The Just War Theory and the Problem of Nuclear Deterrence in R. Paul Ramsey*, New York: Conventual Franciscan Press, 1972.

J. K. Ryan, *Modern War and Basic Ethics*, Milwaukee, Wis.: Bruce Publishing Co., 1940.

J. V. Schall, "Intellectual Origins of the Peace Movement," in Lawler, ed., *Justice and War in the Nuclear Age*, pp. 27–59.

———— "The Defense of Right and Civilization," *Homiletic and Pastoral Review* 82, 11–12 (August/September 1982), 10–23.

T. A. Shannon, ed., *War or Peace? The Search for New Answers*, Maryknoll, N.Y.: Orbis Press, 1980.

R. L. Spaeth, *No Easy Answers: Christians Debate Nuclear Arms*, Minneapolis: Winston Press, 1983.

———— "Disarmament and the Catholic Bishops," *This World* 2 (Summer 1982) 5–17.

W. C. Spohn, "Christian Discernment of the Nuclear Issue," *New Catholic World* 226, 1356 (November/December 1983), 262–266.

W. A. Stein, ed., *Nuclear Weapons: A Catholic Response*, New York: Sheed and Ward, 1961.

———— *Nuclear Weapons and the Christian Conscience*, London: Merlin Press, 1961.

H. Thielecke, *Theological Ethics*, Vol. 2, *Politics*, Grand Rapids, Mich.: Eerdmans Press, 1969, Ch. 26, "War in the Atomic Age," pp. 473–499.

W. S. Thompson, "Strategic Deterrence and Arms Control," *Center Journal* 2 (1982), 37–49.

R. W. Tucker, *The Just War: A Study in Contemporary American Doctrine*, Baltimore: Johns Hopkins University Press, 1960.

G. A. Vanderhaas, *Christians and Nonviolence in the Nuclear Age*, Mystic, Conn.: Twenty-Third Publications, 1982.

L. B. VanVoort, "The Churches and Nuclear Deterrence," *Foreign Affairs* 61 (1983), 827–852.

M. Wakin, ed., *War, Morality, and the Military Profession*, Boulder, Colo.: Westview Press, 1979.

M. Walzer, *Just and Unjust Wars: A Moral Argument with Historical Illustrations*, New York: Basic Books, 1977.

E. I. Watkins, *Morals and Missiles: Catholic Essays on the Problem of War Today*, London: James Clarke & Co., 1959.

G. S. Weigel, *The Peace Bishops and the Arms Race: Can Religious Leadership Help in Preventing War?* Chicago: World Without War Council, 1982.

———— "Beyond the 'Challenge of Peace': *Quaestiones Disputatae*," *Center Journal* 3 (1983), 101–121.

———— "The Catholics and the Arms Race: A Primer for the Perplexed," *Chicago Studies* 18 (1979), 169–195.

C. Weinberger, "The Moral Aspects of Deterrence," *Thought* 59 (1984), 5–9.

F. X. Winters, "After Tension, Detente: A Continuing Chronicle of European Episcopal Views on Nuclear Deterrence," *Theological Studies* 45 (1984), 343–351.

———— "Nuclear Deterrence Morality: Atlantic Community Bishops in Tension," *Theological Studies* 43 (1982), 428–446.

———— "The American Bishops on Deterrence—'Wise as Serpents, Innocent as Doves,'" in Dwyer, ed., *The Catholic Bishops and Nuclear War, The Challenge of Peace*, pp. 23–36.

———— "The Bow and the Cloud," 145 *America* (July 25, 1981), 26–30.

———— "Morality in the War Room," *America* 132 (February 15, 1975), 106–110.

A. Wohlstetter, "Bishops, Statesmen, and Other Strategists on the Bombing of Innocents," *Commentary* 75 (June 1983), 15–35.

J. H. Yoder, *When War Is Unjust: Being Honest in Just War Thinking*, Minneapolis: Augsburg, 1984.

———— *Christian Attitudes to War, Peace and Revolution*, Elkhart, Ind.: Mennonite Co Op Bookstore, 1983.

———— *The Politics of Jesus*, Grand Rapids, Mich.: Eerdmans Press, 1973.

———— *The Original Revolution*, Scottdale, Pa.: Herald Press, 1972.

———— *Nevertheless: A Meditation on the Varieties and Shortcoming of Religious Pacifism*, Scottdale, Pa.: Herald Press, 1971.

———— *Karl Barth and the Problem of War*, Nashville, Tenn.: Abingdon Press, 1970.

P. Zagano, "Media Morality: American Catholic Bishops and Deterrence," *Center Journal* 3 (1983), 177–212.

G. C. Zahn, *War, Conscience, and Dissent*, New York: Hawthorn, 1967.

———— "Pacifism and the Just War," in Murnion, ed., *Catholics and Nuclear War*, pp. 119–131.

Contributors

JOSEPH CARDINAL BERNARDIN, b. April 4, 1928, Columbia, South Carolina; St. Mary's Seminary, Baltimore, A.B.; The Catholic University of America, M.A., 1952. Cardinal Bernardin is Archbishop of Chicago, Illinois.

QUENTIN QUESNELL, b. February 24, 1927, Milwaukee, Wisconsin; St. Louis University, A.B., 1951, A.M., 1953, S.T.L., 1959; Catholic Institute, Paris, dipl. 1961; Pontifical Biblical Institute, Rome, S.S.L., 1962, S.S.D., 1968. Dr. Quesnell teaches in the Department of Religion, Smith College.

JOSEPHINE MASSYNGBAERDE FORD, b. Nottingham, England; Nottingham University, B.A., 1954, Ph.D., 1965; B.D. University of London, 1963. Dr. Ford teaches in the Department of Theology, Notre Dame University.

JOHN HELGELAND, b. October 22, 1940, Pueblo, Colorado: Luther Theological Seminary, D.B., 1966; University of Chicago, Ph.D., 1973. Dr. Helgeland teaches in the Department of Religion, North Dakota State University.

LOUIS SWIFT, b. August 1, 1932, Scranton, Pennsylvania; St. Mary's University, A.B., 1954; Pontifical Gregorian University, S.T.B., 1956; Johns Hopkins University, M.A.T., 1958, Ph.D., 1963. Dr. Swift teaches in the Classics Department, University of Kentucky.

JAMES BRUNDAGE, b. February 5, 1929, Lincoln, Nebraska; University of Nebraska, B.A., 1950, M.A., 1951; Fordham University, Ph.D., 1955. Dr. Brundage teaches in the History Department, University of Wisconsin–Milwaukee.

FREDERICK RUSSELL, b. November 1, 1940, Syracuse, New York; Swarthmore College, B.A., 1962; Johns Hopkins University, M.A., 1964, Ph.D., 1969; University of Chicago, M.A., 1975. Dr. Russell teaches in the History Department, Rutgers University–Newark.

REV. WILLIAM AU, b. January 12, 1949, Phillipsburg, N.J.; St. Mary's Seminary Liberal Arts College, Baltimore, B.A., 1971; St. Mary's Seminary School of Theology, Baltimore, S.T.M., 1975; The Catholic University of America, Ph.D., 1983. Fr. Au is Vice-Chancellor, Archdiocese of Baltimore, and part-time associate, St. Clare Church, Baltimore, Maryland.

MICHAEL NOVAK, b. September 9, 1933, Johnstown, Pennsylvania; Stonehill College, A.B., 1956; Pontifical Gregorian University, B.T., 1958; Harvard University, M.A., 1966. Mr. Novak holds the George Frederick Jewett Chair in Philosophy, Religion, and Public Policy at the American Enterprise Institute, Washington, D.C.

REV. J. BRYAN HEHIR, b. August 22, 1940, Lowell, Massachusetts; St. John's Seminary, A.B., 1962, M. Div., 1966; Harvard University, Th.D., 1977. Fr. Hehir is Secretary, Department of Social Development and World Peace, and Senior Research Scholar, Kennedy Institute of Ethics.

EDWARD LUTTWAK, b. November 4, 1942, Arad, Transylvania; London School of Economics, B.Sc., 1964; Johns Hopkins University, Ph.D., 1975. Dr. Luttwak is a defense consultant and senior fellow at the Center for Strategic and International Studies, Washington, D.C.

GEORGE WEIGEL, b. April 17, 1951, Baltimore, Maryland; St. Mary's Seminary, Baltimore, B.A., 1973; the University of St. Michael's College, Toronto, M.A., 1975. Mr. Weigel is currently President of the James Madison Foundation. During 1984–85, he conducted a major study of contemporary American Catholic thought on war and peace at the Smithsonian's Woodrow Wilson International Center for Scholars.

VIN WEBER, b. July 24, 1952, Slayton, Minnesota; attended the University of Minnesota, 1970–74; President, Weber Publishing Company. Mr. Weber was elected as a Republican to the 97th Congress; he has been reelected since.

ROBERT REILLY, b. October 31, 1946, Chicago, Illinois; Georgetown University, A.B., 1968; attended National Chengchi University (Taiwan) 1973; Claremont Graduate School, M.A., 1978. Mr. Reilly is special assistant to the President for Public Liaison; the views expressed are Mr. Reilly's own and do not necessarily reflect the official views of the United States Government.

REV. PETER HENRIOT, S.J., b. April 14, 1936, Tacoma, Washington; St. Louis University, B.A., 1963; University of Chicago, Ph.D., 1967; University of Santa Clara, S.T.M., 1971. Fr. Henriot is the Director, Center of Concern, Washington, D.C.

ARTHUR WASKOW, b. October 12, 1933, Baltimore, Maryland; Johns Hopkins University, B.A., 1954, University of Wisconsin, M.A., 1956, Ph.D., 1963. Dr. Waskow teaches at the Reconstructionist Rabbinic College, Wyncote, Pennsylvania, and is director of the Shalom Center, a national resource and organizing center for Jewish perspectives on preventing nuclear holocaust.

REV. STANLEY HARAKAS, b. January 13, 1932, Pittsburgh, Pennsylvania; Holy Cross Greek Orthodox School of Theology, B.A., 1957, B.D., 1959; Boston University, Th.D., 1965. Fr. Harakas teaches at Holy Cross Greek Orthodox School of Theology, Brookline, Massachusetts.

JOHN HOWARD YODER, b. December 29, 1927, Smithville, Ohio; University of Basel, Switzerland, Dr. Theol., 1962. Dr. Yoder teaches in the Department of Theology, University of Notre Dame.

ALAN GEYER, b. August 3, 1931, Dover, New Jersey; Ohio Wesleyan, B.A., 1952; Boston University, S.T.B., 1955, Ph.D., 1961. Dr. Geyer is Executive Director, Churches' Center for Theology and Public Policy, Washington, D.C.

REV. BRIAN JOHNSTONE, b. December 5, 1938, Melbourne, Australia; St. Mary's Seminary, Ballarat, B. Theol., 1965; Rome, S.T.L., 1968; Catholic University of Louvain, S.T.D., 1973. Fr. Johnstone teaches in the Department of Theology at The Catholic University of America.

JOSEPH M. BOYLE, JR., b. July 30, 1942, Philadelphia, Pennsylvania; LaSalle College, Philadelphia, B.A., 1965; Georgetown University, Ph.D., 1970. Dr. Boyle teaches in the Department of Philosophy, Center for Thomistic Studies, University of St. Thomas, Houston, Texas.

REV. FRANCIS WINTERS, b. October 12, 1933, Roaring Spring, Pennsylvania; Fordham University, B.A., 1958, M.A.T., 1959, Ph.D., 1973; Woodstock College, Ph.L., 1958, S.T.B., 1963, S.T.L., 1965. Fr. Winters teaches in the School of Foreign Service, Georgetown University.

DAVID JOHNSON, ESQ., b. July 27, 1949, Chicago, Illinois; University of Notre Dame, B.A., 1971; University of Connecticut, M.A., 1974; Fordham University, J.D., 1977. Mr. Johnson is Associate Executive Director, Association of Catholic Colleges and Universities.

ROBERT A. DESTRO, b. September 6, 1950, Akron, Ohio; Miami University, B.A., 1972; University of California, Berkeley, J.D., 1975. Mr. Destro teaches at the Columbus School of Law, The Catholic University of America, and is a member of the United States Commission on Civil Rights. The views expressed are Mr. Destro's own and do not necessarily reflect the views of the United States Commission on Civil Rights.

CATHERINE INEZ ADLESIC, b. November 26, 1960, Pittsburgh, Pennsylvania; The Catholic University of America, B.A., 1983. Ms. Adlesic served on the staff of the Pastoral Letter Clearinghouse, United States Catholic Conference, 1983–84. She currently serves on the staff of Catholic Relief Services, New York City.

CHARLES J. REID, JR., b. December 7, 1953, Milwaukee, Wisconsin; University of Wisconsin–Milwaukee, B.A., 1978; The Catholic University of America, J.D., 1982, J.C.L., 1985. Mr. Reid is currently a graduate student (Sage Graduate Fellow) in the Department of History, Cornell University.

Index